Late one Nagasaki night in 1994, two English teachers were sitting in Panic Paradise Pub imagining the newly-accessible delights finally open to travellers after the collapse of the Soviet Union. Forsaking love, job prospects and the Japanese good life, they put down their saké cups and set off to explore Central Asia. Three and a half years later, having traversed the continent seven times between them, their planned Silk Route pamphlet had mushroomed into this Asian omnibus. We hope you enjoy the ride.

Mark Elliott (34, UK). Radio presenter, chemistry teacher, vacuum salesman, Union Society president: Mark's CV is as straight as the Karakoram Highway. He's played blues harmonica in a Turkmenistan club, and danced rain dances in a Gambian village. He's eaten pig's brains with Borneo dayaks and nibbled chocolate strawberries with US presidents. His poem, *The Grey was eat for Turtle,* was overlooked by the critics but his first travel book is now on its fourth edition in Japan. He is currently challenging a lifetime loathing of Brussels sprouts by taking refuge in Belgium.

Wil Klass (27, USA) worked as an airlines customer service intern, manual labourer at an Alaskan fish cannery, a Malawi guest house manager and as a student at the University of Michigan before teaming up with Mark on *Asia Overland.* He currently plays his pinball in Washington DC and travels virtually – as a producer for US News & World Report Online. He can be reached by e-mail at: ganesh@zahadum.com.

Asia Overland
First edition: 1998

Publisher
Trailblazer Publications
The Old Manse, Tower Rd, Hindhead, Surrey, GU26 6SU, UK
Fax (+44) 01428-607571
E-mail: trailblazer@compuserve.com

British Library Cataloguing in Publication Data
A catalogue record for this book is available from the British Library

ISBN 1-873756-10-0

Editor: Anna Jacomb-Hood
Series editor: Patricia Major

Every effort has been made by the authors and publisher to ensure that the
information contained herein is as accurate and up to date as possible. However, they
are unable to accept responsibility for any inconvenience, loss or injury sustained by
anyone as a result of the advice and information given in this guide.

Printed on chlorine-free paper from farmed forests by
Technographic Design & Print (☎ 01206-303323) Colchester, Essex, UK

Front cover: Karakoram Highway. Negotiating a flooded river in China on the return
journey to Pakistan. © Titus Moser (The Hutchison Library).

ASIA
OVERLAND

MARK ELLIOTT
WIL KLASS

TRAILBLAZER PUBLICATIONS

Acknowledgements

For convenient brevity this book is written in the first person. In a few cases the 'I' or 'we' refers to the experiences of other travellers. In three and a half years of research it is patently impossible for the two of us to have visited every town in 34 countries by ourselves. We have benefited incalculably from the wisdom, hospitality and inspirations of uncountable delightful folk. Some have contributed photos, maps and notes, others a single hotel name or a cup of coffee. All are appreciated and we're painfully aware that not all can be fully recognized here owing to lack of space or because some names we never knew in the first place. Above all we owe unrepayable debts of gratitude to friends and family who have been generous beyond any call of duty in providing love, shelter and unstinting support. In deliberately randomised order a huge thank you to:

Thi Hanh Cao, Michael Ash, Eric Mortensen, John & Janet Anderson, Christian Braun, Julie Sanders, Almas Egemberdiev, Misty Schymtzik, Mr & Mrs. Duane Ebnet (and Hua & Ming at IPAC, Hanoi), Nicki Grihault, Liz Flynn, Mad Polish Tomas, Hans & Demitri, Mohsen Yekeh Fallah, Sam North, Brad Lutz, Stuart and John, Saman Joseph, Mel Copen, Rosita 'the pigeon' Boland, Lisa Cooper, Jennifer in Vilnius, Jurek Sadowski and the Polish tokers, Kimberley Bulkley, Sveta Elchaninova, Nicolai Nikolaiavich Biliznyuk, Vladimir Stapanov, Jonathon Day, Galina Nikolaina and Nastia, Wladimir, Tatania and Julia Nesvetajlo, Ali Erol Bayus, Metin Yazici, Tim Morgan, Erdem Karakoc, Hakan Ayaz and friends, Ivonne Wilken, Jens Ludwig, Zaur Nazarly, Azim Mollazade, Jonathon Cohen, Mishel, Jonathon Garrett, Max and the lovely Natasha, Nursaltan Bairamdurdi, 'don't do it' Blondine, Wada Saab, Luda and Lena, Jacques Gorgechon, Bahtiyor Allayarov, Dave Green, Nurlan Temirbayev, Andy Cox, Katie Lemon, Ahmad Samimi, Hamid and Majid Mousavinia, Nancy Harris, Marius Petan, Yoshitaka Watanabe, Ros 'Bruichladdich' Fordyce, Jamil Hussain, Inga (the angel), Nino Kikilashvili, Jemeli and Lida, Paata Toshkua, Charles van de Leeuw, Sayran, Samir, Fuad Mammadov and family, Rohan Hawthorne, George Kent, Beata Drwiega, Madonna, Zaza and Ilsa, Ie and Ie, Nana, Athol Yates, Greg Dimmock, Dibi Gurung, Dan Iordache, So Miyake (hope you found God), Charlotte and Vicky, Hem and Udaya, Rama (we've still got that book for you when you send us ours), Sanjay Kapoor, Katrine Chang, Natalie Barlow, Mani Raj Manandhar and his magic sandwiches, Daniel Haber, Tom Robbins, Madison, Michael Alcorn, Claire Austin, Jan Gottlieb Larsen, Cybele 'Glug' Renault, Natasha Pairaudeau, Mo Weiming, Gavin Machel, Claus Munch, Jurgen Rotzel, Mei Ling Turner, Elizabeth Tynes, the mysterious Mr Nou, Oleg Sokolov, Pierre-Andre Martinet, Peter Neville Hadley, Jorg Haasenger, Falk Grollmus, Chris Longmore, Philip Verhagen, Mattijs Maussen, Risheng Xia, Joe & Kathy Wood, Jerry Jones, Athit Apichati, John Reynolds, Sushma Rahman, Melissa Chadwick, Will Montgomery, David & Marlene Foster, Jacqueline Blumenthal and Urs Jegher, Onur Ozel, Tom Stone (world walker), Dimple and the Roadhouse crew in Kathmandu, Jamie McG, Sarah-ho Silbert, Jahir Vuma, Dan, Erik and Julie in Burma (I still don't know what bit me that night), Amb. Bill Courtney, Adrienne Benson, Karma Dorjee (Bhutan Tourism), Kiersten Marshall, Kate (Nomads, Mongolia), JNTO, Kristen 'Madame Chair' Edmonds, Europay, Erika Falkenstein, Aziz Huq, Renat Ilyazov, Pam Winfield, Zafar Iqbal, Dong Hoi Kim, Max Moros, Rod Holmes, Hennie Meyer, Justin Mellersh, Andrew Smith, Chan 'Pung!' Park, Jon, Ayla 'Super-sonic' Fulton and Amanda Kufner, Provash Banerjee, Shankar Bhujel, Eddie Kniefel, the Dalai Lhama (makes everything better), Tamsin Sarich, Mort, Barry & Lorraine Rogstad, Danny Sriskandarajah, Sarah Brewster, Amina Tirana, John King, Terumi Tachibana, Shegeo Nakamura, Toshie Satsumoto, 'Itchy-nose', Sokol Shyti, Chisato Tsukimi and the girls, Mick Brown, Neil Taylor, Jennifer Payne, Wilco Oostveen, Kiersten Marshall , Laura Downin, Rebecca Stoeckel, Mr & Mrs. Backus, The Satisfied Mind (Winchester, VA), Mia, Hassen Zerinini, staff of Istanbul's Anadolu pension, Angela Chase, Amit Shukla, Todd Drummond, Will Melara, Brandon Boyle, Lindsey, Dave A and Bastard B, Kathy Anning, Lindsey Austin Samahon, The LoPrestis, Alison Tate, Tim Cummings, Heidi Plat, Michael Madon, Doug Homer, Karen Ellingson, Denis Katzer, Denice Skelly, Bill Allman, Ivan Zoltan, Peter Geiser (Internet travel guides via the newsgroup rec.travel.asia), Carine and Dominique, Carson Klapthor, Heidi S, Jackie Gordon, Tony Lawrence, Gilda Povolo, Cyclone, Rajeev Mishra (Aerotrek Travels, Delhi), Debrah Plumstead, Steve and Cathy (sorry I missed the wedding), Rebecca 'dream girl' Sykes, Ian Godley and family, Zong and Anh (Binh Minh, Hanoi), Mark Cameron, staff of Most Bank (Baku), John Arne and Morten for teaching me to smile at life, Dixie, Phil, Keiko, Harumi, Dave E and Paul M, Zdenek Brabec & Martin, Langen Geleen, William David, Uwe Dannwolf, Francoise Robin, Marianne Heredge, Annie Dillard (for the ability to see), Andrew Dowling & Kirsty Albert, R.E.M. and Dave Matthews, whoever invented coffee, the St. A's gang: Rob Thompson (we miss you in NZ), Jasper Thompson, Paul (our rock) & Donna Downey, and Erik 'Spike' Rogstad (may we always practice the 100% theory). Special thanks to our sensitive editor, Anna Jacomb-Hood, to Jane Thomas in production, and to ever patient publisher Bryn 'Scissors' Thomas.

From Mark Infinite thanks and love to my ever supportive, unbeatable family and to Dani without whom my world would have long ago imploded. **From Wil** Mountains of debt to Greg Backus and Dawn Kuitko who welcomed me into their Virginia home and to Helen Bellanca, who did the same in Oregon. Here's to Katrin Flohrs, who is my proof that beauty can be found on the road, and to my sister, Ingrid, who is my proof that sometimes it is also found at home.

CONTENTS

PLANNING YOUR TRIP

Paths across Asia 7 – Using this guide 7 – Middle East 10 - Trans- Caspian 11
Trans-Siberian options 12 – Heart of Asia 13 – North-East Asia 14
Crossing South-East Asian 16 – Indo-China 17 – Getting to/from Europe 18
Trans-Pacific 20 – Transport costs 21 – Seventeen favourites 22

WEST ASIA

Turkey 23 – Hariem 43 – Iran 47 – Afghanistan 76

THE CAUCASUS

Armenia 86 – Azerbaijan 93 – Georgia 108

CENTRAL ASIA

Kazakhstan 132 – Kyrgystan 144 – Tajikistan 164 – Turmenistan 169 – Uzbekistan 179

CHINA

China introduction 197 – 'Chinese' China 208 – Hong Kong 219 – Yunnan 235
Tibet 242 – Xinjiang 258

THE GREAT NORTH

Belarus 275 – Ukraine 279 – Russia 289 – Mongolia 312

THE SUBCONTINENT

Pakistan 320 – Karakoram Highway 334 – India 342 – Bhutan 375 – Nepal 378 –
Bangladesh 396 – Sri Lanka 409

SOUTH-EAST ASIA

Indonesia 416 – Singapore 427 – Malaysia 431 – Thailand 439 – Burma (Myanmar) 450
Vietnam 467 – Cambodia 488 – Laos 497 – Philippines 512

NORTH-EAST ASIA

Japan 517 – South Korea 538 – North Korea 550 – Taiwan 554

APPENDICES & INDEX

Visa strategy 556 – The 'Visa Shuffle' 557 – Russian words and phrases 560
Index 563

❏ **Update request**
We've tried to ensure that this guide is as accurate and up to date as possible but
things change quickly in Asia. If you notice any changes or omissions please write
to the authors at Trailblazer Publications (address on p2). A free copy of the next
edition will be sent to persons making a significant contribution.

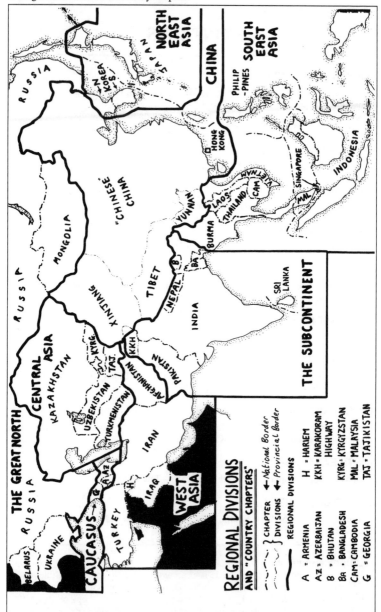

REGIONAL DIVISIONS
AND "COUNTRY CHAPTERS"

⟩ CHAPTER ← National Border
⟩ DIVISIONS ← Provincial Border
⟨ REGIONAL DIVISIONS

A = ARMENIA   H = HARIEM
AZ = AZERBAIJAN   KKH = KARAKORAM
B = BHUTAN   HIGHWAY
BA = BANGLADESH   KYRG = KYRGYZSTAN
CAM = CAMBODIA   MAL = MALAYSIA
G = GEORGIA   TAT = TAJIKISTAN

PLANNING YOUR TRIP

Most information in this book is presented as country chapters arranged in **regional sections** (see opposite). **Trans-regional overview maps** (pp10-20) are as follows:

● **1** Cross Eastern Europe cheaply with short hops across suggested borders: p19.

● **2** Turkey has many cheap international buses. Ferries are pricier: p27.

● **3** Middle East route summary: p10

● **4** The beautiful, hospitable Caucasus region sees few tourists. Route overview: p84. Options around the Caspian: p11.

● **5** Iran is friendlier than you'd expect (but visas can be tough). If you're nervous try our five-day 'rush-through' plan: p52.

● **6** Intrepid travellers crossing Taliban Afghanistan should seek careful advice in Peshawar/Quetta (Pakistan, p333).

● **7** Travel in Central Asia retains a sense of adventure without any actual danger (except Tajikistan). Options: p13. Much is a dull slog but Samarkand, Khiva, Bukhara and alpine Kyrgyzstan justify long detours. Moscow – C Asia – China is great value.

● **8** The rather monotonous Trans-Siberian railway has many variants: p12.

● **9** Burma's closed borders block overland travel between India and SE Asia. Fly or loop via China a) through Xinjiang from C. Asia or Pakistan (easy) or b) across Tibet (seasonal) from Nepal/India (p253).

● **10** Cambodian instability and Vietnam's limited number of border crossings mean flying can avoid long loops on some route sections. Laos's bad roads are even worse in summer rain: p17.

● **11** Transport in south eastern SE Asia is cheap and easy: p16. Sadly no boat to Oz.

● **12** Ferry options between Japan/South Korea and China/Russia/Taiwan: p14.

● **13** Asia-Americas. There is no cheap alternative to flying, (unless you hitch on a yacht) but some airlines offer appealing Pacific Island stopovers: p20.

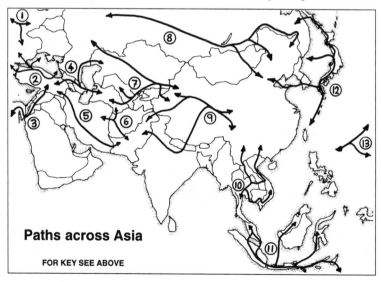

Paths across Asia

FOR KEY SEE ABOVE

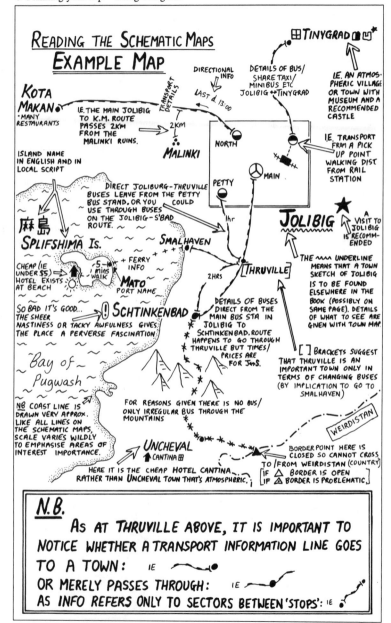

READING THE SCHEMATIC MAPS
EXAMPLE MAP

⊞ TINYGRAD 🖼️ ⛪ ★

DIRECTIONAL INFO

LAST d. 13:00

DETAILS OF BUS/ SHARE TAXI/ MINIBUS ETC JOLIBIG ↔ TINYGRAD

IE. AN ATMOS-PHERIC VILLAGE OR TOWN WITH MUSEUM AND A RECOMMENDED CASTLE

KOTA MAKAN • MANY RESTAURANTS

IE. THE MAIN JOLIBIG TO K.M. ROUTE PASSES 2KM FROM THE MALINKI RUINS.

TRANSPORT DETAILS

2KM

NORTH

IE. TRANSPORT FROM A PICK UP POINT WALKING DIST FROM RAIL STATION

MALINKI

ISLAND NAME IN ENGLISH AND IN LOCAL SCRIPT

PETTY

MAIN

麻島

SPLIFSHIMA Is.

DIRECT JOLIBURG-THRUVILLE BUSES LEAVE FROM THE PETTY BUS STAND. OR YOU COULD USE THROUGH BUSES ON THE JOLIBIG-S'BAD ROUTE.

1hr

★ **JOLIBIG** A VISIT TO JOLIBIG IS RECOMMENDED

SMALHAVEN

THE ～～ UNDERLINE MEANS THAT A TOWN SKETCH OF JOLIBIG IS TO BE FOUND ELSEWHERE IN THE BOOK (POSSIBLY ON SAME PAGE). DETAILS OF WHAT TO SEE ARE GIVEN WITH TOWN MAP.

CHEAP (IE UNDER $5) HOTEL EXISTS AT BEACH

~5~ 1 mins walk

+ FERRY INFO

MATO PORT NAME

[Thruville]

2HRS

SO BAD IT'S GOOD... THE SHEER NASTINESS OR TACKY AWFULNESS GIVES THE PLACE A PERVERSE FASCINATION.

(!) **SCHTINKENBAD**

DETAILS OF BUSES DIRECT FROM THE MAIN BUS STA IN JOLIBIG TO SCHTINKENBAD. ROUTE HAPPENS TO GO THROUGH THRUVILLE BUT TIMES/ PRICES ARE FOR J↔S.

[ ] BRACKETS SUGGEST THAT THRUVILLE IS AN IMPORTANT TOWN ONLY IN TERMS OF CHANGING BUSES (BY IMPLICATION TO GO TO SMALHAVEN)

~Bay of ~ Pugwash ~

NB COAST LINE IS DRAWN VERY APPROX. LIKE ALL LINES ON THE SCHEMATIC MAPS, SCALE VARIES WILDLY TO EMPHASISE AREAS OF INTEREST IMPORTANCE.

FOR REASONS GIVEN THERE IS NO BUS/ ONLY IRREGULAR BUS THROUGH THE MOUNTAINS

WEIRDISTAN

UNCHEVAL ↑ CANTINA ⊞

HERE IT IS THE CHEAP HOTEL CANTINA RATHER THAN UNCHEVAL TOWN THAT'S ATMOSPHERIC.

BORDER POINT HERE IS CLOSED SO CANNOT CROSS TO/FROM WEIRDISTAN (COUNTRY)

[IF △ BORDER IS OPEN
IF ▲ BORDER IS PROBLEMATIC]

N.B.

AS AT THRUVILLE ABOVE, IT IS IMPORTANT TO NOTICE WHETHER A TRANSPORT INFORMATION LINE GOES TO A TOWN: IE •——•
OR MERELY PASSES THROUGH: IE •——•——
AS INFO REFERS ONLY TO SECTORS BETWEEN 'STOPS': IE •——•

Key to symbols used throughout this guide

ACCOMMODATION

↟ CHEAPEST BEDS COST UNDER $5
↟ CHEAPEST BEDS $5-10
↟ $10 OR OVER
■ EXPENSIVE HOTELS (INCLUDED AS LANDMARKS)

AROUND TOWN

X RESTAURANT OR CAFE OF NOTE
⊠ POST OFFICE   ℛ PHONE OFFICE
ⓘ / ⓘ INFORMATION OFFICE: OFFICIAL / UNOFF.
$ / ⑤ MONEY CHANGERS: BANK / STREET
Ⓥ BOOKSHOP   ⊛ BIKE RENTAL
♨ BATH-HOUSE OR HOT SPRING
♪ OPERA OR CONCERT HALL   ♈ THEATRE
▥ MUSEUM   ♣ GARDEN
Ⓟ EMBASSY OR CONSULATE
⊔ CASTLE OR FORT
⊔ PALACE   ↖ VIEWPOINT
⬚ / ∴ RUINS   ☊/Ω CAVE CITY, TOMB, / CAVE
☼ BEACH   ⊛ FERRIS WHEEL (USEFUL ORIENTATION POINT)
⌣ BRIDGE   ⌇ PASS

RELIGIOUS ICONS

卅 TEMPLE / SHRINE   ♱ CHURCH / CATHEDRAL
閈 MONASTERY   ⓘ CHRISTIAN MONASTERY
⍲ CAVE TEMPLE   ⓘ CAVE CHURCH
Ⓖ MOSQUE
Ⓖ MADRASSA / MUSLIM SHRINE OR MAUSOLEUM
Ａ / △ PAGODAS   ◐ TAOIST SITE
⌂ CAO DAI SITE   ♄ ZOROASTRIAN SITE
✿ ACTIVE BUDDHIST SITE (EG IN CHINA)

OTHER CHAPTER-SPECIFIC ICONS ARE INTRODUCED WHERE NECESSARY.

LINES / SHADING

RAILWAY STATION
RAILWAY ┼┼┼┼┼■
DISTANCE Z Y X → Z
SMALL↔BIG ROADS
‒ ‒ ‒ WALKING PATH / TRACK
●—●—● ROAD TRANSPORT BETWEEN TWO MARKED TOWNS
✳ ✳ ✳ ✳ SEASONAL, DANGEROUS OR ROUTE WITH NO TRANSPORT
+ + + + + FERRY
≈≈≈≈ RIVER   ～ COAST OR WATERFRONT
—··—··— PROVINCIAL BOUNDARY
—·△·—·—· NATIONAL BORDER
⊿ BORDER CROSSING MAY/MAYNOT BE POSSIBLE
▲ CROSSING POINT CLOSED
⊿ CROSSING OPEN   ╍╍ BORDER DANGEROUS
▨▨▨ PARK / ZOO   ▨▨▨ MARKET AREA
TOWN ← TOWN MAP / SKETCH OF THIS PLACE

TRANSPORTATION ICONS

Ⓐ BUS STATION
◒ BUS STAND / MINOR BUS STATION
◓ BUS / SHARE TAXI PICKUP POINT OR CITY-BUS STAND
✈ AIRPORT   ⟞⟝ JETTY / PORT
Ⓜ METRO STATION (OR SPECIAL SYMBOL)
—#7— CITY BUS #7 W/ STOPS
Long St.

DESCRIPTIVE / ABBREVIATIONS

★ RECOMMENDED   ★★ ASIA'S BEST
⊞ ATMOSPHERIC.   ~ APPROXIMATELY
A/C AIR CONDITIONING   B+B INCL. BREAKFAST
FREQ FREQUENT $ U.S. DOLLARS
HWY HIGHWAY   H₂O WATER / BATH
NP NATIONAL PARK   REQ REQUIRED
SEP SEPARATE   SEV SEVERAL (PER DAY)
[TOWN NAME] TRANSIT TOWN   ① SO BAD IT'S GOOD
dbl. DOUBLE   rm. ROOM   sng. SINGLE
a/arr. ARRIVAL   d/dep. DEPARTURE

Crossing the Middle East

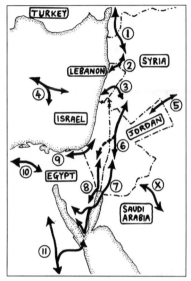

● **1 Syria-Turkey** Several crossing points, most open to tourists. Damascus-Antakya 8hrs, $20.

● **2/3 Lebanon-Syria** The main route is Beirut-Damascus with very frequent share taxis, 1½ hrs. Occasional coastal buses run Beirut-Halab via Tripoli and Latakia. Beirut is rapidly reverting from war zone to party city.

● **4 Cyprus** The E Mediterranean shipping hub but sadly it's impossible to cross between the Greek/independent south and the Turkish controlled north (except occasionally on day trips where you leave your passport at the check point). Thus the cheap overnight boats to Turkey are useless to overlanders. Through tickets Israel-Greece ($70) work out much cheaper than buying separate tickets to and from Cyprus and gave us most of a day in Limassol. Beirut hydrofoils run daily, 3hrs ($100). Most other boats are overnight.

● **5** Through buses **Amman-Baghdad** ($20 14hrs). Good luck getting the Iraqi visa.

● **6 Syria-Jordan (-Israel)** Amman-Damascus freq shared taxis ($7, 7hrs). Jordan-Israel now straightforward **but** Syria won't let you in if you've been to Israel.

● **7 Nuweiba-Aqaba boat** (2/day, $25) lets you avoid Israel. The boat links directly with buses to Cairo (8hrs, $15). Aqaba-Petra-Kerak-Amman buses are surprisingly infrequent but hitching is relatively easy.

● **8 Egypt-Sinai-Israel** Popular route via the Dead Sea, Massada, and Red Sea resorts: Eilat for bustle and nightlife, Dahab for hippy-ish chill scene, Sharm-el-Sheikh for top snorkelling/scuba. $18 border tax southbound only. 2/day buses pass St Catherine's monastery at biblical Mt Sinai.

● **9 Egypt-Israel (north route)** Border taxes $5 eastbound, $18 west. Faster/less interesting than route #8 above. Cairo-Tel Aviv $25 by direct bus. Cheaper in bus/share taxis hops via El Arish and Gaza.

● **10 Cairo-Tripoli (Libya)** Direct buses for $70 but much cheaper in sections using black market Libyan dinars. Libyan visas are obtainable but an Arabic translation of your passport is necessary before you apply. Buses run Tripoli-Tunis (17hrs). Tunisia has cheap charter flights from Europe (Djerba, Monastir).

● **11 Cairo-Luxor** Trains can get very crowded. Buses cost double. Nile boats, from *feluccas* to floating palaces, potter up the bilharzia infested river for very variable prices. Most are pleasure cruises rather than long distance public transport.

● **X Saudi Arabia** Direct buses from Turkey (eg $35 Ankara-Riyadh), Syria, and Jordan. In the unlikely event of getting a Saudi visa, note that women may not drive nor travel without a 'husband'.

For the full story on budget travel in the Near East see Henry Stedman's *Istanbul to Cairo Overland* (Trailblazer).

Routes around and across the Caspian

● **Around the bottom** Pakistan-Iran-Turkey (with a possible loop through Armenia and Georgia) is the fastest, easiest and most comfortable route with arguably the most to see. Land borders between Iran and Turkmenistan/Azerbaijan are not reliably open. Foreigners travelling Iran-Turkmenistan are rarely carried on the 1997-inaugurated Mashhad-Tedzhen railway so must either cut through Afghanistan or fly the Ashgabat-Mashhad hop (Mon, $40 ex-Iran, up to $100

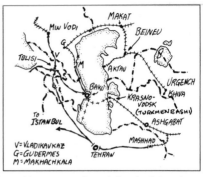

from Ashgabat). The greatest problem with any route through Iran is that at times of political disagreement with the West, visas become very hard to obtain. There are several other options, however.

● **Around the top** Tough. The main advantage is seeing the brilliant but isolated Uzbek museum town of Khiva without having to double back or fly. Getting to Astrakhan (impressive Kremlin and appealing air of decay) is easy enough from Ukraine or Russia but the only practical route from the Caucasus crosses Azerbaijan's uneasy Russian frontier and cuts through a corner of Chechnya. Between Astrakhan and the Aral-wilted cotton stalks of Kungrad the scenery is dreary, camel dotted steppe wilderness. There are no buses, and trains run each section only once daily. The Beineu-Urgench 'service' uses vandalised sardine cans and ranks as the most appalling train ride undertaken by the authors in the research of this book. Locals bring wire to seal shut metal-slat shutters preventing yet more passengers from throwing themselves, their baggage and their grannies through the glass-less train windows. We eventually had 27 people jammed in a compartment designed for 6. Go to the toilet before you leave! If and when a) it runs and b) you can get a berth on it, the infinitely more comfortable Moscow-Volgagrad-Urgench-Samarkand train makes this route altogether more worthy of consideration. Latest reports suggest that the line may be scrapped altogether.

● **Sailing across** The Baku (Azerbaijan) to Turkmenbashi (formerly Krasnovodsk, Turkmenistan) ferry now departs from each port every evening, sometime. Foreigners can get $45, 5th/deck class tickets ex-Baku. In Turkmenbashi we were offered $26 local price berths but many travellers were told flatly that $75, 4th class cabins were the cheapest option. Tales of joining a dockside mêlée and bribing one's way aboard for $10 no longer apply. There are no passenger services to/from Makhachkala, Astrakhan or Aktau though you may be able to arrange ad hoc passage with freighters or oil industry ships. Overnight ferries leave Bandar Anzali (Iran) for Baku Mon, returning Tue. $100+. (The daily bus would be $13 to Tehran if only they'd let you cross the border.) Flying across. Baku->Turkmenbashi flights cost $56 (AZAL, Mon/Thu/Sat). The same flights T->B cost us only $26 (local price) at Turkmenbashi's airport ticket desk but this won't last. Baku to/from Ashgabat $140+. Flying Baku <> Aktau $73, (M, Thu AZAL) doesn't save you the Beineu-Urgench hell ride. Handy from the Russian Caucasus is the Min Vodi-Urgench route ($95, Sat>, <Fri).

Trans-Siberian options

There are two main routes between Moscow and Beijing: **[1] Trans Mongolian** (6 days, 6 nights, allows you a sniff at Genghis Khan), **[2] Trans-Manchurian** (cheaper, 6 days, 7 nights). Direct trains on either route run once or twice weekly. To be sure of a specific date of travel and to party through the monotonous ride with a 'Eurail' style gang of Westerners consider paying the considerable premium (eg 100%) of using through an agent. Add $100+/day for stopovers (Irkutsk/Ulaan Baator). Cheaper to fly. To save money, buy tickets yourself. This is easy in Beijing ($200+ from the CITS at the Beijing International Hotel). With the tickets you can easily sort out the visas. Coming the other way is tougher as you'll have to get the Russian visa in advance. Moscow is an expensive place to hang around; don't worry if you can't get a direct Beijing ticket.

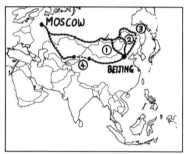

There are other less publicised options:
a) Every other day the **[3] 'Blaggard'** (our name) runs Moscow-Blagovash-chensk. Being a domestic train it conveys cheaper platscart class compartments. From Blag you can cross the Amur river on 6/day summer ferries to Heihe, China. The problem is that the Russians may expect you to have Blagovashchensk written on your visa. Mosc-Beij from $133, 10 days, 9 nights.
b) Don't go via Siberia at all. Cut across China to Kazakhstan/Kyrgyzstan **[4]**).
There are daily services to Moscow from Bishkek (cheapest, $55), Tashkent, Andizhan or Almaty). These routes are more interesting, cheaper and more frequent than Siberian possibilities especially if you travel Urumqi-Almaty in sections (see p143). Moscow-Beijing takes 8-9 days.
c) Do routes [1] or [2] but in sections. Maps and suggested stopovers are given in the Russia chapter. If you're not going 'all the way' there are plenty of trains to choose from until you get to the trans border sections. Then between Ulan Ude and Ulaan Baator there's a daily train ($40). On route [2] there's a Chita to Zabaikalsk (border) train daily and a few to Harbin each week.

NB Open carriage platscart class (defined p271) is around 40% cheaper than 2nd class/kupe but not available on international trains.

Note that the 'real' Trans Siberian links Moscow and Vladivostok. Classy *Rossiya* through trains (kupe or luxe only) run every 2 days though you could go any time by cheaper platscart with a change of trains en route. There is a Vladivostok-Japan ferry but it's very expensive and runs only 10x/year p14.

Further information

Full route details in Bryn Thomas's *Trans Siberian Handbook* (Trailblazer). For the route via Almaty and Urumqi see *Silk Route by Rail* (also from Trailblazer) **Russia Rail** can get you visas, accommodation and tickets. They have a brilliant website run by Athol Yates (author of *Siberian BAM Railway Guide* and *Russia by Rail:*) http://www.russia-rail.com. **Monkey Business**, (mainly westbound) tickets, range of stopover options, studenty atmosphere: Beijing ☎/fax (8610)6329 2244 ext 4406. Hong Kong: ☎ (852)2723 1376, fax: 2723 6653: www.hk.super.net/~shrine/contents.htm. **The Russia Experience** (mainly eastbound) 100604.764@compuserve.com ☎ UK 0181 566 8846. http://travel.world.co.uk/russiaexp.

Heart of Asia

● **[1]** Kazakh-China. 6 direct buses/week with $10 'tax', options p143. Year round.

● **[2]** Kyrgyzstan-China. Torugart Pass p163 is more attractive/awkward than [1]. Direct bus from Artux (nr Kashgar) in 98? New, summer Irkestam route?

● **[3]** Dull, 36hrs, sev buses/day, double price ex-Kashgar. Cheaper on 2-3day charabanc. Varied scenery, even longer/less comfortable via Kuqa Mt Rte p267.

● **[4]** Peter Fleming's 1930's dusty desert route. E of Hotan the Silk Route ruins are v ruined, road v rough. Unfavourably high discomfort/interest ratio.

● **[5]** Karakoram Hwy p339. Glorious (esp Hunza). Easy except mid-winter.

● **[6]** Min 2 days if you can get train reservns to Quetta. Bus to Iran border.

● **[7]** Via Amritsar & at least one other Indian city (Varanasi rec). Options p389.

● **[8]** Nepal-Tibet Officially groups only,

April-Oct (land *or* air). You just *might* be allowed to walk the border alone (+30km thro' winter snow drifts), p253.

● **[9/10]** Both v v tough, potentially dangerous, not officially sanctioned, p256

● **[11]** Regular through bus on paved road. Expensive southbound because of 'invisible' permit.

● **[12]** Train attractive. 5 day odyssey via Tibetan villages p226 unforgettable. Ask in Xiahe or Chengdu (Traffic Hotel) how much of the road has been washed away.

● **[13]** Great train ride. Or loop via Dali and Lijiang (quaint old city). p240.

● **[14]** N Laos slow, unpredictable, extremely beautiful esp the Nam Ou river p509/241.

● **[15]** No roads India-SE Asia. Flights incl Calcutta-Bangkok $110 (Indian Air), $120 (Druk Air), $135 (Thai). Ban-Dhaka $108 (Biman) more ex-Dhaka. For c$45 add a Rangoon stopover. Cal-Dhaka $35. Kathmandu-Ban $220, ($312 with Rangoon stopover).

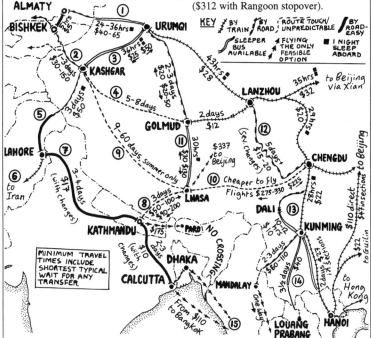

KEY: BY TRAIN / BY ROAD / ROUTE TOUGH/UNPREDICTABLE / BY ROAD-EASY — SLEEPER BUS AVAILABLE — FLYING THE ONLY FEASIBLE OPTION — 1 NIGHT SLEEP ABOARD

MINIMUM TRAVEL TIMES INCLUDE SHORTEST TYPICAL WAIT FOR ANY TRANSFER.

Route	Cheapest ticket*	Operation details	->>	<<-	Notes/ contacts
1 K<->O	335	July - Sept + a few runs in May 10 services/year.	d 16:30 a 07:30	d 11:00 a. 7:30	Or you could hitch fishing boats
2 K<->W		10/year (alternating with the above) plus twice a year to Khomolsk instead.	d. 11:00 a. 14:30	d. 10:30 a. 20:00	☎R-42422-23961 ☎J -11-271-2466 Check carefully.
3 V <-> F/N	350	13 weekly sailings, July - Sept. For 2 weeks to/from Fushiki then two weeks to/from Niigata.	Tu 15:00 arr-Thur 9:00	Fr 16:00 - Su 9:30	Fushiki is near Takaoka. ☎J 3 3475 2843
4 P <-> S	55> <71	Daily, overnight ferry. Tokyo - Pusan rail/ferry combination tickets save about 1000 yen.	d. 18:00 a. 08:30	d. 18:00 a. 08:30	No need to book.
5 P <-> F	a) 55> <71 b) 62> <103	Overnight, 3/week. Irrespective of departure time, you'll arrival at 8:40 am: the boat waits hours offshore for customs to open Daily jetfoil taking only 3 hrs.	Tu, Th, Sun d. 17:40 d. 14:00	M, Wed d. 17:00, Fri d. 19:00 d. 10:00	No student discount. No need to book. Students -20% ☎K 51 465 6111 ☎J-92 281 2315
6 T <-> I	105	Every 5 days each way. NB Arrival times vary substantially - both ports very busy.	d. 18:00 takes 40hrs	d. 14:00 takes 28- 32h	☎Ch 22-319 000 ☎K 2-517-8671
7 W <->I	100	2/week each way, takes 17hrs	Wed, Fri d. 17:00	Tue, Thu d. 17:30	☎ K 2-711 9111 ☎ Ch 896 231 344
8 Q <-> I	100	Weekly boat. Takes approx 21hrs.	Mon d 11:00	Sat d. 17:30	☎ K 2-711 9111 ☎ Ch 532 221152
9 T <-> K/O	153 /172	Weekly boat. Higher price in Feb, Mar, July, Aug and Sept.	Mon, 12:00	Thu, 12:00	☎ J 6 536-6541
10 S <->N	165 /115	Weekly. Cheaper price is from China.	Tue	Thur	☎ J 958 21 0050
11. a) S <-> O/ K	172	Certain Tues from K/O, some Fridays from Osaka South port.	Takes approx 51hrs		☎ J 6 232 0131
11 b) S <-> Y	250	One Tue and certain Fridays each month from Yokohama.	Takes 4 days.		☎ J 3 5202 5781
12. Naha <-> Keelung	130	3 month: d. Naha Fri 20:00 arr Miyako 06:00 next day (2hrs stop) arr Ishigaki 13:30 (stays 4½ hrs), arr Keelung 07:00. PLUS 1/month: Fri, d. Naha 18:00, ar Keelung 18:30 next day (skips Miyako, only 2 hrs in Ishigaki) Keelung to Naha returns non-stop d. 16:00 Sun, arr 14:00 Mon.			☎ J 98 8682191
Naha <-> Kao-shun	150	2/Mondays/month: d. Naha 20:00 arr Miyako 06:00 next day (2hrs stop) arr Ishigaki 13:30 (2½ hrs stop), ar Kaoshun 09:00 d. Kaoshun 16:00 Wed, arr Ishigaki 13:00 d 16:00, arr Miyako 21:30 d 22:30, arr Naha 09:00 Fri.			☎ J 098 868 2191

*Prices in US$ (calculated at $1=120yen=8.2yuan) are for the cheapest berths available. A further student discount is often possible, typically 10 or 20% with ISIC card. Note that tickets sold in Japan are usually more expensive than tickets *to* Japan bought in Korea or China.

International telephone codes ☎ J (Japan) 81, ☎ K (S Korea) 82, ☎ R (Russia) 7, ☎ Ch (China) 86

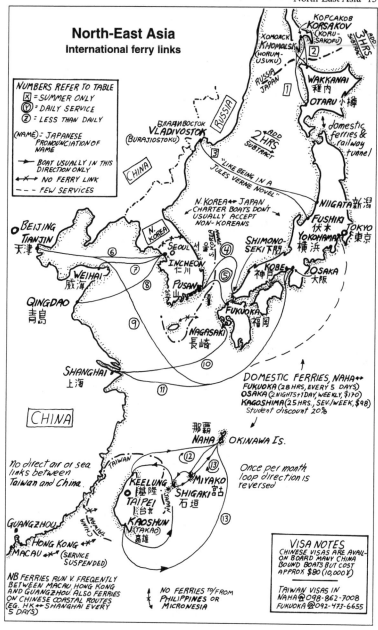

North-East Asia
International ferry links

NUMBERS REFER TO TABLE
- ⓧ = SUMMER ONLY
- ① = DAILY SERVICE
- ② = LESS THAN DAILY

(NAME) = JAPANESE PRONOUNCIATION OF NAME

→ BOAT USUALLY IN THIS DIRECTION ONLY

×→× NO FERRY LINK

– – – FEW SERVICES

KOPCAKOB
KORSAKOV (KORU-SAKOFU)
ХОМОЯСК
KHOMOLSK (HORUM-USUKU)

ADD 3 HRS. SUBTRACT

RUSSIA / JAPAN

WAKKANAI 稚内
OTARU 小樽

domestic ferries & railway tunnel

ВЛАДИВОСТОК
VLADIVOSTOK (BURAJIOSTOKU)

RUSSIA

CHINA

ADD 2 HRS SUBTRACT

"LIKE BEING IN A JULES VERNE NOVEL"

N. KOREA ↔ JAPAN CHARTER BOATS DON'T USUALLY ACCEPT NON-KOREANS

NIIGATA 新潟
FUSHIKI 伏木
YOKOHAMA 横浜
TOKYO 東京

BEIJING
TIANJIN 天津

N. KOREA

S.KOREA

SEOUL 서울
INCHEON 仁川
PUSAN 부산

SHIMONOSEKI 下関
KOBE 神戸
OSAKA 大阪

⑥ ⑦ ⑧ ⑨

WEIHAI 威海
QINGDAO 青島

FUKUOKA 福岡

NAGASAKI 長崎

⑩

SHANGHAI 上海

⑪

CHINA

DOMESTIC FERRIES, NAHA ↔
FUKUOKA (28 HRS, EVERY 5 DAYS)
OSAKA (2 NIGHTS + 1 DAY, WEEKLY, $170)
KAGOSHIMA (25 HRS., SEV./WEEK, $98)
Student discount 20%

那覇
NAHA OKINAWA IS.

No direct air or sea links between Taiwan and China.

TAIWAN

⑫ ⑬

Once per month loop direction is reversed

KEELUNG 基隆
TAIPEI 台北
MIYAKO 宮古
SHIGAKI 石垣

KAOSHUN (TAKAO) 高雄

⑬

GUANGZHOU
HONG KONG
MACAU ×→× (SERVICE SUSPENDED)

NB FERRIES RUN V. FREQUENTLY BETWEEN MACAU, HONG KONG AND GUANGZHOU ALSO FERRIES ON CHINESE COASTAL ROUTES (EG. HK ↔ SHANGHAI EVERY 5 DAYS)

NO FERRIES TO/FROM PHILIPPINES OR MICRONESIA

VISA NOTES
CHINESE VISAS ARE AVAILABLE ON BOARD MANY CHINA BOUND BOATS BUT COST APPROX $80 (10,000¥)

TAIWAN VISAS IN
NAHA ☎ 098-862-7008
FUKUOKA ☎ 092-473-6655

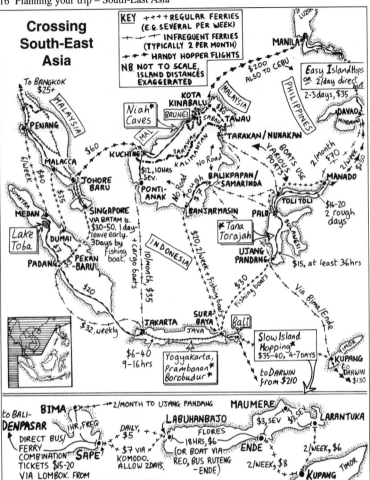

Crossing South-East Asia

KEY
+ + + + REGULAR FERRIES (E.G. SEVERAL PER WEEK)
— + — + — INFREQUENT FERRIES (TYPICALLY 2 PER MONTH)
> + > + > HANDY HOPPER FLIGHTS
N.B. NOT TO SCALE, ISLAND DISTANCES EXAGGERATED

LUZON
MANILA
$200 ALSO TO CEBU
Easy Island Hops or 2/day direct bus 2-3days, $35
PHILIPPINES
DAVAO MINDANAO

KOTA KINABALU
Niah Caves
BRUNEI
MALAYSIA
SABAH TAWAU
TARAKAN/NUNAKAN
BOATS USE VARIOUS PORTS
2/month $70
2/week
MANADO

To Bangkok $25+
MALAYSIA
PENANG
$60
KUCHING
MAL
SARAWAK
KALIMANTAN No Road
$12, 10HRS Sev.
No Road
rough
BALIKPAPAN/ SAMARINDA
TOLI TOLI
$16-20 2 rough days

MALACCA
6/week $40
JOHORE BARU
$35
PONTI-ANAK
BANJARMASIN
PALU
SULAWESI

SINGAPORE VIA BATAM Is. $30-50. 1 day-leave early. 3Days by fishing boat.
+ cargo boats $35
Tana Torajah
UJANG PANDANG
$15, at least 36HRS

MEDAN
Lake Toba
DUMAI
PEKAN-BARU
PADANG
SUMATRA
$20
INDONESIA
10/month $35
$30 Fishing boats
$30 2/week + fishing boat
Via Bima/Ende

$32, weekly
JAKARTA
SURA-BAYA
JAVA
Bali
$6-40 9-16hrs
Yogyakarta, Prambanan, Borobudur
Slow Island Hopping $35-40, 4-7 DAYS
to DARWIN from $210
TIMOR
KUPANG to DARWIN $130

---

to BALI-DENPASAR
BIMA
1HR, FREQ
2/MONTH TO UJANG PANDANG
DAILY, $5
$7 VIA KOMODO. ALLOW 2DAYS.
LABUHANBAJO
FLORES
18HRS, $6 (OR BOAT VIA REO, BUS RUTENG-ENDE)
ENDE
2/WEEK, $8
MAUMERE
$3, SEV
$3, SEV
LARANTUKA
2/WEEK, $6
KUPANG
TIMOR

DIRECT BUS/FERRY COMBINATION TICKETS $15-20 VIA LOMBOK. FROM 9HRS IF LUCKY WITH FERRY CONNECTIONS.
SAPE

Only the most major through routes are shown here. Road transport is easy on the busy Singapore-Penang-Bangkok route but you'll save a little money crossing borders on foot or on short local bus trips. This is also true for the Sing-Malaysia flights – cross the short causeway (bus every 10 mins, $1) to Johore Baru for much cheaper 'internal' fares (eg to Kuching). Internal flights are reasonably priced. Around most of Kalimantan travel is still impossible but the Pontiniak-Kuching road is now open and on the visa waiver scheme. Between Tawau and Tarakan you'll still need a full Indonesian visa (available in K Kinabalu), possibly permits (check current situation with other travellers). Tarakan to Samarinda you may have to do in hops or even via Sulawesi. Crossing N Borneo, Aussies and Kiwis need Bruneian visas unless flying over Brunei (eg Miri-Lauban $35).

With all but one of Burma's border crossings closed to foreigners, the only viable overland routes between China and Thailand pass are: **a) Through Boten (Laos)** The fastest way is via Pakbeng/Chiang Khong, though it's worth an extra day to come down the Nam Ou river to lovely Louang Prabang. (You can get 1 month Lao tourist visas in Bangkok, Chiang Khong (fast), Nong Khai). The cheapest place to apply is Rangoon. Consuls in Kunming, Hanoi or Danang (Viet) give only 5 day transits which you can overstay ($5/day) but not extend. **b) Across Vietnam and through Lao Bao (Laos)** Vietnamese visas *not* available in Kunming or Nanning. Possible in Guangzhou or HK.
c) Through Vietnam and Cambodia (less reliable route). With Camb-Thai border unsafe you'll then need to take the dodgy boat service via Trat (see p496) or cut through Laos from Phnom Penh to Pakxe: beware border insecure. Flying increases your options. Handy hops indicated here.

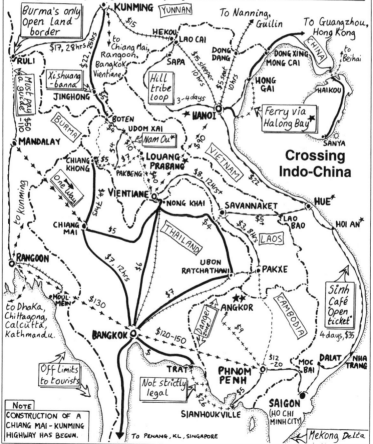

KEY
- BORDER.
- ×·× BY BOAT.
- +++ BEST BY TRAIN.
- ━━ EASY, FREQ BUS/TRAIN
- ─── BY ROAD, INFREQ.
- ---- DIFFICULT/DANGEROUS
- FLYING IS THE ONLY SENSIBLE OPTION.

Burma's only open land border

$17, 28hrs $22 26hrs

to Chiang Mai, Rangoon, Bangkok, Vientiane

RULI

Must pay a guide $50-110

Xishuang-banna

JINGHONG

To Nanning, Guilin

KUNMING   YUNNAN

$15

HEKOU

LAO CAI

SAPA

DONG DANG

$15 sleeper 10hrs

$5 seat 10hrs

Hill tribe loop 3-4days

To Guangzhou, Hong Kong

DONG XING MONG CAI

CHINA

to Beihai

HONG GAI

HAIKOU

HANOI

Ferry via Halong Bay

SANYA

BOTEN

UDOM XAI

Nam Ou*

BURMA

MANDALAY

CHIANG KHONG

$5

$7

LOUANG PRABANG

PAKBENG

VIETNAM

$22

$8, 12hrs*

Crossing Indo-China

One Way

VIENTIANE

NONG KHAI

SAVANNAKET

HUE*

to kunming

CHIANG MAI

$5

THAILAND

$4

$5

LAO BAO

HOI AN*

LAOS

$3, 8hrs

RANGOON

$7, 12hrs

UBON RATCHATHANI

PAKXE

Sinh Café 'open ticket'

4days, $35

MOULMEIN

$130

$7

ANGKOR ★★

Danger

CAMBODIA

to Dhaka, Chittagong, Calcutta, Kathmandu.

BANGKOK

$120-150

$9

$12 -20

MOC BAI

DALAT

NHA TRANG

Off limits to tourists

TRAT

Not strictly legal

PHNOM PENH

SAIGON (HO CHI MINH CITY)

NOTE
CONSTRUCTION OF A CHIANG MAI - KUNMING HIGHWAY HAS BEGUN.

SIANHOUKVILLE

To PENANG, KL, SINGAPORE

Mekong Delta

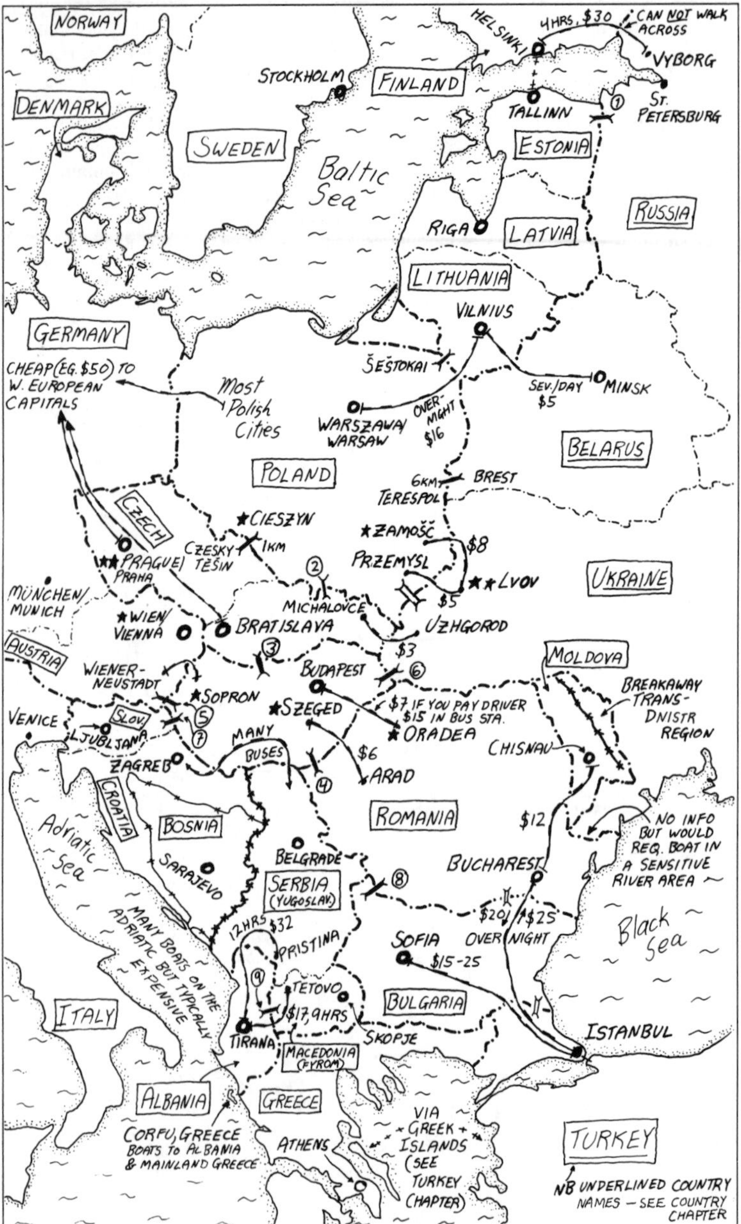
NORWAY
HELSINKI
4 HRS, $30
CAN NOT WALK ACROSS
VYBORG
STOCKHOLM
FINLAND
DENMARK
TALLINN
ST. PETERSBURG
SWEDEN
ESTONIA
Baltic Sea
RUSSIA
RIGA
LATVIA
LITHUANIA
VILNIUS
GERMANY
ŠEŠTOKAI
SEV./DAY $5
MINSK
CHEAP (EG. $50) TO W. EUROPEAN CAPITALS
Most Polish Cities
WARSZAWA/WARSAW
OVER-NIGHT $16
BELARUS
POLAND
6KM
BREST
TERESPOL
CZECH
CIESZYN
ZAMOŠĆ
CZESKY TĚŠIN
1KM
$8
PRAGUE/PRAHA
PRZEMYSL
LVOV
UKRAINE
MÜNCHEN/MUNICH
MICHALOVCE
$5
WIEN/VIENNA
BRATISLAVA
UZHGOROD
AUSTRIA
$3
MOLDOVA
WIENER-NEUSTADT
BUDAPEST
BREAKAWAY TRANS-DNISTR REGION
SOPRON
$7 IF YOU PAY DRIVER $15 IN BUS STA.
VENICE
SLOV.
SZEGED
ORADEA
LJUBLJANA
MANY BUSES
CHISNAU
ZAGREB
$6
ARAD
CROATIA
ROMANIA
$12
NO INFO BUT WOULD REQ. BOAT IN A SENSITIVE RIVER AREA
Adriatic Sea
BOSNIA
BELGRADE
BUCHAREST
SARAJEVO
SERBIA (YUGOSLAV.)
$20
$25
OVER NIGHT
MANY BOATS ON THE ADRIATIC BUT TYPICALLY EXPENSIVE
12 HRS $32
PRISTINA
Black Sea
SOFIA
$15-25
TETOVO
BULGARIA
ITALY
$17, 9 HRS
TIRANA
SKOPJE
ISTANBUL
MACEDONIA (FYROM)
ALBANIA
GREECE
VIA GREEK ISLANDS (SEE TURKEY CHAPTER)
CORFU, GREECE BOATS TO ALBANIA & MAINLAND GREECE
ATHENS
TURKEY
NB UNDERLINED COUNTRY NAMES – SEE COUNTRY CHAPTER

Getting to/from Europe

Domestic travel in Eastern Europe is very reasonable but prices soar when crossing a border. To penny pinch simply walk across. A selection of easy to walk borders and good value bus hops are depicted. We'd welcome additional suggestions (eg. for Romania-Serbia).

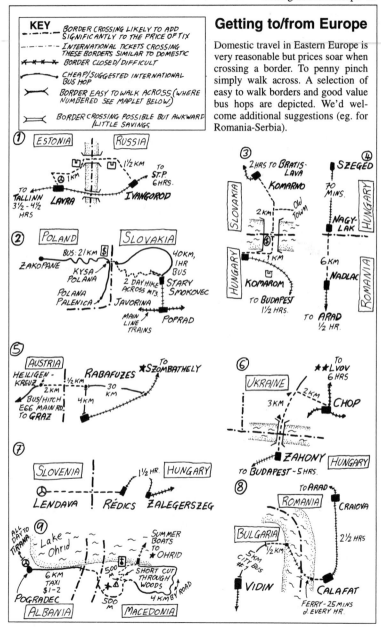

KEY
- ⌐⌐⌐ BORDER CROSSING LIKELY TO ADD SIGNIFICANTLY TO THE PRICE OF TIX
- ----- INTERNATIONAL TICKETS CROSSING THESE BORDERS SIMILAR TO DOMESTIC
- ✖✖✖ BORDER CLOSED/DIFFICULT
- BORDER EASY TO WALK ACROSS (WHERE NUMBERED SEE MAPLET BELOW)
- CHEAP/SUGGESTED INTERNATIONAL BUS HOP
- ✕ BORDER CROSSING POSSIBLE BUT AWKWARD /LITTLE SAVINGS

① ESTONIA — RUSSIA
1 KM — 1½ KM — TO ST.P. 6 HRS.
TO TALLINN 3½ - 4½ HRS — LAVRA — IVANGOROD

② POLAND — SLOVAKIA
BUS: 21 KM $ — ZAKOPANE — KYSA POLANA — POLANA PALENICA — JAVORINA — 2 DAY HIKE ACROSS MTS. — 40 KM, 1 HR BUS — STARY SMOKOVEC — POPRAD — MAIN LINE TRAINS

③ SLOVAKIA — HUNGARY
2 HRS TO BRATISLAVA — KOMARNO — Old Town — 2 KM — 1 KM — KOMAROM — TO BUDAPEST 1½ HRS.

④ SZEGED — HUNGARY — ROMANIA
70 MINS. — NAGYLAK — 6 KM — NADLAC — TO ARAD ½ HR.

⑤ AUSTRIA
HEILIGEN-KREUZ — ½ KM — 2 KM — BUS/HITCH E66 MAIN RD. TO GRAZ — RABAFUZES — 30 KM — 4 KM — ★ TO SZOMBATHELY

⑥ UKRAINE
TO ★★ LVOV 6 HRS — 2 KM — 3 KM — CHOP — ZAHONY — HUNGARY — TO BUDAPEST - 5 HRS.

⑦ SLOVENIA — HUNGARY
LENDAVA — RÉDICS — 1½ HR. — ZALEGERSZEG

⑧ BULGARIA — ROMANIA
TO ARAD — CRAIOVA — 2½ HRS — VIDIN — 5 KM CITY BUS — ½ KM — CALAFAT — FERRY - 25 MINS ∂. EVERY HR.

⑨ ALL DAY TO TIRANA — ~ Lake ~ Ohrid ~ — SUMMER BOATS TO ★ OHRID — 500 — SHORT CUT THROUGH WOODS — 4 KM BY ROAD — 6 KM TAXI $1-2 — 500 M — POGRADEC — ALBANIA — MACEDONIA

Trans-Pacific

Fiji [Fj] would be our choice if allowed just one free trans-Pacific stopover. It's big enough to absorb the tourists, has beaches, backpacker prices, is brilliantly friendly & multicultural and its many islands are close enough to allow cheap island hopping. The other easy stopover choices are French Polynesia [FP] (Tahiti et al) and Hawaii [HI]: beautiful islands but further apart, more Westernised and vastly more expensive than Fiji. Rarotonga [CI] is mid-priced but small, isolated and relatively dull.

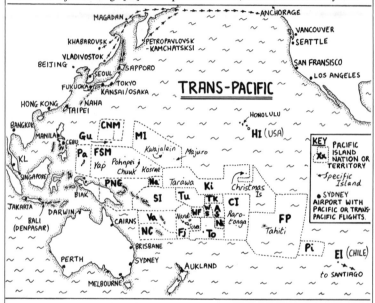

General information (Onward tickets but not visas required except as below)
● Visas required by most for: Kiribati [Ki], PNG, Nauru [Na] (except transfers)
● French island groups New Caledonia [NC], Wallis Futuna [WF], FP are particularly expensive and Australians need visas. French spoken.
● US$ zone (Guam [Gu], Palau [Pa], N. Marianas [CNM], Fed. Micronesia [FSM], Marshall Is [MI], US Samoa [AS] and [HI]). US visa rules apply but not all flights qualify you for the US visa waiver: check. No rock bottom accommodation.
● Camping: possible with permission but not in the Cook Is [CI] or Chuuk [FSM].
● Best guidebooks: David Stanley's *S. Pacific* & *Micronesia* handbooks (Moon).
● Malaria risk: Vanuatu [Va], severe in PNG, Soloman Islands [SI]. Others: none.
● Best landscapes: Rock Islands [Pa], Vava'u [To], Moorea/Bora Bora [FC], Pago Pago harbour viewed from ropeway [AS], hikes in PNG, Niue cliffs & coves [Ni].
● Enigmatic stones: The great 'Moai', Easter Is [EI]; Pohnpei's Nan Madol [FSM].
● Most interesting cultures: Micronesian: Yap [FSM]; Polynesian: Western Samoa [WS], Tonga [To], Kadavu [Fj]; Melanesian: PNG (tribe and language varies valley to valley); Cargo Cults: Tanna [Va]; Indian (with firewalking): Fj; backpacker Fj.
● Paradise resorts: Aitutaki [CI], Bora Bora [FC]

Cost estimates for route sections

We assume travel by cheapest available sleeper class on trains: unreserved seats could save around 30%. Note that all prices are subject to change and that train fares in the ex USSR, variable at the best of times, are set to rise steeply as we go to press. Prices in SE Asia may have fallen slightly. Only the route sections marked ↔ represent an unbroken journey so the cost of accommodation en route must usually be added. Transit visas can also add substantially to the cost and hassle of some routes.

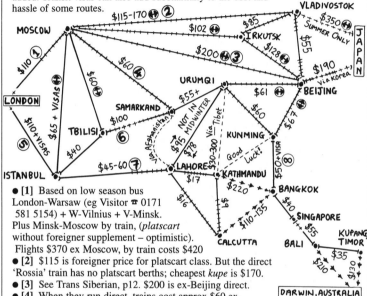

● **[1]** Based on low season bus London-Warsaw (eg Visitor ☎ 0171 581 5154) + W-Vilnius + V-Minsk. Plus Minsk-Moscow by train, (*platscart* without foreigner supplement – optimistic). Flights $370 ex Moscow, by train costs $420

● **[2]** $115 is foreigner price for platscart class. But the direct 'Rossia' train has no platscart berths; cheapest *kupe* is $170.

● **[3]** See Trans Siberian, p12. $200 is ex-Beijing direct.

● **[4]** When they run direct, trains cost approx $60 ex-Samarkand (depending on exchange rate), about $100 ex Moscow. By taking the train first from Samarkand to Chardzhou, Turkmenistan, and buying a ticket from there to Moscow, it was possible in 1996 to do the whole trip for $25 in black market manats (plus a $10 bribe to prevent the train from being 'full'). Be prepared to change trains in Volgagrad or suffer the Beineu Hell Ride (see p11). It's easier to travel via Tashkent, $70+.

● **[5]** Assumes off season buses between London and Bratislava (Slovakia) followed by border hopping. Romanian and Bulgarian transit visas will add $45+ to the cost making flying a sensible option. Normally, fares start at $165 but in late October you can get o/w $80 end-of-season charter bargains **to** Dalaman. Check teletext.

● **[6]** $70 if you pay $45/5th class on the Caspian Ferry. $100 if you're stuck paying the full $75 foreigner price for a cabin. Either figure assumes that you'll get local fares on trains and that you use the Turkmen and Uzbek black markets.

● **[7]** Cheapest using Istanbul-Tehran direct bus but worth a bit extra to stop en route.

● **[8]** Assumes via Namtha/Ban HouayXay, N Laos. But much nicer to go instead via lovely Louang Prabang: $85 with LP-Vientiane flight. Either route will take several days. Direct Kunming-Bangkok flights are typically discounted from $195 to $150. Double that if you stop over in Rangoon en route. The Lao transit visa adds $20+.

Seventeen favourites – Places we'd most like to go back to

● **1 Western Ukraine** Brimming with history. Charmingly untouristed with lots of architectural delights to discover.

● **2 Georgia, N Armenia and NE Turkey** Fierce and friendly, ruggedly beautiful, and packed with forgotten castle towers, ancient churches and mountain hikes. Don't go yet if you want any sort of comfort.

● **3 Iran** Snubbed thanks to its politics, Iran is one of the world's most hospitable places. Incredible scenic variety.

● **4 Mountainous Kyrgyzstan** The Switz-erland of the ex-USSR, without the high prices or the tourists. Few facilities. Few Uzbekistan style police hassles.

● **5 The Xinjiang mountains** Bizarre counterpoint of desert, grasslands, forests and alpine peaks and the surprise of finding Turkic culture alive within China.

● **6 Karakoram Area (N. Pakistan) and Ladakh (India)**. Once forbidden mountain kingdoms set amongst the world's most exaggeratedly sharpened peaks.

● **7 Nepal** Well set up for tourists who love Nepal's trekking and rafting. Kathmandu offers a wonderful variety of cheap accommodation and good food.

● **8 Tibet** A bleak, unforgettable world, defiant in the face of Chinese occupation.

● **9 Sri Lanka** Despite infuriating touts, Sri Lanka's sheer variety: beaches, history, wildlife, are most appealing. Cheap, healthy food and visa-free entry.

● **10 Yunnan** Mountains around Dali are idyllic but Xishuangbanna's over-rated.

● **11 N Laos and NW Vietnam** Great hill tribe exploration area. Lao river trips (eg the Nam Ou) well worth it.

● **12 Yangshuo** A cosy town of great cheap restaurants and hostels tucked into stunning 'willow pattern' scenery.

● **13 Japan** Temples, castles, spirit forests, naked mud baths; poisonous fish as a delicacy...Japan, beneath the neon-concrete veneer is one bizarre country.

● **14 Central Sulewesi** Rice terraces, Torajan ship houses, isolated hikes.

● **15 Eastern Indonesia** Smorgasbord of cultures, beautiful volcanoes and beaches, all ranges of price and service possible. Less relaxing than Thailand but more scope for adventure.

● **XX Burma** The ancient Buddhist culture would put Burma at the top of everyone's list of favourites if it were not for the repressive ruling military dictatorship.

● **YY India** You'll love it and hate it. India has absolutely everything; you'll get sensual and cultural overload.

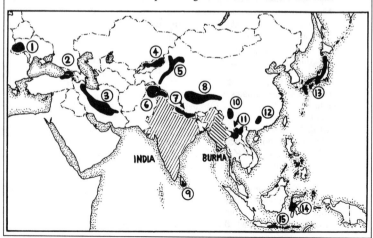

WEST ASIA

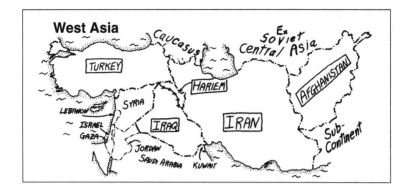

Turkey

Welcome to Europe! Or, perhaps that should be: Welcome to Asia! Coming from east or west, Turkey gives the feeling of arriving in a new continent. Istanbul, in particular, straddles time and continents with unparalleled panache. Few cities can offer such raw history or such evocative clashes of the ancient and modern, of bazaar and boutique. The reason for Turkey's recent tourist popularity is obvious. It has everything from the stunning alpine meadows of the Kaçkar Mountains, to some of Asia's better beaches, ancient cities and archaeological gems, Pamukkale's calcified cascade pools and Cappadocia's unique fairy chimneys. It is all too easy to get soured: by the touts that try to bundle you off to hotels, by the carpet salesmen who lure you in for free tea

❏ **W&M's country ratings – Turkey**
● **Expense $$$** Oscillates with exchange rate.
● **Value for money ✔✔✔** Transport and food are excellent value, hotel singles cost from $2, $5 is more common.
● **Getting around ✔✔✔✔✔** Very extensive and efficient bus system. Travel in the east is slightly more difficult due to the sparser population and security checks.
● **English spoken ✔✔✔** Some English speakers can be found in cities and tourist areas but few in rural areas. German is also useful as many Turks have worked there.
● **Woman alone ✔✔** It's important to be on your guard though sexist attitudes are slowly improving as Turkish women assert themselves. Istanbul is very Western but the east is much more conservative.
● **For vegetarians ✔✔✔** Buffets are a godsend; get used to lots of çorba.

and guilt trips, and by the acne of concrete hotel developments that mar much of the once pristine coastline. Don't be put off. With a little patience, gorgeous unspoiled beaches can still be found in quiet coves. We found many carpet salesmen happy to forget business and give tea for friendship (and English practice). And fortunately the touts are limited to the most obvious tourist hubs (Selçuk and Denizli seem the worst) and are easy to escape.

One travel worry in Turkey is security in south east Anatolia. (Anatolia is the general term for the Asian section of Turkey, *Anadolu* in Turkish.) The PKK (Kurdish Workers' Party) has been leading a sometimes violent campaign for Kurdish independence in their traditional homeland (divided between Iran, Iraq and Turkey). There have been bomb attacks but reports of kidnappings are exaggerated. One 'kidnapped' backpacker quietly admitted later that he'd gone hiking voluntarily with his supposed captors and that the kidnap tale had been something of an anti-PKK propaganda offensive. At the time of writing, however, a major Turkish military operation is in full swing attacking PKK bases across the border in Iraq/Hariem. This makes present dangers hard to assess. Hiking around Mt Ararat remains officially discouraged, and locals in Istanbul portray towns such as Tunceli, Batman and Diyabarbakir as impossibly dangerous. On the spot, however, the area feels much less tense than reports suggest. Be prepared for traffic delays. Along the south-east's most sensitive roads one can see troops across the hill tops and there are regular security checks. Fortunately, soldiers seem friendly towards tourists. One commander delayed

---

❏ Geo-political information – Turkey

Population: 63.5 million – a further 1.3m are working abroad, half in Germany.

Area: 779,500 sq km (3% of this is in Europe).

Capital: Ankara (2.6 million).

Other major cities: Istanbul (6.6m), Izmir (1.8m), Adana (900,000), Bursa (800,000); Gaziantep (600,000); Konya (500,000), Mersin, Kayseri, Eskisehir, Diyarbakir, Antalya (400,000), Samsun, Malatya, Sanliurfa (300,000); Erzerum, Izmit (250,000).

GNP per capita: $2450 (1994).

Currency history: Lira/US$1 Feb 1998: L213,000, Oct 1997: L172,000, July 1996: L83,000, Dec 1995: L61,000, Dec 1994: L39,000, Dec 1993: L15,000.

Major exports/economy: Self sufficient in most foodstuffs. Chrome, cotton, tobacco, nuts and fruit are exported. Turkey has a growing manufacturing base.

Ethnic mix: Turks (85%), Kurds (12%).

Official language: Turkish (90%). Kurdish spoken by 7%. Other Caucasian languages in the north east including 40,000 Georgian speakers and 30,000 Laz.

Religious mix: Islam (99%).

Landmarks of national history: **1453**: Constantinople (now Istanbul) fell to the Ottoman Turks (it was previously the hub of the Byzantine – East Roman empire). **1520-66**: The Ottoman empire reached its peak under Suleyman the Magnificent. **1878**: The empire lost Bulgaria, Serbia and Romania. **1881-2**: Loss of North Africa. **1908**: Young Turks seized power from Sultan. **1923**: Republic declared under Ataturk. **1952**: Joined NATO.

Leaders: President Suleiman Demirel. Prime Minister Mesut Yilmaz.

Pressing political issues: Kurdish autonomy, governing coalition unstable.

our entire bus so he could invite us for tea in the barracks and show off speaking English in front of his troops. Another decided to 'protect' our bus with a tank escort. This slowed us down and surely made us a much more visible potential target. But it's the thought that counts. And delays are even worse when vehicles are grouped into convoys for such military escorts (5hrs+).

It is worth remembering that the vast majority of Kurds are not terrorists – indeed they are extremely charming and hospitable people. If polls are to be trusted, most Turkish Kurds consider themselves Turkish (though not Turks) and do not particularly want independence. On the other hand most *do* want a liberalisation of rules restricting cultural freedom (such as the right to have school classes taught in Kurdish). Recent movement towards such liberalisation is likely to calm the situation in the coming years.

❏ Essential information for travellers – Turkey

- **Visa** Either not required or available on arrival (with a few exceptions).
- **Currency** Turkish Lira. $1=L213,000.
- **Time zone** 2 hours ahead of GMT (same as Bulgaria, Syria; 1½hrs behind Iran; 1hr behind Moscow and Armenia, 3hrs behind Georgia in winter (2hrs in summer).
- **Religious tone** A Western oriented Islamic country with secular institutions.
- **Health factors** Tap water is not recommended.
- **Special dangers** Tensions are still running high in the south east. The dangers are probably overstated but expect to cause suspicion if you're in this area.
- **Social conventions** Show respect to a man with the term *bey* (pronounced 'bay'). For a woman use *hanim* (pronounced 'hah-num'). Shaking hands is common between men but less common between a man and woman.
- **Typical traveller destinations** Istanbul, Ephesus, Pamukkale, Fethiye, Bodrum, Marmaris and the Aegean coast.
- **Highlights** Cappadocia, Istanbul, Mt Nimrud, Kaçkar Mountains (north west), the beach and Chimera at Olympos, 'undiscovered' beach coves.
- **When to go** The Aegean and Mediterranean coasts are temperate year round, averaging around 10°C in January and 25°C in August. Istanbul and the Black Sea coast (where it rains frequently) are about 5°C cooler. Inland areas (ie Ankara and the east) often freeze over during the winter and remain cold until around April.

  The more popular beaches are crammed with package tourists from mid-May till September. October and April are still pleasant and much quieter. Summer gets sizzling hot in the centre of Anatolia but it is the only time to trek in the higher peaks and passes without snow. Since PKK activity has given the south east a bad reputation, you don't have to worry about going during the high season – there isn't one.
- **Pulse of the country** Taksim and Örtaköy (in Istanbul) for modern youth culture, Safranbolu bathhouse for 'real' Turkey, Diyabarkir for a Kurdish pulse.
- **Key tips** The cheapest way to cross Europe is by specially discounted charter flights between Turkey and London.

  Bring enough of your home currency to pay for the entry tax. British passport holders, in particular, have been turned away at certain borders for not having the £10 fee in sterling.
- **Festivals** The mid-December Mevlana festival in Konya with its whirling dervish displays is particularly worth a visit.

Turkey
Geographical areas

SEA OF MARMARA AREA
DENSELY POPULATED AND INDUSTRIAL W/ SCATTERED SIGHTS

BLACK SEA COAST
RAINY COAST WITH STONE BEACHES. INLAND, THE HEAVILY FORESTED HILLS HIDE ATMOSPHERIC VILLAGES.

THE EAST
REMOTE FORTS. GRASSLANDS & STEPPE. SPARSELY POPULATED. MORE MUSLIM INFLUENCE THAN WEST TURKEY.

NORTH AEGEAN
FEWER TOURISTS. SOME NICE SUMMER BEACHES BUT CHILLY IN WINTER.

Kurdish Area
HEAVY ARMY & POLICE PRESENCE BUT TRAVEL IS STILL POSSIBLE.

TOURIST COAST
MANY ONCE LOVELY BEACHES MARRED BY EXTENSIVE DEVELOPMENT. GREEK RUINS.

MEDITERRANEAN COAST - MOSTLY ROCKY WITH SOME BEACHES BACKED BY MOUNTAINS. CASTLES.

CENTRAL TURKEY
DRY WITH LARGE RESEVOIRS IN THE SOUTH. SCATTERED SIGHTS.

GOOD AREAS FOR

RANDOM EXPLORATION Ⓐ ISTANBUL AND THE TOWNS & OLD FORTS ALONG THE BOSPHOROUS.

Ⓑ THE BEACHES & RUINS BETWEEN EPHESUS AND YALIKAVAK.

Ⓒ THE COAST & INLAND FORESTS BETWEEN OLUDENIZ AND OLYMPUS.

Ⓓ CAPPADOCIA - CAVE CITIES & FAIRY CHIMNEYS.

Ⓔ THE GEORGIA BORDER AREA BETWEEN KARS AND ARTVIN. HIKES IN KAÇKAR MTNS (NEED TENT)

PRACTICAL INFORMATION
Visas and formalities

● **Visa strategy** Many Western nationalities can enter Turkey for a three month stay visa free. US citizens can get a three month visa ($20) at most embassies in 24 hours (though the consul in Tashkent will only give one for two weeks). Visas are available on arrival, but when arriving from CIS nations it pays to get one in advance.

Many nationalities who don't need visas must still pay a 'tourist fee' on entry. The amount depends on their nationality – British: £10, Irish: £5, Austrian: AS150, Italian: US$5. Russians, most east Europeans, Spanish and Portuguese have to pay US$10. As of 1997 Belgians will also have to pay and the rules for other European nationalities may change too, so check in advance.

The British and Irish are expected to pay their tourist fee in pounds: certain customs officials, notably at the Turkish-Bulgarian border, have turned back travellers rather than accept other than the specified currency. Even where other currencies are accepted you'll get a poor exchange rate.

Though not explicitly stated on the stamp in one's passport, the tourist fee seems to be good for multiple entries (within the period of validity).

Money

ATMs are remarkably widespread: even in the remoter small towns you'll be able to take money from your bank account in Turkish Lira if you have a cash card on the Cirrus system. There is a 24-hour ATM outside the Istanbul train station but not at the bus station.

Cashing any major currency is easy in western Turkey. In the east stick to US dollars and the German mark. Travellers' cheques often get a lower rate than cash and they are often difficult to change outside major tourist areas (including Ankara). Credit card advances are available commission free in at least a couple of banks in every major city. Most banks advance a minimum of around $100.

Banks are open Monday to Friday 8.30am-12pm and 1.30-5pm. Rates of exchange at Istanbul's money changers in Sultanahmet drop somewhat as soon as the banks have closed for the weekend. They know you have no choice!

The lira devalues at a fairly constant rate, but prices increase in sudden spurts. This means that your costs can vary by as much as 40% depending on your luck with the exchange rate.

Getting there

Istanbul sits at the continental divide and is a logical launching point into Asia or Europe. Turkey is unusually well connected with international ferry and bus services and has three airports to which you can often get bargain charter flights in the season (May-Oct). Below is an overview:

● **Turkey – Greece via the islands** Except Corfu, each of the islands shown has summer services to Turkish ports, and most have at least one daily summer service to Pireus (often overnight, $20+). From September to June services are much more sporadic and some stop altogether (including Kos-Bodrum, and Lesbos-Ayvalik). The hops to/from Turkey are very short (max 90 mins ride) but each route costs $40-45.

Check carefully whether the prices quoted include port taxes – typically $25-30.

● **Boats to Italy** Direct ferries from Izmir to Venice depart Wed (return Sat), $300. It's cheaper to go by land to Albania or Igoumentasia (Greece), and then ferry hop for about $50. The Patras-Brindisi ferry is very overfull in summer. You may wait days.

● **Black Sea ferries** The most reliable service is Trabzon to Sochi, with at least daily service by hydrofoil ($50) and an overnight ferry 3-4 times a week ($35+). Boats to Sukhumi in Abkhazia are liable to cancellation as political pressure grows to

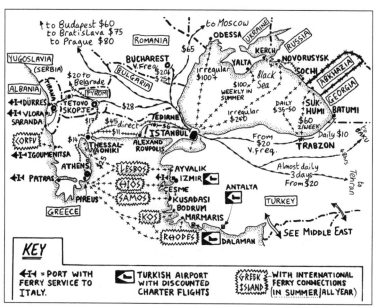

KEY

◄┼◄ = PORT WITH FERRY SERVICE TO ITALY.

TURKISH AIRPORT WITH DISCOUNTED CHARTER FLIGHTS

GREEK ISLAND = WITH INTERNATIONAL FERRY CONNECTIONS (IN SUMMER/ALL YEAR)

enforce a boycott of the self-declared republic. For now you can get Abkhaz visas on arrival for $10.

There are many cruise boats and cargo ships between Istanbul and Ukraine, but these can get expensive and information is hard to find: in Istanbul try calling Blasco (☎ 212 252 4600) or Bumerang Travel (☎ 212 251 7373).

● **Istanbul-Eastern Europe buses** Depending on your nationality the costs of the transit visas can cost as much as the bus fares. Best transport bargains are the buses between Bucharest (main railway station) and Istanbul (Laleli) departing many times a day for as little as $20. Dozens of services to various Russian cities sound cheap but would require a fistfull of transit visas.

● **Other buses** More details on connections to Armenia, Azerbaijan, Georgia and Iran are given in the relevant country chapters. See also the Crossing the Caucasus and Middle East maps.

Transport

● **Bus** The Turkish bus system is one of the best in Asia. Most cities have a single, big, out of town *otogar* (bus station) at which dozens of companies compete for the major routes, and several offer services to even the most remote corners of the country. In choosing a company, check the route you'll be taking and whether you'll have to change buses. Add an hour to any time the company estimates a trip will take.

North to south routes typically take longer than east to west especially in eastern Turkey. A direct service to anywhere from Istanbul, Ankara or Izmir (where competition is greatest) will be significantly cheaper than doing any journey in stages.

The best companies offer plush reclining seats, give free drinks and cakes and don't stop en route to pick up additional passengers. Double deckers have a non-smoking lower deck. On single deckers there is no escape from the fumes. Even the most basic coach offers free mineral water but you may need to ask. Despite the range of services, prices are surprisingly similar so shopping around is worthwhile. Bargaining for a 10-20% discount is almost always possible. Some companies take credit cards.

On an overnight service, the key factor above comfort is how full the service will be. Buses leave (nearly) on time even when they are largely empty so by looking at the passenger manifest when buying a ticket just before departure you can check out the emptiest buses. Varan, Ulusoy, and Metro are among the most reliable and reputable choices. They may also be a little more expensive. But, being well respected they are more likely to be packed full.

All long distance services stop occasionally for meal breaks at restaurants which seem to make their profits from charging to use the toilet.

International buses serving a vast variety of destinations are concentrated in Istanbul. Although you can find services at the *Otogar*, offices for cheaper services to Iran and eastern Europe are clustered round the Lalali tram stop.

Urban buses run frequently. Destination boards mark the area of the city rather than the roads through which a bus passes.

● **Dolmuş** If you want to get to rural areas where inter-city buses don't run or are infrequent, you'll need to locate the dolmuş stand relevant to your destination (towns may have several). A dolmuş may be a van or a minibus and will typically cost about double the bus fare. It will leave whenever the driver feels like going, not necessarily when completely full. Urban bus systems are also supplemented by dolmuş services following the same routes but picking up passengers anywhere along their route.

● **Train** There is a limited rail network and services are much slower and less frequent than buses but they are cheaper. A 50% student discount on the pre-tax price of tickets is given. International tickets are marginally cheaper than in European countries but international buses are cheaper than trains.

Turkey – Bus routes and journey times

This map shows approximate number of hours by bus on Turkey's most useful routes. It assumes the bus is travelling directly between cities (eg. Istanbul-Ankara is typically 6 hours, but some companies go via Bursa, adding 2 hours to the journey). Note that, in the east, roadblocks and detours around areas of PKK activity can add significantly to travel time.

* = ESPECIALLY LIABLE TO LONG DELAYS AT POLICE/ARMY CHECKPOINT

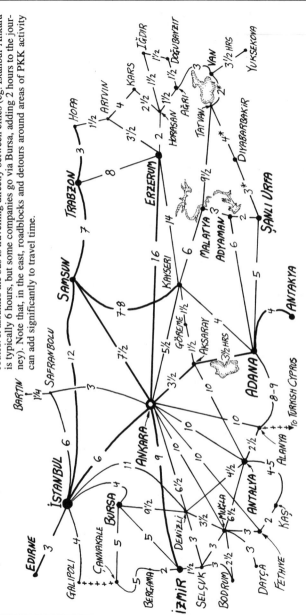

● **Boat** A plethora of ferries criss-cross Istanbul and environs but most other lines you see depicted on the Tourist Bureau's map operate only in the summer. When they run, domestic ferries are good value (as are hops to N Cyprus) and you'll save 50% with a student card. International ferries are subject to very high port taxes.

● **Air** Competition between private airlines (Istanbul Air, Air Alpha, Albatross Air) and the national carrier Turkish Airlines (THY) has driven down internal flight prices. THY also give 25% discounts to ISIC card holders and have an extensive network of flights to central Asia. Many other ex-Soviet airlines ('babyflots') run regular but less reliable, non-scheduled flights into Trabzon and Istanbul from dozens of CIS cities.

● **Hitchhiking** Generally good for men; a smattering of Turkish or German is useful. Women who have hitched alone report problems with attacks that required biting or fighting to escape.

● **Taxis** Taxis are ubiquitous and work on meters – a five minute ride will cost about $1.50, though fares jump by about 50% at night. Some drivers take deliberately circuitous routes.

Accommodation

Show up in practically any city and you'll be able to find inexpensive places to stay clustered in a specific area of town: Sultanahmet in Istanbul, Ulüs in Ankara etc. The cheapest will be a *pansiyon* or small *otel*. The typical cost for a double room in a large city is US$10-12, $5-6 for a single (not all *pansiyons* have single rooms). Costs in smaller towns can be half that but room rates in tourist areas (especially in southern coastal resorts) jump during summer.

Several beaches offer tree house accommodation from $2+. You sleep on mats placed on bare planks built on stilts or in trees which are usually open to the elements: great if it doesn't rain. Some places also rent pre-erected tents and/or camping cabins.

Food and drink

The best way to become familiar with Turkish cuisine is to go to a *bufe* restaurant with a variety of dishes on display. Here you can see what your options are and experiment.

At non-buffet restaurants, the cheapest stomach filler is *çorba*, a lentil soup which

---

❏ **Belly dancing**

It could be a seizure coming on, or it could be an ancient art form. But Turks take their belly dancing seriously. Those whose dance has extra belly, such as Nesrim Topkadi and Sibel Cam, are celebrities in Turkey. The influx of dancers from Egypt, Syria, and (more recently) the former Soviet Union, makes headline news, and is a factor in determining Turkish visa policy – ironic, since belly dancing originated in Egypt. Many Turkish women take at least a few lessons sometime in their lives, if only to condition their body for a healthy child birth, which the dancing is said to aid.

The dance follows certain conventions, but is essentially performed spontaneously. In case the dancer does the most difficult trick, bending backwards while remaining in a belly shaking rhythm, have a coin ready to place on her forehead. If you see belly dancing in a more touristy setting, you should also be forewarned that you might be asked in join in.

Istanbul is the mecca of Turkish belly dancing. Either join the Istanbul By Night tour or go to the Orient Youth Hostel (free shows are held three nights a week); Conrad Hotel, Barbaros Blvd, Besiktas (shows are held daily at 8pm; cover charge is $20+); Keravansaray (Cumhuriyet Caddesi), on the main road to the right of the Hilton Hotel (shows are held daily at 9pm). There are other venues on the same side of the road further down towards Taksim.

is available at any time of day. Like any Turkish meal, it comes with as much fresh French style bread as you can eat. If you're on a budget stick to this free bread rather than ordering rice which will cost almost as much as the meal itself.

Turkish delight, used as an evil temptation by the Witch of Narnia, really is popular in Turkey. Whole stores are devoted to varieties of the pistachioed jellies (*lokum*). *Baklava* (a layered pastry with nuts and syrup), and *kadayif* (shredded wheat with nuts and syrup) are also common desserts.

The word for Western coffee in Turkish is *Neskahve* – a triumph of inter-

---

❑ Meeting the locals

● **The people** Turks are generally friendly and approachable, often they will come up to you. Many speak some English and/or German and are interested in foreigners, especially in the eastern part of the country. To meet college students try heading to Bebek (outside Istanbul) and wander round the campus of Bogazici University, the Harvard of Turkey. Initially, in tourist areas there is a clear financial motive to many 'friendships'.However even salespeople can be genuinely pleased to talk if you make it clear that you've come to chat not to buy.

● **Language** Turkish is closely related to Azeri, Turkmen, Kazakh, Kyrgyz, Uzbek and even the Uigur language of western China. Any Turkish you learn is thus a good preparation for a visit to central Asia.

Some phrases in Turkish:

> Hello – *merhaba*
> How are you? – *nasasim*?
> Reply – *iim*
> Thank you <u>very much</u> – *teshekkur <u>eederum</u>*
> You are welcome – *khezu kinbare*
> Thanks – *saol*
> Reply – *sender saol*
> OK/No problem – *tamam*
> Excuse me – *pardon* (as in French)
> Goodbye – *Allah-ismaladik* (if you're leaving yourself)
>   – *gulé gulé* (if the other leaves)

● **Some conversation starters Music**: Turkish music is distinctive and Turks are proud of it. Popular artists include Mirkelam (his name means 'Words with wisdom') and folk singer Ibrahim Tatlises, a Kurdish Turk. Merely mentioning his name might be enough to start a friendship.

Sport: Soccer teams: Trabzonspor, Galatasaray and Besiktas (the latter two from Istanbul) are good names to throw around in conversation. Weight lifting is also popular.

The Kurdish Question: expect a fascinating and potentially heated debate.

Relations with Greece (*Yunanistan*)

Women: As a Turkish saying goes, the three most important things to a Turkish man are: *At, avrat* and *silah* (a horse, a woman and a gun). The subjects of dating, relationships and sex are more easily discussed here than in any other Muslim country. We didn't try talking to anyone about horses or guns.

Attitude towards eastern Turkey: some Turks view anything east of Ankara as an uncivilised wasteland.

The Greater Turkish nation: Are Yakuts and Mongols actually Turks? Should Turkey support Azerbaijan against Armenia, who are the 'Grey Wolves'? Should army service remain compulsory for men?

national marketing for the Nestlé company even though *Neskahve* is not necessarily always made with Nescafé. Real Turkish coffee, *kahve*, is stronger than Western coffee though it has less caffeine; *kahve* can be served after lunch or dinner (never with a meal) and may be drunk *totli* (sweet), *orta* (medium) or *sade* (without sugar). A coffee house (*kahvehane*) is a typically male affair with backgammon and clouds of tobacco smoke.

Turkish tea, *çay*, is also strong and extremely sweet. *Alma çay* (apple tea) is a tasty alternative and a soothing accompaniment to the *nargile* (hubble bubble water pipe). Also popular is *ayran*, a yogurt, water and salt concoction. Islamic Turkey is unashamed of its Efes beer and older men particularly enjoy the cheap *raki*, a clear aniseed liqueur which, like *pastis* or *ouzo*, magically turns cloudy when mixed with water and produces historic hangovers.

Staying in touch

● **Phone** Frequently malfunctioning public phone booths take either tokens or cards – both are sold by street vendors. Domestic and international calls can be made using either, though feeding in tokens fast enough prevents you hearing much of a long distance call. There are frequently long queues for the card machines.

International country code: +90. Ankara: 312; Antalya: 242; Istanbul: 212 (European Side), 216 (Asian Side); Izmir: 232; Trabzon: 462.

Since 1995, all telephone numbers have been changed to seven digits. If you have an old six figure number a good gamble is to add a 2 (though occasionally it's a 3 or a 4).

● **Mail   American Express offices** that hold customer mail are: **Ankara**: c/o Pamfilya Travel Agency, Keykubat Cad 9/4, Cankaya. **Istanbul**: Turk Ekspress, Cumhuriyet Cad, Hilton International Hotel Lobby (☎ 230 1515). **Fethiye**: c/o Pamfilya Travel, Karagozler Mahallesi, No 31, Kat 1, Fethiye (☎ 614 4474). **Izmir**: c/o Pamfilya Travel Agency, Ataturk Cad,

No 270/1, Alsancak 35220, Izmir (☎ 263 6593). There are also offices in Alanya, Antalya, Kemer, Marmaris and Side.

Activities

● **Swimming** Finding that perfect empty beach is nowhere near as easy as it was 15 years ago. The Black Sea is too rainy and cold for reliable bathing. Most of the west coast's attractive coves and once quaint castle towns have been transformed by package tourists. And the lesser beaches of the north west (eg Çandali) are defaced by the half-built holiday homes of wealthier Turks. The south coast is also heavily touristed. Beautiful Ülü Deniz ('hallo Dennis') is a lagoon in a natural amphitheatre of cliffs, 20 mins drive from Fethiye. It's very commercialised but still has tree houses and the odd çorba restaurant amongst the low-rise tourist disco-diners. It's a great place for scuba diving or paragliding (from mountain crags onto the crowded beach). Nearby are some lovely, lesser known coves which can only be reached by boat. Between Fethiye and Kaş, Patara beach has 20km of sand, much of which remains unexploited.

● **Skiing** Skiing is generally possible from December to April, the peak month being February. Listed below are a few of the better equipped ski slopes. Ski-gear can be rented. Prices are high.

Erciyes (25km south of Kayseri: take a bus via Kayakevi); **Palandöken** (6km out of Erzerum): easy access to some of the country's best skiing; **Saklikent** (north of Antalya): its proximity to the Mediterranean (50km) means that you can ski and swim on the same day. **Uluda** (36km south of Bursa): this is Turkey's biggest ski area but it still gets rather crowded from December to February.

● **Thermal Spas and Turkish baths** Many public bath houses are impressive, ancient marble affairs, light piercing ancient domes and refracting through rising steam. In Istanbul, the best have become tourist attractions in their own right and charge as much as $5 just to wash. In smaller towns, ancient bath-houses (*hamam*) remain functional and cheap. Safranbolu's costs less than $1 and is small but atmospheric. Note that men and women bathe at different times.

There are countless spas in western Anatolia. A free tourist pamphlet introduces 17 of them.

Further information

● **Books** Without a good guide book to add historical context, many of Turkey's classical ruins may seem visually mediocre. Our favourite companion was the *Rough Guide Turkey* though the *Lonely Planet Turkey* is as good as ever. Lonely Planet's *Trekking in Turkey* has some outstanding maps. The *Let's Go Guide to Turkey and Greece* is popular with Eurailers, though we heard many unenthusiastic reviews.

Lords of the Golden Horn by Noel Barber, and *Turkish Sampler: Writings for all Readers* by Muge Galin, provide good background reading. Berlitz/ABC Kitabevi publish an excellent portable dictionary *Ingilizce-Turkce/Turkce-Ingilizce Sozluk*, available in Turkey.

Don't count on buying onward guide books in Turkey: guides to Iran and central Asia are scarce though you might find guides to Europe. Some traveller hangouts have notice boards through which you can arrange swaps and sales, and a few buy and sell books directly (eg the Orient in Istanbul).

● **Tourist information** There are Turkish Tourist offices in Singapore, Tokyo, NY, Washington DC, Sydney and a dozen European cities. All give away excellent country maps, detailed Istanbul and Ankara city plans and colourful brochures on each region. Within Turkey the same freebies are available from an information centre in Sultanahmet (Istanbul) and more patchily at offices in scores of other Turkish cities. They can also be obtained at Istanbul airport and the 'Sarp' Georgian border point. Istanbul has a tourist help line: ☎ 638 2626. Especially helpful for drivers is the Turkish Touring and Auto Association (☎ 231 4631), though their guide book is in Turkish only.

Web sites

Our favourite Turkey site is at www.cs.toronto.edu/~mes/russia/travel.html; it has info on everything Turkish, including skiing, language, humour and an overview of sites.

The Turkish government runs a site at www.turkey.org/turkey/index.htm that gives some useful if overly rosy travel, political and cultural information.

www.turkey.org/turkey/index.htm links to several Turkish travel companies. www.exploreturkey.com has many photos of Turkey, categorised by region; little practical information.

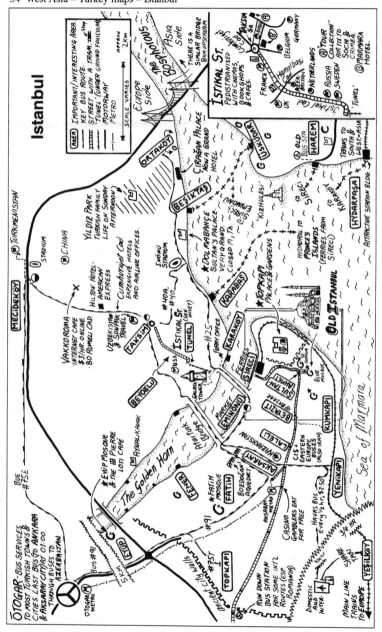

Istanbul

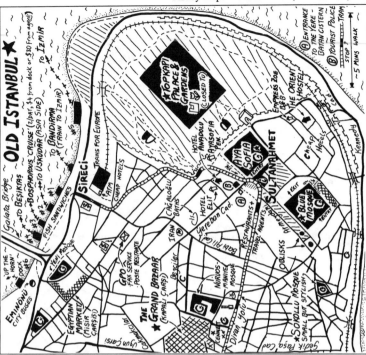

Istanbul – Where Europe meets Asia

Taksim and cosmopolitan Istikal St form the city's modern heart with banks, department stores and stylish jazz clubs. The old city and backpacker centre are in **Sultanahmet**; hostels and some attractive pensions lie in the back streets around the awesome Blue and Aya Sophia mosques. Meet other overlanders at the roof café of the Orient Hostel. Good free maps from the **tourist office** near Sultanahmet tram stop. Travel agents here have flight bargains. Other interesting areas include **Beyazit**: a superb bazaar, hubble-bubble tea houses and an ancient university; **Fener:** historic houses; **Kumkapi** for street side fish restaurants serenaded by minstrels, (especially atmospheric on weekend nights); **Ortaköy:** Istanbul's Camden Market with trendy cafés, boutiques and a youth scene in semi-renovated derelict buildings; **Uskudar,** on the Asia side, has a lively waterfront with cafés and ranks of 1950s US taxi cabs. Note: Topkapi Palace (which houses the world's biggest emerald and Mohammad's cloak) is not in the Topkapi area.

● **Where to stay** Some Sultanahmet choices: *Orient Hostel* ($5/sgl – *Hostel* ($3pp in crowded dorms). *Hotel Anadolu* ($5/sgl – the cheapest rooms we found and better value than the *Youth Hostel* beside Aya Sophia). *Hotel Elit* (worth the $15/sgl for quality rooms and informative staff). *Empress Zoe* ($30+/rm, traditional Ottoman-style B&B). *Ayasofia Pansiyon* ($80+/sgl, very classy B&B, ☎ 212-513-3660). There are cheap but not so cheerful hotels 1-4 blocks W of Istikal St.

● **Excursions** Hopper boats to towns and castles along the Bosphorous (our favourite is Arnavutköy). Princes Islands: a few ferries/day go to main islands – Büyükada (mansions, bike rental) and Heybeliada (beaches, more laid back). Summer services to smaller islands, Burgaz and Kinaliada.

West Turkey

APPROX 100 KM

To ISTANBUL 20 HRS, $11

Jh + 17:30

SINOP

INEBOLU

BARTA

Attractive drive

AMASRA

ÇAKRAZ

BARTIN

KASTAMONU

SAMSUN

KARABÜK HUGE STEEL FACTORY

ZONGULDAK

★SAFRANBOLU AN UGLY FIRST IMPRESSION, BUT BEYOND THE MAIN STREET ARE QUAINT HOMES & AN OLD · ★★OTEL GÜLEN - BASIC BUT V. ATMOSPHERIC, NEAR MOSQUE.

AMASYA DRAMATIC HILLTOP FORTRESS

Barren rolling hills

ÇORUM

TOKAT OLD TOWN

ANKARA ATATURK MAUSOLEUM · CASTLE OVERLOOKING ÜLUS DISTRICT SURROUNDED BY OLD HOUSES. SEV. CHEAP HOTELS IN ULUS.

★BOĞAZKALE 10KM OF CRUMBLING ANCIENT WALL & GATES.

GORDION KNOT CUT BY ALEXANDER.

YOZGAT

To SIVAS

POTALI

STRANGELY, BUSES TO TRABZON TAKE THE LONG ROUTE VIA SAMSUN

KAYSERI

Lake TUZ

GÖREME

AKŞEHIR

AKSARAY

★CAPPADOCIA Fantastic erosion patterns & underground cities.

YALVAÇ 2000 YEAR OLD RUINS OF PISIDIAN ANTIOCH.

NEVŞEHIR

IHLARA

NIĞDE

KONYA FORMER SELCUK CAPITAL -MANY FINE BLDGS. ON MEVLANA CAD. DERVISH MUSEUM.

CASTABALA

ALTINKAYA/SELGE ATTRACTIVE MOUNTAIN BACKDROP

KARAMAN

DILEKKAYA BYZANTINE CITY OF ANAVARZA.

★ASPENDOS HUGE ANCIENT THEATRE.

OLBA ROMAN AQUEDUCT

ADANA

Oil Terminal

ALARHAN ·CARAVANSARAI AND ALARA FORTRESS.

UZUNCABURÇ

MERSIN

TARSUS BIRTHPLACE OF ST. PAUL

CEYHAN

MISIS

YAKA-CIK

SIDE

AYTAP

SILIFKE ★ROMAN BRIDGE

PASLI

3/WEEK $16

ISKENDERUM (HATAY)

ALANYA BEACH LONG BUT LINED WITH SLAB HOTELS. POOR VALUE

TAŞUCU

To MAGUSA, CYPRUS

ANAMUR

AFRO-DISIAS

To CYPRUS

ANTAKYA BIBLICAL ANTIOCH AND A WESTERN TERMINUS OF THE SILK ROAD, BUT THE ONLY REAL INTEREST NOW IS THE MUSEUM.

KIZKALESI

SYRIA

CAPPADOCIA (KAPADOKYA)

A fascinating wilderness of wind-eroded curiosities, ancient cave churches and underground cities spread widely between Aksaray and Kayseri. Bikes or mopeds for local exploration are rented conveniently in **Göreme**, the magical little tourist hub where several cheaper hotels offer rooms in caves. Quaint **Ürgüp**, quiet **Avanos** or big, dusty **Nevşehir** (in rapidly decreasing order of loveliness) also have extensive travel services (cheap rooms, local maps, info, vastly overpriced tours). Nevşehir is a busier transport hub than Göreme which nonetheless has daily buses to many cities in west and south Turkey. Go to/from points east via Kayseri, where the caravanserai and old centre around Ülü mosque are an easy 10mins dolmuş ride (left) from the bus station. **From Istanbul** there's a once daily, tourist-crammed overnighter to Göreme/Nevşehir. Sleep more comfortably on the more frequent, half empty Adana-bound buses which all stop at Aksaray. Some services leave you on the ring road, 15 mins walk from town. Note that Aksaray is also the name of an Istanbul suburb.

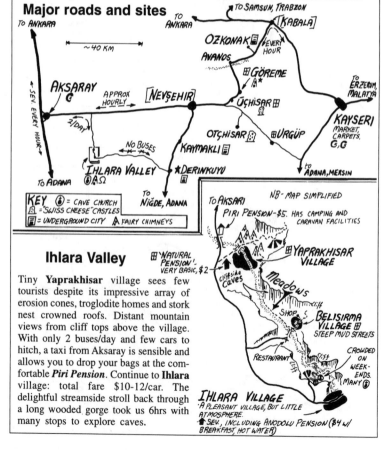

Major roads and sites

Ihlara Valley

Tiny **Yaprakhisar** village sees few tourists despite its impressive array of erosion cones, troglodite homes and stork nest crowned roofs. Distant mountain views from cliff tops above the village. With only 2 buses/day and few cars to hitch, a taxi from Aksaray is sensible and allows you to drop your bags at the comfortable *Piri Pension*. Continue to **Ihlara** village: total fare $10-12/car. The delightful streamside stroll back through a long wooded gorge took us 6hrs with many stops to explore caves.

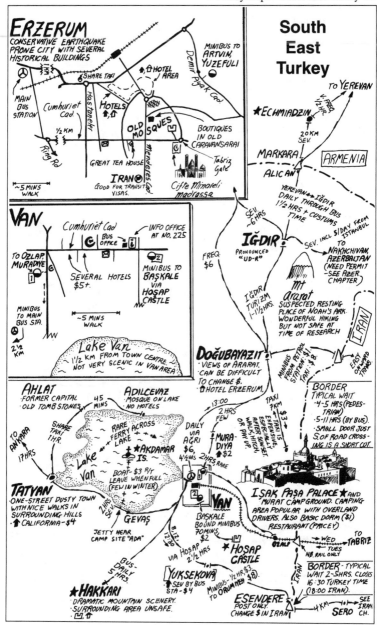

ERZERUM
CONSERVATIVE EARTHQUAKE PRONE CITY WITH SEVERAL HISTORICAL BUILDINGS

South East Turkey

MINIBUS TO ARTVIN, YUZEFULI

Demir Paşa Cad

HOTEL AREA

SHARE TAXI

MAIN BUS STATION

Cumhuriet Cad

Hastaneler

HOTELS

½ KM

Ring Rd

GREAT TEA HOUSE

OLD MO SQUES

Menderes Cad

BOUTIQUES IN OLD CARAVANSARAI

Tabriz Gate

IRAN
GOOD FOR TRANSIT VISAS.

Çifte Minareli madrassa

~5 MINS WALK

TO YEREVAN
★ECHMIADZIN
V. FREQ ½ HR.

20 KM SEV.

MARKARA
ARMENIA
ALICAN

YEREVAN↔IĞDIR DAILY THROUGH BUS 1½ HRS AT CUSTOMS TIME

SEV - 6 HRS

FREQ $6

VAN
Cumhuriet Cad
INFO OFFICE AT NO.225
BUS OFFICE
TO OZLAP, MURADIYE
SEVERAL HOTELS $5+
MINIBUS TO BAŞKALE VIA HOSAP CASTLE
MINIBUS TO MAIN BUS STA.
2½ KM
~5 MINS WALK
Lake Van
1½ KM FROM TOWN CENTRE - NOT VERY SCENIC IN VAN AREA

IĞDIR
PRONOUNCED "UD-R"

SEV. INCL 1/DAY FROM ISTANBUL
TO NAKHCHIVAN, AZERBAIJAN (NEED PERMIT - SEE AZER. CHAPTER)

IĞDIR TURIZM 1-1½ HRS

Mt Ararat
SUSPECTED RESTING PLACE OF NOAH'S ARK. WONDERFUL HIKING BUT NOT SAFE AT TIME OF RESEARCH

IRAN

DOĞUBAYAZIT
· VIEWS OF ARARAT. CAN BE DIRECT TO CHANGE $.
· HOTEL ERZERUM

MINIBUS FROM PETROL STATION $1
TAXI - $8.

EASY ONWARD TRAVEL

AHLAT
· FORMER CAPITAL
· OLD TOMB STONES

45 MINS

ADILCEVAZ
· MOSQUE ON LAKE
· NO HOTELS

SHARE TAXI 1 HR.

TO ANKARA 17HRS

RARE FERRY ACROSS LAKE
★AKDAMAR IS.

Lake Van

BOAT - $3 R/T LEAVE WHEN FULL (FEW IN WINTER)

13:00
2 HRS FEW

DAILY VIA AĞRI $6

4½ HRS

MURA-DIYA $2

2HRS RARE

TAXI 7KM $3

TAXIS EXPENSIVE, ESPECIALLY AFTER SUNSET. WALK, HITCH, OR PAY UP.

BORDER
TYPICAL WAIT
· 4-5 HRS (PEDESTRIAN)
· 5-11 HRS (BY BUS)
· SMALL DOOR JUST S. OF ROAD CROSSING IS A SHORT CUT

TATVAN
ONE-STREET DUSTY TOWN WITH NICE WALKS IN SURROUNDING HILLS
· CALIFORNIA - $4

2HRS

GEVAŞ

JETTY NEAR CAMP SITE "ADA"

VAN

BAŞKALE BOUND MINIBUS 70MINS $2

VIA HOSAP 2½ HRS

8/12 17:30

IŞAK PAŞA PALACE ★ AND MURAT CAMPGROUND. CAMPING AREA POPULAR WITH OVERLAND DRIVERS. ALSO BASIC DORM ($) RESTAURANT (PRICEY)

ÖZLAP

WED TUES NB. RAIL ONLY

TO TABRIZ

IRAN

BORDER - TYPICAL WAIT 2-3HRS. CLOSES 16:30 TURKEY TIME (18:00 IRAN).

HAKKARI
DRAMATIC MOUNTAIN SCENERY.
· SURROUNDING AREA UNSAFE.

BUS- DAILY 5 HRS.

★HOSAP CASTLE

YUKSEKOVA
SEV BY BUS STA.- $4

MINIBUS -½ HR. $3 TO ORUMIEH $8

ESENDERE
POST ONLY. CHANGE $ IN IRAN

4 KM

SERO
SEE IRAN CH.

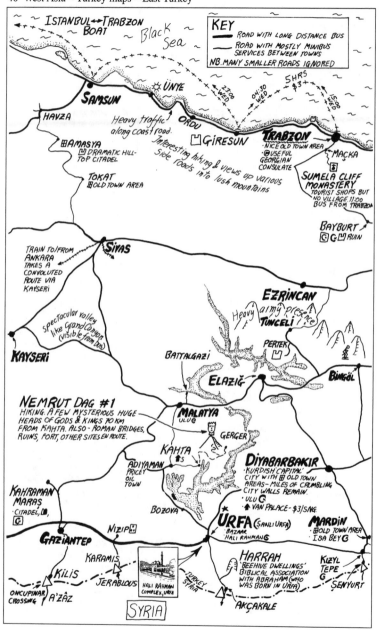

KEY
ROAD WITH LONG DISTANCE BUS
ROAD WITH MOSTLY MINIBUS
SERVICES BETWEEN TOWNS
NB. MANY SMALLER ROADS IGNORED

ISTANBUL↔TRABZON BOAT

Black Sea

ÜNYE

27:00 WED
04:30 WED
5 HRS $3
15:00 SAT

SAMSUN

HAVZA

Heavy traffic along coast road.

ORDU

GIRESUN

Interesting hiking & views up various side roads into lush mountains

TRABZON
·NICE OLD TOWN AREA
·USEFUL GEORGIAN CONSULATE

MAÇKA

AMASYA
·DRAMATIC HILLTOP CITADEL

TOKAT
OLD TOWN AREA

SUMELA CLIFF MONASTERY
TOURIST SHOPS BUT NO VILLAGE. 11:00 BUS FROM TRABZON

BAYBURT
C G RUIN

TRAIN TO/FROM ANKARA TAKES A CONVOLUTED ROUTE VIA KAYSERI

SIVAS

EZRINCAN

Heavy army presence

TUNCELI

PERTEK

Spectacular valley like Grand Canyon (visible from bus)

KAYSERI

BATTALGAZI

ELAZIG

BINGÖL

NEMRUT DAG #1
HIKING. A FEW MYSTERIOUS HUGE HEADS OF GODS & KINGS 70 KM FROM KAHTA. ALSO - ROMAN BRIDGES, RUINS, FORT, OTHER SITES EN ROUTE.

MALATYA
ULU

GERGER

KAHTA

ADIYAMAN
PRICEY OIL TOWN

DIYABARBAKIR
·KURDISH CAPITAL' CITY WITH OLD TOWN AREAS - MILES OF CRUMBLING CITY WALLS REMAIN.
·ULU G
·VAN PALACE- $3/SNG.

KAHRAMAN MARAS
·CITADEL, DB, C

NIZIP

BOZOVA

GAZIANTEP

URFA (SANLI URFA)
·BAZAAR
·HALI RAHMAN G

MARDIN
·OLD TOWN AREA
·ISA BEY G

KARAMIS

KILIS

JERABLOUS

HALI RAHMAN COMPLEX, URFA

TURKEY SYRIA

HARRAH
'BEEHIVE DWELLINGS' BIBLICAL ASSOCIATION WITH ABRAHAM (WHO WAS BORN IN URFA)

KIZYL TEPE
G

SENYURT

ONCUPINAR CROSSING

A'ZÂZ

AKÇAKALE

SYRIA

East Turkey

~100 KM

Black Sea

GEORGIA

LOVELY ROAD

MODERN TOWN IMPRESSIVELY SITUATED:- STACKED UP STEEP SLOPES. MOST HOTELS FULL OF RUSSIAN PROSTITUTES. GÜVEN BETTER $6

BATUMI
SARP BORDER POST
KEMELPASA
SAV. SAT
POSOF
GEORGIA TURKEY
CILDIR

RIZE
HOPA
ARTVIN
ARDESEN

Attractive tea hills
ANCIENT FOOT BRIDGES
AYDER HOT SPRINGS RESORT OF CHALETS IN ALPINE SETTING

ARDANUC GORGE, FORMER GEORGIAN CAPITAL
YUZE-FULI church

ARDAHAN "BIG ⌂ "CENTRAL ASIA ATMOSPHERE IN MARKET.

Cildir Lake

GUMRI
ANIS
SCENIC RUINS OF SMALL FORTIFIED TOWN WITH ARMENIAN CHURCHES. TOURS FROM KARS

KAÇKAR MOUNTAINS GORGEOUS HIKES. FRIENDLY SHEPHERDS BUT NO ROADS! VILLAGES BRING FOOD & TENT. SUMMER ONLY.

Tortum waterfalls (47M HIGH)

KARS
⌂ LARGE CASTLE. "MOST 'ASIAN' FEEL OF ANY TOWN IN TURKEY." SEV. HOTELS IN OLD TOWN BETWEEN ⌂ AND ⊕

ARMENIA

YEREVAN
★ ECHMIADZIN
MARKARA
ALICAN
NAKHCHIVAN AZERBAIJAN

TERCAN
TO ANKARA (20 HRS. SLOW BUT NO MORE RELAXING THAN BUS)

ERZERUM
DULL TOWN WITH MNT. BACKDROP. USEFUL ⊕ IRANIAN CONSULATE.

HORASAN CHANGE HERE GOING BETWEEN KARS ↔ VAN

AGRI

IĞDIR
Mt Ararat (Agri Dag)

BAZARGAN

DOĞUBAYAZIT

NEMRUT DAG #2 BIG CRATER LAKE

AHLAT 12TH CENT. CAPITAL.

MUŞ
HAJI SEREF G

ADILCEVAZ COW LAKE
Lake Van

MURADIYE SMALL WATER FALLS
ÖZALP

WED
TUE
WEEKLY, INCONVENIENT TRAIN TO TABRIZ

SOUTH EAST TURKEY

BITLIS
TATVAN

Many police checks on this road at times of PKK activity

VAN
★ HOSAP
⌂ DRAMATIC CLIFF-TOP RUIN
ÇAVUSTEPE

IRAN

BATMAN
SIIRT

SMALL LAUNCHES TO ★ AKDAMAR ISLAND LEAVE BESIDE 'ADA CAMPING'

road Closed

BAŞKALE
⌂ APALAS (ON TOWN SQ.)

ESENDERE
Share taxis to OVNMINEH

★ HASANKEYF EXTENSIVE 12TH CENTURY RUINED CITY
MIDYAT
ST. GABRIEL MONASTERY
DEYRÜL-ZAFERAN

ŞIRNAK
SILOPI

HAKKARI "Hap Valley"

Sivelan check post
YÜKSEKOVA

NUSAYBIN
EL QAMISHLIYE

Worst Army-PKK tension here

KHABUR
9KM "SECURITY ZONE" CONTROLLED BY TURKISH TROOPS SINCE 1996

SYRIA

HARIEM (N. IRAQ)

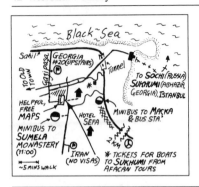

Trabzon

Trabzon is the transport hub of the NE, attractive, prosperous and full of Russian shopper-tourists so check in early to get a cheap hotel room.

The old town, 15 mins walk west of the centre, straddles two small ravines and has several passingly interesting churches, mosques and old homes. Sumella Monastery is a lot more ruined than mist-shrouded postcard views suggest, but makes an easy day trip into the wooded mountains.

❑ In a small town on the Black Sea

Ring the bell by the rusted gate that separates the Otel Gulen from a winding dirt road, and after a few minutes an old man answers. '*Evet, evet,*' he mumbles. Yes, yes. Then some more Turkish which seems to imply 'There you are. What took you so long? Come inside, will you?'

He sits us down in the central room of his house. Wood and the smell of it are everywhere. He pours us tea from the blackened stove and scours the room for food to give us. He finds some peanuts (old, by the taste of them) and stuffs handfuls at us. Then some bread (old) and some kind of candy (old) that is not quite Turkish delight. He pours us more tea and asks a question in Turkish. '*Anlamiorum*', I tell him. 'I don't understand'. He chuckles. Then giggles. Then by the time he starts walking away again he is laughing fully, saying to himself '*Anlamiorum, anlamiorum*' as if I had told him the punch line to a good joke. Water-stained, wood walls hold a cracked mirror, a torn photograph of a proud looking man, and an obligatory portrait of Ataturk. Eventually the hotelier returns and shows me to my room, an octagonal wooden Hobbit hole, small enough to be cosy, large enough for everything to have its place. I've seen beaches, mosques and ancient ruins in this country but to me the Otel Gulen is real Turkey.

Turkish Alphabet – *at first glance seems the same as in English but there are some differences.*

c = English "j"   **ç** = "ch"   **g** = "g" but **ğ** is silent and lengthens the previous vowel

i = "i"/"ee" but undotted **ı** is a grunted short "uh" sound. Capital **i** should be written **İ** (eg İstanbul)

s = "s" but **ş** = "sh"

NB. SIMILAR PRONUNCIATIONS OF THESE LETTERS APPLY IN AZERBAIJAN (except **ğ**), AND CENTRAL ASIA.

Hariem

Iraq has effectively been divided into two countries since 1992. The northern Kurdish sector had been nominally autonomous since 1970 but in 1991 following the Gulf War it became a UN-protected Kurdish safe haven. Initially this was to be for six months but this status has been extended without any granting of full independence. Hariem is a local word meaning something like 'territory', and though it's used locally as the official name of the country, Iraqis and Turks are more familiar with the term Haremi Kurdustan. Its leaders are themselves fiercely divided and there have been factional wars between the major parties: Patriotic Union of Kurdistan (PUK) and Kurdish Democratic Party (DPK/KDP).

In 1996 the KDP did the unthinkable: it made a pact with enemy No 1, Saddam Hussein. Saddam's agents helped the KDP advance eastwards into PUK territory, briefly taking Suleimaniyah. With Iranian backing, the PUK fought back and re-took the city a few days later. An uneasy truce has since returned. Fears that Saddam would take control over the KDP areas do not seem to have come true. Meanwhile Turkey is stridently anti-Kurdish. It has been fighting Kurdish separatist PKK forces in SE Anatolia for years and on several occasions it has made 'anti-terrorist' raids into northern Hariem to root out PKK bases. At present Turkey occupies a Lebanon style 'security zone' along its border. However, US and economic pressure has kept open the border post at Khabur. On the Turkish side you'll see convoys of oil tanker trucks selling off Iraqi petrol very cheaply at a great profit to buyer and seller.

If you can get into Hariem, you'll find it a place of great hospitality and charm. The land is physically as well as culturally different from the rest of Iraq with craggy mountains pierced by green valleys, streams and waterfalls. But beware. You'll be assumed to be a journalist or an aid worker and, as such, may end up a pawn in the political game. One organisation exclaimed: 'Visiting Kurdistan is a totally absurd idea. It hasn't been wise to go there for the last 400 years!' This may be an over-reaction but having solid contacts to look after you is very important. Remember this is a war zone.

❑ **W&M's country ratings – Hariem**
- **Expense $$** Accommodation possible from D35.
- **Value for money** ✔✔ Don't expect too much of a country ravaged by war.
- **Getting around** ✔✔✔ Shared taxis and buses ply major routes regularly.
- **English spoken** ✔✔✔ Most young people have studied English.
- **Woman alone** ✔✔✔ Islamic dress code not enforced. Kurdish women will travel alone. Expatriate women report feeling less threatened here than in Turkey.
- **For vegetarians** ✔✔ Typical Kurdish food is rice, meat and a vegetable or bean dish. Simply dropping the meat part is possible but may cause surprise or disappointment to hosts.

PRACTICAL INFORMATION
Visas and formalities

No visas are required to enter Hariem, though you'll pay a $20 registration fee once you cross into KDP controlled territory from Syria or Turkey. The bigger problem is persuading neighbouring states to let you out. In 1995 it was possible to slip across the Turkish border at Khabur with minimal fuss. Since 1996, however, one is required to show a permit from the Turkish Ministry of Foreign Affairs in Ankara authorising your exit. To get such a permit you'll have to convince them that you're not a journalist (they'd rather this area of the world had as little publicity as possible). It may help if you've spoken to the Turkish embassy in your home country before setting off. British aid workers (eg Save the Children) have three-month multiple exit permits arranged for them in Ankara. Recent reports suggest that the Khabur border controls are now tighter than ever and that most Kurds now reach the outside world through Syria. Aid workers report that crossing from Iran is more straightforward than you'd expect. However getting the necessary paperwork to satisfy the Iranian bureaucracy will be time consuming and you'll find yourself in the potentially more dangerous PUK zone.

If you manage to get into Hariem, it is worth pre-arming yourself with letters written in Sorani explaining who you are and what the hell you're doing there. Kurdish support groups exist in many Western cities. All that we contacted were extremely friendly and happy to oblige with letters of support and contacts to meet. All were surprised but delighted at our interest in visiting their country. Remember to stress that your interest is purely touristic. Some useful addresses:

Kurdish Information Centre (☎ 0171 272 9499) 129 St John's Way, London, N19, UK

Kurdistan Committee, 144 rue des Guildes, 1040 Brussels, Belgium

Kurdish Info Network (☎ 202 483 6444, fax 6476, e-mail akin@kurdish.org), 2623 Connecticut Ave NW #1, Washington DC, USA

KDP, PO Box 7725 London SW1V 3ZD, ☎ 0171 931 7764. In USA ☎ 202 331 9505

The 'Line of Control' between KDP and PUK zones is a guarded frontier. Passports are checked but there are no con-

---

❏ **Essential information for travellers – Hariem**

● **Visa** No visa is required, $20 registration at Hariem border if the neighbouring countries will let you leave.

● **Currency** Dinar. D1=1000fils. The former Iraqi bank notes withdrawn from circulation in Iraq are the legal tender in Hariem. US$1= D22. Bring US$ which can be changed easily throughout the urban areas. Credit cards and travellers' cheques are of no use whatsoever.

● **Time zone** 3 hours ahead of GMT (same as Iraq, 1hr ahead of Turkey and Syria, $1/_2$hr behind Iran).

● **Religious tone** Muslim but as in Turkey the people are relaxed, alcoholic drinks are sold and women do not need to cover their hair, wrists or forearms.

● **Special dangers** The political situation is volatile between the competing Kurdish factions and there is always the possibility of problems with Iraq. Away from the cities there are minefields in some areas. These are generally marked with danger notices – often in English. There is a malaria risk.

● **When to go** Unlike the rest of Iraq, Hariem is almost entirely mountainous with fertile valleys thanks to a relatively high rainfall. Winters are cold and snowy.

● **Highlights** Geli Ali Bakh waterfalls, Shanaderi caves, Hawlier citadel (Arbil), mountain hikes, Zakho (famous ancient bridge and spectacular road to get there).

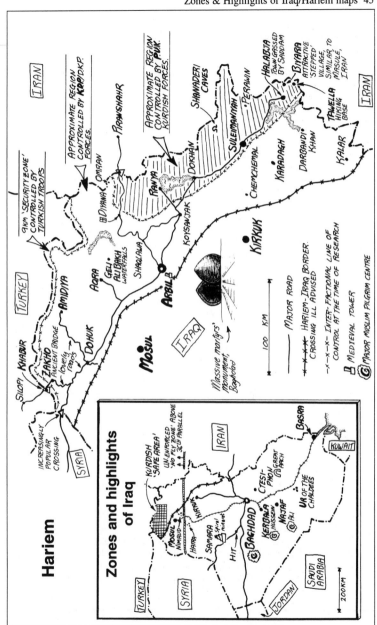

Hariem

Zones and highlights of Iraq

❏ **Meeting the people**

● **Language**

In Hariem the two main Kurdish languages are Sorani and Kermanji. Both are written using the Arabic script with letters the same as in Farsi (as in Iran) except for the additional accent marker (') which softens the letters L, R, I and U.

Some phrases in Sorani Kurdish:

> Greeting – *choni*
> Reply – *chakam supass*
> Thank you <u>very much</u> – <u>*zor*</u> *supass*
> Delicious – *zor batama*
> Beautiful – *juana*
> Very good – *zor basha*

Arbil (Erbil), an ancient city and Hariem's capital, is known to some locals as Hawlier (pronounced How Lair).

sular fees to pay unless you're a merchant liable for duties. There is a certain degree of tension but fighting has died down and buses now cross the line regularly.

Transport

Buses and especially shared taxis run fairly frequently on all main routes from *garaj* or *nakliat* in any town. The road between Arbil and Sulemaniyah has been rebuilt to avoid cutting through Iraq. 2½hrs by share taxi (D300), 3½-4hrs by hourly bus (D120).

There are no trains or commercial flights to neighbouring countries.

Accommodation

If you've made it this far it's unlikely that you won't have met someone willing to put you up. Nonetheless, most town cen-

tres have basic hotels amongst more expensive options. Ask younger locals for directions.

Staying in touch

There is no international mail service. Locals have their letters smuggled out and posted from Baghdad. Nor are there any telephone connections except for highly expensive satellite phones. Warn your friends that you're likely to disappear – though hopefully only for a while.

Further information

● **Books** Read Sherry Laizer's *Martyrs, Traitors and Patriots* (published by Zed) available for £10 plus post and packing from the Kurdish Information Centre in London.

Web sites

Kurdistan has many web pages with history, politics and polemics but little on travel. Try http://www.evitech.fi/~hasand/KURDISTAN.html for an index of sites.

The Kurdish Information Network is at
http://www.xs4all/~tank/kurdish/htdocs/index.html and internet
http://burn.ucsd.edu/~akin

soc.culture.kurdish is a newsgroup for meeting Kurdish people.

Iran

Iran is a little known travellers' gem. Historic oases, beautiful blue-tiled mosques and rugged deserts are the country's trademark but there are also forests, thatched woodland villages, ski slopes and even the odd scraggy beach. Safe, civilised and reasonably efficient, Iran is temporarily one of the cheapest places you can visit thanks to a currency weakened by trade embargoes. It is not the fearful place the Western media tends to portray. The people are honest and hospitable beyond all expectations regardless of any political differences. We found ourselves in Tehran on the anniversary of the 1979 US hostage-taking. A massive demonstration paraded through the streets yelling 'Down with America'. But far from being antagonistic towards Westerners, one jolly set of marchers politely invited us home for tea with them, reminding us that it's Western politicians not people that they hate.

The overthrow of the Shah in 1979 caused great alarm in the West but was highly popular in Iran. The regime that emerged set out to be the first truly Islamic nation since the Arab caliphates of the last millennium. Ayatollah Khomeini was a charismatically unemotional leader who emerged from exile to guide the revolution. At its height, religious fervour led revolutionary guards and other individuals to take the law into their own hands: acid was thrown at women wearing make up and instant floggings were meted out for a variety of misdemeanours. Things are a little more relaxed these days and although folk music, dancing and playing cards remain illegal, chess was decriminalised in 1989. The people are now more worried about the economy than religion.

The horrendous war with Iraq (1980-88) left Iran in economic chaos. Clearing that up has taken years while relations with the West have remained strained. The fatwa calling for the death of British author, Salman Rushdie, is

---

❏ **W&M's country ratings – Iran**

● **Expense $** Despite some foreigner pricing for hotels and internal flights, Iran is inexpensive. In most towns, beds are available for under $2 (except in March or September). It's even cheaper if you use the black market.

● **Value for money ✔✔✔✔✔** Spending a little more allows you to live in style.

● **Getting around ✔✔✔✔** Buses run frequently almost everywhere and there are many overnight services. Tickets are extremely cheap. There are few trains.

● **English spoken ✔✔✔** You can find an English speaker almost everywhere.

● **Woman alone ✔✔** There's less sexual harassment than most expect or fear with very little physical danger but the claustrophobia of having to cover up gets many women down. Some hotels (usually mid range places) and tea shops are reluctant to accept single women.

● **For vegetarians ✔✔** Great fruit, dates in the south, olives in the north, nuts everywhere but most meals and fast foods are meat based. Fish is rare.

still in force while the US accuses Iran of international terrorism and has passed laws sanctioning foreign companies that invest there. In April 1997 a German court ruled Iran responsible for the 1992 shooting of 6 opposition leaders in a Berlin restaurant. In response all EU nations except Greece withdrew their ambassadors and the 'critical dialogue' which had led Germany to become Iran's top trade partner was cancelled. However, May's election returned by a large majority, reformist President Khatami, who has set about a modest repair in relations. Clinton considered the election result 'hopeful' withdrawing long-term US opposition to the Iran-Central Asian pipeline plan.

❑ **Geo-political information – Iran**

Population: 67.5m (1997), 56m (1991), 33m (1975).

Area: 1,650,000 sq km.

Capital: Tehran (6.5 million)

Other major cities: Mashhad (1.7m), Isfahan (1.1m), Tabriz, Shiraz (1m), Ahwaz, Qom (700,000), Kermanshah (600,000), Karaj (450,000), Zahedan, Orumiyeh, Rasht, Hamadan, Arak (350,000), Ardabil, Kerman, Qazvin, Yazd (300,000). In fact only Ahwaz and Zahedan really feel as big as this.

GNP per capita: Estimates vary wildly from $2500 to $730 (1994), $3000 to $1500 (1987).

Currency history: Rial/US$1 – Feb 1998: R3000, 1997: R3010, Dec 1995: R3000 (black market 3800), Summer 1994: R1730 (R2500). For 20 years before deregulation in March 1993 the official rate was between R60 and R80 though the black market rate was often seven to ten times higher.

Major exports/economy: Oil, diversified industry.

Ethnic mix: Persian (63%), Azerbaijiani/Turkic (18%), Kurdish (3%) groups.

Official language: Farsi (sometimes called Persian or Iranian).

Religious tone: Strict Islamic state. Shi'ite Muslim (93%), Sunni (5%).

Landmarks of national history: Approximately **470AD**: Yazd's sacred flame of Zoroastrianism was lit (it's still burning at the Ateshkade). **484AD**: Invaded by White Huns. **637AD**: Battle of Qadisiyeh began Arab assault. **651**: Arab control, Islamification began and intensified under the Seljuk Turks. **1091**: Toghril I (Seljuk Turk) declared himself sultan at Nishapur. **1220/1**: Nishapur, Mashhad, Tus et al destroyed by Genghis Khan. **1256**: Il Khanid dynasty with capitals at first Tabriz, then Soltaniyeh and finally Shiraz. **1393**: Timur (Tamerlane) invaded. **1501**: Esmail, a supposed Shi'ite Imam (direct descendant of the 1st Imam Ali) assumed the mantle of Sultan. **1610-29**: Descendent Shah Abbas adorned the new capital, Isfahan. **1813** and **1828**: Qajar Persian wars with Russia (the Caucasus were lost) which sparked the Great Game (see p138). **1901**: British oil concession later developed Iran as world's top oil producer (overtaking Azerbaijan). **1921**: Pahlavi Shah's coup. **1941**: Anglo-Soviet invasion after Iran backed Hitler (Shah fled, son took over). **1946**: Soviets left north west Iran reluctantly. **1951**: Oil industry nationalised. **1979**: Shah ousted in Islamic revolution. **1980-88**: War with Iraq. **1989**: Ayatollah Khomeini died. **1995**: US trade embargo.

Leaders: President Seyyed Mohammad Khatami. Holds the reins of power more than the spiritual leader Ayatollah Khamenei who lacks the popular support of his powerful predecessor Ayatollah Khomeini. **In power since**: 23 May 1997.

Pressing political issues: People feel economic hardships of the liberalising economy. Unfriendly relations with most Western powers and embargo by US.

❏ Essential information for travellers – Iran

- **Visa** Required; transit visas are the easiest to obtain, though a two week to two month wait is typical while your application is referred to Tehran. Extensions are readily given.
- **Currency** Rial (1 tuman=R10). US$1=R3000 bank rate, R3200-3900 black market.
- **Time zone** $3\frac{1}{2}$hrs ahead of GMT ($4\frac{1}{2}$hrs in summer). $1\frac{1}{2}$ hrs ahead of Turkey and Armenia, $\frac{1}{2}$hr ahead of Azerbaijan, $\frac{1}{2}$hr behind Turkmenistan and Pakistan in summer ($1\frac{1}{2}$hrs in winter).
- **Religious tone** Strict Shiite Islam, religious laws apply.
- **Health factors** Iran has high medical standards, many doctors speak English. Consultations rarely cost more than $2. Dehydration is a danger in the dry summer heat. The tap water is safe almost everywhere except in Zahedan. There is a slight malaria risk.
- **Special dangers** The country is remarkably safe. Photography of government buildings is illegal, infringements are taken surprisingly seriously. Some reports of 'fake policeman' scams in Tehran.
- **Social conventions** Social etiquette is heavily influenced by sharia law (Islamic rules) and the usual Muslim restrictions are adhered to.

  Sexual relationships between unmarried couples are not accepted and friendships between men and women are eyed with suspicion. If travelling with a friend of the opposite sex, whatever your relationship, it is easiest to pretend that you are married. Many couples we met found no challenge to their lie despite having different names and nationalities in their passports. A cheap ring, though not strictly necessary, is worth considering.

  When meeting someone of the opposite sex, shaking hands is not polite. Even looking each other in the eye is discouraged. Between those of the same sex, kissing and holding hands is normal.

  Some hotels but few homes have toilet paper. Most people use the left hand and water jet method. Toilet paper is not commonly sold either, though you can get packs of tissues from market stalls and street vendors.
- **Typical traveller destinations** Isfahan, Shiraz/Persepolis, Kerman.
- **Highlights** Isfahan, Masulé, Yazd, Bam, Chogha Zambil, Gulf coast women's masks, gentle honest hospitality.
- **When to go** Autumn and spring are most pleasant. A sweater is useful for cool desert nights especially on draughty bus rides even in October. Winter is surprisingly cold, with heavy snow in the mountains (the High Alborz become ski slopes, Masulé and even Hamadan get cut off). Expect cold winds in the north east and temperatures below freezing in Tehran, Tabriz and the centre. On the Gulf coast, however, November is still unpleasantly sweaty so mid-winter is the only bearable time to visit. The summer heat is scorching in much of the country but inland the desert keeps it dry and bearable.
- **Pulse of the country** Qom (Islamic heart).
- **Key tips** No Ruz (spring equinox, three weeks around Mar 22) is a particularly busy time: transport/accommodation booked up. Women must take account of Islamic dress codes. Given verbally, prices are generally quoted in *tuman* not *rials* making things sound $\frac{1}{10}$th their real price.
- **Orientation tips** Meidan = Sq. Meidan Sa'at (Time Sq) will usually be graced with a clocktower. Sabsa Meidan (Green Sq) is likely to encircle a small park. Imam Ave, Khomeini Sq etc are likely to be central in any city.

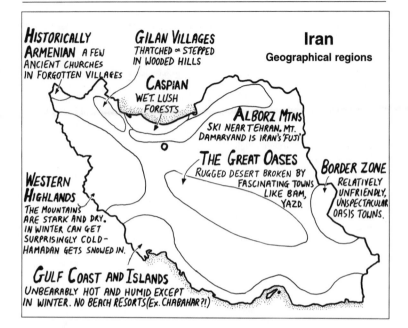

HISTORICALLY ARMENIAN A FEW ANCIENT CHURCHES IN FORGOTTEN VILLAGES

GILAN VILLAGES THATCHED or STEPPED IN WOODED HILLS

Iran
Geographical regions

CASPIAN WET. LUSH FORESTS

ALBORZ MTNS SKI NEAR TEHRAN. MT. DAMAVAND IS IRAN'S 'FUJI'

THE GREAT OASES RUGGED DESERT BROKEN BY FASCINATING TOWNS LIKE BAM, YAZD.

BORDER ZONE RELATIVELY UNFRIENDLY, UNSPECTACULAR OASIS TOWNS.

WESTERN HIGHLANDS THE MOUNTAINS ARE STARK AND DRY. IN WINTER CAN GET SURPRISINGLY COLD– HAMADAN GETS SNOWED IN.

GULF COAST AND ISLANDS UNBEARABLY HOT AND HUMID EXCEPT IN WINTER. NO BEACH RESORTS (Ex. CHABAHAR?!)

PRACTICAL INFORMATION
Visas and formalities

● **Visa strategy** If you're a Muslim (with your Muslim name in your passport) you should have little problem obtaining a pilgrim's visa. A letter of support from an Islamic organisation will reduce the amount of time it takes to obtain one.

For non Muslims the process depends greatly upon your nationality and on recent political relationships between your country and Iran. In good times it is easy to get a transit visa. At bad times no visas at all may be issued. EG At the time of the Rushdie fatwa Brits were refused visas. Then the UK refused to endorse the US stand against Iran's attempted nuclear fuel purchases from Russia. So Brits were back in favour and visas were available in London at short notice. Germans had an easy time while economic ties were strong up until April 1997 when the ambassador was withdrawn. At the end of 1997 relations are improving again. Neutral nation-

als – New Zealanders, Scandinavians, Japanese, Korean – usually have the best chance. Toughest for Americans who should enquire at the Iranian interests section of the Pakistan embassy in the US as there are no direct diplomatic links.

Tourist visas are only available to visitors on pre-booked package tours though Swedes and Australians have been lucky. Most travellers settle for 5 day transit visas which are usually easy to extend (see below). Transit visas cost $50 or local equivalent but you'll usually be required to show a visa for the next country (eg Pakistan or Turkey). Ironically this is a problem for those that don't need visas for either (eg Koreans) who may be required to get a Turkmen visa just to satisfy the condition. You'll also need a letter of introduction from your home embassy or ministry of foreign affairs. Procuring these letters can be free/easy (eg Japanese), expensive and time consuming (eg Brits in the UK) or very tough/impossible (eg French –

at some embassies) according to your nationality.

The best places to apply vary from time to time. New Delhi and Erzerum (Turkey) have proved generally helpful. In China and Central Asia the embassies were friendly but the promised visas never achieved the necessary 'approval' from Tehran.

Women applying for Iranian visas are advised to visit the embassy wearing 'decent' Islamic clothing including a head-scarf. A scarf is also suggested for the visa photographs you present. If you intend to travel through Iran with a friend of the opposite sex you can avoid awkward questions at the embassy by submitting your applications separately. Note that once in Iran, claiming you're married is a good idea and the fact that your names and nationalities are different is not considered odd.

● **At the border** Although border formalities can take four to seven hours, customs forms seem to be taken much less seriously than in the past. At both the Sero (south east Turkey) and Mirjave (Pakistan) borders, we were told that US$1000 was 'too little to bother about' and did not receive a declaration form at all. This proved no problem on exit. At the Bazargan border , guards still write camera details into your passport and sometimes seal shut guitar cases or cassette tapes to prevent you importing infidel music.

Border formalities often involve registering at the health room. We were asked for international vaccination certificates proving we were vaccinated against cholera. By pointing out that these were not officially necessary and assuring the officer that we were indeed healthy, we avoided on the spot injections. If you have suitable paperwork things would be less stressful.

● **Visa extensions** Despite what Iranian embassies in Europe may tell you, many travellers manage a couple of two-week visa extensions. Thus a total stay of about a month is quite possible even if the original visa was only a 5-day transit.

Extensions cost only $0.30 and are possible in any provincial capital, though Shiraz, Tabriz and Rasht are better than Tehran or Bandar Abbas. There is no office in Bam. Kerman's is centrally located and very efficient but will only extend if the visa is within 3 days of expiry. Isfahan's varies from great helpfulness to total rejection. Offices are open mornings only and are closed Fridays. Bring a photocopy of your passport and two photographs, though occasionally these are not used.

It is rumoured that fines for overstaying your visa are relatively small, but no one we met had dared to test the theory.

Money

The rate of exchange at all licensed exchange offices and banks is currently set at R3010 per dollar, though hotels that quote prices in US$ expect the equivalent of R3500 if you pay in rials.

A black market operates somewhat furtively. At the time of writing, the best rates seemed to be outside Iran, especially in Istanbul's Laleli district, at the Turkish border near Dogubayazit, and in Taftan (R3900). Travellers on Istanbul-Tehran buses have reported equally good rates from bus staff. Note that *legally* you may not bring more than R5000 into the country. Within Iran, the rate ranges from R3800 in Tehran (at the bazaar) to R3200 elsewhere but the situation changes constantly.

Travellers' cheques incur a 4% surcharge, and can only be exchanged into rials at the official rate. They are also difficult to cash outside Tehran. A bank in Bandar Abbas that was plastered with stickers exclaiming 'We accept Travellers' Cheques' admitted that we would have to wait about a month for our money! Cash advances on Visa cards are available instantly in bigger cities, but also at poor rates. Bank notes come in two designs for each denomination. Both are valid.

Transport

● **Bus** Iran has well maintained roads and a comprehensive network of long distance buses. In winter take warm clothes on overnight services as the heaters are frequently inefficient. Competition between the many companies keeps prices down to an average of only R500 per hour's travel! You get a numbered seat, and will probably be offered cool drinking water from time to time. We drank this without stomach problems.

'Single seat' buses have only three seats in each row and are consequently more spacious and a little pricier than the normal four wide 'double seat' type. Except during No Ruz and occasionally in September there is no shortage of transport except on very awkward routes. There is a tendency for many services to depart for the same destination at almost the same

time, while at other times there may not be a bus for hours. Most popular slots seem to arrive very early the morning after departure. For example, dozens of buses leave Tabriz for Tehran in the early evening and arrive early morning (3-7 am), but mid afternoon we could find only shared taxis.

Most cities have at least one bus station or *terminal*: some have two or more. Generally the station is filled with the offices of the different companies. Check with a few to find a departure time nearest to your ideal. Touts shout destinations of imminently departing unfilled buses.

Many buses pass through medium-sized towns like Yazd and Qazvin but few of them go to the bus stations there. If you're in a hurry or want to leave after the

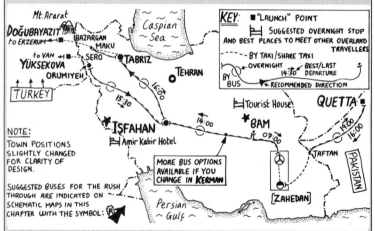

❏ Rushing through Iran

If political machinations limit you to an unextendible 5-day transit visa (occasionally happens), or if you find Iran's beer, fashion and dance restrictions intolerable, here are a few tips to help you make the most of a quick dash between Turkey and Pakistan through this fascinating country.

Key tips A direct Istanbul-Tehran-Zahedan-Quetta trip is quick and cheap but of little interest. T & Z are big, require awkward transfers between bus terminals and are arguably Iran's least attractive cities. Instead stop in gorgeous Isfahan and exotic Bam without spending significantly more time or money. Both places have traveller-friendly hotels where you'll find English speakers and a relaxed atmosphere. You may decide to stay longer after all.

bus station has closed (after 6 or 7pm), it is worth enquiring for the roundabout or junction at which these through buses make pick ups. These may vary for different destinations, but locals invariably seem to know.

In isolated locations it is possible to wave down passing buses if hitchhiking should fail. Buses also stop regularly at police posts at which the driver has to jump out and have his tachograph stamped. Locals often use these opportunities to switch buses: saves going into transit towns. The post outside Sirjan is particularly well used.

City buses require tickets purchased before boarding, usually R40 or R50 per ticket, sold in strips of five or 10. Women enter the rear section of the bus, and are trusted to bring their tickets to the collector at the front door upon exiting. Tehran city bus maps supposedly exist but we were unable to locate any.

● **Taxis** Long distance shared taxis (cars or pickup trucks) operate on many routes and can be very useful for shorter hops, especially to and from the border posts. Most take five passengers so if you occupy the tempting looking front seat, don't be surprised to find the last passenger getting in on your lap.

Urban shared taxis run on fixed routes and charge between R100 and R500 (depending on the distance). A private taxi (ie one for yourself) will be as much as R3000 for a 10 minute ride. Renting a taxi

---

❏ **Rushing through Iran (continued)**
Pakistan border Forget the very unreliable 2/week train. Road crossings are quick with a very short walk. Buses are helpfully timed. Rial black market rates are good on the Pakistan side. Buses **from Quetta** arrive in Taftan as the border opens: easy to reach Bam same day. Buses **to Quetta** leave en masse from Taftan at 7pm. If you sleep in grotty old Zahedan you'll spend all day waiting around at the border. Why not stay in much nicer Bam: the 7am Bam-Zahedan bus (co#8, book pm) gives you enough time to transit Z and cross the border by 7pm.

Turkish border choices Border delays of 2-7hrs are the norm. Typically less at Sero than at Bazargan. Both possible routes are scenic in places: the northern route passes Mt Ararat while on S route you see dramatic Hosap castle. Only Bazargan has a good black market rate.
    Eastbound the key is to reach either Tabriz by 4pm or Orumiyeh by 2.30pm for the last direct buses to Isfahan (avoiding Tehran). You'll need to sleep in Yuksekova or Dogubayazit and start very early. Even so, the deadline on the Tabriz route is very tough given a typical 5hr delay at Bazargan. However Orumiyeh is much nearer to the border than Tabriz and despite some transport frustrations between sleepy Sero and Orumiyeh, you should make it by 2.30pm.
    Westbound either route works but Tabriz is a more interesting place to spend a couple of hours and its bus station is walkably close to the interesting bazaar.

Istanbul-Tehran direct buses Not recommended. Various companies. Services most days dep Tehran's west terminal around 1pm. Takes 3 days. At $20-30, it's cheaper than doing the route in sections **but** a) you miss E. Turkey, b) border delays can last all day c) you start or end your ride in unpleasant Tehran. Same day tickets to Istanbul are possible some mornings but you may be stuck in Tehran for a day or two (better to spend the time in Isfahan). Eastbound you'll face the challenges of Iran after nearly three exhausting days on a bus. If price is really all that matters note that the cheapest direct eastbound tickets are sold in Laleli, Istanbul, not at the bus station.

by the hour (around R5000 per hour) can save you time, especially in Tehran, and it's a great way to become acquainted with a city if you can find a driver who speaks your language. In bigger towns taxis usually wait outside the terminal for buses that arrive late in the evening. They may get a commission from the hotel they take you to on top of their fee, but in our experience are happy to take you to a cheap place (especially if you stick with Iranians who are similarly stranded).

● **Train** Since all but the poorest foreign traveller can afford first class sleeper tickets, Iranian trains provide a luxurious, if slow, alternative to bus travel. Routes are limited, however. There are daily overnight trains from Tehran to Mashhad, Tabriz and Ahwaz. The services to Kerman and Isfahan are much less frequent, while from Isfahan to Mashhad trains run only in the pilgrim season. There are new services from Tehran to Bandar Abbas (so far freight only) and from Mashhad to Turkmenistan. The weekly train from Zahedan to Pakistan has a reputation for being days late.

Railway booking offices tend to keep absurd hours and usually close at 5pm even though most trains leave at night. Try to book at least a day ahead. It is essential to get a ticket in advance, as you can't buy one on the train (or even get onto the platform at major stations without one).

Nilofar Travel Agent in Tehran (see Khomeini Sq area map) is one of the few places that can get advance rail tickets for you, saving a trip to the station.

● **Air** The domestic air system is very extensive, cheap, and you can pay in rials.

❑ A matter of honour

After strenuous and absolute promises from a travel agent named Hossein, I began to wonder whether it was, in fact, possible to buy an international air ticket at local prices. The rule I had heard – repeatedly – was that foreigners pay extra, and do so in US$. But Hossein seemed certain he could get me the local price. Wow! Tehran to Almaty for only R520,000. That would be only $150 in carpet-shop rials. My excitement was tinged with suspicion. Are you sure? I am a foreigner you know. Don't I have to pay dollars? No, no, all was fine. Absolutely. Promise.

So I changed my dollars reluctantly – there is no changing back later even if you change officially, and especially not if you've used a carpet salesman in the bazaar. The next morning I returned to his air-conditioned agency with the wad of rial notes. There was a sudden deafening silence as I walked in. A lot of paper shuffling began as I greeted Hossein, and he shook hands nervously. The smartly uniformed office gave a collective gulp when they saw that I'd already changed the money and explanations were whispered in Farsi. 'No seats available' said the woman at the computer so half heartedly that even she didn't believe it. The confirmation spluttered out of the printer. Plane half empty. But clearly I should have trusted my instincts. 'We make mistake. Real price is $279', said another girl. Impressive how they all spoke English even in a time of crisis. 'Yes' said Hossein. 'I made a mistake'.

Just as I'd feared. But no, not exactly. 'We will still get ticket for the price we agreed' said Hossein. 'Please to go with me to the airline office. We cannot issue for you here'. So it was in the taxi that I discovered the real nature of Iranian honour. Hossein is doing well by local standards, but for all his golden accoutrements and dapper clothes, as a sales rep he earns only $60 a month. Despite this, he had resolved without the merest flinch in his gentlemanly smile to make up the $129 shortfall from his own pocket. 'I made a promise' he said, 'I made a promise, I keep a promise. I am a man.'

I cancelled the ticket and he bought me lunch.

Iran Airtour tickets cost roughly double the Iran Air price and are consequently much easier to book at short notice. International tickets must be paid for in hard currency (see box, p54).

● **Boat** A feature of the Iran-Iraq war was the harrying of warships and oil tankers by tiny armed motor-boats. These have now reverted to peace-time use as mini-ferries darting between Hormuz or Qeshm islands and Bandar Abbas. Even if you daren't jump aboard, it's worth the ticket price to watch everyone else try.

Regular international ferries operate to Baku (Azerbaijan) from Bandar Anzali, and to Sharjah (United Arab Emirates) from Bandar Abbas. Occasional services from Bushehr visit other Gulf ports.

● **Hitchhiking** Within our limited experience, we found hitching on quiet, rural roads to be extremely successful. In cities it worked too but watch out for battered old Paykans which may be unmarked taxis.

● **Car** Restrictions have been lifted so you no longer need to be accompanied across the country by a revolutionary guard escort. Petrol is very cheap ($0.05/litre) and the roads are in good condition. However self-drive rental cars are not available.

● **Bikes** These are an excellent way to get around town though they are difficult to

rent (except in Kerman). Try approaching bicycle shops and arranging your own hire deals.

● **Underground** Construction of Tehran's underground railway started in 1978. It's due to open at last during 1998.

Accommodation

The accommodation situation in Iran is very dependent on the time of year. During the No Ruz holiday (March 20 to April 14) you'll have more luck buying a beer than renting a room. September is busy, too, as it's the cooler end of the holiday season. Accommodation is cheapest in the winter months except on the Gulf Coast where no other time is bearable: a $5 room in summer might cost $3 in November). In modest hotels, bargaining can halve the listed room price except during the peak season.

Price fluctuations on the Caspian Sea coast are more marked. Ski resort accommodation is best booked ahead through city agencies.

In most Asian countries, conventional travellers' wisdom dictates that the smaller the town the cheaper the hotel. The rule doesn't apply in Iran where smaller towns may have only one or two places and both are likely to be pricey.

The cheapest form of hotel is a *mosaferkhané* (R2000-8000 per person). A

❏ In a small village an hour from Isfahan a man rushes up to me, crossing the street without checking for passing tractors, clutching an apparently important document. He hails me politely but urgently and approaches. The whole village appears to have wanted to approach me too but till then a mixture of shyness and polite good manners has prevented any more than an occasional cry of 'Hello Mr' from the odd adolescent. But my new inquisitor is homing in on me and I am soon surrounded. The instant crowd is a scenic mixture of bearded men in turbans and flowing robes as well as little boys and tracksuited youths, two men in tie-less suits and a couple of shy girls hanging back slightly in full chador. The man is rustling through his pamphlet which turns out not to be a Koranic scripture but the manual to an Aiwa video recorder. Scanning the interminable list of instructions he lights randomly upon the feature 'CH' and points to it. The crowd hush to hear the words of wisdom from yours truly, prophet of the god technology. 'Channel?', I guess. How do you play charades with a word like that? But I have spoken, the tension is broken, and I am whisked off for a cup of tea with the privileged questioner. What a country where people vie to play host! I wonder whether he actually had a video at all?

mosaferkhané tends to be clean(ish) but is very basic and rarely has showers (though there is likely to be a public bath, *hamam*, close at hand). Few mosaferkhanés are marked with signs in Roman script – to find one try venturing up hopeful stairways above shop fronts in town centres. Although many do not take women or foreigners (lacking a suitable licence without which they can get shut down), many mosaferkhanés can be more atmospheric than better class hotels.

A *mehmanpazir* is slightly more expensive than a mosaferkhané, and usually has warm showers.

The term 'hotel' in Iran may mean a cheap place, such as a mosaferkhané, that simply had no other way to write a sign in English; or a higher class establishment which is liable to ask for US$ or charge higher foreigner rates.

Roadside restaurants sometimes provide a basic bed for passing travellers. In trailhead villages that don't have formal accommodation, locals will often be prepared to rent a room. Ask in the village store or tea shop for an *otagh*. This found us a basic R5000 room in Masulé, where such requests are relatively common given the delapidation of the single overpriced hotel. It also worked in Kelardasht.

Food and drink

Everyday food for Iranians is typically one of many forms of *khoresht* – stew served with rice. Incarnations of khoresht include *reymé* (meat stew with lentils and lime), *orme sabzi* (vegetable stew) and more luxuriously *fesenjan* (a very rich, almost black coloured walnut and pomegranate based stew with chicken or goose meat). To be served *fesenjan* in someone's home is something of an honour. *Abgusht* is served with a pestle: ask someone show you how to drink, grind and finally eat it!

Sadly, restaurants which serve authentic Persian cuisine are heavily outnumbered by the ubiquitous burger and sandwich shops. Menus in what good Persian restaurants you do find often offer little more than *chello kebab* (pounded minced lamb cooked on skewers and served on rice with a little salad).

The most common drink in Iran is *chai* (tea), served without milk and not quite as strong as in Turkey. As if from a dentist's nightmare, Iranians drink their chai through a rough sugar lump held between the teeth. There are some very atmospheric *chaikhuné* (tea shops) in ancient vaulted cloisters of the city bazaars (and under the classic bridges in Isfahan); at many you can smoke a *hookah* for R1000 (flavoured tobacco only) or sometimes play chess with the locals. Some *chaikhuné* are for men only.

Alcohol is banned under Islamic law, but many locals risk 74 lashes and up to six months in jail by storing a carton of home distilled *arak* surreptitiously behind their bookshelves. Your host might triumphantly pull some out and offer you a drink. If you accept you may wonder why he bothers. It's generally awful. Non alcoholic malt beer, *ma'osha éer*, is also commonly available, including canned Bavaria imported from Holland.

Soft drinks include the ubiquitous Coca Cola and are cheap (R2-300) when sold in returnable bottles. Cans can cost three times this price.

Stands in bigger towns offer a wonderful selection of fresh fruit juices squeezed while you wait; prices depend on whether the fruit is in season or not but expect to pay about R800.

Staying in touch

● **Mail** International mail is great value – postcards cost only R250 to anywhere.

● **Fax** These can be sent from Tehran's Regional Post Centre on Kargar St, south of Mor Sq (R8000 per page to the UK, R12,000 to the USA). If you take a fax to the GPO they will simply post it over there but it should be faxed within a day or two.

● **Phone** Local calls are free from shops and lobby phones in better hotels. Pay phones take cards or hard to find R5 coins. Long distance and international calls can be made only from special telephone offices and there is a three minute minimum for calls abroad. That said, calls are good value at R2800 a minute to Europe and R3510 to North America. You'll have to wait an unspecified time for the call to be put through: as much as an hour if they are busy.

Dress

Women who uncover their hair, or allow others tantalising glimpses of wrist or calf, may be considered on a par with prostitutes in Iran, which demands women cover up 'for their own protection'. Most

---

❏ Meeting the locals

● **The people** Prepare yourself for some of the friendliest people you are likely to meet anywhere. Invitations to dine or stay with local people are embarrassingly generous and common. You'll soon lose that Western suspicion of ulterior motives and realise that most invitations are based on a genuine desire to help and entertain, though undoubtedly your host will enjoy practising his English, question you on your religion and try to fathom your moral standpoint. Despite initial fears, we have found that frank discussion doesn't get you locked up. While enthusiasm for the Islamic Revolution has diminished over the last ten years most people still agree that freedom of speech is better now than under the Shah. Women like to explain the joys (or otherwise) of the *hejab* (dress code) to Western women. Everyone seems keen to express the benefits of Islam, but mutual respect between religions is considered a key. Atheists, however, may find that becoming a tactical Christian saves a lot of discussion.

Perhaps the most important decision travellers to Iran have to make is decided if they are red or blue. Perspolis (Reds) and Esteghlal (Blues) are the two top soccer teams (both from Tehran) and Iranians divide by this question.

The *Meidan* (main square) and bazaar are the central gathering points in each town. Particularly at weekends, students seek out tourists there and offer guided walks etc in order to practise their English.

To avoid frustration we found it helped to regard the Islamic rules as a sort of game, joking with locals (who do have a sense of humour) about the crazy quirks. Who can fail to laugh at the concept of a Tehran 'nightclub': no booze, no music, no dancing so they play table tennis. 'Of course if a woman came in we'd have to stop and tell her to leave or else we'd all be liable to arrest'.

Chess and backgammon are the most popular games (though it's illegal to play the latter in public).

With so little legal entertainment, it is hardly surprising that the population is growing rapidly. And perhaps boredom contributes to the friendly openness of strangers who delight in spending time with you – in Iran making friends seems easier than almost anywhere else.

● **Language** The Iranian language is Farsi and despite the Arabic script it is not Arabic.

Some phrases in Farsi:

> Hello – *salam* (or more formally *salam elekum*)
> How are you? – *chetori?*
> Reply – *man khu bam*
> Thank you – *kheli mamnu* (also *merci* from French, *teshekur* from
>   Turkish and more formally *motte shakeran*)
> Delicious – *hosh ma-zé*
> Beautiful – *ga-shang* (for things), *kosh ger* (for people)
> I'm sorry/excuse me – *be bak shi*

Western women find this rule understandably infuriating and sweaty. Conforming can be as easy as wearing jeans (not tight), a baggy long sleeved blouse/coat and a head scarf. Veils are not necessary, as long as the hair is covered. However, wearing the ubiquitous one piece *chador* (black head and shoulder drape) will win you respect. These chador can be made up very cheaply and quickly upon arrival and are compulsory for entry to a few holy sites (eg in Mashhad, Shiraz and Qom). If you get one, consider keeping it for Pakistan where unwanted advances tend to be much more common.

Men have it easy, but shorts and sleeveless shirts should be avoided.

Wash your feet and socks regularly if you plan to go into mosques or people's homes: you'll need to remove your shoes.

Further information

● **Books** Check to see if the new edition of Lonely Planet's *Iran* guide (due July 98) has come out as the first edition makes travel sound much tougher than it now is. Philip Ward's *Touring Iran*, is so far out of date (1971) and so quirky that it makes a refreshing alternative travelling companion. His delight in the country (and what he had for breakfast) is infectious though nowadays you have less need to wonder whether you will be captured by 'Kurdish Brigands' (on the Iranian side of the border at least). Odyssey has recently produced an Iran guide.

● **Maps** Decent maps of most Iranian cities and regions, produced by Gita Shenasi, are patchily available from book shops in larger towns. The cost will be between R700 and R2000. A wonderfully detailed if unwieldy Tehran map is available from stalls on Ferdowsi St near the UK embassy.

Most streets have been renamed, some more than once, though many old names remain in common parlance. If you can't find an address, suspect either that your map is old, or more likely, that people are still using the old names.

● **Information offices** The best (and easiest to find) tourist office in Iran is the one in Isfahan – the staff are very helpful and the maps are excellent and free. Elsewhere ask for the *Ershad-e-Islami* office.

Some tourist offices give out a large and detailed road map of Iran which includes some useful icons, such as those for mosques and petrol pumps but all copies of this Iran road map we saw were in German with confusing transliterations of town names. If you're lucky you might get a copy sent to you by writing to the Ministry for Islamic Guidance, Wali-e-Asr St, Dameshq St 11, Tehran.

CUNEIFORM WORLD'S OLDEST ALPHABETIC SCRIPT

D A R H E U Ş

Marks end of word

DEVISED BY THE BABYLONIANS, REFINED (AS ABOVE) BY PERSIANS. THIS WORD (KING "DARIUS") APPEARS FREQUENTLY ON THE MONUMENTS HE SPONSORED E.G. PERSEPOLIS AND BISITUN, IRAN.

❏ Farsi, Arabic and Urdu scripts

Transliterating Farsi, Urdu or Arabic is much easier than you might imagine. Words are written from **right to left**. Letters run into one another and take slightly different forms according to which of 4 positions each occupies: starting the word (ie right end), finishing it (left end), in the middle, or standing as a single letter. Many letters are topped or tailed with dots. The number and position of such dots will help identify letters using our table of fully written out forms:

LETTER	A	B	Ch	D	Ē	Eh	F	G	Gh	H	Ī	J	K	Kh	L	La	M	N	Ō	P	Q	R	S	T	Th
NO OF DOTS	-/•	1↑	3↑	-	*	-	=H	1↑	-		1↑	-/-	-/2	1↑	-		1↑	-	-	-	1↑	-/*	3↑	2↑	-/-/3↑	-/2↑ 3↑

LETTER	Ū	V	Y	Z	Zh
DOTS	*	=0	=Ī	1↑/1↑/1↑	3↑

↑ = DOT(s) ABOVE LETTER

⊞ = PRONUNCIATION = TOUGH. SOME TRANSLITTERATIONS REVERSE Q↔Gh

* AS **ı** (Ā OR ANY LONG VOWEL) OR AS **ı** WITH Ī OR Ō

ALONE	START	MIDDLE	END	SOUND	ALONE	START	MIDDLE	END	SOUND	ALONE	START	MIDDLE	END	SOUND	ALONE	START	MIDDLE	END	SOUND
NO DOTS									Ā/ANY LONG VOWEL E/I/O/u					L					L
ه	ط	ه	ه	H/Eh	ک	ک	ک	ک	K	گ	گ	گ	گ	G	لا			لا	La

AT END OF A WORD AFTER "I/Y" — SEE "2DOTS" — Ī/Y

					ONE DOT					**TWO DOTS**					**THREE DOTS**				
					ب	ب	ب	ب	B	ت	ت	ت	ت	Ī/N	پ	پ	پ	پ	P
					ن	ن	ن	ن	N	ت	ت	ت	ت	T	ث	ث	ث	ث	Th/S
س	س	س	س	S											ش	ش	ش	ش	Sh
ر	ر	ر	ر	R	ز	ز	ز	ز	Z	ق	ق	ق	ق	Q	ژ	ژ	ژ	ژ	Zh
م	م	م	م	M	ف	ف	ف	ف	F										
و	و	و	و	Ō/V						**HARD TO PRONOUNCE OR TO DIFFERENTIATE**									
ح	ح	ح	ح	H	ج	ج	ج	ج	J	**THE TWO DOTS MAY BE WRITTEN AS — OR .**					چ	چ	چ	چ	Ch
					خ	خ	خ	خ	Kh	EG ق = ق̇									
ص	ص	ص	ص	S	ض	ض	ض	ض	Z						**MAY BE WRITTEN AS ؛ OR .**				
ع	ع	ع	ع	A	غ	غ	غ	غ	Gh						EG ٿ̈ = ٿ̇				
د	د	د	د	D	ذ	ذ	ذ	ذ	Z										
ط	ط	ط	ط	T	ظ	ظ	ظ	ظ	Z										

There are no letters for short vowels. Though these can be indicated by special markers (as in Arabic), in Urdu and Farsi this is rarely done. Look at the example:

Right to left this is Ch L O K B A B. Say Chlo Kbab fast and it sounds more like real Farsi than 'Chelo Kebab' (the popular Iranian dish). Normal English transliteration usually adds the short vowels. This problem of transliteration explains why the spelling of names on maps may vary. **Beware**: the end of a

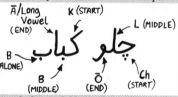

Ā/Long Vowel (END)   K (START)   L (MIDDLE)   B ALONE   B (MIDDLE)   Ō (END)   Ch (START)

group of letters need not necessarily be the end of a word. Notice the gap between the A and B of kebab. The space is necessary because, if the letters were joined, the A would become indistinguishable from an L. Letters A, D, La, O, R, 2Zs, and Zh all suffer from this unconnectability and thus have no 'start' or 'middle' forms.

The long vowel **ا** is usually pronounced A in the middle of a word but can be transliterated in different ways (eg kebab and kebob are equally valid). The same character at the start of a word might be any vowel, A, E, I, O, U and can combine with an O or I/Y to make a single OU or I/YI sound eg Iran:

LONG VOWEL AS Ā → ایران ← N   R   Ī LONG VOWEL   **IRAN** ایـــــــوان

Note that horizontal length of letters can be varied without affecting readability.

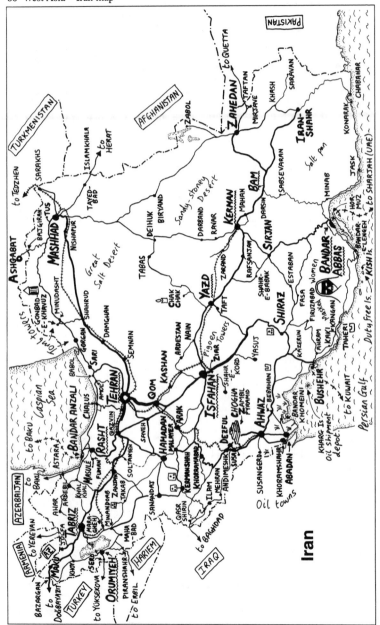

Iran

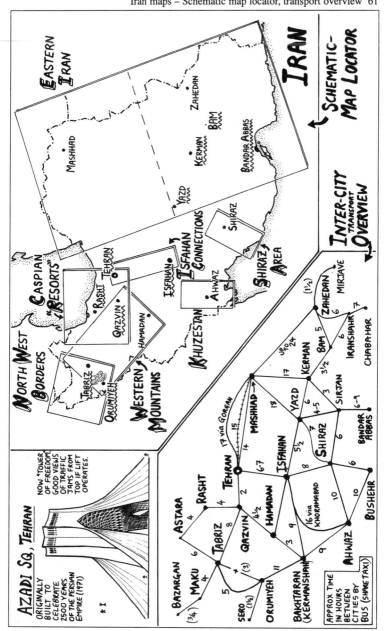

IRAN

SCHEMATIC–MAP LOCATOR

EASTERN IRAN

MASHHAD
ZAHEDAN
BAM
KERMAN
YAZD
BANDAR ABBAS

NORTH WEST BORDERS

CASPIAN "RESORTS"

RASHT   TEHRAN

QAZVIN   HAMADAN

TABRIZ
ORUMIYEH

WESTERN MOUNTAINS

ISFAHAN CONNECTIONS

ISFAHAN
AHWAZ

KHUZESTAN

SHIRAZ
SHIRAZ AREA

INTER-CITY TRANSPORT OVERVIEW

AZADI SQ. TEHRAN

ORIGINALLY BUILT TO CELEBRATE 2500 YEARS OF THE PERSIAN EMPIRE (1971)

NOW "TOWER OF FREEDOM" GOOD VIEWS OF TRAFFIC JAMS FROM TOP IF LIFT OPERATES.

BAZARGAN
MAKU   6
(3/4)   5   (3)
SERO   ORUMIYEH
(1/2)   11
BAKHTARAN (KERMANSHAH)

ASTARA   4   RASHT
4
TABRIZ   8   QAZVIN   2   TEHRAN
6   4 1/2   HAMADAN
3
9   16 via KHORRAMABAD
9   AHWAZ

BUSHEHR
10
BANDAR ABBAS
6
SHIRAZ   6
8   5 1/2   7
ISFAHAN   6-7   YAZD   6   SIRJAN   3
14   17   KERMAN   4-5
15   19   6   3 1/2
MASHHAD   17 via GORGAN   IRANSHAHR   7
CHABAHAR
BAM   5
up to 24
ZAHEDAN   6   MIRJAVE
(1 1/2)

APPROX TIME IN HOURS BETWEEN CITIES BY BUS (SHARE TAXI)

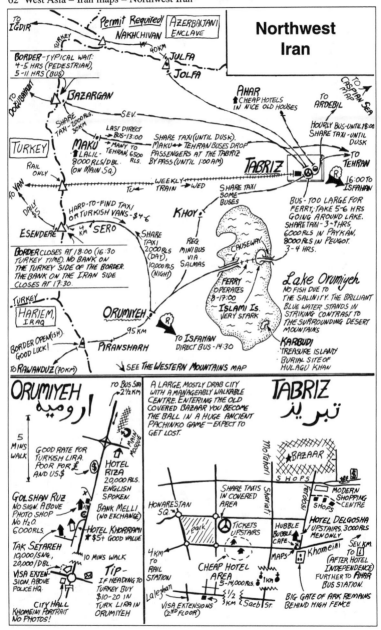

Northwest Iran

TO IGDIR

Permit Required! NAKHCHIVAN — AZERBAIJANI ENCLAVE

TURKEY

BORDER – TYPICAL WAIT: 4-5 HRS (PEDESTRIAN), 5-11 HRS (BUS)

JULFA
JOLFA
40KM

AHAR — CHEAP HOTELS IN NICE OLD HOUSES

TO DOĞUBAYAZIT

BAZARGAN

TO ARDEBIL

TO CASPIAN SEA MAP

SHARE TAXI – 2000 RLS 30KM

SEV.

HOURLY BUS – UNTIL 18:00 SHARE TAXI – UNTIL DUSK

LAST DIRECT BUS – 13:00

SHARE TAXI (UNTIL DUSK). MAKU → TEHRAN BUSES DROP PASSENGERS AT THE TABRIZ BYPASS (UNTIL 1:00 AM)

TURKEY

MAKU — LALIL – 8000 RLS/DBL (ON MAIN SQ.)

MANY TO TEHRAN, 6500 RLS.

TABRIZ

TO TEHRAN

Rail only

WEEKLY TRAIN → WED

16:00 TO ISFAHAN

TO VAN

SHARE TAXI SOME BUSES

BUS – TOO LARGE FOR FERRY; TAKE 5-6 HRS GOING AROUND LAKE. SHARE TAXI – 3-3½ HRS 6000 RLS IN PAYKAN, 8000 RLS IN PEUGOT. 3-4 HRS.

DAILY $2

HARD-TO-FIND TAXI OR TURKISH VANS – $4-6

KHOY

ESENDERE
SERO
4 KM

SHARE TAXI 2000 RLS (DAY), 10,000 RLS (NIGHT)

REG. MINIBUS VIA SALMAS

CAUSEWAY

BORDER CLOSES AT 18:00 (16:30 TURKEY TIME). NO BANK ON THE TURKEY SIDE OF THE BORDER. THE BANK ON THE IRAN SIDE CLOSES AT 17:30.

FERRY OPERATES 8-17:00

ISLAMI IS. VERY STARK

Lake Orumiyeh

NO FISH DUE TO THE SALINITY. THE BRILLIANT BLUE WATER STANDS IN STRIKING CONTRAST TO THE SURROUNDING DESERT MOUNTAINS

TURKEY
HARIEM, IRAQ

ORUMIYEH

95 KM

KARBUDI 'TREASURE ISLAND' BURIAL SITE OF HULAGU KHAN

BORDER OPEN(ISH). GOOD LUCK!

PIRANSHAHR

TO ISFAHAN DIRECT BUS – 14:30

TO RAWANDUZ (70 KM)

SEE THE WESTERN MOUNTAINS MAP

ORUMIYEH   اروميه

TO BUS STN 2½ HRS

5 MINS WALK

GOOD RATE FOR TURKISH LIRA. POOR FOR £ AND US$

MAIN MOSQUE

HOTEL RIZA 20,000 RLS. ENGLISH SPOKEN.

GOLSHAN RUZ NO SIGN. ABOVE PHOTO SHOP NO H₂O. 6000 RLS

BANK MELLI (NO EXCHANGE)

HOTEL KHORRAMI $5+ GOOD VALUE

TAK SETAREH 10,000/SNG., 20,000/DBL.

10 MINS WALK

VISA EXTENSION. ABOVE POLICE HQ.

CITY HALL KHOMEINI PORTRAIT NO PHOTOS!

Tip – IF HEADING TO TURKEY BUY $10-20 IN TURK LIRA IN ORUMIYEH

TABRIZ   تبريز

A LARGE, MOSTLY DRAB CITY WITH A MANAGEABLY WALKABLE CENTRE. ENTERING THE OLD COVERED BAZAAR YOU BECOME THE BALL IN A HUGE ANCIENT PACHINKO GAME – EXPECT TO GET LOST.

Motahari

BAZAAR
SHOPS

MODERN SHOPPING CENTRE

SHARE TAXIS IN COVERED AREA

Shariati

Ferdosi

SHOPS

HONARESTAN SQ.

park

TICKETS UPSTAIRS

HUBBLE BUBBLE CAFE

HOTEL DELGOSHA UPSTAIRS. 3000 RLS MEN ONLY

Khomeini

MAPS

SEV. KM. TO (i) (AFTER HOTEL INDEPENDENCE) FURTHER TO AHAR BUS STATION.

4 KM TO RAIL STATION

CHEAP HOTEL AREA 5-14,000 RLS.

1 KM

BIG GATE OF ARK REMAINS BEHIND HIGH FENCE

Laleghan

½ 3 KM Saeb St.

VISA EXTENSIONS (2ⁿᵈ FLOOR)

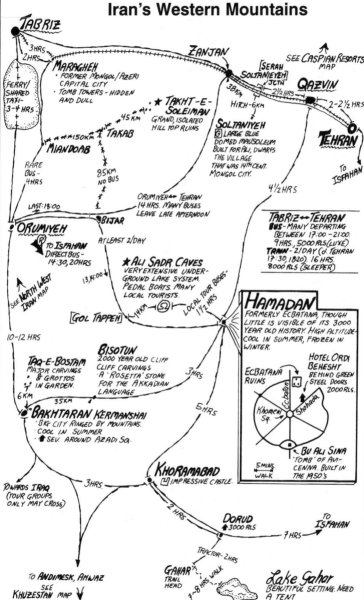

Iran's Western Mountains

TABRIZ

3 HRS
2 HRS

FERRY / SHARED TAXI - 3-4 HRS

MARAGHEH
· FORMER MONGOL/AZERI CAPITAL CITY
· TOMB TOWERS - HIDDEN AND DULL

ZANJAN

[SERAH SOLTANIYEH] JCTN

38 KM

HITCH - 6 KM

2½ HRS

QAZVIN

SEE CASPIAN RESORTS MAP

2-2½ HRS

★ **TAKHT-E-SOLEIMAN**
GRAND, ISOLATED HILL TOP RUINS

45 KM

SOLTANIYEH
Ⓖ LARGE BLUE DOMED MAUSOLEUM BUILT FOR ALI, DWARFS THE VILLAGE THAT WAS 14TH CENT. MONGOL CITY.

150 KM ← **TAKAB**

MIANDOAB

85 KM NO BUS

TEHRAN

TO ISFAHAN

RARE BUS - 4 HRS

LAST: 18:00

ORUMIYEH ↔ TEHRAN 14 HRS. MANY BUSES LEAVE LATE AFTERNOON

BIJAR

4½ HRS

ORUMIYEH
↓ TO ISFAHAN DIRECT BUS - 14:30, 20 HRS

AT LEAST 2/DAY

SEE NORTH WEST IRAN MAP

TABRIZ ↔ TEHRAN
🚌 BUS - MANY DEPARTING BETWEEN 17:00 - 21:00. 9 HRS, 5000 RLS (LUXE)
🚆 TRAIN - 2/DAY (d. TEHRAN 17:30, 1820). 16 HRS. 8000 RLS (SLEEPER)

★ **ALI SADR CAVES**
VERY EXTENSIVE UNDERGROUND LAKE SYSTEM. PEDAL BOATS. MANY LOCAL TOURISTS.

13, 14:00

[GOL TAPPEH]   14 KM   Ω   LOCAL TOUR BUSES 1½ HRS

LOCAL BUSES

HAMADAN
FORMERLY ECBATANA, THOUGH LITTLE IS VISIBLE OF ITS 3000 YEAR OLD HISTORY. HIGH ALTITUDE - COOL IN SUMMER, FROZEN IN WINTER.

10-12 HRS

TAQ-E-BOSTAM
MAJOR CARVINGS & GROTTOS IN GARDEN.

6 KM

BISOTUN
2,000 YEAR OLD CLIFF CLIFF CARVINGS A 'ROSETTA' STONE FOR THE AKKADIAN LANGUAGE

35 KM

3 HRS

5 HRS

BAKHTARAN KERMANSHAI
· BIG CITY RINGED BY MOUNTAINS.
· COOL IN SUMMER
· 🕌 SEV. AROUND AZADI SQ.

ECBATANA RUINS

HOTEL ORDI BEHESHT BEHIND GREEN STEEL DOORS 2000 RLS.

Khomeini Sq.   Shahada

Bu Ali Sina 'TOMB' OF AVICENNA. BUILT IN THE 1950's

5 MINS WALK

TOWARDS IRAQ (TOUR GROUPS ONLY MAY CROSS)

3 HRS

KHORAMABAD
🏰 IMPRESSIVE CASTLE

2 HRS

DORUD
⛺ 3000 RLS

7 HRS

TO ISFAHAN

TRACTOR - 2 HRS

TO ANDIMESK, AHWAZ SEE KHUZESTAN MAP ↓

GAHAR
TRAIL HEAD

7-8 HRS WALK

Lake Gahar
BEAUTIFUL SETTING. NEED A TENT

Caspian 'resorts' – escape the sunshine

The Caspian coast attracts crowds of local tourists drawn *away from* the summer sun to savour the rain of Iran's wettest region. Beaches are non-descript and hard to find. We did see bathers but preferred day hikes into the lush forests of the Alborz foothills. Minibuses shuttle along the traffic clogged coast road where holiday towns sprawl amorphously making hotel seeking tough without a car. Accommodation is mostly in upmarket B&Bs. Despite prices of 200,000rls (more in Ramsar or Nowshehr), almost everywhere was full in Aug. In Oct the few places still open were empty and charged from 20,000rls. Chalus and Rasht aren't resort towns and have cheap hotels.

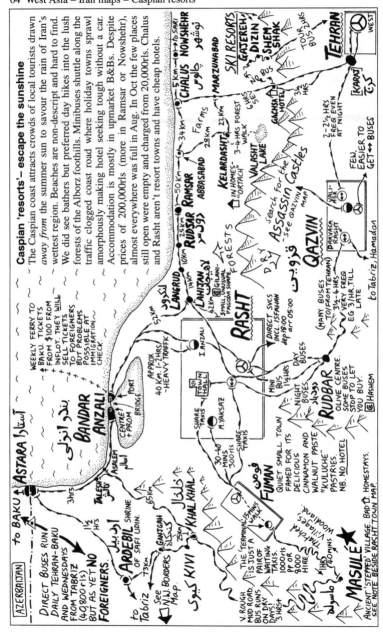

Masulé

This compact, atmospheric 1400-year old village is stacked so steeply that the roof of one mud house forms the road for the neighbour above. View from above for a fascinating pastiche of life scenes. Traditional bakeries, quaint ramshackle teashops, and the little Onebne Mohammad Ali shrine all add character; and there are great walks in the mountains. The approach from Fuman passes attractive thatched roofed hamlets (hiring a taxi one way is worthwhile for photo stops). Only one hotel, **Monfarel**, grotty and very overpriced at 20,000rls local price let alone 70,000 (B&B, 10,000rls) for foreigners. Ask around town for an *otagh* (private B&B) for 5000rls. Or 10km before Masulé at Lave Sheshme springs you can stay in streamside *cabins* for 5000rls. A cool refuge in summer, Masulé gets cut off by snow in winter and can be freezing cold as early as October.

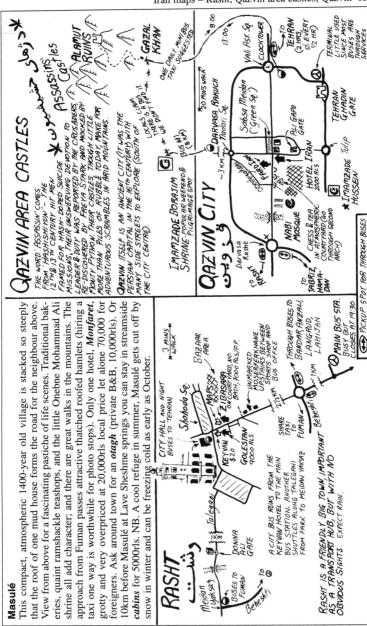

QAZVIN AREA CASTLES

The word "ASSASSIN" comes from "HASHISHIYUN" – THE 12TH & 13TH CENTURY HIT MEN FAMED FOR HASH-DOPED SUICIDE MISSIONS, THEIR UNSWERVING DEVOTION TO LEADER & DUTY WAS REPORTED BY THE CRUSADERS. RE-DISCOVERED BY FREYA STARK AND MOCKED BY MONTY PYTHON, THEIR CASTLES TODAY MAKE FOR MORE THAN PILES OF RUBBLE TODAY, MAKE FOR ADVENTUROUS SCRAMBLES IN ARID MOUNTAINS.

ALAMUT RUINS

Assassins Castles

GAZAL KHAN

ONE DAILY MINIBUS. TAXI SUGGESTED

QAZVIN ITSELF IS AN ANCIENT CITY (IT WAS THE PERSIAN CAPITAL IN THE 16TH CENTURY) WITH MANY SIDE STREETS TO EXPLORE (SOUTH OF THE CITY CENTRE).

LOCALS CLAIM IT WAS THERE (IS A BUS) BUT WE DIDN'T FIND IT

IMAMZADE BORAJIM SHRINE – POPULAR WEEKEND & PILGRIMAGE SPOT

QAZVIN CITY

TO TEHRAN (2 HRS) CLEVERY 1/2 HR)

TERMINAL USED SINCE MOST BUSES ARE THROUGH SERVICES

8:00 / 13:00

CLOCKTOWER

Vali Asr Sq.

20 MINS WALK

DARVASA RANICH

Sabsa Meidan ("Green Sq.")

Nadari Sq.

Ali Qapo GATE

3KM TEHRAN

(FREEWAY)

Obadallah

NABI MOSQUE

CHESS & TEA IN ATMOSPHERIC COURTYARD (GO THROUGH SECOND ARCH)

HOTEL IRAN 2000 RLS

TEHRAN GHADIN GATE

IMAMZADE HUSSEIN

IMAMZADE TULIP

Darvasa Rashti

TO TABRIZ, HAMADAN

RASHT

Meidan (Yaksar)

DONNA ALI GATE

BUSES TO FUMAN

TO Beheshti

Talegani

1KM

CITY HALL AND NIGHT BUSES TO TEHRAN

BAZAAR AREA

Shohoda Sq.

MASJED

ZURSAPA ONCOURTYARD NO. BATH, 3000 RLS/P.P.

KEYVAN $20

GOLESTAN 9000 RLS

SHARE TAXI TO FUMAN

UNMARKED MOSEREEKHANE UPSTAIRS BETWEEN SPORTS SHOP AND BUS OFFICE

THROUGH BUSES TO BANDAR ANZALI, LANGRUD, LAHIJAN

MAIN BUS STA. BUSY BUT CLOSES AT 19:30

3 MINS WALK

2 1/2 KM

1KM

A CITY BUS RUNS FROM THE MAIN BUS STATION. ANOTHER SHUTTLES ALONG TALEGANI FROM PARK TO MEIDAN YAKSAZ.

TO THE KEYVAN HOTEL

RASHT IS A FRIENDLY BIG TOWN, IMPORTANT AS A TRANSPORT HUB, BUT WITH NO OBVIOUS SIGHTS. EXPECT RAIN.

PICKUP SPOT FOR THROUGH BUSES

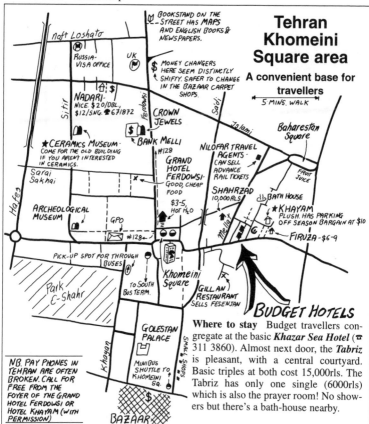

Tehran Khomeini Square area

A convenient base for travellers

Naft Loshato

Russia-Visa office

UK

BOOKSTAND ON THE STREET HAS MAPS AND ENGLISH BOOKS & NEWSPAPERS.

MONEY CHANGERS HERE SEEM DISTINCTLY SHIFTY. SAFER TO CHANGE IN THE BAZAAR CARPET SHOPS.

NADARI- NICE. $20/DBL., $12/SNG. ☎ 671872

CROWN JEWELS

Sadi

Islami

Baharestan Square

★CERAMICS MUSEUM- COME FOR THE OLD BUILDING IF YOU ARENT INTERESTED IN CERAMICS.

BANK MELLI #128

NILOFAR TRAVEL AGENTS- CAN SELL ADVANCE RAIL TICKETS

FRUIT JUICE

Sarai Sakhai

GRAND HOTEL FERDOWSI- GOOD, CHEAP FOOD

SHAHRZAD 10,000 RLS.

BATH HOUSE

★KHAYAM PLUSH. HAS PARKING OFF SEASON BARGAIN AT $10

ARCHEOLOGICAL MUSEUM

Hafes

GPO

$3-5, Hot H₂O

Mellat

FIRUZA -$6-9

#128

PICK-UP SPOT FOR THROUGH BUSES

Park E-Shahr

Khomeini Square

TO SOUTH BUS TERM.

GILLAN RESTAURANT SELLS FESENJAN

BUDGET HOTELS

GOLESTAN PALACE

Khayan

Small Shops

MINIBUS SHUTTLE TO KHOMEINI SQ.

NB. PAY PHONES IN TEHRAN ARE OFTEN BROKEN. CALL FOR FREE FROM THE FOYER OF THE GRAND HOTEL FERDOWSI OR HOTEL KHAYAM (WITH PERMISSION)

Small Shops

BAZAAR

Where to stay Budget travellers congregate at the basic *Khazar Sea Hotel* (☎ 311 3860). Almost next door, the *Tabriz* is pleasant, with a central courtyard. Basic triples at both cost 15,000rls. The Tabriz has only one single (6000rls) which is also the prayer room! No showers but there's a bath-house nearby.

5 MINS. WALK

TEHRAN is huge. Ali Asr St alone runs 17km from the railway station rising slowly uphill towards the expensive suburb of Tajrish. Near Tajrish you can visit the ex-Shah's summer palace and the scenic streamside teashops of Darband, where the dry Alborz mountain foothills form the city's northern limit. The rest of Tehran is a smoggy city where traffic-snared expressways push right through the drab residential areas as the city grinds through day long rush hours. Tehran's few tourist attractions tend to be open at inconveniently rare intervals. Crown Jewels: Tue+Thur, 2-4pm. Towchal Cable Car: Thur+Fri only. Archaeological Museum: closed Tue.

Getting around Buses cover most of the city except the swanky north-east corner (where many embassies lie). Taxis are extremely reasonable (5000rls/hr). For buses, pre-purchased tickets from kiosks cost 500rls for 10; journeys cost 1-3 tickets. Shared taxis stick to larger roads and take routes which are fairly predictable given a good map, though one way streets confuse matters slightly. Shared taxis (typically orange Paykans) cost 400rls for a ride sector, though if you get out after a block or two 100-200rls is OK. The underground railway should be open during 1998.

Tehran transport

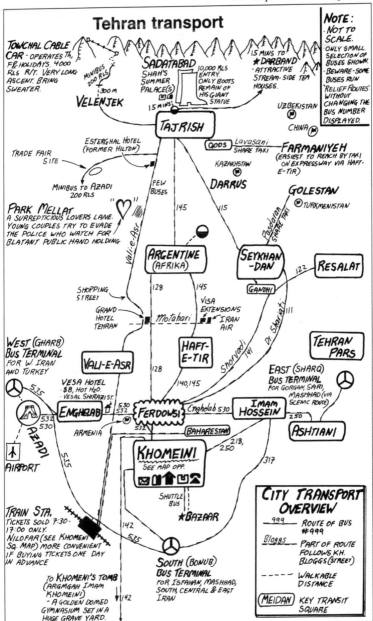

NOTE:
- NOT TO SCALE.
- ONLY SMALL SELECTION OF BUSES SHOWN.
- BEWARE - SOME BUSES RUN 'RELIEF ROUTES' WITHOUT CHANGING THE BUS NUMBER DISPLAYED.

TOWCHAL CABLE CAR - OPERATES Th, F & HOLIDAYS. 4000 RLS R/T. VERY LONG ASCENT. BRING SWEATER.

MINIBUS 200 RLS
1300 M
VELENJEK

SADATABAD SHAH'S SUMMER PALACE(S)
10,000 RLS ENTRY. ONLY BOOTS REMAIN OF HIS GIANT STATUE.

15 MINS TO ★**DARBAND** ATTRACTIVE STREAM-SIDE TEA HOUSES.

15 MINS

UZBEKISTAN
CHINA

TAJRISH

ESTERGHAL HOTEL (FORMER HILTON)

QODS Lavasani SHARE TAXI

FARMANIYEH (EASIEST TO REACH BY TAXI ON EXPRESSWAY VIA HAFT-E-TIR)

TRADE FAIR SITE

MINIBUS TO AZADI 200 RLS

KAZAKHSTAN
DARRUS

GOLESTAN
TURKMENISTAN

PARK MELLAT A SURREPTICIOUS LOVERS LANE. YOUNG COUPLES TRY TO EVADE THE POLICE WHO WATCH FOR BLATANT PUBLIC HAND HOLDING

FEW BUSES

145   115

Pasdaran SHARE TAXI

Vali-e-Asr

ARGENTINE (AFRIKA)

SEYKHAN-DAN

RESALAT

122

SHOPPING STREET

128   145

GANDHI

Dr. Shariati

111

GRAND HOTEL TEHRAN

Motahari

VISA EXTENSIONS IRAN AIR

TEHRAN PARS

WEST (GHARB) BUS TERMINAL FOR W. IRAN AND TURKEY

VALI-E-ASR

HAFT-E-TIR

128

Shariati 141

EAST (SHARQ) BUS TERMINAL FOR GORGAN, SARI, MASHHAD (VIA SCENIC ROUTE)

VESA HOTEL - $8, HOT H2O. VESAL SHIRAZI ST.

140,145

ENGHELAB

535   532   530

530   532

FERDOWSI

Enghelab 530

IMAM HOSSEIN

250

ASHTIANI

AZADI
AIRPORT

532

ARMENIA

535

BAHARESTAN

KHOMEINI SEE MAP OPP.

218, 250

317

SHUTTLE BUS

★**BAZAAR**

TRAIN STA. TICKETS SOLD 7:30-17:00 ONLY. NILOFAR (SEE KHOMENI SQ. MAP) MORE CONVENIENT IF BUYING TICKETS ONE DAY IN ADVANCE

142

535

SOUTH (BONUB) BUS TERMINAL FOR ISFAHAN, MASHHAD, SOUTH, CENTRAL & EAST IRAN

TO KHOMENI'S TOMB (ARGMGAN IMAM KHOMENI) - A GOLDEN DOMED GYMNASIUM SET IN A HUGE GRAVE YARD.

↓142

CITY TRANSPORT OVERVIEW

999	ROUTE OF BUS #999
Bloggs	PART OF ROUTE FOLLOWS KH. BLOGGS (STREET)
- - - -	WALKABLE DISTANCE
MEIDAN	KEY TRANSIT SQUARE

Isfahan Connections

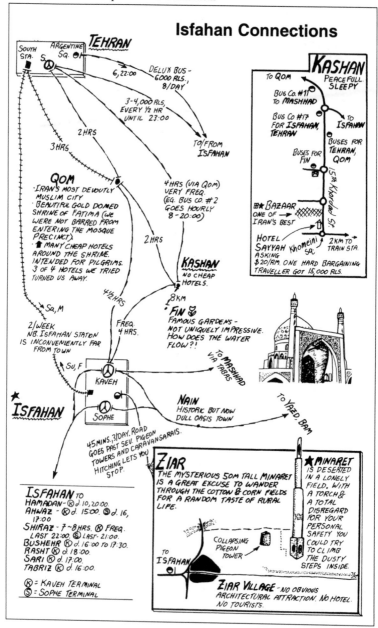

TEHRAN

SOUTH STA.
ARGENTINE SQ.

DELUXE BUS - 6000 RLS. 8/DAY
6, 22:00

3-4,000 RLS, EVERY ½ HR UNTIL 23:00

TO/FROM ISFAHAN

2 HRS
3 HRS

4 HRS (VIA QOM) VERY FREQ. (EG. BUS CO. #2 GOES HOURLY 8-20:00)

2 HRS

KASHAN
NO CHEAP HOTELS.

QOM
· IRAN'S MOST DEVOUTLY MUSLIM CITY
· BEAUTIFUL GOLD DOMED SHRINE OF FATIMA (WE WERE NOT BARRED FROM ENTERING THE MOSQUE PRECINCT)
· MANY CHEAP HOTELS AROUND THE SHRINE. INTENDED FOR PILGRIMS. 3 OF 4 HOTELS WE TRIED TURNED US AWAY.

Sa, M

2/WEEK
NB. ISFAHAN STATION IS INCONVENIENTLY FAR FROM TOWN

4½ HRS

FREQ. 4 HRS.

8 KM

FIN
FAMOUS GARDENS - NOT UNIQUELY IMPRESSIVE. HOW DOES THE WATER FLOW?!

TO MASHHAD VIA TABAS

Su, F

KAVEH

SOPHE

★ **ISFAHAN**

NAIN
HISTORIC BUT NOW DULL OASIS TOWN

TO YAZD, BAM

45 MINS, 3/DAY. ROAD GOES PAST SEV. PIGEON TOWERS AND CARAVANSARAIS. HITCHING LETS YOU STOP.

KASHAN
PEACE FULL. SLEEPY
To QOM
Bus Co. #11 To MASHHAD
Bus Co #17 FOR ISFAHAN, TEHRAN
TO ISFAHAN
BUSES FOR TEHRAN, QOM
BUSES FOR FIN
15th Khordad St.
▥★ Bazaar ONE OF IRAN'S BEST
HOTEL SAYYAH Khomeini Sq. ASKING $20/RM. ONE HARD BARGAINING TRAVELLER GOT 15,000 RLS.
2 KM TO TRAIN STA.

ISFAHAN TO
HAMADAN - Ⓚ d. 10, 20:00.
AHWAZ - Ⓚ d. 15:00. Ⓢ d. 16, 17:00
SHIRAZ - 7~8 HRS. Ⓚ FREQ. LAST 22:00. Ⓢ LAST - 21:00.
BUSHEHR Ⓚ d. 16:00 to 17:30.
RASHT Ⓚ d 18:00.
SARI Ⓚ d. 17:00.
TABRIZ Ⓚ d. 16:00.

Ⓚ = KAVEH TERMINAL
Ⓢ = SOPHE TERMINAL

ZIAR
THE MYSTERIOUS 50M TALL MINARET IS A GREAT EXCUSE TO WANDER THROUGH THE COTTON & CORN FIELDS FOR A RANDOM TASTE OF RURAL LIFE.

★ MINARET IS DESERTED IN A LONELY FIELD. WITH A TORCH & A TOTAL DISREGARD FOR YOUR PERSONAL SAFETY YOU COULD TRY TO CLIMB THE DUSTY STEPS INSIDE.

COLLAPSING PIGEON TOWER

TO ISFAHAN

ZIAR VILLAGE - NO OBVIOUS ARCHITECTURAL ATTRACTION. NO HOTEL. NO TOURISTS.

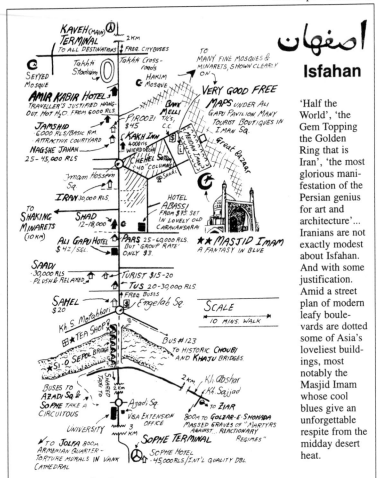

اصفهان

Isfahan

KAVEH (MAIN) TERMINAL
TO ALL DESTINATIONS

2 KM
FREQ. CITYBUSES

Takhti Cross-roads

SEYYED MOSQUE

Takhti Stadium

HAKIM MOSQUE

TO MANY FINE MOSQUES & MINARETS, SHOWN CLEARLY ON ↘

AMIR KABIR HOTEL
TRAVELLER'S JUSTIFIED HANG-OUT. HOT H₂O. FROM 6000 RLS.

BANK MELLI T/c's, C.C.

VERY GOOD FREE MAPS UNDER ALI GAPU PAVILION. MANY TOURIST BOUTIQUES IN IMAN SQ.

JAMSHID
6000 RLS/BASIC RM. ATTRACTIVE COURTYARD

PIROOZI $45

KAKH INN 4000rls WIERD DÉCOR

NAGSHE JAHAN
25- 45,000 RLS.

CHEHEL SOTUN "40" COLUMNS

Saadi

MEIDAN IMAM

Great Bazaar

Imam Hossein Sq.

IRAN 30,000 RLS.

HOTEL ABASSI FROM $75. SET IN LOVELY OLD CARAVANSARAI

TO SHAKING MINARETS (10 KM)

SHAD 12-18,000

ALI GAPU HOTEL $42/SGL

PARS 25-60,000 RLS. BUT 'GROUP RATE' ONLY $3.

★ ★ MASJID IMAM
A FANTASY IN BLUE

SAADI 30,000 RLS PLUSH & RELAXED

TURIST $15-20

TUS 20-30,000 RLS.

SAHEL $20

FREQ. BUSES

Engelab Sq.

SCALE
10 MINS. WALK

Kh. S. Motahhari

☆★ TEA SHOP?

SI-O-SEPOL BRIDGE

BUS #123
TO HISTORIC CHOUBI AND KHAJU BRIDGES.

BUSES TO AZADI SQ. & SOPHE TAKE A CIRCUITOUS

2 KM ↑↓ SHARED

UNIVERSITY

Azadi Sq.

2 Km. Kh. Abshar
Kh. Sajjad

TO ZIAR

VISA EXTENSION OFFICE

800M TO GOLZAR-E-SHOHADA MASSED GRAVES OF "MARTYRS AGAINST... REACTIONARY REGIMES"

TO JOLFA 800M ARMENIAN QUARTER – TORTURE MURALS IN VANK CATHEDRAL

SOPHE TERMINAL

SOPHE HOTEL 45,000RLS/INT'L QUALITY DBL

'Half the World', 'the Gem Topping the Golden Ring that is Iran', 'the most glorious mani-festation of the Persian genius for art and architecture'... Iranians are not exactly modest about Isfahan. And with some justification. Amid a street plan of modern leafy boule-vards are dotted some of Asia's loveliest build-ings, most notably the Masjid Imam whose cool blues give an unforgettable respite from the midday desert heat.

Which bus station?
There is a wide range of services from both terminals to most destinations, but the north (Kaveh) station is easier to reach and has more departures. The south (Sophe) terminal has a very helpful info desk. If you arrive in Isfahan but still seem to be in the middle of a craggy desert, you're at Sophe.

Quick tours
There are a couple of English speaking (almost) taxi drivers that tout quietly outside the Amir Kabir hotel. 4-5000rls/hour. Good value for visiting Vank, Golzar-e-Shohoda, distant bridges etc but first visit Meidan Imam (main sights easier to explore on foot) and get one of the free maps. Sunset is great from the Si-O-Sepol Bridge teahouse. Good breakfast too.

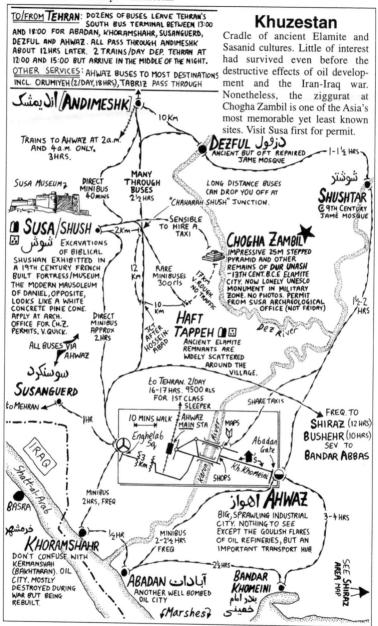

TO/FROM TEHRAN: DOZENS OF BUSES LEAVE TEHRAN'S SOUTH BUS TERMINAL BETWEEN 13:00 AND 18:00 FOR ABADAN, KHORAMSHAHR, SUSANGUERD, DEZFUL AND AHWAZ. ALL PASS THROUGH ANDIMESHK ABOUT 12HRS LATER. 2 TRAINS/DAY DEP. TEHRAN AT 12:00 AND 15:00 BUT ARRIVE IN THE MIDDLE OF THE NIGHT.
OTHER SERVICES: AHWAZ BUSES TO MOST DESTINATIONS INCL. ORUMIYEH (2/DAY, 18HRS), TABRIZ PASS THROUGH

Khuzestan

Cradle of ancient Elamite and Sasanid cultures. Little of interest had survived even before the destructive effects of oil development and the Iran-Iraq war. Nonetheless, the ziggurat at Chogha Zambil is one of the Asia's most memorable yet least known sites. Visit Susa first for permit.

اندیمشک (ANDIMESHK

10 Km

TRAINS TO AHWAZ AT 2a.m. AND 4a.m. ONLY. 3HRS.

Susa MUSEUM

DIRECT MINIBUS 40MINS

MANY THROUGH BUSES 2½ HRS

دزفول DEZFUL
ANCIENT BUT OFT REPAIRED JAME MOSQUE

1-1½ HRS

شوشتر

SHUSHTAR
@ 9TH CENTURY JAMÉ MOSQUE

LONG DISTANCE BUSES CAN DROP YOU OFF AT "CHAHARAH SHUSH" JUNCTION.

SENSIBLE TO HIRE A TAXI

-2Km-

شوش SUSA/SHUSH

EXCAVATIONS OF BIBLICAL SHUSHAN EXHIBITTED IN A 19TH CENTURY FRENCH BUILT FORTRESS/MUSEUM. THE MODERN MAUSOLEUM OF DANIEL, OPPOSITE, LOOKS LIKE A WHITE CONCRETE PINE CONE. APPLY AT ARCH. OFFICE FOR CH.Z. PERMITS. V. QUICK.

CHOGHA ZAMBIL ★
IMPRESSIVE 25M STEPPED PYRAMID AND OTHER REMAINS OF DUR UNASH –13TH CENT. B.C.E ELAMITE CITY. NOW LONELY UNESCO MONUMENT IN MILITARY ZONE. NO PHOTOS. PERMIT FROM SUSA ARCHAEOLOGICAL OFFICE (NOT FRIDAY)

12 Km

RARE MINIBUS 300rls

17 KM V. ROUGH V. NO TRAFFIC

1½-2 HRS

Dez River

10 KM

ALL BUSES VIA AHWAZ

DIRECT MINIBUS APPROX 2HRS

JCT AFTER HOSSEIN-ABAD

HAFT TAPPEH
ANCIENT ELAMITE REMNANTS ARE WIDELY SCATTERED AROUND THE VILLAGE.

سوسنگرد SUSANGUERD

to MEHRAN

to Tehran. 2/DAY 16-17 HRS. 9500 RLS FOR 1ST CLASS SLEEPER

SHARE TAXIS

1HR

IRAQ

10 MINS WALK

Enghelab Sq.

≈3 ≈5 Km

AHWAZ MAIN STA

MAPS

Karun River

Abadan Gate

SHOPS

Kh. Khomeini

FREQ. TO SHIRAZ (12 HRS) BUSHEHR (10HRS) SEV TO BANDAR ABBAS

Shatt-al-Arab

BASRA

MINIBUS 2HRS, FREQ

½HR

MINIBUS 2-2½HRS FREQ

اهواز AHWAZ
BIG, SPRAWLING INDUSTRIAL CITY. NOTHING TO SEE EXCEPT THE GOULISH FLARES OF OIL REFINERIES, BUT AN IMPORTANT TRANSPORT HUB

3-4 HRS

خرمشهر KHORAMSHAHR
DON'T CONFUSE WITH KERMANSHAH (BAKHTARAN). OIL CITY. MOSTLY DESTROYED DURING WAR BUT BEING REBUILT.

2½ HRS

آبادان ABADAN
ANOTHER WELL BOMBED OIL CITY

Marshes

بندر امام خمینی BANDAR KHOMEINI

SEE SHIRAZ AREA MAP

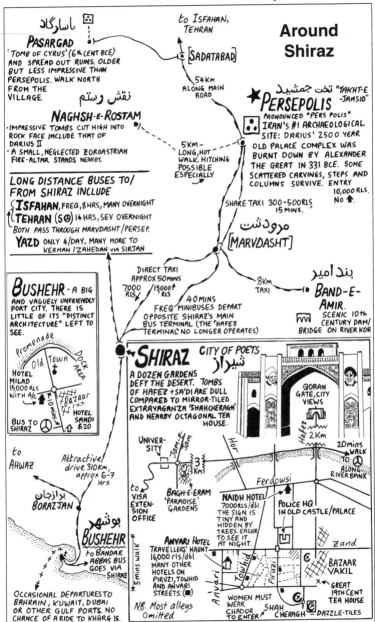

Around Shiraz

PASARGAD پاسارگاد
'TOMB OF CYRUS' (6TH CENT BCE) AND SPREAD OUT RUINS. OLDER BUT LESS IMPRESSIVE THAN PERSEPOLIS. WALK NORTH FROM THE VILLAGE

to ISFAHAN, TEHRAN

[SADATABAD]

54KM ALONG MAIN ROAD

NAGHSH-E-ROSTAM نقش رستم
- IMPRESSIVE TOMBS CUT HIGH INTO ROCK FACE INCLUDE THAT OF DARIUS II
- A SMALL, NEGLECTED ZOROASTRIAN FIRE-ALTAR STANDS NEARBY.

5KM-LONG, HOT WALK. HITCHING POSSIBLE ESPECIALLY

★ **PERSEPOLIS** تخت جمشید "TAKHT-E-JAMSID"
PRONOUNCED "PERS POLIS"
IRAN'S #1 ARCHAEOLOGICAL SITE: DARIUS' 2500 YEAR OLD PALACE COMPLEX WAS BURNT DOWN BY ALEXANDER THE GREAT IN 331 BCE. SOME SCATTERED CARVINGS, STEPS AND COLUMNS SURVIVE. ENTRY 10,000 RLS. NO ↑.

SHARE TAXI 300-500 RLS. 15 MINS.

LONG DISTANCE BUSES TO/FROM SHIRAZ INCLUDE
{ **ISFAHAN**, FREQ, 8 HRS, MANY OVERNIGHT
{ **TEHRAN** (S0) 14 HRS, SEV OVERNIGHT
BOTH PASS THROUGH MARVDASHT/PERSEP.

YAZD ONLY 4/DAY. MANY MORE TO KERMAN/ZAHEDAN VIA SIRJAN

[MARVDASHT] مرودشت

DIRECT TAXI APPROX 50 MINS 7000 RLS / 15000 RLS

40 MINS FREQ MINIBUSES DEPART OPPOSITE SHIRAZ'S MAIN BUS TERMINAL (THE "HAFEZ TERMINAL" NO LONGER OPERATES)

8KM TAXI

BAND-E-AMIR بند امیر
SCENIC 10TH CENTURY DAM/BRIDGE ON RIVER KOR

BUSHEHR - A BIG AND VAGUELY UNFRIENDLY PORT CITY. THERE IS LITTLE OF ITS "DISTINCT ARCHITECTURE" LEFT TO SEE.

Promenade
Old Town
DOCK AREA
HOTEL MILAD 15000 RLS WITH A/C
BAZAAR
10 MIN
HOTEL SANDI $20
BUS TO SHIRAZ

to AHWAZ

Attractive drive 310KM, approx 6-7 Hrs

BORAZJAN برازجان

BUSHEHR بوشهر
to BANDAR ABBAS BUS GOES VIA SHIRAZ

OCCASIONAL DEPARTURES TO BAHRAIN, KUWAIT, DUBAI OR OTHER GULF PORTS. NO CHANCE OF A RIDE TO KHARG IS.

★ **SHIRAZ** CITY OF POETS شیراز
A DOZEN GARDENS DEFY THE DESERT. TOMBS OF HAFEZ + SA'DI ARE DULL COMPARED TO MIRROR-TILED EXTRAVAGANZA "SHAHCHERAGH" AND NEARBY OCTAGONAL TEA HOUSE.

QORAN GATE, CITY VIEWS

Hafez 2 KM

20 MINS WALK ALONG RIVER BANK

UNIVERSITY

Jam-e Hor

to VISA EXTENSION OFFICE

BAGH-E-ERAM 'PARADISE' GARDENS

3 KM

Ferdowsi

NAIDH HOTEL 7000 RLS/DBL. THE SIGN IS TINY AND HIDDEN BY TREES. EASIER TO SEE IT AT NIGHT.

POLICE HQ IN OLD CASTLE/PALACE

Zand

ANVARI HOTEL TRAVELLERS' HAUNT 16000 RLS/DBL MANY OTHER HOTELS ON PIRUZI, TOWHID AND ANVARI STREETS.

5 mins walk

Anvari Towhid Piruzi

WOMEN MUST WEAR CHADOR TO ENTER

SHAH CHERAGH - DAZZLE-TILES

BAZAAR VAKIL

GREAT 19TH CENT TEA HOUSE

NB. Most alleys omitted

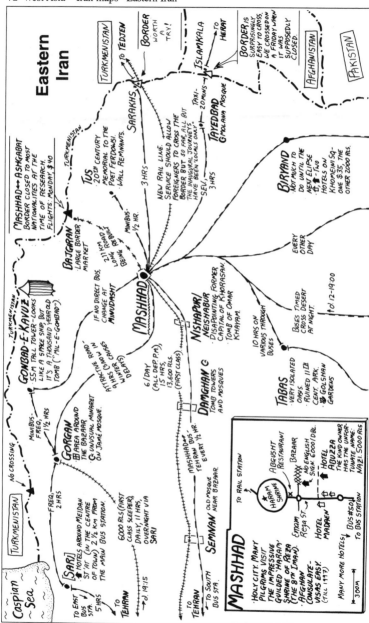

Eastern Iran

TURKMENISTAN

TO TEDJEN

BORDER WORTH A TRY!

TO HERAT

ISLAMKALA

BORDER IS SURPRISINGLY EASY TO CROSS, WE CROSSED ON A FRIDAY WHEN IT WAS SUPPOSEDLY CLOSED.

AFGHANISTAN

PAKISTAN

TAXI - 20 MINS.

TAYEDBAD GMOLANA MOSQUE

MASHHAD→ASHGABAT BORDER CLOSED TO MOST NATIONALITIES AT THE TIME OF RESEARCH. FLIGHTS MONDAY $40

SARRAKHS.

NEW RAIL LINE. SERVICE SHOULD ALLOW FOREIGNERS TO CROSS THE BORDER BUT SO FAR, ALL BUT THE INAUGURAL JOURNEY'S HAVE BEEN LOCALS ONLY.

TURKMENISTAN

TUS. 20TH CENTURY MEMORIAL TO THE POET FERDOWSI. WALL REMNANTS.

3 HRS

SEV. 3 HRS

BIRJAND NOT MUCH TO DO UNTIL THE NEXT ECLIPSE ⊙ - TWO HOTELS ON KHOMEINI SQ- ONE $35, THE OTHER 2000 Rs.

BAJGIRAN LARGE BORDER MARKET. 211 KM ROAD - LONG REBUILT.

GONBAD-E-KAVUZ 55M TALL TOWER - LOOKS LIKE A SPACE SHIP BUT IT'S A THOUSAND YEAR OLD TOMB ("MIL-E-GONBAD").

MINIBUS - ½ HR.

MASHHAD

IF NO DIRECT BUS, CHANGE AT MIMUDASHT.

MINIBUS FREQ.

ATTRACTIVE ROAD ' (3HOUR.) IN 9 HRS. (WINTER DELAYS).

GORGAN ✦ AREA AROUND THE BAZAAR. ⓖ UNUSUAL MINARET ON JAME MOSQUE.

EVERY OTHER DAY

⊙ 12-19:00

NISHAPUR/ NEISHABUR - DISAPPOINTING FORMER CAPITAL OF KHORASAN. - TOMB OF OMAR KHAYAM.

TABAS VERY ISOLATED OASIS. RUINED II.Ⅲ. CENT. ARK. ⓖ GOLSHAN GARDENS

BUSES TIMED CROSS DESERT AT NIGHT.

10 HRS ON VARIOUS THROUGH BUSES

6 / DAY (ALL DEP. P.M.) 13 HRS, 13,600 RLS. (FIRST CLASS)

DAMGHAN ⓖ TOMB TOWERS AND MOSQUES

MASHHAD– TEHRAN BUS' EVERY ½ HR.

FREQ, 2 HRS

[SAR] ⓖ HOTELS AROUND MEIDAN SQ. IN (THE CENTRE OF TOWN) 2½ KM FROM THE MAIN BUS STATION.

TO EAST BUS STN 5 HRS

TO TEHRAN

6000 RLS (FIRST CLASS SLEEPER) DAILY, 11 HRS, OVERNIGHT VIA SARI

⊙ 14:15

Caspian Sea

TURKMENISTAN

No crossing

TURKMENISTAN

SEMNAN OLD MOSQUE NEAR BAZAAR.

TO TEHRAN

TO SOUTH BUS STA.

MASHHAD

- HOLY CITY. MANY PILGRIMS VISIT THE IMPRESSIVE GUILDED 'HARAM' SHRINE OF REZA (THE 8TH IMAM).
- AFGHAN CONSULATE - VISAS EASY. (TILL 1997)

MANY MORE HOTELS

TO RAIL STATION

AUGUST RESTAURANT

BAZAAR

HARAM SHRINE

NO ENGLISH SIGN.

HOTEL AGUZZA THE KIND OWNER HAS THE UNFORTUNATE NAME: NAZI. 5000 Rs.

Emam Reza St.

HOTEL MADRAN

BUS #SQ

↓ GOLSHAN

TO BUS STATION

300M

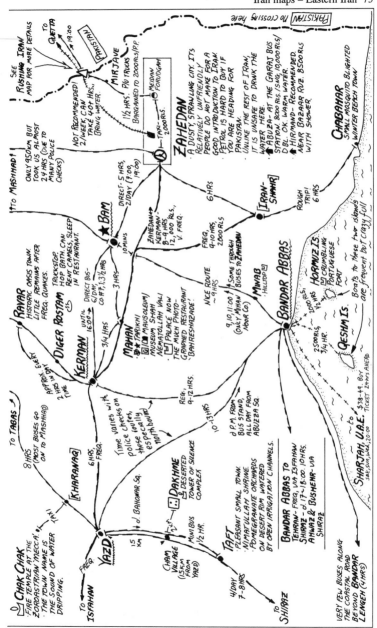

Yazd

Oh, for a good ladder in this atmospheric mud built city of glimpses! Behind the modern street facades the maze of adobe walls hide a marvellously medieval oasis skyline of beige and blue tiled domes, ubiquitous wind towers and minarets backed by snow flecked mountains.

'Alexander's prison' (improbable site of a tourist info office) had been over-restored, but trying to find it gets you deep into the old town kuches (alleys). Guides await to show you the city ($2 for half-day, ☎ 61056).

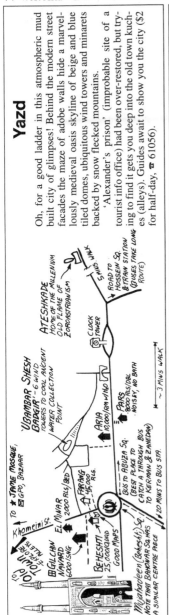

Kerman

Though convenient for a stop between Isfahan and Zahedan, Kerman is much less interesting than Yazd and lacks Bam's spectacular Ark. Many of its interesting older buildings were destroyed by recent earthquakes, though fragments remain around the bazaar.

NB. A crackdown at the time of research prevented foreigners using many of the cheapest hotels; the *Omid* and *Mahdi* seem the most reliable for now.

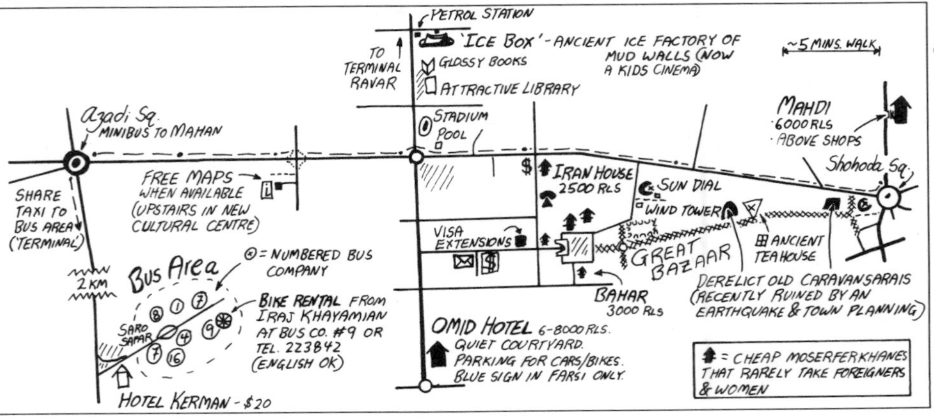

Map labels — Yazd

TO ★ JAME MOSQUE, ★ GPO, BAZAAR

Khomeini St.

'UBAMBAR SHESH BADGIR' – 6 WIND TOWERS TO COOL ANCIENT WATER COLLECTION POINT

ATESHKADE HOME OF THE MILLENNIUM OLD FLAME OF ZOROASTRIANISM

~ 5 MINS WALK

ROAD TO HOSSEIN SQ. & TRAIN STATION (BUSES TAKE LONG ROUTE)

CLOCK TOWER

~ 3 MINS WALK

ARIA 10,000/QM WHO

PARS 8000 RLS/DBL NOISY, NO BATH

FRANG 45,000 RLS

ELMNAR 2000 RLS/QUAD

GULCHIN NAVARD 6000 S/NG GOOD MAPS

BEHESHTI 25,000/QUAD

Mohadesseen (Beheshti) Sq. NOTE THAT BAHONAR SQ. HAS A SIMILAR CENTRE PIECE

BUS TO ABUZA SQ. (BEST PLACE TO CATCH A THROUGH BUS TO KERMAN & ZAHEDAN)

120 MINS TO BUS STA.

Map labels — Kerman

Shohada Sq.

~ 5 MINS WALK

MAHDI 6000 RLS ABOVE SHOPS

ANCIENT TEAHOUSE

'ICE BOX' – ANCIENT ICE FACTORY OF MUD WALLS (NOW A KIDS CINEMA)

SUN DIAL

WIND TOWER

GREAT BAZAAR

DERELICT OLD CARAVANSARAIS (RECENTLY RUINED BY AN EARTHQUAKE & TOWN PLANNING)

PETROL STATION

GLOSSY BOOKS

ATTRACTIVE LIBRARY

STADIUM

POOL

IRAN HOBE 2500 RLS

BAHAR 3000 RLS

VISA EXTENSIONS

OMID HOTEL 6-8000 RLS QUIET COURTYARD. PARKING FOR CARS/BIKES. BLUE SIGN IN FARSI ONLY.

TO TERMINAL RAVAR

♥ = CHEAP MOSERERKHANES THAT BARELY TAKE FOREIGNERS & WOMEN

Azadi Sq.

MINIBUS TO MAHAN

SHARE TAXI TO BUS AREA (TERMINAL)

~ 2 KM

⊕ = NUMBERED BUS COMPANY

FREE MAPS WHEN AVAILABLE (UPSTAIRS IN NEW CULTURAL CENTRE)

BIKE RENTAL FROM IRAJ KHAYAMAN AT BUS.CO. #9 OR TEL. 223842 (ENGLISH OK)

Bus Area

SARD SHMR

HOTEL KERMAN – $20

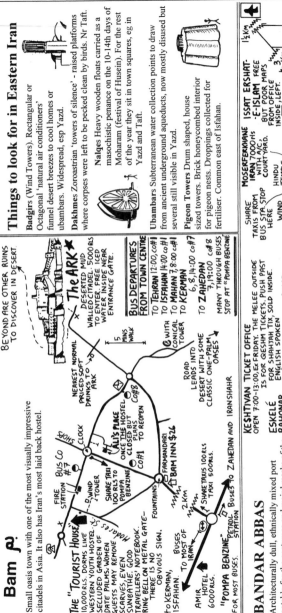

Things to look for in Eastern Iran

Badgirs (Wind Towers). Rectangular or Octagonal 'natural air conditioners' funnel desert breezes to cool homes or ubambars. Widespread, esp Yazd.

Dakhmes Zoroastrian 'towers of silence' - raised platforms where corpses were left to be pecked clean by birds. Nr Taft.

Nalges Heavy wooden floats carried as a masochistic penance on the 10-14th days of Moharam (festival of Husein). For the rest of the year they sit in town squares, eg in Yazd and Taft.

Ubambars Subterranean water collection points to draw from ancient underground aqueducts, now mostly disused but several still visible in Yazd.

Pigeon Towers Drum shaped, house sized towers. Brick honeycombed interior for pigeon nests. Droppings collected for fertiliser. Common east of Isfahan.

Bam

Small oasis town with one of the most visually impressive citadels in Asia. It also has Iran's most laid back hostel.

BANDAR ABBAS

Architecturally dull, ethnically mixed port notable for the costumes and weird masks of the women and the photogenic morning mayhem at the jetty for Hormuz bound boats. The city is a long strip with Bazaar Shadori the rough centre.

Afghanistan

Afghanistan has had many images: a 'high' point on the old hippie trail, a place of drugs, hospitality, and historical intrigues (in the Great Game, for example) as well as a backdrop to Eric Newby's *A Short Walk in the Hindu Kush*. The 1979 Soviet invasion, spray painted this image with blood and ever since the Mujahadeen factions which forced the Soviet retreat, have continued the agony. More people have been killed since the victory than during Soviet occupation. For much of the 1990s the country has been divided into the personal fiefdoms of local warlords. The central government at best controlled a small area around Kabul, and has now been toppled by the Talibaan movement. The Talibaan are predominantly ethnic Pushtus trained in the madrassas of Pakistan who have been ruthlessly effective at restoring law and order to the areas they control. Travellers along the former 'extortion highway' from Kandahar to the Pakistan border no longer have to pay bribes at dozens of militia check points. Transport services in Talibaan areas are beginning to resume and life has taken on a degree of normality. But it's a very puritanical brand of Islamic normality and a severe step backwards for women who are forced to wear *burqa* and are not permitted to work. Even football, popular in fundamentalist Iran, is considered un-Islamic by the stricter Talibaan and is banned.

Under the pressure of rapid Talibaan advances, the squabbling factions of ethnic Uzbeks and Tajiks in the northern areas, patched together an anti-Talibaan alliance based at the relatively unscarred, prosperous city of Mazar-i-Sherif. Then in July 1997 Uzbek warlord, Malik Pahlawan, turned the tables on former leader and one time communist collaborator, Dostum. In a flurry of backstabbing intrigues Malik grabbed Mazar-i-Sherif and invited in the

---

❏ **W&M's country ratings – Afghanistan**
● **Expense $$** Being here is either extremely cheap, or (should you need airlifting out) desperately expensive.
● **Value for money** ✔✔ The food is of poor quality and there's no electricity in most places.
● **Getting around** ✔✔ From Quetta to Turkmenistan via Kandahar and Herat is possible, other routes are dangerous though not necessarily suicidal. Crossing between lines of enemy factions is possible – taxi drivers arrange complex truce papers.
● **Woman alone** Probably extremely difficult: wear Islamic dress even more conscientiously than you would in Iran. The advantage of wearing the full *burqa* would be that you'd be invisible as a Westerner, given the right shoes and walk.
● **For vegetarians** ✔✔ Buy vegetables from the markets and ask your hotel to cook them for you.
● **English spoken** ✔✔✔ Many returned refugees learnt English while in exile. Any Farsi, Pushtu or Urdu is a great asset in villages.

Talibaan. Yet after just a few days' occupation and a heavy handed attempt by the Talibaan to disarm the populace, the city revolted. Hundreds of Talibaan fighters were captured or killed and the remainder retreated rapidly. Malik is now allied with Massoud (the Tajik faction leader in the anti-Talibaan alliance) so it's probable that the whole plan was a complex Talibaan trap from the outset. The intrigues and civil war continue.

We last visited in 1996 before Kabul had fallen to the Talibaan. At that time one could travel relatively freely in the Talibaan-controlled west, and there seems no reason that this would have changed. A Czech traveller we met had crossed between Talibaan and alliance lines – apparently taxi drivers can negotiate documents of safe passage between areas under the control of different factions. If things look too dangerous they'll turn back. With most of the south under Talibaan control, travel should now be easier than before.

❏ Geo-political information – Afghanistan

Population: 20.5 million (1997), 20m (1993), 13m (1979), 16m (1973).

Area: 652,000 sq km.

Capital: Kabul (1.4 million, 1988).

Other major cities: Kandahar (230,000), Herat (180,000), Mazar-i-Sherif (130,000).

GNP per capita: $150 (1994), $175 (1987).

Currency history: Afghani/US$1 Feb 1998: Af22,000, Oct 1997:Af20,300, July 1996: Af15,500, Nov 1995: Af4500, Aug 1995: Af5000, 1990: Af500, 1987: Af61.

Major exports/economy: Re-export of supposed aid shipments (worth $5.2 million in 1992).

Ethnic mix: Pashtun/Pathan (majority), Tajik, Hazara, Turkmen, Uzbek, Baluchis.

Official languages: Dari and Pushtu.

Religious tone: Fervently Islamic, 80% Sunni Islam, 19% Shi'ite.

Landmarks of national history: **1747**: Small Afghan state created by Ahmed Durrani (capital at Kandahar). **1839, 1878** and **1919**: Anglo-Afghan Wars, failed attacks from British India; a feudal monarchy until WWII. **1973**: King deposed, **1979**: Soviet invasion. **Valentines Day 1989**: Last Soviet troops withdraw. **28 April 1992**: Islamic State proclaimed.

Leaders: The Talibaan's low profile leader is Mola Mohammad Omar. The main anti-Talibaan alliance is led by Massoud (Tajik), with Malik (Uzbek), Galiani and Hekmatyar (former prime minister). Forces of former president Rabbani and warlord Dostum (Uzbek) may also be re-grouping. There are other regional leaders.

Pressing political issues: The continuing civil war, the degree of Islamic regulation and the legal status of football.

PRACTICAL INFORMATION
Visas and formalities

● **Visa strategy** Only Pakistan and Saudi Arabia have yet to recognise the Talibaan as the official government of Afghanistan. However the former government forces have long since been driven out of Kabul. Thus quite who you'll find manning the Afghan embassies abroad, is a bit of a lottery. Paying such consuls for a visa may give you a sense of comfort, but the chances of the document being useful for the areas you visit are limited. On the other hand, Talibaan guards did not specifically show annoyance at our possession of Afghan visas issued by non Talibaan consuls. To get such a visa the most co-operative consulates seem to be Mashhad (Iran) and New Delhi with Quetta and Peshawar (Pakistan) oscillating from helpful to door-slammingly bad. In 1996 you could arrive at Talibaan controlled borders with no Afghan visa, report to the Talibaan office at the border and ask for a message of invitation to be written into your passport. We've heard no recent reports of this method failing or succeeding. It's worth noting that Turkmen visas are easily available in Herat, and Pakistan visas are equally easy in Kandahar.

● **At the border** Borders to Uzbekistan and Tajikistan are presently closed to travellers but, surprisingly, we found that the Iranian and Turkmen borders were open. However, Iran's relationship with the Talibaan deteriorated significantly during 1997 (ambassador expelled from Kabul in June). Pakistan's borders may not be officially open to Westerners but several travellers have managed to cross surreptitiously. By wearing a Pathan hat and *shelwar kamise* men will be less conspicuous. A beard would also help. Women can wear a burqa which completely hides the face making sneaking across easy if (as sometimes happens) there is no-one to check your papers. Small men might also get across in a burqa. Allah help you if you're caught!

Money

Despite the fragmentation of the country there is still a national currency though its value fluctuates according to the political situation. Money changers are easy to find in town markets but will require cash, preferably US$. Some of the best rates are with changers in Pakistan (especially in Peshawar market).

Transport

● **Air** Aid flights were operating frequently to Mazar-i-Sherif but no reports since August 1997.

● **Road** Transport is running again in western Afghanistan and in most places is

---

❏ **Essential information for travellers – Afghanistan**

● **Visa** Theoretically required but travel to parts of the country is possible without any visa at all.

● **Currency** Afghani; US$1=AF22,000. The rate fluctuates according to military and political developments. Bring US$ cash.

● **Time zone** $4\frac{1}{2}$ hours ahead of GMT (1hr ahead of Iran, $\frac{1}{2}$hr behind Pakistan, and Turkmenistan).

● **Health factors** Purify the water. However, even with scrupulous care, many travellers get giardia.

● **Special dangers** The fierce civil war continues. Don't stray from well used roads and paths: there are many land mines. Listen closely to all news and traveller tales. White cairns denote that land mines have been cleared.

● **Former traveller destinations** Kabul, the surreal lakes and canyons of Band-i-Amir, Bactria, Bamian, Herat, the 40 steps at Kandahar.

● **Highlights now** Hospitable people; the resilience of the bazaar atmosphere; the war wreckage at roadsides; survival.

● **When to go** The summers are very hot and winters very cold.

● **Key tips** Afghanistan is volatile – obtaining information shortly before entering is very important. The best places to get a feel for the situation in Pakistan are: Quetta (Muslim Hotel), Peshawar (Tourist Motel) or from Afghans (in the markets); in Iran: Mashhad (Hotel Abuzar); in Turkmenistan: Kushka. The Talibaan controlled areas were the safest at the time of writing. Borders can be tricky: see 'At the border' section.

by truck or pick-up. Prices are generally very reasonable and it is worth paying the extra for the front seats to avoid being crushed. Russian Volga taxis also ply some roads, leaving when full.

Hitchhiking is possible and less nerve-racking than you'd imagine.

Accommodation

Most hotels in Kabul were seized by Mujahadeen factions as HQ buildings. Whether any budget accommodation has reopened there since Talibaan occupation is not clear. In Kandahar, Ghazni and Herat, however hotels can be found for under $2 a night.

A metal trough with three metal cylinders of water or three taps may signify that you're looking at an unmarked restaurant or hotel. You'll probably meet friendly locals who'll help you find somewhere to stay as the people are very hospitable: one traveller reported receiving free lodgings at the border post with Iran. However there may not always be a hotel so a blanket or sleeping bag and a mat would be useful.

Further information

● **Information** In the UK, try the Afghan Information Office, 290 Penton-ville Rd, London N1 9NR.

● **Books** No current guidebook has useful information on Afghanistan – try finding a pre-1979 book (such as Lonely Planet's *Asia On The Cheap*, the precursor to *West Asia on a Shoestring*). A few old Afghanistan-only guidebooks are still collecting dust in Kathmandu (we found two among the stacks in Mandala Book Point).

Among the myriad of background literature, an off-beat favourite is *The Afghan Amulet* (Michael Joseph, 1994). Author Sheila Paine's passionate desire to hunt down a specific piece of embroidery leads her to wander nonchalantly into the war

> ### ❏ Meeting the locals
> ● **Language**
> **Some phrases in Dari** (spoken in Kabul and the north):
> Thank you – *tesh-eek-kul*
> Friend – *andiwar*
> This food tastes good – *xh-eh-lee hober*
> Where is a cheap hotel room? – *arr-zan kujah ast*?
> Is this area safe? – *amin ja xh-hoo-beh*?
> 'Xh' is said as a hard back-of-the-throat rolling 'r' sound.
>
> **Some phrases in Pushtu** (spoken in the south):
> Thank you – *teh-eek-kur*
> Greetings – *stereh ma shee*
> Reply – *teh stereh meh shee*
> Good – *seh*

zone (Afghanistan is only a part of the odyssey): it's a fascinating story though there's a little too much detail on what she ate! A highly recommended, though difficult to find, book is *Les Cavaliers* by French journalist-explorer Joseph Kessel. More widely available are Eric Newby's *A Short Walk in the Hindu Kush*; *Caught In The Crossfire* by Jan Goodwin – the story of an American woman's travels with the Mujahadeen during the Afghan war – and *The Fragmentation of Afghanistan* by Dr. Barnett R. Rubin (Yale University Press), a recent book about political events. There are several glorious, full colour coffee-table books by Roland and Sabrina Michauld which capture the pre-1979 landscape and culture: look out for *Caravans to Tartary*.

● **Maps** Nelles produces a map of Afghanistan but it is difficult to find in Asia. Another option is getting an ONC map (Operational Navigational Chart).

Web sites
We didn't find any sites with useful information on what readers of this book really what to know about Afghanistan (ie. how to get in and stay alive). Try the list of links at frankenstein.worldweb.net/afghan/FaqNew/homes2.html

Afghanistan

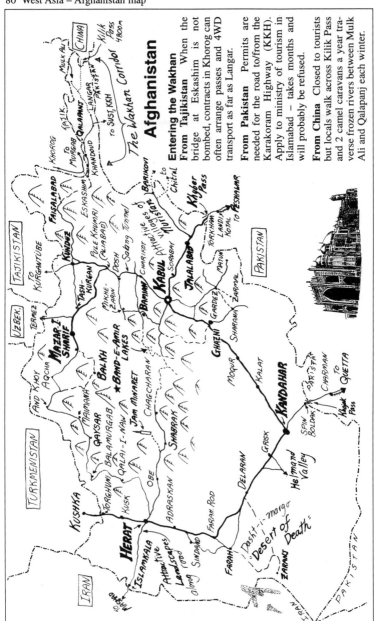

CHINA
Kilik Pass 4800m

MULK ALI

TAJIK.

LANGAR
to SUST, KKH

QALAMUT
to MURGAB

The Wakhan Corridor

KHOROG
To MURGAB

KHANDOUD

ESKASHIM

PULE KHUMRI (ALIABAD)

Sabng Tunnel

KHANDOUD

FAISALABAD

KUNDUZ

to Chitral

BARIKOT

Khyber Pass

TORKHAM

TASH-KURGAN

DOSH

MIKHE-ZARIN

BAMIAN

Charikot Attractive villages of Nuristan

SORABAY

KABUL

JALALABAD

LANDI KOTAL
TO PESHAWAR

MAYUM

GARDEZ

ZARANI

GHAZNI

SHARANA

MOQUR

KALAT

TAJIKISTAN
TO KURGANTUBE

UZBEK.

TERMEZ

MAZAR-I-SHARIF

BALKH

BAND-E-AMIR LAKES

Jam Muharet

CHAGCHARAN

SHABRAK

OBE

ANDKHOY

AQCHA

MAIMANA

QAYSAR

BALAMURGAB

QALAI-I-NAU

IBRAHIMI

KUSK

KUSHKA

TURKMENISTAN

ADRASKAN

FARAH ROD

FARAH

SINDAND

Attractive Landscapes Along 1700

ISLAMQALA

HERAT

QUSHM

IRAN

DELARAM

GIRSK

Helmand Valley

SPIN BOLDAK

KHOJAK Pass

CHARMAN
TO QUETTA

KANDAHAR

Dasht-i-marga "Desert of Death"

ZARANJ

PAKISTAN

PAKISTAN

Entering the Wakhan

From Tajikistan When the bridge at Eskashim is not bombed, contracts in Khorog can often arrange passes and 4WD transport as far as Langar.

From Pakistan Permits are needed for the road to/from the Karakoram Highway (KKH). Apply to ministry of tourism in Islamabad – takes months and will probably be refused.

From China Closed to tourists but locals walk across Kilik Pass and 2 camel caravans a year traverse frozen rivers between Mulk Ali and Qalapanj each winter.

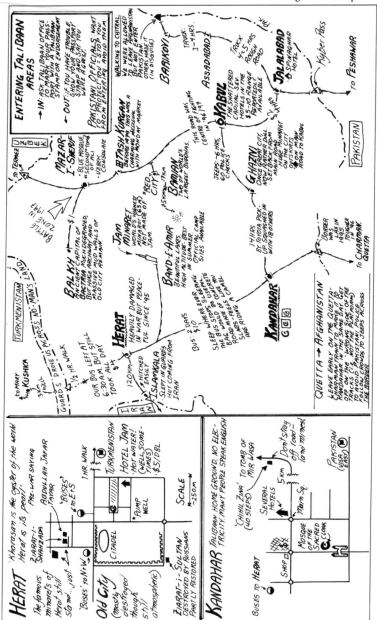

ENTERING TALIBAAN AREAS
- IN: ASK TALIBAAN OFFICE TO MARK TOWN PASSPORT WITH TALIBAAN STAMP FOR ENDORSEMENT
- OUT: IF YOU HAVE TROUBLE SHOW VON THIS PASSPORT WERE ALLOWED

PAKISTANI OFFICIALS: WANT TO PROTECT YOU - STOP YOU FROM ENTERING, AVOID THEM

WALKING TO CHITRAL - WE WERE ALLOWED TO LEAVE AFGHANISTAN + ENTER PAKISTAN - OTHERS MAKE IT (IN DISGUISE)

BARIKOV!

TRUCK 3 - HRS.

Khyber Pass

JALALABAD — SPINGHAR HOTEL

To PESHAWAR

TRUCK 4.5-5 HRS. ROUGH ROAD

ASSADABAD!

KABUL — THE SHATTERED CAPITAL. SEV. HOTELS IN THE $5-10 RANGE AVAILABLE

THIS ROAD WAS CENTRE OF FIGHTING IN '96/'97

To TERMEZ — UZBEK

BATTLE ZONE IN 1997

MAZAR-I-SHERIF — BLUE MOSQUE "SECOND" TOMB OF ALI. UZBEK. CONSULATE.

TASH KURGAN — BEFORE MAZAR IS A CHARMING MEDIEVAL TOWN WITH MONDAY MARKET

BALKH — ANCIENT CAPITAL OF BACTRIA MUCH DEGRADED BUT HUGE ARCHWAY AND MASSIVE MUD WALLS OF OLD CITY REMAIN

Jam Minaret — $1 WORLD'S HIGHEST MINARET (65?) NOT MADE OF JAM.

BAMIAN — HOME OF WORLD'S LARGEST BUDDHAS

"RED CITY"

SHAHR-I-ZOHAK

GHAZNI — ONCE GREAT CITY. NOW RATHER DULL SET BACK FROM THE CITY ON OUTSKIRTS ON MINARET ON THE ROAD TO KABUL

JEEPS: 6 HRS. 60 POLICE CHECKS

BAND-E-AMIR — BEAUTIFUL LAKES HIGH IN MOUNTAINS BEST IN SUMMER. OFFICIAL CAMP SIZES AVAILABLE

1 HR BY TOYOTA PICK-UP. SQUISHED IN WITH 18 OTHERS

KANDAHAR — G G G

DINNER WAS MILD IN 1995 — TOUGHER QUETTA

To CHAMAN, QUETTA

PAKISTAN

QUETTA → AFGHANISTAN
LEAVE EARLY ON THE QUETTA-CHAMAN TRAIN TO MAKE IT TO KANDAHAR IN THE SAME DAY. GET ONE OF THE JEEPS ON THE WRONG SIDE OF THE TRACKS TO AVOID PAKISTANI POLICE. FOLLOW CROWDS TO JEEPS ACROSS THE BORDER

To MARY — **KUSHKA** — 3 km GUARD'S DROVE US ACROSS NO-MAN'S LAND. 1/2 HR. WALK. OUR BUS LEFT AT 6:30 AM. BUT IT TOOK ALL DAY

TURKMENISTAN

IRAN

HERAT — HEAVILY DAMAGED IN WAR BUT PEACEFUL SINCE '95

120 km

ISLAMQALA — SLEPT IN GUARDS HUT COMING FROM IRAN. HITCHED EASILY

Bus: 2 DAYS $10 SLEEP WHERE WE'RE SLEEPING. USE FREE ROAD MEALS. BAAD-MEZ-FREE. SLEEP IN THE WINDS OF CAMEL ROAD ARE RIDING

HERAT — "Khorasan is the oyster of the world, Herat is its pearl" PRE-WAR SAYING — ABDULLAH JAFAR

The famous minarets of Herat still stand... just

"BUSES" TO N.W.

ZIARAT-I-SHAHZADA

Old City (mostly destroyed though still atmospheric)

CITADEL

ZIARAT-I-SULTAN DESTROYED BY RUSSIANS PARTLY RESTORED

TURKMENISTAN JAM

1 HR WALK

"BUSES" TO E'S

PUMP WELL

HOTEL JAM — HOT WATER! (HELL, SOMETIMES) $5 / DBL.

SCALE — 150m

KANDAHAR — TALIBAN HOME GROUND. NO ELECTRICITY. MANY PEOPLE SPEAK ENGLISH

5 km — DON'T STAY OFF ROAD - (land mines)

TOMB OF MIR WAIS

"CHIHIL ZINA" TO (40 STEPS)

SEVERAL HOTELS

MAIN SQ.

MOSQUE OF THE SACRED CLOAK

SHOP

BUSES TO HERAT

PAKISTAN (VISA EASY)

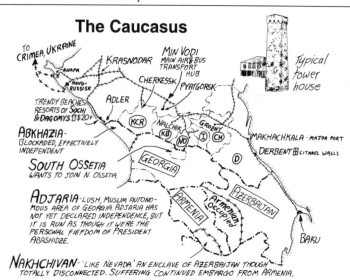

The Caucasus

TO CRIMEA, UKRAINE

ANAPA

Novo-RUSSISK

TRENDY BEACHES RESORTS OF SOCHI & DAGOMYS ☆ $20+

ADLER

KRASNODAR

CHERKESSK

MIN VODI
MAIN AIR & BUS TRANSPORT HUB

PYATGORSK

Typical tower house

ABKHAZIA – BLOCKADED, EFFECTIVELY INDEPENDENT

(KCR)
(KB) NALCHIK
(NO)

GROZNY
(I) (CH)

MAKHACHKALA - MAJOR PORT

DERBENT ⊞ CITADEL WALLS

GEORGIA

(D)

SOUTH OSSETIA WANTS TO JOIN N. OSSETIA.

ADJARIA – LUSH, MUSLIM AUTONOMOUS AREA OF GEORGIA. ADJARIA HAS NOT YET DECLARED INDEPENDENCE, BUT IT IS RUN AS THOUGH IT WERE THE PERSONAL FIEFDOM OF PRESIDENT ABASHIDZE.

ARMENIA

Armenian occupied

AZERBAIJAN

BAKU

NAKHCHIVAN – `LIKE NEVADA.' AN ENCLAVE OF AZERBAIJAN THOUGH TOTALLY DISCONNECTED. SUFFERING CONTINUED EMBARGO FROM ARMENIA.

The Greater Caucasus – Armenia, Azerbaijan and Georgia

For the sake of this book, the 'Caucasus' implies the three recently-independent countries of Armenia, Azerbaijan and Georgia: beautiful mountainous states on the divide between Asia and Europe. The Russian Federation's Caucasian empire is also fascinating with even higher mountains and several ancient tower house villages but is beyond the scope of this edition. The whole region has been battered by geo-politics for a millennium. Recent wars and blood feuds have not encouraged mass tourism. Nonetheless, the people are as warm hearted to guests as they are fierce to enemies. A venture into this wildly rugged land is a joy and an adventure.

Remember: a) the locals are **not** ethnic Russians, though most can speak Russian; b) listen closely for potential trouble spots: crossing between Georgia and Abkhazia, or between Armenia and Azerbaijan (both pairs have fought vicious and un-concluded wars) is potentially suicidal; c) exercise elementary tact when talking politics and religion: though few people seem very pious Georgia and Armenia are cradles of Christianity while Azerbaijan, Adjaria, Chechnya and much of Dagestan are proudly (if alcoholically) Muslim. Travel in mountain areas is hampered by deteriorating roads and (especially in Georgia and the North Caucasus) by bribe hungry police road blocks. A stock of cigarettes to hand out may be useful, but in many cases there's an almost set fee. Relatively high bus fares through North Ossetia and on the Georgian military highway reflect the bribes extorted from the driver. In Chechnya factional roadblocks add complexity.

Russian Caucasus – some notes

(CH) Chechnya War-torn republic. Grozny rail line closed, but Astrakhan-Derbent trains still run via bomb battered Gudermes.

(D) Dagestan Some spill-over of Chechnyan conflict but generally safe. Lovely mountain areas and gorges, great walking, transport slow/unreliable. Tindi atmospheric town. Kurush is Europe's highest village.

THE CAUCASUS

The Caucasus nations (Georgia, Armenia and Azerbaijan) form a spectacular bridge between the Caspian and Black Seas crashing together in a knot of soaring mountains. Caucasus is Persian for 'glittering ice' but the region also comprises a surprising variety of warmer climatic zones from semi-tropical forests to deserts. Stirred into the scenic blend are half forgotten castle ruins and some of the world's most ancient churches. For millennia the area has been a migration and invasion cross-roads leaving a human landscape that's a confusing and fascinating patchwork of fiercely independent, disarmingly hospitable people.

Wars have long enlivened the region's history. The three nation states that have emerged bruised and sore from the shadow of the USSR, initially continued in this tradition. Armenia and Azerbaijan have yet to settle their 1991-3 war over Nagorno Karabakh, and Armenian forces remain in control of some 20% of Azeri territory. Georgia also remains divided following the breakaway of Abkhazia, and hundreds of ethnic Georgians remain displaced as internal refugees. The scars remain but need not frighten off potential visitors. In recent years the situation has cooled markedly. Some clearly defined areas are still worth avoiding (the Abkhazian border, the Azeri-Armenian ceasefire line) but the worst trouble spots are now across the border in the Russian north Caucasus (Dagestan, Chechnya and Ingushetia) not covered by these chapters.

Economically, Islamic Azerbaijan is set to develop as a major power and its cosmopolitan capital Baku is already sniffing an oil boom. Meanwhile the historic Christian kingdoms of Armenia and Georgia are stabilising after years of economic freefall. Prices are low, there's lots to see, and for now, relative discomfort and lack of information has discouraged all but a trickle of intrepid visitors from realising the area's charms.

Russian Caucasus – some notes (cont)

(I) Ingushetia Part of Chechnya till 1992. 50% of population are refugees. New capital, Magas, under construction 5km from Nazran. Mountainous south has many Swanetian style tower houses but is hard to reach.

(KB) Kabardina Balkaria Highest mountains of all. Terskol for skiing, cable car/climbs to Mt Elbruz, Europe's No 1 mountain. In the days of the USSR it was possible to hike across the Becho Pass to Becho near Mestia (Swanetia, Georgia). The name of the capital, Nalchik, means horseshoes, for the ring of foothills surrounding it.

(KCR) Karachay-Cherkess Rep Great climbing, hiking (summer) and skiing around Teberda and Dombay (bus from Min Vody).

(NO) North Ossetia More tower houses, tombs, gorges (notably Dargavs). Spa/sanitorium at Karmadon. Vladikavkaz (capital) has a $10 hotel opposite the university, bus No2 from bus station.

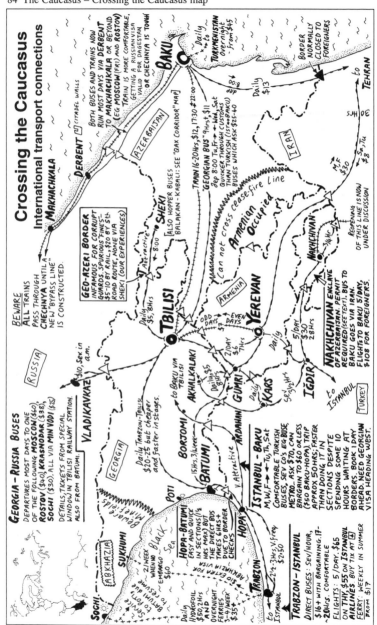

Crossing the Caucasus
International transport connections

PRACTICAL INFORMATION
Visas – general rules

Armenia, Azerbaijan and Georgia have their own reciprocal visa treaty. Given the relative ease of procuring visas and the fairly uncomfortable experiences we've had at several borders, we recommend that you get a visa for each country you intend to visit/transit. However, those who enjoy a challenge may note that the visa for any one country theoretically permits a five-day transit of either of the others. In practice this is of limited use. Armenia and Azerbaijan's mutual enmity keeps their common border tightly shut so using one visa in the other country would require the guts of a lemming. Other combinations work better, but unlike in Central Asia, you can't wander to and fro across borders at will on a single entry visa because border posts examine and stamp your passport. A single entry visa is naturally invalidated once you're stamped out of the issuing country so in effect the only reliable transits allowed by the agreement are:

Direction of transit	Visa used
Turkey → Armenia → Georgia	Georgian
Turkey → Georgia → Azerbaijan	Azeri
Azerbaijan → Georgia → Turkey	Georgian
Georgia → Armenia → Turkey	Armenian

Heading in the 'wrong' direction would be possible given a double/multi-entry visa. Alternatively you could try to persuade the guards not to stamp you out of the country. The latter is unlikely/dangerous (though we once managed it) as you could find yourself stuck in no man's land with some major bribes to pay. If you do make it to any of the capital cities without a visa, it is usually quite straightforward to apply for one at the consular department of the ministry of foreign affairs.

Through transport/border crossings

The map opposite gives an overview of the main transport routes. Travellers debate the relative merits of cross-border buses compared to 'do-it-yourself' options. In our experience, the Georgia-Turkey border is relaxed and quick to cross on foot, especially at Sarp where transport connections are easy. The same border causes delays of at least 5 hours for most through buses making a 30km Hopa-Batumi journey a nonsensical overnight ride. The Geo-Armenian border is relatively relaxed, and the several Georgian-run through buses are a sensible choice.

We've crossed the Geo-Azerbaijan border in three places and each time found the guards to be difficult, twice imposing arbitrary fines. The 'fine' on the overnight Tbilisi-Baku train was cheaper: 'only' $10 which we bargained to $5, and travelling by train is probably the best of a bad set of choices if you're rushing through. Crossing in local public transport hops is cheaper and quicker than taking the long distance Turkish buses which spend hours at the border especially east-bound (all the passengers have to get through customs, many bribing extra to prevent their bags being properly examined). However, if there's a 'problem' it can be reassuring to have the bus driver negotiate with the guards on your behalf. Georgian run buses have less to hide so pass through the borders in a few minutes. The driver on the cheap, twice weekly Georgian-run Tbilisi-Baku service will help foreigners through even though formalities take longer than for the rest of the passengers. Drivers on the shorter Balakan-Lagodekhi hop sometimes leave without you.

Further information

There is no overall Caucasus guidebook. Curzon Press (UK) publishes a series of background books including *Storm over the Caucasus,* about the Nagorno Karabakh conflict, by Baku-based journalist, Charles van de Leeuw. A new map of the region has recently been published by GiziMap (Afonya 1, Budapest, Hungary) available in most Western countries under the Bartholomew's imprint. It's more accurate than the Iranian produced Gita Shenasi map which shows roads across mountain passes where in reality there are only rough footpaths. Neither map shows cease-fire lines.

Armenia
(Hayastany Hanrapetoutioun)

Under King Tigran II (1st century BC), Armenia was one of the world's major powers with conquests as far afield as the Mediterranean coast. However, it's suffered a very turbulent history ever since. Amongst its better known invaders were Romans, Arabs, Persians, Mongols and Turks. Stalin also added his characteristic touch. The majority of historical Armenia actually lies within the easternmost part of modern Turkey. This area was depopulated in 1915, with around 1.5 million Armenians killed or deported, an act of genocide which Hitler studied diligently. Yet somehow, like neighbouring Georgia, Armenia survived as an island of Christianity in a sea of Islam.

❏ **W&M's country ratings – Armenia**
● **Expense $$$** Transport is expensive relative to neighbouring states.
● **Getting around ✔✔** There are some fuel shortages, buses run to most places but not frequently.
● **English spoken ✔** Carry a Russian phrase book if you don't speak Armenian.

Armenia's recent history hasn't been much kinder. An appalling 1988 earthquake devastated the region. Before damage was fully repaired a de facto war broke out with Azerbaijan (even though both republics were still technically within the USSR). Locals of either camp will gladly expound at great length upon the many causes. But the most important was the status of the ethnic Armenian population of Nagorno Karabakh. This mountainous area of Azerbaijan declared independence in 1991 with tacit support from Armenia and has occupied a surrounding skirt of Azeri territory ever since. Today it forms a virtual adjunct of an enlarged Armenia. Peace talks designed at resolving the situation look less likely than ever at resolving the issue. The new pres-

---

❏ **Essential information for travellers – Armenia**
● **Visa** Required, US$50-$80 (one month). At the airport a 21-day tourist visa is $100. You can enter on a Georgian visa.
● **Currency** Dram. US$1=D495.
● **Time zone** 3 hours ahead of GMT (4hrs in summer) 1hr ahead of Turkey.
● **Highlights** Peaceful mountain grasslands, ancient churches (like Georgia, Armenia has been Christian for around 1500 years), gorges and river valleys in the south east.
● **When to go** Great seasonal temperature variations, Yerevan and the lowlands are extremely hot in summer, but the mountains which constitute most of the country are ideal in August.
● **Pulse of the country** Holocaust museum in Yerevan, Echmiadzin spiritual centre.

ident of Nagorno Karabakh (Arkadii Ghukasyan), was elected by massive majority (89%) in Sept 1997 pledging no return to Azerbaijan. And the new prime minister of all Armenia (Robert Kocharyan), himself a Karabakh citizen, is hardly enthusiastic about returning his homeland to Azeri rule. Wherever we visited, otherwise balanced Armenian/Azerbaijani men told us vehemently that they'd be prepared to die to keep/return Karabakh. Yet passions are slowly cooling, and in October 1997 Azerbaijan announced that it is to start clearing minefields despite the lack of any formal peace deal. For now, however, you can only reach Karabakh via Armenia. Meanwhile, Armenia's economy continues to slump (down 8% again in 1997) and the re-election of president Petrosyan amid calls of ballot fixing resulted in riots during 1996.

All this is necessary background. It need not put you off visiting this attractive and extraordinarily hospitable land. Ancient churches still pepper hillsides – some are over1000 years old. Tourism remains negligible even though visas are easy to procure (by CIS standards). Yet the wide open, flower filled pastures around Sepanovan, complete with mountain rimmed horizons and overpowering bird song must be one of the greatest paradises a hiker could discover. Could there be a more peaceful war-zone?

❏ **Geo-political information – Armenia**

Population: 3.4m (1997), 3.6m (1995), 3.3m (1989), 2.5m (1970).

Area: 29,000 sq km.

Capital: Yerevan (1.3 million).

Other major cities: Gümri (200,000), Kirovakan (now Vanadzor, 170,000).

GNP per capita: $186 (1994).

Currency history: Dram/US$1 Feb 1998: D495, Nov 1997: D495, June 1995: D420, Nov 1994: D424, Feb 1994: D230, Dec 1993: D77. Currency introduced Nov 1993 at D1=RR83 (Russian Roubles).

Major exports/economy: Wine, agriculture, copper. Azerbaijanis claim that Armenia is rushing to extract gold from the occupied area of Nagorno Karabakh.

Ethnic mix: Armenian (94%), Kurdish (2%), Russian (1.5%). In 1989 there were 3% Azeris but most have fled since the outbreak of the Karabakh dispute.

Official language: Armenian (96%). Unique language with script created in 391AD. Russian (2%).

Religious mix: Christian (Armenian Orthodox). World's oldest Christian country.

Landmarks of national history: 95BC: First united under Tigran II but invaded by Rome in 55BC. 301AD: Adopted Christianity. 387: Divided between Persian and Byzantine (East Roman) empires, thereafter kicked about by Arabs, Mongols, Ottomans and Persians with the Russians taking the eastern half from Persia in 1828. 1915: Genocide – 1½ million Armenians deported from Turkish Armenia, half died and the others fled to the USA, France etc. 1919 and 1921: Flashes of independence crushed by Soviet troops. 1988: Devastating earthquake and the beginning of an embargo by Azerbaijan. 1992: All-out war with Azerbaijan. 1994: Ceasefire with Armenia still controlling a lot of Azeri territory.

Leaders: President Levon Ter-Petrosyan, Prime Minister Robert Kocharyan. The President of the self-proclaimed republic of Nagorno Karabakh is Arkadii Ghukasyan. **In power since**: President since 29 Dec 94. Re-elected 22 Sep 96.

Pressing political issues: Uneasy ceasefire with Azerbaijan. Continuing embargo with Azerbaijan and Turkey.

PRACTICAL INFORMATION
Visas and formalities
● **Visa strategy** Getting an Armenian visa doesn't require much paperwork but you will have to wait about three weeks for it to be issued. Usually an invitation is not required (though having one may save you money on the visa fee). You may also enter from Georgia on a Georgian visa (3 days maximum). The border guards seemed surprised that we knew the rule but allowed us into Armenia (and out again) after a certain amount of argument. Other travellers have been turned back. If you enter this way you could continue to the capital and get a visa at the Ministry of Foreign Affairs, 10 Bagranemi St, Yerevan: the Ministry also grants extensions to real Armenian visas.

● **Permits** To visit Nagorno Karabakh you need permits from the Permanent Representative of Nagorno Karabakh in Yerevan. Although the area is officially part of Azerbaijan it's controlled by Armenia and can be visited only from there

and Russian currencies were accepted, though at a poor rate. Exchange booths are rarer than in Georgia. Nonetheless, market traders are usually happy to change dollars (and sometimes roubles) at a fair price. Travellers' cheques can be exchanged in Yerevan at Arm-econombank, 223/1 Vramshapoo Arka St.

Transport
● **Bus** Though fuel is still relatively expensive (due to the Azerbaijan blockade) buses are running: services even operate into occupied areas of Azerbaijan.

● **Train** Train services from Georgia restarted recently with 3 services per week. The lines between Azerbaijan proper and Nakhchivan pass through southernmost Armenia and are unlikely to restart until the resolution of the Karabakh dispute.

● **Hitchhiking** There are few vehicles but hitching proved perfectly feasible and we were dropped off at places that might have been difficult to find without help.

Money
The Dram is reasonably stable. In the northernmost towns we found Georgian

Accommodation
There's cheap accommodation from $1 a night. Few places have hot water.

❑ Feasting with Kirakasian

Kirakasian was late to milk the cows. Dragged along by his two tiny daughters he was singing drunkenly until he noticed me – I'd already alarmed fellow passengers by jumping off the bus at this beautiful but isolated spot. Once Kirakasian had peered at me, squeezed me and generally convinced himself that I was neither alien nor Ukrainian, he started waxing excitedly about the hospitality he was going to unleash. He was a poor man but this afternoon we would eat. Oh, how we would eat! He would feed me *matsonye*. He drooled incomprehensibly, his Russian almost as bad as mine; clearly matsonye was a supreme treat. As we walked he pulled a vodka bottle from his plastic bag and we made the first of many toasts.

He lived on a co-operative farm on which only he and Shishłozoya, his gold-toothed Belorusian wife seemed to co-operate. And not too well today for Kirakasian was late and drunk. Their home was the tanker section of a huge former milk delivery lorry: cylindrical, with a window hole cut in one end. Fork-lift pallets on the floor levelled things up a little. After a period of great anticipation filled with offerings of tea, orange squash and more vodka the arrival of the matsonye was heralded. The daughters gazed expectantly through the doorway as their mother unveiled the plate proudly and Kirakasian spooned a huge portion onto my grubby plate. It was stringy milk-curd. I did my best to show awed appreciation. As I struggled with the sour, disconcertingly lumpy mass, my host decided to treat me to his finest words of English: 'Sit down. Thank you. Heil Hitler'.

❑ Meeting the locals

● **The people** Passions still run very high over the Armenian-ness of Nagorno Karabakh and most of the men we encountered were quick to announce their willingness to die in its defence should hostilities resume. These same tough guys were some of the world's merriest drunks: as in Georgia, preparing a list of subjects to toast (family, peace, friendship etc) is handy.

● **Language – Some phrases in Armenian**

Greetings – *von tek*   Reply – *lavem*
Thank you – *shenora galem*
Cheers – *Vorchj linek, Tzer genadtze*

● **Armenian script**

Staying in touch

To phone out: dial 8, wait for the tone, dial 10 followed by the code for the country you are calling and then the number. International country code +374, Yerevan: 2, Echmiadzin: 52, Vanadzor: 57.

Further information

Tour Armenia will be published in early 98 by TransWorld Resources, 146 Deer Creek Rd, Fedonia, TX 76842. In Yerevan there are info booths at the Hotel Armenia (☎ 560-844) and Hotel Ani (☎ 520-724).

Web sites

www.cilicia.com has a useful overview of tourist attractions in Armenia and of the Armenian communities of Jerusalem, Venice and Istanbul. Also sells books.

The largest Internet provider in Armenia is at www.arminco.com. Links to several Armenia-related homepages, including the excellent travel information at www.arminco.com/mirror/WinArm/tour.html.

wotan.wiwi.hu-berlin.de/~houssik/arax/ links to a travel agency in Armenia.

For current visa information see www.armeniaemb.org.

ourworld.compuserve.com/homepages/Joerg_Zeitschel/armenia.htm has updating information on the ever-increasing flight selections offered by Armenian Airlines.

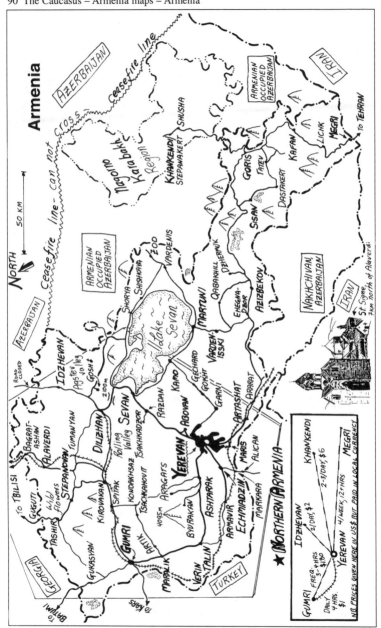

Northern Armenia

TO ALKHALKALAKI

GEORGIA
ARMENIA
TURKEY

BORDER CROSSING has no exchange on the Armenian side. A kiosk on the Georgia side will trade roubles, US $.

SHARED TAXI

GUMRI
† Sev. by train sta.
FREQ: 3-4 HRS
$1.60

TO KARS

Mt Aragac 4094M – HIGHEST IN ARMENIA

BYURAKAN

TASHIR – Small town – formerly Grand. Buildings look sad & overgrown. Mail collected only on Saturdays.
† Bus sta. 2 blocks south of the post office
† In town centre - $2.

GUGUTI
THROUGH BUSES TO TBILISI

★ ARAGATS Castle on mountain side.

GEORGIA
ЗОРА

TO TASHIR, †

TO TBILISI
THROUGH BUSES

SADAKHLO 4 HRS, $3
GEORGIA

TO TBILISI
THROUGH TRAINS

BAGRATASHAN
5-6 HRS DAILY

ALAVERDI † 3KM (SANAHIN)
† 7KM (ST. SIGNE, HALBAT)
† IN TOWN
YEREVAN-IDZHEVAN, 2
1 DAY/ $2

AZERBAIJAN

IDZHEVAN – Armenian hill-side tourist resort town. High rise hotel spoils the otherwise magnificent view.

STEPANOVAN † - A small town with a surprisingly busy airfield - flights to Min. Vodi, Yerevan. Money changers at the market.

3KM TO A † HOTEL IN AN UNLIKELY TRAILOR PARK.

KIRO-VAKAN
MARKET † MAIN SQ.

TSAKHKADZOR VILLAGE ⊞ – Ski resort - creaky old chairlift threadbare during the summer. Hikers hike up into the mts.

DILIZHAN ⊞ Resort framed by the Lesser Caucasus.
★ AGHARTZIN MONASTERY- 5KM Hike up into the mts. No cheap hotel but many good (unofficial) camping spots.

SEV.

RAZDAN

SEV.

SEV. 3KM

SEVAN ⊞ JUTTING OUT ONTO THE LAKE

KAMO

Lake Sevan

PAGAN TEMPLE, GARNI

FAIRY TALE

⊞ GECHARD ★ Cave monastery (working). Other caves & hiking in the area. Taxi - R/T from Yerevan $40.

HITCH TAXI TAXI *#* *#*

GOKHT

YERITASAR-DAKAN

KIROVAKAN ⊞
2/DAY $2

★ ASHTARAK †††

#104
#104

GARNI 3RD CENT. B.C. Pagan Temple-of-the-Sun. Looks like it should be in the middle of Athens instead of looking over a river canyon. No hotel.

#137,135

KAMAKERI
MAIN
TRAIN STA.

YEREVAN
FREQ. 1/2HR 15

#111,1/2HR

★ ZVARTNOTS † Church ruins

#115,117
#115, -117

20KM SEV.

★ ECHMIADZIN † Centre of the Armenian church.
††† Many in town, incl. the St. Echmiadein Cathedral.
† St. Haypsime - edge of town.
† Sev. in city centre

MARKARA
ALICAN

ARMENIA
TURKEY

TO IĞDIR

TURKEY

★ ARTASHAT †† Ruins of 2nd cent. B.C. capital. Views of Mt. Ararat.

Mt. Ararat

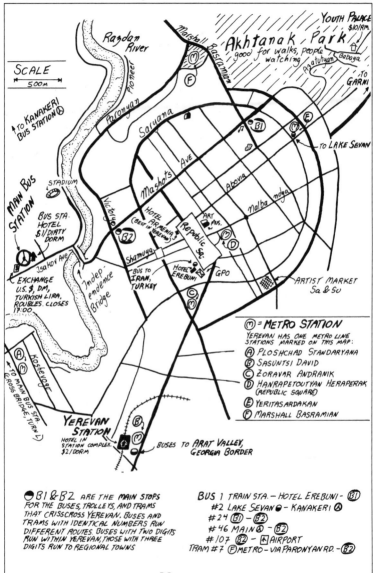

Yerevan

Azerbaijan

Azerbaijan has made no attempt to lure tourists to its beautiful mountains, forests or deserts. It has earthquake battered ruins to discover and there are several unusual but hard to visit curiosities: mud volcanoes, chimera (flames leaping spontaneously from the ground), a town of 6000 people built on stilts in the Caspian sea (Neftyany Kamni), sturgeon farms for the Caviar industry (at Neftchala and Mingaçevir) and an oil rig building plant off the Baku-Gobustan road where massive surreal steel silhouettes make modern art of the skyline. Ganja, Guba, Shemakha, Sheki, Barda, Nakhchivan and Lenkoran are all former capitals of khanates or small kingdoms, Gobustan has some of the world's foremost Neolithic rock carvings and the whole country is wrapped in the poetry, culture and hospitality of the Caucasus.

Elegant Baku is one of west Asia's most cosmopolitan capitals. Jazz was played here when banned elsewhere in the Soviet Union, and today the city has one of Asia's coolest jazz cafés as well as dozens of other stylish venues catering mainly to business people and expats riding the new oil boom. Oil money is also funding reconstruction of Baku's medieval Old Town where four 15th century caravanserais have been turned into atmospheric restaurants or clubs.

The rest of the country, however, lags noticeably behind. Though not as severe as in Georgia, there are frequent power cuts, water supply problems and a general air of neglect. Many refugees from the as yet unresolved Nagorno-Karabakh conflict remain in camps. Some 20% of the territory remains under Armenian control including Shusha, one of the cultural centres of the country. Borders with Armenia are firmly shut adding to the isolation of the disconnected Nakhchivan enclave. Relationships with Russia are strained by disagreements over the division of Caspian Sea oil rights, oil pipeline routings and Azerbaijan's refusal to allow CIS troops to man its borders. Several years of virtual Russian blockade were only eased during 1997. Iran is also a wary neighbour, afraid that a strong regime in Baku might encourage pro-indepen-

❑ **W&M's country ratings – Azerbaijan**
● **Expense $$** Food and transport are cheap. Most places have budget accommodation though it's more expensive in Baku.
● **Value for money** ✔✔✔ The country is not as chaotic as Georgia and the hotels are slightly less run down than in Kyrgyzstan.
● **Getting around** ✔✔✔✔ Regular services operate on most routes though they are not especially frequent. Tickets are relatively easy to buy.
● **English spoken** ✔✔ Some Russian or Turkish would help enormously as few people speak much English, except in Baku.
● **Woman alone** ✔✔✔ Local men are 'quaintly chivalrous'.
● **For vegetarians** ✔✔ Not a great place for vegetarians. Mutton is prevalent. Most of the caviar now goes for export.

dence leanings in Southern Azerbaijan (ie Tabriz and Iran's north west provinces). This led ironically to Islamic Iran lending some tacit support to Christian Armenia during the Karabakh war. Even the US initially banned government aid to Azerbaijan thanks to a strong Armenian lobby in Congress. This will soon be out-weighed by petro-dollars following the $7,400,000,000 'deal of the century' signed with a consortium of Western oil companies.

❏ **Geo-political information – Azerbaijan**

Population: 7.8m (1997), 7.4m (1993), 7m (1989), 6.6m (1983). An estimated 10 million+ Azeris live in Iran.

Area: 86,600 sq km.

Capital: Baku (1.2 million, 1.7m for metropolitan area).

Other major cities: Ganja (280,000), Sumgait just north of Baku (240,000).

GNP per capita: $500 (1994), $3350 (1987).

Currency history: Manat/US$1 Feb 1998: M3900, Oct 1997:M3950, Feb 1996: M4500, Feb 1995: M4300, July 1994: M1200, Feb 1994: M118.

Major exports/economy: Oil, gas, silk, caviar. Cotton and wine production hit by Karabakh conflict (water diverted).

Ethnic mix: Azeri (90%), Dagestani (3.2%), Russian (2.5%), Armenian (2%).

Official languages: Azerbaijani. Talysh spoken in south.

Religious mix: 83% Muslim (mainly Shi'ite).

Landmarks of national history: **7th century AD**: Invaded by Arab caliphates hence conversion to Islam. **12th century AD**: 'Golden Age' – notably in Ganja. **1176**: Shemakha was ruined by an earthquake. **16th century**: Invaded by Persia and became a province. **1747**: Khanate of Baku founded. **1828**: Treaty of Turkmenchai divided Azerbaijan between Russia and Persia (the division remains today) – one of the triggers that started the Great Game (see p138). **1859**: The regional capital was transferred from Shemakha to Baku. **1870s**: Oil fields developed and by 1900 Baku had become the world's leading oil producer. **28 May 1918**: Independence (the capital was at Elisavetpol, later called Kirovabad and now renamed Ganja). **1920**: Occupied by the Red Army and became a Soviet Republic. **Feb 1988**: Decision of Nagorno Karabakh Soviet to request a transfer from Azerbaijan to Armenia was refused in Baku, big protests followed in Armenia and Karabakh spurring an anti-Armenian backlash in Azerbaijan (at least 26 were killed in Sumgait). **Jan 1990**: The nationalist Popular Front of Azerbaijan (PFA) launched attacks on Soviet installations attempting to open the border with Iranian Azerbaijan. **Jan 1990**: A state of emergency followed and Soviet troops massacred hundreds of people in Baku – a very formative moment in Azeri national consciousness. **18 Oct 1991**: Formal independence. **Nov 1994**: Deal of the century oil contract ratified promising hope for future economic advancement.

Leader: President Heydar Aliev (a generally respected former communist party first secretary who took power after the elected but increasingly unpopular leader Abulfaz Elchibey fled in the face of advancing rebel troops.) Confirmed by a 97% vote at the general election in October 1993.

Pressing political issues: The continued occupation of 20% of the country by Armenia and the large refugee population; the refusal to give in to Russia's demands to station her troops at Azeri border posts; worries over the oil pipeline routing and whether the Caspian is a sea or a lake (if the latter, all bordering countries share revenues from the oil, gas etc extracted).

PRACTICAL INFORMATION
Visas and formalities

● **Visa strategy** Most Western nationals require visas. Typical cost is about US$50 for a single entry, $100 double entry, $250 multi-entry or $30 for a 5-day transit. A letter of invitation is required for business or 'entry' visas. Tourist visas require confirmed hotel bookings or a letter from a tourist agency showing your itinerary. If you have no contacts in Azerbaijan and don't want to book a tour, you can fax directly to the Hyatt Regency Hotel in Baku (☎ 981-234, fax 980-817). State your name and proposed dates of stay (ie when you want the visa for). They faxed us back a room booking confirmation within 24hrs. If you can't afford the $336/night room tariff, fax a cancellation as soon as your visa is issued: there's no cancellation fee up to 48hrs before the booking date. You may also be able to use Hyatt's international booking system, though a fax from Baku looks more 'official'. Clearly, Hyatt won't appreciate too many such cancellations, so this system may not last long.

Visas take at least 3 days to issue (a week for multi entry). The Brussels embassy was prepared to issue a tourist visa without invitation/hotel booking if we waited two weeks.

Transit visas valid 5 days are available in the Istanbul consulate if you show possession of a Turkmenistan visa. Arriving from Turkmenistan (where there is as yet no Azerbaijan or Georgian Embassy) you may be allowed to get a visa on arrival. We have not met anyone who's done so since 1994, but officials in Baku assured us that it is still legal. Your passport will be taken from you at the airport – don't worry that's normal procedure. You will then have to report to the visa extension office (see below) to collect the visa. You'll receive a

---

❑ **Essential information for travellers – Azerbaijan**

● **Visa** Required by all; available on arrival only if you are coming from a country where there is no Azeri consul. A transit visa (about $30) is available if you have a visa for onward travel (and maybe a letter from the embassy of your own country). Five days' stay permitted on Georgian visa.

● **Currency** Manat. US$1=M3900.

● **Time zone** 4hrs ahead of GMT (+5 in summer). 2hrs ahead of Turkey year round and, bizarrely, 1hr behind Georgia in winter (same in summer).

● **Religious tone** Gently Islamic.

● **Health factors** No malaria except a very mild risk on the Iran border. However, mosquitoes around the Caspian are very unpleasant: note that no good repellent is sold locally. The tap water is drinkable in emergencies.

● **Special dangers** The war with Armenia has not been concluded but there is a ceasefire. Passions still run high and 20% of Azerbaijan is still occupied. Bombs on the Baku metro killed many in 1994 so your bags are regularly searched. This can be extremely time consuming.

● **Typical traveller destinations** There aren't any travellers, only oil men and bankers who stay in and around Baku.

● **Highlights** Ruined castle villages in the Caucasus, old town Baku, Sheki.

● **When to go** Like Chicago or Wellington, Baku is famous for its winds (*khazri*), which blow every few days mitigating the unpleasantly humid summer heat, disrupting Caspian shipping or adding a bite to the mild chill of winter. Winters are much colder inland and some mountain villages get snowed in. The centre of the country is dry with irrigated farmland, veering on semi desert. The southern forests are often wet with heaviest rains in October, November and March, best for hiking in May. Rainfall in the orchards around Guba is lighter and less constant and peaks later in the spring.

seven day non-extendible 'emergency visa' ($40) unless you can conjure up a local friend to act as sponsor ('receiving party') in which case, a one month stay is negotiable. If you're unable to get an Azeri visa elsewhere, entering Azerbaijan on a Georgian visa is theoretically legal using the reciprocal visa treaty (but see p85). Heading west, the Georgian consul in Trabzon, Turkey obligingly issues double-entry Georgian transit visas, so if you have trouble on the Azeri side of the notoriously awkward Geo-Azerbaijan border you can at least get back into Georgia again.

● **Extensions** You'll need a sponsor or local friend to get an extension, and they must come with you in person to the ministry office at 2 Kontrol St in Baku (open 10am-1pm, Mon-Fri for submissions; collect after 5pm). Extension fees are $10 for one day, $20 for 2 days, $30 for 3 days, $40 for up to a month, $80 for one to three months. With powerful contacts you might get a one year multiple entry exit visa ($250!). If you apply when your visa has already expired the minimum fee is $50.

● **Permits** According to the Foreign Ministry, entry to the Nakhchivan enclave requires a special permit only available through OVIR in Baku. However, at OVIR itself, the official responsible politely told us in English that a tourist visa was sufficient without permit. While it may be possible to enter Nakhchivan without such a permit there'll probably be considerable police harassment to deal with and bribes to pay as permits are carefully checked on arrival at Nakhchivan airport. You may even be sent back to Baku. If necessary ask the Foreign Ministry to write a letter to OVIR requesting such a permit be issued.

Police in Lenkoran, Astara and Gabala have been known to politely turn back permitless travellers, even though there seems to be no official permit requirement. Until recently permits were needed to visit lake Goy Gol (south of Ganja) though the requirement has apparently now been dropped. Venturing too near to the Armenian border will cause suspicion.

Money

The currency is the manat but prices are generally quoted in Mammad (1000 manat) or Shirvan (10,000 manat). These names are taken from the pictures on the bank notes: Mammad Rasulzade (the 1918 democrat) and the Shirvanshah's palace (still standing in Baku Old Town). The 500 manat is less frequently called a Nizami. Shirvan Mammad Nizami would thus mean 11,500 manat.

Baku's more expensive restaurants, night-clubs and ex-pat supermarkets often quote prices in dollars but they assume that you'll pay in manat (usually at a slightly unfavourable rate). If you want to pay in US$ that's OK too.

Changing money is easy in cities, especially Baku, and there's a relatively low split between buy and sell rates for US$, Russian roubles and DM. Other currencies can only be exchanged in major Baku banks. MOST Bank in Baku (9am-1pm, 2-6pm, Mon-Sat) cashes travellers' cheques (3% commission) into US$ and gives US$ cash advances on Visa and MasterCard: free via ATM (cash machines), 1.5% commission if you use the counter service.

Transport

● **Bus** Long distance buses are typically faster but less comfortable than trains and marginally more expensive. Most towns maintain a bus station with a timetabled web of routes including stuffed-full services to many of the smaller villages. In addition there's usually at least a couple of early evening departures to Baku with pre-bookable seats. These arrive very early next morning and frequently leave from a locally known but unmarked road junction, not necessarily near the bus station.

Several Turkish companies run comfortable Istanbul-Hopa-Tbilisi-Baku buses taking about 48hrs and costing $75, easily bargained to around $60. $10 less to/from Hopa. The trip involves two very lengthy border delays (up to 5hrs each). They'll also take passengers on the Tbilisi-Baku leg for $25-40 but you'd be better off taking the 2/week Georgian buses or the overnight train, either costing only $10. In Baku, Turkish bus offices are clustered around the Sahil metro/26 Commissars area. Igdir Turizm has 5 daily services directly between Istanbul bus station and Nakhchivan for $25-30. A daily bus to Tehran departs at 8am from outside the Port office in Baku.

● **Train** Overnight trains run on all major lines. Classes are the same as in all ex-Soviet trains. A comfortable night's sleep in the shabby but functional *platscart* cars costs $4-5 ie less than the cheapest Baku hotel room. It's usually fairly easy to find berths for same day departure. Note that the railways follow the river valleys and stations are often a considerable distance from the town centres they're supposed to serve (eg 20km from Sheki). In 1997 train services resumed to Russia with a service most days to either Makhachkala, Rostov or Moscow (2/week via Chechnya).

A slow, regular, seat-only service operates on the suburban/Apsheron peninsula lines conveniently serving Mardakan and the fire temple at Surakhany approximately every 40 mins.

● **Metro** Nizami station has some fine mosaics, but generally the Baku metro is less attractive, less comfortable and runs less frequently than its Moscow role model. Avoid carrying luggage on the metro if you're in a hurry. Since the 1994 metro bombing, all bags are checked with metal detectors at the entrances. Carrying a large bag will almost inevitably lead to a more thorough search, often escalating to a full document and money check. Twice this delayed us for over half an hour.

Jafar Jabbarly and 28 Mai stations are

❏ **Meeting the locals**

● **The people** Throughout Azerbaijan I was a source of much intrigue. 'Anglia number one' whooped a vodka-proffering businessman on one train, thereby exhausting his English conversation. 'Sit dow, sit dow' were the only words of a pair of engineers in Sheki who wanted visas to watch Manchester United play at Wembley and invited me to stay a few days in their hillside apartment. In villages, herds of children followed me up mountains and round the ruined castles. In Baku station the Soviet tradition of rudeness was markedly absent as the ladies at the information office scurried round to get me a ticket though it really wasn't their job. One English speaking hotel cashier took pity on me: 'No cheap in Baku. This is oil city. You are a teacher? Teachers all over the world are poor, come back at 6pm.' He was quite happy to sneak me into one of their $125 a night rooms once the manager had gone. 'Please leave before 7am tomorrow or for me, trouble!'

● **Language** Azeri is similar to Turkish (numbers are the same except for 3 and 1000). Russian is widely spoken, and is a sign of education, though increasingly English is becoming popular amongst the young and ambitious. Signs are usually bilingual, in Russian and in Azeri using the new Azeri version of the alphabet. This is based heavily on Turkish pronunciations with the following additional letters: ə (a), J (y), Q (g/k), and X (kh). The ğ which is silent in Turkish is lightly gargled in Azeri. Hippocrene Books publishes an Azeri-English-Azeri dictionary. A cheaper locally printed dictionary (5000m) and phrase book (8000m) are sold in Baku bookshops. **Some words in Azeri**:

> Greeting – *salam*
> How are you? – *nasliznik*
> Reply (good) – *yakhshi*
> Thank you – *chok sawol*
> Delicious – *dadlidir*
> Beautiful – *güzel*

South of Massali, most people speak Talysh.

different platforms of the same station, both of which are entered through the 'Jafar Jabbarly' entrance in the square of the main railway station. Since all routes (except the one stop Khatai spur) now use the 28 Mai platform, there can be a considerable crush of passengers there. Commonly displayed metro maps misleadingly imply that through trains run from Khatai to Memar Acami which is no longer the case.

● **Air** Many plane tickets are subject to foreigner surcharges. If you have a student card proving that you study in the CIS you can get a small discount but not the cheap local prices. Baku has dozens of airline offices, but a good first stop is the friendly AmEx travel agent (13 Samet Vurgun). For flights to Nakhchivan ($116!!) you'll have to visit the main office of AZAL (2 blocks SE of the station). Flights to Turkmenbashi (Krasnovodsk), Turkmenistan cost $56 from the ground floor of the Hotel Azerbaijan. The private Imair sells tickets through Improtex (#16 Samet Vurgun) – including Tashkent ($145, Sat), Minsk ($140, Thur) and Urumqi, Xinjiang ($300, Wed & Sat). Airport tax ($15) is usually included in any quoted fare. There are many buses from metro station Azizbayov (Azizbekov) to Baku airport, as well as regular services every 15 mins from the bus station (#154) and rail station (#16).

There are international flights from Ganja to Moscow and Sharjah, UAE.

● **Boat** Berths on the Caspian Sea ferry to Turkmenistan cost $75-100, but as of 1997 foreigners are now permitted to take the $45 '5th class' seats (locals pay $26). Cars cost from $78. On our first visit in 1995, one could wait days for a departure. Now there is a fairly reliable overnight service leaving 'after dinner' every evening (supposedly 6pm but usually later). Foot passengers must buy tickets at the Port Office (not post office) near the Apsheron Hotel. However the ferry departs from a separate dock, a km beyond (10 mins walk following freight-rail tracks from the Gajibekova overpass or a 10,000manat, 5 min taxi hop from the train station – ask for *Turkmenistanski Peron*).

The weekly Inflot ferry (☎ 935132) to Bandar Anzali (Iran) leaves at 6pm on Tuesdays and costs a prohibitive $100 for foreigners ($50 for Iranians, $33 for Azeris) in seat-only class, $130-$200 for a berth. The office is on the top floor of the port office. Even with an Iranian visa nobody is sure that the Iranians will let you in so take the (much cheaper) bus.

Note that for the boat to Neftyany Kamni, you'll need a letter of introduction from the state oil company, SOCAR.

● **Hitchhiking** This works OK though there are relatively few available spaces in cars, and traffic in rural areas is light.

Accommodation

Almost all towns have at least one basic hotel. Typically there is a dysfunctional bathroom en-suite but only very rarely any hot water or heating/air-conditioning. In small towns the usual price is one or two Shirvan per person (ie $2.50-5). In Baku there is a much greater range including the international standard *Hyatt* and *Europa* hotels, though the only real budget hotel is the out of centre *Tulpan* (3 Shirvan/double, shared squat toilets, no showers at all).

Homestays are great value (we paid $2 in Zakatala including meals) but can only be arranged through chance encounters: they're not formally organised except at Baku railway station where the booth refuses to serve foreigners.

Locals are extremely hospitable and offering any payment will be considered insulting if you're a guest.

Staying in touch

Several Baku hotels will let you make free calls within the city. Otherwise telephone boxes require jetoni which cost 500M from phone offices (eg in the GPO) and some kiosks, but 1000M from most street vendors. There are special phone offices for long distance calls. International calls can be made from top hotels or using phone cards at special booths at the GPO (approx $4/min if you buy the card, double if you pay touts to use a few units). International phone code +994. Baku: 12, Ganja: 222, Nakhchivan: 136.

Mail is not entirely reliable. Only half of our letters arrived and different post offices charged us substantially differing rates for the same weight. There is a poste restante service at the GPO in Baku and the new AmEx office (fax 983512) 13 Samet Vurgun, Baku, is happy to hold mail though has yet to do so.

Activities

● **Hiking** There are many good areas for hiking if you're self sufficient. The trailheads above Guba or the Qax Corridor lead into the Caucasian foothills through a patchwork of chestnut and hazel glades with scrub and semi-arid slopes leading up to majestic white capped peaks on the Russian border. A hike between Lerik and Jardimly (far south) takes you through attractive forests and villages famed for hospitality and longevity. The lovely mountain lakes above Xanlar and Dashkasan (see Ganja Road map) are no longer out of bounds as tensions with Armenia start to cool slightly.

● **Swimming** The Caspian Sea has risen 2m in the last 20 years, leaving many of the better beaches underwater, or scarred with the half submerged wreckage of former buildings and promenades. The once attractive brown sand swathe at Zagulba (Apsheron Peninsula, 15 mins N of Mardakan) is now disfigured with twisted metal and overshadowed by ugly apartment blocks (as well as the luxury Oasis Hotel). Zagulba's limpid green lagoon is in fact a pool of raw sewage dribbling out into the sea through broken rusted pipes. Coves further north are supposedly better, and Nabran (near the Russian border) is said to be the country's nicest beach.

● **Work** English tutors are paid an average US$8 per hour. Students on the British Council teaching programme or at any English language institute are keen to meet foreigners and may offer tours in exchange for conversation practice. The British Council also has a vocational institute that hires occasional professional lecturers. The oil business is drawing expatriates, and there is an undoubted need for pollution experts to help clean up the mess!

Further information

● **Books and magazines** We found no travel guide whatsoever to Azerbaijan apart from a few pages in out of date guides to the USSR. Baku bookshops do have the attractive coffee table book *Azerbaijan: Fortresses and Castles* by Mamedov and Giyas, but at M250,000 it is hardly an impulse purchase. Highly recommended reading is *Azerbaijan International* a glossy English language magazine which raises a spectrum of cultural, political and business issues about Azerbaijan: $48 quarterly ($28 in USA). $12 ($7 in USA) for a sample copy from PO Box 5217, Sherman Oaks, CA 91413, USA (fax 1-818-997-7337). Email: ai@artnet.net. It is cheaper though to look at their web site (see box).

● **Maps** An excellent 1:500,000 map of the country with Cyrillic/Azeri romanisation can be found in Baku (10,000-30,000M, depending on where you buy it): better and cheaper than any equivalent in the West.

● **Information** The staff of the Hotel Azerbaijan in Baku speak English and are helpful. The US Embassy, Azadlyq Pr 83, has free copies of *Caspian Chronicle* which lists forthcoming events in Baku.

Web sites

www.azer.com is the homepage of the magazine, *Azerbaijan International*; it has a searchable index.

solar.rtd.utk.edu/oldfriends/azerbaijan/index.html links to several Azerbaijan pages.

ourworld.compuserve.com/homepages/azerbaijan is the very basic homepage of the Azeri embassy in Washington DC.

Main towns

Azerbaijan

Geographical regions

THE HIGH CAUCASUS

(KAVKAZ) FORGOTTEN CASTLE RUINS AND STRENUOUS HIKES AMID HIGH MOUNTAINS. WHITE PEAKS ALONG RUSSIAN BORDER

BEACHES

HILL TOWNS

ATTRACTIVE RURAL VILLAGES AMID FRUIT ORCHARDS (N.E.) OR GROVES OF NUT TREES (N.W.)

SEMI-DESERT

IRRIGATED AGRICULTURAL PLAINS AND VALLEYS

"LESSER CAUCASUS"

BEAUTIFUL MOUNTAIN LAKES AND HIKES BUT PEAKS ARE SENSITIVELY CLOSE TO THE CEASE-FIRE LINE.

NAGORNO-KARABAKH

BEAUTIFUL MOUNTAINS BUT QUASI-INDEPENDENT, OCCUPIED BY ARMENIAN FORCES. NO ACCESS FROM AZ.

THE OIL COAST

OIL WORKINGS AND SOME HEAVY INDUSTRY AMID SPOOKILY LIFELESS LANDSCAPES OF BARREN HILLS AND "MUD VOLCANOES"

NAKHCHIVAN

DISCONNECTED ENCLAVE OF ARID PLAINS RISING TO DRAMATIC MOUNTAIN BACK-DROPS. PERMITS REQUIRED—ONLY AVAILABLE IN BAKU. BEWARE, BUS FROM BAKU GOES VIA IRAN. SEE YEZIDABAD (MINI MASADA) AND MOMINYE-KHATUN

MOUNTAINS DRY PLAIN

TALYSH REGION

LUSH FORESTED MOUNTAINS. TEA FARMS IN LOWLANDS. LOCALS ARE PARTICULARLY HOSPITABLE, SPEAK TALYSH, AND LIVE TO OVER 100 YRS OLD (IN VILLAGES AROUND LERIK)

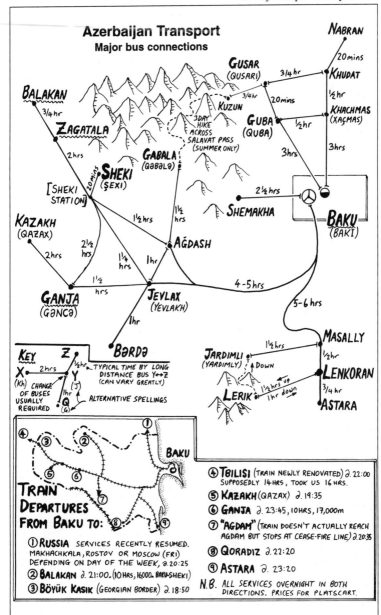

Azerbaijan Transport
Major bus connections

NABRAN
20mins
KHUDAT
GUSAR (QUSARI) ¾ hr
¾ hr 20mins ½ hr
KUZUN KHACHMAS (XAÇMAS)
3 DAY HIKE ACROSS SALAVAT PASS (SUMMER ONLY) 20mins GUBA (QUBA) ½ hr
BALAKAN ½ hr
¾ hr
ZAGATALA 3hrs 3hrs
2hrs GABALA (QƏBƏLƏ)
[SHEKI STATION] SHEKI (ŞEXI) 2½ hrs
20mins 1½ hrs SHEMAKHA
KAZAKH (QAZAX) 1½ hrs BAKU (BAKI)
2½ hrs AĞDASH
2hrs 1¼ hrs 1hr
1½ hrs JEVLAX (YEVLAKH) 4-5 hrs
GANJA (GƏNCƏ)
1hr 5-6 hrs
BƏRDƏ MASALLY
JARDIMLI (YARDIMLY) 1½ hrs ½ hr
KEY DOWN LENKORAN
X Z
2hrs ½ hr TYPICAL TIME BY LONG DISTANCE BUS Y↔Z (CAN VARY GREATLY) LERIK 1½ hrs UP ¾ hr
(Kh) CHANGE OF BUSES USUALLY REQUIRED Y 1hr down ASTARA
1hr (J) ALTERNATIVE SPELLINGS
Q (G)

TRAIN DEPARTURES FROM BAKU TO:

BAKU

④ ③ ② ①
⑤ ⑥
⑦
⑧ ⑨

① **RUSSIA** SERVICES RECENTLY RESUMED. MAKHACHKALA, ROSTOV OR MOSCOW (FRI) DEPENDING ON DAY OF THE WEEK, ∂ 20:25

② **BALAKAN** ∂ 21:00. (10 HRS, 16000. BAKU-SHEKI)

③ **BÖYÜK KASIK** (GEORGIAN BORDER) ∂ 18:50

④ **TBILISI** (TRAIN NEWLY RENOVATED) ∂ 22:00 SUPPOSEDLY 14 HRS, TOOK US 16 HRS.

⑤ **KAZAKH** (QAZAX) ∂ 19:35

⑥ **GANJA** ∂ 23:45, 10 HRS, 17,000m

⑦ **"AGDAM"** (TRAIN DOESN'T ACTUALLY REACH AGDAM BUT STOPS AT CEASE-FIRE LINE) ∂ 20:35

⑧ **QORADIZ** ∂ 22:20

⑨ **ASTARA** ∂ 23:20

N.B. ALL SERVICES OVERNIGHT IN BOTH DIRECTIONS. PRICES FOR PLATSCART.

Central Baku

Grand oil boom architecture (1890-1915), brilliant 'living' old town, and cosmopolitan Fountains Square. Bring mosquito repellent.

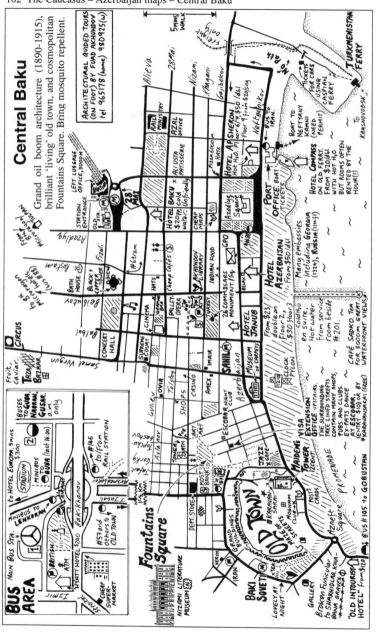

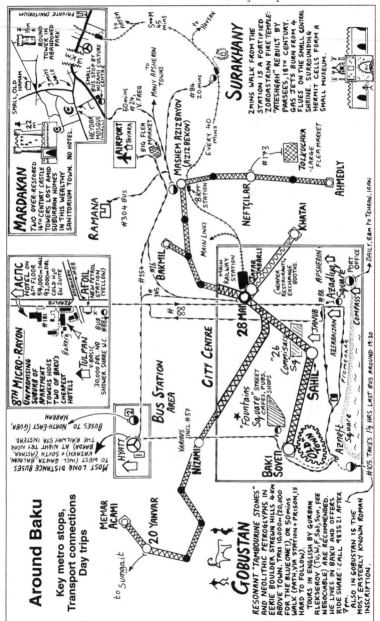

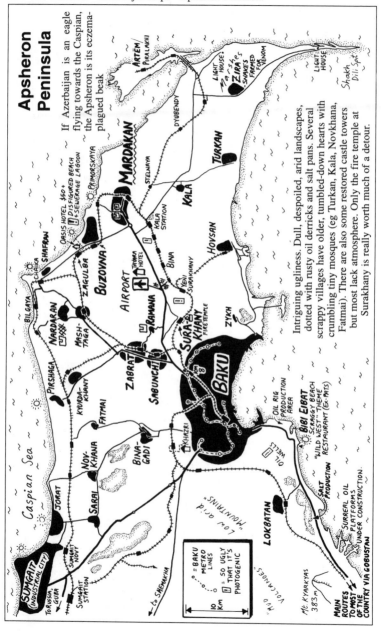

Apsheron Peninsula

If Azerbaijan is an eagle flying towards the Caspian, the Apsheron is its eczema-plagued beak.

Intriguing ugliness. Dull, despoiled, arid landscapes, dotted with rusty oil derricks and salt pans. Several scrappy villages have older, tumbled-down hearts with crumbling tiny mosques (eg Turkan, Kala, Novkhana, Fatmai). There are also some restored castle towers but most lack atmosphere. Only the fire temple at Surakhany is really worth much of a detour.

Caspian Sea

SUMGAIT (INDUSTRIAL CITY)
TORRUSIA, GUBA
SUMGAIT NOVY
SUMGAIT STATION

JORAT
SARAI
NOV-KHANA
BINA-GADI
KHIZRI
LOKBATAN
Low arid "MOUNTAINS"
to SHEMAKHA

BILGAYA
CHAIKA
SHAGAN
PIRSHAGA
MASH-TAGA
NARDARAN
ZAGULBA
KYURDA-KHANY
FATMAI

ARTEM / PIRALLAKHI
Marshes
ZIRA SNAKES FARMED FOR VENOM
LIGHT HOUSE
LIGHT HOUSE
Shakh Dili Spit

DYUBENDY
STELNAYA
TURKAN
KALA
KALA STATION
HOVSAN

MARDAKAN
PRIMORSKAYA
OASIS HOTEL $60+
DISFIGURED BEACH + SEVERAGE LAGOON

BUZOVNA
AIRPORT
TAYAK HOTEL
BINA
YENI SURAKHANY
RAMANA
ZABRAT
SABUNCHI
SURA-KHANY FIRE TEMPLE
ZYKH

BAKU
Km 8
OIL RIG PRODUCTION AREA
BIBI EIBAT
Scraggy beach "WILD WEST" THEME RESTAURANT (Ex-PATS)
OIL WELLS
SALT PRODUCTION
SURREAL OIL PLATFORMS UNDER CONSTRUCTION

MUD VOLCANOES
Mt KYARKYAS 383m
MAIN ROUTES TO MOST OF THE COUNTRY VIA GOBUSTAN

10 Km

= BAKU METRO LINES
= SO UGLY THAT IT'S PHOTOGENIC

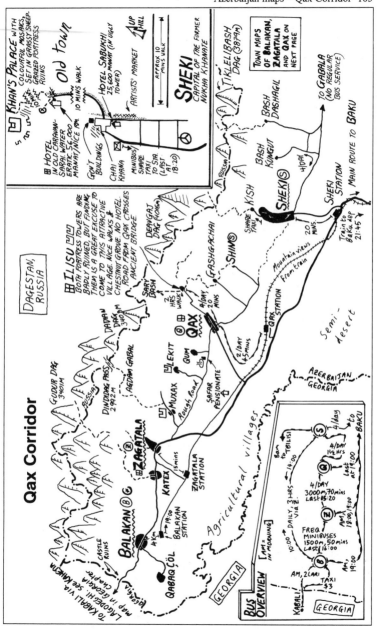

Qax Corridor

Old Town (Sheki inset)

KHAN'S PALACE WITH COLOURFUL MOSAICS, SET IN GRASSY SHEEP-GRAZED FORTRESS RUINS

HOTEL SABUKHI 25,600 MANAT (IN UGLY TOWER)

ARTISTS' MARKET

Approx 10 MINS WALK

10 MINS WALK

SHEKI
CAPITAL OF THE FORMER NUKHA KHANATE

HOTEL IN OLD CARAVAN-SARAI, WATER ERRATIC, SO FOOD MANAT/NICE POOL

GOV'T BUILDINGS

CHAI KHANA

MINIBUS SHARE TAXI TO STN. (LAST AT 18:20)

UP HILL

TIKLELIBASH DAG (3874M)

BASH DASHAGIL

BASH KUNGUT

TOWN MAPS OF BALAKAN, ZAGATALA AND QAX ON NEXT PAGE

TO GABALA (NO REGULAR BUS SERVICE)

DAGESTAN, RUSSIA

ILISU
BOTH FORTRESS TOWERS ARE BADLY RUINED, BUT FINDING THEM IS A GREAT EXCUSE TO COME TO THIS ATTRACTIVE VILLAGE. NICE WALKS & CHESTNUT GROVE. NO HOTEL. ROAD FROM QAX CROSSES ANCIENT BRIDGE.

RUSSIA

KISH

SHEKI(S)

SHARE TAXI 20 MINS

DERVIGAT DAG (1010M)

GRASHGACHAI

SHIN(S)

SAFAR BASH

2 HRS WALK

4/DAY 20 MINS

4/DAY 45 MINS

GUDUR DAG 3401M

DADAN DAG 3402M

AGDAM GABAL

BESSIGA

DINDIGA PASS 2992M

SARY BASH

MUXAX

LEKIT

GUM

Rough Road

SAFAR PENSIONATE

QAX

GAX STATION

Mountain views from train

2/DAY 45 MINS

SHEKI STATION

MAIN ROUTE TO BAKU

Train to BAKU 21:45

Semi-desert

ZAGATALA

KATEX

15 MINS

ZAGATALA STATION

Agricultural villages

AZERBAIJAN
GEORGIA

CASTLE RUINS

BALAKAN

1 HR

QABAQ ÇÖL

BALAKAN STATION

4 HRS

TO KABALI VIA LAGODEGHI; SEE GEORGIA MAP IN GEORGIA CHAPTER.

GEORGIA

BUS OVERVIEW [AM = IN MORNING]

TO TBILISI
8 AM

10:00 DAILY, 3 HRS, VIA Z.

S → 4/DAY → to BAKU

4/DAY 1½ HRS — Last at 17:00

4/DAY 3000M, 70 MINS LAST 15:20

AM, 18:00, 19:00

FREQ MINIBUSES 1500M, 50 MINS LAST 16:00

AM, 19:00

AM, 2 LARI

TAXI $3

KABALI

GEORGIA

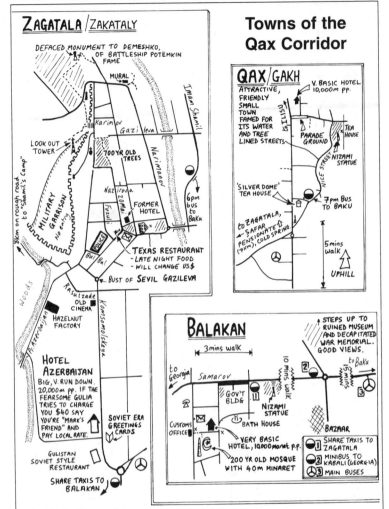

Zagatala (Zagataly)

A single city bus shuttles every half hour from the bus station to the charming old town (top of this map). Zagatala's 1830 fortress famously imprisoned the mutineers of the battleship *Potemkin* (1905). Now the sturdy walls enclose disappointing apartment blocks and a closed garrison. The ***Hotel Azerbaijan*** is dismal. We were offered an excellent ***homestay*** (5000m pp including meals) by locals at the bus station. The friendly owner of the ***Texas Restaurant*** can also make recommendations if you speak some Russian.

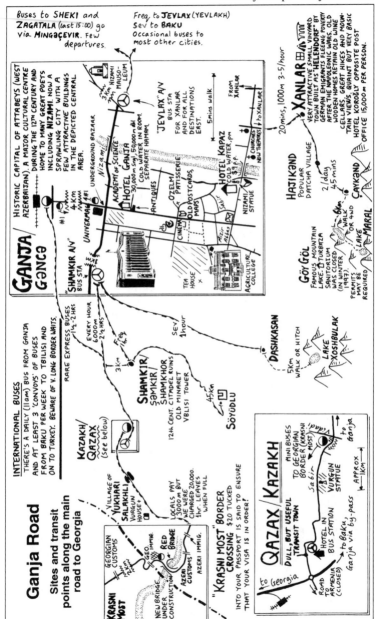

Georgia
(Sakartvelo)

The home of the Golden Fleece, an ancient Christian Kingdom, birthplace of Stalin, land of music and blood feuds. Georgia is overflowing in history, myth and character and is home to some of the planet's most hospitable, most passionate and at times its craziest people.

The land is small but encompasses 5000m peaks, lush sub-tropical forests, rolling semi-desert and the wide Kahetian vineyard valleys. It was the first nation to freely elect a socialist government (1919) and the first Soviet republic to hold multi party elections (1990). Economically dynamic, it seemed the republic most likely to achieve success after the collapse of the USSR. Such hopes were quickly dashed. Two independence struggles (Abkhazia and South Ossetia) and a brief civil war (when deposed though much admired ex-president Gamsurkhurdia tried to force a comeback in 1992/3) set the tone for several years of turbulence. Anarchy and mob rule left the economy looted to devastation. Regaining stability took four years of strong-arm rule by former Gorbachev side-kick Schevardnadze. However, by 1997 the economy was showing the second highest growth rate in the CIS, albeit from the lowest of starting points. Tbilisi today is a world away from the lawlessness of 1993 when a BBC correspondent reported a man shooting out a friend's window merely to wake him up. Bomb damaged buildings are largely patched up and a small café scene is burgeoning on the now peaceful streets even though incomes as low as $3/month make such luxuries unaffordable for many.

All is not rosy. Many thousands of ethnic Georgians remain displaced from Abkhazia which has declared itself an independent nation. Tourism, once an economic mainstay of both Georgia and Abkhazia (the 'Soviet Riviera'), is stagnant. Abkhazia is blockaded by Georgia (beware of landmines near the border) and also now by Russia, the rebels' former backers. (Once Georgia

---

❏ **W&M's country ratings – Georgia**

● **Expense $** Accommodation is available for $1-3 except in Tbilisi, transport is cheap. Food is cheaper than in Turkey.

● **Value for money** ✔✔ Cheap hotels are dismal and the transport slow.

● **Getting around** ✔✔ Even locals seem confused by the bus system. Hitching is bearably easy. Trains are amazingly slow.

● **English spoken** ✔✔ Knowledge remains limited but in Tbilisi you're likely to find someone who is helpful and capable of conversation.

● **Woman alone** ✔✔✔✔ Georgian women play a full part in urban society. Beware of old fashioned mountain men who traditionally find brides by literally grabbing the woman of their fancy.

● **For vegetarians** ✔✔✔ Feasts require meat but poverty has reduced meat consumption. Homemade cheese is a daily staple and vegetables and fruit are widely available at markets.

reluctantly agreed to join the CIS and accept Russian troops on its soil, Russia's Abkazian stooges proved disposable.) UN and Russian peacekeeping mandates expire as we go to press with no sign of a lasting peace treaty.

South Ossetia, though officially abolished as a Georgian autonomous region, is actually more autonomous than ever, and Georgian government rule barely applies there. There are no recent reports of violence, however, and buses still run to the Ossetian capital, Tskhinvali.

As yet, few travellers visit Georgia. Some we talked to reported brushes with police, intimidation on trains and a general sense of insecurity. However, in our three visits we have enjoyed an overwhelmingly positive impression.

❑ **Geo-political information – Georgia (figures include Abkhazia)**

Population: 5.1m (1997), 5.4m (1989), 4.9m (1973).

Area: 69,700 sq km.

Capital: Tbilisi (1.4 million, 1990).

Other major cities: Kutaisi (240,000), Rustavi (160,000) Batumi (140,000), Sukhumi (110,000 – before the war). Zugdidi's normal population of 50,000 is estimated to be temporarily doubled due to the refugees.

GNP per capita: $960 (1994), $5135 (1989)

Currency history: Lari/US$1 Feb 1998: L1.24 Dec 1997: L1.30, June 1996: L1.25. Introduced September 1995, $1=L1.31.

Major exports/economy: Wine, fighter planes. The new Azeri oil pipeline should provide transit revenues. The economy has collapsed since independence (it's now only 17% of its 1989 level). Power shortages mean more than 35% of industry has closed down; the huge Rustavi steel works operate at a fraction of capacity.

Ethnic mix: Georgian (70%), Armenian (8%), Russian (6%), Ossetian (3%).

Official languages: Georgian (71%). Other languages: Russian is widely spoken, Osetinski (3%), Mingrelian (up to 500,000), Laz (2000 in Adjaria), Bats (3000 est), Svan (35,000) – mostly old people (verbal only), Abkhaz (91,000 – 94% as mother tongue).

Religious mix: Georgian Orthodox (65%), Muslim (11% – mainly in Adjaria), Russian Orthodox (10%), Armenian Orthodox (8%).

Landmarks of national history: Complex history of several regional Georgian kingdoms including Colchis (where Jason and the Argonauts sought the Golden Fleece – locals in the Mingrelia and Swanetia regions still pan for gold using sheepskins), Iveria (or Iberia), and Kartli (from which Georgia's present name, Sakartvelo, derives). **330AD**: 14yr old St Nino walked in from Cappadocia bringing Christianity. **645**: Tbilisi fell to the Arabs and became an emirate. **978**: Kutaisi became the capital of Bagrat's unified Georgia. **1089-1125**: David Agmashenebeli ('the Builder') defeated the Turks and launched a Christian Golden age. **1220-26**: Mongol attacks. **1386**: Tamerlane sacked Tbilisi. **1540s**: Persian invasions. **1800**: Annexed by the Russian empire. **26 May 1918**: Independence under Noe Jordania lasted until the Soviet invasion in Feb 1921. **April 1991**: Independence again.

Leaders: President Eduard Shevardnadze, Prime Minister Otar Patsatia. De facto president of Abkhazia: Vladislav Ardzinba, Prime Minister Sergei Bagapsh. Chairman of South Ossetian parliament: Ludvig Chibirov.

Pressing political issues: Settling Abkhazian civil war. Status of independently minded Adjaria and South Ossetia. Controlling the Mkhedrioni, a feared network of paramilitary mafiosi. Rebuilding the economy.

PRACTICAL INFORMATION
Visas and formalities

Georgian visas are easy to get. One month tourist visas cost $30, and are usually issued with no fuss, no need for invitation letters. If the embassy where you apply does demand any awkward papers, it's easy to get a 3-day transit visa: $15 issued on the spot in Trabzon, Turkey or Baku (Room 1324, Hotel Azerbaijan). It's painless to convert this to a full tourist visa for a total stay of up to 2 months ($30) at the Visa Extension Office in Tbilisi (see p120-1). Note that there's no Georgian consulate in Vladikavkaz so if arriving from Russia you'll need to apply in Moscow (easy, double charge for same day service). We tested the 5-day reciprocal visa rule, using an Azerbaijan visa to transit Georgia from Turkey. This worked successfully, though partially thanks to a letter in Russian from the Azeri consul confirming that such a transit was indeed permitted.

Money

In 1995 the Lari replaced the old Georgian currency, the Coupon ('Kuponi'). Coupons were introduced at a rate of 687 to the US$ in May 1993, but a nosediving exchange rate soon made Georgia one of the easiest places in the world to become a millionaire. In contrast the Lari has remained very stable.

Exchange booths are found all over Tbilisi, and less commonly in other cities, and they compete keenly to change US$ or

---

❏ **Essential information for travellers – Georgia**

● **Visa** Required but generally possible to get when you arrive in Tbilisi. There are few Georgian embassies.

● **Currency** Lari. US$1=L1.24. Travellers' cheques are only exchangeable at one bank in Tbilisi.

● **Time zone** 5 hours ahead of GMT year round. 3hrs ahead of Turkey in winter, 2hrs in summer. Same as Azerbaijan in summer but bizarrely 1hr ahead in winter despite lying to the west.

● **Religious tone** Ancient Christianity tempered by recent communist history.

● **Health factors** The water is OK in mountain areas (though not from open streams) but should be boiled in the cities.

● **Special dangers** War and minefields in Abkhazia, banditry on Russian border.

● **Social conventions** Toasting is very important. The word for cheers varies according to whom you are toasting. *Gaumarjos* is a safe start while *Sakartvelos Gaumarjos:* 'to Georgia' or *Gagvimarjos* ('to us') will impress. Toasting should be preceded by a little speech in honour of your toasted subject. Beware that to toast someone with beer is a way to subtly insult them.

Some children are given *urjani* wrist bands made of a special wood to ward off the bad eyes of jealous adults.

● **Highlights** The people; champagne at $0.80; ancient mountaintop churches and castles dotted all over the country, the spectacular Caucasus mountains, Mtskheta (fortified cathedral complex); the botanical gardens near Batumi.

● **When to go** In Tbilisi or the High Caucasus summer days often start clear but end in thunder and torrential downpours. Autumn and spring also have their share of rain, and nights can get chilly. In winter Swanetia gets cut off by snow and is prone to avalanches which the attractive, ancient tower houses were built to withstand. Snow ploughs attempt to keep the Georgian Military Highway open year round to ensure access to Russia and the Gaudari ski area (peak season Dec-April).

● **Pulse of the country** The pantheon (Tbilisi), mountain villages.

DM cash. Other currencies are more rarely accepted. Travellers' cheques can be cashed at Ivertbank (18 Iashvili, Tbilisi). Cash advances though MasterCard should become available at Intellect Bank during 1998.

Transport
● **Train** Georgian trains are slow enough to allow an overnight sleep despite the small distances covered. In fact our Batumi-Tbilisi train took 17hrs including breakdowns. There is a daily overnight service from Tbilisi to each of the following:

Zugdidi (dep 8pm, 4L); Poti (dep 9.30pm, 4L, supposedly will connect with a resumed ferry service to Sochi, Russia); Akhaltsikhe (dep 11.40pm, 4.5L kupe – no platscart); Batumi (7pm, 5L); Baku, Azerbaijan (dep 5.30pm, 15L). Prices for platscart berths in Lari. Trains to Yerevan, Armenia depart on odd days (9L) and there's an inconvenient and very slow seat-only train to Telavi on even days at 4pm (1.7L).

● **Bus** Long distance buses are faster and more frequent than trains. The big red 'Ikarus' buses charge slightly more than

---

❏ In the mountains men are men

I was under strict instructions: 'Remember, this is not Tbilisi. Here you don't dance (except the mountain dances). You don't sing (except the mountain songs). You must be a man. You must drink.'

I was on tour with two Georgian women who had adopted me during the 17 dawdling train hours from Batumi. They accommodated me in their 12th floor Tbilisi apartment, where for four years the lifts hadn't worked. (Even operating lifts are best avoided in Georgia given the frequency of power cuts). There we passed endless wine-soaked musical evenings, feasting on delicacies which must have cost most of their $30 monthly incomes (and that's 10 times above the official average). They had been offended that I tried to pay for anything, though my occasional gifts were, sometimes, grudgingly accepted.

When they suggested a trip to the mountains I worried for them as I feared they would bear the expense. And what about hotels, food etc? No problem, they assured me. We would hitch hike and stay with friends.

The hitching was effortless but the friends had moved away. No problem (there never was a problem for the saintly serene Inga), we would stay with the friends' family. With the same effortlessness with which she dispensed hospitality in her own home, she unquestioningly accepted the hospitality of others. This, to my uncultured amazement, was delightedly given. 'The guest should not be grateful to the host, but the host to the guest'. The proverb is a living reality in Georgia.

The family were shepherds, self sufficient in milk and cheese, and we feasted on home made delicacies. Wine, an appetiser for the vodka, was proffered in mugs to be downed like medicine in a single draught. I tried to be a man. But my eventual attempt to skip the fifteenth toast was not the main cause of the strife that was brewing. Nor was the mounting financial burden of our heavy vodka consumption. It was this: they had been caught with no meat. How could they entertain us with no meat?! The men folk felt themselves disgraced. The womenfolk felt their men were pissed. But we had arrived too late to kill a sheep, and father and son would have to endure the shame till the next night. We stayed several days enjoying bareback horse rides, walks with the sheep in the mountains and plenty more sheep on our plates.

When we finally came to leave, the hosts thanked us for coming by loading us with presents. We hitched back to Tbilisi laden with food hampers having spent not a lari on the whole trip. The drivers paid for dinner, naturally.

the train but less than half the price of the faster minibuses. Some buses operate to fixed schedules but, increasingly, drivers operate 'depart when full' services to improve profitability. Timetabled buses generally depart only in the morning or early afternoon to arrive before dark, while minibuses and 'when full' services depart up until early evening and often use separate bus stations. Bus destinations are usually written in Kartuli so learning the alphabet (see p119) is worthwhile.

Accommodation

Georgia's recent history has wreaked havoc on its hotels. Some were looted, burnt out or abandoned during the civil strife of the early 1990s. Most of the big Intourist hotels remain full of refugees from the Abkhazian conflict, though for around $20 they'll usually find a space for you. In major cities, private B&Bs are becoming more popular – they typically charge $10 a night but are hard to locate. Other hotels are either extremely basic and run down, but are likely to cost only $1-3 a night.

All this said, you might never have a chance to pay for a hotel. We were in Georgia for less than five minutes before we met a local – a customs official working at the border – who eventually took us to a hotel and paid for it. Elsewhere families rushed to play host. Then, when at last we tried to check into a hotel in a town where we knew nobody, the hotelier exclaimed: 'Why not stay in my home? That way you won't have to pay me anything!'

Food and drink

It can be difficult to buy food or drink in Georgia, not due to any shortage but because the locals are so overbearingly generous with everything: notably wine, vodka, and the dreaded *chache*, which makes vodka look like a soft drink. In one restaurant I was greeted by the owner who initially bemoaned the lack of tourists. But considering that he charged me nothing for the extensive meal, fruit and flowing booze, I should hope for his sake that few do come.

Common foods are *khajapuri* (cheese filled bready circles), *rhingkale* (lamb and herb filled dumplings), and *pais* (beans with herbs). Harder to find is *satsivi* (a delicious garlic, walnut and herb sauce chicken dish somewhat reminiscent of Iranian *fesenjan*). In winter *churchkhela*

❑ **Camping in Georgia**

We had come to the Georgian Black Sea to go camping. Our first attempt didn't work. A local family spotted us walking on the road with our backpacks and insisted we stay with them. But the next night we were determined. We informed the family that we were planning to return to Batumi and began walking towards the main road. Out of eyeshot from our hosts who stood waving us goodbye, we doubled back and eventually found a secluded spot in the woods next to the coast.

All went well until a policeman spotted our bonfire that night on the beach. He asked in a sort of Anglo-Germanic-Russified-Georgian language where we were staying. We pretended we didn't understand, but he persisted in asking. Eventually we gave in and reluctantly showed him our campsite. He was horrified.

'You stay my house!' he yelled. We tried convincing him that we were very happy camping, but he argued more forcefully than us. Judging from his handcuffing gesture, if we didn't stay in his house he was apparently going to arrest us and do something else to us that provoked him to make large sweeping motions with his hands.

We knew we had no choice, and proceeded to his humble dwelling. He scoured his cupboards, and returned with a bottle of vodka and some food – a typical ending for nights spent camping in Georgia.

dangle from many a kiosk – vaguely obscene nobbly batons of extruded brown rubbery grape extract coating strings of walnuts.

Restaurants are few and far between except in Batumi, Tbilisi and occasionally at the roadside, (most notably in the small castle town of Surami between Kutaisi and Khashauri where almost all east-west long distance buses stop for snacks). Bigger towns have markets full of produce. In Tbilisi the best are beside metro stations Didube, Isani and Akhmetelisi Teatri. In small rural towns, people tend to be largely self sufficient in food so groceries can be relatively hard to buy. The ubiquitous vodka-and-Snickers kiosks don't offer a very balanced diet.

Staying in touch

Tbilisi's Communications Centre in the PO near the Hotel Iveria is extremely helpful and efficient. You can send faxes ($3 a page) and receive replies ($0.30 a sheet). Phone rates are very reasonable ($2 a minute to the UK).

❏ Meeting the locals

● **The people** Georgia is a place of passion, of poetry and of music (everyone we met seemed to play the guitar or the three stringed *panduri* lute). Tbilisi has several pantheons – graveyard memorials to the nations' poets, artists and savants. Each of our adopted friends could recite a stanza by any poet whose grave they might stumble across, referring to the artist on first name terms as if they were talking about old friends. And these were not professional guides. People acted as though characters in a William Morris utopia: educated helpfulness and unconditional hospitality seems to have become the genuine joy of the giver. We have heard reports of travellers feeling intimidated on rail journeys and, in general, mountain people are reputed to be much less open to strangers. Venturing alone to out of the way villages (especially in Swanetia or Ossetia) without connections is discouraged even by urban Georgians. Yet by luck or judgement we found the people there to be even more hospitable than their lowland compatriots, the only problem being how to accept hospitality from two families at once – and how to handle all the booze.

● **Language** Georgian is nothing like Russian, though many people in Georgia speak both languages. For Kartuli alphabet see p119.

Some phrases in Georgian:
> Hello – *gamar jobat*
> Thank you – *didi madloba* (reply: *ara-prees*)
> Greeting – *rogor rakhat*?
> Reply – *gargi* (good)
> It's delicious – *gemrielia*
> It's beautiful – *lamazia*

● **Some conversation starters Politics:** Shevardnadze versus Gamsakhurdia (the ousted first president); Gamsakhurdia's rebellion and death; Aslan Abashidze – the 'king' of Adjaria (autonomous, Muslim south west Georgia); Stalin (Josep Dzhughashvili) – attitudes to the world's most infamous Georgian; Who are the 'evil horsemen' (Mkhedrioni) and are they likely to strike again?

Arts: Famous painters include Pirosmani (self-taught painter of stick figures), Gudiashvili (ask why his characters have no ears), Kakabadze.

Writers: Shota Rustaveli (*Knight in the Tiger Skin*), Baratashvili, Chachavadze.

Opera and ballet stars: Vartang Tjchabukiani, Paata Burjtchuladze.

Sports: Dynamo Tbilisi football team and their heyday against Liverpool. Kinkladze and other Georgian stars abroad.

❑ While God was busy dividing the world amongst primordial tribes, the Georgians were out boozing. Flattering the not yet omniscient deity that they had been drinking in His honour, God decided to give them the most beautiful land of all, the land that he had been saving for himself, today's Georgia. **Popular saying**

International phone code +995 (but if this doesn't work try 7, the old Soviet number). Tbilisi: 8832. Batumi: 222. Phone lines to Abkhazia are cut.

Activities

● **Hiking** There are excellent opportunities in the high Caucasus but no facilities. A local guide would be sensible both to help you find the way and to introduce you in the various wilder villages en route: the three to four day walk from Kazbegi to Khevsureti is recommended. Local shepherds do not use tents but have an extremely heavy woollen *nabadi* cloak which doubles as a sleeping bag and mat and stands on its own given the chance.

● **Swimming** The best beaches were around Gagra (Abkhazia) but they are now impossible to reach from the rest of Georgia. Kobuleti and Batumi have pebble beaches which are popular with locals. Nice for sunsets over the Black Sea, less so for bathing.

● **Work** There is a great demand for English teachers. Although earnings average only $4 an hour, this is a considerable sum in Georgia and as yet there are few other foreigners competing for the jobs.

Further information

● **Maps** Georgia maps are available in bookshops and at kiosks in all the bigger towns. The easiest to find show only geographical features – look closely because an apparently identical map exists with roads, rail and village names. The fact that most maps in Georgia are in Kartuli is thoroughly daunting at first. But the alphabet is easy enough and learning it is a great excuse to meet people to ask for help. Kartuli maps are useful for matching with bus destination notices. City maps of Tbilisi are available in English, Russian and Kartuli. An excellent French city centre cartoon map is also sold. Maps for other towns seem to be unavailable.

● **Books** At present, the only dedicated guide to Georgia is Roger Rosen's *Odyssey Guide – Georgia*. A new edition is due soon but the current guide was written before much of the Soviet-style state apparatus had crumbled away, lacks good regional maps, and assumes you have a car. Rosen gives thorough background to the architecture and extremely complex history of the country. Not available in Georgia.

Please don't call it Soviet Georgia, by Mary Russel, is an entertaining travel narrative written the year before independence. Due early 1998, Peter Nasmyth's *Georgia – In the Mountains of Poetry* promises to be interesting. Street vendors in Tbilisi's prospect Rustaveli have a good selection of secondhand books on Georgian history and culture, and reprints of *Teach Yourself Georgian*.

Web sites

The links and information at voyager.rtd.utk.edu/~zlotchen/georgia is the best place to start gathering information on Georgia.

www.sanet.ge/webpages.html has a curious selection of sites, including home-pages for Georgian rugby, recipes, wine and links to the US embassy in Tbilisi.

www.parliament.ge/index.html is the homepage of the parliament of Georgia; it has lots of information but mostly economic/governmental and somewhat turgid.

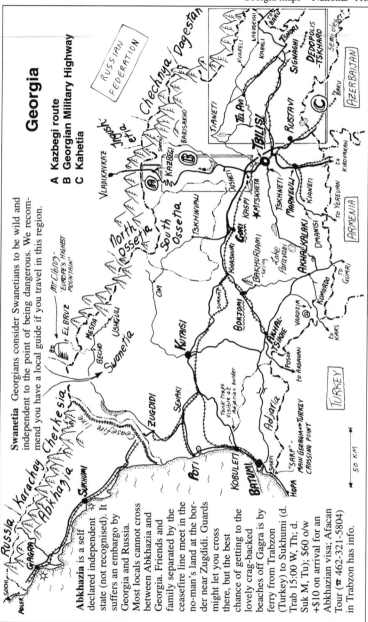

Georgia

A **Kazbegi route**
B **Georgian Military Highway**
C **Kahetia**

Swanetia Georgians consider Swanetians to be wild and independent to the point of being dangerous. We recommend you have a local guide if you travel in this region.

RUSSIAN FEDERATION

Mt Elbrus - "EUROPE'S HIGHEST MOUNTAIN"

50 KM

Abkhazia is a self declared independent state (not recognised). It suffers an embargo by Georgia and Russia. Most locals cannot cross between Abkhazia and Georgia. Friends and family separated by the ceasefire line meet in the no-man's land at the border near Zugdidi. Guards might let you cross there, but the best chance of getting to the lovely crag-backed beaches off Gagra is by ferry from Trabzon (Turkey) to Sukhumi (d. Trab 15:00 W, Th; d. Suk M, Tu); $60 o/w +$10 on arrival for an Abkhazian visa; Afacan Tour (☎ 462-321-5804) in Trabzon has info.

Tank traps visible at Adjarian border

"SARP" MAIN GEORGIA↔TURKEY CROSSING POINT

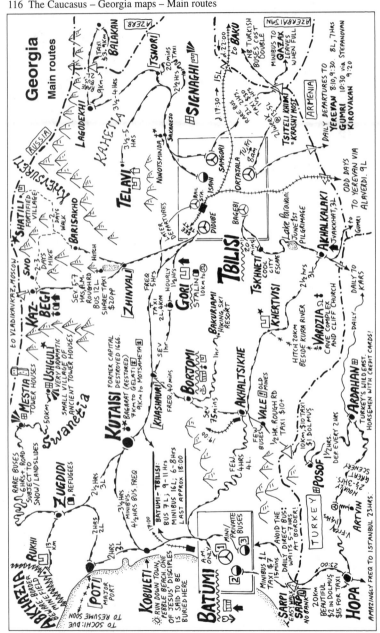

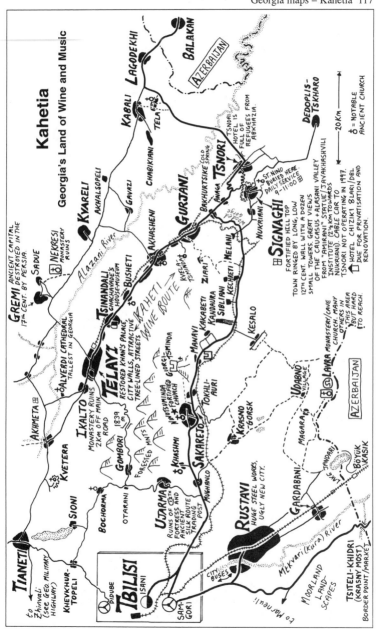

Kahetia

Georgia's Land of Wine and Music

☩ = NOTABLE
ANCIENT CHURCH

BALAKAN

AZERBAIJAN

LAGODEKHI

KABALI

TELA

DEDOPLIS-
TSKHARO

TSNORI hotel is
full of refugees
from Abkhazia.

ACHALSOPELI

KVARELI

NEKRESI
MONASTERY RUINS

GAVAZI

CHABIKIANI

AKHASHENI

GURJANI

Bakhurtsike cold
spring

TSNORI
ANAGA

NUKRIANI gorge

ST. NINO
BURIED HERE:
DAILY SERVICE
9-11:00

20Km

GREMI ANCIENT CAPITAL
DESTROYED IN THE
17TH CENT. BY PERSIA.

SADVE

Alazani River

BUSHETI

MELANI

KVELA
TSMINDA

ZIARI

KECHETI

KAHETI
WINE ROUTE

TSINANDALI
CHAVCHAVADZE'S
HOUSE-MUSEUM

ALVERDI CATHEDRAL
TALLEST IN GEORGIA

TELAVI RESTORED KHAN'S PALACE,
CITY WALLS, ATTRACTIVE
TREE-LINED STREETS

KESALO

NUKRIANI

SIGNAGHI
FORTIFIED HILL TOP
TOWN RINGED BY LONG, LOW
12TH CENT. WALL WITH A DOZEN
SMALL TOWERS. GREAT VIEWS
OF THE CAUCASUS + ALASANI VALLEY
FROM "AMIRANI" STATUE (JAVAKHASHVILI
INSTITUTE (2½ km TOWARDS
NUKRIANI). CABLE CAR TO
TSNORI NOT OPERATING IN 1997.

☩ Hotel CHIZIKI BLAKI/DBL.
DUE FOR PRIVATISATION AND
RENOVATION.

IKALTO MONASTERY RUINS
2km OFF MAIN
ROAD

AKHMETA

KAKABETI

SIBLIANI

KANDAURA

MANAVI

GOMBORI 1839

FORESTED MNTS

☩ KHASHMI

NINOTSMINDA
FORTIFIED
CHURCH GIORGI
TSMINDA

SAKARETO

TOKHLI-
AURI

KRASNO
GORSK

UDABNO
VILLAGE

LAVRA MONASTERY/CAVE
CHURCH. MANY
OTHERS IN
THIS AREA
BUT HARD
TO REACH.

AZERBAIJAN

KVETERA

SIONI

BOCHORMA

OTARANI

UJARMA
RUINS OF 8TH FORTRESS AND
ANCIENT SILK ROUTE
TRADING POST

MUHANLO

MAGARA

BÖYÜK
KASIK

TIANETI

to
Zhinvali
(SEE GEO MILITARY
HIGHWAY)

KHEVKHUR-
TOPELI

DIDUBE TBILISI
ISANI

SAM-
GORI

RUSTAVI
HUGE STEEL WORKS,
UGLY NEW CITY.

GARDABANI

CITY
BUSES

To Marneuli

Mtkvari (Kura) River

MOORLAND
LANDSCAPES

TSITELI-KHIDRI
(KRASNY MOST)
BORDER POINT/MARKET.

To JANDARI

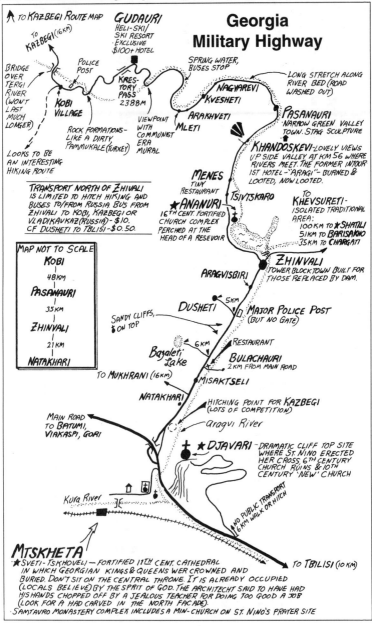

Georgia Military Highway

↑ to KAZBEGI ROUTE map

TO KAZBEGI (16KM)

GUDAURI HELI-SKI/ SKI RESORT EXCLUSIVE $100+ HOTEL

BRIDGE OVER TERGI RIVER (WON'T LAST MUCH LONGER)

Police Post

KRESTORY PASS 2388M

KOBI VILLAGE

SPRING WATER, BUSES STOP

LONG STRETCH ALONG RIVER BED (ROAD WASHED OUT)

NAGVAREVI
KVESHETI

LOOKS TO BE AN INTERESTING HIKING ROUTE

ROCK FORMATIONS - LIKE A DIRTY PAMMUKALE (TURKEY)

VIEWPOINT WITH COMMUNIST ERA MURAL

MLETI

ARAKHVETI

PASANAURI NARROW GREEN VALLEY TOWN. STAG SCULPTURE

KHANDOSKEVI - LOVELY VIEWS UP SIDE VALLEY AT KM 56 WHERE RIVERS MEET. THE FORMER INTOUR 1ST HOTEL - 'ARAGI' - BURNED & LOOTED, NOW LOOTED.

MENES TINY RESTAURANT

TRANSPORT NORTH OF ZHIVALI IS LIMITED TO HITCH HIKING AND BUSES TO/FROM RUSSIA BUS FROM ZHIVALI TO KOBI, KAZBEGI OR VLADIKAVKAZ (RUSSIA) - $10. CF DUSHETI TO TBILISI - $0.50.

★ANANURI 16TH CENT. FORTIFIED CHURCH COMPLEX PERCHED AT THE HEAD OF A RESEVOIR

TSIVTSKARO

TO **KHEVSURETI** - ISOLATED TRADITIONAL AREA: 100 KM TO ★SHATILI 51KM TO BARISAKNO 35KM TO CHARGATI

ZHINVALI TOWER BLOCK TOWN BUILT FOR THOSE REPLACED BY DAM.

ARAGVISBIRI

MAP NOT TO SCALE

KOBI
48KM
PASANAURI
35KM
ZHINVALI
21KM
NATAKHARI

DUSHETI   5KM

MAJOR POLICE POST (BUT NO GATE)

SANDY CLIFFS, ON TOP

6KM   RESTAURANT

Bazaleti Lake

BULACHAURI 2KM FROM MAIN ROAD

TO MUKHRANI (16KM)

MISAKTSELI

NATAKHARI

HITCHING POINT FOR **KAZBEGI** (LOTS OF COMPETITION)

MAIN ROAD TO BATUMI, VIAKASPI, GORI

Aragvi River

★DJAVARI - DRAMATIC CLIFF TOP SITE WHERE ST. NINO ERECTED HER CROSS 6TH CENTURY CHURCH RUINS & 10TH CENTURY 'NEW' CHURCH

Kura River

NO PUBLIC TRANSPORT 6KM WALK OR HITCH

TO TBILISI (10 KM)

MTSKHETA
★SVETI-TSKHOVELI — FORTIFIED 11TH CENT. CATHEDRAL IN WHICH GEORGIAN KINGS & QUEENS WER CROWNED AND BURIED. DON'T SIT ON THE CENTRAL THRONE. IT IS ALREADY OCCUPIED (LOCALS BELIEVE) BY THE SPRIT OF GOD. THE ARCHITECHT SAID TO HAVE HAD HIS HANDS CHOPPED OFF BY A JEALOUS TEACHER FOR DOING TOO GOOD A JOB (LOOK FOR A HAD CARVED IN THE NORTH FACADE).
SAMTAVRO MONASTERY COMPLEX INCLUDES A MIN-CHURCH ON ST. NINO'S PRAYER SITE

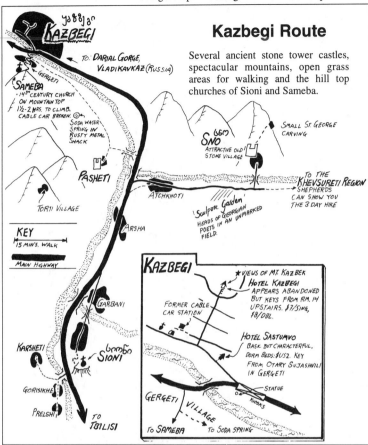

Kazbegi Route

Several ancient stone tower castles, spectacular mountains, open grass areas for walking and the hill top churches of Sioni and Sameba.

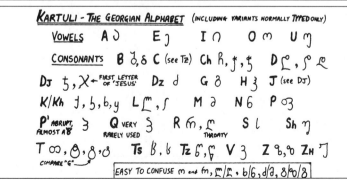

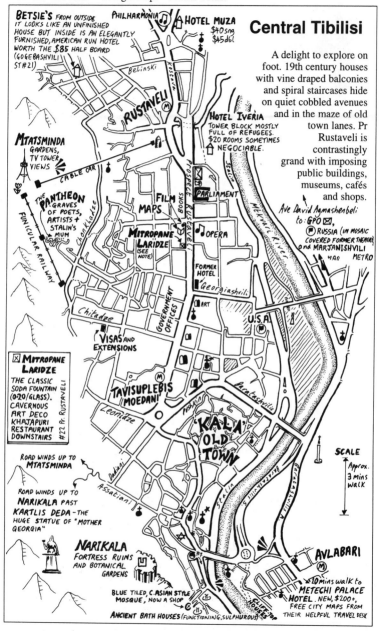

Central Tibilisi

A delight to explore on foot. 19th century houses with vine draped balconies and spiral staircases hide on quiet cobbled avenues and in the maze of old town lanes. Pr Rustaveli is contrastingly grand with imposing public buildings, museums, cafés and shops.

BETSIE'S FROM OUTSIDE IT LOOKS LIKE AN UNFINISHED HOUSE BUT INSIDE IS AN ELEGANTLY FURNISHED, AMERICAN RUN HOTEL. WORTH THE $85 HALF BOARD (GOGEBASHVILI ST#21)

PHILHARMONIA

HOTEL MUZA $40 sng $45 dbl

Belinski

RUSTAVELI Ⓜ

HOTEL IVERIA TOWER BLOCK MOSTLY FULL OF REFUGEES. $20 ROOMS SOMETIMES NEGOCIABLE.

MTATSMINDA GARDENS, TV TOWER VIEWS

CABLE CAR

THE **PANTHEON** GRAVES OF POETS, ARTISTS + STALIN'S MUM

FUNICULAR RAILWAY

Chonkadze

FILM MAPS

BOOKS

Prospect Rustaveli

Stalin

PARLIAMENT

Mtkvari River

Ave David Agmashenbeli to: GPO ✉,

Ⓜ RUSSIA (IN MOSAIC COVERED FORMER THEATRE) and MARJANISHVILI METRO

чао

OPERA

MITROPANE LARIDZE (SEE NOTE)

FORMER HOTEL **Georgiashvili**

ART

U.S.A

Chitadze

GOVERNMENT OFFICES

VISAS AND **EXTENSIONS**

☒ **MITROPANE LARIDZE** THE CLASSIC SODA FOUNTAIN (0.20/GLASS). CAVERNOUS ART DECO KHAJAPURI RESTAURANT DOWNSTAIRS #22 Pr. RUSTAVELI

TAVISUPLEBIS MOEDANI Ⓜ

Leonidze

Pushkin

Baratashvili

KALA OLD TOWN

Stalin

SCALE Approx. 3 mins walk

ROAD WINDS UP TO **MTATSMINDA**

ROAD WINDS UP TO **NARIKALA** PAST **KARTLIS DEDA** –THE HUGE STATUE OF "MOTHER GEORGIA"

Dadiani

Assatiani

NARIKALA FORTRESS RUINS AND BOTANICAL GARDENS

BLUE TILED, C. ASIAN STYLE MOSQUE, NOW A SHOP

ANCIENT BATH HOUSES (FUNCTIONING, SULPHUROUS)

AVLABARI Ⓜ

→ 10 mins walk to **METECHI PALACE HOTEL**. NEW, $200+, FREE CITY MAPS FROM THEIR HELPFUL TRAVEL DESK

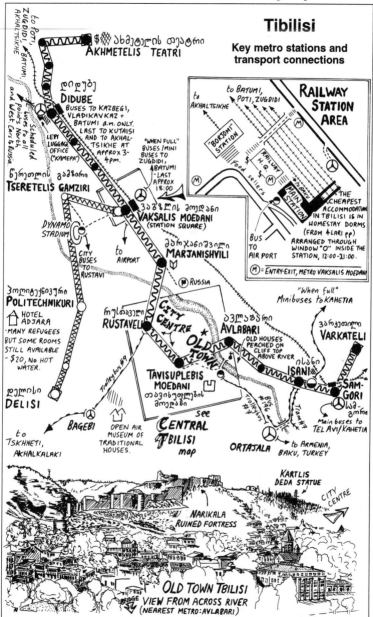

Tibilisi

Key metro stations and transport connections

to POTI, ZUGDIDI, BATUMI, AKHALTSIKHE

to POTI, ZUGDIDI, BATUMI and West. Cars to Russia

Schedules buses to all points North

$※ აბჟეტელის თეატრი
AKHMETELIS TEATRI

დიდუბე
DIDUBE
BUSES TO KAZBEGI, VLADIKAVKAZ + BATUMI a.m. ONLY. LAST TO KUTAISI AND TO AKHALTSIKHE AT APPROX 3-4pm.

LEFT LUGGAGE OFFICE ("KAMERA")

"WHEN FULL" BUSES/MINI BUSES TO ZUGDIDI, ABATUMI - LAST APPROX 18:00.

წერეთლის გამზირი
TSERETELIS GAMZIRI

DYNAMO STADIUM

CITY BUSES TO RUSTAVI

to AIRPORT

ვაგზლის მოედანი
VAKSALIS MOEDANI
(STATION SQUARE)

მარჯანიშვილი
MARJANISHVILI

Ⓜ Russia

RAILWAY STATION AREA

to AKHALTSIKHE

to BATUMI, POTI, ZUGDIDI

"BORJOMI" STATION

Ⓜ

Food sellers

RAILWAY H.Q.

MAIN STATION

THE CHEAPEST ACCOMMODATION IN TBILISI IS IN HOMESTAY DORMS (FROM 4 LARI pp) ARRANGED THROUGH WINDOW "0" INSIDE THE STATION, 12:00-21:00.

BUS TO AIR PORT

Ⓜ = ENTRY-EXIT, METRO VAKSALIS MOEDANI

პოლიტექნიკური
POLITECHNIKURI
⌂ HOTEL ADJARA
·MANY REFUGEES BUT SOME ROOMS STILL AVAILABLE - $20, NO HOT WATER.

რუსთაველი
RUSTAVELI

CITY CENTRE

OLD TOWN

★

"When full" Minibuses to KAHETIA

ავლაბარი
AVLABARI
OLD HOUSES PERCHED ON CLIFF TOP ABOVE RIVER

ისანი
ISANI

ვარკეთილი
VARKATELI

სამ-გორი
SAM-GORI
samgori Ⓜ

Main buses to TEL AVI/KAHETIA

დელისი
DELISI

BAGEBI

to TSKHNETI, AKHALKALAKI

Trolley bus #9

თავისუფლების მოედანი
TAVISUPLEBIS MOEDANI

OPEN AIR MUSEUM OF TRADITIONAL HOUSES.

see ₵entral ₸BILISI map

Bus #6

Trolleys

Trams

ORTAJALA

to Armenia, BAKU, TURKEY

KARTLIS DEDA STATUE

CITY CENTRE

NARIKALA RUINED FORTRESS

OLD TOWN TBILISI
VIEW FROM ACROSS RIVER
(NEAREST METRO: AVLABARI)

BRIDGE

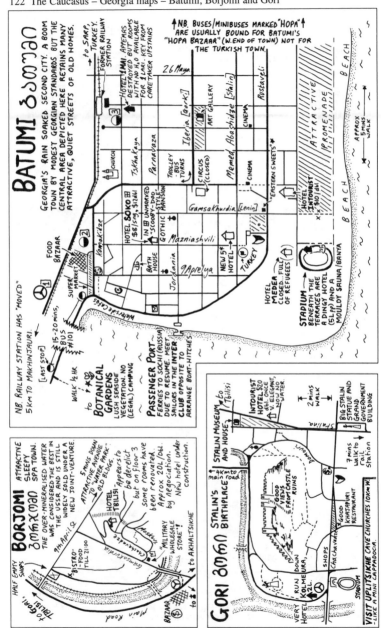

CENTRAL ASIA

A century ago the Russians were advancing inexorably across the desert and steppe of today's Kazakhstan and seemed set on invading British India. During what became known as the Great Game (see p138), the desert potentates of Central Asia were seldom out of the news. Stranger-than-fiction spy tales renewed the mystery in names like Bukhara and Samarkand. But then the 'dashed Ruskies' became 'darned Commies' and these majestic Silk Road cities disappeared into 70 years of Soviet obscurity.

Following the 1991 collapse of the USSR, five new Asian nations were created. Each has rapidly developed a distinct political style: from free-market Kyrgyzstan, the 'Switzerland of Central Asia' to authoritarian Turkmenistan whose leader's statues rapidly filled the spaces left by toppled Lenins.

Independent travellers are only slowly noticing these 'new' destinations. One described travel in the region as 'slogging through the mud to get to the gems'. The gems include historic oases, dramatic, unspoilt mountain landscapes dotted with nomad yurts and alpine lakes, and some of the world's highest peaks. But there is plenty of slogging, too. Towns are predominantly fashioned from dismal Soviet concrete. Hotels are mostly run down. The intricacies of getting visas can be a headache. And the shards of post Soviet bureaucracy have produced some haphazardly conceived rules. Police corruption is undisguised, though it affects locals much more than visitors – indeed we suffered less than we had pessimistically expected.

Travellers looking for an easy, relaxing vacation are best advised to head elsewhere. But for those who want a pioneering sense of adventure without significant danger, or for those who enjoy duelling with bureaucracy and post-communist fall-out, now is a unique and fascinating time to visit.

❏ **Social conventions in Central Asia**
- Learn to drink large quantities of vodka and to enjoy mutton if you want to make friends the local way.
- A handy toast is *mir, druzhba* – peace, friendship (in Russian), or *dustliq* in the other languages in the region.
- Hospitality seems to be heartfelt without ulterior motives.
- Take time. Hurrying is not in the local culture. Local women meeting men consider punctuality to be a sign of forwardness. An hour or more late is normal according to one Kyrgyz women who was shocked to find her female German friends departing for a rendezvous before the planned meeting time had even elapsed.
- A guest is a guest for three days. After complete mollycoddling, on the fourth day you may be given chores to do. This is a form of flattery as you are being informally accepted as a member of the family.

Central Asia

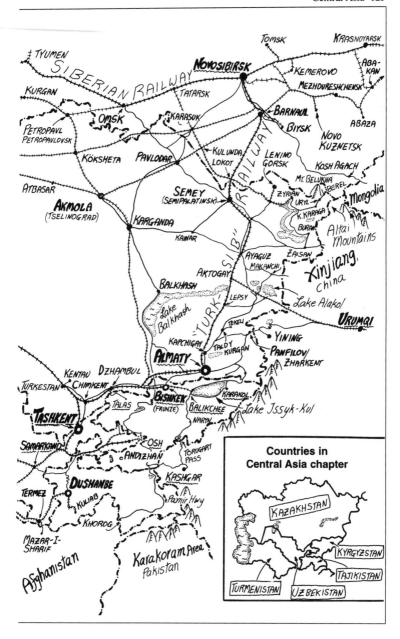

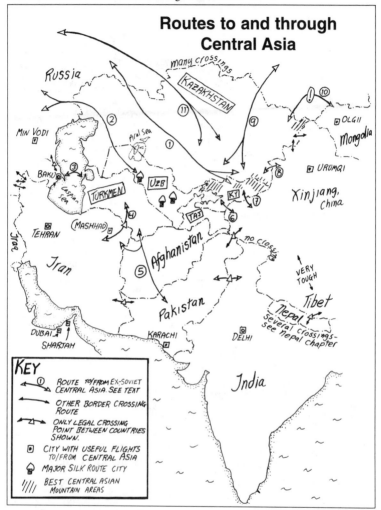

Routes to and through Central Asia

KEY

⟵① ROUTE TO/FROM EX-SOVIET CENTRAL ASIA. SEE TEXT

⟷ OTHER BORDER CROSSING ROUTE

⟷ ONLY LEGAL CROSSING POINT BETWEEN COUNTRIES SHOWN.

▣ CITY WITH USEFUL FLIGHTS TO/FROM CENTRAL ASIA

⌂ MAJOR SILK ROUTE CITY

//// BEST CENTRAL ASIAN MOUNTAIN AREAS

● **1 Silk Rail** The Central Asian mainline. Convenient, comfortable, v. freq trains to Moscow (3 daily from Tashkent, 2 from Almaty ($65), daily from Bishkek ($55), Dushanbe, Andizhan, Kyzyl Orda, Akmola and other N Kazakh cities.) The route is hypnotically repetitive: scrubby flat steppe in Kazakhstan, green expanses of rolling farmland in Russia. On Moscow-bound services a provodnik comes around before Orenburg taking orders for onward tickets. Even as a foreigner you'll pay local fares (plus 10% booking fee) which saves money as well as time and hassle in Moscow. Tickets thus reserved are delivered to your berth after Samara (but remember to change Russian roubles before departure to pay for them).

● **2 Silk Rail 2** Moscow-Samarkand. ($52). That this route passes the three greatest Silk Route gems seems too good to be true. However, trains are sporadic (at best a few/week) and can be exceedingly hard to book (especially northbound). Doing the trip in hops is possible but rather arduous. See 'Across or around the Caspian', p11. Trailblazer's *Silk Route by Rail* guide details this route. Recent rumours suggest that the Beinen-Urgench section may be scrapped altogether.

● **3 Trans Caspian** The Caspian ferry (Baku-Krasnovodsk) costs from $45 and operates daily. Flights are $59 and give a better view of the oil derricks and stark beauty of the Turkmen coast. See 'Across or around the Caspian'.

● **4 The Oil Route** A new rail line connects Mashhad (Iran) with Tedjen (Turkmenistan). There is also a direct road to Ashgabat. At the time of research these borders were still closed to citizens of Western countries, but the rail line is slated to re-open to foreigners in the next year or two. In the meantime, if you get stuck there is a Mashhad-Ashgabat flight every Monday for only $40 (Turkmen A/L), though some travellers have been charged $100.

● **5 Routes through Afghanistan** Obviously volatile due to the continued Afghan civil war, but at the time of writing the Quetta (Pakistan)-Kandahar (Afgh)-Kushka (Turkmen) road is not only open but undergoing an expensive, much needed upgrade. Surprisingly we were also allowed to cross from Iran into Afghanistan and managed to get Turkmen visas very easily in Herat. (Heading the other way from Turkmenistan into Iran might prove more difficult). See Afghanistan chapter.

● **6 Irkestam Route** Osh-Sary Tash-Irkestam (Kyrg)-Archal (Xinjiang)-Kashgar. This 'new' route opened in summer 1996. The high pass, closed by snow all winter, allows trucks to go directly between the Fergana Valley (Uzb) and Kashgar (Xinjiang, China) between May and October. Check the latest details in Osh or at Kashgar's Info Café.

● **7 Torugart Pass** An attractive mountain route. Crossing has become considerably easier since Nov 1995 with the introduction of a twice daily minibus between the border posts (105km) but remains awkward, slow and potentially pricey. See Torugart section in Kyrgyzstan chapter. An Artux-Bishkek direct bus has been announced.

● **8 Urumqi-Almaty options** Now very straightforward though not particularly attractive. Direct buses run 6/week ($50), direct trains 2/week. Taken in sections the trip can be more comfortable, cheaper and still easy enough to organise (possibilities expanded in Kazakhstan chapter).

● **9 To/from Siberia** Trains crisscross the Kazakh-Russian border in many places, with direct services along the Turk-Sib line from Bishkek, Almaty and Tashkent to a variety of different Siberian cities on different days. Weekly trains run all the way Tashkent-Irkutsk in summer. Sosnovka, Kyrgyzstan (see Around Bishkek map) is a particularly good spot for hitching to Siberia.

● **10 Mongolia-Central Asia** Mongolia and Kazakhstan don't share a common border. Contrary to some travel rumours it is not even possible to cross between Kosh Argach (Russia) and Olgii (Mongolia). Even if this opens, mountains prevent a convenient loop south into Central Asia. For now the only option is the $200 Olgii-Oskamen (Ust Kamenogorsk, Kazakhstan) - Almaty flight (Friday), though it's usually 'locals only'.

● **11 To Kharkov, Ukraine** If we showed them tickets for the three-day, weekly slow train Tashkent-Kharkov ($35) the Ukrainian embassy in Tashkent was prepared to give us transit visas. Catch 22: to buy the ticket we had to show the visa. There's also a Karaganda (Kaz)-Kharkov train.

● **Other border points** We have no personal experience of the other two Kazakhstan-China crossing points. Tajik borders with Afghanistan are just fine if you have a large private army, but you'll need to equip them with wire cutters and anti landmine specialists to get across the mountains into China.

PRACTICAL INFORMATION
Visas and formalities

Each country has its own visa policy, interpreted very differently by different consuls. Visas can be hard to procure because, not only are there so few embassies but most consuls require applicants to provide a letter of invitation or evidence of a pre-booked tour. Fortunately there are exceptions, and, furthermore the 1992 CIS visa agreement (which we've dubbed the Visa Shuffle) allows you to enter any one of 7 CIS nations on the visa of any other. All the central Asian nations except Turkmenistan are signatories to this agreement, so a visa from one will get you into most of the other countries – see p557 for full details. Even a Russian, Belarus or Armenian visa will do.

Your first objective, therefore, is to get a visa of any kind to get into the region. The simplest visa to procure is usually that of Kyrgyzstan (easy in the USA or Turkey) or a Kazakh transit visa (cheap and easy in Beijing, though very expensive indeed in Urumqi). Turkmen visas are also easiest to get in Istanbul and you'll get a Kyrgyz visa on the spot once you get to Ashgabat.

Once you're within the region, applying for other central Asian visas is relatively straightforward. Furthermore, there are few if any passport checks between nations so although a visa may be only intended for a single entry, in practice you can use it to flit to and fro. This is fortunate considering the way roads wind back and forth across borderlines.

Money

Each former Soviet country has its own currency, though some locals tend to refer nostalgically to their money as *roublei*. Wherever you go, there is a tendency for expensive hotels, government departments and corrupt policemen to price their services in US$, even in Kyrgyzstan and Kazakhstan where the currencies are stable. This has been made officially illegal in some places, but the result is merely to charge the equivalent at today's rate.

US$ cash is the easiest to exchange, though DM and Russian roubles are widely convertible too. Exchange booths (*Obmen - Valyut*) are ubiquitous in cities and town markets, and typically keep long hours. In rural areas you can normally find private individuals who are happy to buy your dollars. Travellers' cheques can be changed only at a few big city locations and with a typical commission of 3-5% on an already poor exchange rate. It is usually to your advantage to change $ travellers' cheques for US$ cash in a bank then convert to local currency at an exchange booth. Cash advances on credit cards are becoming possible in main cities but may incur a 5% commission. A few shops, restaurants and top hotels take plastic. MasterCard seems most commonly accepted.

● **Bring post 1991-US$ bills** As elsewhere in the ex-USSR, mass forgery means that not all US$ bills are equally acceptable. Notes dated before 1991 lack the security stripe for which most cashiers and exchange booths automatically check. They are thus impossible to change in many places or at best are worth 10-20% less. If you do get stuck with older notes, try using them at embassies for visa fees.

Transport

● **Bus** Schedules painted on bus station walls are usually leftovers from the Soviet era and shouldn't be relied upon. Although bus schedules do still exist in reduced form, some operators now take a more capitalist approach. In Bishkek bus station, one driver went round asking passengers where they wanted to go. He finally announced he had a bus, leaving in five minutes, to the destination that had proved the most popular.

● **Train** See ex-USSR chapter. Most trains are reasonably reliable and comfortable. However, in Uzbekistan, there's an annoying tendency to cover the windows in metal slats; and trains numbered above 500 are local services using vandalised sardine cans instead of the normal rolling stock.

Unlike in Russia, few of the stations have computerised reservation systems.

There are usually plenty of tickets available from the starting station. However, stops en route have a very limited quota of advance sale tickets and it's worth booking a day or two ahead to get one. Once this quota has been sold, one has to wait till minutes before the train arrives when the number of available berths is cabled ahead to the ticket office and a mad scramble ensues. If you just can't get a ticket, it's worth going to the end of the train and talking to the *provodnik* of the *obshchii* unreserved car. If you offer slightly more than the ticket price, you'll likely get aboard, though in somewhat crowded discomfort.

● **Hitch-hiking** Across the region, pot-bellied traffic police (GAI/DAN/DAI) lounge about at road blocks, whistling at trucks to stop. Their ostensible purpose is to promote safety which they do by extorting bribes from drivers: about $2 for a car, up to $30 for a big Kamaz truck. One lorry driver estimated that bribes constituted at least a third of his operating costs.

Police stops may be the bane of drivers' lives but they are a hitch hiker's saviour. These particular police don't seem to bother hassling foreigners and often take a delight at helping you find a ride. Once a policeman gave the driver a choice of taking us or paying twice the usually bribe. Another time the cops opened a bottle of vodka to bless our journey.

Accommodation

● **Big city hotels** (Russian: *gastinitsa*, Turkic languages: *mekhmankhana*) are mostly run down, overpriced or both. The capital cities have one or two exceptional business hotels apiece (at $200+), handy for information and orientation.

● **Bed and breakfast** – still very rare. Best options in Bukhara and Khiva.

● **Camping/roughing it** A few camp sites exist, while in the mountains a tent gives you great freedom to sleep almost anywhere. Asking permission to camp on a local farmer's land is polite and often results in offers of hospitality. Camping in city parks is not recommended because of the drunks as well as official ire. Some but

not all rail and bus stations have warm waiting rooms where you can curl up on the floor at night.

Food and drink

Mutton, mutton, mutton. Even if you like lamb, you may tire of the sheepy bits that end up on your plate at almost any meal. One family cooked up a delicious fish for grandma but served us lamb... 'you are guests, you must eat meat'. Wherever you go in the region, you'll see *shashlyk* (skewers of lamb barbecued on rusty roadside braziers), and *plov* (a pilaf of rice, yellow carrot and mutton fat cooked in huge greasy pans that would look comfortable in a Caribbean steel band). At home people eat *laghman* (noodle soup with, yes, mutton). Central Asia is tough on vegetarians. See the box in the ex-USSR chapter, p273.

For budget meals head for an *ashkhana*, (a central Asian *stolovaya* canteen) or eat at street stall (especially at lunch times) where a plov need not cost more than $0.60. After dark most of these cheap places will be closed.

Since the days of Genghis Khan, boozing has been seen as a social necessity. *Koumys* (fermented mares' milk) is a speciality and the traditional drink of the region, though increasingly hard to find in the cities. Deliciously ironic in this supposedly Islamic region, is the prevalence of Israeli vodka. Muslim or not, alcohol remains an important social focus and refusing to join toasts would be extremely poor form.

Beware of local vodka. If buying a present for friends it's worth paying slightly more for a more respected brand (eg Russkaya, Solichnaya) or impress with an imported bottle. The extra investment pays off as you'll surely have to drink some and methanol is bad for the eyes.

Local *shampanski* is cheap (around $2/bottle) and is often better than the ubiquitous, over sweet Italian Spumante, which sells in more of the kiosks. Local beer is almost unanimously dreadful.

With the dry, summer heat and the likelihood of hangovers to combat, drinking large quantities of water or soft drinks is crucial. *Gaz voda/gazli suu* is soda water sold from resurrected street corner vending machines. The source of water is dubious (straight from the mains supply) but we remained healthy having drunk 3-4 litres a day. In many cases if you buy draft 'Pepsi' you'll actually receive the same gaz voda with a squirt of syrup. Old style government stores sell cheap, returnable glass bottles full of gassy mineral water, usually costing less that one twentieth of the price of imported plastic bottles sold at kiosks and import shops.

The region has some splendidly atmospheric teahouses (*chaikhanas*) though the tea (*chai*) itself rarely shapes up to much. The cold, tea coloured liquid (*kvas* or *mors*) dispensed irregularly from yellow tanker trailers parked on street corners is a non alcoholic drink made unappetisingly from old bread, but a passable acquired taste. If the same tankers are marked *pivo* they're dispensing beer. Drinks are ordered by glass: a *stakan* is the smaller (250ml) glass, *bokal* the larger, pint mug. Jam and pickle jars often replace the chipped old glasses.

Language
Each language except Tajik is Turkic, and a knowledge of Turkish may prove helpful. Numbers are the same, though Turkish travellers find Turkmen barely comprehensible. Russian remains commonly understood, most locals are fluent and there seems to be no stigma to using the former colonial language. Conversely, however, those ethnic Russians that remain don't seem too keen on being greeted in local languages.

Lonely Planet has a phrase book covering all the local languages. Hippocrene publishes a *Concise Uzbek-English-Uzbek Dictionary* by K Khakimov, as well as a *Kazakh-English* (but not English-Kazakh) one by K Krippes. Arabic script was used till the end of the 1920s, then Latin script until 1940 when Cyrillic was imposed. Uzbekistan, Turkmenistan and (half heartedly) Kazakhstan are now reverting to their own variants of the Latin alphabet, though being able to read Cyrillic remains useful throughout the region.

Further information
● **Books** For a regional guidebook the main choice is between Lonely Planet's predictable volume and *Central Asia – A Practical Handbook* by Giles Whittell (Cadogan). The latter is well written and researched and Whittell's enthusiasm is appealing without blinkering his observations. Other guidebooks include *Silk Route by Rail* (Trailblazer) for those taking the Moscow-Samarkand-Almaty-Beijing railway. For hikers, *Trekking in Russia & Central Asia* (The Mountaineers) gives hiking and climbing info for certain hard-to-reach parts of the C.I.S. without much information on how to get there.

For general reading try Colin Thubron's *The Lost Heart Of Asia* or Tiziano Terzani's *Goodnight Mister Lenin* by (Picador). The latter is a journalist's view of the collapsing Soviet Union in 1990. He visits Dushanbe, Samarkand, feels oppressed in Tashkent, tries to uncover the Kyrgyz versus Uzbek ethnic violence in Uzgen etc. If you wonder why Central Asian taxi drivers sometimes expect you to have $100 bills for every occasion, blame high rollers like Terzani. For accessible historical background read *Central Asia: A Traveller's Companion* by Kathleen Hopkirk (John Murray Press), or *Siberia, Outer Mongolia, Central Asia: Crossroads of Civilizations* by Christine de Weck (Vantage Press).

● **Maps** As yet there is no Western produced map depicting exclusively ex-Soviet central Asia. The best selection of detailed topographical maps in the region is available at the Geographical Institute in Bishkek (see Bishkek map). For city maps, try bookstores and the lobbies of bigger hotels. The most useful versions show bus and tram routes. Beware that some older Soviet maps deliberately missed out whole blocks of a city; some modern versions have copied these without corrections.

❏ Dealing with officialdom

Not every official is a baddy, and we have been helped out of some potentially unpleasant situations by 'straight cops' and helpful *provodniks* (railway carriage attendants). However, the locals claim with some justification that 'people protect you from the police rather than vice versa'. Certain agents from OVIR (foreigner registration department), border guards and ordinary police can see you unashamedly as a way to supplement their incomes. Airport officials may ominously demand a fee to 'ensure your baggage gets aboard'. Uniformed police may suddenly decide to inspect your *dokumenti* and claim that some arcane stamp is missing. 'Fake policemen' are worst of all.

In any such situation, try to smile. Remain friendly, calm and unintimidated. Some times paying up is (eventually) the only choice – trust your instincts if you spot a masochist. However, some bribes can be avoided. Every situation is obviously different but the following techniques have worked for us:

● Diverting attention from a potentially awkward conversation by asking questions of your own, eg about travel, where you can find a cheap hotel in your destination etc. Ask about his family. Show interest in him.
● Deliberately misunderstanding what is being said. Once we spoke Japanese at a confused officer till he got bored and left. Another time we assumed that a policeman was giving us 'helpful advice'. We thanked him, shook him warmly by the hand, and walked off.
● Sharing some food, chocolate etc. I carry Earl Grey teabags. Once when stopped for a bribe on a train I offered to make a cup of this *Anglitsky Chai*. Going to the *samovar* for boiling water provided a break from an unpleasant inquisition and when I returned the conversation became more friendly.
● If all else fails, it's worth having cheap but attractive items that you're prepared to give away (eg large foreign coins) in place of a dollar denominated bribe.
● Have a lot of US$1 bills and if forced to show your money, display these first. On one occasion this resulted in me being jokingly labelled 'Georg Vashington' – too poor to pay.

Don't let these examples scare you unduly. In four trips to the region, we have only had to pay a total of $20. If you fly out of Tashkent, however, you'll probably pay much more.

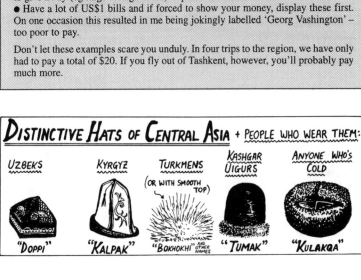

DISTINCTIVE HATS OF CENTRAL ASIA + PEOPLE WHO WEAR THEM:

UZBEKS — "DOPPI"

KYRGYZ — "KALPAK"

TURKMENS (OR WITH SMOOTH TOP) — "BOKHOKHI" AND OTHER NAMES

KASHGAR UIGURS — "TUMAK"

ANYONE WHO'S COLD — "KULAKQA"

Kazakhstan

Looking like a two-day old beard of grass and scrub on the face of the earth, the vast, ragged steppe-landscape that dominates Kazakhstan cannot be described as exciting. It's amazing how this country, the ninth largest in the world, can have so much land and yet so little of traveller interest. Swallowed up in this monotonous environment lies the exhausted Aral Sea, the Semipalatinsk nuclear testing area, Russia's main space centre (near Leninsk) and a sprinkling of unappealing industrial towns. Even the Caspian coast is not at its most charming with Aktau's (Aqtau) original design as a utopian resort long since buried under the Soviet concrete of an isolated oil town. The Silk Road cities Turkestan, Talas (now Dzhambul) and Otrar have all been of major historic importance but little of antiquity remains. The country's main attractions lie in the mountains; the majestic forested Altay to the north east, and the snow-capped Tien Shan which looms above Almaty, the pleasant ex-capital. Fortunately, the good transport links with Uzbekistan, China and Russia, mean the Almaty area is the part of Kazakhstan you're most likely to visit.

Kazakhstan is the least Muslim of the Central Asian republics. While Islam was becoming concentrated into fundamentalism in the medieval khanates of Uzbekistan, the Kazakh steppes remained home to nomads whose transience never fitted with strict religious practice. Today, Kazakhs are a minority in their own heavily Russified land, and Islam remains diluted. Only a small portion of the population is still nomadic; ironically it is easier to stay with nomadic Kazakh families in Xinjiang, China than in Kazakhstan itself.

In December 1997 the government officially transferred the capital from Almaty to Akmola as a political gesture. Akmola (Aqmola) is more centrally located and therefore it was hoped the move would encourage a more inclusive government. But for diplomats and government workers the move to the faceless, industrial city in the heart of the bleak steppe is as welcomed as a transfer to purgatory. Thus far, however, relatively few practical steps have been taken to complete the move by the proclaimed 2000 deadline.

Kazakhstan has remained very close to Russia since its independence. But it has also fostered good relations with the West by instituting some free mar-

❏ **W&M's country ratings – Kazakhstan**
● **Expense $$$** Finding cheap accommodation is difficult. Other travel items are reasonable.
● **Value for money ✔✔** Much of the country is run down.
● **Getting around ✔✔** Everything is far apart, the roads are worse the further one gets from Almaty.
● **Woman alone ✔✔✔✔** The most open and Western of any Central Asian country.

ket reforms, inviting foreign aid groups such as the Peace Corps, allowing a measure of free speech, and (more importantly) awarding a billion dollar contract to the US company Chevron to develop its oil fields. The West, in turn, has supported Kazakhstan and its only leader since independence, Nursultan Nazerbaev. The *Business Central Europe* newspaper described Nazerbaev as 'the closest Central Asia has to a benevolent dictator.' Deciding he wanted to save his country from the unnecessary trauma of a general election in 1996, he held a referendum on his leadership a year earlier, giving a chance for people to let him continue in power until 2000 without such distractions. The 95% 'yes' vote he won came mysteriously close to his own predictions.

❏ **Geo-political information – Kazakhstan**

Population: 16.9m (1997), 16.9m (1994), 16.5m (1989), 14.2m (1975).

Area: 2,717,000 sq km.

Capital: Akmola ('white tomb') (200,000).

Other major cities: Almaty (Alma Ata) (1,150,000), Karaganda (610,000), Chimkent (410,000), Semey (Semipalatinsk), Pavlodar, Oskamen (Ust Kamenogorsk) (330,000).

GNP per capita: $1,460 (1994), $5300 (1988).

Currency history: Tenge/US$1 – Feb 1998: T75, Oct 1997: T75, July 1996: T67.1, Nov 1995: T64, Sept 1994: T51, at introduction in Nov 1993: T4.75.

Annual inflation rates: End of 1995: 60%, Averages 1994: 1900%, 1993: 1571%, 1992:1513%, 1991: 90%, 1990: 4.2%.

Major exports/economy: Mining, oil, gas. The country received nearly $400m US aid for scrapping its nuclear arsenal. It leases its Baikonour spaceship launch site to Russia.

Ethnic mix: Kazakh (43%), Russian (37%), Ukrainian (5%), Tatars, Uzbeks (2%), Belarusian (1%). There are intriguing ethnic pockets of Koreans (1%), Lezghins, Chechens and others originally deported here en masse by Stalin. The biggest such group were the ethnic Germans (formerly settled in the Volga basin) who constituted about 6% of the population pre-independence but have been leaving in droves.

Official languages: Kazakh (spoken by 40%). Russian remains the everyday language of business.

Religious mix: Muslim (47%), Russian Orthodox Christian (44%), Protestant (2%) – though these figures don't indicate the generally apathetic attitude prevalent towards religion.

Landmarks of national history: Part of various empires (Persian, Parthian, Kushan, Turkic). **1820-50**: Russian encroachment. **1873-97**: 400,000 Russian settlers arrived and by 1916 one million more. **1917-20**: Brief semi-independence under the Alask Orda government. **1941**: Stalin's forced migration of Volga Germans, Koreans etc. **1954-6**: Virgin Lands programme to make the steppe a Soviet bread basket. **1957**: First Soviet rocket into orbit from Baikonour. **1991**: Independence.

Leader: President Nursulatan Nazarbaev, central Asia's benevolent dictator. Rule extended to year 2000 by overwhelming referendum.

Pressing political issues: Ecological disasters of retreating Aral Sea, over-fertilisation of farm land, atomic bomb test site near Semipalatinsk. Persuading the Russians to honour the pipeline link deal to pump Kazakh oil to the Black Sea.

PRACTICAL INFORMATION
Visas and formalities
● **Visa strategy** An official invitation letter from a tourist agency, Kazakh individual or company is required for a tourist, personal or business visa. This letter will need to be stamped by the local OVIR office. In addition the inviter has to persuade the Ministry of Foreign Affairs to send a (different) letter of approval direct to the embassy that will eventually issue the visa. All this is very tough to organise alone. Fortunately Kan Tengri (see Travel Agents, below) can arrange all the paperwork on your behalf. Send them the dates you plan to visit and your passport details. Then transfer $50 per person to their account: 001284002/689070742, Zao Bank Turanalem, Almaty, Kazakhstan, (Swift ABKZKZKX). Or in the USA to account: 04-0498-797, Bankers Trust, NY, (Swift: BKTR US 33). The invitation is issued within a week of receiving the money. This is all very awkward when you're on the road. Fortunately there are other options, the most appropriate of which depends upon the direction you're travelling.

From China Five-day Kazakh transit visas are issued with no fuss in Beijing. In Urumqi there's a very slim chance of getting a two-day transit visa but this can be very expensive and is by no means assured.

Note that the dates you choose for visa validity cannot be changed. We once arrived at the border one day after the stated period had finished and were unceremoniously turned back. Luckily we had a double entry Chinese visa or we'd still be stuck in no-man's land.

If you're coming up the Karakoram Highway it would be best to apply in Tehran where five day transits are possible if you claim you plan to fly to Almaty then continue to China (you'll need to show a Chinese visa).

❏ Hidden Almaty
'How many stores do you think are on this intersection?' asked an American living in Kazakhstan. Sipping at the beers he'd bought us we surveyed the area. We saw an import-export outlet which was not surprising as stores selling Western goods have spread through Almaty over the last few years. We looked a little more and saw a bank, a bakery, and a kiosk selling Mars bars and Marlboros. Up some stairs there seemed to be a bar, or perhaps it was a restaurant or a public toilet.

'Five,' we guessed. The American took a sip of his Heineken.

'More than fifty.'

Much is hidden. Many businesses here do not rush to advertise themselves and operate from basements, apartment rooms and improbable suburban homes. Capitalism is re-inventing itself throughout central Asia from bottom up. Big store-fronts are expensive and attract that other booming sector – the mafia. Even the World Bank offices were hidden away on a building site, the Tajik embassy is reached by scrambling along a stream bed, and the Afghan consul operates from a totally unmarked residential flat. Almaty is like that – thoroughly unassuming. Quiet traffic slides down tree-lined avenues. Quiet people run through their routines camouflaged by the stone-grey buildings which are neither menacing nor initially inviting. But there is a sense of intrigue. Almaty's two Russian churches, daunting eternal flame, and over-hyped Medeo ice rink will not hold your attention for long but those who enjoy getting to know a place well could start at any Almaty street corner and ask themselves how many stores they see. The question might take longer to answer than you think. We set aside two days for Almaty, half expecting to leave after one. Two weeks later we were still enjoying delving into unmarked corners, hiking off into dacha suburbs and discovering streets that had been deliberately omitted from Soviet era maps.

From the west Kazakh visas are hard to get hold of, but Kyrgyz visas are easy to procure in Turkey or Turkmenistan and allow you to transit without a Kazakh visa for three days. Alternatively, a Kyrgyz visa can get you as far as Tashkent where two-week Kazakh visas are available on the spot for $70 if the consul 'likes you' and you don't need a receipt.

From Russia Your Russian visa allows you three days' stay in Kazakhstan.

● **Visa extension and shuffle** Don't worry about arriving in such a huge country with a short visa. Transit visas can only be extended by two days (grudgingly by OVIR, $12). However, in Almaty it's easy to get a Kyrgyz visa which bizarrely allows you to stay a further three days in Kazakhstan (see Visa Shuffle, p557). Alternatively Kan Tengri, Kuppava and other agencies can sponsor you for a full visa once you're in the country (allow at least a week waiting in Almaty for this).

● **Visa on arrival** Impossible by land, and potentially expensive at Almaty airport. The standard charge is $120 but you are expected to have an invitation in your hand. Ironically without the invite you'll be given a much cheaper ($30) three-day transit, though a few travellers were charged $150 for this. The approach is risky as some airlines will refuse to let you board if you don't have the visa in advance. Certain ticket staff in the Urumqi branch of China Airlines refuse to sell you a ticket to Almaty without a visa, but we found that others would oblige. The situation is very changeable; in Urumqi ask other travellers in the Hongshan Hotel for the latest information.

❏ **Essential information for travellers – Kazakhstan**

● **Visa** Required. Transit visas are possible at a few embassies but other kinds of visa are expensive and an officially recognised invitation is required. The visa shuffle operates here.

● **Currency** Tenge=100teen. US$1=T75. Bring US$ cash in new bills.

● **Time zone** Eastern Kazakhstan including Almaty is 6 hours ahead of GMT (1hr ahead of Kyrgyzstan and Uzbekistan, 3hrs ahead of Moscow). In winter it's two hours behind Beijing time, though in summer the gap is only one hour as China has no daylight savings time. Central/western Kazakhstan is 5hrs ahead of GMT (same as Turkmenistan in winter, one hour ahead in summer). Some far western cities use GMT+4 (+5 in summer).

● **Religious tone** Minimally Islamic.

● **Special dangers** The cities at night are more dangerous than elsewhere in Central Asia and there's a small risk of muggings and robberies.

● **Social conventions** *Ke*, added to the end of a surname, is a sign of respect. Whistling is considered rude, as is talking to someone through a doorway.

● **Typical traveller destinations** Transit though Almaty.

● **Highlights** Hidden Almaty, mountains along Kyrgyz border.

● **When to go** Being so far inland, Kazakhstan's climate doesn't get any of the moderating benefits of the oceans. Summers are very hot (up to 40°C) in the steppes but ideal for the mountain walk to Kyrgyzstan. Skiing and skating are possible in winter with facilities at Chimbulak and Medeo close to Almaty. However the poor heating systems in all but the most expensive hotels make Kazakhstan's Siberian-style blizzards seem less appealing. Snow is common from November to March. The best time to visit is the autumn (September and October) when the air is clear and the temperature pleasant. Spring sees moderate temperatures too, though statistically about half the days are rainy. Thunderstorms are common in May.

Money

The Tenge is now relatively stable. Obmen/valyut kiosks will change US$, DM or Russian Rouble cash as long as the notes are freshly ironed. For a small loss you can reconvert, but watch out for pre-1990 US$ bills which will be hard to spend. Alem Bank gives dollar cash advances on Visa or Diners Club (3% commission) and cashes travellers' cheques (2%). Travellers' cheques can also be cashed at the Dostyk and Hyatt/Rachat Palace hotels in Almaty. For MasterCard cash advances you need to go to the Halyk Savings bank. Banks are typically open Monday to Friday, 9am-12 noon only.

Transport

● **Buses** Long distance bus services operate along most roads; they are faster and more frequent than trains on the busy Tashkent-Bishkek-Almaty route, as well as to Urumqi.

Buses, trolleys, and trams crisscross Almaty. A route map is invaluable though routes are sometimes improvised. Note that route numbers for buses and trolleys have no relationship to each other (eg bus 6 does not follow trolley 6 nor tram 6). Services after about 10pm are very few and far between – don't believe the optimistic last bus times written on bus-stop signs. Those that come with their lights off

are 'temporarily privatised' and charge up to 10 times the normal fare.

● **Train** Apart from the south-east corner of the country, trains are more comfortable and relatively more reliable than buses; only one third of the Kazakhstan railway network needs overhauling, compared to half the road network. Rail tickets are marginally more expensive in Kazakhstan than in Kyrgyzstan or Uzbekistan, and much more so than in Turkmenistan.

● **Taxi** It is possible to get an unofficial taxi by standing at the side of almost any city street and waving your arm. Almost by magic, a car will pull over next to you. Yell your destination at the driver in the best Russian accent you can muster. If he is going that way he will beckon you into the car, if not he'll simply drive off. The fares appear rather random but in most cases are reasonable. If you know the Russian numbers and the phrase for 'How much?' (*Skolka stoy-et*) you can negotiate beforehand. After taking these cars a few times you might begin to wonder who these people are who give strangers rides; some are private entrepreneurs doing this for a living; others are ordinary people who want to supplement their income on their way to work or when going shopping.

There are also official taxis. If you speak Russian (or can get someone to speak for you) you can reserve one (☎

❏ **Meeting the locals**

● **Language** Russian is spoken by the majority, though Kazakh has become the official language.

Some phrases in Kazakh:

Greeting – *salamat sisba* (literally, 'Are you healthy?')
Reply – *salamat sisba*
How are you? – *khalingiz khalay?*
Thank you <u>very much</u> – <u>*koop*</u> *rakhmet*
Excuse me – *keshiringiz*
Great! – *keremet!*
<u>It's</u> expensive – <u>*min-ow*</u> *kimbat*
Delicious – *damdi*
Interesting – *kyzyk*
Beautiful – *ademi*
Really? – *solai ma?/shin ba?*

078). They will call back with the licence plate number when the taxi is on its way. Taxis are not unreasonable if you can get them to use the meter (about $4 for 20 minutes).

Staying in touch

● **Mail** Based on our unscientific tests, sending mail from Kazakhstan seemed more reliable than from Kyrgyzstan. Postage is cheap, though the specific price seems suspiciously random.

● **Phone** Placing a local telephone call in Kazakhstan requires an act of great faith even when you can find a pay phone that works. Most calls never go through. Strangely, international calls are much more reliable than local ones – because of this, one hotel in Almaty routes local calls via Vienna. The whole system is being replaced.

The most expensive option for an international call is using the special international pay phones in Almaty; they accept credit cards as well as phone cards sold specifically for the purpose at around $7 per minute's credit. Two such phones are in the lobby of the Kazakh Business Centre and in the Hotel Otrar. If you are in the Hotel Otrar anyway, you can call more cheaply from their business centre (eg $5/minute to Canada). For a less reliable but cheaper service place calls at a Public Call Office (eg 129 Pantilov Ul, Almaty). Costs are approximately $2/minute to Europe.

International operator: 079 (English is usually spoken). International enquiries: 071. The international code remains: +7 (old USSR code). Almaty: 3272 (3275 for satellite phones), Karaganda: 3212, Uralsk (Oral): 31122.

Food and drink

Beshbarmak (literally 'five fingers) is a typical, central Asian dish; it's usually a rice and mutton concoction which is eaten with the hands.

Local specialities are based on horse meat or mutton; *kasi, suret, chukchuk, plov* and *shashlyk*. Russian food is more common here than in the rest of central Asia – *manti* and *borshch* are cheap options. Spicy Korean salads and kimchee-esque Korean salads are available cheaply in the market in Almaty.

Almaty's Eidelweiss pub brews the best beer in central Asia while the bizarre *kvas*-flavoured Zhigulevskoe beer may be Asia's worst.

Activities

● **Almaty nightlife** Almaty has some of the best nightlife in central Asia, though this is mostly because nowhere else has any. Gorky Park has lawns, sports fields and occasionally hosts bizarrely named 'American Original' parties. Several casinos provide a convenient way for you to give your money to the mafia.

Dr Bangs is a hip, student run disco. Edelweiss is a pine decor pub and German micro-brewery; it's signposted in English from Gogol St.

Classical concerts are held most weekend evenings, invariably starting at 6pm giving people a chance to get home before the buses go private at around 10pm. Between September and June there are full scale ballet and opera productions.

The original circus building has been sold off as a car showroom and pizzeria, though the troop does still perform occasionally elsewhere.

Web sites

ils.unc.edu/kiree/kazakhstan.html calls itself the 'Kazakhstan homepage', and has basic travel information.

The Kazakhstan page of Interactive Central Asia Resource Project is at www.rockbridge.net/personal/bichel/kazakh.htp.

Further information

● **Books** *Abai* by Mukhtar Auezov is a major (if over long) novel depicting life on the Kazakh steppe.

● **Travel agents and general assistance Intourist Southern** (☎ 332013, fax 331234), is at the front of the Hotel Otrar. On our first visit they had some extremely competitive airfares (eg Bangkok for $175 via Tashkent). Their discounting agreement with Uzbekistan Airlines was later suspended but, if renewed, good deals may once again emerge. If not, the cheapest deals out of Almaty are sold at the old air terminal building in Bishkek, Kyrgyzstan.

The very helpful **Mir Travels & Insurance Co** (☎ 613618) has now transferred its visa/travel support services to a Mr Daribay (☎/fax 222615). He can provide a visa invitation for only $35 per person (the process takes 10 days) though he's sometimes hard to contact. Visa support (see Visas and formalities) and trekking services are also available through **Kan Tengri** (☎ 677866/024 fax 509323, e-mail: kazbek@kantengri.almaty.kz), 48 Abai, 480072 Almaty. They also have their own mountaineers' camp. **Kuppava** (☎ 535966, fax 437626), Apt 145, 129 Shevchenko will help solve a variety of problems – visas, car/motorbike hire, finding apartments and work. Note that there's no sign on their door nor on the unlikely apartment block in which it is hidden. They plan to open a new office shortly. The staff at the lesser known **Sana3 Travels** at Room 507, 46 Mynbaeva speak relatively poor English.

❑ The Great Game

Moustache-twirling gentleman-spies from Russia and British India spent the 19th century dashing about the uncharted Central Asian deserts, wooing murderous Uzbek khans and surreptitiously mapping unknown Himalayan passes. For the British, the 'Great Game' aimed to foil Russian encroachment towards their Indian colonies. They were partially successful: Persia (Iran) was maintained as an uncolonised buffer states while Afghanistan was given the Wakhan Corridor to keep imperial borders apart. However, Central Asia fell to the 'Ruskies' despite insanely valiant missions by real life James Bonds such as Stoddart and Connolly who were left to languish in the infamous Zindan – a scorpion and insect stocked bug pit, now a museum in Bukhara.

Peter Hopkirk's many enthralling books are spellbinding accounts of the stranger-than-fiction intrigues of the day which twice came close to all-out war when British agents spied Russians at **Bozai Gumbaz** (Afgh) and **Pandjeh** (now Turkmenistan). Russia effectively controlled Xinjiang from its embassy in Kashgar. Now you can stay there (it's the Seman Hotel #1) or at the Qini Bagh Hotel which incorporates the former British consulate. You can once again ride the Trans Caspian Railway (Krasnovodsk to Ashgabat) which the Russians built as a supply line as they advanced into the then ferociously independent land of the 'wild Turkomens' whose final defeat and massacre came at the decisive battle of **Geok Tepe** (limited ruins). When dazzled by the splendours of **Hunza** (KKH, Pakistan) imagine Younghusband storming the Mir's castle (still standing) armed only with public school bravado and a handlebar moustache. Read Rudyard Kipling's *Kim*.

With the dissolution of the USSR, the fascination of a new Game resumes, this time played out in Baku hotel rooms rather than on camel patrols in the high Pamirs. The main players today are Russia and Turkey with Iran and the Western powers far from impartial. The prize, on top of the perennial quest for regional influence, is control of the vast oil and gas reserves of the Caspian basin.

Internet: http://www.deltanet.com/users/llambert/great_game.html

Kazakhstan

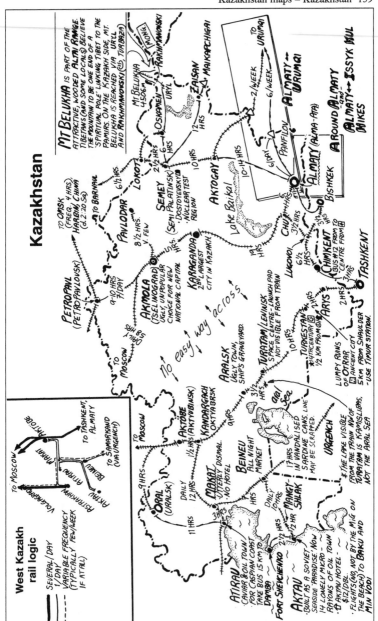

MT BELUKHA IS PART OF THE ATTRACTIVE, WOODED ALTAI RANGE. TIBETANS (AND SOME LOCALS) BELIEVE THE MOUNTAIN TO BE ONE END OF A SPIRITUAL 'POLE' LINKING TIBET TO THE PAMIRS. ON THE KAZAKH SIDE, MT. BELUKHA IS REACHED VIA URYL AND RAKHMANOVSKI (ⓖ), TURBAZA)

West Kazakh rail logic
SEVERAL/DAY
1/DAY
VARIABLE FREQUENCY (TYPICALLY FEW/WEEK IF AT ALL)

'no easy way' across

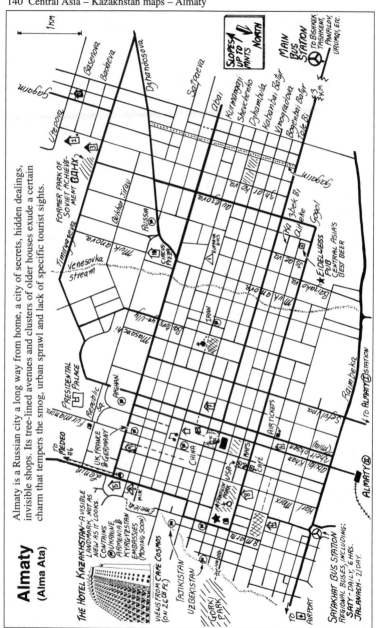

Almaty is a Russian city a long way from home, a city of secrets, hidden dealings, invisible shops. Its tree-lined avenues and clusters of older houses exude a certain charm that tempers the smog, urban sprawl and lack of specific tourist sights.

Almaty
(Alma Ata)

THE HOTEL KAZAKHSTAN-A VISIBLE LANDMARK, NOT AS NEW AS IT LOOKS. CONTAINS UKRAINE, ARMENIA & KYRGYZSTAN EMBASSIES (MOVING SOON)

VIEWS FROM CAFE COSMOS (ON 26 th FL)

TAJIKISTAN
UZBEKISTAN
GORKI/ PARK

SAYAKHAT BUS STATION
REGIONAL BUSES, INCLUDING:
SATY-DAILY, 6 HRS.
JALABASH-2/DAY.

TO AIRPORT

UK, FRANCE & GERMANY
CHINA

TO MEDEO #6

SLOPES UP TO MNTS
NORTH

MAIN BUS STATION
TO BISHKEK, TASHKENT, PANFILOV, URUMQI, ETC.

FORMER PARK OF SOVIET ACHIEVEMENT БАНК

EDELWEISS PUB CENTRAL ASIA'S BEST BEER

PRESIDENTIAL PALACE

AIR TICKETS

TO ALMATY 1 STATION

ALMATY 2

Venesovka stream

CIRCUS

RUSSIA

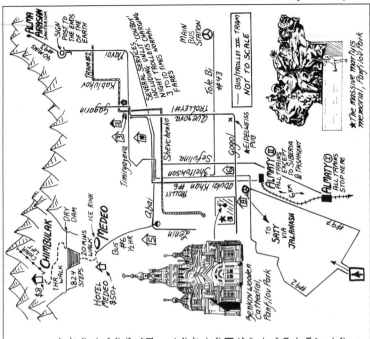

★ The massive martyrs memorial, Panfilov Park

Getting around Almaty

South seems the natural top of Almaty as all streets tilt gently towards the impressive southern mountains. Beware older maps: many contain mistakes, most glaring of which is the omission of four N-S streets between Seifulina and Auezova. Old maps also lack new street names: changes are ongoing, though as yet Lenin and Karl Marx survive. Rivers marked are very small, but at the time of research Venesovka stream was being canalised and many of the smaller roads were blocked, their bridges removed. Metro construction began 1989; should be partly running by 1998.

● **Where to stay** Cheapest places ½hr (trolley #1) from centre. We stayed for $2 in a *nurses' residence* [1] hidden behind the fire station on Gagarina but this is hard to find/arrange. Easier and cleaner is **Hotel Raketa** [2]: $8pp if you arrive late, negotiable earlier (unmarked at 212 Zharkova). If this fails try the dingy **Altynden** [3] ($9). More central hotels: *Turkistan* [4] ($25+, dingy and unfriendly but handy for bus station); *Kazakhstan* [5] (once top spot, reports claim min. rates now cut to $25pp); *Zhetysu* [6] ($45+, drab, unfriendly, and usually full); *Issyk* [7] ($55+. Attractive, quality rooms, leafy area, several cafés nearby); *Otrar* [8] ($80+. Intourist Southern office occasionally discounts air tickets); *Dostyk* [9] ($160+ stylish marble low-rise former aparachik lodge, now serves a $17 Sunday brunch popular with diplomats. Travellers' cheques cashed.); *Hyatt Rachat Palace* [10] ($330+). *Homestays* are possible for $2-20 through touts outside Kazakhstan or Zhetysu hotels.

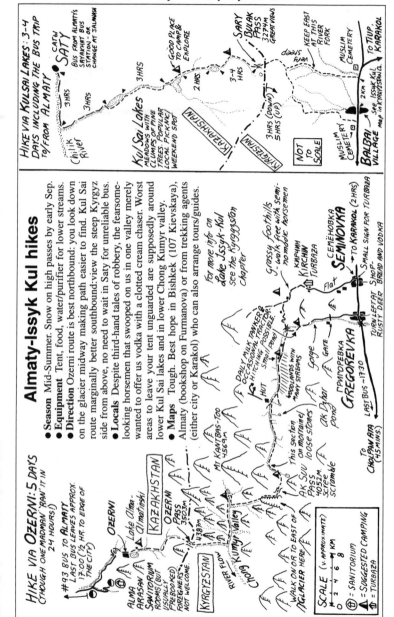

Almaty-Urumqi
route options

METHOD. SECTIONAL COSTS, BENEFITS, ETC.	MIN TIME	COST

RAIL

ALMATY II STATION
21.45

AA ————————————— ~36 HRS ————————————— U
Tu, Su
9.30 BT

Direct, comfortable but slow. Border guards untrustworthy

36 HRS. | US$65

ROAD – DIRECT BUS

AA ——— 6/WEEK $50 (DOLLARS OR LOCAL CURRENCY) ——— U
6.00
M-Sa
5.00 BT
Su-F

Direct but difficult to sleep.

24-30 HRS | $50 (+$10 FOR POLICE)

– VIA YINING

SENSIBLE
WESTBOUND ONLY –

SLEEPER
BUS FREQ.
100 元, 16-
20 HRS

AA ——— $7, 8 HRS ——— P ——— $30 ——— Y ——— 5.30 BT ——— SLEEPER BUS $13 ON
6.00 M, W, Th   8.00 M, W, Th, Sa   BT   100 元

28 HRS. | $32 42 (+$10)
*WITH CHANGE IN P

Comfortable sleeper bus. Stopover in Yining

2 DAYS
2 NIGHTS

– IN SECTIONS

SEV.
15-19 HRS.
ASK 100-300元
PAY 90-100元

U ——— RED BUS 2O
BED BUS 16-
DOK DEEP
HRS AFTERNOON ——— Y

U ——— 100 元
15 YINING ——— Q

MINIBUS
FREQ.
1 HR.

Q ——— MINIBUS
20 元
(LOCALS PAY
4元) ——— KH

KH ——— SHARE
TAXI
20元 ——— △

△ ——— TAXI
HOP
OR
BUS
$10 (OR HITCH) ——— SHRG. TRN.

P ——— LOCAL BUS–
$7, 8 HRS
6/DAY (INCL.
NIGHT BUSES) ——— △

△ ——— TAXI 4
(UP TO 4
PEOPLE)
$50-40,
5 HRS WITH
STOPS ——— AA

cheap, flexible and easy

2 DAYS
2 NIGHTS
(ASSUMING
YOU SLEEP
IN P)

25-28
HRS.

~ $30+
(+$10)

FLIGHT

KAZAKHSTAN AIRLINES – MONDAY & FRIDAY

Small chance of Kazakh visa on arrival in AA

2 HRS.
(PLUS A
FEW DAYS
TO BOOK)

$113

XINJIANG AIRLINES – TUESDAY & FRIDAY

$205

NOTES

- NO VISAS ISSUED AT BORDER.
- BORDER CLOSED ON SUNDAY AND ON ANY HOLIDAY OF EITHER NATION.
- BT = BEIJING TIME (GMT +8)
- $10 ROAD TOLL. SEE P

[AA] **Almaty** Try to arrive early to find a cheap bed.

[P] **Panfilov/Zharkent** Locals around bus stn offer *homestays* ($3). West of town a 'police post' demands $10 'tax' for 'Zharkent Free Trade Zone'. In a taxi, speaking Russian it took an hour to avoid paying.

[KH] **Khorgas (border)** Banks/shops on Chinese side only. No walking over border. Bargain for bus to Urum.

[Q] **Qingsuihe** If no U to Kh bus available, you could get off a U-Y bus here and flag down passing Y-Kh minibuses. NB eastbound all Y to U buses full by Q.

[Y] **Yining** Usually called Guljur by Russians/Kazakhs.

[S] **Sairam Hu** Spluttering trucks on the hairpins up to this attractive lake can delay eastbound buses for hours.

[U] **Urumqi** Latest info: travellers at Hongshan Hotel.

[D] **Druzhba/Dostyk** Train waits several hours for bogie-changing and customs search.

[AI] **Alashankou** Border crossing by rail only.

Kyrgyzstan

Kyrgyzstan is an adventurer's dream; spectacular lakes, forested valleys and mountains reaching over 6000m. It's untouristy yet accessible. The high grasslands are dotted in summer with nomad tents and wild, moustachioed horsemen in silly hats who, vodka bottle in hand, welcome the weary traveller to decollectivised collectives. Unlike neighbouring Tajikistan there is no looming war, visas are easy, the authorities are laidback, and accommodation is cheap.

The people are hospitable beyond all expectations. A money changer in the bus station gave us the key to his Bishkek flat to use as we liked. At first we were suspicious, but this is Kyrgyzstan. The bus driver of a rural service found us a homestay in a hotel-less village. The giver of a hitch-hiked ride insisted we come home so that he could kill a sheep in our honour. When, after three days of feasting, we'd eaten it, he loaded us with presents and thanked us for having dropped by. While we have heard a few tales (always third hand) about dangerous mountain men and bandits in the hills, our experiences were uniquely positive. Apart from the unscrupulous taxi drivers at the Torugart Pass (don't let them put you off), everyone we encountered was helpful and quietly intrigued to meet Westerners yet rarely imposing – a charming combination.

The population in the Stalin-delineated republic of Kyrgyzstan is by no means all ethnically Kyrgyz. Osh, the second city, is traditionally Uzbek and Uzbeks remain the majority. Many feel increasingly discriminated against, believing that since independence, government jobs go preferentially to ethnic Kyrgyz. In 1990, scores of people died in riots in Osh and Uzgen.

Telling Uzbek men from Kyrgyz is easy as long as they're wearing their hats (see p131). The Uzbek *doppi* is a square, usually black, skull cap embroidered with white arabesques, while the jolly Kyrgyz *kalpak* is a tall, tassled, cream-white dunce's cap with black lining folded jauntily out at the base like an origami boat. Despite its height some keep it on even while driving.

The people, the relaxed atmosphere and the vast mountain wilderness make Kyrgyzstan one of our favourite travel destinations.

❏ **W&M's country ratings – Kyrgyzstan**

● **Expense $$** Cheap accommodation is available even in Bishkek. The currency is stable.

● **Value for money** ✔✔ Hotel rooms and food are usually of poor quality. Shampanski is good value.

● **Getting around** ✔✔✔ The buses operate vaguely to a schedule but there are often only one or two a day in rural areas, and there are almost no trains. However it is easy to hitch.

● **Woman alone** ✔✔✔✔ The Kyrgyz people are laidback, but care is required in the more strongly Muslim Fergana Valley and in the very remote areas where locals have an (often unfair) reputation for wildness.

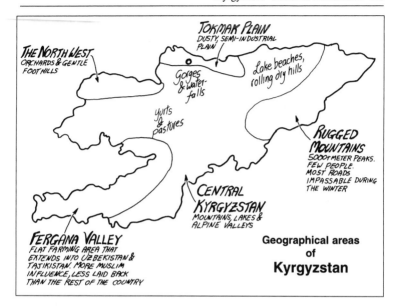

Geographical areas of Kyrgyzstan

TOKMAK PLAIN DUSTY, SEMI-INDUSTRIAL PLAIN

THE NORTH WEST ORCHARDS & GENTLE FOOTHILLS

Lake beaches, rolling dry hills

Gorges & water-falls

yurts & pastures

RUGGED MOUNTAINS 5000+METER PEAKS. FEW PEOPLE. MOST ROADS IMPASSABLE DURING THE WINTER

CENTRAL KYRGYZSTAN MOUNTAINS, LAKES & ALPINE VALLEYS

FERGANA VALLEY FLAT FARMING AREA THAT EXTENDS INTO UZBEKISTAN & TAJIKISTAN. MORE MUSLIM INFLUENCE, LESS LAID BACK THAN THE REST OF THE COUNTRY

PRACTICAL INFORMATION
Visas and formalities

● **Visa strategy** Kyrgyz embassies are usually obliging and helpful. Like other CIS countries, having an invitation or pre-booked tour is theoretically a visa requirement (they are worried about who is responsible for you). But in reality this condition is often waived. You just have to persuade the consul that you know what you're up to. This means having a few names up your sleeve, ie where you plan to stay and go. Play safe and tell them that you will be staying in the Ala Too Hotel in Bishkek and then plan to visit Issyk Kul.

Even if you don't expect to go to Kyrgyzstan at all, a Kyrgyz visa can be very useful for transiting other CIS countries for which visas are harder to obtain. See visa shuffle.

If you need an invitation letter, Tien Shan Travel, Dostyk Trekking or Kyrgyz Concepts can help out. Letters from Tien Shan cost $52 for one person, $37 each for two people or $15 each for 10 or more on the same letter. They are prepared to send a letter to a single individual on trust, but **please** pay them when you arrive or this system will break down. You'll have to transfer money to their account in advance for a group invitation. See 'Agencies' below for addresses.

● **On arrival** If you've somehow got as far as Bishkek without a Kyrgyz visa, you can get one (usually within 48 hours) at the Ministry of Foreign Affairs behind the Frunze House museum. When you enter, don't stop to ask questions at the guard post in the entrance hall – you will always be told to come back another time. Instead march confidently past, keeping right at the end of the hall. The offices beyond are typically crowded and slightly chaotic but it helps to pester someone to find you an English speaker.

If you're arriving by air, it is possible to get a visa on arrival but you must arrange this in advance. Call the Tourist Office (Bishkek ☎ 214854) before you go and then fax them your passport details; they can send a representative to the airport to smooth things out for you.

• **Visa Extensions** Extensions of up to a month are possible on tourist visas, and six months on business visas. Visit the Foreign Ministry (same procedure as in 'On arrival' above). If you have any problems, the Tourist Office (see above) can usually help out.

Money

US$ (and often DM) cash can easily be changed in *obmen valyut* kiosks at markets all over the country. If there is no kiosk, enterprising individuals may be found but the profit margins on currency deals have fallen making people less keen to oblige.

Credit card advances are better done in Almaty but may be possible at Orient Bank, 161 Moskovskaya. At the time of writing, changing travellers' cheques is only possible at AKB Bank (5% commission). Banks are open from 9am-1pm and from 2-6pm.

Transport

• **Bus** Bus travel is reasonably priced, approximately $1 for a two hour journey. Big red Ikarus buses pick passengers up only from bus stops, and, by local standards, are not too overcrowded. Small yellow buses stop for anyone and anything – one drove into a potato field to collect the potential passenger's eight sack harvest. Even the smallest villages usually have at least one service a day; typically this

---

❑ **Geo-political information – Kyrgyzstan**

Population: 4.5m (1997), 4.5m (1991), 4.3m (1989), 2.9m (1970).
Area: 198,500 sq km (only 7% arable).
Capital: Bishkek (650,000, 1990).
Other major cities: Osh (220,000).
GNP per capita: $610 (1994).
Currency history: Com/US$1 – Feb 1998: 17.7, Oct 1997: 17.5com, June 1996: 11.2com, Dec 1995: 11.2com, July 1995: 10.2com, Oct 1994: 11.8com. Introduced 10 May 1993 at $1=4com.
Major exports/economy: See box p148. Industry has collapsed. Tourism's potential is yet to be exploited. Gold mines are being developed in the mountains.
Ethnic mix: Kyrgyz (52%), Russian (21.5%), Uzbek (13%), Ukrainian (2.5%), Tartar, Kazakh, German, Dungan and Uigur (each about 1%). (Definitions are blurred – many 'Uzbeks' are actually of Uigur descent).
Official languages: Kyrgyz.
Landmarks of national history: **995**: Randomly selected origin date of Manas (the Kyrgyz epic). **1293**: The Kyrgyz people were pushed out of their homeland (around Abakan, Siberia) by the Mongols. **1869**: Karakol founded on Lake Issyk Kul (Russian settler town). **1881**: Treaty of St Petersburg fixed mountainous border with China. **1888**: Explorer Przhevalski died at Pishpek (Bishkek). **1918**: Became part of the Turkestan ASSR within the Russian Federation. **1936**: Became a constituent republic of the USSR with the ancient Uzbek cities of Osh and Uzgen tacked on. **1941-5**: Stalin deported Volga Germans to Kyrgyzstan and other republics. **1990**: Inter-ethnic riots in Uzgen and Osh. **1991**: Independence.
Leader: President Askar Akayev (respected free market democrat, academic elected unopposed).
Political issues: Kyrgyzstan has been the keenest central Asian state to follow IMF guidelines on privatisation. But the rapid all-out economic reforms are not enough to protect a nation of mountains and few natural resources from the loss of Soviet economic integration and today's economy is buttressed by large amounts of foreign aid from the US, EU etc. The reconciliation of Kyrgyz and Uzbek communities is a priority.

leaves early in the morning for a transportation hub or market village and returns in the evening. Small buses are interesting for their colourful clientele. And where else do you get to travel in a bus where a butter knife is used as the ignition key?

● **Train** Trains are not ideally suited to a country that's 90% mountains. The only entirely domestic routes in Kyrgyzstan are on the Bishkek-Tokmak plain; west to Kaindy/Lugovoi and east to Balikchee. The Balikchee train takes six to seven hours – double the time of a slow bus but a little cheaper. Beware of the Bishkek to Dzhalalabad (near Osh) line. The train follows three sides of a huge square, via the Fergana valley and southern Kazakhstan, and arrives 28 hours later after nine border crossings. Construction of an Osh-Balikchee line is due to start in 1998.

● **Hitching** Hitching proved very easy and led frequently to free meals, accommodation and/or shots of vodka with the drivers. Only once were we asked for any sort of payment; a souvenir US$1 bill. The best spot for long distance rides is the Sosnovka GAI police post, less than an hour south of Kara Balta. Every vehicle must stop there and negotiate the 'toll' (ie bribe), providing hitchers with an ideal opportunity to leap aboard. Most southbound trucks are heading for Andizhan market where they buy tomatoes at one or two US cents/kilo. Northbound the trucks are heading via lake

---

❑ **Essential information for travellers – Kyrgyzstan**

● **Visa** Required. Typical cost US$30-$60 for a one month stay. Visas are usually easy to get but there are few embassies. This is a visa shuffle country.

● **Currency** Com (pronounced 'Som'). US$1=11.2Com. It's hard to exchange travellers' cheques and get an advance on credit cards. (Since our research, the value of the Com has slumped to US$1=17.7Com.)

● **Time zone** 5 hours ahead of GMT (6hrs ahead in summer). This is the same as Uzbekistan, 1hr behind Almaty, 2hrs ahead of Moscow. In winter it's 2hrs behind Beijing time, the same as Pakistan. In summer it's 1hr behind Beijing and 1hr ahead of Pakistan.

● **Religious tone** Islam at its least noticeable. Slightly more devout in the south (eg around Osh).

● **Special dangers** Kyrgyz people taking too much care of you.

● **Typical traveller destinations** Issyk-kul. Mazarbaeker Lake and Pik Pobeda for mountaineers.

● **Highlights** Kyrgyz hospitality, valleys south of Bishkek, yurt dotted grasslands around Susamir, camping at Issyk-kul and walking in nearby mountains. The stunning alpine scenery of Lake Sary Chelek and the drink called *Shoro*.

● **When to go** Kyrgyzstan's great attractions – its mountains and lakes – become very hard to reach (and bitterly cold) in winter. Despite rather sweltering lowland heat in the cities and Fergana Valley, early to mid summer is a very sensible time to visit. For Issyk Kul, August is peak holiday season. While prices are high and beaches crowded, this is the only time when swimming is really comfortable. By September, chilly water means that the resorts are appealingly deserted, even though there are still spells of warm sunshine. September is a great time for hill walking despite the dusting of snow that may already grace even the lower peaks, but it's already too late for the hikes to/from Kazakhstan. Contrary to popular belief the Torugart Pass is ploughed clear of snow throughout the winter, but at 3750m warm clothes are essential even in mid-summer due to the high chance of being left stranded outdoors for unpredictable periods of time. The Irkestam pass is closed between October and May because of the snow.

● **Pulse of the country** Horsemen and yurts in grassy valleys.

Balkhash (Kazakhstan) to one of the Siberia cities where tomatoes are worth 40 times the price. The licence plate is a good indication of which Siberian city they are going to.

Accommodation

Cheap basic accommodation (between $1 and $6) is easy to find all over Kyrgyzstan, though the choice is limited to one or two places in most towns. Standards are poor

VIEW IS THE BASIS OF THE KYRGYZSTAN FLAG

(often the water system is defunct in the cheapest places). Foreigner mark ups are rare except in Bishkek and even there cheap beds can be found. Around Lake Issyk-Kul you should count on paying $10+ for homestays near the beach during August, though attractive, cheap turbazas exist in the nearby hills and there are cheap hotels in Karakol and Balikchee.

Food and drink

'Have they killed a sheep for you yet?' is a common first question among the (few) travellers in Kyrgyzstan. Local hospitality reaches its zenith in the sacrificing of a sheep and offering the guest the head to carve. The facial parts are then distributed according to an etiquette consisting of obvious metaphors eg a piece of tongue for a great talker, a piece of ear for everyone you respect – so cut it small! This said, we were never presented with any sheep eyes to munch (which makes us wonder if sheep-head-eating is a gullibility test for the naive) though we did join in the skinning.

In addition to the usual Central Asian mutton selections, *ashlianfu* (cold noodles in a spicy vinaigrette sauce) is a speciality in Karakol.

The Kyrgyz economy

'For several years the economy has lost at least 10% annually' a Western economist in Bishkek explained to us. 'Analysts looking at Kyrgyzstan's economic statistics would tell you that the people must be starving, desperate and ready for revolution. And then they arrive in Kyrgyzstan and find everyone smiling, smartly dressed and planting the God-damn flower-beds. It doesn't add up!'

Kyrgyzstan's economic forecast is gloomy. The country's largest factory makes coin-operated vending machines – Kyrgyzstan has no coins at all in circulation. IMF liberalisation measures have been obediently adopted and tax breaks are available to entice foreign capital. Yet, somehow, foreign investors haven't rushed to export the 58 tempting products listed in the government export pamphlet. These include: 'cable (old), half-finished pocks, waste products of autimony factories [sic], arsenious slag, wool waste, pancreas (frozen), hen's dung and Mummies' (!?). Gold extraction and adventure tourism seem the only obvious potential but access to both is hampered by the nation's isolation.

Meanwhile, the country retains the most liberal regime in the region. The press is free (relatively), and Kyrgyzstan remains the darling of the IMF for its attitude if not its prospects. At last, in 1997, growth was reported.

Local drinks include a supposedly healthy millet brew called *makhsin* (it goes by the brand name *Shoro* in Bishkek); it grows on you once you come to terms with the mouthful of muesli sediment in each glass. Its alcoholic cousin is *bowozo* (also available in Turkey). *Bowozo* is meant to be drunk quickly. Traditional fermented mare's milk, *koumyss*, is sold in early summer; a proverb calls *koumyss* 'the blood of the Kyrgyz people'. You can recognise *koumyss* sellers by the churn in which they agitate the brew with a wooden plunger.

Staying in touch

International calls can be made from the business centre at the Dostyk Hotel (expensive and often interrupted), as well as from the central GPO in Bishkek. Public call offices are rare. International country code: +996. Balikchee: 33144, Bishkek: 3312, Naryn: 33522, Osh: 33222.

Activities

● **Hiking and trekking** As yet there aren't enough tourists to give Kyrgyzstan the network of trekkers' guest houses that you'd find in Nepal. You'll be on your own so take supplies and a good tent. The shepherds, horsemen and the isolated farmstead families we stumbled across were all delightfully hospitable, despite sometimes fearsomely wild appearances. Nonetheless, in the remote valleys of the Almaty-Issyk Kul treks there have been occasional (probably exaggerated) reports of hikers' camps being raided by drunk locals or bandits.

For a price, Dostyk Trekking (see Information offices) will arrange any reasonable tour or trek for you. The staff also offer trekking advice to individuals and are extremely helpful. **Speleotrek** (☎ 3312-264751, fax 3312-264761), Gogolya Str 8/41, 720021 Bishkek, organises caving and trekking trips.

● **Mountaineering** Tien Shan Travel has its own base camp at 2600m; the camp has a sauna and dining room. Sample climb prices, including helicopter flights (to/from Bishkek):

Khan-Tengri peak	$1560	21 days
Pobeda peak	$1800	26 days
Lenin peak	$1200 without helicopter flight 22 days	

□ **Meeting the locals**

● **Language** Unlike the other republics, Kyrgyzstan has as yet made no attempt to change its script from the Cyrillic one used in Soviet days.

Some phrases in Kyrgyz:

      Thank you – *rachmat*
      Greeting (Arabic) – *salam elekum*
      Response (Arabic) – *elekum a salam*
      Delicious – *daamdoo*
      Beautiful – *suloo*
      Bicycle – *molasapet*

● **Some topics of conversation**: *Rosa vs Santa Barbara.* The former is a Mexican soap opera, the latter from the US; both are insanely popular in Kyrgyzstan. Life stops so that one, the other, or both of these can be watched. They are the only foreign programmes in which voices are properly dubbed. Other movies and shows have a single voice reading an approximate translation in characterless monotony.

Impressions of China – after decades of isolation, the Kyrgyz are beginning to discover their large neighbour, but opinions are not positive. The term 'Kitaiski' (Chinese) is used as a general derogatory term. (eg 'Kitaiski spichki' = 'bloody matches' – when they won't light).

Uzbek vs Kyrgyz – the subject is far from taboo but generates strong reactions especially amongst the Uzbek community in Osh.

Further information

● **Books** Chingez Aitmatov is a celebrated Kyrgyz author and now prominent diplomatic figure. His most famous novels, *White Steamer* (which gives a great impression of Issyk Kul) and *Golgotha,* have been translated into several Western languages.

● **Maps** Dostyk Trekking (see address below) sells detailed maps of areas in Kyrgyzstan. However, identical maps are cheaper at the Geographical Institute (Room 510), 107 Kievskaya. Once you've found the place and talked your way in you'll have to cajole the friendly but slow moving ladies in that office to show you the bundles of cartographic masterpieces. The detail, quality and selection is surely the best in Central Asia and covers all of Kyrgyzstan and some other neighbouring areas in a variety of scales; $3 to $10, plus cheaper tourist maps, city plans etc.

● **Information offices and travel agencies** The **Ministry of Tourism** (17 Togolok Moldo, Bishkek) now has a helpful Tourist Office with an information line (☎ 214854, fax 212845). The service operates from 8am to 8pm Monday to Friday, plus weekend mornings. Shahsanem Abakir speaks pretty good English. Their German office (Postfach 1500, D-53105 Bonn) can also provide leaflets for potential tourists.

Branches of **Kyrgyz Intourist** at the Dostyk and Ala Too Hotels are occasionally helpful, though the latter told us (incorrectly) that we'd be unable to cross the Torugart Pass without a rented jeep. Other useful agencies include:

Dostyk Trekking (☎ 427471, fax 419129, e-mail: nicolai@dostuk.bishkek.su), 42-1 Vosiemnatset Linea (18th Line), Bishkek. The office is in an unmarked house in a most unlikely semi-rural backstreet – see inset of the Bishkek map. Their treks are recommended.

Kyrgyz Concepts (☎ 267508, fax 620746), 225 Chui, Bishkek, can be hard to contact by phone. They claimed they could find us an apartment, a car and a job, and they were prepared to assist with visa problems.

Tien Shan Travel (☎/fax 270576, e mail: tienshan@asiemm.bishkek.su), 126 Tsherbakova, 720042 Bishkek. They can help with mountaineering, trekking, heli-skiing and visa queries.

Kyrgyzstan

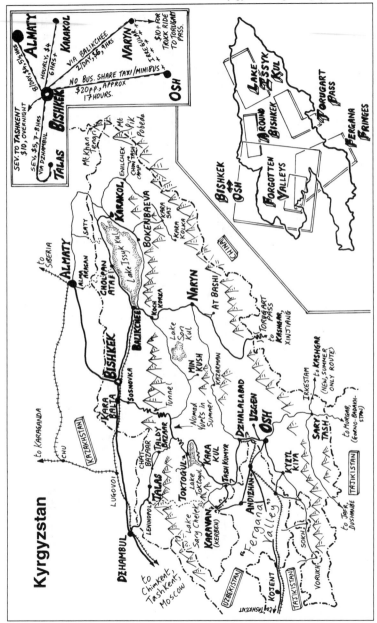

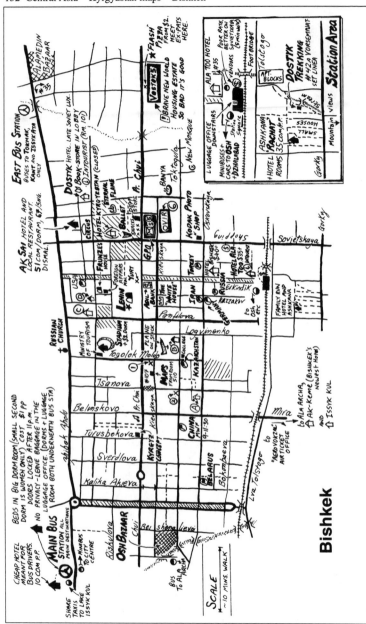

Bishkek

Bishkek – Useful bus and trolley routes

Many buses run E–W on Chui, Moskovskaya, and fewer along Zhibek Zholu, Toktogula and Kievskaya. N–S routes are more limited, mostly Sovietskaya, Mira and Togolok Moldo. Prospect Erkindik has no buses at all but its parkland atmosphere makes it the most pleasant street to stroll. The useful #35 bus is relatively rare. Much more frequent minibuses follow the same basic route but run along Chui without the diversion to Moskovskaya and the train station.

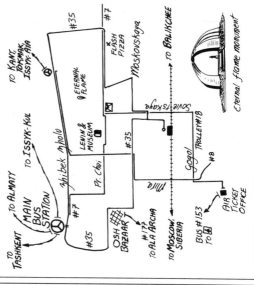

KEY

Where to stay

Cheapest choices are at the *bus station* though budget travellers more often seem to head for the *dorms* beneath the stadium. A slight step up is the little known *Rachat* across the railway tracks from the station. Other lower range options include:

[A] *Hotel of Autotransport Ministry*. 100com for an ageing suite. Four dorm beds cost the same each (!?). An arrow points to it from Isanova Ul but the building is unmarked. Bang on the pink gates. Quiet, set in a rose garden.

[B] *Hotel Polyut*. $7 with bargaining. Soviet era tower with occasional hot water. Many lurking prostitutes.

[C] *Hotel Business School*. $15/dbl, hot water, clean rooms. Bar. Upstairs at 237 Panfilova Ul. Popular with overlanders.

[D] *Hotel Sary Chelek*. Sad old building not worth the 400com/sgl, or 200/dbl. They have two basic triples at 150/room.

Where to eat

At lunch time there are several places to get a cheap hearty *plov* eg stalls opposite the GPO, a street vendor just south of the Hotel Dostyk etc. Classier but not much more expensive is the *Dzhalalabad Chaikhana* [1] in an attractive pavilion with wooden facade which becomes a bar at night. A *yurt tent restaurant* near the Lenin serves over-priced shashlyk. There are several attractive outdoor cafés in the nearby parks. Shoro is available from many street sellers particularly at Osh Bazaar where all kinds of groceries are on sale.

For meeting expats without spending a fortune try *Flash Pizza* on the Vostok 5 estate. Their pizza includes mint instead of oregano but tastes remarkably good. It's better value than *Primavera* [2] downstairs at 175 Toktogul ($1 cover charge) or the various restaurants on Sovietskaya and in the bigger hotels.

Around Bishkek

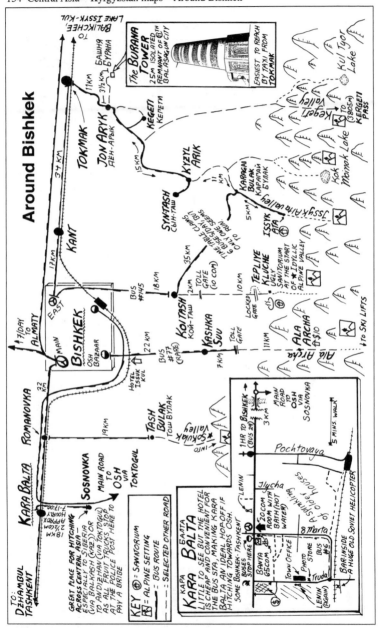

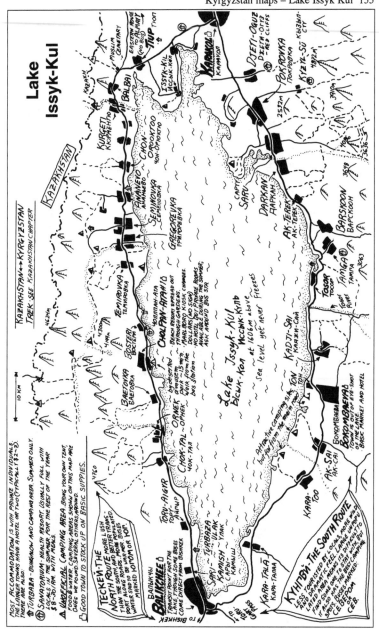

Lake Issyk-Kul

KAZAKHSTAN ↔ KYRGYZSTAN
TREK - SEE KAZAKHSTAN CHAPTER

MOST ACCOMMODATION IS WITH PRIVATE INDIVIDUALS.
THE LARGER TOWNS HAVE A HOTEL OR TWO (TYPICALLY $2-3).
THERE ARE ALSO:

Ⓢ SANATORIUM - HEALTH RESORT USUALLY FULL WITH LOCALS IN THE SUMMER. OPEN FOR THE REST OF THE YEAR $8-30/RM. WITH MEALS.

Ⓣ TURBAZA - BUNGALOW AND CAMPING AREA SUMMER ONLY.

△ UNOFFICIAL CAMPING AREA. BRING YOUR OWN TENT, FOOD & WATER. CAMPING AREAS SHOWN ON THIS MAP ARE ONES WE FOUND. SEVERAL OTHERS AROUND.

☐ GOOD TOWN TO STOCK UP ON BASIC SUPPLIES.

KAZAKHSTAN

10 KM

Lake Issyk-Kul
Исык-Кол Иссык-Куль

at 1606m above sea level, yet never freezes

CHOLPAN-ATA
Чолпон-Ата
Beach resorts spread out through gardens. Marlboro kiosk changes dollars (no sign). No hotel but prime rooms, ask around bus stn.

CEB.

TECKEM-THE NORTH ROUTE
MORE LUSH & GREEN THAN THE SOUTH AND BETTER-POPULATED LAKE. THROUGH SOME BOSES COME CREST FROM DISHKEK. TRANSIT POINT FOR THE LAKE PORT & FAD TO & VAR. WATER MARKED KOTOM OR HOT.

KYHTBH - THE SOUTH ROUTE
LESS TOURISTED BY LOCALS, MORE WILD AND DRAMATIC. FEEL LARGE UNTIL YOU FIND AREA MEANS STAY DIFFICULT. IF ALSO BUSES OR SITES. BUT IN SOME ONE TO STAY FOR THE BEST CAMPING - CEB.GETOM

to Bishkek

Getting around

Big Ikarus buses run approx hourly Bishkek-Balikchee-Cholpan Ata-Karakol picking up en route only at major stops (or not at all when bus is full). Small buses stopping everywhere run sporadically between neighbouring villages and a few per day Balikchee-Karakol via either shore (only 3/day on the south route, one continuing to Bishkek). No buses after 5.30pm. Share taxis between Bishkek and Balikchee are worth the $2 extra: an hour faster and much more frequent than buses. Twice daily trains on this route cost only 15 com but are very slow (5hrs+) and leave you far from central Balikchee (contrary to some maps). Cholpan Ata has direct bus services to Almaty (6am, 9am) and Tashkent (12 noon).

BISHKEK BALIKCHEE CHOLPAN ATA
BUS:3-4HRS   1½-2 HRS   3½ HRS   KARAKOL
SHARE TAXI: 6-7 HRS
2HRS,50 COM

To: NARYN
(↓BISHKEK-9:00)

The Atlantis of Kyrgyzstan

The underwater city of Chiga can be visited on scuba dive tours organised very expensively by Bilim (95a Kievskaya #17, Bishkek ☎ 226503, e-mail bilim@dhl.bishkek.su). We found no dive operations anywhere on the lake to cater to casual visitors.

Balikchee

Formerly named Ribache (and the rail station still thinks it is) and then for a couple of confusing years known as Issyk Kul. This long, dull strip of transit town is backed by scraggy mountains. There are passable lakeside walks if you're stuck here.

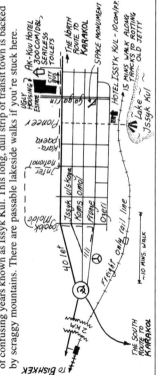

To BISHKEK →
2 KM
THE SOUTH ROUTE TO KARAKOL

40 let
Togobek Molda
Issyk W/skaya
Koms omol
Frunze
Oseri
Flight only rail line
Inter national
Kara-Opera
Pioneer
~10 MINS WALK

UGLY HOUSING ESTATE
Ak-Kuu HOTEL 300 COM/DBL., SEATLESS TOILETS
CITY BUS
THE NORTH ROUTE TO KARAKOL
SPACE MONUMENT
15 MINS WALK ALONG ROTTING TRACKS TO OLD JETTY
HOTEL ISSYK KUL – 10 COM/P.P.
~ Lake Issyk Kul ~

Karakol

Formerly Prezhevalsk. Pleasant town; base for mountaineering expeditions via Enylchek (220km SE) to 'disappearing' glacier-lake Mazarbaeker and peaks Pobeda (7439m) and Khan Tengri (6995m). Much nearer is beautiful Altin Arashan turbaza, a day's walk from Teplokliyuchenka. Local trekking agents can arrange lodges, meals and guide from $12/person/day (Valentin Akkerberg ☎20361; Valentin Derevyanko, Hotel Karakol or ☎ 22368).

HOTEL KARAKOL 80 COM/SNG.
Mail
Gagarina
Toktogula
Kalinina
International
BACK ROUTE TO ALMATY (NO BUSES)
FLIGHTS (2/WEEK)
TO ALMATY, OSH.
ABOVE BUS STA. BIG, CLEAN ROOMS 10 COM. P.P. NO H₂O. ENTER UP UNMARKED STAIRWAY IN SIDE OF BUS STA. BUILDING.
UGLY HIGHRISE HOUSING ESTATE
CHEAP FOOD
~5 MINS WALK
MAIN SQ. – MINIBUSES TO VILLAGES EAST (INCL. TEPLOKLYUCHENKA) PLUS TO LAKE SIDE AND TO PREZHEVALSK MONUMENT (ПЛЯЖ/ДАЧИ)
WOODEN HOMES ON THESE STREETS
DISNEY-ESQUE RUSSIAN CHURCH
Gorkogo
CITY BUS ROUTE
TO MNTS
N

Kyrgyzstan's Fergana fringes

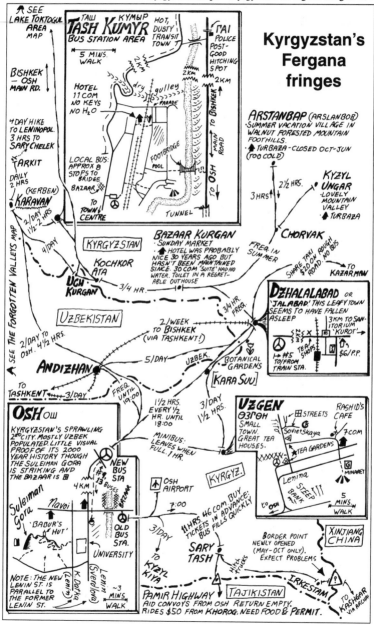

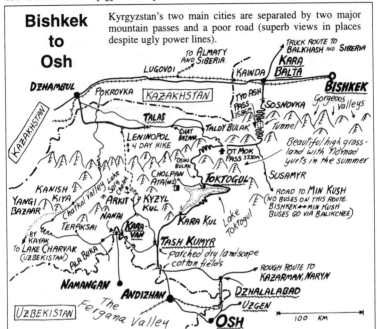

Bishkek to Osh

Kyrgyzstan's two main cities are separated by two major mountain passes and a poor road (superb views in places despite ugly power lines).

- **Local bus hops** There is no direct public bus. The scheduled early morning Bishkek-Toktogul bus didn't materialise for us even though the bus station had sold us a ticket (later refunded with a 'what do you expect' shrug). Daily buses Toktogul-Dzhalalabad and T-Osh (via Andizhan) leave very early. Also a few windowless cattle-trucks run to no particular timetable. Hitching is faster, more comfortable and lets you appreciate the scenery. S of Tash Kumyr buses are more frequent/reliable.
- **Direct shared taxi** $20 pp squashed in a Lada for 17+ bumpy hours from Bishkek train station to Karavan, Osh or Dzhalalabad. Same price for minibuses.
- **Hitching** Traffic is heavy with grindingly slow Siberian produce trucks. Toktogul-Kara Balta took us 20hrs with stops. Cars are rare and usually full but much faster. Hitches are easiest to arrange at bigger police posts such as Sosnovka, Oshu Bulak (near Toktogul) and Tash Kumyr where most vehicles stop to pay bribes. Several drivers fed us en route and none seemed to expect payment.
- **Alternate route** Sev/day Bishkek-Talas buses loop through Dzhambul (Kazakhstan – no visa checks, unspectacular). Hitch Talas-Toktogul via peaceful Ot Mok Pass (not scarred with power lines though less dramatic than the Tyo Ash Pass).
- **Train** Bishkek-Dzhalalabad trains take an uninteresting loop via Tashkent (crowded, 28hrs, no Uzbek visa check, 2/week, days vary). More trains from Andizhan.
- **Flying** From Karavan, Osh and Kazarman the foreigner price to Bishkek is approx $70. By luck we got the local price ($25) for a flight from Karakol (on Issyk Kul) to Osh. (2/week).
- **Walking** 4-5 day summer hike. Leninopol-Sary Chelek hike summarised in sketch opposite. Better trekking maps sold in Bishkek (107 Kievskaya). High passes but no need for climbing gear.

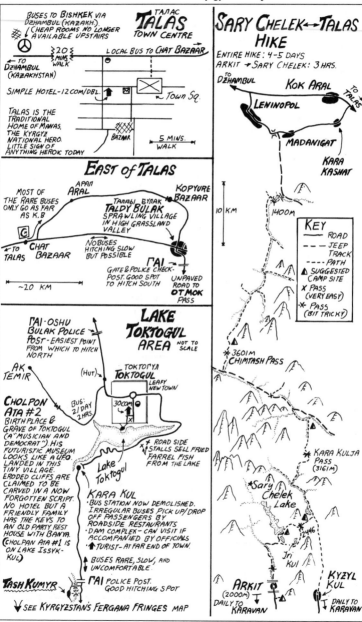

TALAS TOWN CENTRE ТАЛАС

BUSES TO BISHKEK VIA DZHAMBUL (KAZAKH.) CHEAP ROOMS NO LONGER AVAILABLE UPSTAIRS

LOCAL BUS TO CHAT BAZAAR

→ TO DZHAMBUL (KAZAKHSTAN)

20 MINS WALK

SIMPLE HOTEL - 12 COM/DBL.

Town Sq.

TALAS IS THE TRADITIONAL HOME OF MANAS, THE KYRGYZ NATIONAL HERO. LITTLE SIGN OF ANYTHING HEROIC TODAY

BAZAAR

5 MINS. WALK

EAST of TALAS

MOST OF THE RARE BUSES ONLY GO AS FAR AS K.B

АПАН ARAL

KOPYURE BAZAAR

Талды Булак TALDY BULAK SPRAWLING VILLAGE IN HIGH GRASSLAND VALLEY

→ TO TALAS CHAT BAZAAR

NO BUSES HITCHING SLOW BUT POSSIBLE

~20 KM

ГАI GATE & POLICE CHECK-POST. GOOD SPOT TO HITCH SOUTH

UNPAVED ROAD TO OTMOK PASS

LAKE TOKTOGUL AREA NOT TO SCALE

ГАI-OSHU BULAK POLICE POST - EASIEST POINT FROM WHICH TO HITCH NORTH

AK TEMIR

(HUT)

ТОКТОГУЛ TOKTOGUL LEAFY NEW TOWN

CHOLPON ATA #2
BIRTHPLACE & GRAVE OF TOKTOGUL ("A MUSICIAN AND DEMOCRAT"). HIS FUTURISTIC MUSEUM LOOKS LIKE A UFO LANDED IN THIS TINY VILLAGE. ERODED CLIFFS ARE CLAIMED TO BE CARVED IN A NOW FORGOTTEN SCRIPT. NO HOTEL BUT A FRIENDLY FAMILY HAS THE KEYS TO AN OLD PARTY REST HOUSE WITH BANYA. (CHOLPAN ATA #1 IS ON LAKE ISSYK-KUL)

BUS 2/DAY 2 HRS.

300 COM

Lake Toktogul

ROAD SIDE STALLS SELL FRIED FARREL FISH FROM THE LAKE

KARA KUL
· BUS STATION NOW DEMOLISHED. IRREGULAR BUSES PICK UP/DROP OFF PASSENGERS BY ROADSIDE RESTAURANTS
· DAM COMPLEX - CAN VISIT IF ACCOMPANIED BY OFFICIALS
· TURIST AT FAR END OF TOWN

BUSES RARE, SLOW, AND UNCOMFORTABLE.

TASH KUMYR

ГАI POLICE POST. GOOD HITCHING SPOT

↓ SEE KYRGYZSTAN'S FERGANA FRINGES MAP

SARY CHELEK ↔ TALAS HIKE

ENTIRE HIKE: 4-5 DAYS
ARKIT → SARY CHELEK: 3 HRS.

→ TO DZHAMBUL

KOK ARAL

TO TALAS

LENINOPOL

MADANIGAT

KARA KASHAT

10 KM

1400M

KEY
— ROAD
– – – JEEP TRACK
· · · · PATH
▲ SUGGESTED CAMP SITE
✕ PASS (VERY EASY)
✱ PASS (BIT TRICKY)

✱ 3601M CHIMTASH PASS

✱ KARA KULJA PASS (3161M)

Sary Chelek Lake

2446

Iri Kul

ARKIT (2000M) DAILY TO KARAVAN

KYZYL KUL DAILY TO KARAVAN

Sary Chelek

Alpine lake, nature reserve and gem of Kyrgyz tourist posters, Sary Chelek has craggy, tree-speckled vistas and wonderful forest hikes yet barely sees a foreigner. There is no lakeside village, no hotel and only a handful of tastefully hidden dachas near the short south shore 'beach'. Official theory is that you'll stay at the moth-eaten Sary Chelek turbaza in Jilgen village, then drive up and back during the day, paying the park fee ($10, or 5 com for locals) at the lower gate, 2km before Arkit. However, without a car, there's a problem. The daily bus from Karavan (via Jilgen) arrives around 6pm in Arkit and the gatekeepers are liable to send you back to the turbaza to sleep. That's a 12km walk and there's no bus back again until the same time next day – catch 22. Three possible solutions:

● **A)** Argue. Not knowing any of the above, we were carried through the lower gate in a packed bus, then prevented from camping on Arkit's idyllic little streamside meadows by the upper gatekeeper. However, after 2 hrs of negotiating he let us stay in his hut, accepting the $10 park fee himself. We camped the next night at the lake side (cool but not freezing in June).

● **B)** Take the 10.10am Karavan-Jilgen bus then walk/hitch the same day.

● **C)** Get off just before the lower gate. You'll see a couple of stark canyons with streams running through them where camping would be possible. Wait till morning and pay up or try sneaking through. The wardens sleep in their huts but locals pass nonchalantly through side gates with their animals. Returning from camping at the lakeside, we passed through both gates around dawn while they slept.

Other delightful valleys accessible from Karavan also offer great walking and lovely scenery for self sufficient travellers and are utterly untouristed (the bus driver to Raikomol told us we were the first foreigners he'd carried in 26 years). Our tent caused some astonishment and a quizzing from a drunken ex-KGB grand-dad but more often invitations to eat/sleep in local homes. The lively weekly markets are mêlées of donkeys and kalpak hats, but otherwise there is nowhere to buy food – so stock up in Karavan. The regional transport map opposite shows the villages accessible by bus from Karavan/Tash Kumyr.

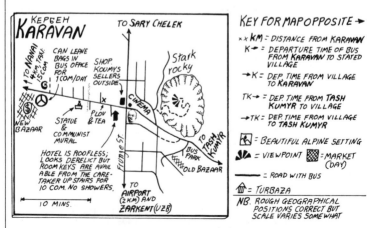

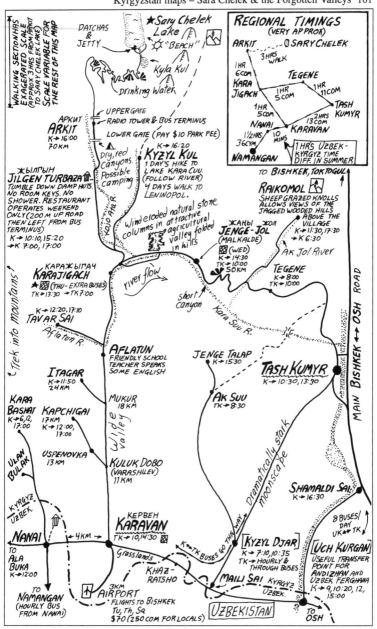

★ Sary Chelek Lake

DATCHAS & JETTY

"BEACH"

Kyla Kul

Drinking water

REGIONAL TIMINGS
(VERY APPROX)

ARKIT ········ ◎ SARY CHELEK
3 HRS WALK

1 HR 6 COM
KARA JIGACH

TEGENE

1 HR 5 COM
1 HR 11 COM
TASH KUMYR

1 HR 5 COM
NANAI
2 HRS 13 COM
10 MINS
KARAVAN

1½ HRS 36 CYM

NAMANGAN

1 HRS UZBEK-KYRGYZ TIME DIFF IN SUMMER

WALKING SECTIONS HAS EXAGERATED SCALE (APPROX 3 HRS FROM ARKIT TO SARY CHELEK LAKE) SCALE VARIABLE FOR THE REST OF THIS MAP

UPPER GATE
RADIO TOWER & BUS TERMINUS
LOWER GATE (PAY $10 PARK FEE)

АРКИТ
ARKIT
K → 16:00
70 KM

Dry, red canyons. Possible camping

K → 16:20
KYZYL KUL
1 DAY'S HIKE TO LAKE KARA CUU. (FOLLOW RIVER)
4 DAYS WALK TO LENINOPOL.

ЫЛГЫН
✷ JILGEN TURBAZA 🏛
TUMBLE DOWN DAMP HUTS. NO ROOM KEYS. NO SHOWER. RESTAURANT OPERATES WEEKEND ONLY (200 M UP ROAD THEN LEFT FROM BUS TERMINUS)
K → 10:10, 15:20
→ K → 7:00, 17:00

TO BISHKEK, TOKTOGUL

Wind eroded natural stone columns in attractive agricultural valley folded in hills

RAIKOMOL 🏔
SHEEP GRAZED KNOLLS ALLOWS VIEWS OF THE JAGGED WOODED HILLS ABOVE THE VILLAGE
K → 11:30, 17:30
→ K 6:30

ЖАҢЫ
JENGE-JOL
(MALKALDE)
(WED)
K → 14:30
TK → 10:00
50 KM

Ak Jol River

river flow

КАРАЖЫГАЧ
KARAJIGACH
★ 🏚 (THU- EXTRA BUSES)
K → 13:30 → TK → 7:00

short canyon

Kara Suu R.

TEGENE
K → 8:00
TK → 10:00

K → 12:20, 17:10
TAVAR SAI

Aflatun R.

Trek into mountains

AFLATUN
FRIENDLY SCHOOL TEACHER SPEAKS SOME ENGLISH

JENGE TALAP
K → 15:30

TASH KUMYR
K → 10:30, 13:90

MAIN BISHKEK ↔ OSH ROAD

ITAGAR
K → 11:50
24 KM

MUKUR
18 KM

AK SUU
TK → 8:30

KARA BASHAT
K → 6, 12, 17:00

KAPCHIGAI
17 KM
K → 12:00, 17:00

Wide valley

ULAN BULAK

USPENOVKA
13 KM

KULUK DOBO
(VARASHILEV)
11 KM

Dramatically stark moonscape

SHAMALDI SAI
K → 16:30

8 BUSES / DAY
UK → TK

КЕРВЕН
KARAVAN
TK → 10, 14:30

K → TK BUSES GO THIS WAY

KYZYL DJAR
K → 7:10, 10:35
TK → HOURLY & THROUGH BUSES

UCH KURGAN
USEFUL TRANSFER POINT FOR ANDIZHAN AND UZBEK FERGHANA
K → 9, 10:20, 12, 15:00

КYRGYZ-UZBEK.

NANAI
TO ALA BUKA
K → 12:00

← 4 KM →

Grasslands

KHAZ-RATSHO

3 KM
✈ **AIRPORT**
FLIGHTS TO BISHKEK
Tu, Th, Sa

MAILI SAI
KYRGYZ-UZBEK.

TO NAMANGAN
(HOURLY BUS FROM NANAI)

UZBEKISTAN

TO OSH

$70 (250 COM FOR LOCALS)

Torugart Pass

Edging up from the Xinjiang badlands to an other-worldly mountain ringed plateau at Chatyr Kul, the Torugart Pass is a much more attractive gateway to Central Asia than Khorgas (Almaty-Urumqi). Travel companies claim that you must be met at the border by an authorised agent/rental jeep. We crossed both ways without. Chinese officials assured us that since 1995 tourists need only their visas (locals must telex their travel plans to the border post). The hard-to-book weekly bus from Kashgar's Wuz Binguan direct to Bishkek has been suspended but a daily minibus now clatters the 105km between the old and new Chinese border posts at Tuergate/Archal.

● **Costs** Min $30 if hitching. Naryn to the Kyrgyz borderpost is potentially expensive: there's no bus, a truck ride is your best hope (offer $10-15). Taxis want extortionate sums (up to $1200 northbound) though patient bargaining may get this down to $100/car (northbound) or $50 (south). Bishkek travel firms rent vehicles but $380 for a minibus including Tash Rabat excursion is not cheap even if you fill the 8 seats.

● **When open** Officially open year round (snow ploughs keep it clear). Nights are very cold even in August. In Dec we were left to freeze in the snow for 4hrs. Borders closed Sa, Su, any national holiday of either nation or Russia (guards are Russian).

● **Visas** No visas issued at or anywhere near the borders. The Visa Shuffle works – we met travellers who entered Kyrgyzstan on Kazakh transit visas (available quickly in Beijing) as well as on Russian and Uzbek tourist visas. Chinese visas are very tough to obtain in Bishkek, easier in Almaty.

● **Time** All times quoted here are BT, XT or KT. BT (Beijing Time) is 2hrs before XT (Xinjiang time as quoted by non-Han Chinese). KT (Kyrgyz Time) is BT-3, XT-1. This time change causes delays when heading into China. In summer KT=XT.

Tips – Northbound (Kashgar to Naryn) **Timing:** Possible in 24hrs taking taxis but allow two days. Chinese formalities (11am-1.30pmBT) outgoing, painless. Kyrgyz immigration (4pm KT till cleared), takes 1hr+. **Transport:** Buses from Kashgar's Artux bus stand bound for Kangsa, Ulugchat or Bayankuluti take 1-2hrs to Archal. It may be worth paying a taxi (100yuan, 70mins) or sleeping at Archal the night before to ensure you make it for the minibus to Tuergate which leaves at 10am XT sharp. A second minibus usually runs at 11amXT but don't rely on it. The minibus drops you at the Kyrgyz gate by a queue of trucks. You may not walk across the 400m to the Kyrgyz immigration office so dash immediately and ask the lead truck driver for a ride (no money expected). After a long, cold wait the gate finally opens to trucks after 4pm KT (5XT). Trucks clear customs fast – don't expect them to wait. Only by arriving with the first truck will you have a slim chance of hitching with one of the stragglers. If not, stay the night in Torugart. In the morning the taxi drivers seem a little more open to bargaining, travel is safer and views are worth the wait.

Tips – Southbound (Naryn to Kashgar) **Timing:** 3 days, 2 if you're lucky. Don't leave Naryn on a Thur, Fri or Sat or you may get stuck one extra day. Officially the Kyrgyz border opens 9am-12pmKT, though some travellers have been allowed to pass in the late afternoon. Chinese incoming formalities take a couple of minutes, and desks stay open at least until the scheduled minibus arrives. **Transport:** The truckstop 9km beyond Naryn (this may move) is the best spot to hitch to Torugart. Naryn seems better than At Bashi for Torugart taxis. The Tuergate-Archal minibus is scheduled ridiculously for noon BT, (ie 9amKT, when the Kyrgyz immigration is only just opening). Fortunately it was 3hrs late when we crossed giving us time to find a ride across the 12kms of no-man's land. Otherwise wait a day and sleep at Tuergate. From Archal minibuses run till about 6pmXT heading for Artux or Kashgar (10yuan).

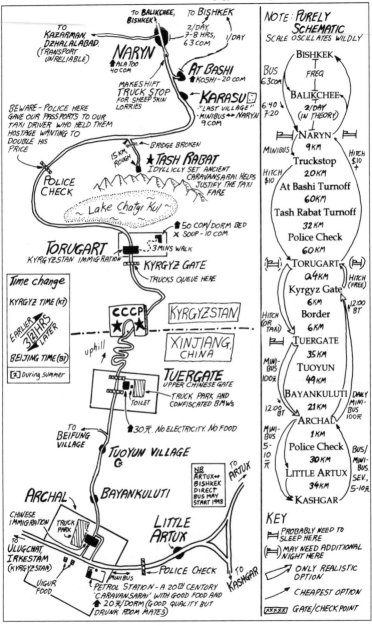

Tajikistan

① KOJENT (LENINABAD)
② BEKABAD (UZB.)
③ BUSTON

Note: In Gorno Badakhstan (eastern two-thirds of Tajikistan) permits are required and food shortages are possible. See below.

The three countries of Tajikistan

Tajikistan has three distinct regions. The northern 'periscope' is dominated by Khojent and is virtually indistinguishable from neighbouring Uzbekistan. Here one can use Uzbek money (or Russian roubles), the main roads are safe and transport links are with Tashkent and Kokand not Dushanbe. There's good hiking in the NE corner.

The western lobe is a series of wide valleys and home to two thirds of the population and much of the unrest. The Penjikent-Dushanbe highway is particularly bad for extortion. There's a special rivalry between Dushanbe and Kuliab mafiosi.

The eastern lobe, Gorno-Badakhstan is an isolated, autonomous area of enormous barren peaks and deep cut valleys. The only major road linking it to Dushanbe is frequently cut by rebel forces (eg in 1996 with the occupation of Tavildera). The few supplies that reach the region come via Osh in Kyrgyzstan along the stark, frigidly dramatic Pamir highway. Badakhstan is one of the most fundamentalist Islamic areas of the ex-USSR and its Pamiri people consider it an independent country.

Tajikistan

Tajikistan is Central Asia's odd man out. While its neighbours speak Turkic languages, Tajik is Persian based. The country has none of Kazakhstan's oil potential, none of Turkmenistan's gas, none of Kyrgyzstan's enlightened commercialism and, thanks to Stalin's creative cartography, it doesn't even control its own cultural capital (Samarkand) which now falls within Uzbekistan. Like Kyrgyzstan, the landscape includes some of the world's most breathtakingly stark, unspoilt mountain scenery. But, unlike its stable northern neighbour, it has spent its first years of independence in turmoil and civil war.

Despite military assistance from Russia and a team of border troops from CIS nations, the Dushanbe government has little effective control over most of the country. Militias and semi-private army units control their own mini fiefdoms. Armed checkpoints demand random fees from road users. Travellers who refuse to pay the bribes risk being branded as drug smugglers or terrorists. A June 1997 treaty legalising the (mostly Islamic) opposition parties offered the most promising signs of peace this decade. But, at the time of writing, the return of the opposition leader, Said Abdullo Nuri, from exile in Iran has been delayed by a wave of bombings including one at the Vakhash Hotel, Dushanbe where Nuri's 'Council for Reconciliation' will be based. It is telling that there are Tajik refugees in Afghanistan rather than the other way round.

The 2000-year-old Silk Road city of Khojent is one of the few 'safe' zones of Tajikistan but is a great disappointment; a calm, crashingly dull Soviet city as unprepossessing as the neighbouring Uzbek towns of the Fergana Valley. The nation's real attraction is the towering Pamir mountain range in the far east where the Tien Shan, Karakoram and Himalayan ranges crash spectacularly into one another. Few Western visitors have glimpsed this region since the days of the Great Game; with food shortages and hostilities still rumbling along the Afghan border, there's no imminent threat of a tourist flood. The lower but arguably more attractive Fann and Ramid mountains see no tourists either.

❑ **W&M's country ratings – Tajikistan**

● **Expense $$$ to $$$$$** Modest in the west, except at gunpoint. Prices are near European level in Badakhstan where most of the merchandise is trucked in on dangerous routes.

● **Value for money** ✔ The food is poor and difficult to buy (many people are self-sufficient). The cost of internal flights is reasonable.

● **Getting around** ✔ Tajikistan is cut off from most links; there is no public transport in the east.

● **Woman alone** ✔✔✔ The only single woman traveller we met had hitched some of the world's most dangerous roads alone. Her assurances that all was fine may have been overstated; she'd spent several days in jail 'for her own protection'.

PRACTICAL INFORMATION
Visas and formalities

● **Visa strategy** If you happen to be in Ashgabat, Turkmenistan, you can get a Tajik visa on the spot with no need for invitations or special paperwork. However, there are few other consulates; there are none in Kyrgyzstan or in Uzbekistan, and the embassy in Almaty (Kazakhstan) doesn't issue visas. If Ashgabat is not on your route, you have two main options:

1) Using the **visa shuffle** (see p557). Tajikistan is a shuffle signatory and transits through the 'periscope' are no trouble on Kyrgyz, Uzbek or other shuffle visas. However, some travellers have been turned back from the border on the Samarkand-Penjikent road, despite valid Uzbek visas that should have allowed them through. If you do make it to Dushanbe, you can apply for a real Tajik visa at the 'Consolstsvo MID' office, Rudaki Sq (☎ 211560).

❏ **Geo-political information – Tajikistan**

Population: 6.13m (1997), 6.15m (1995), 5.1m (1989), 3.4m (1975).

Area: 143,000 sq km.

Capital: Dushanbe (602,000).

Other major cities: Khojent (160,000).

GNP per capita: $1000 estimate (1994).

Currency history: Tajik Rouble/US$1 – Feb 1998: TR750, Oct 1997: TR750, Dec 1996: TR470, Jan 1996: TR295, autumn 1995: TR140, summer 1995: TR45 (bank), TR60 (street). The Tajik rouble was introduced reluctantly and without IMF backing on 11 May 1995 at TR1=100 Russian Roubles as there were not enough rouble banknotes in circulation and Russia refused to provide more.

Major exports/economy: Cotton and aluminum. Intriguingly Switzerland is the biggest trading partner outside the former USSR.

Ethnic mix: Tajik (65%), Uzbek (25%), Russian (3% and falling through emigration – was 8% in 1989). Pamiris are included in census statistics as ethnic Tajiks, a classification they dispute.

Official languages: Tajik. Russian is commonly used in business and government, Uzbek is common in the north and west. Pamiri dialects are not recognised as separate though they are different from Tajik.

Religious mix: Sunni Muslim (80%), Shi'ite Muslim (5%). The Ismaili Muslims in Badakhstan are influential.

Landmarks of national history: **1876**: Bukhara (which held nominal control over the region) became a Russian protectorate. The Pamirs were not claimed by any state until the Russians decided to add the region (today's Gorno Badakhstan) to their collection. **1922**: Enver Pasha and the Basmachi briefly liberated Dushanbe. **1924**: Russia annexed the region as an autonomous republic in the Uzbek SSR. **1927**: Railway built via Termez. **1929**: Became a full republic within the USSR. **1985**: Gorbachev's anti-corruption drive was opposed by Tajik leaders as Russification. **1991**: Independence though communists remained in power. **1992**: The government was overthrown by a secular/Islamic coalition, but after nearly 20,000 deaths returned to power. **1993**: Purges and disappearances. Fighting continued, fragmented government forces supported by Russian troops. **1997**: Peace treaty.

Leader: Emomali Rakhmonov since Nov 1992. Officially elected in Nov 94.

Pressing political issues: Civil war. Winning IMF approval for currency, political tensions between regional factions in politics (Khojent, Dushanbe and Kuliab political cliques) and the army. Keeping the aluminium smelter running.

2) Getting a specially **endorsed Russian visa** from Russian embassies where there is no Tajik visa office. You'll theoretically require a letter of invitation endorsed by the Tajik Ministry of Foreign Affairs. These are almost impossible to get without business contacts. However, two travellers managed to persuade a Russian consul to include the names 'Penjikent' and 'Dushanbe' on the city list of a normal Russian visa just by talking to him nicely.

● **Permits** These are required for Khorog, Murgab and all of Gorno-Badakhstan and can be obtained only with an invitation letter from a specialist agency. We suggest heading first to Dushanbe and trying to make some high powered contacts there (eg in the bar/lobby of the Intourist hotel).

On the Pamir Highway from Sary Tash (Kyrgyzstan) visas and permits are carefully checked at a minimum of nine roadblocks, so bluffing your way through is most unlikely to work.

Transport
Badakhstan has no public transport whatever. The only regular transport on the Pamir highway is supply trucks and these only run in any numbers when an aid shipment is dispatched (from Osh,

---

❏ Essential information for travellers – Tajikistan
● **Visa** Required, and many areas require a special permit. The visa shuffle is allowed but it's more difficult to use than in Kazakhstan or Kyrgyzstan.
● **Currency** Tajik Rouble. US$1=TR750. Hard currency cash is essential.
● **Time zone** 6 hours ahead of GMT (3hrs ahead of Moscow).
● **Religious tone** Suppressed undercurrent of fundamentalist Islam. Many Ismaili Muslims in Badakhstan. The most fundamentalist of the central Asian republics.
● **Health factors** A slight malarial risk, but this is confined to the Afghan border areas. Drinking untreated water is not recommended.
● **Special dangers** The civil war; the marksmen on the Afghan side of the border who use passing vehicles for target practice; occasional curfews and disturbances in Dushanbe.
● **Typical traveller destinations** None. Pendjikent (from Samarkand) and the Pamirs (for mountaineers) would be the most obvious choices.
● **Highlights** The spectacular Dushanbe-Khorog flight; the moonscapes of the Pamir Highway; surviving the above; the Varzhob and Ramid mountains.
● **When to go** The weather in the Khojent periscope is much the same as in the Fergana valley of Uzbekistan with hot, dry, just-bearable summers, and winters that are cold and also dry (the minimum temperature is around -15°C but the average is rarely below freezing point). Summer temperatures and humidity are higher in the south west and the rare rainfall is most likely in August. Badakhstan is hit by icy winds, even in the summer – very warm clothes are needed on the Pamir highway at night. July and August are the only feasible months for mountaineering as it becomes rapidly colder later in the year (-63°C being the record low). There is regular heavy snow in the Pamirs and on higher passes, snowfalls may linger year round.
● **Pulse of the country** Tajikistan is more like three countries than one (see p164).
● **Key tips** Tajikistan is unstable. Reliable local contacts are important for getting permits, for helping you visit interesting areas, and for keeping you safe and supplied while there. Don't expect the Aga Khan Foundation workers to take care of you. While they are extremely nice people, their role is to develop high yield agricultural projects not to nanny out of depth tourists.

❑ **Meeting the locals**

● **Language** Tajik is related to Farsi, the language of Iran. It is written in Cyrillic (Russian) letters; the move to Arabic script proposed at independence proved unpopular. Note that there are many dialects in Tajik. The phrases given below are also used in Samarkand (ethnically Tajik though physically in Uzbekistan):

How are you? – *jifu shi mo/khoroton ji tu*
Reply – *narz* (literally, 'OK')
Thank you very much – *rakhmuti kalom*
Beautiful – *kushroi* (thing), *zebo* (person)
Delicious – *bamaza*

Kyrgyzstan). The Aga Khan Foundation would know when trucks are leaving, but they are not a tourist service, nor are they too keen to help travellers in this hostile land. US$50 would be a typical price (after negotiation) for the cold, desperately uncomfortable but fascinating three-day trip from Khorog to Osh. The Penjikent to Dushanbe road has many bandit check points where you'll have to pay 'protection' fees; these may add up to $100.

● **Bus** Services operate between Samarkand (Uzbekistan) and Penjikent.

● **Train** Khojent is linked to the main Uzbek rail network. There are also trains from Dushanbe to Tashkent and Moscow, but they have to take a crazy, time-consuming loop, heading south for Termez (Uzbekistan) to get around the Zerafshan mountains before they can head anywhere you might want to go.

● **Air** The flight between Dushanbe and Khorog ($30 for locals, $70 foreigners) is rightly reckoned to be one of the world's most spectacular (and hair-raising). Khorog is in a valley banked with mountains. Tajikistan International Airlines ran a London-Dushanbe-Delhi flight in 1994/5 but stopovers were hard and expensive to organise. This service is not operating at present.

Further information

● **Books and newspapers** The Central Asia guides published by Cadogan and Lonely Planet include useful sections on Tajikistan. Coverage in Vacation Work's *Russia and the Republics* is more limited. One of the best sources of up to date information is the weekly newspaper, *New Europe*.

● **Maps** West Col have optimistically published hiking maps to the Fann and Pamir mountains of Tajikistan; these are available in good Western map shops. The whole country is covered by very detailed, but hard to find, Russian military-made topographical maps in 1:100,000 (150 sheets, $1500) and 1:200,000 (42 sheets, $336) scales. Prices are for the full set if bought from Omni (US ☎ 910-227-8300, http://www.omnimap.com).

Certain sheets covering 'the periscope' and other areas along the Kyrgyz borders are available from the cartographic agency at 107 Kievskaya, Bishkek, Kyrgyzstan for about $4/sheet. We met one traveller who had photocopied Curzon's original 19th century maps from a copy of Cobbald's *Pamir* at the US Library of Congress. He claimed they're still useful.

Web sites

Probably the best source of current information on Tajikistan is from the Soros Foundation, one of the few organisations who do extensive work in the country. It's at www.soros.org/tajkstan.html.

Turkmenistan

Don't expect too much from Turkmenistan. It's a stark, arid desert pocked with scrubby saxaul bushes and a few unappealing Soviet towns. The cacophonous Sunday market in the sands outside Ashgabat still teems with splendidly photogenic, deeply wrinkled old tribesmen with long white wispy beards, and hats that look like a whole sheep's been plonked on their heads. But today their $100-camels arrive by truck not caravan and are sold from prosaic concrete enclosures. Merv is astoundingly desolate; a once proud city of a million souls reduced to a single blue dome and a few yards of mud wall. Nisa and Kunya Urgench, the other main historical places, are not much more extensive. The Kopet Dag mountains are dustily appealing, but their position on the Iranian border makes hiking there a 'suspicious activity'. Chardzhou sits on the banks of the Amu Darya, but as one guide book proclaims: 'Never has a great river so completely failed to bring charm'. Determined to prove this wrong, we searched diligently for hidden points of interest or atmosphere. All we found was a palace (Dvoretz Himit) that looked more like an abandoned cinema and a castle (Gala) whose amorphous mud-mound form rose dully above a rubbish tip amongst the drab rows of slab-tower apartments.

For all this, Turkmenistan is fascinating in its head-on clash of economic opportunity (natural gas) with old school authoritarianism. An eerie, full blown personality cult surrounds the ex-communist president, Saparamud Niyazov. Re-naming himself Turkmenbashi (leader of the Turkmens), his Yeltsin-esque, grey-haired image stares at you from bank notes, billboards and plaques everywhere, with the ubiquitous slogan; *Halk Watan Turkmenbashi* (peace, motherland, Niyazov). Hastily chiselled Niyazov statues have been erected on the very plinths from which Lenin was toppled in 1991-2.

Niyazov hopes to use Turkmenistan's potential gas and oil wealth to create another Kuwait. As yet the money hasn't arrived but this hasn't stopped the spending spree. The modern hotels, mosques and a new presidential palace springing up around the capital show an eccentric disregard for economic rationale while currency controls and bread rationing continue in the communist mould.

❏ **W&M's country ratings – Turkmenistan**
● **Expense $$** Food and transport are extremely cheap; hotels are either cheap or very overpriced for foreigners.
● **Value for money** ✔✔✔✔ The black market rate makes everything reasonable, though low end accommodation is still poor value.
● **Getting around** ✔✔ You can get anywhere eventually but there's a lot of desert to cross; transport is slow and crowded.
● **Woman alone** ✔✔✔ Similar to Uzbekistan.

PRACTICAL INFORMATION
Visas and formalities

● **Visa strategy** The best place to get an entry visa is Istanbul, or in Turkmenistan itself. The **Ministry of Foreign Affairs** (Consular Dept), Room 6, Makhtumkuli 83, Ashgabat, grants 10-day visas for $20. Once there, it is also possible that you can find a travel agent to sponsor you for a longer stay. But how do you get into the country to begin with?

Turkmenistan is not part of the visa shuffle but if you are arriving from Soviet Central Asia you can often slip across the loosely guarded border with Uzbekistan. OVIR in Khiva warned us of $20 fines and possible expulsion back to Uzbekistan if we tried to enter Turkmenistan without a

---

❏ Geo-political information – Turkmenistan

Population: 4.2m (1997), 3.75m (1991), 3.5m (1989).

Area: 488,100 sq km (slightly larger than California).

Capital: Ashgabat/Ashkabad (407,000).

Other major cities: Chardzhou/Charjev (164,000), Tashauz/Dashkhovuz (114,000).

GNP per capita: $2660 (1994) but wages are pitiful, $4120 (1988).

Currency history: Manat/US$1 – Feb 1998: M5300 (M7600), Oct 1997: M5300 (M7600). Multiple rates according to the purpose of exchange. The official cash rate is quoted with the black market rate in parentheses – June 1996: M2400 (M4500), July 1995: M195 (M300), Oct 1994: M75 (M150), Mar 1994: M10 (M70). At introduction in Nov 1993: M1.99 (M35).

Major exports/economy: Oil, gas and cotton. Building statues of Niyazov.

Ethnic mix: Turkmen (74%), Russian (9.5% but many have emigrated – Ashgabat retains a 30% Russian minority), Uzbek (8.5%), Kazakh (2.9%) plus Ukrainian, Tartar, Armenian, Baluchi, Kurd and some 60 other nationalities.

Notion of a Turkmen nationality: Created in 1924 when locals had to choose whether to declare themselves either Turkmen (Turkomen) or Uzbek.

Official language: Turkmen, though Russian is still very widely understood.

Religious mix: 87% Muslim, mostly Sunni of the Hanafi sect which is not noted for fundamentalism. Also a declining population of Eastern Orthodox Christians.

Landmarks of national history: 505BC: Supposed founding of Merv (Alexander the Great took it in 320BC), later one of the world's biggest cities. **200BC-300AD**: Nisa capital of Parthian empire. **651AD**: Arabs took Merv. **995AD**: Khorazm united with Kunya Urgench (Gurganj) as capital. **1220-2**: Devastation by Genghis Khan. **1380s**: Devastated again by Timur. **1881**: Russian massacre of the Tekke Turkomen warriors at Geok Tepe. **1917-19**: British agents propped up the anti-Bolshevik regime. **1924**: Turkmen SSR created. **1940**: Latin script replaced by Cyrillic (Arabic script used till 1920s). **1948**: Ashgabat completely destroyed in an earthquake. **March 1991**: Referendum vote 95% to maintain USSR. **Oct 1991**: 95% vote for independence! **Jan 1994**: Referendum extended president's rule to year 2002 (out of 2 million votes, only 212 votes were against him!).

Leader: Saparmurad Turkmenbashi, née Niyazov. Autocrat.

Pressing political issues: Growing dissatisfaction and economic collapse (Niyazov's reaction to the first demonstrations was to lay the foundation stone of a new palace and to have himself nominated as President for life). Making bread and petrol free to citizens. Routing of gas and oil exports to countries that can pay (ie not Ukraine). World disapproval for close ties to Iran. Caspian Sea pollution, diversion of a large part of the Amu Darya river into irrigation contributes to that river's inability to replenish the Aral Sea; desertification.

visa but we suffered no such fines, nor did other travellers we met. Transit visas are available in New Delhi if you're coming from the subcontinent; from the west, full entry visas were available (at the time of research) without an invitation in Istanbul and Ankara though this may change as it breaks with official policy.

Ten-day visas were once available at Ashgabat (but not Krasnovodsk) airport for $20 without the need for an invitation. At the time of writing, invitations did seem to be required for an airport visa; check with your airline for the latest policy.

● **Extensions** Visa extensions are possible but usually a letter of support or invitation from a business or Turkmen citizen is required. Present three copies of your letter and one copy of your passport (so they don't need to hold the original during the three to five day processing period). It will cost: $30 for one month (maximum), $20 for 20 days, $10 for up to 10 days. The Ministry of Foreign Affairs has helpful English speaking staff and seems flexible; as we had no local sponsor they suggested we write a letter explaining why we would like more time and said that they would consider our request.

● **Permits** Internal travel permits are needed to visit the southern town of Kerki and for the hikes in the Kopet Dag mountains that go near to Iran. The Iranian border is open to locals but foreigners need a permit to cross. These seemed almost impossible to procure wherever we tried. When the Iran-Turkmen railway was inaugurated, foreigners were briefly allowed to use it. Within a week or two this decision was reversed but recent reports suggest that the train will be reopened to foreigners soon.

Money

Turkmenistan is one of the last former Soviet countries to continue to have a black market. The value of the Turkmen currency, the manat, is slipping constantly making quotation of prices in manats largely meaningless. Street changing remains a cloak and dagger affair. You are unlikely to be openly approached – the blatant dealers that used to operate outside the Hotel Ashgabat have been (perhaps temporarily) disbursed. Be discreet. Ask people you meet when you're alone and don't change too much when you first arrive till you know the real rate. You probably won't

---

❏ **Essential information for travellers – Turkmenistan**

● **Visa** Required. Acquired with variable difficulty. The visa shuffle is not applicable – Turkmenistan refused to sign it.

● **Currency** Manat. US$1=M5300 (bank); M7600 (black market). Falling fast.

● **Time zone** 5 hours ahead of GMT (NB Unlike most neighbouring countries Turkmenistan does not add one hour during the summer).

● **Religious tone** Muslim beliefs are fundamental but there are few mosques or outward signs of religious activity.

● **Typical traveller destinations** None. Too few travellers.

● **Highlights** The atmospheric desolation of the former Silk Road towns at Merv, Kunya Urgench, Geok Tepe and Nisa; the grand hats and flowing grey beards of the old Turkoman men; escaping from the heat. Ashgabat's Sunday market.

● **When to go** Summers sizzle – after all, Turkmenistan is 90% desert. While we were in Ashgabat (July) the thermometer seemed to register over 50°C, though being so dry it was much more acceptable than a 36°C day in sweaty Baku (Azerbaijan). A towel is useful to soak up all your sweat in trains where little air circulates, especially if you have to sit in stations for long periods. December and January are the coolest months: snow possible in Tashauz.

● **Pulse of the country** The heat, dust, colour, concrete and life of the Tolguchka Sunday market, Ashgabat.

need much anyway – despite getting a dreadful rate for my $10 note, it was enough to get into downtown Krasnovodsk (officially renamed Turkmenbashi) from the airport, pay for a night's hotel accommodation and buy a train ticket to Ashgabat.

Cashing travellers' cheques (5% commission) and credit card cash advances (6%) are possible at Vneshcom Bank, 22 Zhitnikova, Ashgabat; they will give you dollars so you can use the black market.

Transport

● **Bus** Bus services don't exist on the long trans-desert routes (eg Ashgabat to Tashauz). Services between nearby cities are reasonably regular but worth booking a few hours ahead.

● **Train** Railways are slow but regular; going by train is the sensible way to cover longer distances. Ticket prices are cheap – almost too cheap – resulting in horrendous fights for tickets. Instead of fighting for tickets or bribing your way on board one trick is to pay a fixer to get the tickets for you. He requires only an hour or so and mark-ups need not be ridiculously high (eg $2 on a $10 Chardzhou to Volgagrad ticket). In Chardzhou, particularly, there seems to be collusion between the very dapper touts and the ticket office. Locals there were as surprised as I was that in *only* 9 hours I'd managed to wade through the scrum and procure a ticket for the dismal Tashkent bound service, without a tout's help.

● **Air** Internal flights carry a hefty foreigner surcharge, though on rare occasions you'll run into someone who doesn't know the rules; the Krasnovodsk Airport ticket-ing desk was one. Azerbaijan Airlines operates a thrice weekly (Monday, Thursday, Saturday) flight from Krasnovodsk to Baku ($26 if bought at the airport, $56 at foreigner rates).

● **Boat** The ferry from Krasnovodsk (Turkmenbashi) to Baku is running again after a period of very irregular operation. Though departure times are extremely variable they seem to leave most evenings eventually. We were offered the tickets at $26 (local price), but most travellers report paying $75.

● **Taxi** As in Kazakhstan, every car in a city seems to double as a share taxi. Prices are extremely reasonable once you figure out the scale, and pay accordingly. A 10-minute ride costs less than US$0.10 when shared, or 40 cents+ on your own.

Accommodation

Most hotels are expensive or have high foreigner surcharges. However, in every town we visited there was at least one place to stay for under $5. Dormitories (*obshchii*) are more prevalent in Turkmenistan than the other Central Asian republics. Single women may be given an empty dormitory, or refused dorms altogether – 'for their protection'.

Food and drink

Much as in the rest of Central Asia, food is lamb based. There is a great variety of fruit and vegetables available at the markets in season. Bread, butter, rice and flour are officially rationed as part of the government's stated policy to make them free to all citizens. In the summer the searing dry heat means you should drink more than you feel you need. Fortunately there are

---

❏ **Language**
The Cyrillic script is still in common use, but there is a concerted move to a Turkmen version of the Roman alphabet.
   Some phrases in Turkmen:
         Hello (Arabic) – *salam elekum*
         How are you? – *gurgun me?*
         Reply – *gurgun*
         Thank you – *sagbol* (same for goodbye)

Turkmen Romanization includes 2 unique letters
$\int$ *(lower case* $\mathfrak{c}$*) = "Sh"*
W *(w) = "v" as in German*

drink vendors at every turn in the town centres. Watery draught Pepsi ($0.03) is easy to find though it can be orange and occasionally green. *Mors* is a watery version of *kvas* (fermented bread water); it looks like beer and is served in chipped pint mugs from yellow tankers parked at street corners. *Chalbar* is camel's milk sold from churns on trains. Beer and cheap vodka are widely available. However, Turkmenistan leans towards Islam slightly more than most other CIS republics so public drunkenness is rare.

Staying in touch
● **Fax** You can send international faxes from the Hotel Grand Turkmen for $11/page but it costs only $3 from the telephone office near Ruski Bazaar.
● **Phone** Calls from a phone office to the USA or Europe are about $2/minute.
    International country code: +993. Ashgabat: 3632, Tashauz: 360.

Shopping
Carpets are integral to Turkmen culture (the traditional motifs of the five major tribes are incorporated into the national flag) and are amongst the best in the world. Many carpets, known as *Bukharan*, probably originate from Turkmenistan where prices are low for the quality of workmanship. Carpets and artefacts purchased at the state-owned hard currency store are easy to export legally (simply show the receipt to customs officials). However, export restrictions have recently been tightened on souvenirs purchased through private sources. The process involves obtaining an export certificate from the **Ministry of Culture**, Museum Department (☎

253417), 14 Pushkin, Ashgabat. This takes three days. You then have to pay duty (in US$) at the **Customs Office Operations Section** (☎ 470209), Ul Atabayeva and Stepan Razin, Ashgabat. Both offices are open Monday to Friday, 9am-1pm and 2-6pm. The tax per sq metre of carpet is five times the national minimum monthly salary! There are few customs checks if leaving by land to Uzbekistan – hint, hint.

Activities
● **Hiking** This is possible from Chuli (10 hours to the mountain top) but in general the desert makes hiking less appealing, and since the mountains are close to the Iranian border they tend to be militarily sensitive.
● **Swimming** There are beaches at Cheleken on the Caspian for adventurous plungers who enjoy desolate chemical factories as a backdrop.
● **Work** Farmers should watch the trade press for interesting contracts bringing in the Turkmen grain crops. The pay is not spectacular but flights and prestigious accommodation are provided.

Further information
● **Maps** These are hard to find anywhere. An Ashgabat city map is given free to American citizens from the US Embassy and very tiny ones (though surprisingly detailed) are sold from a few kiosks.
● **Travel agents Sputnik Travel** (☎ 3632-251279, fax 3632-298960), 162 Kamina, Ashgabat, will help with travel arrangements but it's best to visit, rather than phone, them. **Intourist** (☎ 360-24737), Dashauz Hotel, Sovietskaya 4, Tashauz – Er Mohammad speaks some English.

Web sites
There is little budget travel info but the Turkmenistan-travel page on the Soros foundation web site, www.soros.org/turkstan/turktrvl.html, is a good place to start.

www.rockbridge.net/personal/bichel/turkmen.htp is the Turkmenistan page of the Central Asia Interactive Resource Project.

mh102.infi.net/~embassy/tourism.html has basic tourism information, including a flight schedule and list of holidays.

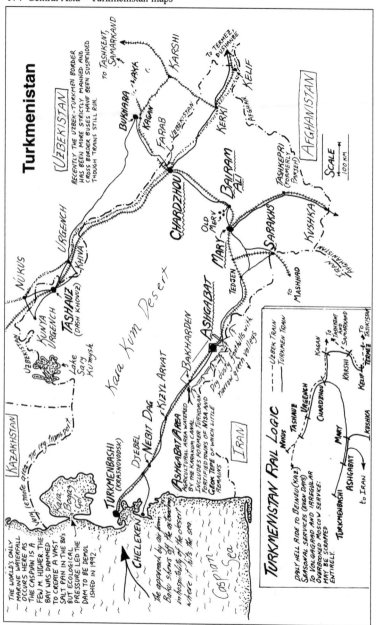

Turkmenistan

[UZBEKISTAN]

RECENTLY THE UZBEK-TURKMEN BORDER
HAS BEEN MORE STRICTLY MANNED AND
CROSS BORDER BUSES HAVE BEEN SUSPENDED
THOUGH TRAINS STILL RUN.

to TASHKENT, SAMARKAND

NAYA

KARSHI

To TERMEZ, DUSHANBE

BUKHARA

KAGAN

FARAB

UZBEKISTAN

KERKI

KELIF

AFGHAN R.

[AFGHANISTAN]

SCALE
100 KM

URGENCH

KHIVA

CHARDZHOU

BAIRAM ALI

TASHKEPRI (FORMERLY PANDEI)

NUKUS

TASHAUZ
(DASH KHOVUZ)

Old MERV

MARY

SARAKHS

KUSHKA

IRAN
TURKMENISTAN

KUNYA URGENCH

UZBEKISTAN

Lake Sary Kumysh

Kara Kum Desert

TEDJEN

to MASHHAD

to TAJIKISTAN

[KAZAKHSTAN]

very remote area – no reg. transport

ASHGABAT

BAKHARDEN

Day dusty foothills with
narrow green valleys

KIZYL ARVAT

NEBIT DAG

DJEBEL

ASHGABAT AREA
AGRICULTURAL AREA WATERED
BY THE KARAKUM CANAL
INCLUDES FORMER TURKOMAN
FORTIFIED TOWNS OF NISA AND
GEOK TEPE OF WHICH LITTLE
REMAINS

IRAN

TURKMENBASHI
(KRASNOVODSK)

Kara
Bogaz
Gol

CHELEKEN

The approach by air from
Baku shows off the astonishing
inhospitality of the desert
where it hits the sea.

Caspian Sea

THE WORLD'S ONLY
MARINE WATERFALL
OCCURS HERE AS
THE CASPIAN IS A
FEW M. HIGHER. THE
BAY WAS DAMMED
TO CREATE A VAST
SALT PAN IN THE 80'S
BUT ECOLOGICAL
PRESSURE LED THE
DAM TO BE DEMOL-
ISHED IN 1992.

TURKMENISTAN RAIL LOGIC

– – – – Uzbek Train
━━━━━ Turkmen Train

NNOS

TASHUIE

URGENCH

CHARDZHOU

KAGAN

To
TASHKENT
AND
SAMARKAND

KARSHI

KELIF

To
TERMEZ
TAJIKISTAN

MARY

KUSHKA

TURKMENBASHI

ASHGABAT

to IRAN

DAILY HELL RIDE TO BEINEU (KAZ)
SEASONAL SERVICES (EVEN DAYS)
TO VOLGAGRAD AND IRREGULAR
OVERBOOKED MOSCOW SERVICE
MAY BE SCRAPED
ENTIRELY.

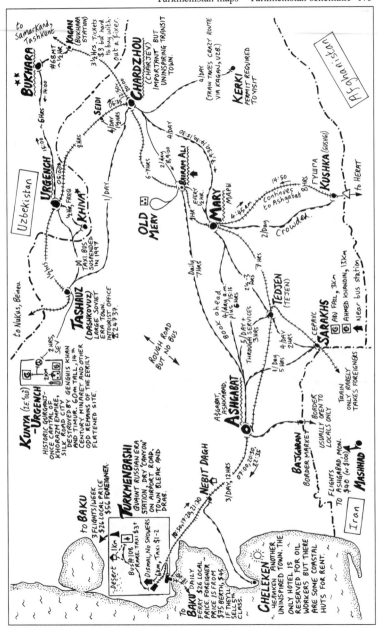

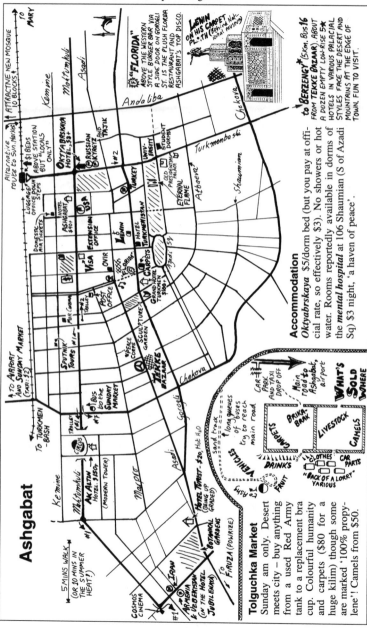

Ashgabat

"FLORIDA" ABOVE THE WESTERN STYLE BURGER BAR VIA A SIDE DOOR ON KOROGLI ST. IS THE PLUSH FLORIDA RESTAURANT AND ASHGABAT'S TOP DISCO.

LENIN ON HIS CARPET PLINTH (Political and National Musings)

to **BERZENGI★** (5km, BUS 16 FROM TEKKE BAZAAR.) ABOUT A DOZEN EMPTY LOW-RISE 5★ HOTELS IN VARIOUS PALACIAL STYLES FACE THE DESERT AND MOUNTAINS AT THE EDGE OF TOWN. FUN TO VISIT.

Accommodation

Oktyabrskaya $5/dorm bed (but you pay at official rate, so effectively $3). No showers or hot water. Rooms reportedly available in dorms of the *mental hospital* at 106 Shaumian (S of Azadi Sq) $3 night, 'a haven of peace'.

Tolguchka Market

Sunday am only. Desert meets city – buy anything from a used Red Army tank to a replacement bra cup. Colourful humanity and carpets ($80 for a huge kilim) though some are marked '100% propylene'! Camels from $50.

What's Sold Where

CAMELS · BRIKA BRAK · LIVESTOCK · CAMELS

DRINKS · CLOTHES · CAR PARTS

"BACK OF A LORRY" VARIOUS · FRUIT · VEHICLES

CAR PARK AND TAXI DROP OFF

Main road to Ashgabat, airport

long queues of buses try to reach main road

Sand track (being up graded)

to ASHG.

Around Ashgabat

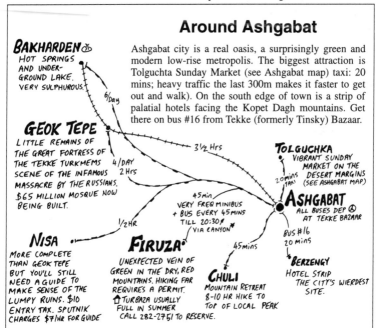

Ashgabat city is a real oasis, a surprisingly green and modern low-rise metropolis. The biggest attraction is Tolguchta Sunday Market (see Ashgabat map) taxi: 20 mins; heavy traffic the last 300m makes it faster to get out and walk). On the south edge of town is a strip of palatial hotels facing the Kopet Dagh mountains. Get there on bus #16 from Tekke (formerly Tinsky) Bazaar.

BAKHARDEN
HOT SPRINGS AND UNDER-GROUND LAKE. VERY SULPHUROUS.

6/DAY

GEOK TEPE
LITTLE REMAINS OF THE GREAT FORTRESS OF THE TEKKE TURKMEMS
SCENE OF THE INFAMOUS MASSACRE BY THE RUSSIANS. $65 MILLION MOSQUE NOW BEING BUILT.

4/DAY
2 HRS

3½ Hrs

TOLGUCHKA
VIBRANT SUNDAY MARKET ON THE DESERT MARGINS (SEE ASHGABAT MAP)
20 mins TAXI

45min
VERY FREQ MINIBUS + BUS EVERY 45 MINS TILL 20:30 VIA CANYON

ASHGABAT
ALL BUSES DEP AT TEKKE BAZAAR

½HR

NISA
MORE COMPLETE THAN GEOK TEPE BUT YOU'LL STILL NEED A GUIDE TO MAKE SENSE OF THE LUMPY RUINS. $10 ENTRY TAX. SPUTNIK CHARGES $7/HR FOR GUIDE

FIRUZA
UNEXPECTED VEIN OF GREEN IN THE DRY, RED MOUNTAINS. HIKING FAR REQUIRES A PERMIT.
TURBAZA USUALLY FULL IN SUMMER CALL 282-2751 TO RESERVE.

CHULI
MOUNTAIN RETREAT 8-10 HR HIKE TO TOP OF LOCAL PEAK

45mins

BUS #16
20 mins

BERZENGY
HOTEL STRIP THE CITY'S WIERDEST SITE.

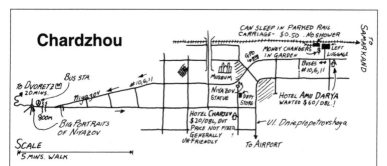

Chardzhou

CAN SLEEP IN PARKED RAIL CARRIAGE - $0.50. No SHOWER

TO SAMARKAND

MONEY CHANGERS IN GARDEN

GPO

LEFT LUGGAGE

BUSES #10,6,11

Bus STA.

To Dvoretz 2
20 mins.

Niyazov

#10,6,11

MUSEUM

NIYAZOV STATUE

DEPT STORE

HOTEL AMU DARYA
WANTED $60/DBL !

HOTEL CHARJEV $20/DBL. BUT PRICE NOT FIXED. GENERALLY UN-FRIENDLY

Ul. Dniepropetrovskaya

800m

BIG PORTRAITS OF NIYAZOV

To AIRPORT

SCALE
5 MINS. WALK

There's little reason to visit Chardzhou but bus and train schedules are such that you're likely to be stranded here for at least half a day. One time-killing suggestion is to take the #6 or #10 bus 11 stops beyond the bus station to Gala Castle (mud ramparts with a view over the mediocrity of the Chardzhou Soviet cityscape) and Dvortz Palace (less attractive than your average cinema).

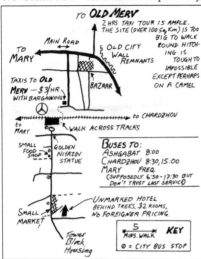

Bairam Ali

Bairam Ali is a modern limpit town clinging to the southern most wall remnants of old Merv – an ancient Silk Route centre and once one of the world's largest cities. Taxis to Merv charge by the hour for tours (2 hours should be sufficient). Ask for Sultan Sanjar (the one remaining large 12th century mausoleum) and Kys Kala (mud walls of the old castle). View the entire scene from the hillock at Iskanderkala and wonder how a city of over a million people could have ever existed on those piles of lifeless mud.

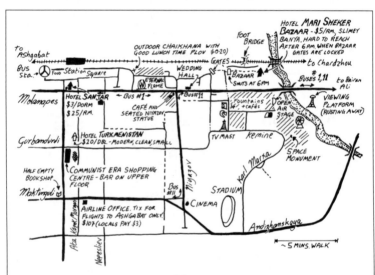

Mary

Mary is usually touted as the staging point for visits to Bairam Ali/Old Merv, yet Bairam Ali itself has a cheaper and better hotel (though rather inconveniently located). If coming from Afghanistan, you could break the train ride from Kushka here and take a side trip to Bairam Ali.

Uzbekistan

Uzbekistan is the hub of Central Asia. It contains all the major cultural centres including the three greatest Silk Route survivors: Bukhara, Samarkand and Khiva. No visit to the region would be complete without a peep at Samarkand's Registan – Central Asia's 'Taj Mahal'. Uzbekistan also has lesser known ruins scattered amongst its scrubby, flat, wilting cotton fields, and an eastern shoulder of attractive, accessible mountains.

The post-Soviet regime is the pre-Soviet one in a new *doppi*. It has taken a middle line between the authoritarianism of Turkmenistan and the liberal free market openness of Kyrgyzstan. While foreign investment has been encouraged (notably the Korean Daewoo company), a strong authoritarian streak remains and there's a tight muzzle on political opposition. There's no sign of open discontent, and the firm hand has so far 'prevented' a Tajik-style civil war. However, even as a traveller, one senses a quietly oppressive atmosphere. Encounters with the police are nerve-rackingly unpredictable; officers may be delightfully helpful one minute, then confiscate your dollars the next. As yet, the Soviet-thinking government is not quite prepared to let tourists wander at will. Rules can change suddenly, as the government periodically re-thinks how to make the fastest profit from its tourist potential. Yet perversely, the KGB-shadowed conspiratorial edge of being an independent traveller here adds to the intensity of a visit to this memorable land.

❏ **W&M's country ratings – Uzbekistan**
● **Expense $$$** Day to day prices have risen steeply in recent years. Foreigner pricing on hotels remains, but travelling on US$8-10 per person a day is possible.
● **Value for money ✔✔** The hotels are government-run but the quality of the food is improving with more private enterprise.
● **Getting around ✔✔✔** Higher prices mean fewer crowds, bus services are extensive and generally at least daily.
● **Woman alone ✔✔✔** More male oriented than Kazakhstan or Kyrgyzstan, some hassles to be expected.

PRACTICAL INFORMATION
Visas and formalities
● **Visa strategy** Uzbekistan knows it has enormous tourist potential yet it is an oppressive police state whose instinct is to retain the rigid old Soviet visa rules. The official position is that you must have an invitation or pre-booked tour before a visa will be issued. If you go through a travel agent the necessary paperwork will be handled for you. Raisa Gareyeva, a Bukharan travel agent (Bukhara ☎ 37277, e-mail raisa@salom.bukhara.silk.org), can arrange an invitation letter for $15.

A few Uzbek embassies issue tourist visas outright without any special or expensive requirements. The embassies in Almaty (Kazakhstan) and, a little less reliable, Ashgabat (Turkmenistan) are the best bets. This is fortunate because your overland travel to Uzbekistan could probably include one of these places without much inconvenience. Some other consulates (such as Istanbul) twist the pre-booking regulations by accepting meaningless tourist vouchers. Tourist vouchers are supposed to be proof of the pre-payment of hotel accommodation but entrepreneurial agents, notably Sunpak Travels, have come up with 'formality vouchers'. These are pieces of paper that satisfy the ridiculous visa regulations while offering you nothing at all when you arrive – compare the prices with that of a real tour.

Basic visa fees (excluding the voucher and sundry fees) are $40 for a week, $50/2 weeks, $60/1 month.

In Ashgabat, Turkmenistan it is possible to pay double the fee and receive the visa next day – if the consul's in a good mood. Everywhere else you'll wait at least a week. Allow up to three weeks if you need vouchers. Changing the entry and exit dates is not usually possible.

Most foreign nationals are permitted to venture only within a 30km radius of the towns listed on their visas (and on the roads between them). A Canadian went to OVIR at Tashkent Airport to ask whether his CIS visa (a Russian visa with Tashkent listed as a possible destination) would be valid for Samarkand. 'Nyet' said the immigration officer. The Canadian was charged $30 for the Samarkand endorsement plus

---

❑ Geo-political information – Uzbekistan

Population: 23m (1997), 21m (1991), 13.7m (1970), 9.2m (1960).

Area: 447,000 sq km (slightly larger than California).

Capital: Tashkent (2.1 million, 1990).

Other major cities: Samarkand (370,000), Namangan, Andizhan (300,000), Bukhara (230,000).

GNP per capita: $2650 (1994), $2720 (1988).

Currency history: Cym/US$1 – Feb 1998: 81.3cym, Oct 1997: 75.3cym (160cym on the black market), July 95: 31cym (28cym on the black market – bizarrely less than the bank rate). Introduced in July 1994 at initial rate $1=7cym (35cym) replacing the cym coupon (which was then 35,000cym=$1).

Major exports/economy: Cotton, gas and oil, uranium, gold.

Ethnic mix: Uzbek (71%), Russian (8% and falling), Tajik (5%), Kazakh (4%), Tatar (2%), Karakalpak (2%), Armenians (1%). 80% of the once famous Bukharan Jews have now emigrated to the USA or Israel.

Official languages: Uzbek (74%) official. Also spoken: Russian (14%), Tajik (5% – significant in Samarkand and Bukhara).

Religious mix: Muslim (mainly Sunni) (88%), Eastern Orthodox Christian (9%).

Historical background: Despite the long and complex history of the Khanates (Bukhara, Khiva, Khorazm, Kokand) that have come and gone, Uzbekistan is a new idea, created in 1924 by the Bolsheviks. Initially including Tajikistan, and still hanging on to little known Karakalpakstan, Uzbekistan was famous for corruption in the Soviet era sending Russia cotton in quantities significantly below the quota for which the republic had been paid.

Leader(s): President Islam Karimov since 1983 confirmed by 86% (rigged?) vote after independence. His term has been extended till 2000 by an unanimous referendum (99.6% of a 99.3% turnout). The Popular Democratic Party is just the Communist Party renamed.

Pressing political issues: Aral Sea depletion and resultant health problems, reduced cotton crops and loss of fishing. Fear of Islamic fundamentalism led to the closure of Tajik language schools, the continued ban on many opposition groups and reports of torture. Tashkent is bidding for the 2008 Olympic games.

$70 for a hotel voucher giving him one night in a double room at the Hotel Samarkand.

In theory, visas (but not transit visas) issued to British, French, German and US citizens are valid for the whole country. An American, travelling with the Canadian mentioned above, was told she didn't have to pay extra to go to Samarkand. However, the visa rules are unknown to the majority of police in Uzbekistan, especially in rural areas. We met two French and one German who were fined and sent back to Tashkent for being in a city not listed on their visas (even though their visas clearly stated validity for the whole country).

We strongly recommend that travellers to Uzbekistan have all the towns they plan to visit listed, even if the consulate insists it isn't necessary. Getting this done can take some persuasion. When we applied in

Almaty, we tried listing every town on our Uzbekistan map. The consul refused to write them all down citing lack of space, but after a good deal of begging and pleading he managed to find space for eight.

And what happens if you go to a town not listed on your visa? Some officials don't seem to care much. Others – such as one OVIR agent on the road from Samarkand to Shakrisabz – have turned travellers away altogether. Hotels have been known to refuse guests without the correct town names, even if they are from an exempted nation.

One traveller took the precaution of typing the names of all the Uzbek towns and cities he knew onto a computer. He printed and miniaturised the list and stapled a copy into his passport opposite the Uzbek visa. He never claimed the list was officially endorsed, but the police that he

---

❑ Essential information for travellers – Uzbekistan

● **Visa** Required; an invitation is usually (though not always) needed. Going to Tashkent is possible on the Visa Shuffle but visiting other towns may result in some problems or small fines.

● **Currency** Cym (pronounced 'sum'). US$1=81.3cym (official), up to 160cym (black market).

● **Time zone** 5 hours ahead of GMT (same as Kyrgyzstan; 1hr behind Almaty).

● **Religious tone** More devoutly Muslim than neighbouring Kyrgyzstan or Kazakhstan, partly as a statement of national identity.

● **Social conventions** In Bukhara it is an insult for hosts to clean their house for three days after a guest leaves – otherwise they are indicating that they want to eliminate the memories of the guest's stay. The right hand held across the chest can show respect, or it can mean 'peace' (having a similar effect to 'shanti' in India).

● **Typical traveller destinations** Samarkand, Bukhara, Tashkent.

● **Highlights** Bukhara's atmospheric old town and tea pool; Khiva; Samarkand's spectacular Registan, blue domed mausolea and riverside tea houses.

● **When to go** The best time to visit is September – warm days, chilly evenings and some clear, brilliant blue skies. Winter temperatures can drop below zero on occasions but it may feel much worse due to the lack of efficient heating. Midsummer is stiflingly hot, though taking things slowly one need not rule out a trip at this time. The nearby Kyrgyz mountains make a handy escape from the dusty unpleasantness of the Fergana Valley summers.

● **Pulse of the country** Andizhan market, sipping tea at the Lyab-I-Khauz pool in Bukhara, picking cotton at sunset with a gang of conscripted students in the Fergana valley.

● **Key tip** Ask the consul to list all the cities that you might want to visit on your Uzbek visa (see box overleaf for suggested list); even if you are assured your visa is valid for all of Uzbekistan, it possibly isn't.

encountered seemed mollified by its presence despite the fact that it was typed in English!

● **Visa shuffle** Crossing Uzbekistan on the visa shuffle is more problematic than it is in any other shuffle signatory for two reasons: Firstly, corrupt and ignorant police. They make the experience quite uncomfortable, and potentially expensive if you succumb to their sometimes very intimidating threats of prison and requests for presents. I was locked for over an hour in the provodnik's cabin on a train to Samarkand; my belongings were double and triple searched. They finally released me having decided that I really was as mad as I seemed (I had been smiling, joking and happily bluffing that I would gladly go to jail for the nebulous crimes I hadn't committed). Secondly, you may also have difficulties getting hotel rooms without a real visa.

Both Tashkent airport (regularly) and Samarkand railway station (sometimes) are plagued by OVIR tourist police agents who impose $20 fines on those arriving without genuine Uzbek visas. We were fined despite having valid visa shuffle visas (if you don't have any CIS visas at all you've got real problems – see At the border, below). If this happens to you, don't immediately get angry as they may simply be 'registering' you. Check their identity; the real tourist police usually speak fairly reasonable English and should be able to explain what is happening and will give a receipt. If you want to stay more than the legal three days on the shuffle try to avoid getting registered until you're nearly ready

to leave. Keep an eye on the map for where you might have recently arrived from, in case you're questioned.

Official policy seems to demand that your visa shuffle transit be via Tashkent, without getting off the train or bus at any other point. Yet Tashkent is the most unpleasant place for police spot checks so avoiding it can be both sensible and desirable, especially when you're going between Samarkand and southern Kyrgyzstan/China. About half the travellers we met who have taken this route have been fined, but none more than the standard $20. However, we have also met at least two travellers who crossed Uzbekistan (three and five days respectively) using Kyrgyz visas without encountering any problems.

Some Kyrgyz bus routes pass through chunks of Uzbek territory on domestic routes, this is no problem on the shuffle.

At the border

We met a mild-mannered history professor who was refused entry because he arrived at Tashkent airport without any form of CIS visa. (He was deported to Almaty.) Many other travellers have reported scams, extortion and randomly enforced new rules being dreamed up on their arrival and departure from Tashkent airport. The moral is to have at least one CIS visa shuffle visa before arriving. Even then you may have to buy expensive vouchers before being allowed in.

Entering by land you will probably not meet a border guard, but don't lose the customs declaration form that you got when

---

❑ **Useful towns to have listed on an Uzbek visa**
● Tashkent, Samarkand and Bukhara (main cities).
● Khiva (Urgench on your visa allows a daytrip but not a stay in Khiva's great Orkanchi Hotel).
● Shakrisabz (if you want more than a day trip from Samarkand).
● Angren (in case you try the mountain route Tashkent-Fergana).
● Termez (for the Afghan border).
● Munyak and Nukus (if you want to see the Aral Sea ship-graveyard).
● Andizhan (generally accepted for the rest of the Fergana Valley but you might also ask for Namangan if you're heading to Sary Chelek in Kyrgyzstan).

first entering the CIS. Its loss is taken very seriously, especially if you fly out of Tashkent airport.

● **Registration** You are required to register your address with OVIR at least once during your stay in Uzbekistan; until you have done so there will be a constant cat and mouse game to play with OVIR and potential fines to pay. Bigger hotels will register for you and should give you a slip of paper to prove it (though you may have to nag). However, if you stay with people you meet, you're meant to register this with OVIR too. This registration can be a time consuming process (we heard up to two weeks!). Private citizens who rent you rooms or apartments do so semi-legally so they don't want you doing this anyway. Ensure that for at least one night you do have an official registration, especially if you're flying out of Tashkent airport where they take every rule very seriously. Leaving overland, however, there were no checks so we were never asked to show registration documents. Registration fees are from $20 for up to one month's stay ($40 for two months, $60 for three).

Registration of your proposed destination is also necessary when you wish to buy long distance bus or train tickets out of Tashkent. This rule doesn't seem to apply in any other cities (except irregularly in Andizhan). The registration process is easy as long as your visa is in order, but it will add an extra 10 to 30 minutes to the time needed to buy tickets. If you haven't registered with any hotel they may question you as to where you've been staying – we claimed we'd just arrived from Kazakhstan when in fact we'd been in town for several days. The OVIR officers we encountered were friendly, spoke English and were very helpful, even offering to assist us at the chaotic ticket windows in the bus station.

Money

On each visit to Uzbekistan the exchange situation has changed considerably. In 1994 the first currency (the cym coupon) had us juggling zeros. In July, the beautiful new cym banknotes appeared. By September the black market was offering almost a 50% saving though only with fairly intense bargaining. On our next visit in

---

❑ Sleeping with a stranger

I arrived in Kokand at 2am. The plov I'd wolfed down in Samarkand must have been suspect and I found myself a bilious wreck, unceremoniously dumped off the bus in the station forecourt. Two Uzbek travel companions, with whom I seemed to have had a long conversation despite the lack of a mutual language, were keen to drag me on to Namangan on a bus which they assured me would be coming along even at such a late hour. But I felt too weak and collapsed onto my bedroll, intending to sleep where I was.

Rustani, one of the night's last cigarette vendors, was packing up his pitiful stalls, while his jolly wife Afir in pinafores, scarves and aprons, had almost emptied her stainless steel buckets of soggy old *piroshkis* (doughnut-style fried snacks with a smear of savoury filling). They gathered around the strange sight of the collapsed Westerner and within seconds I was being led across the tracks to the couple's home.

Like most older Uzbek homes it was based around a courtyard filled with vines, fruit trees and a vegetable plot. I soon discovered that this couple were living on the bread line, renting one inside room in return for assistance to the invalid owner. Their bed which doubled as a dining table, and was rapidly set with cloth and cushions, bread, fruit and vodka to welcome me, sat outside gazing up at a sea of stars. Forcing food into my tired, sick body was an effort but somehow the situation allowed no refusal. As the evening wore on Afir disappeared and her space on the bed beside her husband was mine for the night. To sleep.

1995, banking reforms had wiped out the black market altogether and banks were prepared to re-convert cym. However by January 1997 dual rates had been introduced and the black market was offering almost double the foreigner' rate. Ask other travellers for the most recent rates before you exchange. Relative security and some of the best rates are offered by small, non tourist-orientated shops (such as the food stands near Samarkand bus station). Beware of the dodgy looking touts that hiss improbable rates at you in the tourist areas.

Travellers' cheques can be cashed for cym at the National Bank for Foreign Economic Activity, Tashkent, or at its branches in nine other cities. In Termez the bank is on Al Termezi 7.

Credit card cash advances are possible at the Hotel Uzbekistan in Tashkent and at the National Bank of Uzbekistan (5% fee).

Banks are open Monday to Friday, 10am-12 noon.

Transport

● **Bus** Bus prices have risen sharply but this has made the queues for the ticket windows much shorter. Booking a day ahead is possible from special windows in bigger bus stations.

Inspectors have cracked down on overloading with spot checks on buses leaving the bus stations. However, surplus passengers often arrange a place where the driver picks them up a few minutes later; these are worth knowing about if you have to get aboard a full bus and are prepared to stand. Ticket sellers at the Tashkent bus station require you to register your destination with OVIR in an office which is up the stairs to the left of the ticket windows (see Registration above). If the office is closed, you may have to get a local to buy your ticket for you. Despite the procedure the bus tickets do not cost more for foreigners.

● **Train** Fares are extremely reasonable; a Tashkent to Moscow (3400km) ticket costs about $50. There is a special foreigners' ticket window in Tashkent in a building altogether separate from the station (see the map). Travellers report that the $20 foreigner booking fee is to be withdrawn – this had made rail travel extremely expensive for short domestic hops.

● **Air** Flights have foreigner pricing and the airport tax is US$10.

Accommodation

Foreigner pricing exists in the hotels that you are allowed to use, though in some cases bargaining is possible. When you check in, your passport will usually be held or at least examined by wary staff. Foreigners need to be officially registered, and since many cheaper hotels simply do not have the facility to do this they refuse foreigners a room. You could try disguising yourself and your passport – stationery shops sell cheap Soviet-era plastic passport covers making it possible for yours to be mistaken for a local one. If you can look and behave Russian and the clerk is lax enough not to open the passport (this is rare as they should fill in the details in the ledger) then you just might sneak in, as we did once in Samarkand. But don't count on it.

❏ Registan

The minarets of Samarkand's Registan are a cross between overgrown classic pillars and squat, gentrified, medieval smokestacks turned artistic masterpiece by the vivid blue-tiled mosaics that are Samarkand's trademark. The purpose of the minarets was to 'hold up the sky' rather than to broadcast a call to prayer, but one tower does retain its staircase. A sign at the door declares that entry is forbidden. Trespassers will be fined 150cym. The policeman on guard beckoned us over and asked if we wanted to go up. 'Are we allowed?' we asked surprised. 'Nyet' he grunted, 'Not allowed. But fine is very small. You can pay it to me first.' He pocketed the cash and bundled us in.

● **B&Bs** Realising the great tourist potential of the Silk Road cities, a few registered private bed and breakfast style mini-hotels have opened recently, often as part of a traditional Uzbek home. Where these exist (eg **Mubinjon** and **Sasha and Lena's** in Bukhara, and *'Hotel' Orkhanchi* Khiva) they tend to be great value for money, even if not the cheapest option available – from $10 full board at the latter (you can bargain if they're not full).

● **Private apartments/rooms** In Samarkand we were offered an apartment in a grey suburban towerblock for $3 per night per person. From the furtive way we were smuggled in and out this hardly seems to be a legal option. We were accommodated by hospitable locals in several places. Bedding down on railway waiting room floors proved possible at Tashkent and Urgench but not so in Samarkand or Bukhara.

Shopping

The *cholpan*, a heavy dressing-gown-like robe distinctive to Bukhara, makes a cheap (from $5, hand made), warm and very colourful if bulky souvenir. Carpets are great value, but theoretically incur a 100% export duty – keep the receipt or else you'll have to have it valued at the **Ministry of Culture** (17 Pushkin St, Tashkent). Also beware that antiques may not be legally exported and by Uzbekistan's definition anything pre-1945 is an antique. If you leave by train to Kazakhstan you probably won't have to pay duty as there are no customs checks.

Staying in touch

● **Mail** Postal rates have been increased in recent years and are not a particular bargain. Packages should be sent registered since delivery is not reliable, though this does not seem to be a common practice –

❏ **Meeting the locals**

● **The people** Uzbekistan has a great tea-house culture. Old men (rarely women, though foreign females become honorary men) sit in fly-blown chaikhanas for hours at a time, discussing philosophy and politics, and reminiscing, like pensioners everywhere, about the good old days. You'll see more than a few old boys sporting a breast-full of Soviet army medals.

In a true tea house, patrons lounge on tea beds; carpet-decked bed frames topped in the centre with a squat table for the battered teapots and plates of *plov*. Traditional homes use similar bed frames, though without the table, and at night many sleep on them. Eating on the teabed (or indeed anywhere) comes with a certain etiquette: don't walk cross the central area (creep behind those who are already seated); pass tea with the right hand; you should also receive the cup with your right hand, placing your left hand over your heart to show gratitude; begin and end any formal meal by drawing your hands across your face – watch your hosts; address men by the formal Uzbek *dishanob* and women *chonim*.

● **Language**

Some phrases in Uzbek:
Typical Muslim greeting – *salaam elekum*
Reply – *elekum a-salaam*
Hi – *salam*
Thank you very much – *katta rakhmat*
How are you? – *ishlaringé Khalai?*
Reply – *yakhshi* (literally, 'good')
Beautiful – *chivoli*
Delicious – *bamaza* (literally 'there is taste')
How much does it cost? – *kanja pul?*

UZBEK ROMANIZATION

Similar to the Kazakh system there is a marked fondness for **q** ="k" and **x**="kh". More confusingly there is a "vowel shift": notably **o** is usually pronounced "a". E.G. in Uzbek, Tashkent is spelt **TOSHKENT** (or TOSKENT) Fergana is **FARGONA**.

Tajik (rather than Uzbek) is spoken by many in Samarkand and Bukhara.

a package we sent to Japan from Khiva was number 000001 ($3 for 400g).

● **Faxes** These can be sent from the business centre in Hotel Uzbekistan, Tashkent ($5/page) or from Hotel Tashkent ($7/page). In Samarkand faxes can be sent from the expensive ($16/page!) and usually closed private booth on the street corner beside the public telephone office.

● **Telephone** Calls abroad are cheapest from public telephone offices though you have to wait for the call to be connected and leave a deposit. $2/min to the UK, $2.70 to the USA. A three-minute minimum fee is sometimes demanded but was waived when we complained.

Dial 8, wait for a tone, then dial 10 to place an international call. International country code: +7. Bukhara: 36522; Samarkand: 3662; Tashkent: 3712; Urgench: 36222.

Activities

Expats run the Tashkent Hash (Sunday afternoons, starting from Hotel Uzbekistan's car park) and play soccer (Saturday or Wednesday afternoons – call the UK embassy ☎ 533685). Horse-riding is possible at Tashkent hippodrome, and skiing in the Chimgon Mountains – though it is difficult to get skis that fit and bindings that aren't broken. Swimming and windsurfing are popular on the Chirvak reservoir, and the Pskem and Chatkal valleys are great for hiking and white-water rafting.

Further information

● **Books** Odyssey publishes a very thorough Uzbekistan guide. Uzbek novels include Abdullah Khodiri's *Passed Days* and Melgrob Danchen Chaiyon's *Scorpion from the Mehrab* (the mehrab shows Muslims the direction of Mecca for prayer, and the book is something of a satirical piece on the role of Islam).

● **Maps** Detailed Tashkent street maps and large sheet maps of the country are available from a shop near Tashkent's Chorsu market, and from some hotels and bookshops. Excellent city maps of Samarkand are sold from the small souvenir stand inside the Registan's central (Tilla Kari) madrassa, and increasingly from other bookshops. Maps of Bukhara vary wildly in quality; the best has the maze of old town streets marked reasonably accurately, while others leave a shaded patch with only a few main routes.

TIMUR

CENTRAL TASHKENT

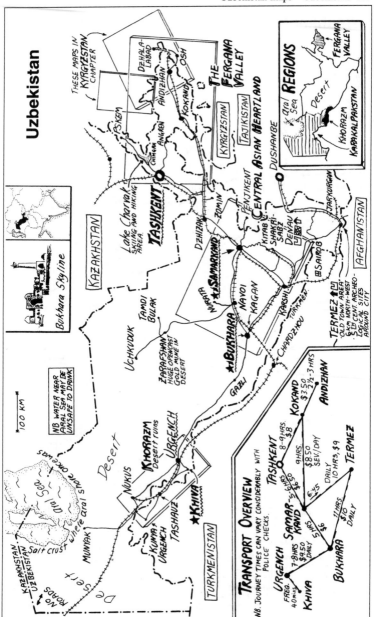

Uzbekistan

Tashkent

This historic Silk Route city was flattened by a 1966 quake – few antiquities remain, even in the 'old city'. The gardens around Timur's statue are the pleasant focus of the modern Tashkent, though there are few specific attractions. Maps available at Chorsu Market.

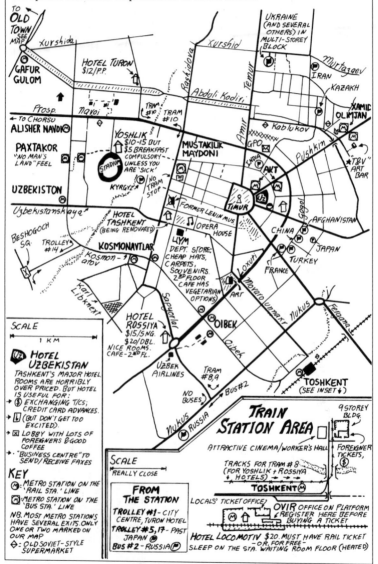

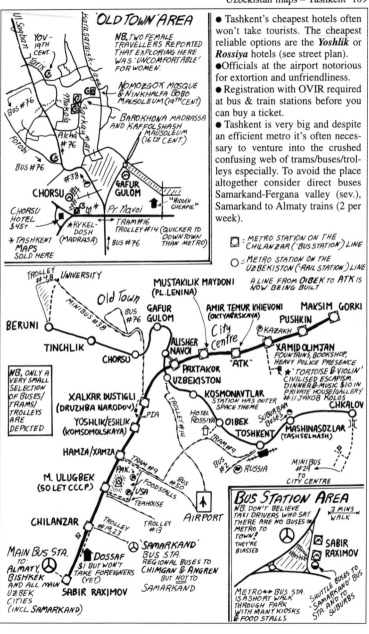

- Tashkent's cheapest hotels often won't take tourists. The cheapest reliable options are the *Yoshlik* or *Rossiya* hotels (see street plan).
- Officials at the airport notorious for extortion and unfriendliness.
- Registration with OVIR required at bus & train stations before you can buy a ticket.
- Tashkent is very big and despite an efficient metro it's often necessary to venture into the crushed confusing web of trams/buses/trolleys especially. To avoid the place altogether consider direct buses Samarkand-Fergana valley (sev.), Samarkand to Almaty trains (2 per week).

'OLD TOWN' AREA

Ulsabah
YOV- 19TH CENT.

NB. TWO FEMALE TRAVELLERS REPORTED THAT EXPLORING HERE WAS 'UNCOMFORTABLE' FOR WOMEN.

BUS #76

NOMOZGOX MOSQUE & NINKHALFA BOBO MAUSOLEUM (19TH CENT.)

Masala

Alcha #76

BAROKHONA MADRASSA AND KAFFOL SHASH MAUSOLEUM (16TH CENT.)

Foroh

BUS #76

#38

GAFUR GULOM

CHORSU

Pr. Navoi

"HIDDEN CHEAPIE"

CHORSU HOTEL $45+

★KYKEL-DOSH (MADRASA)

TRAM #16 TROLLEY #14 (QUICKER TO DOWNTOWN THAN METRO)

BUS #76

★ TASHKENT MAPS SOLD HERE

☐ = METRO STATION ON THE CHILANZAR ('BUS STATION') LINE

○ = METRO STATION ON THE UZBEKISTON ('RAIL STATION') LINE

A LINE FROM OIBEK TO ATK IS NOW BEING BUILT

TROLLEY #18 UNIVERSITY

Old Town

MINIBUS #38

MUSTAKILIK MAYDONI (PL. LENINA)

GAFUR GULOM

AMIR TEMUR KHIEVONI (OKTYABRSKAYA)

MAKSIM GORKI

PUSHKIN

BERUNI

BUS #76

City Centre

KAZAKH

TINCHLIK

ALISHER NAVOI

"ATK"

XAMID OLIMJAN

CHORSU

FOUNTAINS, BOOKSHOP, HEAVY POLICE PRESENCE

PAXTAKOR

★ 'TORTOISE & VIOLIN' CIVILISED ESCAPISM. DINNER & MUSIC $10 IN PRIVATE HOUSE/GALLERY #11 JAKOB KOLOS

UZBEKISTON

NB, ONLY A VERY SMALL SELECTION OF BUSES/ TRAMS/ TROLLEYS ARE DEPICTED

XALKAR DUSTIGLI (DRUZHBA NARODOV)

KOSMONAVTLAR STATION HAS OUTER SPACE THEME

CHKALOV

PIA

TROLLEY #14

YOSHLIK/ESHLIK (KOMSOMOLSKAYA)

HOTEL ROSSIYA

OIBEK

SUBURBAN BUSES

MASHINASOZLAR (TASHSELMASH)

HAMZA/XAMZA

TOSHKENT

TRAM #9

TRAM #9

BUS #2

RUSSIA

M. ULUGBEK (50 LET CCCP)

PAK.

BUS #50

MINIBUS #29 TO CITY CENTRE

FOODSTALLS

USA

TEAHOUSE

AIRPORT

CHILANZAR

TROLLEY #19,23

TROLLEY #13

DOSSAF $1 BUT WON'T TAKE FOREIGNERS (YET)

'SAMARKAND' BUS STA. REGIONAL BUSES TO CHIMGAN & ANGREN BUT NOT TO SAMARKAND

MAIN BUS STA. TO: ALMATY, BISHKEK AND ALL MAIN UZBEK CITIES (INCL. SAMARKAND)

SABIR RAXIMOV

BUS STATION AREA

NB. DON'T BELIEVE TAXI DRIVERS WHO SAY THERE ARE NO BUSES OR METRO TO TOWN! THEY'RE BIASSED

3 MINS WALK

SABIR RAXIMOV

METRO ↔ BUS STA. IS A SHORT WALK THROUGH PARK WITH MANY KIOSKS & FOOD STALLS

SHUTTLE BUSES TO 'SAMARKAND' BUS STA. AND TO SUBURBS

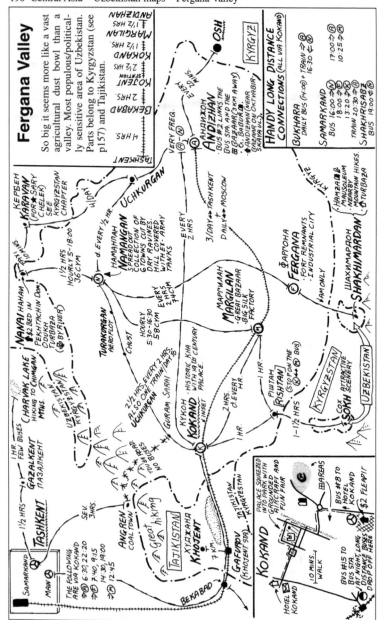

Fergana Valley

So big it seems more like a vast agricultural dust bowl than a valley. Most populous/politically sensitive area of Uzbekistan. Parts belong to Kyrgyzstan (see p157) and Tajikistan.

HANDY LONG DISTANCE CONNECTIONS (ALL VIA KOKAND)

BUKHARA DAILY BUS (14-00) + TRAIN ⇒Ⓑ 16:30

SAMARKAND
BUS 16:00 ⇒Ⓝ   17:00→Ⓑ
18:00 ⇒Ⓔ   10:25 →Ⓝ
13:20 →Ⓑ
TRAIN 20:30 ⇒Ⓑ

SHAKHRISABZ BUS 14:00 ⇒Ⓔ

KYRGYZ

OSH

ANDIZHAN · BUS #2 LINKS THE BUS STA. AND THE BAZAAR (3KM AWAY) Cs. BAGIR ♦ ANDIZHAN (NEAR BAZAAR ON OKTYABIR SKAYA VL.)

ANDIZHAN
MARGILAN 1½ HRS
KOKAND 2½ HRS
KOSTENT STATION
BEKABAD 2 HRS
1 HRS
TASHKENT

VERY FREQ. Ⓑ→Ⓝ

EVERY ½ HR. ⇄TASHKENT

d. EVERY ½ HR.

KEPSEH KARAVAN (FOR SARY CHELEK) SEE KYRGYZSTAN CHAPTER

UCHKURGAN

HAMAHAH 1½ HRS HOURLY 5-18:00 36CYM

NAMANGAN SO MODERN
COLLECTION OF
CTOWNS CUT BY
DRY RAVINES.
HILL COVERED
WITH EX-ARMY
TANKS

3/DAY ⇄TASHKENT
DAILY ⇄ MOSCOW

EVERY
2 HRS

NANAI HAHAM
2 BED IN
PEKHTACHIN DOM
ODUKH
TURBAZA
(Ⓑ BY RIVER)

CHARVAK LAKE HIKING TO CHIMGAN MTNS.

UZBEKISTAN
KYRGYZSTAN

1 HR.
FEW BUSES

GAZALKENT
ГАЗАЛКЕНТ

½ HRS

TASHKENT
ТАШКЕНТ

SAMARKAND
MAW ⊕

THE FOLLOWING ARE VIA KOKAND
⇒Ⓑ 6:30, 22:20
⇒Ⓝ 7:40, 9:15
⇒Ⓝ 14:30, 14:00
⇒Ⓔ 12:45

UZBEKISTAN
KYRGYZSTAN

ⓔ 10 MINS

½ HRS
HOURLY 5-30-16:30
58CYM

TURAKURGAN
HERDFLOT

CHUST

2½ HRS EVERY 2 HRS
ALSO ONE TRAIN/DAY
UCHKURGAN

GURAM SARAI

EVERY
2 HRS
74CM

MARPILAN
MARGILAN
GREAT BAZAAR
BIG SILK
FACTORY

1 HR

ФАРТОНА
FERGANA
FORT REMNANTS
INDUSTRIAL CITY

HAMZAⓔ⊞
MAUSOLEUM
NEARBY
MOUNTAIN HIKES
⇣TURBAZA

ШАХИМАРДОН
SHAKHIMARDAN

KYKOH - HISTORIC KHA
WITH A 18 CENTURY
PALACE.

KOKAND
INSET

2 HRS,
d. EVERY
HR.

ПИШТАН
RISHTAN
(STOP ON THE
Ⓚ ⇄ Ⓝ BUS)

KYRGYZSTAN
UZBEKISTAN

Cox ATTRACTIVE
SOKH SCENERY

1 HR.

1-1½ HRS

ANGREN
COALFIELD

SEV.
3 HRS.

THE FOLLOWING
ARE VIA KOKAND

TAJIKISTAN
ХУЏЖАНД
KHOJENT

FAM ONLY

1 HR.

Ⓚ

GAFUROV
(KHOJENT STA.)

7 KM.

BEKABAD

TAJIKISTAN
KYRGYZSTAN

KOKAND

PALACE SQUEEZED
INTO PARK WITH
ⓔ CROCHARD AND
FUN FAIR

⊞BARGAS

BUS #8 TO
HOTEL
KOKAND

$2 FLEAPIT

10 MINS
WALK

HOTEL
KOKAND

BUS #15 TO
BUS STA.
AT NIGHT, LONG
DISTANCE BUSES
DROP OFF HERE

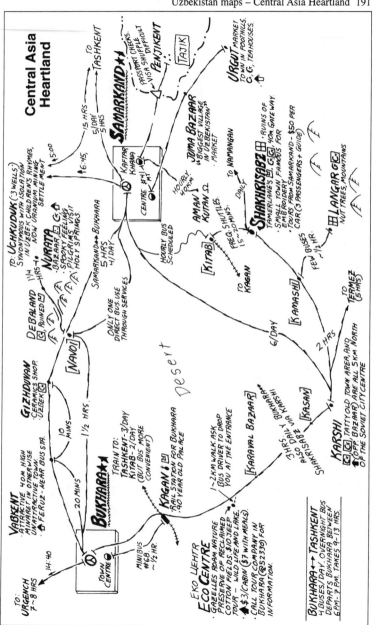

Central Asia Heartland

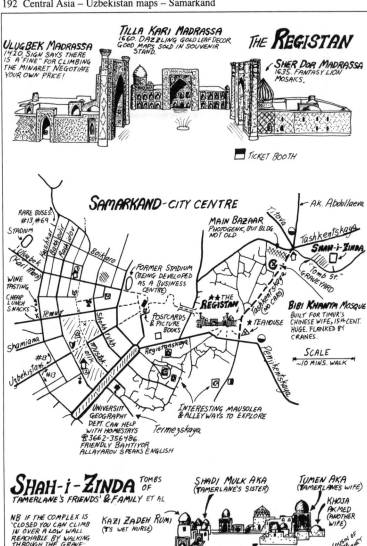

ULUGBEK MADRASSA
1420. SIGN SAYS THERE IS A "FINE" FOR CLIMBING THE MINARET. NEGOTIATE YOUR OWN PRICE!

TILLA KARI MADRASSA
1660. DAZZLING GOLD LEAF DECOR. GOOD MAPS SOLD IN SOUVENIR STAND.

THE REGISTAN

SHER DOR MADRASSA
1635. FANTASY LION MOSAICS.

 TICKET BOOTH

SAMARKAND - CITY CENTRE

RARE BUSES #13, #69
STADIUM
WINE TASTING
CHEAP LUNCH SNACKS
Yashnal Bashlolio Bashlolio
Boiloro
Ulugbek (Karl Marx)
Temur
Shohrukh
Tmysbek alik
Shamiana
Uzbekistans #13 #13
Registanskaya
Termezskaya

FORMER STADIUM (BEING DEVELOPED AS A BUSINESS CENTRE)
POSTCARDS & PICTURE BOOKS

MAIN BAZAAR PHOTOGENIC, BUT BLDG. NOT OLD

T. Titova
AK. Abdullaeva
Tashkentskaya
SHAH-i-ZINDA
"TOMB ST." GRAVEYARD

★★ THE REGISTAN

Tashkentskaya (NO CARS)

TEAHOUSE

BIBI KHANYM MOSQUE
BUILT FOR TIMUR'S CHINESE WIFE, 15TH CENT. HUGE. FLANKED BY CRANES.

Penikentskaya

SCALE
~10 MINS. WALK

INTERESTING MAUSOLEA & ALLEYWAYS TO EXPLORE

UNIVERSITY GEOGRAPHY DEPT. CAN HELP WITH HOMESTAYS ☎3662-356486. FRIENDLY BAHTIYOR ALLAYAROV SPEAKS ENGLISH

SHAH-i-ZINDA TOMBS OF TAMERLANE'S FRIENDS' & FAMILY ET AL

NB IF THE COMPLEX IS 'CLOSED YOU CAN CLIMB IN OVER A LOW WALL REACHABLE BY WALKING THROUGH THE GRAVEYARD BESIDE THE ENSEMBLE.

KAZI ZADEH RUMI (T'S WET NURSE)

OFFICIAL ENTRANCE

THE ORIGINAL 'STAIRWAY TO HEAVEN'

SHADI MULK AKA (TAMERLANE'S SISTER)

TUMEN AKA (TAMERLANE'S WIFE)

KHOJA AKMED (ANOTHER WIFE)

TOMB OF KASIM ABBAS COUSIN OF THE PROPHET
REACHED THROUGH THE ONCE JEWEL ENCRUSTED WOODED DOOR OF PARADISE.

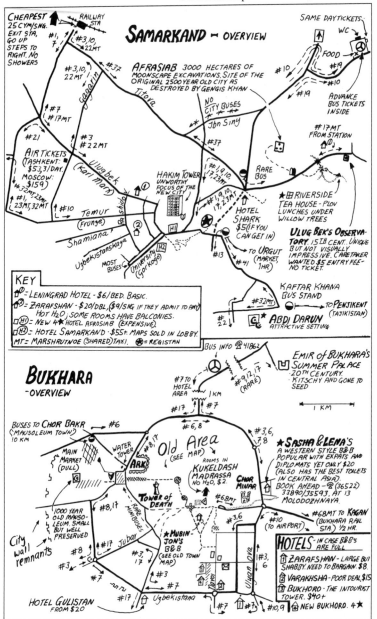

CHEAPEST 25 CYM/SNG. EXIT STA, GO UP STEPS TO RIGHT. NO SHOWERS

RAILWAY STA

#1, 7

#3,10, 22MT

SAMARKAND – OVERVIEW

SAME DAY TICKETS

WC

FOOD

#10

#19

#3,10, 22MT

#32

AFRASIAB 3000 HECTARES OF MOONSCAPE EXCAVATIONS. SITE OF THE ORIGINAL 2500 YEAR OLD CITY AS DESTROYED BY GENGIS KHAN

#10

#19

ADVANCE BUS TICKETS INSIDE

#7 #17MT

Gagarin

Titova

NO CITY BUSES

Ibn Siny

#37

#17MT FROM STATION

#21

#3 #22MT

#7 #17MT

Ulugbek (Karl Marx)

#1,9,10, 17,23MT

RARE BUS

AIR TICKETS (TASHKENT: $53.3/DAY. MOSCOW: $159)

#1, 23MT, 32MT

#32MT, 23MT

#10

Temur (Frunze)

Shamiana

Uzbekistanskaya

MOST BUSES

University (Gorkogo)

Registan

Hakim Tower UNWORTHY FOCUS OF THE NEW CITY

#1,9,10, 17,23MT

HOTEL SHARK $5 (IF YOU CAN GET IN)

#13

#41

to URGUT (MARKET, 1HR)

★ RIVERSIDE TEA HOUSE - PLOV LUNCHES UNDER WILLOW TREES

ULUG BEK's OBSERVATORY 15TH CENT. UNIQUE BUT NOT VISUALLY IMPRESSIVE. CARETAKER WANTED $5 ENTRY FEE- NO TICKET.

KAFTAR KHANA BUS STAND

#32MT

to PENJIKENT (TAJIKISTAN)

#22

ABDI DARUN ★ ATTRACTIVE SETTING

KEY

= LENINGRAD HOTEL - $6/BED. BASIC.
= ZARAFSHAN - $20/DBL, ($9/SNG IF THEY ADMIT TO ANY) HOT H₂O; SOME ROOMS HAVE BALCONIES.
H1 = NEW 4★ HOTEL AFROSIAB (EXPENSIVE)
H2 = HOTEL SAMARKAND $55+. MAPS SOLD IN LOBBY.
MT = MARSHRUTNOE (SHARED) TAXI. ★ = REGISTAN

BUS INFO ☎ 41862

EMIR of BUKHARA's SUMMER PALACE 20TH CENTURY. KITSCHY AND GONE TO SEED

#9,12,17 (RARE)

#7 to HOTEL AREA

1 KM

BUKHARA - OVERVIEW

#17

#7

BUSES TO **CHOR BAKR** (MAUSOLEUM TOWN) 10 KM

#6

#6, 8

#3, 6, 7, 8

#3, 6, 7, 8

MAIN MARKET (DULL)

WATER TOWER

ARK

Old Area (SEE MAP)

ROOMS IN KUKELDASH MADRASSA NO H₂O, $2.

CHOR MINAR

★ **SASHA & LENA's** A WESTERN STYLE B&B POPULAR WITH EXPATS AND DIPLOMATS YET ONLY $20 (ALSO HAS THE BEST TOILETS IN CENTRAL ASIA). BOOK AHEAD – ☎ (36522) 33890/35593. AT 13 MOLODOZHNAYA.

1000 YEAR OLD MAUSO- LEUM. SMALL BUT WELL PRESERVED

Tower of Death

#68MT

#68MT TO KAGAN (BUKHARA RAIL STA.) ½ HR.

#8,17

RARE MINIBUSES

Jubar

#8,17

#3, 6

#10 (to AIRPORT)

City wall remnants

#8

#3

★ **MUBIN- JON's B&B** (SEE OLD TOWN MAP)

#3, 17

#3

#7

#7

Ulgan Ova

#3, 6

HOTELS - IN CASE B&B's ARE FULL

ZARAFSHAN - LARGE BUT SHABBY. NEED TO BARGAIN. $8.
VARAKHSHA - POOR DEAL. $15
BUKHORO - THE INTOURIST TOWER. $40+
NEW BUKHORO. 4★

HOTEL **GULISTAN** FROM $20

#17

Uzbekistana

#7

#10,9

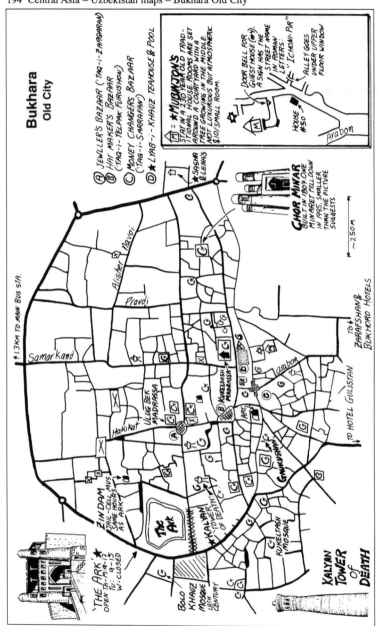

Bukhara
Old City

A Jeweller's Bazaar ('Taq-i-Zargaran')
B Hat Maker's Bazaar ('Taq-i-Telpak Furushov')
C Money Changers Bazaar ('Taq-i-Sarrafav')
D ★ Lyab-i-Khauz Teahouse & Pool

🏠 = ★ MUBINJON'S STAY IN A 100-YEAR OLD TRADITIONAL HOUSE. ROOMS ARE SET AROUND A COURTYARD WITH A TREE GROWING IN THE MIDDLE. NOT LUXURIOUS BUT ATMOSPHERIC. $10/SMALL ROOM.

DOOR BELL FOR GUEST HOUSE (#9). A SIGN HAS THE STREET NAME IN ROMAN LETTERS:- "ICHONI-PIR"

ALLEY GOES UNDER UPPER FLOOR WINDOW

HOUSE #50

Arabon

SASHA & LENAS

↑ 1.3 KM TO MAIN BUS STA.

Alisher Navoi

Pravdi

Samarkand

CHOR MINAR BUILT IN 1807. ONE MINARET FELL DOWN IN 1995. SMALLER THAN THE PICTURE SUGGESTS.

~250 m

TO ZARAFSHAN & BUKHORO HOTELS

Hakikat

Ulug Bek Madrassa

Kukeltash Madrassa

ART.

Arabon

Gaukushan

TO HOTEL GULISTAN

Zindam TRAIL-CELL MUS SAME HOURS AS ARK

The Ark

Kalyan 'Tower' of Death

Kukeltash Mosque

'THE ARK' OPEN M-TU-TH-F-SA: 9-15 W: CLOSED

Bolo Khauz Mosque 18TH CENTURY

KALYAN TOWER OF DEATH

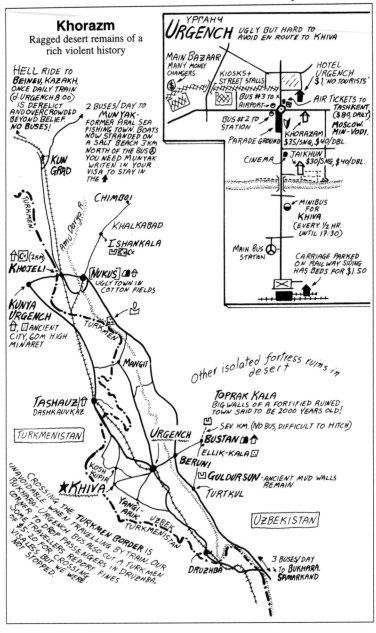

Khorazm
Ragged desert remains of a rich violent history

УРГАНЧ
URGENCH UGLY BUT HARD TO AVOID EN ROUTE TO KHIVA

MAIN BAZAAR MANY MONEY CHANGERS

KIOSKS + STREET STALLS

BUS #3 to AIRPORT

BUS #2 to STATION

PARADE GROUND

CINEMA

HOTEL URGENCH $1, 'NO TOURISTS'

AIR TICKETS to TASHKENT ($89, DAILY) MOSCOW, MIN-VODI.

KHORAZAM $35/SNG, $40/DBL.

JAIKHUN $30/SNG, $40/DBL.

MINIBUS FOR KHIVA (EVERY ½ HR. UNTIL 17:30)

MAIN BUS STATION

CARRIAGE PARKED ON RAIL WAY SIDING HAS BEDS FOR $1.50

HELL RIDE TO BEINEU, KAZAKH. ONCE DAILY TRAIN (d. URGENCH 8:00) IS DERELICT AND OVERCROWDED BEYOND BELIEF. NO BUSES!

2 BUSES/DAY TO MUNYAK - FORMER ARAL SEA FISHING TOWN. BOATS NOW STRANDED ON A SALT BEACH 3KM NORTH OF THE BUS ④ YOU NEED MUNYAK WRITTEN IN YOUR VISA TO STAY IN THE ↑

KUN GRAD

CHIMBOI

KHALKABAD

ISHANKALA

Amu Darya R.

TURKMEN.

↑Cx (2KM)
KHOJELI

NUKUS
UGLY TOWN IN COTTON FIELDS

KUNYA URGENCH
ANCIENT CITY, 60M HIGH MINARET

TURKMEN

MANGIT

TASHAUZ
DASHKAUVKAZ

TURKMENISTAN

URGENCH

Other isolated fortress ruins in desert

TOPRAK KALA
BIG WALLS OF A FORTIFIED RUINED TOWN SAID TO BE 2000 YEARS OLD!

SEV. KM. (NO BUS, DIFFICULT TO HITCH)

BUSTAN

ELLIK-KALA

BERUNI

GULDURSUN - ANCIENT MUD WALLS REMAIN

TURTKUL

UZBEKISTAN

KOSH KUPIR

★KHIVA

YANGI-ARIK

UZBEK TURKMENISTAN

CROSSING THE TURKMEN BORDER IS UNAVOIDABLE WHEN TRAVELLING BY TRAIN. OUR BUKHARA-URGENCH BUS ALSO CUT A TURKMEN CORNER TO DROP PASSENGERS IN DRUZHBA. SOME TRAVELLERS REPORT FINES OF $5-20 FOR CROSSING VISAS, BUT WE WERE NOT STOPPED.

DRUZHBA

3 BUSES/DAY TO BUKHARA, SAMARKAND

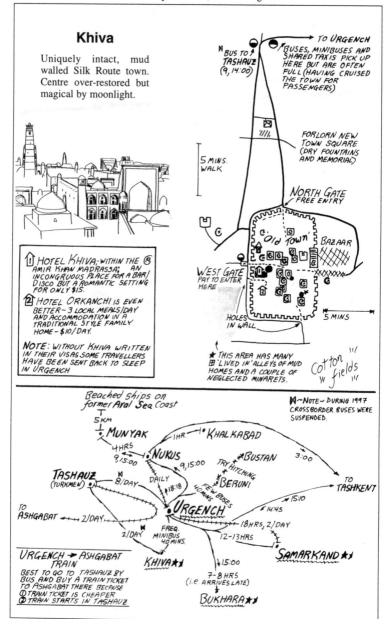

Khiva

Uniquely intact, mud walled Silk Route town. Centre over-restored but magical by moonlight.

1 HOTEL KHIVA: WITHIN THE AMIR KHAN MADRASSA; AN INCONGRUOUS PLACE FOR A BAR/DISCO BUT A ROMANTIC SETTING FOR ONLY $15.

2 HOTEL ORKANCHI IS EVEN BETTER – 3 LOCAL MEALS/DAY AND ACCOMMODATION IN A TRADITIONAL STYLE FAMILY HOME – $10/DAY.

NOTE: WITHOUT KHIVA WRITTEN IN THEIR VISAS SOME TRAVELLERS HAVE BEEN SENT BACK TO SLEEP IN URGENCH

TO URGENCH
BUS TO TASHAUZ (9, 14:00)
BUSES, MINIBUSES AND SHARED TAXIS PICK UP HERE BUT ARE OFTEN FULL (HAVING CRUISED THE TOWN FOR PASSENGERS)

5 MINS. WALK

FORLORN NEW TOWN SQUARE (DRY FOUNTAINS AND MEMORIAL)

NORTH GATE FREE ENTRY

Old Town
BAZAAR

WEST GATE PAY TO ENTER HERE

HOLES IN WALL

5 MINS

★ THIS AREA HAS MANY ⊞ 'LIVED IN' ALLEYS OF MUD HOMES AND A COUPLE OF NEGLECTED MINARETS.

Cotton fields

Beached ships on former Aral Sea Coast

⋈ ~NOTE~ DURING 1997 CROSSBORDER BUSES WERE SUSPENDED.

5 KM
MUNYAK
1 HR. KHALKABAD
4 HRS 9,15:00
NUKUS 9,15:00
BUSTAN 3:00
TRY HITCHING
TASHAUZ (TURKMEN) 8/DAY ⋈
DAILY 18:18
BERUNI FEW BUSES 40 MINS
TO ASHGABAT 2/DAY
URGENCH
TO TASHKENT
15:10
14:45
18 HRS, 2/DAY
2/DAY FREQ. MINIBUS 40 MINS.
12-13 HRS
SAMARKAND ★⤧
KHIVA ★⤧
15:00
7-8 HRS (i.e. ARRIVES LATE)
BUKHARA ★⤧

URGENCH → ASHGABAT TRAIN
BEST TO GO TO TASHAUZ BY BUS AND BUY A TRAIN TICKET TO ASHGABAT THERE BECAUSE
① TRAIN TICKET IS CHEAPER
② TRAIN STARTS IN TASHAUZ

PEOPLE'S REPUBLIC OF CHINA

When you think of a person from China you probably imagine a 'Han' Chinese. Though the Han do form the vast majority (92%) in the world's most populous nation, the remaining 8% of a billion people is still a considerable number: there are 67 registered ethnic groups in the PRC. Many of the larger minorities are not immediately recognisable as ethnically different (eg the Manchu and the Muslim Hui). However, other groups have more in common with neighbouring countries than with the ruling Han Chinese. The Uigurs of Xinjiang are 'Eastern Turks', the hill tribes of Yunnan are also found across Burma, Laos and northern Thailand, and Tibet is an ancient nation which has been submerged within China only since the 1950s. Hong Kong, reabsorbed in July 1997, is also a cultural world apart. Recognising these differences, regionally specific information and maps for these four regions have been given their own chapters with a 'Chinese China' (our catch-all name for the remainder where Han Chinese are the majority) dealing with the heartland of the 'Middle Kingdom'. Much of the information is relevant to travel anywhere within the political borders of the PRC (eg visa, currency, accommodation and travel overview) and this is presented in this chapter.

In the propaganda brochure *China in Brief* a shadowy Big Brother voice declares proudly: 'The People's Republic of China is a socialist state under people's democratic dictatorship... democracy is practised within the ranks of the people, dictatorship is exercised over the enemies of the people.... The people are defined as...all patriots who support socialism and the unification of the motherland.' Do you qualify for democracy? Few Chinese people seem to mind unduly. Economics is more on their minds: ask any of the migrant workers who call the ticket lounge of a large eastern train station their home. And yet, despite 70 million people officially classified as below the poverty line, the sense we had was that most people are feeling wealthier. A peasant farmer in Guanxi told us 'Of course I was sad [about the Tiananmen Sq massacre] but it had to be like that. Otherwise revolution. And every time there is revolution in China we lose another 30 years. Better to work, to get better day by day.' But in Tibet and Xinjiang, many would disagree.

❏ 'China' in different languages		
Language	**Name**	**Origin of name**
Chinese	Zhongguo	Mandarin reading of the characters 'central country'.
Japanese	Chugoku	Japanese reading of the same characters
English	China	The Ch'in empire controlled NW China when medieval Europe first took an interest in the area.
Turkish	Cin	Pronounced 'Jin', an alternate transliteration of Ch'in.
Russian	Kitai	The N Chinese Khitaians were allies of the Mongols.

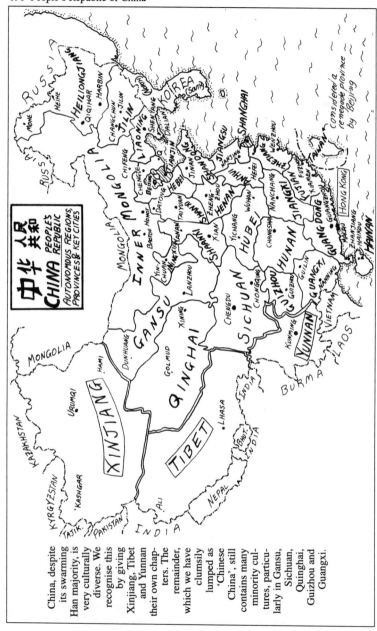

China, despite its swarming Han majority, is very culturally diverse. We recognise this by giving Xinjiang, Tibet and Yunnan their own chapters. The remainder, which we have clumsily lumped as 'Chinese China', still contains many minority cultures, particularly in Gansu, Sichuan, Quinghai, Guizhou and Guangxi.

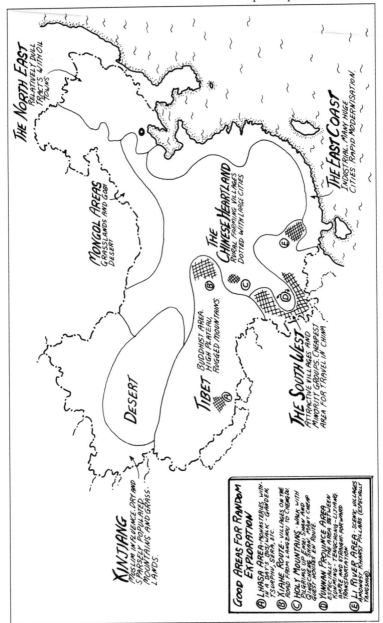

THE NORTH EAST — RELATIVELY DULL TRACTS WITH OIL TOWNS

THE EAST COAST — INDUSTRIAL, MANY HUGE CITIES. RAPID MODERNISATION.

MONGOL AREAS — GRASSLANDS AND GOBI DESERT

THE CHINESE HEARTLAND — RURAL FARMING VILLAGES DOTTED WITH LARGE CITIES

DESERT

XINJIANG — MUSLIM INFLUENCE. DRY AND SPARSELY POPULATED MOUNTAINS AND GRASS LANDS.

TIBET — BUDDHIST AREA. HIGH PLATEAU, RUGGED MOUNTAINS.

THE SOUTH WEST — ATTRACTIVE VILLAGES AND MINORITY GROUPS. CHEAPEST AREA FOR TRAVEL IN CHINA

GOOD AREAS FOR RANDOM EXPLORATION

(A) LHASA AREA — MONASTERIES WITH-IN A DAY'S BUS/WALK - GANDEN TSUPHU, SERA, ETC.

(B) XIAHE ROUTE - VILLAGES ON THE ROAD FROM LANGZHOU TO CHENGDU.

(C) HOLY MOUNTAINS - WALK WITH PILGRIMS UP EMEI SHAN AND QINGCHENG SHAN. MANY CHEAP GUEST HOUSES EN ROUTE.

(D) YUNNAN PROVINCE AREA — ESPECIALLY THE AREA BETWEEN KUNMING - TENGCHONG - LIJIANG AMPLE AND STRAIGHT FORWARD TRANSPORTATION.

(E) LI RIVER AREA - SCENIC VILLAGES AMONGST KARST PILLARS (ESPECIALLY YANGSHUO)

❏ Geo-political information – China

Population: 1221 million (1997), 1160m (1990), 910m (1974).

Area: 9,326,000 sq km.

Capital: Beijing (7 million [11 million for the municipality]).

Other major cities: Shanghai (7.9 million [13m]), Tianjin (5.8m [9.4]), Shenyang (4.5m), Wuhan, Guangzhou, Chongqing, (3-4m), Harbin, Chengdu, Xian, Nanjing (2.5m+), Zibo, Dalian, Jinan, Changchun, Qingdao, Taiyuan (2m+), Guiyang, Zhengzhou, Kunming (Yunnan), Lanzhou and Tangshan (1.5m+); Anshan, Qiqihar, Fushun, Nanchang, Hangzhou (once the world's biggest city), Changsha, Shijiazhuang, Fuzhou, Jilin, Baotou, Huainan, Luoyang, Datong, Urumqi (Xinjiang), Handan, Ningbo, Nanning, and Heifei (all 1m +).

GNP per capita: $590 (1997) but unequally distributed, $530 (1994) $290 (1987).

Currency history: Yuan/US$1 – Feb 1998: Y8.28, Oct 1997: Y8.29, Feb 1996: Y8.29, 1995: Y8.35, 1994: Y8.44 (before 1994 there was a dual currency with foreigners forced to purchase FECs), 1993: Y5.75, 1990: Y5.22, 1980: Y1.53.

Major exports/economy: Increasingly diversified economy though 70% of the population are still agricultural workers.

Ethnic mix: Very complex. The 1990 census gave Han as 92% with over a billion people, Zhuang (15m), Manchu (10m), Hui (8m), Miao, Uigur, Yi (7m), Tujia (6m), Mongol (4.8m), Tibetan (4.6m) and nine more groups with populations over a million including Dai, Kazakh and Korean.

Official languages: Mandarin Chinese, though many others appear on bank-notes and are used officially in the relevant provinces.

Religious mix: Religious tolerance since 1977 before which places of worship were systematically destroyed. The vast Confucian majority profess no religious beliefs. Hui, Uigur and Kazakhs are predominantly Muslim. Most Tibetans and some Mongols are Buddhists. There's a growing Christian community as a result of heavy Korean missionary work.

Landmarks of national history: The Dynasties [with imperial capital] **1650-1027 BCE**: Shang. **1027-770BCE**: Zhou [Luoyang]. **481BCE**: Warring States period. **221BCE**: Unification under the Qin dynasty. Great wall started, history rewritten, all old books burnt [Xianyang]. **206BCE**: Han, Confucius's ideas incorporated into government, growth of the Silk Route [Chang'an – today's Xian]. **221CE**: Three Kingdoms period (Wu, Wei and Shu), turmoil and inter- kingdom rivalries, Buddhism spread. **317**: Divided by invasions from the North. **589**: Reunification under the Sui dynasty following the Sinification of the invaders. Grand canal built and Great Wall re-fortified [Luoyang]. **618**: Tang dynasty. **From 840**: Persecution of Buddhists. **960**: Song dynasty [Kaifeng and Hangzhou], Ch'in rule in the north. **1210**: First Mongol attack under Genghis Khan. **1279**: Final Mongol victory over all China, Kublai Khan's Yuan dynasty and 'pleasuredomes' [Beijing and Xanadu]. **1368**: Ming dynasty [Nanjing then Beijing], Great Wall rebuilt. **1431**: Zheng He 'discovered' the rest of the world. **1644**: Qing (Manchu) dynasty. **1851-66**: Taiping rebellion. European colonial powers developed spheres of influence. **1911**: Sun Yat Sen launched Chinese Republic [Nanjing]. **1933-45**: Japanese occupation [Changchun]. **1949**: People's Republic declared [Beijing], old government fled to Taiwan. **1960**: Break of relations with USSR following Krushchev's detente with the USA. **1965**: Mao's Cultural revolution, temples and anything old targeted for demolition. **1976**: Mao died, rise of Deng Xiao. 'Gang of four' including Mao's wife considered responsible for the excesses. **1989**: Tiananmen Sq protests. **1997**: Deng Xiaoping died, Hong Kong returned to Chinese rule.

PRACTICAL INFORMATION
Visas and formalities
● **Visa strategy** Visas are required for most nationals. The cost is theoretically the same as the amount Chinese citizens are charged to visit your country. In reality, prices as well as conditions for application vary considerably depending on the embassy/consulate at which you apply: Hong Kong is the easiest and is good for longer stays; Rangoon (Burma) is the cheapest; Kathmandu (Nepal) and Bishkek (Kyrgyzstan) are among the worst. Chinese embassies in Eastern Europe are particularly notorious for stringent visa requirements.

A double entry visa is useful for any long trip through the country, if you can find an embassy (such as Hong Kong or London) that will issue one. Double entry visas cost twice as much as a single but, unlike double entry visas elsewhere, your period of stay begins afresh on your second entry. Handy for testing uncertain borders, eg into Burma.

The Chinese are very keen that the country is seen to be stable so you will not be welcome in places where there is a hint of unrest. On visa application forms you'll be asked where you want to go; whatever you say makes no difference to the visa you're finally issued so try to be uncontroversial. Normally Beijing, Shanghai and Canton are safe choices, though during the 1995 Beijing Women's Conference fear of media-grabbing activists meant that visas became hard to get for those listing Beijing. Lateral thinking and an awareness of political developments is very useful when applying.

● **Extensions** Some embassies only grant short visas, occasionally as short as 10 days. But don't worry, extensions are given – usually readily – at the Aliens Department of the **Public Security Bureau** (PSB) located in almost every town. A 30-day extension at the PSB in Beijing takes three days, or 24 hours if you pay double; the Chengdu PSB issues them within minutes. In general, smaller towns are easier places to get extensions, especially if the PSB's address isn't listed in a Lonely Planet guide. Theoretically, only one extension is possible but we met travellers who had received up to four. Note that some PSBs will not issue an extension unless the visa is within five days of expiring. Additional entries (re-entry permits) can not be added to a visa.

Money
Renminbi (people's money) consists of the *yuan* (commonly referred to as *kwai*) which is divided into ten *jiao* (normally called *mao*). The tiny *fen* notes (marked only in Chinese) are virtually worthless (one tenth of a *mao*).

The exchange rate is stable and there is no longer a black market. Anyone approaching you with an offer to change money is likely to be a con artist, though street traders may help if you arrive at a border post at night. The dual currency system that once required foreigners to use special FECs (Foreign Exchange Certificates) has been suspended. If you've just arrived, be sure you're not palmed off with FECs (these can easily be recognised by the English writing on the notes).

Travellers' cheques and credit card cash advances give better rates than cash but only the largest branch of the Bank of China in each major town can oblige. Minimal commission is charged for travellers' cheques. Cash advances are either free or subject to a 2 or 4% commission. In

❏ **Chinese student cards**

Though less useful than it once was, a student card can save you a lot of money. An ordinary ISIC student card is not enough. It must be a Chinese student card in a red wallet liberally stamped with communist stars. Such items are commonly forged and sold to travellers for around Y20 – you can save twice this just at the Terracotta Warriors.

Fake student cards are available in Xi'an, Beijing (harder to find recently), Yangshuo, Chengdu and Lanzhou. The travellers' grapevine will show you the exact places – we cannot name them without undermining them.

small border towns there is rarely a bank that can do such transactions so US$ cash is useful. Upmarket hotels can change travellers' cheques but usually only do so for registered guests (nonetheless they're worth a try if you're stranded on a Sunday with no alternative). With the exception of Hong Kong dollars, the currencies of China's immediate neighbours are generally not convertible in China, except with street traders in the relevant border zones.

With increasing frequency, stores and hotels are accepting credit cards though some add a surcharge. Sometimes when Visa/MasterCard signs are shown the establishment claims to accept such cards only when they have been issued on Chinese accounts.

Transport
● **Bus** China's momentous, if slightly claustrophobic, contribution to overnight road travel is the bed bus (*wopu*). Unlaundered blankets are usually provided, though a sleeping mat is recommended for berths that are less than clean or have protruding springs. Put your day-pack (and extra clothes in winter in case of heater breakdowns) under your knees – both for safety and to compensate for the lack of legroom. Each major town has at least one long distance bus station (plus smaller ones for local services), but increasingly you'll find convenient long distance services that operate from railway station concourses. Foreigner pricing applies only from cities that have yet to deregulate. Where there is competition, departure times are less reliable for private services than for the government ones but you are in a stronger bargaining position. Don't leave it till you've got aboard the bus to ascertain the real price; a sense of fair play (towards the conductor, not you) seems to

❏ **Chinese rail classes**

Class		Notes
软卧	Soft sleeper	An unnecessary luxury.
硬卧	Hard sleeper	Three-tiered bunks in an open carriage. The uppermost berth is 15% less expensive than the lower ones but is cramped and stiflingly hot in summer.
软席	Soft seat	Plush reclining seats.
硬席	Hard seat	Your chance to get to know the local farmyard while on the move. Sleeping mats are useful to pad your behind.

prevent fellow passengers telling you the real price until after you've struck a deal. Thereafter, they'll merrily tell you how much extra you paid and join you in cursing the swindler for having rooked you!

● **Train** Wonderfully unhelpful Soviet-style service is still observable all over China but is fast disappearing into anthropological myth. While some ticket staff would still rather swallow their chopsticks than sell you a ticket, there's a new friendly breed who speak polite English and actually give the odd straight answer. As we were about to leave ticketless following an exchange with one unhelpful clerk, a new face appeared at the window squeaking politely in English. 'You want a ticket for Kunming? Tomorrow? OK, no problem'. This new openness, together with the abolition of foreigner pricing on train tickets, is likely to reduce the importance of ticket buying agents. Agents, found in traveller restaurants and guesthouses, are still useful back up as they can often conjure up tickets even in the high season (the summer and Chinese holidays) when trains really might be booked solid for days ahead. See Chinese rail classes (opposite).

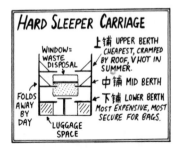

HARD SLEEPER CARRIAGE

WINDOW= WASTE DISPOSAL

上铺 UPPER BERTH CHEAPEST, CRAMPED BY ROOF, V HOT IN SUMMER.

中铺 MID BERTH

FOLDS AWAY BY DAY

下铺 LOWER BERTH MOST EXPENSIVE, MOST SECURE FOR BAGS.

LUGGAGE SPACE

● **Boat** Slow, romantic sounding riverboats cruise many of China's bigger rivers and the sections of the Grand Canal that remain passable. Most travellers find 24 hours enough though many journeys are much longer. There are four classes on regular river boats – second to fifth (apparently, having a first class was considered too bourgeois). Second class is a double room

with public showers and lockable toilets (in contrast to the other showers and toilets that are in one big room with everybody else watching). Third class is in an eight-berth room, while fourth class is in a 14-berth room. Fifth class provides only space on the floor. Foreigners staying in third class can usually get away with using the second class restrooms.

● **Hitching** Some travellers claim that suspicion of foreigners and the low ownership of cars combine to make China a relatively difficult place to hitch. However, we managed to hitch several rides – including one on a tractor and another in an army jeep; both times without trying and for free. The paid hitch is the established method of travel in remoter areas; know how much you want to pay as zeros can easily get added to the asking price.

● **Air** Many regional airlines have split from the former monolithic CAAC. After a spate of crashes and a history of abysmal service, things seem to have improved over the last three years though prices are now quite high. It is usually cheaper to buy tickets for internal flights abroad (or in Hong Kong) than in China where a substantial foreigner surcharge remains.

● **Bicycle** Most urban transportation systems in China are crowded and confusing; where possible rent a bicycle. Even in Beijing, though the distances are great, roads are set up for cycling. There are bike parking lots, bike lanes, bike interchanges and repair stations. Most hotels catering to backpackers will have bicycle rental nearby. If you can't find an official bicycle renter ask at a large bicycle storage lot. One such lot in Tianjin agreed to rent bicycles to us for a late night ride if we promised to bring them back before their real owners returned in the morning.

Beware of the bike rental scam. Having paid a hefty deposit, you ride off not realising that you're being followed. You carefully lock the bicycle using the lock provided. When you return the bike has vanished, 'stolen' back by the renter's agent who had a copy of the key. Easily prevented by using your own padlock.

Accommodation

China is not accommodation friendly. Though there are a myriad of atmospheric little places offering cheap rooms, it is likely you'll be forced to stay in a more expensive concrete block. Only certain hotels are open to foreigners. And, since local municipalities decide the minimum level of comfort that a tourist should be allowed to endure, they often rule against cheap private places in favour of hotels which, coincidentally, they own.

Foreign pricing is common, averaging 100% more than locals pay, though 'overseas Chinese' sometimes qualify for special intermediate rates. Many cheaper state-owned hotels are undergoing renovation, which in turn pushes up prices.

Fortunately, cheap hotels in smaller towns are more likely to accept foreigners (especially if there is nowhere else). In cities used to tourists, it is common for certain hotels to become the established travellers' pads; these may prove the most convenient base from which to explore as there will be travel agents, bike rental, English speaking staff and there's a good chance of a dormitory. If you prefer to avoid the 'Lonely Planet' circuit, look elsewhere. See the Types of Accommodation box.

Staying in touch

● **Mail** Sending mail is reliable, even from rural areas.

● **Phone** Calls to the USA or Europe from a public telephone office cost Y37.5 per minute. Country code +86, Beijing 10.

Further information

● **Books** Lonely Planet's *China* is the backpackers' bible with its wealth of maps, lashings of Chinese script and extensive listings of cheap accommodation. Going anywhere not mentioned by LP is a sure way to avoid other travellers. The main alternatives are a Rough Guide and Ruth Lor Malloy's slightly less practical *China Guide*. For German speakers the Reise Know-how China Manual is very useful.

❏ Types of cheap accommodation (for characters see p206)

A *zhaodaisuo* is generally the cheapest kind of accommodation available and ranges from a few rooms in a family home above a shop front to large but basic concrete slab buildings. Signs are likely to be marked only in Chinese. In cities where such places are forbidden to foreigners, you'll be forced into the generally much bigger and sometimes very grand *binguan*, *fandian* or *jiudian*.

If the only place available looks very grand don't necessarily be put off. Even some of the plushest hotels have a building B; an annex with festering old rooms at the price you want to pay. Price lists are generally displayed.

Ask first for a *duorenfang* (dormitory). In traveller-primed hotels there seems to be a general policy of putting foreigners in separate dorms from Chinese guests, so if there are no other Westerners (or Japanese) you may have a room to yourself. Sexes are not separated in this way. If the receptionist claims that there are no dorms that may be because they define dormitory differently. It may still be possible to get one bed in a shared triple if prices are quoted *chuangwei* (per bed) rather than *baofang* (whole room). Look closely at the squiggles on the price board. *Danrengfang* (single) rooms are typically more expensive than a triple (*sanrenfang*) as singles are usually luxury rooms with attached toilet and bathroom facilities.

You will have to pay in advance. Often, a Y10 or Y20 deposit is also required – you'll get it back providing you check out by noon and return the room card. This card is held in lieu of a key; show it to the attendant on your floor, and she'll open your door and refill the thermos with boiling water for tea. Lifts stop working late at night and there may be an unofficial midnight curfew.

❏ China challenge – without a guide book

China is a confusing and rapidly changing place for which a detailed, up to date guide book is a worthy investment. You can buy new guides in Hong Kong, or in Karimabad (Hunza) if you're coming up the Karakoram Highway. Otherwise your best shot is a second-hand copy from another traveller. More daring, but perfectly feasible, is to get off the guide book circuit altogether. The notes in this volume should be sufficient to get you to the main sites. With locally available maps it's then possible to strike out into random territory. Some tips:

● Certain small towns like Dali, Yangshuo and Xiahe, plus specific hotels and restaurants in bigger cities, are de-facto traveller hubs. The most notable ones are indicated on the 'East China Highlights' map (p212) with a double underline. In any of these places you'll find other travellers who can help you get your bearings and suggest interesting excursions, pass on the latest travel gossip etc.

● Without baggage it's much easier to explore towns and seek out cheap rooms. Fortunately there are luggage rooms at almost all the railway stations and big hotels will often hold baggage for non-residents at Y5/day or less.

● If you can't find a cheap hotel somewhere, it may be cheaper to jump on an overnight train or 'bed-bus' than spend the night in an overpriced tower.

● Chinese road atlases are available cheaply from Xinhua bookshops, both for the whole country and in more detail per province. These are in Chinese which is handy for showing to the folks at a bus or train station. Buy a bi-lingual national map so at least you can work out the pronunciation of the main city names. Locals can help with pronouncing other names and may be thoughtful enough to warn you if a visit sounds like a silly idea.

There are hundreds of China related books for background reading. Particularly interesting are travelogues written in the 1980s at the time that travel restrictions were first being lifted; it's amazing how much a country can change in 10 years. Try *Behind the Forbidden Door* (Tiziano Terzani, 1985) and *A ride along the Great Wall* (Robin Hanbury-Tenison, 1987). Also recommended is Martin Palmer's *Travels through Sacred China*.

● **Maps** City maps are readily available from hawkers at train stations in most big cities and at some bus stations and airports. They often include some English words and picture icons which suggest places of interest. There are usually several versions available; look for one with numbered bus routes. Prices are usually marked at Y1.5 or Y2, but unless you go to a bookshop you'll pay an extra Y1 commission to the vendor.

Web sites

Peter M. Geiser's China Internet Guide is at www-students.unisg.ch/~pgeiser/china/china.htm.

The *China Daily* newspaper online: www.ihep.ac.cn/~cbnet/cd.html.

An independent traveller gives his advice and experience about travel in China at www.star.de/sturm/china/china1.html.

China is the sort of place everyone comes away from with a different impression. Virtual travelogues include: www.speedlink.com/collin/china/html/china.html

The Museum of the Absurd, www.mianbao.com, takes a look at the lighter side of China, including a toilet photo gallery.

Chinese words and phrases

Locals are unlikely to understand your attempts at pronouncing Chinese. Even if you speak fluently many seem to assume you're speaking English and so don't listen. Buy a phrase book with Chinese characters: show people the written words. If you have no phrase book our selection of words will be most useful if you first make a couple of photocopies. Cut these up and paste together the words you need to make pidgin Chinese sentences (eg 'cheapest double room, private shower'). For all its other complexities, Chinese is grammatically very simple, so you have a fair chance of hitting on a sentence that someone understands. As we've tried to show (see 'Verbs' below) pasting in an extra character is all you need to change tenses, negatives etc.

PRONOUNS 我 I/ME 你 YOU 他 HE/HIM 她 SHE/HER 它 IT Add 们 for plural - eg 我们 WE/US (*TO SHOW RESPECT)
wǒ   nǐ (nín)   tā   tā   tā   men   wǒ men

VERBS

EAT→ MEAT
我 吃 肉
wǒ chī ròu
I EAT MEAT (AM EATING, WILL EAT, DO EAT)

NOT
我 不 吃 肉
wǒ bù chī ròu
I DON'T EAT MEAT

CAN
我 不 能 吃 肉
wǒ bù néng chī ròu
I CANNOT EAT MEAT

HAVE
我 吃 了 肉
wǒ chī le ròu
I ATE MEAT

IN PAST
我 吃 过 肉
wǒ chī guò ròu
I HAVE EATEN MEAT (ONCE UPON A TIME)

NOT (PAST)
我 没 吃 肉
wǒ méi chī ròu
I DIDN'T EAT MEAT

TODAY
我 今 天 吃 肉
wǒ jīn tiān chī ròu
TODAY I (WILL) EAT MEAT

我 明 天 吃 肉
wǒ míng tiān chī ròu
TOMORROW I WILL EAT MEAT

QUESTIONS

你 吃 肉 吗 ← QUESTION MARKER
nǐ chī ròu ma?
DO YOU EAT MEAT?

我 吃
wǒ chī
YES. (I EAT)

我 不 吃
wǒ bù chī
NO. (I NOT EAT)

ALTERNATIVELY
你 吃 不 吃 肉 NO "MA"
nǐ chī bù chī ròu?
DO YOU EAT MEAT (OR NOT)?

QUESTION WORDS

~ ~ 什 么
~ ~ shén me
WHAT IS ~ ~

~ ~ 几 点
~ ~ jǐ diǎn
WHAT TIME IS ~ ~?

~ ~ 在 哪 儿
~ ~ zài nǎr
WHERE IS ~ ~?

多 少 钱
duō shǎo qián
HOW MUCH (COST)?

TIME

点
diǎn
HOUR/O'CLOCK

五点四十分
wǔ diǎn sì shí fēn
5:40 MINUTE

今 天
jīn tiān
TODAY

明 天
míng tiān
TOMORROW

昨 天
zuó tiān
YESTERDAY

星 期 一 ← One'
xīng qī yī
MONDAY 2 FOR TUESDAY, 3 WED...ETC EXCEPT SUNDAY

月
yuè
MONTH

一 月 二 月 etc..
yī yuè   èr yuè
JAN. FEB.

DAY(SUN)
五月十日
wǔ yuè shí rì
MAY 10TH

一星期
yī xīng qī
ONE WEEK

星 期 日
xīng qī rì
SUNDAY

1	一
2	二
3	三
4	四
5	五
6	六
7	七
8	八
9	九
10	十
11	十一
12	十二

HOTEL

Cheapest type
招待所 /
ZHAODAISUO

宾 馆
BĪNGUAN

酒 店
JIǓDIAN

饭 店
FANDIAN

ROOMS

多人房
duō ren fang
DORM ROOM

单/双/三人房
dān/shuāng/sān ren fang
SINGLE/DOUBLE/TRIPLE ROOM

床 位
chuáng wèi
PAY PER BED

包 房
bāo fáng
PAY FOR WHOLE ROOM

MOST CHEAP
最 便 宜 (房)
zuì pian yi (fáng)
CHEAPEST (ROOM)

(私人) 浴室/ 淋 浴/厕所
(sī ren) yù shì lín yù cè suǒ
(PRIVATE) BATH/SHOWER/TOILET

热 水
rè shuǐ
HOT WATER

我可以看看房间吗
wǒ kě yi kàn kàn fang jiān mā?
MAY I LOOK AT THE ROOM?

HANDY WORDS

太谢谢(你了)	对不起	仁慈的	良好的	幸福的
(tài) xiè xiè (nǐ le)	duì bù qǐ	rén cí de	liáng hǎo de	xìng fú de
THANKS (V. MUCH)	SORRY	KIND	GOOD	HAPPY

很美的	很有意思	非常的	朋友	我不懂	高价的
hěn měi de	hěn yǒu yì sì	fēi cháng de	péng yǒu	wǒ bù dǒng	gāo jià de
BEAUTIFUL	INTERESTING	UNUSUAL	FRIEND	I DON'T UNDERSTAND	EXPENSIVE

TRANSPORT

BUS OR TRAIN →

卧铺	上/中/下铺	硬/软席	到	开	行李寄存处
wò pu	shàng/zhōng/xià pu	yìng/ruǎn xí	dào	zǒu	xíng lǐ jì cún chù
SLEEPER	UPPER/MID/LOW BERTH	HARD/SOFT SEAT	ARRIVAL	DEP.	LEFT LUGGAGE OFFICE

慢/直快/特快/国联车	售票处	定票处	问讯
màn/zhí kuài/tè kuài/guó chē	shòu piào chù	dìng piào chù	wèn xùn
SLOW/FAST/EXPRESS/INT'L TRAIN	TICKET OFFICE	RESERVATION OFFICE	INFO

我只要…张硬卧铺去～	我只要租一辆自行车
wǒ yào… zhāng yìng wo pu qu	wǒ yào zū yí lang zì xíng chē
I'D LIKE (NUMBER) HARD SLEEPER TIX TO～	I'D LIKE TO RENT A BICYCLE

MAPS

我想买一张(市/交通)地图	MAP
wǒ xiǎng shi yì zhang (shì/jiāo tōng) dì tú	
I WANT TO BUY A (CITY/TRANSPORT) MAP	

Map Kanji

江/河 RIVER	湖 LAKE	岛 ISLAND
山 MOUNTAIN	峰 PEAK	山口 PASS
村 VILLAGE	县 RURAL COUNTY/COUNTY TOWN	
公园 PARK	物 ZOO	古城 OLD TOWN

PLACES

Street Names:

路	街	大街	道	大道	广场 SQUARE
lù	jiē	dà jiē	dào	dà dào	guǎng chǎng

北 běi	～～北路
	～～beilu
西 xī 东 dong	= THE NORTH SECTION OF ～～ ROAD
南 nán	

教堂	寺院/庙	清真寺	博物馆
jiào tang	sì/yuàn/miào	qīng zhēng sì	bó wù guǎn
CHURCH	TEMPLE	MOSQUE	MUSEUM

书店	(中国)银行	领事馆	大使馆	公安局外事科
shū diàn	(zhōngguó) yín háng	lǐng shì guǎn	dà shǐ guǎn	gōngan jú wài shì kē
BOOK SHOP	BANK (OF CHINA)	CONSULATE	EMBASSY	P.S.B. (FOR VISA EXTENSION)

邮局	存局候领栏	飞机场	汽车站	火车站	码头
yóu jú	cún jú hòu lǐng lán	fēi jī chǎng	qì chē zhàn	huǒ chē zhàn	mǎ tóu
POST OFFICE	POST RESTANTE	AIRPORT	BUS STATION	TRAIN STATION	FERRY PIER

With its confusing plethora of vowels and its four tones, Chinese is a nightmare to pronounce. There is an increasing use of 'pinyin' (Chinese words in Western letters, as used below the characters on these pages), but the letters don't correspond exactly with their equivalents in Western languages. Most different are:

c - ts   *ie* - like yeah!   *j* - ds   *q* - roughly ch   *x* - roughly SH
e - sounds like the grunt you might make after being punched gently in the stomach.
i - similar to e in some words but is normally a more conventional ee sound.

Accent markers over vowels graphically show the tones: flat, falling, rising, falling+rising.

Chinese China

Confucius and Kung Fu, calligraphy on misty mountain tops, funky facial hair on philosophers who ponder the oneness of the universe. Attractively quirky stereotypes like these were bulldozed by Mao's cultural revolution and are now being paved over with the concrete and glass of 'red capitalism'. After decades of revolutionary mood swings and centuries of hardship, the ordinary people of China are finally getting a double-edged taste of economic development. The TV aerials and power lines that mar tourist photos of bucolic villages are signs of real, if modest, improvements for the rural majority. However, their spending power is decreasing as prices rise. In the cities, rapid 'progress' brings a widening gulf between rich and poor. A building boom has produced shiny hotel towers, modern offices and expensive restaurants to service a dynamic new class of businessmen. But growth is at the expense of the narrow *hutong* alleys, traditional walled courtyards, and low, tile-roofed homes which once gave cities like Chengdu and Beijing much more character. Some of the temples which were torn down in the 1960s are being replaced and parts of the Great Wall that had been reduced to rubble by time and neglect have been dramatically reconstructed. The results are sometimes awesome, at other times tacky. Visit any one of the 'holy' mountains for a mixture of both. One can glimpse the divine beauty which drew the original pilgrims and there are still quiet, lesser known trails and shrines. But cable cars and concrete steps do detract from the spiritual atmosphere, as do the myriad litter-bug local tourists.

Now is an exciting time to visit China. The practical aspects of travel are easier than ever before. Many Chinese are discovering that foreign devils aren't always demons. And that helps visitors to realise that the apparent rudeness that has been a trademark of China is a mixture of linguistic style and embarrassment as much as innate temperament.

❏ **W&M's country ratings – China**
- **Expense $$$** The larger coastal cities and the north east of the country are relatively expensive.
- **Value for money ✔✔✔** Buses and food are bargains. Accommodation is often low quality – renovations bring huge price hikes.
- **Getting around ✔✔✔** Transport services are comprehensive and increasingly easy to use.
- **English spoken ✔✔** Much more is spoken in Shanghai and Guangzhou than elsewhere. None in rural areas.
- **Woman alone ✔✔✔✔** More difficult in rural areas.
- **For vegetarians ✔✔✔✔** You can often go into the kitchen and point out non-meat ingredients, but after you see the kitchen you might lose your appetite anyway. Some vegetarian restaurants have very fanciful menus.

❑ **Essential information for travellers – China**

● **Visa** Required. Generally between $20 and $40 for a 30-day stay but conditions vary greatly between embassies. Extensions are generally granted easily.

● **Currency** Yuan. US$1=Y8.28.

● **Time zone** 8 hours ahead of GMT (same as Hong Kong); 1hr ahead of Indochina and central Mongolia, 1 hr behind Korea, 2 hrs behind Vladivostok.

● **Special dangers** Petty theft is especially rampant; late-night violent crime is becoming a problem in the largest cities.

● **Health factors** Where possible drink bottled or boiled water (the latter is available on trains and in hotels). There's a small risk of malaria in the southern coastal areas.

● **Social conventions** Travellers can gain acceptance by following some cultural rules. Faux pas include pointing with your index finger and placing food debris in your rice bowl (though on the floor may be fine). Clicking your fingers, whistling, and tapping your chopsticks on the table are considered especially rude.

For male visitors, inviting a Chinese women to your room is likely to raise alarms as well as eyebrows and may result in an unwelcome visit from the Public Security Bureau (PSB). One such couple were dragged off to jail on the (false) grounds that his visa was forged. Female travellers seem to be permitted to have Chinese boyfriends.

If a restaurant is crowded, it is OK to sit down at a table with other people.

● **Typical traveller destinations** Beijing and the Great Wall, Xian, Shanghai, Guilin.

● **Highlights** Yangshuo, spending the night on the Great Wall, Xiahe and the route to Chengdu, people-watching on holy mountain treks, Sichuan Opera.

● **When to go** The Chinese eastern seaboard covers the spectrum of climates, so there is no one best time to visit. Beijing is warm and humid in the summer with frequent short but heavy downpours. It's dry and freezing cold in the winter. During the spring and autumn the temperature runs between the two extremes.

North of Beijing, a sweater is usually necessary in the summer – especially at higher altitudes. If you are spending a night on the Great Wall you'll need warm clothes and a sleeping bag, even in August. Winter in the north is bitterly cold – lakes and rivers freeze and deserts collect snow on their dunes – but it can be very beautiful if you're suitably dressed, though bus windows tend to frost over impairing the view.

The southern areas are hot and humid in summer with occasional typhoons on the coast between July and September. Mid winter (January/February) you may need a good sweater, even in Guilin.

● **Pulse of the country** City parks, rural villages.

● **Key tips** If you ask the price and one finger is held up, this might mean Y10 not 1. If one finger crosses the other, this is certainly 10. Stretching your thumb and first finger forward means 7 not 2.

PRACTICAL INFORMATION
Food and drink

The four major cuisines in China are: Beijing, Shanghai, Sichuan and Cantonese. The Shanghai and Cantonese cuisines are dominated by seafood. In Beijing they prefer noodles and in Sichuan they like it spicy. The intrepid will enjoy experimenting with different meals throughout the country, especially if they don't mind eating snake, aardvark, goose intestines and the like.

Activities

● **Work** There is a rapidly expanding demand for English teachers. Official positions are categorised as FT (foreign teacher) or FE (foreign expert). FTs need relatively few qualifications. Their hours and conditions vary substantially but all earn a minimum Y1200/month (less than $150). This is just about enough to survive on given subsidised housing and certain other perks. FEs earn $300/month but need at least three years' teaching experience, a master's degree and/or a TEFL diploma. Non-teaching FEs with similar levels of

---

❏ Meeting the locals

● **The people** Few Chinese have a conversational command of English. More than xenophobia or political constraint, it is this linguistic barrier which makes it so relatively hard to form friendships with the locals you meet. Conversely, try as you might, it's unlikely that your beginners' Chinese will be understood or even recognised as Chinese at all. Fortunately, many cities have an intriguing weekly gathering called an 'English Corner' where enthusiasts meet to practice their language abilities. These meetings tend to be in the local 'Renmin Park' on Sundays. It's also worth visiting universities as students are often hungry for English conversational practice. Many universities are closed to visitors, but there are frequently food stalls near the guarded gates where it's easy to strike up a conversation over a bowl of noodles. Chinese universities are increasingly home to small, helpful communities of Westerners who study Chinese while teaching English. One of our more inventive methods of meeting people was to play frisbee in Tiananmen Square. Some locals did eventually join in, including a rather bemused soldier once he'd decided not to arrest us. Sadly no-one stayed around to chat afterwards. But then, would you?

● **Conversational topics** It's quite possible to discuss **political issues** though blunt criticism of the Chinese government is not recommended. Many people are happy to talk about the Tiananmen Square massacre, economic change, chairman Mao etc. Discussing **families** can be fascinating in the light of the one child policy (this doesn't apply to minority ethnic groups) and the migration (is it chosen or forced?) which has uprooted and broken up many extended families in the last 50 years. **Sport** makes for lighter conversation but though soccer and swimming are popular, you may need to do your homework to be able to discuss your nation's up and coming table tennis supremos.

● **Language** There are many 'Chinese' languages. Though most are mutually unintelligible when spoken, the writing system, in which characters have meanings rather than set sounds, is common to all. See 'Chinese Phrases' (p206-7) for basic linguistic logic and some useful words. By 'Chinese' we imply 'Mandarin' (*putonghua*), the national and most commonly used language.

Some phrases in Mandarin Chinese (the pinyin Chinese transliteration is in parentheses):

Thank You – *Sheh sheh [Xie Xie]*
Hello/How are you – *Nee how (ma) [Ni Hao (ma)]*
Yes – *She [Shi]*
No – *Boo She [Bu Shi]*
How much – *Dor shau chan?*
Not possible* – *Meh yoh [mei yo]*

* A very common phrase which means that anything from 'sorry that's not available' to 'get lost Big Nose'.

skill are hired as business consultants, proof-readers and engineers. Apply through Chinese embassies; or through **CEAIE**, 37 Damucang Hutong, Beijing, 10086; or try the **China Teaching Program**, Western Washington University, 530 Old Main, Bellingham, WA 98225, USA. Casual teaching jobs are technically illegal, especially on a tourist visa. But in reality they can be relatively easy to arrange. We were offered a ten-week, Y80/hr tutoring job by someone we met while walking down the street.

● **Volunteering** The government discourages all but the most highly skilled foreign volunteers – to do otherwise would be a face-losing admission that China is not a developed country. Few NGOs operate in China and the only opportunities for unskilled volunteers are in small, Western-run programmes, which usually require you to pay a large fee to join. One such group is the **Fudan Museum Foundation** (US ☎/fax 215-699-6448), 1522 Schoolhouse Rd, Ambler, PA 19002, USA, which accepts archaeological volunteers.

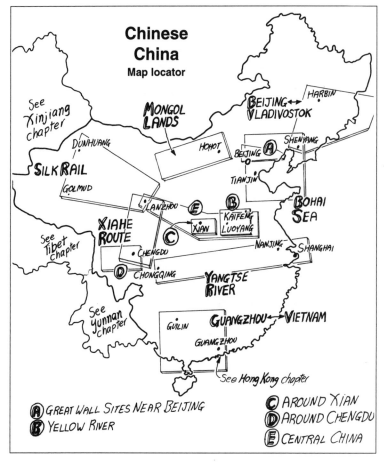

Chinese China
Map locator

See Xinjiang chapter

MONGOL LANDS

HARBIN

BEIJING↔VLADIVOSTOK

SHENYANG

DUNHUANG

HOHOT

BEIJING Ⓐ

SILK RAIL

GOLMUD

TIANJIN

LANZHOU Ⓔ

BOHAI SEA

XIAHE ROUTE

Ⓑ KAIFENG LUOYANG

XIAN

Ⓒ

See Tibet chapter

CHENGDU

NANJING

SHANGHAI

Ⓓ CHONGQING

YANGTSE RIVER

See Yunnan chapter

GUILIN

GUANGZHOU↔VIETNAM

GUANGZHOU

See Hong Kong chapter

Ⓐ GREAT WALL SITES NEAR BEIJING
Ⓑ YELLOW RIVER

Ⓒ AROUND XIAN
Ⓓ AROUND CHENGDU
Ⓔ CENTRAL CHINA

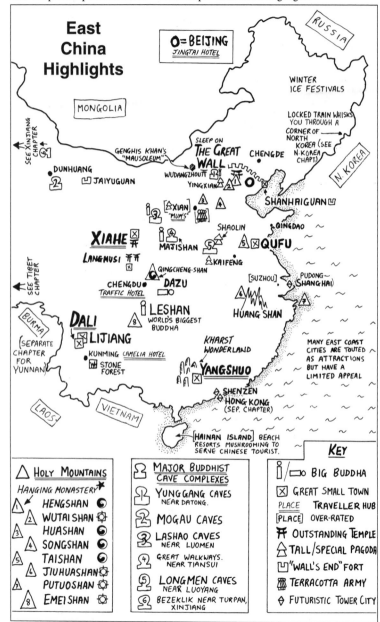

East China Highlights

O = BEIJING
JINGTAI HOTEL

MONGOLIA

RUSSIA

WINTER ICE FESTIVALS

SEE XINJIANG CHAPTER →

LOCKED TRAIN WHISKS YOU THROUGH A CORNER OF NORTH KOREA (SEE N. KOREA CHAPT.)

GENGHIS KHAN'S "MAUSOLEUM"

SLEEP ON THE GREAT WALL

CHENGDE

N. KOREA

DUNHUANG

JIAYUGUAN

WUDANGZHOU

YINGXIAN

SHANHAIGUAN

SEE TIBET CHAPTER →

XIAHE

LANGMUSI

XIAN "MUM'S"

MAJISHAN

SHAOLIN

QINGDAO

QUFU

KAIFENG

QINGCHENG-SHAN

DAZU

CHENGDU TRAFFIC HOTEL

[SUZHOU]

PUDONG SHANGHAI

BURMA

DALI

LIJIANG

LESHAN WORLD'S BIGGEST BUDDHA

HUANG SHAN

KUNMING _CAMELIA HOTEL_

STONE FOREST

KHARST WONDERLAND

MANY EAST COAST CITIES ARE TOUTED AS ATTRACTIONS BUT HAVE A LIMITED APPEAL

YANGSHUO

LAOS

VIETNAM

SHENZEN

HONG KONG (SEP. CHAPTER)

[HAINAN ISLAND] BEACH RESORTS MUSHROOMING TO SERVE CHINESE TOURIST.

△ HOLY MOUNTAINS

HANGING MONASTERY ✷

1. HENGSHAN ●
2. WUTAI SHAN ✿
3. HUASHAN ●
4. SONGSHAN ●
5. TAISHAN ●
6. JIUHUASHAN ✿
7. PUTUOSHAN ✿
8. EMEI SHAN ✿

MAJOR BUDDHIST CAVE COMPLEXES

1. YUNGGANG CAVES NEAR DATONG.
2. MOGAU CAVES
3. LASHAO CAVES NEAR LUOMEN
4. GREAT WALKWAYS. NEAR TIANSUI
5. LONGMEN CAVES NEAR LUOYANG
6. BEZEKLIK NEAR TURPAN, XINJIANG

KEY

🛕/▭ BIG BUDDHA

⊠ GREAT SMALL TOWN

PLACE TRAVELLER HUB

[PLACE] OVER-RATED

₸ OUTSTANDING TEMPLE

⌂ TALL/SPECIAL PAGODA

凵 "WALL'S END" FORT

▦ TERRACOTTA ARMY

⊹ FUTURISTIC TOWER CITY

Chinese rail network

Beijing to Vladivostok
(North East China)

• Cheap accommodation non existent in most large towns but many overnight trains.
• Pre-1992 NE China-USSR border was closed. There are now more than 20 border crossings but guards remain paranoid. If you can't get through one, try another.

SUIFENHE ←→ POGRANICHI
SENSITIVE CROSS 1ML. 10KM
ACROSS BUT TRAINS RUN ONLY
1-2 WEEK ONWARD TRAINS
FROM SUIFENHE TO HARBIN
LEAVE WITHOUT RUSSIAN
CARRIAGES IF THEY ARE LATE!

TO: MOSCOW (1 WEEK) → KHABAROVSK (11 HRS)

■ПОГРАНИЧНЫЙ POGRANICHI
ALSO: GRODEKOVO

2½/DAY
3 HRS

ПОКРОВКА ■POKROVKA

УССУРИЙСК USSURISK
PLEASANT GREEN STREETS

2½ HRS → TO JAPAN

DIRECT TO HARBIN 48 HRS

ВЛАДИВОСТОК
⊞VLADIVOSTOK

6 HRS

RUSSIA

CHINA

КРАСКИНО KRASKINO (MAKHALINO)

СЛАВЯНКА SLAVYANKA ☆ BEACH

1 HR

1 HR

ДУННИН ■DONGNING 东宁

СУНЬФЫНЬХЕ ⊞■SUIFENHE 绥河 绥芬河

СУЙ SUIYANG

北山 △BEISHAN

MUDIANGJIANG 牡丹江

DONGJING 东京城 ⊞

ХУНЬЧУНЬ HUNCHUN

ЯСАН ■KHASAN

TRAIN ACROSS BORDER TO 50 KM
LE BUILT BY CHINA?
½ CHINA PASSES THROUGH N. KOREA

NOTE:
■ = BORDER TOWN
⊞ = ATMOSPHERIC ONLY RELATIVE TO OTHER TOWNS ON THIS MAP

黑河 HEIHE ⊞河
WHENCE RIVER
BOATS CROSS TO
BLAGOVASH-
CHENSK
БЛАГОВЕШ-
ЕНСК (RUSSIA)

7 HRS
半夜 ■BEIAN 北安
13-14 HRS

19:42

18:35

HARBIN 哈尔滨
☆ WINTER
ICE FESTIVAL

Jingpo Lake 镜泊湖
'FOREST WALKS'

6 HRS 5/DAY (INCL. NIGHT)
15 HRS

SHENYANG -15 HRS
18:17 SHENYANG - 24 HRS
10:00 DALIAN - 24 HRS
17:07 BEIJING - 24 HRS

2½ HRS

3 HRS

1 HR.

4 HRS

CHINA

1½-2 HRS

DOORS LOCKED WHILE TRAIN PASSES THROUGH N. KOREA

Tümen River

TO PYONGYANG
(2~3 DAYS)

NOTE THE AREA AROUND THE KOREA-RUSSIA-CHINA BORDER IS A FREE TRADE ZONE

图们 ■ TUMEN 图们

SMALL KOREAN VILLAGES IN CHINA

YANJI 延吉

1 HR

HARBIN←BEIJING 16-22 HRS

TO BEIJING (9-11 HRS)

CHANGCHUN 长春 ⊞
• CAPITAL OF WW II
JAPANESE PUPPET
STATE OF MANCHUQUO

10 HRS (VIA) OVERNIGHT
JILIN 吉林

SEE BOHAI SEA MAP

SHENYANG 沈阳
●
HARBIN→BEIJING 5 HRS

⊞ MANCHU
IMPERIAL PALACE
(GUGONG 故宫)
TOMBS (8条)
MAO STATUE
☆ALL $20+

~10 HRS
SOME STEAM TRAINS

BAIHE 白河 ■
2 HRS
7 HRS
WALK
1½ - 2 HRS

BAISHAN 白山

TONGHUA 通化

TO DANDONG

⊞ Tianchi Lake
VOLCANIC LAKE
'NE ASIA'S
LOCH NESS?'

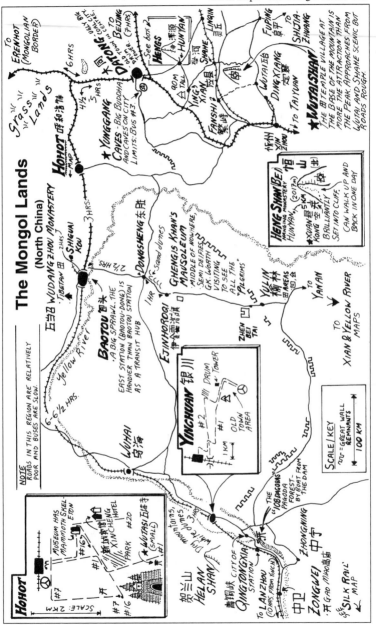

Central Beijing

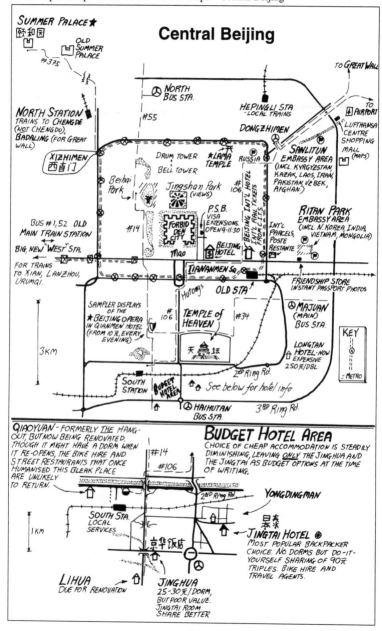

SUMMER PALACE ★
颐和园
#375
OLD SUMMER PALACE

NORTH BUS STA.
#55

HEPINGLI STA. - LOCAL TRAINS

TO GREAT WALL
TO AIRPORT
LUFTHANSA CENTRE SHOPPING MALL (MAPS)

DONGZHIMEN

NORTH STATION
TRAINS TO CHENGDE (NOT CHENGDU), BADALING (FOR GREAT WALL)
XIZHIMEN 西直门

Drum Tower
Bell Tower
★ LAMA TEMPLE
RUSSIA
SANLITUN EMBASSY AREA (INCL. KYRGYZSTAN, KAZAK, LAOS, IRAN, PAKISTAN, UZBEK, AFGHAN.)

Beihai Park
Jingshan Park (VIEWS)
#14
#106

P.S.B. VISA EXTENSIONS OPEN 9-11:30

RITAN PARK EMBASSY AREA (INCL. N. KOREA, INDIA, VIETNAM, MONGOLIA)

BUS #1, 52 OLD MAIN TRAIN STATION
BIG, NEW 'WEST' STA.
FOR TRAINS TO XIAN, LANZHOU, URUMQI.

FORBIDDEN CITY
Mao
BEIJING HOTEL
BEIJING INT'L HOTEL INT'L RAIL TICKETS FROM C.I.T.S.
INT'L PARCELS, POSTE RESTANTE

TIANANMEN Sq.
FRIENDSHIP STORE INSTANT PASSPORT PHOTOS

SAMPLER DISPLAYS OF THE ★ BEIJING OPERA IN QIANMEN HOTEL (FROM 10元, EVERY EVENING)
Hutongs
OLD STA.
#106
TEMPLE of HEAVEN
天坛
#34

♀ MAJUAN (MAIN) BUS STA.

LONGTAN HOTEL - NOW EXPENSIVE 250元/DBL.

3KM

2ND Ring Rd.
SOUTH STATION
BUDGET HOTEL AREA
See below for hotel info
♀ HAIHUTAN BUS STA.
3RD Ring Rd.

KEY
= METRO

QIAOYUAN – FORMERLY <u>THE</u> HANG-OUT, BUT NOW BEING RENOVATED. THOUGH IT MIGHT HAVE A DORM WHEN IT RE-OPENS, THE BIKE HIRE AND STREET RESTAURANTS THAT ONCE HUMANISED THIS BLEAK PLACE ARE UNLIKELY TO RETURN.

BUDGET HOTEL AREA

CHOICE OF CHEAP ACCOMMODATION IS STEADILY DIMINISHING, LEAVING ONLY THE JINGHUA AND THE JINGTAI AS BUDGET OPTIONS AT THE TIME OF WRITING.

#14
#106
2ND Ring Rd.
YONGDINGMAN
景泰

1KM

SOUTH STA. LOCAL SERVICES
京华饭店

JINGTAI HOTEL ✪
MOST POPULAR BACKPACKER CHOICE. NO DORMS BUT DO-IT-YOURSELF SHARING OF 90元 TRIPLES. BIKE HIRE AND TRAVEL AGENTS.

LIHUA
DUE FOR RENOVATION

JINGHUA
25-30元/DORM, BUT POOR VALUE. JINGTAI ROOM SHARE BETTER

The Great Wall 长城

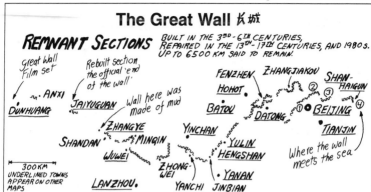

REMNANT SECTIONS

BUILT IN THE 3RD-6TH CENTURIES, REPAIRED IN THE 13TH-17TH CENTURIES, AND 1980s. UP TO 6500 KM SAID TO REMAIN.

Great Wall Film set

Rebuilt section the official 'end' of the wall

Wall here was made of mud

ANXI

DUNHUANG

JIAYUGUAN

FENZHEN ZHANGJIAKOU SHAN-HAIGUN

HOHOT

BATOU DATONG BEIJING

ZHANGYE YINCHAN TIANJIN

SHANDAN MINQIN YULIN Where the wall meets the sea

WUWEI HENGSHAN

ZHONG-WEI YANAN

LANZHOU. YANCHI JINBIAN

300 KM
UNDERLINED TOWNS APPEAR ON OTHER MAPS

Tourist literature claims the Great Wall is the only man-made object visible from outer space. Rubbish! For much of its length the Great Wall is so overgrown it's not even visible from the Great Wall itself. However, in the parts where it stands out from the mist-shrouded mountains, the Wall ranks among Asia's most dramatic sights. Most travellers visit it at one of the reconstructed sections near Beijing (see below). Transportation from Beijing is easiest with tour buses, and doesn't cost much more than going by yourself. At the most popular sections, Badaling and Mutiyan Yu, the heavy stream of tourists rarely seem to venture far along the Wall and leave well before sunset missing the best part: sleeping in the atmospheric, ruined watch towers is technically illegal, drafty and cold even in mid-summer, but what a sunrise!

WALL SITES NEAR BEIJING
SAVE MONEY WITH A STUDENT CARD

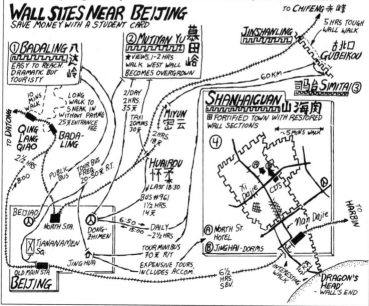

TO CHIFENG 赤峰

① BADALING 八达岭
EASY TO REACH. DRAMATIC BUT TOURISTY!

② MUTIYAN YU 慕田峪
★ VIEWS. 1-2 HRS WALK WEST WALL BECOMES OVERGROWN

JINSHANLING
5 HRS TOUGH WALL WALK

古北口 GUBEIKOU

60 KM

司马台 SIMITAI ③

10 MINS WALK

LONG WALK TO SNEAK IN WITHOUT PAYING 25元 ENTRANCE FEE

QING LANG QIAO

BADA-LING

TO DATONG

2½ HRS.

8.00

PUBLIC BUS

TOUR BUS FREQ. 20-50元 R.T.

BEIJIAO

NORTH STA.

TIANANAMEN Sq.

JING HUA

OLD MAIN STA.
BEIJING

2/DAY 2 HRS. 35元

TAXI 20 MINS 30元

MIYUN 密云

2 HRS. 18元

HUAIROU 怀柔

LAST 18:30

BUS #961 1½ HRS. 14元

6:50 — DAILY
15:00 ~ 2½ HRS.

TOUR MINIBUS 70元 R/T

DONG-ZHIMEN

EXPENSIVE TOURS INCLUDES ACCOM.

SHANHAIGUAN 山海关
⊞ FORTIFIED TOWN WITH RESTORED WALL SECTIONS

④

~5 MINS WALK

Xi Dajie

CITS

Nan Dajie

TO HARBIN

Ⓐ NORTH ST. HOTEL
Ⓑ JINGHAI-DORMS

6½ HRS. SEV.

INTERESTING WALK

DRAGON'S HEAD - WALL'S END

Around the Bohai Sea

SHENYANG 沈阳
· BEILING TOMB, MINI FORBIDDEN CITY (GUGONG 故宫)

SEE TO "BEIJING TO VLADIVOSTOK" MAP

14-15 HRS, 2/DAY

4-5½ HRS

承德 **CHENGDE**
SPREAD OUT REPLICAS OF TIBET'S POTALA AND OTHER MINORITY TEMPLES. SOUNDS CORNY BUT GOOD.

4½-6 HRS.

SEE PREVIOUS PAGE

BEIJING

NORTH STATION

OLD MAIN STATION

5 HRS. 6 - HRS.

SHAN-HAIGUAN

1 HR.

丹东 **DANDONG**
BORDER CITY WITH N. KOREA INFLUENCE

N. KOREA

TO PYONGYANG 2/WEEK

Good for random exploration

9~10 HRS

TIANJIN NO CHEAP HOTELS. SEE OLD REMNANTS (BUILT BY SIX COLONIAL POWERS) BEFORE THEY ARE TORN DOWN. ✪ INFORMAL BIKE RENTAL FROM UNDER GROUND CAR PARK NEAR R.R. STA. LOCALS LOVE "THE WONDERFUL ½ HR. DIANSHI", - A TV TOWER

2-2½ HRS.

天津

1 HR.

BEIDAIHE 北戴河
O-COLONIAL ERA RESORT
田△ WAIJIMO REYUAN - 7KM

大连 **DALIAN**
· BUS #13 PORT → TRAIN STA.
· COLONIAL STYLE BLDGS.

TIANJIN PORT
MINIBUSES WAIT AT DOCKS (WATCH YOUR VALUABLES!)

To JAPAN and KOREA (SEE NE ASIA CHAPTER), MANY DOMESTIC SERVICES

LUSHUN (PORT ARTHUR)
· OLD BRITISH COLONY
· CHINESE NAVAL BASE.
· BUS #3 (FROM R.R. STA. FOR CHEAP TOUR).

KOREA

FREQ 5-7 HRS.

Bohai Sea
渤海
Mouth of Yellow River

◎四★ **PENGLAI**
蓬莱

1 HR. 2 HRS.

龙口 LONG-KOU

YANTAI 烟台
△ JINBE-NEAR PORT

1½ HRS.

WEIHAI 威海

KOREA

ZIBO TOMBS

潍坊 **WEIFANG**

4 HRS

3-3½ HRS

6 HRS 5/DAY 4 HRS 5 HRS

JINAN 济南

FROM JINAN STA.

MINIBUS

1½ HR.

SHENQI BINGUAN

TAISHAN 泰山
· MOST SACRED OF CHINA'S SACRED MTS.
· CALLIGRAPHIC CARVINGS, HEAVEN'S GATE.

3 HRS

QINGDAO 青岛
(OR TSINGTAO) - HOME OF THE BEER ORIGINALLY BREWED BY GERMANS
· ATTRACTIVE REMNANTS OF GERMAN COLONIAL TOWN AMIDST SCARS OF MODERISATION

5 MINS.

BUS #3 TO END

TAISHAN BINGUAN

4 HRS

CITS UPSTAIRS

TAIAN 泰安
· ATTRACTIVE TOWN
· DAI MIAO 开
▲ NEAR TRAIN STA., MAPS OUTSIDE STA.

1 HR

MENGLIANGGU
孟良崮

MENGYIN 蒙阴

YAN-ZHOU

20 MINS.

★⊙田 **QUFU** 曲阜
· BIRTH PLACE OF CONFUCIUS (KONG)
· CHARMING SMALL TOWN WITH SEV.
· VISIT KONG LIN 孔林, KONG FU 孔府 OR THE HUGE 凹/开 COMPLEX OF
★ KONG MIAO 孔庙

SEE "GRAND CANAL" MAP

SEE "YELLOW RIVER" MAP

to SHIJIAZHUANG

MANY

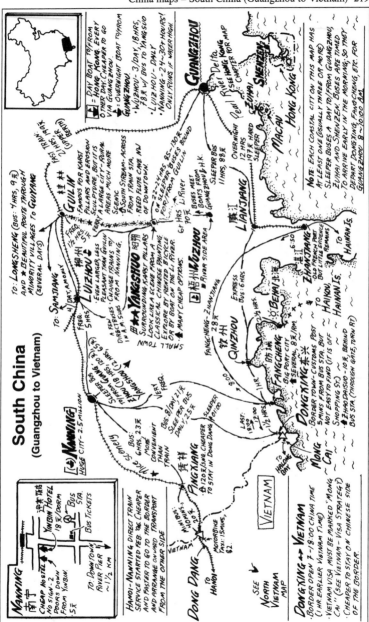

Guangzhou 广州

Bustling, charmless gateway to Hong Kong. Good food – the more unusual ingredients for which are sold in cages at the Qinping Market. Touts at the bus station offer rooms for 20 yuan, but once there the cheap rooms are 'full'. ('No problem. 120 yuan room OK'. Hmm...). Cheapest reliable option is the **Youth Hostel** on Shamian Island (60 yuan/dorm).

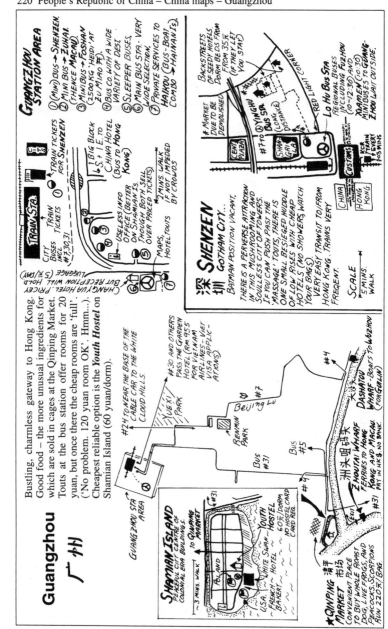

GUANGZHOU STATION AREA

① (MINI) BUS → SHENZEN
② MINI BUS → ZUHAI. (THENCE MACAU)
③ MINIBUS → FOSHAN (2500 KG. 'HEIDI' AT ZU MIAO 祖庙)
④ BUS CO. WITH A WIDE VARIETY OF DESTINATIONS
⑤ SLEEPER BUSES,
⑥ MAIN BUS STA. - VERY WIDE SELECTION.
⑦ PRIVATE SERVICES TO HAIKOU (BUS-BOAT COMBO → HAINAN'Ts).

TRAIN STA.
CITY BUSES INCL #7,30,31
TRAIN TICKETS
TRAIN TICKETS FOR SHENZEN

① USELESS INFO OFFICE (BETTER ON SHAMIAN IS. THOUGH, BOTH SELL OVER PRICED TICKETS)

1 BIG BLOCK E.S. + 1 E. TO CHINA HOTEL (BUS to HONG KONG)

MAPS, HOTEL TOURS

~2 MINS. WALK IF NOT IMPEDED BY CROWDS

HANGYUA HOTEL. PRICEY BUT RECEPTION WILL HOLD LUGGAGE (5 元/DAY)

GUANGZHOU STA AREA

SHENZEN 深圳
GOTHAM CITY...

BATMAN POSITION VACANT.

THERE IS A PERVERSE ATTRACTION IN THIS MUSHROOMING AND SOULLESS CITY OF TOWERS. IF YOU CAN PUSH PAST THE 'MASSAGE' TOUTS, THERE IS ONE SMALL BESIEGED HUDDLE OF LOW RISES WITH CHEAP HOTELS (NO SHOWERS WATCH YOUR BAGS).
VERY EASY TRANSIT TO/FROM HONG KONG. TRAINS VERY FREQENT.

SCALE
5 MINS. WALK

BACKSTREETS OF SEEDY HOTELS, DORM BEDS FROM 35元

RED LIGHT CORNER

MARKET DUE TO BE DEMOLISHED

CEN PLAZA

#710 ② YINGHU BUS STA (LONG DISTANCE)

SHAN GRI LA

Lo Hu BUS STA

REGIONAL BUSES INCLUDING FUZHOU (10-12.30) AND XIAMEN (10.30) MINIBUSES TO GUANG-ZHOU WAIT OUTSIDE.

CUSTOMS

KCR TRAINS EVERY 1-3 MINS

CHINA
HONG KONG

SHAMIAN ISLAND
PEACEFUL CITY CENTRE OF COLONIAL ERA BUILDINGS.

~3 MINS. WALK

To QINPING MARKET

#31

POLAND

U.S.A.
FRENCH BAKERY
WHITE SWAN HOTEL

YOUTH HOSTEL
60元/DORM
NO HOSTEL CARD REG.

#24 TO/NEAR THE BASE OF THE CABLE CAR TO THE WHITE CLOUD HILLS.

YUEXI PARK

#30 AND OTHERS PASS THE GARDEN HOTEL (RM. 955 FOR VIETNAM - VIET VISA APPLIC-ATIONS)

Beijing Lu

RENMIN PARK

Bus #31

Bus #5

Bus #31

#4

#4

ZHOUTAI WHARF
FERRIES TO HONG KONG AND MACAU
PAY IN HK$, NO BANK.

DASHATOU WHARF - BOATS TO WUZHOU (FOR GUILIN)

洲头咀码头

大沙头

EXIT

#31

★ QINPING MARKET 清平市场
CONVENIENT PLACE TO BUY WHOLE ROAST DOG, LIVE FROGS, AND PEACOCKS, SCORPIONS RUN 220元/BAG.

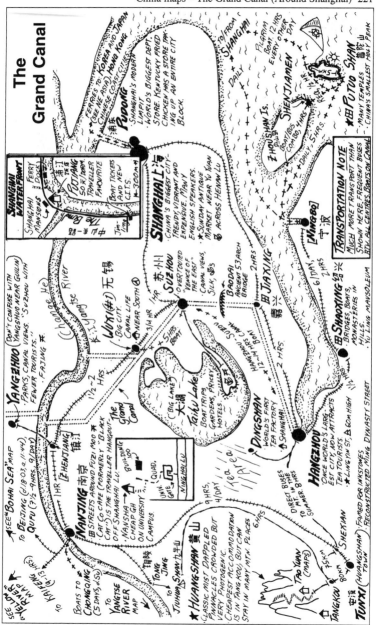

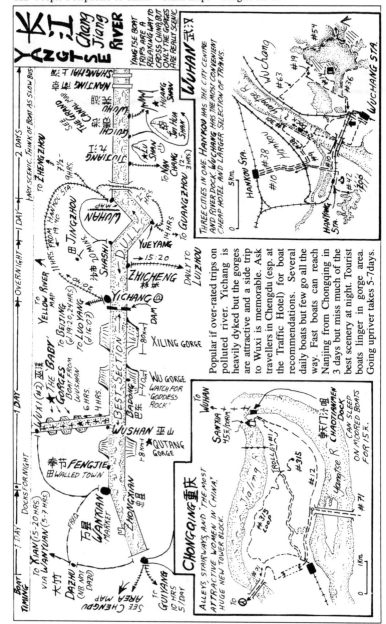

YANGTSE River 长江 Chang Jiang

Yangtse boat trips are a relaxing way to cross China, but only the gorges are really scenic.

WUHAN 武汉

Three cities in one. Hankou has the city centre and river dock. Wuchang has the most convenient cheap hotel and larger selection of trams.

THE GRAND CANAL See China map

SHANGHAI 上海

NANJING 南京 See China map

To ZHENGZHOU — 2 DAYS
1 HR. SCENIC. TRUNK OF BOAT AS SLOW BUS

庐山 Lu Shan

Huang Shan
黄山

九华山 Jiu Hua Shan

JIUJIANG 九江 7½-8 HRS
To NAN CHANG 2-3 HRS

田 JINGZHOU

WUHAN MAP
(11 HRS. FROM HANKOU STA. 19.40)

SHASHI 沙市 10 MIN.

To GUANGZHOU (3 HRS.)

DULL

YUEYANG 14 HRS
Daily to Luizhou

15:20

ZHICHENG

YICHANG @
DAM
To Beijing (19.20, 24 HRS) O.K.
To LUOYANG (16.01)

XILING GORGE
80m↑

WU GORGE
WATCH FOR 'GODDESS ROCK'

BADONG 巴东
↓140m↑

BEST SECTION

WUSHAN 巫山
↓8m↑
QUTANG GORGE

WUXI (#2) 巫溪
★ THE 'BABY' GORGES
Boat from Wushan 6 HRS.
4 HRS.

奉节 FENGJIE
田 WALLED TOWN

ZHONGXIAN 忠县

WANXIAN 万县 MARKET

FRQ

石柱 DAZHU (NB NOT DAZU) 大竹

To XIAN (15-20 HRS) VIA WANYUAN (5-7 HRS)

SEE CHENGDU AREA MAP

To GUIYANG 10 HRS 5/DAY

To Yellow River MAP

CHONGQING 重庆

Alleys, stairways and the most attractive women in China. Huge new Tower block.

To WUHAN
SANMIA 三码头 45¥/DORM

朝天门码头 CHAOTIANMEN DOCK
Can sleep on moored boats for 15¥.

Yangtse R.

(TROLLEY #1) #12

#315
#315 LOOP

Jialing R.

#71

To Yellow River MAP

BOAT TIMING

1 DAY — DOCKS FOR NIGHT — 1 DAY — OVERNIGHT — 1 DAY — OVERNIGHT — 1 DAY — 2 DAYS

Popular if over-rated trips on polluted river. Yichang is heavily dyked but the gorges are attractive and a side trip to Wuxi is memorable. Ask travellers in Chengdu (esp. at the Traffic Hotel) for boat recommendations. Several daily boats but few go all the way. Fast boats can reach Nanjing from Chongqing in 3 days but miss much of the best scenery at night. Tourist boats linger in gorge area. Going upriver takes 5-7 days.

WUHAN 武汉 (inset map)

Wuchang
#54
#19
#63
#36
WUCHANG STA.

HANKOU STA.
#10 #38
Han Shui R. 汉水
#8
HANYANG STA.
#42
#71

0 ___ 5km

CHONGQING (inset map)

0 ___ 1 Km

Central China

TO BEIJING
Daily 20 HRS,
23号 HARD
SLEEPER

TO BEIJING
Sev/DAY,
19 HRS.

TO SHANGHAI
25 HRS.

SEE
YELLOW
LANDS MAP

TO SEE
MONGOL LANDS MAP

SEE
YELLOW
RIVER
MAP

TO GUANGZHOU
2/DAY, 34-36 HRS.
255号 HARD SLEEPER

LUOYANG

TO SEE
YULIN 榆林
⊕田 8KM N

13 HRS

延安 YAN AN
CIVIL WAR
ERA COMMUNIST HQ.
CAVES, HUANG LING
TOMB ON MT. QUAO.

[BAOJI]

TO CHENGDU
5/DAY, 17-20 HRS.

SEE MAP BELOW

XIAN 西安

TO TAIYUAN
9 HRS.

MENGYUAN 孟源

50元

10/DAY
1½ HRS.

TO YELLOW RIVER
MAP

[DONGGUAN]
HOTEL
AT TOP
50元

HUASHAN
VERY ATTRACTIVE.
STEPS RUN ALL THE
WAY UP TO TOP... 5 HRS

17/DAY
25 MINS

10/DAY
1½ HRS.

[LINTONG]
MINIBUSES
7KM

2½ HRS

BUS# 306
FROM STA.
45 MINS

THE
TERRACOTTA
WARRIORS

XIAN

TO YAN AN

½ HR.

咸阳 XIN YANG
FORMER CAPITAL

10/DAY
20 MINS

BANPO
BUS# 11

TERRACOTTA WARRIORS
IN TOWN MUSEUM

ALTERNATIVE (SMALLER)
PREHISTORIC
VILLAGE MUSEUM

TO LANZHOU
13-16 HRS.

Terracotta Warriors

Considered one of China's top sights. Tours cost around Y90 + the entrance fee (Y60, 20 for students) and also take you to a succession of other rather dull, expensive museums. Better to go by yourself.

TO URUMQI

LANZHOU 兰州

SEE
SILK RAIL MAP

LUMEN 龙门
BIG
BUDDHA

LASHAO CAVES

[WUSHAN]

SEE
NAME ROUTE
MAP

TIANSUI 天水
BIG
BUDDHA

MINIBUS
1 HR.

★MAJISHAN
CAVES & CAT WALKS
AROUND CLIFF-
FACE BUDDHA
- SEE PHOTOGRAPH

MINIBUS
AT STA.

Xian

Former imperial capital of Chang'an, eastern hub of the Silk Route, world's biggest city in the 7th century (pop. almost one million). Massive 14th century city walls still largely intact, but recent modernisation has ripped away most of the atmospheric old streets. In the surrounding country, however, are many tombs, palaces and the remains of the city's glory days. Bicycle (from Mum's Home Cooking) is recommended for exploration.

TO ZOO

NORTH GATE

21

EAST GATE

BUS
#35,36

SOUTH GATE

21

BIG
GOOSE
PAGODA
#5

★WEST GATE

21

LITTLE
GOOSE
PAGODA

BUS
#10

(FORMERLY)
RENMIN
⊕ HOSTEL

RENT BIKES,
MEET OTHER
TRAVELLERS
AT THE RESTAUR-
ANTS ("MUM'S"
DAD'S HOME
COOKING) OPP.
THE HOSTEL
(STILL KNOWN
AS RENMIN
DESPITE OFFICIAL
NAME CHANGE)

Yellow River

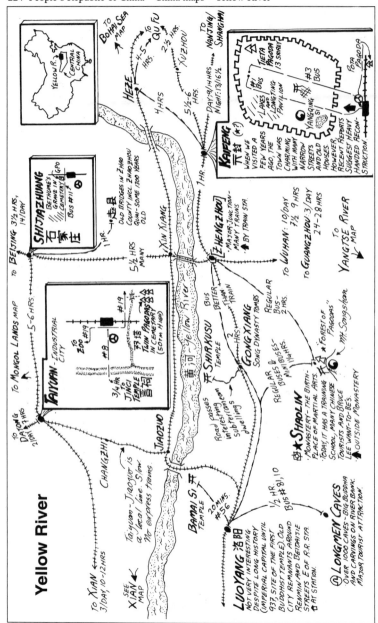

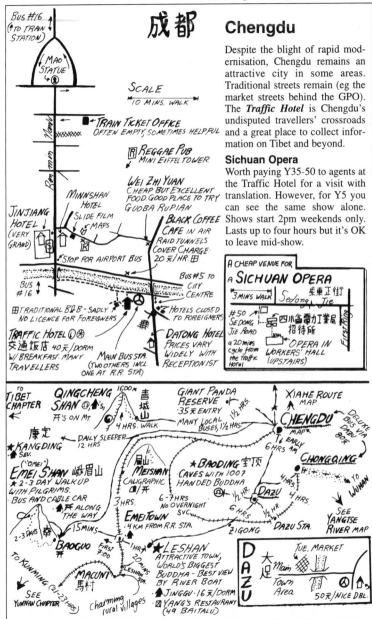

Chengdu

Despite the blight of rapid modernisation, Chengdu remains an attractive city in some areas. Traditional streets remain (eg the market streets behind the GPO). The *Traffic Hotel* is Chengdu's undisputed travellers' crossroads and a great place to collect information on Tibet and beyond.

Sichuan Opera

Worth paying Y35-50 to agents at the Traffic Hotel for a visit with translation. However, for Y5 you can see the same show alone. Shows start 2pm weekends only. Lasts up to four hours but it's OK to leave mid-show.

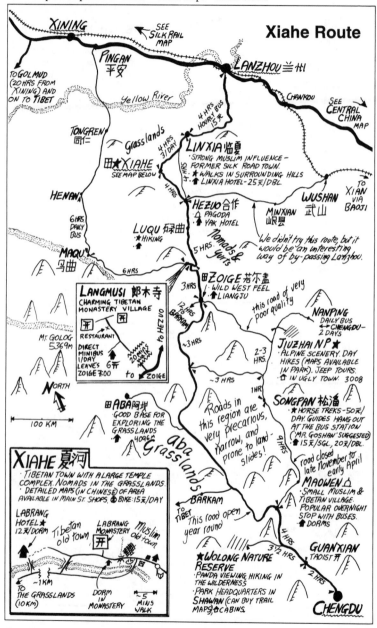

Xiahe Route

XINING

SEE SILK RAIL MAP

PINGAN 平安

TO GOLMUD (20 HRS FROM XINING) AND ON TO TIBET

LANZHOU 兰州

Yellow River

CHANKOU

SEE CENTRAL CHINA MAP

TONGREN 同仁

Grasslands

4 HRS 3/DAY

4 HRS HOURLY BUS 15元

田★XIAHE SEE MAP BELOW

LINXIA 临夏
· STRONG MUSLIM INFLUENCE – FORMER SILK ROAD TOWN.
★ WALKS IN SURROUNDING HILLS
🏠 LINXIA HOTEL – 25元/DBL.

XIAN VIA BAOJI

HENAN

HEZUO 合作
⛩ PAGODA
🏠 YAK HOTEL

WUSHAN 武山

MINXIAN 岷县

LUQU 绿曲
★ HIKING

Nomads & yurts

We didn't try this route, but it would be an interesting way of by-passing Lanzhou.

MAQU 马曲

6 HRS DAILY BUS

5 HRS.

6 HRS

田★ZOIGE 若尔盖
· WILD WEST FEEL
· LIANGJU

3 HRS

this road of very poor quality

NANPING
DAILY BUS
←CHENGDU– 2 DAYS

LANGMUSI 郎木寺
CHARMING TIBETAN MONASTERY VILLAGE
🏠 RESTAURANT
DIRECT MINIBUS 1/DAY LEAVES 6元 ZOIGE 7:00

12 HRS to BARKAM

to HEZUO

20 HRS MARCH

JIUZHAI N P ★
· ALPINE SCENERY. DAY HIKES (MAPS AVAILABLE IN PARK). JEEP TOURS.
🏠 IN UGLY TOWN. 3008

MT. GOLOG 5369M

to ZOIGE

~3 HRS

2-3 HRS.

~3 HRS

1HR

SONGPAN 松潘
★ HORSE TREKS – 50元/ DAY. GUIDES HANG OUT AT THE BUS STATION ('MR. GOSHAN' SUGGESTED)
🏠 15元/SGL., 20元/DBL.

NORTH

100 KM

田★ABA 阿坝
· GOOD BASE FOR EXPLORING THE GRASSLANDS
🏠 HORSE

Aba Grasslands

Roads in this region are very precarious, narrow, and prone to land slides!

4 HRS

road closed late November to early April

MAOWEN 🏠
· SMALL MUSLIM & TIBETAN VILLAGE.
POPULAR OVERNIGHT STOP WITH BUSES.
🏠 DORMS

Xiahe 夏河
· TIBETAN TOWN WITH A LARGE TEMPLE COMPLEX. NOMADS IN THE GRASSLANDS.
· DETAILED MAPS (IN CHINESE) OF AREA AVAILABLE IN MAIN ST. SHOPS. 🚲 BIKE: 15元/DAY

LABRANG HOTEL ★ 12元/DORM

Tibetan old town

LABRANG MONASTERY 开

Muslim old town

TO TIBET
This road open year round

BARKAM

4 HRS

3½ HRS

GUANXIAN TAOIST 开

2 HRS

TO THE GRASSLANDS (10KM)

DORM IN MONASTERY

~5 MINS WALK

★WOLONG NATURE RESERVE
· PANDA VIEWING, HIKING IN THE WILDERNESS
· PARK HEADQUARTERS IN SHAWAN (CAN BUY TRAIL MAPS) 🏠 CABINS

CHENGDU

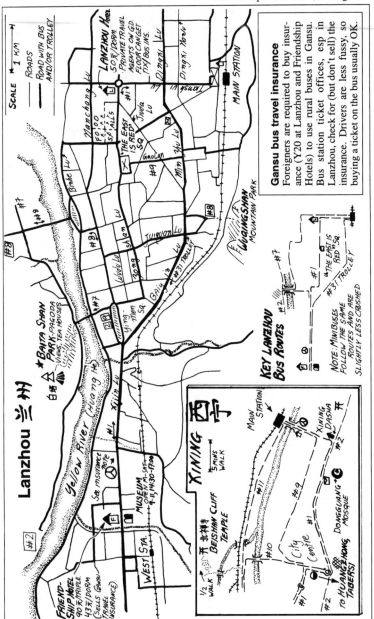

Lanzhou 兰州

Gansu bus travel insurance

Foreigners are required to buy insurance (Y20 at Lanzhou and Friendship Hotels) to use rural buses in Gansu. Bus station ticket offices, esp in Lanzhou, check for (but don't sell) the insurance. Drivers are less fussy, so buying a ticket on the bus usually OK.

KEY LANZHOU BUS ROUTES

NOTE: MINIBUSES FOLLOW THE SAME ROUTES AND ARE SLIGHTLY LESS CRASHED

XINING 西宁

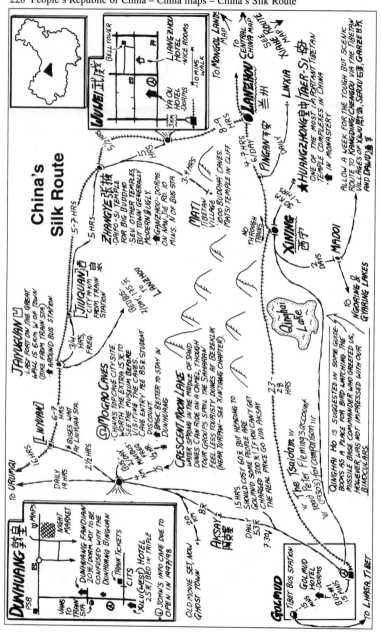

China's Silk Route

WUWEI 武威
BELL TOWER
LIANGZHOU HOTEL – NICE ROOMS
YAOU HOTEL – DORMS
~10 MINS. WALK
3KM

DUNHUANG 敦煌
VANS TO TRAIN STA.
PSB
B
CITS
TRAIN TICKETS
NIGHT MARKET
MAPS
DUNHUANG FANDIAN 20元/DORM. NOT TO BE CONFUSED WITH THE DUNHUANG BINGUAN
XILU(WEST) HOTEL 2.5元/BED IN TRIPLE
Ⓙ JOHN'S INFO CAFE DUE TO OPEN IN 1997/98

TAIYUGUAN 巴
'LAST FORT ON THE GREAT WALL IS 6KM W. OF TOWN (BIKE FROM TRAIN STA.)
☆ AROUND BUS STATION.

[LIUYUAN]
6-7 HRS
BUSES WAIT AT LIUYUAN STA.
1½ HR.
(1 HR.)
2½ HRS

TO URUMQI
(3 HRS.)

DAILY 14 HRS

BUS ¥50 45 KM TO MOGAO

JIUQUAN 酒泉
CITY 14KM FROM TRAIN STATION
3/4 HRS, FREQ.
BED 186元, 25元
2/DAY/25元

LANZHOU 蘭州

ZHANGYE 张掖
DAIFO-SI TEMPLE FOR BIG BUDDHO. SEE OTHER TEMPLES BUT TOWN GENERALLY MODERN & UGLY.
• GANZHOU-DORMS ON NAN JIE RD. 10 MINS. N OF BUS STA.
5-7 HRS
5 HRS
5½ HRS
5 HRS

Ⓜ MOGAO CAVES
CHINA'S TOP CAVE CITY-SITE. WORTH THE EXTRA 15元 TO SEE THE MUSEUM BEFORE VISITING THE CAVES. CAVE ENTRY FEE 85元 STUDENT DISCOUNT.
• BASIC. BETTER TO STAY IN DUNHUANG

CRESCENT MOON LAKE
WATER SPRING IN THE MIDDLE OF SAND DUNES. CAN RIDE ON A CAMEL, THOUGH TOUR GROUP'S SPOIL THE SAHARAN FEEL. LESS TOURISTY DUNES AT BEZEKLIK (NEAR TURPAN – SEE XINJIANG CHAPTER).

MATI TIBETAN VILLAGE
1000 BUDDHA CAVES. MATI TEMPLE IN CLIFF
3-4 HRS

OLD MOVIE SET, NOW GHOST TOWN

AKSAY 阿克塞
DAILY 53元
7-3元
8元
2.0 KM

15 HRS – SHOULD COST 60元. SOME PEOPLE ARE CHARGED 300元. IF YOU CAN'T GET GOLMUD VIA AKSAY THE REAL PRICE GO VIA AKSAY

Ⓥ The Tsaidam w/ read Peter Fleming's account (1935) VII for comparison!!!

GOLMUD 格尔木
TIBET BUS STATION
GOLMUD HOTEL – DORMS
BUS #1 15 MINS
BUS #1 15 MINS
TO LHASA, TIBET

Qinghai Lake

QINGHAI HU IS SUGGESTED IN SOME GUIDE-BOOKS AS A PLACE FOR BIRD WATCHING. THE MISSILE BASE COMMANDER WHO GREETED US, HOWEVER, WAS NOT IMPRESSED WITH OUR BINOCULARS.

TO NGORING & GYARING LAKES

23-28 HRS

XINING 西宁

MADOI

2 DAYS

PINGAN 平安
8-9 HRS
4-7 HRS 6/DAY
DAILY

★ HUANGZHONG皇中 / TAER-SI 塔尔寺
ONE OF THE MOST IMPORTANT TIBETAN TEMPLE COMPLEXES IN CHINA

LINXIA

NO THROUGH TRAINS

ALLOW A WEEK FOR THE TOUGH BUT SCENIC ROUTE TO KANGDING/CHENGDU VIA THE TIBETAN VILLAGES OF KANWU 甘玉, SERXU 石渠, GARZE 甘孜 AND DAWU 道孚

MONGOL LANDS MAP
CENTRAL CHINA MAP
XIAHE ROUTE SEE ROUTE

Hong Kong

The pictures of Hong Kong that you've probably seen are the neon-clad skyscrapers straddling Victoria Harbour. However there's much more to Hong Kong than this: traffic free Cheung Chau Island is as quaint a place as you'll find in China; the Bird Market has a special atmosphere; there are walled villages (Kam Tin, though a bit touristy) and there's good camping at Clearwater Bay. Not perhaps as exotic as Tibet, but Hong Kong has its own style, great restaurants and a unique economic dynamism. Things haven't changed noticeably since the July 1997 handover to Chinese rule and the stockmarket's rollercoaster ride in October 1997. The 'one country, two systems' philosophy has so far been honoured; Hong Kong retains its own currency, visa policy and even its own writing system as, unlike mainland China, the letters were never simplified. Though many ex-patriot foreigners remain, Hong Kong is, and has always been overwhelmingly Cantonese.

❏ **W&M's country ratings – Hong Kong**
- **Expense $$$$** Expensive compared to the rest of China, most prices are equivalent to Western Europe. Hotels pricey. Bangkok better value for air tickets.
- **Value for money ✔✔✔** Local ferries and Big Macs are great value.
- **Getting around ✔✔✔✔✔** Services are often crowded but they are regular and very easy to figure out.
- **English spoken ✔✔✔✔** Very easy to get by.
- **Woman alone ✔✔✔✔** Take the same precautions as in any big city.
- **For vegetarians ✔✔✔✔✔** Plenty of food for all tastes.

❏ **Essential information for travellers – Hong Kong**
- **Visa** Not required for most Western nationals (most Eastern Europeans do need visas). The period of stay, one or three months, depends on your nationality.
- **Currency** Hong Kong Dollar. US$1=HK$7.73. Credit card cash advances, cashing travellers' cheques and ATM withdrawals are all easy.
- **Time zone** 8 hours ahead of GMT; same as China and Irkutsk; 1hr ahead of Indochina; 2hrs behind Eastern Australia.
- **Health factors** We drank the water. There is no reported malaria risk.
- **Social conventions** A 10% tip in bars and restaurants is customary, even if a 10% service charge is already added. For taxis, tip by rounding the fare up.
- **Typical traveller destinations** Victoria Peak, markets, shopping malls.
- **Highlights** Outer islands, New Territory beaches, bamboo scaffolding.
- **When to go** Summers are very hot and humid, spring and autumn are generally warm during the day and cool in the evening and winter days are sometimes cool enough for a sweater or light jacket but it can be cold at night.
- **Pulse of the country** The Star ferry.
- **Key tips** All the info and maps you need available free from HKTA.

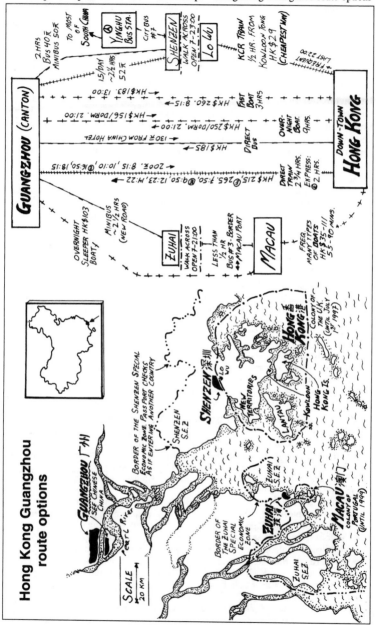

Hong Kong Guangzhou route options

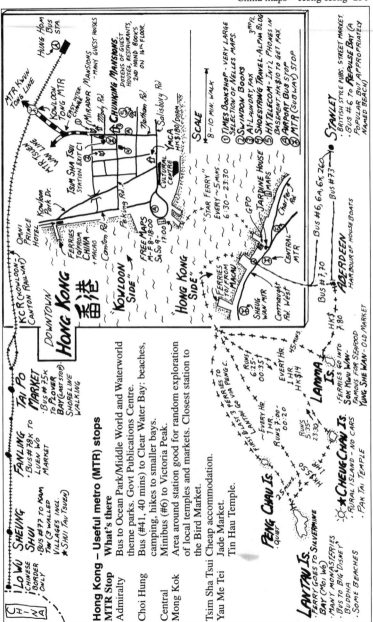

Hong Kong – Useful metro (MTR) stops

What's there

MTR Stop

Admiralty — Bus to Ocean Park/Middle World and Waterworld theme parks. Govt Publications Centre.

Choi Hung — Bus (#41, 40 mins) to Clear Water Bay: beaches, camping, hikes to smaller bays.

Central — Minibus (#6) to Victoria Peak.

Mong Kok — Area around station good for random exploration of local temples and markets. Closest station to the Bird Market.

Tsim Sha Tsui — Cheap accommodation.

Yau Me Tei — Jade Market. Tin Hau Temple.

PRACTICAL INFORMATION
Visas and formalities
The **Immigration Department** (☎ 2824 6111, fax 2877 7711), 2/F Immigration Tower, 7 Gloucester Road, Wan Chai, will arrange visa extensions and processes applications for work visas.

Money
All major currencies are exchangeable but poor rates are given for Thai Baht. Banks generally give the best rates; the airport rate is one of the worst. Beware of high commissions and/or psychological tricks from change booths (such as quoting rates of, say, HK$7.07, which you mistake for the standard 7.70). **Patel's** (on the ground floor in Chungking Mansions) have good rates and charge no commission to cash travellers' cheques. Chinese Yuan are exchanged at HK$0.9.

Transport
● **Air** International departure tax: HK$50. (NB A new airport is scheduled for completion in summer 1998.) Flights are booked solid around Chinese New Year (usually in February).
● **Bus** Airport buses run to and from different parts of Hong Kong between 7am and midnight. Useful buses include: **A1** (HK$12) to Tsim Sha Tsui (Chungking and Mirador mansions, YMCA, China ferries); **A2, A20** (HK$17) to Central (Island ferries); **A3** (HK$17) to Causeway Bay.
● **Ferry** Hong Kong has an extensive network of ferries. Prices are very reasonable – the hop between Central and Kowloon is HK$1.40. Ferries to the outer islands are very crowded at weekends and holidays.

Accommodation
Whoever named Chungking Mansions had never seen a mansion. Chungking and its next door neighbour, Mirador Mansions, are the seediest pair of towerblocks in downtown Kowloon. Fortunately, no-one has yet demolished them and they remain warrens of tiny guest houses, restaurants and the odd travel agent – the undoubted centre for budget travellers. Tsimshatsui MTR station is right outside.

Recommendations in Chungking include the *Sky Dorm* (block A, 3F) for dorm beds and the *London Guest House* (block B, 6F) for singles. In Mirador Mansions, which is slightly cheaper (cheapest dorms are HK$60), try the *Welcome Guest House* (7F), or *Garden Hostel* (3F). One problem is the queues for the very slow lifts. Choosing a hostel on a lower floor makes it easier to take the stairs.

Hong Kong's **youth hostels** are cheap-

❏ **Geo-political information – Hong Kong**
Population: 6.4 million (1997), 5.8m (1993), 5.5m (1991), 850,000 in 1931.
Area: 1078 sq km.
GNP per capita: $17,800 (1993), $9,300 (1988).
Currency history: HK$/US$1 – Feb 1998: HK$7.73, 1997: 7.70, 1996: 7.74.
Ethnic mix: Chinese (97%), European (2.2%), Sikhs and Indians.
Official languages: English and Cantonese. Native speakers: Cantonese (88%), Other Chinese (9%), English (3%).
Religious mix: Buddhist/Taoist (74%), Christian (9%) Muslim, Hindu, Sikh.
Landmarks of national history: **1842**: Ceded to Britain following the Opium War. **1898**: Lease on New Territories signed for 99 years. **1941-45**: Occupied by Japan. **26 Sept 1984**: Sino-British Declaration on restoration to China. **1 July 1997**: Reverted to China (the separate currency remains).
Leader: Tung Chi Hwa.
Pressing political issues: The economic fallout following the stock market crises in Korea and South East Asia; maintaining the 'one country, two systems' code; genocide of chickens.

Yunnan and South West China

Laid-back, friendly Yunnan is a marked contrast to the harsh bustle of east coast China. The prices are much lower, the people smile more and the cities are smaller and more manageable.

Dali, set high on Lake Erhai with a great mountain backdrop, has developed into a muesli and banana-pancake traveller hangout to rival Yangshuo. Nearby Lijiang has (or had until the 1995 earthquake) China's most attractive old town. The steamy jungles of Xishuangbanna have become surprisingly popular with raucous gangs of Han Chinese tourists, but its Dai and other hill-tribe villages remain very well preserved; arguably they are more interesting than similar villages in Thailand and grander (if less idyllic) than in Laos. Even Kunming, despite the ongoing bulldozing and the construction of ever more gleaming tower blocks, retains an airy, attractive old quarter and a modicum of charm. But the real Yunnan is in the mountains – green, lush and inviting.

❏ **W&M's country ratings – Yunnan**
● **Expense $$** Significantly cheaper than elsewhere in the People's Republic of China; travel on as little as $6/day is possible.
● **Value for money** ✔✔✔✔ Good food and passable accommodation for little money.
● **Getting around** ✔✔✔✔ Buses go almost everywhere, but the roads are windy and slow.
● **English spoken** ✔✔ No trouble in the traveller centres but a big problem in rural areas.
● **Woman alone** ✔✔✔✔ Few hassles reported.
● **For vegetarians** ✔✔✔ Lots of great food but ascertaining the ingredients can be tough.

PRACTICAL INFORMATION
Visas and formalities
● **Permits** Almost everywhere is now 'open' apart from the far west road to Gongshan and the route from Deqen into Tibet via Markam. Permits are necessary for both these routes and are unlikely to be granted unless you are on a tour. Though Deqen itself had been announced permit free, some travellers reported they'd been fined. Check latest details in Zongdian.

Money
Travellers' cheques can be cashed easily in Kunming and Dali, but may be difficult elsewhere. In border towns such as Mohan and Ruli, restaurants and some shops will change money for you. In Mohan the rate for buying Lao *kip* is extremely good.

Transport
● **Bus** The bus system is extensive, services are reasonably frequent, and there's little or no sign of foreigner mark-ups. Long-distance routes are covered by sleeper buses.
● **Train** Long-distance train services include the Kunming to Chengdu line, through a long series of tunnels, and a newly inaugurated link to Hanoi (though

cheaper to take a train only to the border).
● **Air** Yunnan has its own airline. It costs Y520 to fly between Kunming and Jinghong (compared to 25 hours on the tiring, if beautiful, bus ride).

Accommodation

Yunnan is much more relaxed than the rest of China and you're not usually restricted to 'foreigner approved' hotels. You'll rarely have to pay more than Y10-15 for a basic bed, except in Kunming where dorms cost from Y30.

Food and drink

Dai cuisine is understandably popular because of its use of the fine fruity flavours of Thai cooking, without the chilli-hot sting. In some villages where traditional Dai houses accept visitors, you are asked (or gesticulated at): 'Eat?' Agreement results in a multi-dish feast well worth the Y40 or so it may cost per person. There are more commercial Dai restaurants in Jinghong, some with rather tacky 'cultural shows' and dances. Of course the Dai are only one of many tribes – each has its own distinct cuisine; this could mean you'll eat roots and insects in one place, bamboo shoots and spices in another.

In backpacker centres (Dali, Jinghong and Kunming) there are cafés with the usual egg and toast breakfasts and other tourist fare. Locally made cigarettes are said to be the best in China; better ones have flower petals added for fragrance. There's a small scene for naughty smokes.

Staying in touch

● **Fax** Faxes can be sent and received at the Journey to the East café in Kunming (near the 'Pink Palace' foreign students'

❏ **Essential information for travellers – Yunnan**
● **Visa** Visa required. See China chapter, p201.
● **Currency** Yuan. US$1=Y8.28.
● **Time zone** 8 hours ahead of GMT (1hr ahead of Laos, 1½hrs ahead of Burma.
● **Religious tone** Mildly Buddhist at heart; Tibetan style in the north, Burmese in the south.
● **Special dangers** A few lone trekkers have been robbed in the otherwise idyllic Tiger Leaping Gorge, but generally Yunnan is very safe.
● **Social conventions** Most ethnic groups have their own foibles – be observant and sensitive. Talking to locals while wearing sunglasses is rude. Shorts and sleeveless shirts (especially if worn by women) are often unacceptable. Mirrors have a negative connotation in part of southern Yunnan.
● **Typical traveller destinations** Kunming, Stone Forest, Dali, Lijiang, Tiger Leaping Gorge, Xisuangbanna.
● **Highlights** As above, random hill walks, the villages round Simao, the Zongdian route to and from Tibet (this is difficult).
● **When to go** The tropical forests of southern Yunnan (on the same latitude as Calcutta) are best visited November to February when the weather is cooler, though summer is bearable. Rain forests need rain; this can fall at any time, though it's unlikely to do so for prolonged periods. Kunming has cool winter nights and slightly sweaty days. Although Dali and Lijiang are surrounded by mountains, the winters are mild and the travellers' scene remains year round. Zongdian is appreciably colder. The best time to attempt the road into Tibet is April: the snows of winter should have cleared, but the summer rain has yet to cause landslides.
● **Pulse of the country** Hilltribe village markets.
● **Key Tips** Random exploration is easy using locally produced 'traffic maps' on which the thin red lines denote roads with bus services. A tent is useful for walks into the mountains. Jinghong is a good place to extend Chinese visas.

dormitory building of the university in the north west part of the city). International code: +86, Kunming code: 871.

Shopping

The weekly hilltribe markets such as Menglun's (Sunday mornings) are similar colourful spectacles to those in north Thailand, and offer tempting if useless souvenir fodder.

Activities

● **Hiking** There are few set hiking routes, but excellent wandering opportunities. Northern Yunnan has many ad hoc camping sites; there are fewer in the southern rain forests. The most popular trek along the Tiger Leaping Gorge has suffered from reported muggings in the last few years.

Further information

● **Books** *Southwest China Off the Beaten Path* (Passport) was our favourite regional guide but sadly it now seems to be out of print. A second-hand copy is still worth seeking out, though most China guidebooks cover Yunnan in adequate detail. Indeed Yunnan is a relatively easy place to explore without a guidebook at all.

For background information, read anything by Joseph Rock, a famous biologist who lived in Yunnan. Compare Samuel R Clarke's 1891 *Among the Tribes in South-West China* with Zhong Xiu's 1983 *Yunnan Travelogue: 100 Days in Southwest China* – both of which are sold throughout China.

The Journey to the East café in Kunming has English books (but only a few are guides) for sale and swap. In Dali try the Coca Cola café. New guide books are hard to find anywhere.

● **Maps** Xinhua bookshops sell Yunnan road atlases (Y3.60), divided by county. Normal county names (.....*zhan*) are four characters long. However, ethnic minority areas are named according to the 'autonomous' tribal groups present, so the longer the county name the more likely it is that the area has an interesting cultural mix and that it could be interesting for random exploration. Yunnan and Kunming city maps are sold by swarms of vendors outside Kunming's main railway station. The very detailed, bilingual *Cross-Border Communications* map includes the northern parts of Laos, Vietnam, Thailand and

---

❑ Meeting the locals

● **The people** Yunnan has a very diverse mix of colourful, hill tribes. As Nanzhou, it was the original home of the Thai people who later emigrated south, especially after the 13th century Mongol raids. Their close relatives, the Dai, remained. Tribal people still wander fairly freely between Yunnan, Laos and Burma. Kunming and the cities are predominantly populated by Han Chinese who have been mellowed by the warmer climes, but costumed minority folk can often be seen downtown selling their artefacts. The bigger hilltribe groups in Yunnan are:

Group	Approximate number
Yi	6 million (total population)
Miao	5.5 million (total population)
Bai	1.5 million
Hani	1.2 million
Dai (Thai)	1 million
Lisu	600,000
Lahu	400,000
Naxi	300,000
Jingpo	100,000

● **Languages** Most tribal groups have their own language. These overlap with the languages of Laos and northern Thailand so Lonely Planet's *Thai Hilltribe Phrasebook* is useful.

Burma as well as Yunnan – thus it's useful for onward travel. If you can figure out the Chinese, it also has the major air and train timetables, and gives tourist information.

● **Information** Wei's Place in Kunming is a popular café with a travellers' notebook.

Jinghong has a helpful CITS office offering free Xishuangbanna maps; travellers meet at Mei Mei's Café or the Good Companions Guest House. Dali is Yunnan's Kathmandu with scores of chilled out travellers.

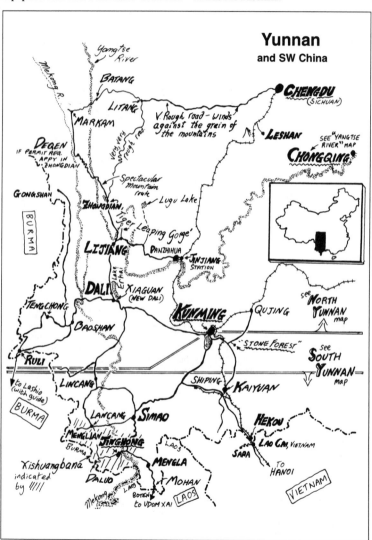

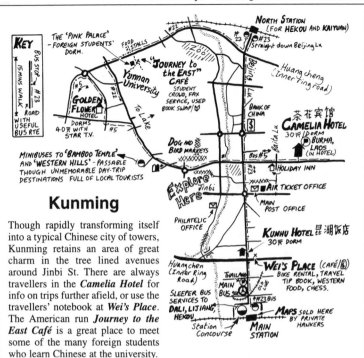

KEY

15 MINS WALK ← → BUS STOP #23

ROAD WITH USEFUL BUS RTE

THE 'PINK PALACE' - FOREIGN STUDENTS' DORM.

FOOD STALLS

NORTH STATION (FOR HEKOU AND KAIYUAN)

Straight down Beijing Lu

"JOURNEY to the EAST" CAFÉ — STUDENT CROWD, FAX SERVICE, USED BOOK SWAP/☕

Yunnan University

ZOO

Huang cheng (inner ring road)

Beijing Lu

GOLDEN FLOWER HOTEL

DORMS 40元 WITH STAR T.V.

To Lake

BANK OF CHINA $

茶花宾馆 **CAMELIA HOTEL** 30元 DORM BURMA, LAOS (IN HOTEL)

Beijia Lu

MINIBUSES TO 'BAMBOO TEMPLE' AND 'WESTERN HILLS' - PASSABLE THOUGH UNMEMORABLE DAY-TRIP DESTINATIONS FULL OF LOCAL TOURISTS

DOG AND BIRD MARKETS

BUS #5

HOLIDAY INN

Explore Here

Jinbi

AIR TICKET OFFICE

MAIN POST OFFICE

PHILATELIC OFFICE

Kunming

Though rapidly transforming itself into a typical Chinese city of towers, Kunming retains an area of great charm in the tree lined avenues around Jinbi St. There are always travellers in the *Camelia Hotel* for info on trips further afield, or use the travellers' notebook at *Wei's Place*. The American run *Journey to the East Café* is a great place to meet some of the many foreign students who learn Chinese at the university.

Huangchen (Inner Ring Road)

SLEEPER BUS SERVICES TO DALI, LIJIANG, HEKOU.

Station Concourse

THAILAND

MAIN BUS STN

KUNHU HOTEL 昆湖饭店 30元 DORM

WEI'S PLACE (CAFÉ/☕) BIKE RENTAL, TRAVEL TIP BOOK, WESTERN FOOD, CHESS.

#23 BUS

MAPS SOLD HERE BY PRIVATE HAWKERS

MAIN STATION

Onward travel is relatively easy: some long distance buses can be pre-booked at the bus station but many sleeper buses (especially to Dali/Ljiang, Hekou and other destinations) leave when full from the main railway station concourse in the early evening (no booking).

SHILIN 石林
STONE FOREST

STONE FOREST

SHILIN BING YUAN

SHOPS

$ DORM 40元

OFFICIAL ENTRY: PAY 33元

SNEAK IN FREE VIA VILLAGE

SHILIN FANDIAN

BUS PARK

Not to scale

Surreal park full of sharp rocky pinnacles, swarming with tourists by day but magical by moonlight.

The easiest way to arrive is on minibus day tours from the Camelia Hotel (3-4 hrs, dep 8.30am) then ditch the group to explore on your own. Public buses run only in the early morning. Trains (2/day on the Hekou/Kai Yuan-bound line from north station) drop you still an hour short of the park, at Yiliang. The nearest town to the stone forest is Lunan (10km, Y2 by bus) but there's accommodation and food in Shilin village.

If you're heading to Guiyang, there's no need to double back to Kunming – take a Shilin-Qujing bus (4/day, Y20, the last is at 1.30pm).

North Yunnan

CHENGDU
ⓘ TRAFFIC HOTEL - INFO FOR GOING SOUTH

SEE CHINESE CHAPTER

PERHAPS THE BEST TRAIN IN CHINA. CLEAN, FREE GIFTS, IN-FLIGHT STYLE SAFETY DEMO.
↓ TO KUNMING : 25 HRS, 197元 HARD SLEEPER.
↓ TO JINJIANG : 16-17 HRS.

DEQEN PERMIT?
CONFLICTING CLAIMS OVER WHETHER YOU NEED A PERMIT. SOME TRAVELLERS REPORT 70元/DAY FINES FOR NOT HAVING ONE. I INQUIRE IN ZHONGDIAN (PREFECTURE OFFICE ALMOST OPP. P.O. - 2ND FL. 9-11, 14:30-17:00)

SEE TIBET CHAPTER

TO MARKAM
1½-2 DAYS HITCH

DEQEN 德钦

★ GREAT RIDE. HIGHEST MTS. IN YUNNAN (4300M PASS) BUS EVERY OTHER DAY

TO **CHENGDU** - VERY TOUGH ROUTE. ALLOW AT LEAST ONE WEEK. BRING WARM CLOTHES

YONGNING 永宁   11 KM   HOT SPRINGS
落水   LUGU LAKE 泸沽湖

EVERY 2 DAYS

ZHONGDIAN 中甸
♠★ TIBET HOTEL - 20元
STAR TV
TOWN HAS A TIBETAN ATMOSPHERE

2/DAY
11 HRS

TIGER LEAPING GORGE PLEASANT HIKE, THOUGH LESS DRAMATIC THAN TOURIST HYPE.

→ HADA

4-5 HRS

NINGLANG 宁蒗

QIAOTOU

1-2 DAYS   3HRS WALK
● DAJU

8-9 HRS

★**LIJIANG** 丽江
· OLD TOWN. ONE OF THE MOST BEAUTIFUL CHINESE CITIES (THOUGH NEW SECTIONS UGLY).
· ★ BLACK DRAGON POND. NEARBY NIXA TRIBE HAVE A MATRIARCHAL SOCIETY.
· MILD CLIMATE IN THE WINTER DESPITE MOUNTAINOUS SETTING
♠ RED SUN 18元. WALLS CRACKED BY 1995 EARTHQUAKE BUT STILL STANDING.

[JINJIANG]   4:52, 15:05, 17:40, 23:50
23:48, 7:15

11 HRS

6-7 HRS MANY DIRECT BUSES FROM OUTSIDE KUNMING RAIL STA. EVENINGS

PANZHIHUA (FORMERLY DUKOU)
★ SO BAD IT'S GOOD. SUPREMELY UGLY - LIKE BLADE RUNNER GONE WRONG

GUDONG 古永
· ⓘ TEMPLE

10 KM
VOLCANOES
100 M WALK   7 KM   20 MINS HIKE
MAZHANG

VOLCANIC LAKE

20 KM

腾冲

★田**TENGCHONG**
♠ TENGCHONG GH - 18元/ 3 BED DORM. SELLS MAPS.

ROAD TO **GONGSHAN** 贡山 IS CLOSED UNLESS YOU CAN GET A PERMIT.

TO KUNMING (9 HRS)

★ WEEKLY MARKET ON OTHER SIDE OF THE LAKE. BOAT 30-70元 FROM DALI

5 HRS, 22元 (VERY BUMPY!)

田 **DALI** 大理
· LAKE, MTNS, AND YUNNAN ATMOSPHERE.
· POPULAR TRAVELLER HANGOUT - USED BOOKS, BIKE RENTAL, GREAT FOOD.
· DON'T CONFUSE WITH NEW DALI (XIAGUAN) - AN UGLY JUNCTION TOWN AT WHICH SOME "DALI" BUSES TERMINATE.
♠ ★ OLD DALI INN. ALSO NEW HOTEL BY S GATE (10元, HAS SWIMMING POOL)
· TAHE - 7KM AWAY, RUINS OF PROTO-THAI CAPITAL OF NAMACHAO

25元
5~8 HRS   保山
田 **BAOSHAN**
· ♠ OTHER SIDE OF ⓘ AND THEN 300M LEFT. 8元/DORM, 15元/SNG.

MINIBUS FROM N. CORNER

6½-8HRS   30元

RULI 瑞丽
· BORDER BOOMTOWN. MAJOR DRUG SMUGGLING CENTRE. FULL OF BROTHELS.
♠ 90元/TRIPLE. NO DORMS.

14~17 HRS   90元

SLEEPER 11HRS, 90元
LOCAL, 45元
13HRS, 45元
MOST GO OVERNIGHT

-3 KM   45 MINS   15元
MUSE

临沧
SLEEPER: 24HRS, 175元
LOCAL: 2 DAYS, 90元

昆明 **KUNMING**

BURMA
POSSIBLE TO CROSS BORDER BUT NEED A GOV'T ESCORT TO GO TO/FROM LASHIO ($30~40)

WANDING

SOUTH YUNNAN MAP

South Yunnan

S. Yunnan's main attraction is Xishuangbanna: a region of intriguing minority villages set in patchy rainforest and rubber plantations. Unspectacular Jinghong, is the laid back hub town - great Dai cuisine, a small travellers' scene, and good for Chinese visa extensions. Jinghong's CITS is remarkably helpful giving free maps and genuine advice on how to avoid the villages most plagued with busloads of Han Chinese package tourists. Landscapes en route to dull Mengla are particularly attractive. There are other interesting minority areas around Simao and Menglian which are less 'discovered'. 'MENG' in a town name is a clue that nearby villages will be full of wooden stilt homes.

HEKOU > VIETNAM
Vietnam is a short walk across a narrow rail bridge near the town centre. Hekou is more interesting than Lao Cai but Sapa (Viet) a short ride beyond is nicer than either.

MOHAN > LAOS
15min walk or 5Y tractor ride across no man's land. Border opens 8am (with the time difference the Lao side thus opens 1hr later). Mohan is an ugly single street of concrete shops but restaurants here have cheap, comfortable rooms and change $ for kip at very good rates (no banks). It's worth staying here (visit Shangyang) to get an early start heading south as Boten is only a handful of ragged wooden shacks and transport to the rest of Laos is very limited - a couple of 4wds in the morning only.

DALUO > BURMA
At the time of writing, this border remains closed. This is sure to change as work has started on a major international route to Chiang Rai (Thailand) via Kengtung in Burma's Shan States using this route. Ask in Kunming or Jinghong for the latest.

Tibet

A deeply spiritual, magical place on the proverbial roof of the world, Tibet has intrigued travellers for centuries and inspired them long after they've returned home. But getting there isn't easy. And once there, police regulations, political turmoil and very limited transportation add to the rigours of the extreme altitude, the thin air, and the icy winds that tear across the rugged, barren terrain.

Independent for most of its long history, Tibet was invaded by China in 1950. For nine years there were many local uprisings while the Dalai Lama, Tibet's spiritual and political leader, sought a peaceful solution. By 1959 the Chinese had had enough. The army moved in, in full force, and the Dalai Lama fled with many followers across the mountains to India where he now leads a government in exile from Dharamsala.

China has ruled with an iron fist ever since. Beijing sees Tibetan culture as feudal, backward and anachronistic. One approach to modernising Tibet was to destroy most of the Buddhist temples and religious buildings. Of over 6000 monasteries operating before the Chinese invasion, only 31 survive today. Guides and Chinese publications blame this on Mao's 'little mistake', the Cultural Revolution. In fact most of the destruction came later. Several temples are now being rebuilt, but whole atmospheric quarters of historic old Lhasa continue to be torn down in the name of sanitation and progress. Many Tibetans continue to suffer imprisonment, torture and blackmail and there is widespread corruption and spying, even within monasteries. Meanwhile the culture is being systematically diluted by sheer numbers of outsiders. Tibetans are now a minority in their own land, following widespread Chinese immigration.

The issues are not completely black and white. The Chinese settlers aren't cruel or evil. The government has simply made resettlement attractive for them by offering high salaries and added benefits such as the right to bear two chil-

---

❑ **W&M's country ratings – Tibet**

● **Expense $$ - $$$$** Cheap in terms of survival needs but permits, paying for tours, and occasional fines can make it pricey.

● **Value for money** ✔ Prices may vary but standards remain low. You don't come for comfort.

● **Getting around** ✔ Difficult unless you are prepared to wait, hitch, wait some more, pay fines, rent your own transport and/or join tours. Walking is the best way to get around. The Kathmandu-Lhasa route is comparatively straightforward!

● **English spoken** ✔ Sometimes in Lhasa, rarely in large towns and almost never in the countryside.

● **Woman alone** ✔✔✔✔ Safe relative to the rest of the world.

● **For vegetarians** ✔ Extremely difficult outside Lhasa.

dren (most Chinese are only allowed one). And though some Chinese police can be ruthless, the young soldiers seem clueless and simply follow orders while Tibetans themselves are often corrupt.

This said, it is difficult not to view the Chinese occupation as a tragedy on a massive scale. So should you visit? Few Tibetophiles back the idea of a tourist boycott. While travelling, it is possible to ensure that most of what you spend ends up in Tibetan pockets. Locals seem to realise that most foreigners are on 'their side' and take the tourist presence as proof that they have not been forgotten. If you do go to Tibet the single most important thing you can do is to ensure you don't jeopardise the Tibetans you meet. You can leave – they usually cannot. There is a lot of spying, much of it by other Tibetans. Even if you trust someone, be careful who's around when you speak on sensitive subjects. Don't write to Tibetans about politics and be careful what you write about to friends or to yourself – not even your journal is sacred (change names, etc). If you do talk about politics, make it clear that you are not a journalist as Tibetans occasionally risk talking to you hoping their words will reach a larger audience in the West.

We don't want to suggest that the responsibility for all Tibetans is on your shoulders. Tibetans have been living under Chinese rule for a long time now and are expert at it. They are trying to stay alive and to follow the Dalai Lama's non-violent teachings. Simply remember who you are speaking to and their political situation. When in doubt, keep quiet and be sensitive to anyone who dodges a question. There's no need to be paranoid – just be aware.

Signs in Lhasa hotels tell you not to photograph demonstrations. Take note – photographs could cause minor problems for the Chinese if published, but major ones for you if you are caught with them.

This chapter is designed to help you straddle obstacles to travel here, though no book can keep pace with a situation that is in constant flux. In Tibet, every travel rule has many exceptions and whatever one person says is impossible, another manages to achieve. Other travellers will inevitably be your best guide.

❏ Difficult times to travel to Tibet

Consistently, the worst time to visit is around 10 March – the anniversary of the 1959 Tibetan uprising. As early as December, authorities prevent travellers entering Tibet from Nepal (there are no flights from late November to mid-March, though it is possible to leave by land). Typically, around January one needs special (hard to get) permits to fly from Chengdu, and the land routes from Golmud and Chengdu tighten up. The situation eases around mid-March.

At other times of year, the situation is more of a guessing game. Keeping updated on the news (eg on the 'Panchen lama' issue) can increase your odds of timing your trip successfully. But it could take as little as one anti-Chinese demonstration in one small town to close Tibet to foreign travellers. Festival times make authorities particularly nervous. Lhasa, Shigatse and Samye are traditional trouble spots.

Other difficult times include Losar (Tibetan New Year) in February; around 10 June (the anniversary of a large 1989 demonstration) and around 15 December (International Human Rights day and the anniversary of various demonstrations).

❑ Essential information for travellers – Tibet

● **Visa** Same as China, but special permits may be required.

● **Currency** Yuan. US$1=Y8.28.

● **Time zone** 8 hours ahead of GMT (same as Beijing time, 2hrs ahead of Xinjiang time, 2¼hrs ahead of Nepal, 2½hrs ahead of India).

● **Religious tone** Deeply Tibetan Buddhist: the spiritual leader, the Dalai Lama, lives in exile in India. Also some *Bön* (Tibetan-style Shamanism).

● **Health factors** Altitude sickness. If you're hitching on trucks check the altitude of your route – truck drivers are already acclimatised and won't slow down to give you the chance to do the same. Water is not usually difficult to find on summer walks (as always, drink upstream from animals). Tap water is not safe to drink.

● **Social conventions** To win respect, bring butter and a spoon to monasteries and spread it piously onto the butter candles burning there.

Though not required, it is a nice gesture to offer a *khata* (see box, p247) and token Y1 where Tibetans are doing so.

● **Typical traveller destinations** Lhasa, and the road from Kathmandu to Lhasa.

● **Highlights** Anything Tibetan especially nomads, secluded monasteries and wilderness areas; not being fined.

● **When to go** Politics generally play a greater role than the climate in planning a trip to Tibet (see Difficult times to travel to Tibet box). Temperatures in the winter months vary from cold in the morning and evenings to really cold at night, but in the afternoon it can be quite warm. Winter can be a good time to visit Tibet if you don't plan to do major trekking because it is pilgrimage season and Lhasa is full of nomads (and empty of travellers of the backpack variety).

The weather starts warming up in late April/early May: an ideal time for the difficult roads in eastern Tibet (to/from Sichuan). Police are rumoured to be more lenient with the first travellers of spring.

The summers are warm, yet high altitude areas are still cold (the Yadong/Chumbii valley area can have snow in July). Western Tibet receives an occasional monsoon visit in June and July; eastern Amdo and Khams receive some rain in the late Spring which could temporarily wash out roads to/from Chengdu, but otherwise there is little rain.

Throughout the year, but especially in the winter, there is an enormous difference between the air temperature and the temperature in the sunshine; on a particularly cold and sunny day, it is possible to stand on the shadeline and be sunburnt and frost-bitten at the same time.

● **Pulse of the country** Lhasa Potala Palace.

● **Key tips** If you have a tent, stove, food, water, good sleeping bag and good pair of hiking boots you will greatly increase your freedom in Tibet. Patience and flexibility are equally essential.

Don't wait until Kathmandu to get your Chinese visa if you're heading into Tibet from Nepal.

Bear in mind that individual travel to Tibet is possible, but can be difficult.

● **Festivals** A kind of Tibetan Olympics (with horseraces and archery) held in Gyantse in May/June for two weeks.

Shoton – a week of opera contests is held in August/September. There are many other festivals.

PRACTICAL INFORMATION
Visas and formalities

● **Permits** Permit requirements for Tibet vary town by town, day by day and with the slightest change in the political breeze. Lhasa city and region is 'open' so you don't officially need any special papers to visit. But you've got to get there first. The General Tibet permit is effectively a way of charging tourists a whacking Y400-700 entry fee. You'll need the permit to buy a flight into (though not out of) Lhasa and, in most cases, to enter by land from Nepal (see below). The easiest way to procure the permit is to join a group tour. However, contrary to the claims of certain travel agents and dictionaries, a group can consist of one person. To take the bus from Golmud, the permit is not required per se, but the vastly inflated foreigner price of the south-bound ticket simply reflects the permit fee. All other routes into Tibet are officially closed. To use them you'd need a separate Closed Area permit which could, theoretically, be issued for a nominal fee by a PSB office. In reality, such permits are almost never issued without high powered contacts, wads of cash and super-human charm. Even then there's no guarantee that the paper will work. For around $1600, a group of five chartered a Land Cruiser for the Lhasa-Markam-Kunming drive and got what they thought to be official permits. However they were prevented from proceeding by police in Markam who declared that the permit listed the wrong towns and dates. Try to check your permit with someone who can read Chinese before you pay for it.

Many of the towns, villages and monasteries of greatest tourist interest (eg Shigatse) are not 'closed'. But falling outside the Lhasa region they're not quite 'open' either. To keep your visit legitimate you could get an 'Open town permit'; these are issued easily and cheaply during calm periods. However, such permits are rarely checked, except at times of political unrest.

● **Entering Tibet from Nepal** If you do get a visa in advance, you have a small chance of being allowed across the border independently at Kodari, even during the winter. Most individuals are turned back but it costs little to try given the cheap Nepali bus services. Being let out of Nepal is no trouble, but Chinese guards normally demand to see a Tibet 'visa endorsement' which is only available to those on a tour. However, every year a few people do talk their way through. A patient and polite persona can work wonders. A friend of ours spent two days chatting and drinking with Chinese border guards claiming he wanted to learn Mandarin. Eventually, they asked him if he'd like to visit the People's Republic to learn more. 'Sure' he said (in Chinese through a dictionary). They gave him a Tibet permit for Y10 and let him in. We met others who were refused entry the very same day having made the mistake of demanding their 'rights'. Saying 'I have a Chinese visa, you say Tibet is China, so you have to let me in', doesn't work.

Note Coming independently **from** Tibet into Nepal seems to be no problem.

● **Travel without a permit** If you have the wrong permit, or no permit at all, one way to avoid the authorities is to stick to rural areas and walk. A tent, good map, warm clothes, water and food are required and it is not advisable to go alone. The walking option only works once inside Tibet – do not try to cross the heavily guarded borders of China illegally.

If you travel by road through towns and villages you are doomed to a cat and mouse game with the police. The two major places foreigners are caught are at hotels and road blocks. At hotels, police often have informers, and foreigners have been known to have their rooms raided at 3am. Chamdo, Markam, Baij, Zhamo and Ali have particularly bad reputations for police diligence. Try to arrive after dark and pass through these towns as quickly as possible – again, camping would be the safest option. Trouble at road blocks can be avoided by either hiding in the vehicle (it's surprisingly easy to get lost amongst the huddle of coats and Tibetans in the back of a truck) or by getting out a mile or so before the checkpoint and walking around it. The second option requires a sensibly slow pace of travel as you're unlikely to find a driver who knows all the check points and is patient enough to wait for your subterfuge. Occasionally Chinese drivers have been known to deliberately hand travellers over to the authorities.

The penalty for travelling with the wrong (or no) permit depends on where you are caught and by whom. It is likely you'll be reprimanded, be made to write a letter of apology and/or be fined. The maximum fine, regardless of what any police officer says, is Y500. Fines are often as low as Y10 or Y20. Even if **you** are not charged, drivers providing transport without the right paperwork can be fined Y500 per foreigner, and risk losing their licences. In some rare cases, foreigners breaking permit rules have had a spell in jail, but in all the cases we know of, the traveller was either in a very sensitive military area or was caught committing the same offence twice.

If you're not to be jailed the police will probably send you back from whence you came – assuming they know what direction that is. With a little reverse psychology some travellers have managed to get police to turn them back in the very direction they were heading. Other police will always send travellers away from Tibet, making

sneaking back in more difficult – but ideal if you were heading out anyway. Of course, being ordered out of town is not as easy as all that. You may have to wait days for a bus to materialise during which time you are usually free to wander around. Expulsions from Chamdo and Markam are likely to be on the Chengdu bus via Batang and Litang – a very attractive route in itself.

● **Tours** We rarely recommend joining a group tour but, as a pragmatic way to get into Tibet, there may be no other choice. See box below. Tours ex-Kathmandu enter Tibet by air or road between April and October. The cost, including flight in, permits, two nights in Lhasa and road transport back, starts from $360. The Chinese embassy in Kathmandu issues 'group permits' only – it does not issue full Chinese visas. Converting these papers into a full (individual) Chinese visa in Lhasa takes a lot of hassle, the co-operation of your tour-group leader and at least $60. Thus it is much better to have a proper Chinese visa before you arrive in Nepal if you are planning to breakaway from the group to explore Tibet and China on your own.

● **Visa extensions** It's better to get an extension on your Chinese visa elsewhere in China – it is much easier and doesn't leave evidence of your Tibet trip in your passport. The ease of getting extensions in

---

❑ **Companies offering tours to Tibet**

● **Richa Tours and Travels** (Nepal ☎ 215331, fax 229304), PO Box 1657, Thamel, Kathmandu (in Namche Bazaar opposite the Maya Pub) offers eight-day overland tours from Kathmandu to Lhasa for $380; there's a guaranteed departure every Saturday but they need five days' advance notice.

● **Himalayan Adventures** (Nepal ☎ 229459, fax 411453), PO Box 9001, Kathmandu.

● **Tibet Friendship Travel Service** (☎/fax 0891-34533), No 18 Norblingka Rd, Lhasa, is a Chinese-run travel agency that does tours of Tibet.

● **Tenzing Himalayan Expeditions** (Australia ☎ 3-437 5399), 304 Willoughby Rd, Naremburn, NSW 2065, Australia, is a Tibetan-owned travel agency.

● **Trans Himalaya** (UK ☎ 0181-459 7944), 30 Hanover Rd, London NW10 3DS, UK.

● **Inner Asia Expeditions** (US ☎ 415-922-0448), 2627 Lombard St, San Francisco, CA 94123, USA.

Tibet fluctuates with the political situation but is generally best in the summer. Lhasa seems the best place to try: enquire at the PSB.

Money

There are few money changing offices – it's better to change a lot when you have a chance because it's easy to re-exchange money when you're leaving China (if you keep the exchange certificate).

Travellers' cheques are exchangeable in Lhasa and Shigatse at the Bank of China and at the Nepal border. You might be able to get a credit card advance (with 4% commission) at the Bank of China in Lhasa but don't count on it.

Transport

There is a severe lack of transport of any kind in Tibet. Distances are huge and the population small, so paid hitchhiking is the only transport on many routes. For long journeys you'll need to be totally self-sufficient with plenty of food, water and warm clothes (it can be difficult to get the driver to stop once you're moving and there have been cases of travellers dying of hypothermia in the back of trucks). Don't assume that there will be villages and shops along the way. You might go for days without seeing much sign of habitation, especially on the Kashgar-Lhasa route.

● **Bus** Bus services operate on some routes but these may be as infrequent as three times a month.

● **Trucks and paid rides** Agree (and write down for future reference) the sum you want to pay and pay it in stages, with the final amount to be handed over on arrival. The asking price varies wildly (as much as 2000%) so be prepared to wait a few days if you want a better deal. Check travellers' tales for up to date news on the longer routes. For example, sections of the Kashgar-Tibet road have been under repair and may be closed for 10-day periods to allow work to continue uninterrupted.

Keep in mind that, in Tibet, truck drivers are gods and they know it. Be kind and patient and you will go far.

The standard price for five people in a Landcruiser from Lhasa to Kathmandu (including permits and stops along the way) is $200 each.

● **Air** Lhasa has Tibet's only airport, although there is talk of constructing another one at Tarchen (200km from Mt Kailash). Lhasa has direct flights to/from Chengdu (daily, $190), Beijing (weekly, $340) and Kathmandu (two a week except between late November and early April, $190). There are also plans to begin flights to Guangzhou. It is unlikely that you'll be allowed to simply buy an air ticket and go to Tibet without showing some kind of permit/tour booking.

❏ **Khatas**

Khatas are white scarves, the best of which are silk and splendid. Khatas are offered respectfully to people of honour, teachers, departing friends and statues – you could place one on the Jowo statue in the Jokang in Lhasa or at the Karmapa at the Tsurphu monastery. Earn merit by placing one around the neck of another person and don't be surprised if they immediately put it back on you (the Dalai Lama is expertly kind in this regard) – it is a blessing. Khatas can also be offered as a thank you or as a congratulation eg to couples getting married. In Bhutanese archery competitions, if someone has played so wholeheartedly as to pass out drunk, their inebriated body is often blessed in khatas for a job well done.

Khatas can always be bought near monasteries and usually from the monks inside. The Han Chinese khata sellers in front of the Jokang have the best quality silk khatas (even Tibetans buy them) but they are ruthless hagglers. It is OK to take off a khata that you've been given after a while and re-use it.

● **Bicycle** A self-styled Tour de Tibet is a wonderful alternative to the public transport hassles. Decent Chinese mountain bikes are sold in Lhasa for Y550-800 – and it is often possible to resell them in Kathmandu for a similar price. One couple rode their bicycles all the way to Australia and sold them there for a profit. The Lhasa-Golmud and Lhasa-Nepal roads are open to foreigners; cycling on them is legal when politics permit. The Kathmandu trip is typically done in 16-18 days, though most take rest and/or sightseeing days. The Lhasa-Chengdu roads are closed and it's unlikely you'll be granted a permit for them. We know of one permit-less traveller who had his bike confiscated in Kham.

Good sunglasses are really important for protection from the glare and the strong dusty winds.

With a bike you have a better chance of talking your way through police checkpoints than if you are a lone hiker with no obvious means of transport.

Accommodation

Most of the towns that foreigners can visit on an open permit have at least one hotel. Hotels you can legally stay in have a sign of some sort in Roman letters. Expect to pay Y15 for a bed in a dorm and Y50 for a single. It is possible to stay in monasteries, nomad tents and sometimes in homes outside cities, but stay for a short length of time only. It is too dangerous for locals to put you up, especially in small towns.

There are no official campgrounds but the terrain in much of Tibet is ideal for pitching a tent – self sufficiency is a must.

Food and drink

Life for most Tibetans is *tsampa* (roasted barley flour) – add Tibetan tea and you have a nice breakfast (and, alas, often lunch and dinner). Tsampa is eaten with the right hand, scooped in balls. Also popular are *tukpa* which is noodle soup with meat and *momos* which are meat or vegetable dumplings. Yak meat is also common – it's chewy and has less taste than you'd expect.

Tea is the standard drink – Tibetans literally drink dozens of small glasses in one day. Tibetan tea, *peu cha* (salty yak butter tea), is said to be very rehydrating though that doesn't make it taste better. *Cha nga mo* (sweet tea) is similar to Indian chai and is found mostly in central Tibet. There are fierce discussions in Lhasa as to which tea shop has the best *cha nga mo*. We are partial to Tea Shop Number Six.

Staying in touch

● **Mail** The mail system is remarkably reliable considering Tibet's remoteness; one traveller sent six boxes containing religious texts by sea mail to the USA and all made it. Lhasa is the best place to send mail from.

● **Fax** Faxes are easy to send from Lhasa. Small upmarket travel agents offer the best rates. The price per minute is OK but it becomes expensive if your fax takes several minutes to go through, which is possible given bad lines.

● **Phone** There is no direct dial but call backs are possible (eg in Lhasa at the Kirey Hotel). International code: +86, Lhasa code: +891.

Further information

● **Books** We recommend having a guidebook: the most authoritative and one of the best guidebooks to anywhere is Victor Chan's *Tibet Handbook* (Moon Publications). However, being thicker than

---

❑ **First steps in Tibetan**

Many Westerners were unconsciously exposed to Tibetan at an early age: Tibetan was the language spoken by the Ewoks in the Star Wars movies. Or, at least the Ewoks' words were Tibetan – the overall meaning was utter nonsense:

    Luke Skywalker: 'Where is Princess Leia?'
    Ewok (in Tibetan):   'Paddy field, yak, refrigerator'.

❏ Meeting the locals

● **The people** To lump different groups together as 'Tibetan' is as difficult and generalising as labelling different Western nationalities as European. Tibetan-ish folk are spread all over the Himalayas from Ladakh to Bhutan, Sikkim to Sichuan, Nepal to Yunnan, Qinghai to Himachal and, of course, in Tibet. There is no definitive way to determine exactly who is and isn't Tibetan. Eric Mortensen, Harvard Tibetologist, believes there are two key factors: 1) whether the individual follows Tibetan Buddhism (he excludes Mongols who are 'recent converts'); 2) whether he/she eats, and actually enjoys tsampa. By this definition, semi-Tibetans would thus include Nepali Sherpas (who originated in Tibet's Kham region), the Bhutanese (who would fiercely deny the connection), and the Ladakhis of far northern India (whose language is similar to the Tibetan spoken in Lhasa).

● **Language** Tibetan is part of the Tibeto-Burmese language family. There are several mutually unintelligible dialects though all use the same beautiful Tibetan script. The Tibetan script is a distant relative to Sanskrit. It looks confusing and is harder to read than it looks: seemingly half of the letters are silent, depending on their position in a word. Tibetan is also a difficult language to speak, although Tibetans are patient folk and will listen intently as you sputter out your phrases.

A Mandarin phrase book is also useful for communicating with ethnic Chinese. Many Tibetans understand some Chinese too, but the language has an understandably negative connotation.

Some phrases in Tibetan (pronunciations are for the Lhasa dialect):

Greeting – *Tashi delay*
How are you? (literally 'Is your body comfortable?') – *Gu zu day po*
Reply – *Day po* or *La yin*
Goodbye (said to person who is staying) – *Kali shu* or *Shu ah*
Goodbye (said to person who is going) – *Kali pay* or *Pay oh*
The food is good – *Kala shimbo du*
Slowly slowly – *Kali kali* (for speeding drivers and talkers)
How much? – *Kormo katse ray?*
Too expensive – *Kong chenpo ray* (best said with a smile)
Where is ___? – ___ *ka bar ray?* (with slightly rolled 'r')
 a toilet – *San jo* a monastery – *Gompa*
 a nunnery – *Ani-gompa* an hotel – *Dunkhang*
Where are you going? – *Ka bar pep ga?*
I am going to ___ – *Nga ___-la dro gee yin.*
I don't like meat – *Nga shia ga bo mey*

● **Alphabet**

a   'a   Ba   Ca   Cha   Da   Dza   Ga   Ha   Ja   Ka   La   Kha   Ma   Na

Nga   Nya   Pa   Pha   Ra   Sa   Sha   Ta   Tha   Tsa   Tsha   Wa   Ya   Za   Zha

VOWEL MODIFIERS: E ⌒   I ⌒   O ⌣   U ⌣
(■ = ANY LETTER)

a telephone book it is not an item you will want to lug around with you. An excellent alternative is *Trekking in Tibet* by Gary McCue (The Mountaineers), which is very useful even if you aren't going trekking (despite the title, it has less trekking information than the Handbook). Also good is Steven Batchelor's *Tibet Guidebook*; sadly it is no longer published in English but it is available in French (in Kathmandu's Pilgrim's bookshop and, of course, in France). Lonely Planet's latest edition of the *Tibet Travel Survival Kit* has marginal history information and seems to have dropped some of its more useful information on the long distance routes to and from China – we prefer the older editions.

Tibet has long fascinated writers. Dozens of Tibet travelogues, histories, religious treatises and coffee table photobooks are available, especially in Kathmandu. One of the more gripping tales is Heinrich Harrer's *Seven Years in Tibet* – a film based on the book was released in 1997. The Chinese government publish several books giving their version of political and social developments in Tibet, eg *100 Questions about Tibet* (Beijing Review, 1989). Such books are hard to find outside Nepal or China though occasionally they're available free from Chinese embassies abroad.

● **Maps** Though not available anywhere near Tibet, the best maps for trekking/walking/do-it-yourself exploring are the ONC pilotage charts; the topographic information is excellent, though the place names are often completely wrong. The Nepa trekking maps (Nepali Rs125/US$2.15) are a good alternative. They are widely available in Kathmandu and include south central Tibet (with the Lhasa-Kathmandu road) and the Kailash route. For an overview, Bartholomew's Tibet and the Mountains of Central Asia is recommended. Within Tibet, Lhasa's Xinhua bookstore sells maps of Lhasa and the surrounding region. In Dharmsala, an excellent Lhasa city map is available from Amnye Machen publishers.

When looking at a map remember that Chinese and Tibetan names for places are often completely different.

● **Information:** **Australia**: (☎ 6-285 4046, fax 6-282 4301, E-mail: OffTibet@peg.apc.org), 3 Weld St, Yarralumla, ACT 260, Canberra. **Switzerland**: (☎ 1-201 3336, fax 1-201 2160, E-mail: tibetzurich@tibchzh.link ch1.ch.), Waffenplatzstrasse 10, 8002 Zurich. **UK**: (☎ 0171-722 5378, fax 0171-722 0362, E-mail: tibetlondon @gn.apc.org.), 1 Culworth St, London NW8 7AF. **USA**: (☎ 212-213-5010, fax 212-779-9245, E-mail: OTNY@igc.apc. org.), 241 East 32nd St, New York 10016.

There are also offices in France, Hungary, India, Japan and Russia.

Tibetan votive money

Web sites

Peter M Geiser's Internet travel guide to Tibet is at www-students.unisg.ch/~pgeiser/tibet/tibet.htm.

Links and information are supplied by the Tibet Support Group at www.tibet.org. The International Campaign for Tibet, another group supporting human rights, is at www.peacenet.org/ict. The government-in-exile's official homepage is at www.tibet.com.

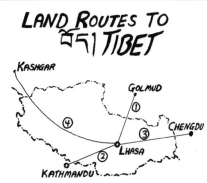

LAND ROUTES TO
ཙྱི TIBET

KASHGAR
GOLMUD
① CHENGDU
④ ③
② LHASA
KATHMANDU

Open routes

(Routes that are theoretically possible on a General Tibet Permit):

● **1) Golmud-Lhasa** Offers the highest chance of getting into Tibet by land, though it's the least interesting route. Direct buses (some sleepers) run daily taking 32-40 hrs. **From** Lhasa to Golmud foreigners are usually charged 250 yuan though we've heard up to 750 yuan. **To** Lhasa, it's 1080 yuan – supposedly includes a 'permit' but you're unlikely to ever see one. We did meet one Japanese traveller who paid the local price (128 yuan) and got through by disguising himself as a Tibetan. However police at two stops en route usually check ID and may eject from the bus any Lhasa-bound foreigner who's paid too little. A lonely place to wait.

● **2) Kathmandu-Lhasa** Spectacular route over high mountains, past temples and forts. Going to Nepal the biggest obstacle is the mountain passes between Nyalam and the border; be prepared for a long snowy walk in the winter and spring. Going to Tibet also be prepared for border guards who turn back independent travellers on a whim, especially in times of political unrest. Takes three to four days of constant travel, though there is lots to see on the way. See the Lhasa-Kathmandu map.

Closed routes

(You'll have to hide from police checks unless you can get a very hard to arrange special permit. Routes are physically as well as politically dangerous):

● **3) Chengdu-Lhasa** Spectacularly beautiful route with some of the world's most memorable mountainscapes. However, even those paying $1600 for a Landcruiser tour reported difficulty at police checks – Markam is the toughest. If you could avoid the police there are several weekly buses running each segment of this route as well as a rare bus going directly between Lhasa and Chengdu (350 yuan, 9-20 days!), stops off for the night at hotels where you are sure to be discovered).

● **4) Kashgar-Lhasa** Crosses high but barren passes of 5000m+. The only transport between Kargilik and Ali is in the back of trucks with a real danger of altitude sickness and frostbite. There is barely a hut along the way so you'll need to be self sufficient for 8-60 days depending on your hitching luck. About 20 travellers made it last year with fewer than usual being turned back at Ali. Enquire locally about pilgrim trucks in autumn. Unproven rumours worthy of the Gt Game claim PSB spies operate in Kashgar traveller cafés to thwart suspected Lhasa-bound backpackers.

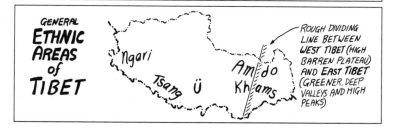

GENERAL
ETHNIC
AREAS
of
TIBET

Ngari

Tsang Ü Amdo Kham

ROUGH DIVIDING
LINE BETWEEN
WEST TIBET (HIGH
BARREN PLATEAU)
AND EAST TIBET
(GREENER, DEEP
VALLEYS AND HIGH
PEAKS)

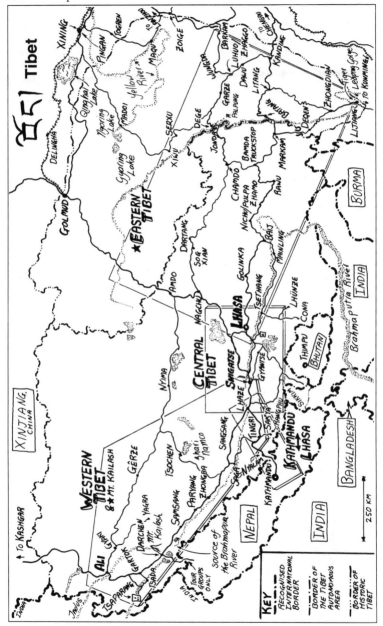

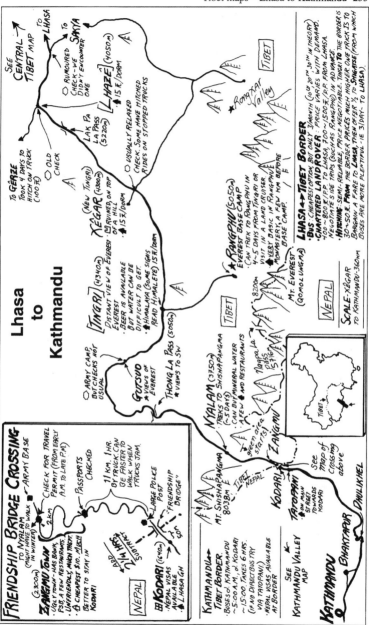

Lhasa to Kathmandu

See CENTRAL TIBET MAP

TO LHASA

RUMOURED TO SAYA - CHECK - WE DIDN'T ENCOUNTER ONE

[LHAZE] (4050m)
◇ 15 ₤/DORM

TIBET

★ Rangxar Valley

TO GÉRZE - TOOK 4 DAYS TO HITCH ON TRUCK (100₤)

◇ OLD CHECK

LAK PA LA PASS (5220m)

◇ USUALLY RELAXED CHECK. SOME HAVE HITCHED RIDES ON STOPPED TRUCKS

XEGAR (NEW TINGRI) (4300m)
◻ RUINED ON TOP OF A HILL
▲ 15 ₤/DORM

[TINGRI] (4340m)
• DISTANT VIEW OF EVEREST
• BEER IS AVAILABLE BUT WATER CAN BE DIFFICULT TO GET.
★ HIMALAYA (SOME SIGNS READ HIMALEYE) 15 ₤/DORM

★ RANGPHU (5050m) EVEREST BASE CAMP
• CAN TREK TO RANGPHU IN 4-5 DAYS FROM TINGRI OR VISIT IN A LANDCRUISER
▲ VERY BASIC IN RANGPHU MONASTERY, A FEW KM BEFORE BASE CAMP.

◇ ARMY CAMP BUT CHECKS NOT USUAL.

GUTSVO
★ VIEWS OF EVEREST

THONG LA PASS (5050m)
★ VIEWS TO SW

8200m

Mt. EVEREST (QOMOLUNGMA)

NEPAL

SCALE: XEGAR TO KATHMANDU ~ 360km

LHASA ↔ TIBET BORDER
BUS: CHEAPEST OPTION BUT ONLY 3/MONTH (10+20+30TH IN THEORY) - PRICE VARIES WITH DEMAND.
CHARTERED LANDROVER: 400~800 ₤/PP TO LHASA, 700~1500 ₤/PP FROM LHASA. NEGOTIATE SIDE TRIPS (SUCH AS RANGPHU) IN ADVANCE.
HITCHING: SEMI-RELIABLE. PRICE NEGOTIABLE. TINGRI TO THE BORDER IS 30~50 ₤. FROM THE BORDER PRICES MUCH HIGHER. ONE WAY TRICK IS TO BARGAIN A FARE TO LHASA, THEN OFFER ½ TO SHIGATSE (FROM WHICH BUSES ARE MORE PLENTIFUL - IE 3/DAY - TO LHASA).

NYALAM (3750m)
• TREKS TO SHISHAPANGMA (~5 DAYS)
• CAN BUY MINERAL WATER
▲ A FEW AND RESTAURANTS

Nagpa La PASS 5116m

TIBET

GREEN RICE STARTS

ZANGMU

TIBET / NEPAL

Mt. SHISHAPANGMA 8038m

KODARI

See Map of crossing above

TATOPANI
• ON MAIN STREET TOWARDS KODARI

See KATHMANDU VALLEY MAP

DHULIKHEL

BHAKTAPUR

KATHMANDU

KATHMANDU ↔ TIBET BORDER
• BUSES OF KATHMANDU ~500 A.M., OF KODARI ~1500. TAKES 6 HRS.
  (IF NO DIRECT BUS TRY VIA TATOPANI)
• NEPAL VISAS AVAILABLE AT BORDER

FRIENDSHIP BRIDGE CROSSING

TO NYALAM (MIGHT HAVE TO WALK IN WINTER)

■ ARMY BASE

ZANGMU TOWN (2300m)
• UGLY TOWN - HAS BANK, PSB, A FEW RESTAURANTS.
• UNFRIENDLY, MUCH THEFT.
• A CHEAPEST S/O. MUCH BETTER TO STAY IN KODARI

2 km

CHECK FOR TRAVEL PERMIT (FROM EARLY A.M. TO LATE P.M.)

PASSPORTS CHECKED

11 KM. BY TRUCK. CAN BE FASTER TO WALK WHEN TRUCKS JAM.

● LARGE POLICE POST

"FRIENDSHIP BRIDGE"

ADD 2¼ HRS. (SUBTRACT)

⊞ KODARI (1670m)
• NEPAL VISAS AVAILABLE
• LHASA GH

NEPAL

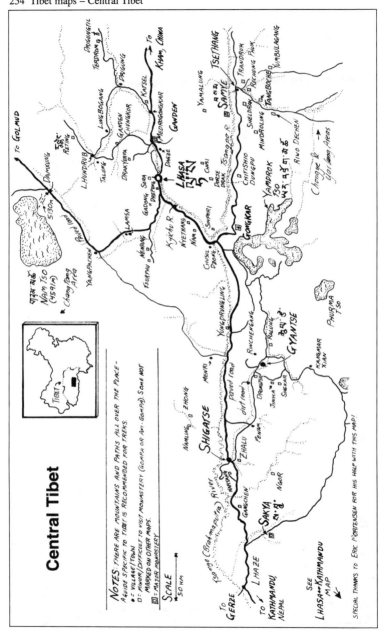

Central Tibet

NOTES: THERE ARE MOUNTAINS AND PATHS ALL OVER THE PLACE-
A GUIDE SPECIFIC TO TIBET IS RECOMMENDED FOR TREKS.

• = VILLAGE/TOWN
☐ = MINOR/DIFFICULT TO VISIT MONASTERY (GOMPA OR ANI-GOMPA). SOME NOT
MARKED ON OTHER MAPS.
▣ = MAJOR MONASTERY

SCALE
├─────┤
50 KM

SPECIAL THANKS TO ERIK MORTENSEN FOR HIS HELP WITH THIS MAP!

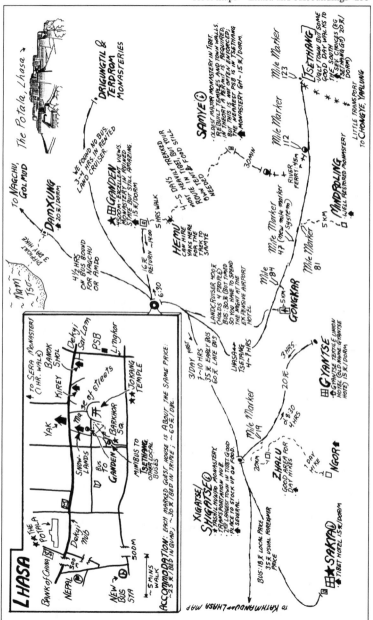

The Potala, Lhasa →

DRIGUNGTIL & TERDROM MONASTERIES

I'VE FOUND NO BUS. 3-4 HRS. IN RENTED LAND CRUISER.

TO NAGCHU, GOLMUD →

DAMXUNG 20元/DORM

DIFFICULT HIKE ~ 3 DAY HIKE

Nam ~ 150

★★ **GANDEN** MONASTERY — EXCELLENT VIEWS. SOMEWHAT "RE-RUINED" STATE BUT STILL AMAZING. 15元/DORM

5 HRS WALK

4½ HRS. ON BUS BOUND FOR NAGCHU OR AMDO

6:30

16元 RETURN ~14:00

HEMU CAN HIRE YAKS HERE TO TREK TO SAMYE

4-5 DAYS TREKKED MOST OF ROUTE BUT STILL NEED TO OWN RENTED FOOD NEEDED

SAMYE ⊕ — OLDEST MAJOR MONASTERY IN TIBET. REBUILT TEMPLES, AND SOME WALLS. ALIEN PERMIT IS REQUIRED. BUT THIS IS NOT OFTEN ENFORCED. THE NEAREST PSB IS IN TSETHANG. MONASTERY GH ~ 15元/DORM

30MIN

TSETHANG — UGLY TOWN BUT SOME GOOD DAY WALKS TO THE SOUTH. SEE CHANGES (EG SEE YARLUNG GH ~ 20元)

Mile Marker 123

LITTLE TRANSPORT TO CHONGYE, YARLING

Mile Marker 112

MINDROLING — WELL RESTORED MONASTERY

RIVER 45m ← ✦

Mile Marker 47 (NEW MILE MARKER SYSTEM)

Mile Marker 81

Mile Marker 98½

LANDCRUISER 400元 (HOLDS 4 PEOPLE) BUS 30元 (BUT TIMED SO YOU HAVE TO SPEND THE NIGHT EN ROUTE) EN ROUTE AT BRASHE AIRPORT HOTEL

5 KM

GONGKAR

← 5 KM

LHASA→TSETHANG 4-7 HRS

LHASA (inset)

★ **THE POTALA**

Bank of China 卐

NEPAL 500 卐

Dekyi SHAR LAM

Dekyi NUB

← TO SERA MONASTERY (1 HR. WALK)

BANOK SHOL

KIREY

PSB

YAK

SNOW-LANDS

MA ze of streets

Barkhor SQ.

★★ **JOKANG TEMPLE**

Lingkor

Bus to GANDEN

New Bus Sta

← 5 MINS walk

MINIBUS TO TSETHANG; OTHER LOCAL BUSES

500M

ACCOMMODATION: EACH MARKED GUEST HOUSE IS ABOUT THE SAME PRICE: ~ 25元/BED IN QUAD; ~ 30元/BED IN TRIPLE; ~ 60元/DBL.

to KATHMANDU→LHASA MAP

3-DAY FAST! 7-10 HRS 35元 EARLY BUS 60元 LATE BUS

KATHMANDU↔LHASA MAP

3 HRS

20元

Mile Marker 119

GYANTSE — ⊕ GYANTSE TEXTILE UNION HOTEL (OLD NAME GYANTSE HOTEL) 15元/DORM

at 8:30 4 HRS

20元

★ **NGOR**

1 DAY HIKE

ZHALU GOOD AREA FOR DAY HIKES

20MIN

XIGATSE/SHIGATSE ⊕ — TASHILHUNPO MONASTERY. TRANSPORTATION HUB. 2ND LARGEST TOWN IN TIBET. GOOD PLACE TO STOCK UP ON FOOD. SEVERAL.

BUS: 18元 LOCAL PRICE. 35元 USUAL FOREIGNER PRICE

★ **SAKYA** ⊕ — TIBET HOTEL 15元/DORM

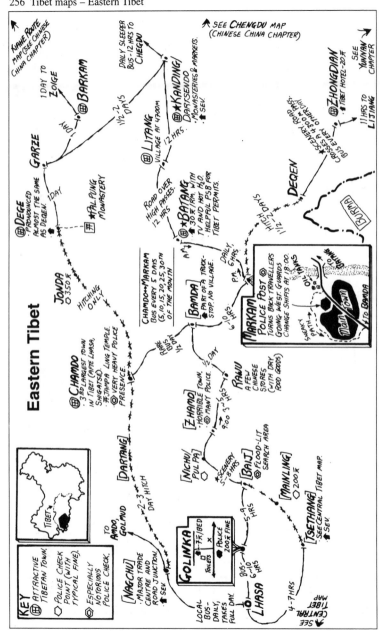

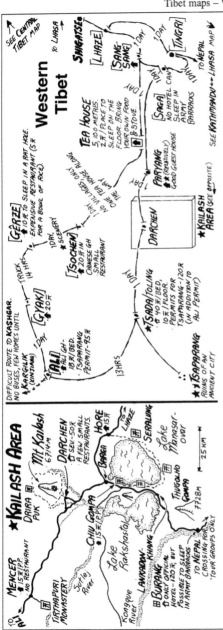

Spectacular mountain scenery and ancient Tibetan kingdoms dotted with ugly Chinese truck stop villages. One of the highlights of the area is Mt Kailash, holy to Hindus, Jains and Tibetan Buddhists. Trekking possibilities abound (circumnavigate Mt Kailash (53km) just 108 times for instant enlightenment). Monasteries offer simple lodgings – they've been hosting pilgrims for 1000+ years.

There is very little public transport in Western Tibet, so getting around requires hitching or pre-arranged transportation. As hitching in this area is illegal you'll have to find creative ways around the check points (the ones in Ali, Lhaze and around Saga are the most difficult). If caught you may be fined (Y100-500) but not get sent back. Hitching is unpredictable – Lhasa to Kailash can take from eight days to one month. We hitched Lhaze to Gerze in four days (Y100, though some trucks wanted Y2500!) and from Gerze to Ali in three days (Y75).

Arranging your own transport gives you much greater flexibility. Prices vary with your itinerary, group size, and bargaining skills. A typical price for a six-person group going on a three-week return trip from Lhasa to Gerze, Ali, Tsaparang, and Kashgar typically costs $700 + accommodation + food (bring plenty of your own). A two-week tour only from Lhasa to Kailash and back typically runs $250 + accommodation. Once you find a respectable driver, it is a good idea to put the agreed upon price and travel details in writing lest the deal change along the way. Find travel partners and more information on the noticeboards in the Lhasa backpacker hangouts. Groups leave regularly.

Xinjiang and Western China

Xinjiang contains some of the world's most forbidding deserts and some of Asia's most scenic mountains. The parched Turpan Basin, in the centre of Xinjiang, is China's hottest spot as well as being its deepest depression. It is kept habitable by ancient underground irrigation channels which allow melons and grapes to grow in the midst of the desert. To the north and west are the alpine meadows of Bodega Shan, the truly 'Heavenly Lake', and the hilly Altai Mountains where Kazakh horsemen still roam. To the south of Turpan, ancient Silk Road settlements languish in a sand-swept amnesia. A string of industrial cities mars the main road between Urumqi and Yining.

In recent years, Han Chinese have been pouring into the unlikely boomtown of Urumqi. The rest of Xinjiang is still dominated by various ethnic groups: Turks, Kyrgyz, Kazakhs and Uigurs (Xinjiang's largest group, numbering some four million). The Altai mountains are the ancestral home of each of these groups. A place many contrasts, Xinjiang is more than just a western adjunct of the PRC.

❑ **Essential information for Xinjiang**

● **Time zone** Officially the whole of China is on Beijing Time (BT), 8 hours ahead of GMT. However, using BT in Xinjiang means an inconveniently late winter sunrise, ie around 9.30am. Thus some locals prefer to use an unofficial Xinjiang Time (XT). This is 2hrs behind BT, 6hrs ahead of GMT, and one hour ahead of Pakistan. It's an hour ahead of Kyrgyzstan in winter but is the same in summer. Typically XT is used by most of the Uigur population and by many bus stations, but banks, railway stations, post offices, government officials and a lot of the Han Chinese population dutifully stick to BT. There's no steadfast rule for who uses which, so always check whether a quoted time is XT or BT.

● **Health factors** Boiled water is safest; there are no reports of malaria.

● **Special dangers** Summer heat is intense but dry, so beware of dehydration.

● **Typical traveller destinations** Kashgar, Turpan, Urumqi, Heavenly Lake.

● **Highlights** As above plus Dragon's Pool, Kuqa-Yining road, Sayram Lake.

● **When to go** Xinjiang starts getting cold in Oct/Nov, and backpacker-oriented services (cycle hire, dorm rooms, cafés) are closed from Nov to April/May. In winter, Urumqi is appreciably colder than Kashgar and settled snow had already compacted into ice by late November. Some higher mountain passes close (eg Narat-Korla, the new route to Kyrgyzstan via Irkestam), though the Torugart Pass and Kuqa-Yining road are kept open by snowploughs. If you cover up well (warm clothes and thermal underwear etc are available cheaply) you'll be rewarded with the memorable sight of snow on the sand dunes of the Taklamakan Desert and ice ponds forming between them. Summers are searingly hot, but being so dry, they are surprisingly bearable even in the Turpan basin – China's hottest hot spot.

● **Pulse of the country** The weekly markets – Hotan and Kashgar (Sunday) and Kuqa (Friday) are the biggest, but there are many more.

PRACTICAL INFORMATION
Transport
● **Bus** Buses incur foreigner pricing in Kashgar, but not in the bus stations at Urumqi or Yining where only a small percentage of services still require you to queue at the ticket windows. The main road between Kashgar and Urumqi has many long distance buses (including several sleeper services), but from intermediate points there may be only one or two long-distance services a day. This need not be daunting as mini-buses ply the area, and long-haul buses collect from the bus stations of larger centres. As relatively few people get off at these intermediate stops waiting times are unpredictable, but as a foreigner you are more likely to get a space as the driver knows he can easily overcharge you. On smaller roads, minibuses or BJC jeeps will stop unless desperately over full. Bargain hard if the price is more than about Y2 per 10km (locals pay about Y1), though prices do increase on the rougher roads.

● **Train** As for the rest of China, trains are a sensible way to cover great distances. Hard sleeper tickets can be difficult to buy from intermediate stations between Urumqi and Lanzhou (the only major route). A branch line from Daheyan (near Turpan) to Korla should eventually be extended to Kashgar, though an estimated 1998 opening date seems optimistic.

● **Air** Travel by plane is sensible considering the distances and the rough terrain; a bonus is the spectacular desert and mountain view. Foreigner pricing makes flying relatively expensive ($250 one way Urumqi-Chengdu, $400 to Guangzhou). The $300 fare for flights (Wednesday and Saturday) to Baku on Azerbaijan's private airline IMAir is a handy last resort if you're heading west but have carelessly arrived in Urumqi without a Central Asian or Pakistani visa. The Azeris will let you in without a visa (see Azerbaijan chapter).

Urumqi's airport tax is Y50. Refuse to pay the Y20 insurance since it is not compulsory, despite the airline's probable insistence.

● **Tours** Some corners of Xinjiang are so remote that public transport simply won't get you there. The ruined desert cities are precisely that and you'll generally have to pay a taxi to get out to them. This need not be dreadfully expensive; we paid $20 for a day's tour from Turpan (for as many people as we could jam in a mini-van) to see Gaocheng and the Bezeklik caves with a fascinating English-speaking Uigur nationalist driver. Negotiation is crucial; an Australian tourist we met the same day had paid $200 for the same tour. $20 was also the starting price for tours from Kuqa to the lonely Silk Road ghost towns. Tours are unnecessary for visits to Turpan or to Heavenly Lake from Urumqi.

Accommodation
In smaller towns there is almost invariably a place to stay in or near the bus station,

---

❏ **W&M's ratings – Xinjiang**
● **Expense $$** Much cheaper than Eastern China.
● **Value for money** ✔✔✔ You get what you pay for.
● **Getting around** ✔✔ Buses are cramped, distances long and the roads poor and dusty. Services are rare on minor roads.
● **English spoken** ✔✔ In Urumqi and Kashgar you can find English speakers (often Pakistani traders). In smaller towns communication is tough so a phrase book is recommended. Russian is handy in Yining, Kashgar and border areas.
● **Woman alone** ✔✔✔ Expect more hassle from drunk men than in the rest of China, but travelling here is much easier than in Pakistan.
● **For vegetarians** ✔✔ Uigur food is heavily mutton based but in most towns there is at least one Chinese-run restaurant with meat-free options. Markets have a selection of dried fruits and nuts.

though you may need to look carefully for the Chinese characters for *zaodaishuo* (招待所). Basic places charge around Y10 a bed, double what locals pay. Foreigner-only dorms are available in Urumqi and Kashgar (Y25/15), though most close in winter when beds in a triple start at Y30/20. If hotels in the small towns along the southern Silk Road tell you that the cheapest room is Y250, refuse to take it. The same hotel will probably be able to

find you a bed for a tenth of the price and won't want you to die outside in the winter snow, whatever their apparent attitude.

Activities

● **Hiking and horse treks**   The area around Heavenly Lake is ideal for hiking – open walking in high Alpine meadows in between beautiful patches of forest. Often Kazakh nomads will put you up for the night in their yurt tents and the first night

---

❏ Meeting the locals

● **The people**   The Uigurs are coyly friendly and the slightest attempt on your part to speak their language is very warmly received. It's also much easier to pro-nounce than Chinese, so bargaining in Uigur wins you brownie points and a dis-count at the same time.

You'll hear constant reminders that Uigurs are Musselmen (Muslims) but that doesn't prevent a generosity with beer and vodka that allows language barriers to magically melt. However, passions rise quickly and brawling is not uncommon even over minor disagreements (like a bicycle collision). Perhaps the fairly com-mon Kashgari practice of rolling hashish into the curiously angular cigarettes (hand rolled from newspaper) is tolerated to calm such tempers.

Few speak English, but those who do are keen to meet you. The small food stalls outside Kashgar University are a good place to find Uigur and Kazakh stu-dents (you will probably be prevented from getting into the campus by surly guards). The students can be very frank about their negative views towards the Chinese and have some strange ideas about Hitler who has something of a local following!

● **Language**   Uigur is a Turkic language. It is widely spoken in most of Xinjiang, except in Urumqi (where Chinese is more common), and the far northern areas (Kazakh).

Note that Uigurs often refer to the Chinese Yuan as Som; this is not to be con-fused with Som (the currency of Kyrgyzstan).

Written Uigur usually takes the Arabic script.

Some phrases in Uigur:

Greeting – *yakshi ma*; (or more formally) *yakshi misus*
Reply – *yakshi* (good)
Thank you <u>very much</u> – *küpr rakhmet*
How much is it? – *khaj pul*?

Numbers (for bargaining):

1	bir	8	sekis	60	atmesh
2	iki	9	tokuz	70	yetmesh
3	ooch	10	on	80	seksen
4	turt	20	jigime	90	toksuz
5	besh	30	otuz	100	yuz
6	alte	40	kirik		
7	yete	50	elled		

It's easy to put the number together eg 435 = turt yuz otuz besh.

(on the lakeside) can be arranged for about Y20 (with meals!) by the surprisingly honest but persistent 'you-come-my-yurt' touts at Urumqi's Hongshan Hotel. Horse treks can be arranged by host families for an average Y50 a day with guide, but walking may be more comfortable as the horses stumble frequently on the rocky stream beds and narrow paths.

Further information

● **Books** The only dedicated English language book shop (at the Holiday Inn, Urumqi) offers a station platform selections of novels with a few picture books on Xinjiang, but no practical guidebooks. The bilingual *Tourist Guidebook to Kuqa* sold at the Xinhua book shop in that town has a map with no key to the numbered sites. Various similar pamphlets on Xinjiang exist. If you're coming from Pakistan certain guidebooks are available in Karimabad, Hunza (eg the Lonely Planet *China* book), though you can frequently trade Pakistan guides for China ones with travellers in Kashgar.

The mysteries of Xinjiang have inspired several great travel books. Chief among them are the various adventures of Swedish explorer Sven Hedin (recently reprinted in Kathmandu, Nepal but only available to lucky browsers in used bookstores elsewhere). Another classic is Peter Fleming's *News from Tartary* – amusing for the bumbling success of his trans-Taklamakan venture and his 1930s ideas on travelling light. Compare this with the description of the same trip by Ella Maillart (his Swiss-French companion) in

Forbidden Journey. National Geographic covered Xinjiang with customary excellence in its March 1996 issue. The best and most up-to-date guide to the region is Peter Neville Hadley's *China: The Silk Routes* which also includes some details on Central Asia.

● **Maps** Detailed local maps are difficult to find. There is a Xinjiang road atlas (新疆维吾尔自治区地图册) which sells for Y9.80 in Xinhua book shops in bigger towns. It includes city maps but is entirely in Chinese. The tourist maps of Xinjiang in English are fine for a basic idea of the area but show few of the smaller roads. City maps in English are available in Kashgar, Kuqa (upstairs in Tongba Hotel), Urumqi (at the Hongshan Hotel or from the post office at the rail station), and Yining (at the Post Hotel).

● **Information** There's a **Tourist Information Centre** (☎ 0991-224449) at 16 Jianguo Road, Urumqi. Free information is also offered by the travel agents at the Hongshan Hotel in Urumqi, though this is often with the clear aim of selling you a tour. In Kashgar, the **CITS** office, in an annex of the Qini Bagh Hotel, gives city maps away half heartedly. The dormitories at both mentioned hotels, and conceivably also at the Seman Hotel (block 2), Kashgar, are the surest places to meet other travellers, arrange book swaps etc. Try also John's Café which has conveniently situated branches in Kashgar, Urumqi and Turpan; another may open in Dunhuang. The cafés are open only from April to October but they do have traveller noticeboards.

❏ Onward visas for Central Asia

There is no Kyrgyz representative in Urumqi, and the chances of getting a Kazakh visa are slim and potentially expensive. The Kazakh Airlines office has a consular official but he very rarely issues visas to non-Xinjiang residents, even if the office is open between floods, bankruptcy and moves. Your best hope is to pay an exorbitant $230 to Mr Jie Ensi at **Nature Travel**, Room 209, Hotel Xinjiang. This gets you their cheapest two-day visa and nominal 'tour' of Almaty – long enough to give you time to apply for a Kyrgyz visa there. See the visa appendix for details of our experience, but don't rely on getting **any** visas in Xinjiang.

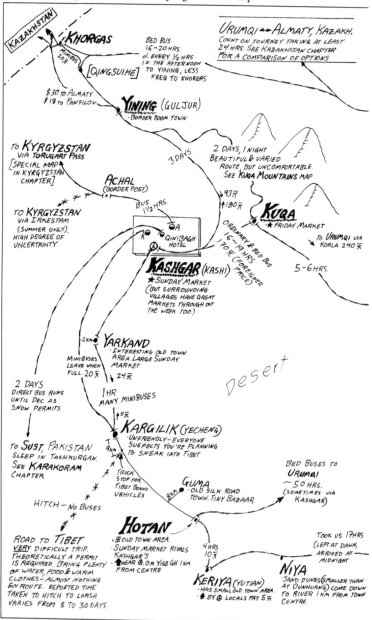

KAZAKHSTAN

KHORGAS

PLUMING 20元

[QINGSUIHE]

BED BUS
16~20 HRS.
d. EVERY ½ HRS
IN THE AFTERNOON
TO YINING, LESS
FREQ TO KHORGAS

URUMQI ↔ ALMATY, KAZAKH.
COUNT ON JOURNEY TAKING AT LEAST
24 HRS. SEE KAZAKHSTAN CHAPTER
FOR A COMPARISON OF OPTIONS

$30 TO ALMATY
$19 TO PANFILOV

YINING (GULJUR)
·BORDER BOOM TOWN

TO KYRGYZSTAN
VIA TORUGART PASS
[SPECIAL MAP
IN KYRGYZSTAN
CHAPTER]

3 DAYS

2 DAYS, 1 NIGHT
BEAUTIFUL & VARIED
ROUTE BUT UNCOMFORTABLE.
SEE KUQA MOUNTAINS MAP

ACHAL
(BORDER POST)

BUS 1½ HRS.

↓93元
↑180元

KUQA
·FRIDAY MARKET

TO KYRGYZSTAN
VIA IRKESTAM
(SUMMER ONLY).
HIGH DEGREE OF
UNCERTAINTY

○A

○ QINIBAGH
HOTEL

ORDINARY & BED BUS
16~19 HRS
130元 (FOREIGNER
PRICE)

TO URUMQI VIA
KORLA 240元

5-6 HRS.

KASHGAR (KASHI)
★SUNDAY MARKET
(BUT SURROUNDING
VILLAGES HAVE GREAT
MARKETS THROUGHOUT
THE WEEK TOO.)

·2KM

YARKAND
·INTERESTING OLD TOWN
AREA LARGE SUNDAY
MARKET

Desert

MINIBUSES
LEAVE WHEN
FULL. 20元

↓24元

2 DAYS
DIRECT BUS RUNS
UNTIL DEC. AS
SNOW PERMITS

1 HR
MANY MINIBUSES

↑11元

KARGILIK (YECHENG)
·UNFRIENDLY-EVERYONE
SUSPECTS YOU'RE PLANNING
TO SNEAK INTO TIBET

TO SUST, PAKISTAN
SLEEP IN TASHKURGAN.
SEE KARAKORAM
CHAPTER

↓9KM

TRUCK
STOP FOR
TIBET BOUND
VEHICLES

GUMA
·OLD SILK ROAD
TOWN. TINY BAZAAR.

8KM

BED BUSES TO
URUMQI
~50 HRS.
(SOMETIMES VIA
KASHGAR)

HITCH – NO BUSES

ROAD TO TIBET
VERY DIFFICULT TRIP.
THEORETICALLY A PERMIT
IS REQUIRED. BRING PLENTY
OF WATER, FOOD & WARM
CLOTHES – ALMOST NOTHING
EN ROUTE. REPORTED TIME
TAKEN TO HITCH TO LHASA
VARIES FROM 8 TO 30 DAYS.

HOTAN
·OLD TOWN AREA.
·SUNDAY MARKET RIVALS
KASHGAR'S.
·NEAR ⊕. OR YISO GH 1 KM
FROM CENTRE

4 HRS
10元

TOOK US 17HRS
(LEFT AT DAWN,
ARRIVED AT
MIDNIGHT

KERIYA (YUTIAN)
·HAS SMALL OLD TOWN AREA.
·BY ⊕. LOCALS PAY 5元

NIYA
SAND DUNES (SMALLER THAN
AT DUNHUANG) COME DOWN
TO RIVER 1 KM FROM TOWN
CENTRE.

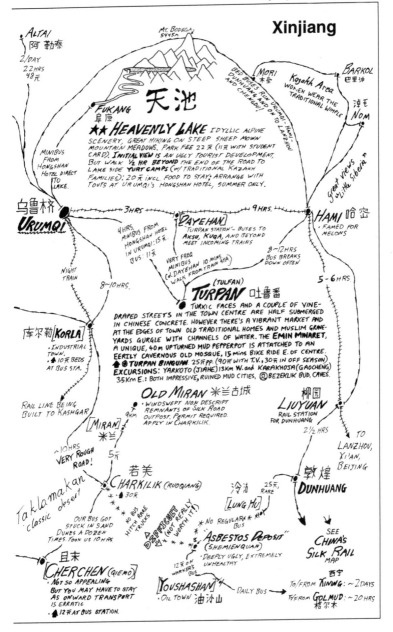

Xinjiang

ALTAI 阿勒泰
2/DAY
22 HRS
48元

MT. BODEGA
5445m

MORI 木全

BARKOL 巴里坤

凉毛 NOM

Kazakh Area
WOMEN WEAR THE
TRADITIONAL WIMPLE

RED BUSES RUN URUMQI-HAMI
AND ONTO LANZHOU
DUNHUANG AND CHENGDU

FUKANG 阜康

天池

★★ HEAVENLY LAKE IDYLLIC ALPINE
SCENERY, GREAT HIKING ON STEEP SHEEP MOWN
MOUNTAIN MEADOWS. PARK FEE 22元 (11元 WITH STUDENT
CARD). INITIAL VIEW IS AN UGLY TOURIST DEVELOPMENT,
BUT WALK ½ HR BEYOND THE END OF THE ROAD TO
LAKE SIDE YURT CAMPS (W/ TRADITIONAL KAZAKH
FAMILIES): 20元 INCL FOOD TO STAY; ARRANGE WITH
TOUTS AT URUMQI'S HONGSHAN HOTEL, SUMMER ONLY.

Great views "LITTLE SIBERIA"

MINIBUS
FROM
HONGSHAN
HOTEL DIRECT
TO LAKE.

乌鲁木齐
URUMQI

3 HRS

DAYEHAN 大河沿
TURPAN STATION" - BUSES TO
AKSU, KUQA, AND BEYOND
MEET INCOMING TRAINS

9 HRS.

HAMI 哈密
• FAMED FOR
MELONS

4 HRS. MINIBUS FROM
HONGSHAN HOTEL
IN URUMQI: 15元
BUS: 11元

VERY FREQ
MINIBUS
(d. DAYEHAN 10 MINS
WALK FROM TRAIN 4元A)

8-12 HRS
BUS BREAKS
DOWN OFTEN

NIGHT
TRAIN

8-10 HRS.

(TULFAN)
TURPAN 吐鲁番

5-6 HRS

TURKIC FACES AND A COUPLE OF VINE-
DRAPED STREETS IN THE TOWN CENTRE ARE HALF SUBMERGED
IN CHINESE CONCRETE. HOWEVER THERE'S A VIBRANT MARKET AND
AT THE EDGES OF TOWN OLD TRADITIONAL HOMES AND MUSLIM GRAVE-
YARDS GURGLE WITH CHANNELS OF WATER. THE EMIN MINARET,
A UNIQUE, 40m UPTURNED MUD PEPPERPOT IS ATTACHED TO AN
EERILY CAVERNOUS OLD MOSQUE, 15 mins BIKE RIDE E. OF CENTRE.
♠ ⊕ TURPAN BINGUAN 25元PP. (90元 WITH T.V., 30元 IN OFF SEASON)
EXCURSIONS: YARKOTO (JIAHE) 13KM W. and KARAKHOJA (GAOCHENG)
35KM E.: BOTH IMPRESSIVE, RUINED MUD CITIES, ⊛ BEZEKLIK BUD. CAVES.

库尔勒 KORLA
• INDUSTRIAL
TOWN.
♠ 10元 BEDS
AT BUS STA.

RAIL LINE BEING
BUILT TO KASHGAR

OLD MIRAN 米兰古城
• WINDSWEPT NON DESCRIPT
REMNANTS OF SILK ROAD
OUTPOST. PERMIT REQUIRED.
APPLY IN CHARKILIK.

9 KM

柳园
LIUYUAN
RAIL STATION
FOR DUNHUANG

2½ HRS

[MIRAN]
米兰

~10 HRS
VERY ROUGH
ROAD!

5元

若羌
CHARKILIK (RUOQIANG)
• 30元

TO
LANZHOU,
XI'AN,
BEIJING

敦煌
DUNHUANG

冷湖
[LUNG HU]

25元,
RARE

Taklamakan
classic desert

OUR BUS GOT
STUCK IN SAND
DUNES A DOZEN
TIMES. TOOK US 10 HRS.

NO BUS
HITCH RARE
TRUCKS

DIFFERENT (NOT REALLY)

No REGULAR
BUS

"ASBESTOS DEPOSIT"
(SHEMIENQUAN)
• DEEPLY UGLY, EXTREMELY
UNHEALTHY

SEE
CHINA'S
SILK RAIL
MAP

且末
CHERCHEN (QIEMO)
• NOT SO APPEALING
BUT YOU MAY HAVE TO STAY
AS ONWARD TRANSPORT
IS ERRATIC
• 12元 AT BUS STATION.

12元 ON
WORKER'S
BUS

[YOUSHASHAN]
油沙山
• OIL TOWN

DAILY BUS

西宁
TO/FROM XINING: ~2 DAYS

格尔木
TO/FROM GOLMUD: ~20 HRS

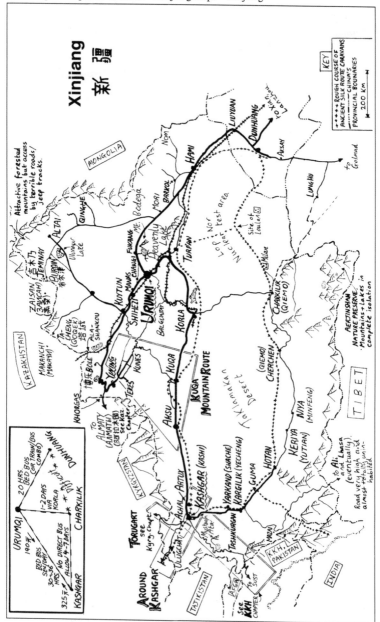

Xinjiang
新疆

KEY
+++ ROUGH COURSE OF
ANCIENT SILK ROUTE CARAVANS
— CHINA'S
PROVINCIAL BOUNDARIES
200 Km

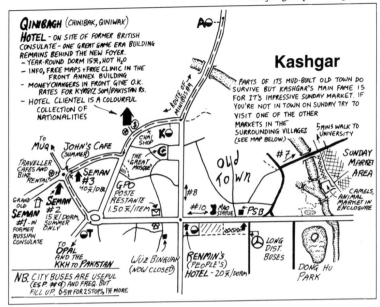

QINIBAGH (CHINIBAK, QINIWAK)
HOTEL - ON SITE OF FORMER BRITISH CONSULATE - ONE GREAT GAME ERA BUILDING REMAINS BEHIND THE NEW FOYER.
- YEAR-ROUND DORM 15元, HOT H₂O
- INFO, FREE MAPS + FREE CLINIC IN THE FRONT ANNEX BUILDING
- MONEYCHANGERS IN FRONT GIVE O.K. RATES FOR KYRGYZ SOM/PAKISTAN Rs.
- HOTEL CLIENTEL IS A COLOURFUL COLLECTION OF NATIONALITIES

Kashgar

PARTS OF ITS MUD-BUILT OLD TOWN DO SURVIVE BUT KASHGAR'S MAIN FAME IS FOR IT'S IMPRESSIVE SUNDAY MARKET. IF YOU'RE NOT IN TOWN ON SUNDAY TRY TO VISIT ONE OF THE OTHER MARKETS IN THE SURROUNDING VILLAGES (SEE MAP BELOW)

5 MINS WALK TO UNIVERSITY

SUNDAY MARKET AREA

CAMELS, ANIMAL MARKET IN ENCLOSURE

ROUTE OF MINIBUS #9

CHAI SHOP

To MUQ
JOHN'S CAFE (SUMMER)
TRAVELLER CAFES AND BIKE RENTAL
THE GREAT MOSQUE
SEMAN #3 40元/DBL

OLD TOWN

#7
#8
#10 MAO STATUE PSB

GRAND OLD SEMAN #1 - IN FORMER RUSSIAN CONSULATE
SEMAN #2 15元/DORM, SUMMER ONLY
GPO POSTE RESTANTE 1.50元/ITEM

To OPAL AND THE KKH to PAKISTAN

WÜZ BINGUAN (NOW CLOSED)
RENMIN'S (PEOPLE'S) HOTEL - 20元/DORM
LONG DIST. BUSES
DONG HU PARK

NB. CITY BUSES ARE USEFUL (ESP. #9) AND FREQ. BUT FILL UP. 0.5元 FOR 2 STOPS, 1元 MORE

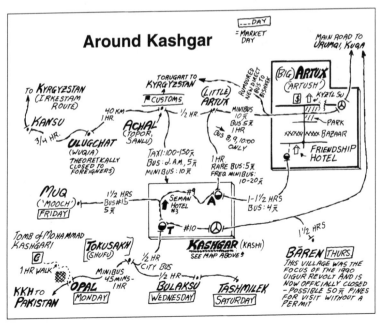

Around Kashgar

- - - DAY = MARKET DAY

MAIN ROAD TO URUMQI, KUQA

(BIG) **ARTUX** (ARTUSH)
KYZYL SU
PARK
XXXXX/XXXX BAZAAR
FRIENDSHIP HOTEL

RUMOURED NEW DIRECT BUS TO BISHKEK

To KYRGYZSTAN (IRKESTAM ROUTE)
TORUGART TO KYRGYZSTAN
CUSTOMS
(LITTLE) ARTUX

KANSU
3/4 HR.
40 KM 1 HR.
½ HR.
MINIBUS 10元 BUS 5元 1 HR
BUS 8,9,10:00 ONLY

ULUGCHAT (WUQIA) THEORETICALLY CLOSED TO FOREIGNERS
ACHAL (TOPOR, SANLU)
TAXI: 100-150元
BUS: 0 A.M., 5元
MINIBUS: 10元
1 HR. RARE BUS:5元 FREQ MINIBUS: 10-20元

MUQ ('MOOCH') FRIDAY
1½ HRS BUS#15 5元
SEMAN HOTEL #3
#9
A
#10
1-1½ HRS BUS: 4元

Tomb of MOHAMMAD KASHGARI
G
1 HR WALK
TOKUSAKH (SHUFU)
½ HR CITY BUS
KASHGAR (KASHI) SEE MAP ABOVE
1½ HRS
BÄREN THURS
THIS VILLAGE WAS THE FOCUS OF THE 1990 UIGUR REVOLT AND IS NOW OFFICIALLY CLOSED - POSSIBLE 50元 FINES FOR VISIT WITHOUT A PERMIT

KKH to PAKISTAN
OPAL MONDAY
MINIBUS 45 MINS- 1 HR
½ HR
BULAKSU WEDNESDAY
TASHMILEK SATURDAY

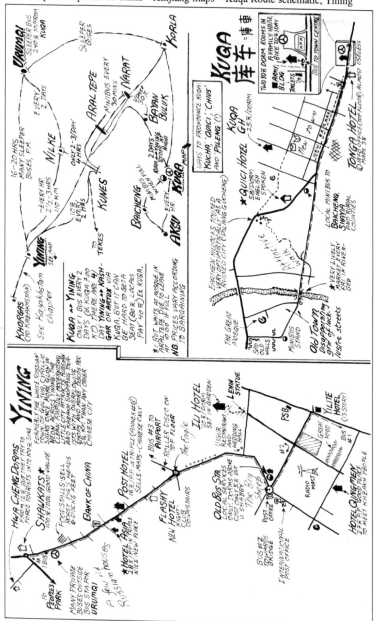

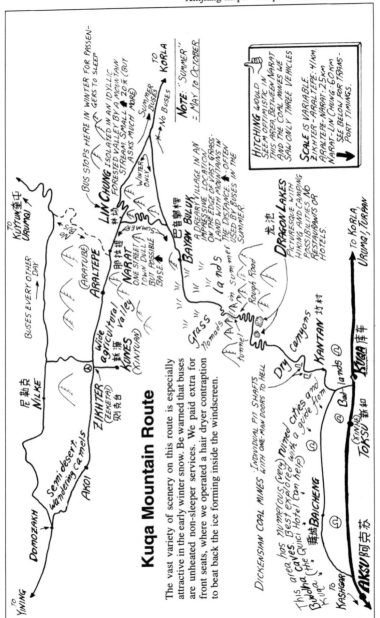

Kuqa Mountain Route

The vast variety of scenery on this route is especially attractive in the early winter snow. Be warned that buses are unheated non-sleeper services. We paid extra for front seats, where we operated a hair dryer contraption to beat back the ice forming inside the windscreen.

NOTE: "SUMMER" = MAY TO OCTOBER.

HITCHING WOULD SEEM OPTIMISTIC IN THIS AREA. BETWEEN NARAT AND THE COAL MINES WE SAW ONLY THREE VEHICLES.

SCALE IS VARIABLE. ZIKHTER-NARAT: 41KM ARALTEPE-NARAT: 25KM NARAT-LIN CHUNG: 60KM SEE BELOW FOR TRANSPORT TIMINGS.

TO KUYTUN 奎屯 URUMQI

BUSES EVERY OTHER DAY

TO YINING

TO KORLA

SUMMER → buses
No buses

BUS STOPS HERE IN WINTER FOR PASSEN-GERS TO SLEEP

LIN CHUNG 林场 ISOLATED IN AN IDYLLIC FORESTED VALLEY BY A MOUNTAIN STREAM SMALL ⚑ 20元 (BUT ASKS MUCH MORE)

WINTER ONLY

SUMMER

Semi desert: wandering camels

AKOI

DOMOZAKH

NILKE 尼勒克

ZIKHTER (ZEKEPU) 奥克台

Wide agricultural valley

ARALTEPE (ARATUBE)

那拉提 NARAT

KUNES (XINYUAN) 新源

ONE STREET TOWN DULL BUT POSSIBLE BASE.

BAYAN BULUK 巴音布鲁

A DREARY VILLAGE IN AN IMPRESSIVE LOCATION ON THE EDGE OF VAST GRASS-LAND WITH MOUNTAINS IN THE DISTANCE. ⚑ OFTEN USED BY BUSES IN THE SUMMER.

Grass lands

nomads in summer

Rough Road

DRAGON LAKES 龙池

PICTURESQUE WITH HIKING AND CAMPING POSSIBILITIES. NO RESTAURANTS OR HOTELS.

tunnel

TO KORLA, URUMQI, TURFAN

KANTAN 村村

Dry canyons

Badlands

KUQA 库车

TOKSU (XINHE) 新和

DICKENSIAN COAL MINES : INDIVIDUAL PIT SHAFTS WITH ONE-MAN DOORS TO HELL

This area has numerous (very) Dirty cities and (best explored with a guide from the Quici Hotel [can help])

Buddha caves KUQA

BAICHENG 拜城

AKSU 阿克苏

TO KASHGAR

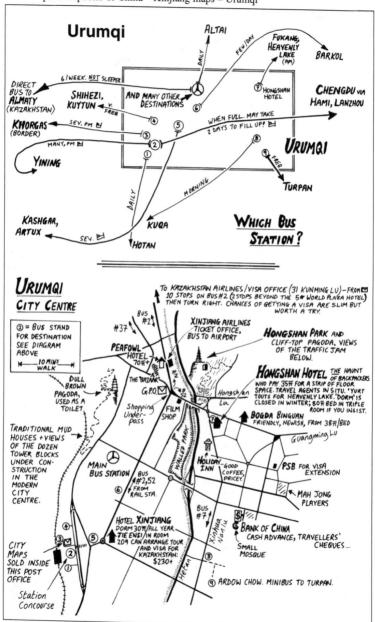

Urumqi

ALTAI

FUKANG, HEAVENLY LAKE (PM)

BARKOL

DAILY

FEW/DAY

DIRECT BUS TO ALMATY (KAZAKHSTAN)

6/WEEK. NOT SLEEPER

SHIHEZI, KUYTUN

AND MANY OTHER DESTINATIONS

⑦ Hongshan Hotel

CHENGDU via HAMI, Lanzhou

V. FREQ

④

⑤

⑥

WHEN FULL, MAY TAKE 2 DAYS TO FILL UP!

Urumqi

KHORGAS (BORDER)

SEV. PM

③

②

⑧

V. FREQ

MANY, PM

①

Turpan

Yining

DAILY

MORNING

KASHGAR, ARTUX

SEV.

KUQA

↓HOTAN

WHICH BUS STATION?

URUMQI CITY CENTRE

② = BUS STAND FOR DESTINATION SEE DIAGRAM ABOVE

|← 10 MINS WALK →|

TO KAZAKHSTAN AIRLINES/VISA OFFICE (31 KUNMING LU)–FROM 10 STOPS ON BUS #2 (2 STOPS BEYOND THE 5☆ WORLD PLAZA HOTEL) THEN TURN RIGHT. CHANCES OF GETTING A VISA ARE SLIM BUT WORTH A TRY.

BUS #2

#37

XINJIANG AIRLINES TICKET OFFICE, BUS TO AIRPORT

HONGSHAN PARK AND CLIFF-TOP PAGODA, VIEWS OF THE TRAFFIC JAM BELOW.

PEAFOWL HOTEL 70元

DULL BROWN PAGODA, USED AS A TOILET

THE BAZAAR

G.P.O.

Shopping Underpass

FILM SHOP

Hongshan Lu

HONGSHAN HOTEL THE HAUNT OF BACKPACKERS WHO PAY 35元 FOR A STRIP OF FLOOR SPACE. TRAVEL AGENTS IN SITU. 'YURT' TOUTS FOR HEAVENLY LAKE. 'DORM' IS CLOSED IN WINTER; 80元 BED IN TRIPLE ROOM IF YOU INSIST.

BOGDA BINGUAN FRIENDLY, NEWISH, FROM 38元/BED

Guangming Lu

TRADITIONAL MUD HOUSES + VIEWS OF THE DOZEN TOWER BLOCKS UNDER CONSTRUCTION IN THE MODERN CITY CENTRE.

MAIN BUS STATION

⑥

BUS #2, 52 FROM RAIL STA.

WALLED PARK

HOLIDAY INN

GOOD COFFEE, PRICEY.

PSB FOR VISA EXTENSION

MAH JONG PLAYERS

CITY MAPS SOLD INSIDE THIS POST OFFICE

Station Concourse

④

③

⑤

②

①

HOTEL XINJIANG DORM 30元/ALL YEAR JIE ENSI IN ROOM 209 CAN ARRANGE TOUR AND VISA FOR KAZAKHSTAN: $230+

BUS #7

Xinhua Nanlu

Hecan

Xinhua Nanlu

BANK OF CHINA CASH ADVANCE, TRAVELLERS' CHEQUES...

SMALL MOSQUE

⑧

⑨ ARDOW CHOW. MINIBUS TO TURPAN.

THE GREAT NORTH

This chapter includes an overall introduction to the ex-USSR then deals more specifically with Belarus, Ukraine and Russia, plus Mongolia. For the other countries of the ex-USSR see Central Asia (p123) and the Caucasus (p82).

What happened to the USSR?
In 1991 the USSR, bogeyman to generations of propaganda-fed Westerners, ceased to exist. In theory, it had always been a 'voluntary' union of SSRs (Soviet Socialist Republics). In reality, for 70 years no republic had dared to declare independence from dominant Russia. Indeed a cold war childhood had given many of us the mistaken idea that the USSR and Russia were one and the same thing. Even after the momentous split of 1991, the Russian Federation remains the world's biggest nation. But that split also created 14 new countries including nuclear-armed Kazakhstan, now the world's ninth largest country. For some ancient nations like Georgia, independence was long awaited and much celebrated. Others like Turkmenistan and Belarus ('White Russia') seemed unsure whether they wanted independence at all.

The CIS
The sudden, almost unexpected implosion of the USSR left some glaring logistical problems. Particularly in Central Asia, most inter-republic borders had been artificially drawn and periodically redrawn without any conception that they might one day become frontiers. Roads and railways had been built regardless, and wander to and fro across these arbitrary lines. Russian bauxite, smelted in Tajikistan was taken to Belarus to make consumer goods. Petroleum

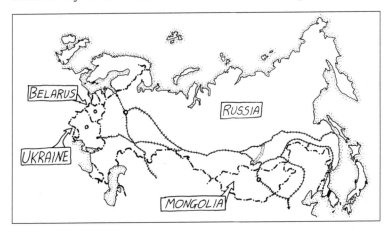

extracted in Kazakhstan would be refined in Russia then shipped back to run Ukrainian buses on Kazakh streets. Thus from an economic viewpoint, a total break-up of the USSR was simply impractical. And from a political angle, Russia wasn't about to lose its hegemony without a fight.

The compromise was the Commonwealth of Independent States (CIS), a loose confederation of former Soviet republics whose leaders meet occasionally in the nominal capital Minsk (Belarus). The CIS has passed many resolutions, friendship accords and customs agreements (eg the Visa Shuffle, see p557) though these have little binding power and states can simply decline to sign. Enthusiastic members (Russia, Belarus, Kazakhstan) see the commonwealth as a watered down USSR, and have signed free trade accords (now including Kyrgyzstan). Belarus's tragi-comic president has even tried to seek political re-union with Russia, though Yeltsin rejected this as an economic liability. Other nations like Ukraine are reluctant members and Azerbaijan maintains only nominal membership following the CIS's apparent favouring of Armenia during the Nagorno Karabakh conflict. The Baltic states (Estonia, Latvia and Lithuania) never joined. Georgia originally refused, too, but was forced to re-consider after civil war and separatist rebellions crippled its ambitious plans for a total split with the ex-USSR. Few doubt that the conflicts were sponsored by Russia to prevent Georgia leaving the fold.

Except in Azerbaijan, the borders of all CIS states with the outside world are now manned by CIS (Russian-commanded) guards. Azerbaijan's refusal has caused great friction with Russia and an occasional partial blockade.

The CIS – Is it safe?

Chechnya is certainly not ready to open a Club Med just yet. Tajikistan is so secure that its refugees spill over into Afghanistan to avoid trouble. However, elsewhere across the ex-USSR you'll find the situation calm with overwhelming kindness and hospitality the most abiding characteristic. A few separatist wars still smoulder in isolated pockets but these clearly defined areas are easy to avoid. The supposedly 'exploding crime rate' starts from such a low base that you're probably safer here than in most Western countries. Indeed the problem is less likely to be from criminals than from crooked police and border guards. Travel here is not yet easy. The concept of the wandering backpacker is still a novelty. But that is as much of an attraction as a problem.

Features common to all CIS nations

Seven years after the break up, each republic retains its share of ugly Soviet grey concrete. Private enterprise has led initially to a flush of kiosks selling imported cigarettes, sweet Italian wine, Israeli vodka and ubiquitous Snickers bars. If you don't know the exchange rate in a country with a black market, simply ask the price of a Snickers and add 10% for the rough US$ rate.

In each republic, Russian remains commonly understood. In the Kyrgyz mountains we found villagers still glued to Moscow TV. For basic Russian phrases see p296, a more detailed word list and the Cyrillic alphabet is found in the language appendix, p560. Toasting a family and friends with vodka remains a major social focus even in the Muslim republics.

Visas and formalities

● **Visa and registration offices** Each ex-Soviet country now has its own very different visa regulations but they have in common the offices which implement the rules. In general the *konsolstvo* (consular) department of the Foreign Affairs ministry (**MID**, pronounced meed) are the people to see for visa extensions. In some countries the old Soviet requirement of 'registering with the police' still applies, but rather than a police station you should visit **OVIR** (pronounced Aveer). Although these are the Russian acronyms, even where the official office titles have been changed, people will know what you mean.

● **Period of stay** Visas for Central Asian states are valid between the **exact** dates that you choose when applying. On the last day, a 'one month' visa expires even if you entered only the day before. You may need to plan far in advance.

● **Visa Shuffle** For details of the reciprocal visa agreement between Armenia, Belarus, Kazakhstan, Kyrgyzstan, Russia, Tajikistan and Uzbekistan, see p557-9.

● **Customs Declaration Form (CDF).** Important notes. See p559.

Transport

● **Trains** The impressive, wide gauge railway system built up in Soviet times remains generally comfortable and punctual. Unlike trains elsewhere, there is no supplement for sleeper berths as the three main ticket classes, *platscart*, *kupe* and *luxe* (see diagram) all have fold down sleeping space. All give you a reserved, numbered place. If few enough people got on, sleeping would even be possible in the cheapest, unreserved *obschii* class as the berths are arranged exactly as in *platscart*. But in reality they're always packed. The suburban *electrichka* services use uncomfortable, seat only carriages which are often appealingly old. Rumours that the trains are dangerous seem highly

exaggerated. Although there have been high profile cases of passengers being robbed by gangs, this is no more common than in Western Europe. Indeed the dangers of petty theft are actually lower than in other countries thanks to the *provodnik* (male) or *provodnitsa* (female) attendant – a guard, ticket collector and general do-gooder who is attached to every carriage and keeps a strict eye open for passengers who should not be aboard. It's worth befriending the provodnik/nitsa and the other passengers in your car by sharing food, making tea for each other (boiling water is free from a samovar in each carriage) and trying to communicate through words, gesticulation or pictures. This is especially true for single travellers on long journeys: at some point you'll need to use the toilet or may want to buy snacks from

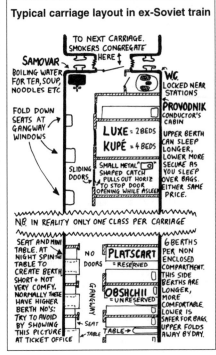

Typical carriage layout in ex-Soviet train

TO NEXT CARRIAGE. SMOKERS CONGREGATE HERE ↑

SAMOVAR BOILING WATER FOR TEA, SOUP, NOODLES ETC

WC. LOCKED NEAR STATIONS

FOLD DOWN SEATS AT GANGWAY WINDOWS

PROVODNIK CONDUCTOR'S CABIN

LUXE = 2 BEDS
KUPÉ = 4 BEDS

UPPER BERTH CAN SLEEP LONGER, LOWER MORE SECURE AS YOU SLEEP OVER BAGS. EITHER SAME PRICE.

SLIDING DOORS

SMALL METAL "CATCH" SHAPED CATCH PULLS OUT HORIZ TO STOP DOOR OPENING WHILE ASLEEP

NB. IN REALITY ONLY ONE CLASS PER CARRIAGE

SEAT AND MINI TABLE. AT NIGHT SPIN TABLE TO CREATE BERTH SHORT + NOT VERY COMFY. NORMALLY THESE HAVE HIGHER BERTH NO'S: TRY TO AVOID BY SHOWING THIS PICTURE AT TICKET OFFICE

NO DOORS

PLATSCART = RESERVED

OBSHCHII = UNRESERVED

GANGWAY

SEAT

TABLE ←

TABLE →

6 BERTHS PER NON ENCLOSED COMPARTMENT. THIS SIDE BERTHS ARE LONGER, MORE COMFORTABLE. LOWER IS SAFER FOR BAGS. UPPER FOLDS AWAY BY DAY.

hawkers on the platforms. In major stations, the train can stop for 15 to 30 minutes. Check with the carriage attendant how long you have; passengers are occasionally left behind.

Accommodation

In the days of the USSR, almost all foreign tourists were forced to stay in vastly overpriced, prematurely aged concrete tower hotels run by the state tourism organisation, Intourist. Most of these grey, depressing, unanimously unfriendly carbuncles still exist and many retain an anthropologically fascinating tribe of rude staff and surly waiters: service with a shrug. You may also spot a specimen of the dwindling species of *dezhurnaya* – floor ladies who are paid to hover around a specific storey of the hotel and swap your room card for the door key. For a few dollars they can mend, find or wash anything and may help with money changing where there's a black market. Your first stay in such a hotel (*gastinyitsa*) is one of those cultural moments to savour – a living memento of the USSR. But the second night can get you down. Don't lose the room card.

Many bigger bus stations, river terminals and railway stations have very basic rooms attached, sometimes just a communal room lined wall to wall with beds. These are often reluctant to take foreigners though they can be persuaded. It might be safest to lock your bags in left-luggage (*kamepa*) overnight.

Some scenic rural areas still have *turbaza*s – a sort of holiday camp for nature lovers, and *alplaga*s – mountain hut bases for climbers. Many of these have fallen into disrepair but many more still operate, though often in summer only.

In the main areas that once attracted Soviet tourists there are remarkably few hotels. This is because most comrades holidayed with their work units in private residences or sanitoria owned by their union. Since 1991, some of these places do now take non-union guests but typically only by reservation. It may also be possible to talk your way into one of the sad looking apartment blocks that double as university or professional hostels. We rented a room in a nurses residence in Almaty, slipping $2/day to the caretaker and agreeing to sneak in and out to avoid the *direktor*.

The best deals, though not necessarily the cheapest, are homestays or the much rarer private B&Bs. Renting a room in a private apartment (*chaznie kvartiera*) is also a good way to see how locals live. The best way to arrange homestays varies greatly between cities – tips are given in country chapters/on relevant maps. Try simply asking those you meet (staff at some mid range hotels helped us). Local people are extremely hospitable: sometimes your problem is persuading them **not** to take you home. As a *ghosty* (guest), you'll sleep and eat for free, but there's likely to be an outpouring of hospitality (ie vodka) which though delightfully generous, can be a little exhausting.

Food and drink

If you are looking for a cheap, sit down meal don't head for a restaurant. 'Restaurants' in the former USSR were seen as places for weddings and other very special occasions. Soviet era establishments may still maintain ludicrous floor shows and cheesy bands. This can be fun for a surrealistic night out, but check the prices carefully when ordering. The bill has a tendency to include all kinds of extras and can easily reach $30 or more per person. Cheaper meals are to be found from *stolovaya* (in Russian), or *ashkana* (in Turkic languages). Alternatively, there's usually fresh produce at the markets and fried snacks from street vendors and on railway platforms. Each region of the ex-USSR has its distinctive cuisine, though *Borshch* (Russian beet and cabbage soup) still features in most far flung republics. Common to most regions is the belief that guests must be fed meat. This can be hard on vegetarians.

The other unifying dietary factor is vodka. Half-litre bottles are obligingly sealed with only a cardboard disc, so locals have the perfect excuse to say: 'Well it's open now, better finish it'. Regardless of religion, vodka is a way of life through most of the CIS, and seems all the more so to a visitor whose presence provides an added excuse for a round or three of toasts. Vodka is not supposed to be sipped. For the duration of a conversation, charged glasses sit untouched on the table. Then a toast is proposed and the glasses are downed and re-filled. Men are expected to keep pace, though women are often offered an alternative of *shampanski* sparkling wine.

Further information

● **Current Affairs** *New Europe* is an excellent weekly English-language newspaper focusing on Central and Eastern Europe and the entire ex-USSR. Subscription is a daunting $350/year: 480 Mesoghion Av, 15342 Athens, Greece. Fax 301-601-4600. A condensed version appears on http://www.new.europe.com.

● **Books** Lonely Planet, Vacation Work and Cadogan have guidebooks to all or parts of this area. Check publication dates: information dates quickly in this fast-changing region. For background the best read is Stephen Dalziel's *Rise and fall of the Soviet Empire*.

● **Maps** Hilderbrand and Kummerly & Frey both produce good CIS maps. The latter has a detailed Central Asia inset but the road and rail key switch confusingly between maps.

❏ Meat Avoidance Techniques for veggies in the ex-USSR

It is possible to survive in the ex USSR without eating meat. There is always bread, cheese, Mars Bars, vodka and even the occasional vegetable. However, getting immersed in local culture is tough for veggies. All hospitality revolves around food and drink. Hosts feel a duty to provide. It is your duty, as a guest, to eat. And the food for guests is meat.

Politely declining any meat dishes placed before you is not a realistic option. Your host will initially think your '*nyet, spaceeba*'s are a sign of good manners and will insist more vigorously that you do eat – it is polite to decline a few times. However if you persist in refusing his food, the host will be confused or hurt.

More creative options (ie lying) don't work either when you lack a common language. 'I'm very sorry but it is against my religion to eat meat', may at best be considered a poorly metered haiku. 'I have an allergy to meat' is a concept somewhat difficult to communicate through sign language and pictionary. Claiming an upset stomach doesn't help much either. 'Bad feel?' one host responded. 'Ah. If Bad feel, eet meat. Eez gud forr you.' The best solution is to throw yourself into the culture regardless but employ as many Meat Avoidance Techniques (MAT) as possible. Some I have tried:

● **MAT 1 The Carnivorous Friend** Discretely dump your unwanted morsels onto his/her plate in return for a few bones.

● **MAT 2 The Early Afternoon Meeting** Arriving between mealtimes reduces the odds of meat being served to 80%. Difficult to use since you will rarely control the timing of an invitation.

● **MAT 3 The Over Complement of Non-Meaty Items** Gorge on them, wonder whether you might have more, then suddenly find yourself full.

● **MAT 4 The Abundance of Vodka** Make so many toasts to your host's good hospitality that he (or, more likely, you) won't notice what you are and are not eating.

● **MAT 5 The Disappearing Act** In one restaurant where I was the guest of a local policeman, I managed to make several fatty sausagesque patties disappear from my plate each time my host left the table to order more food. (Apologies to the staff who later found them in the flower pot).

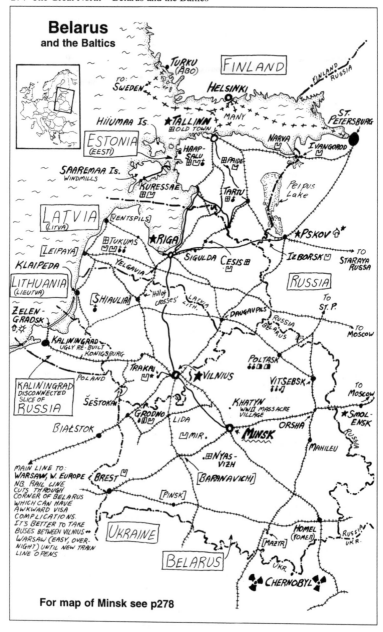

Belarus
and the Baltics

TURKU (ABO)
FINLAND
TO SWEDEN
HELSINKI
FINLAND RUSSIA
MANY
Hiiumaa Is.
★TALLINN
OLD TOWN
ST. PETERSBURG
ESTONIA (EESTI)
HAAP-SALU
PAIDE
NARVA
IVANGOROD
SAAREMAA Is.
WINDMILLS
KURESSAE
TARTU
Peipus Lake
LATVIA (LTVA)
[VENTSPILS]
★RIGA
★PSKOV
[LEIPAYA]
TUKUMS
SIGULDA CESIS
IZBORSK
TO STARAYA RUSSA
KLAIPEDA
YELGAVIA
LATVIA LITH.
RUSSIA
LITHUANIA (LIEUTVA)
SHIAULIAI
Hill of crosses
DAUGAVPILS
RUSSIA BELARUS
TO ST. P.
ZELEN-GRADSK
TO MOSCOW
KALININGRAD
UGLY RE-BUILT KONIGSBURG
POLTASK
TRAKAI
★VILNIUS
VITSEBSK
TO MOSCOW
KALININGRAD
DISCONNECTED SLICE OF RUSSIA
POLAND
ŠEŠTOKAI
KHATYN
WWII MASSACRE VILLAGE
★SMOL-ENSK
GRODNO
LIDA
ORSHA
RUSSIA
BIAŁSTOK
MIR.
★MINSK
MAHILEU
MAIN LINE TO:
WARSAW, W. EUROPE
NB. RAIL LINE CUTS THROUGH CORNER OF BELARUS WHICH CAN HAVE AWKWARD VISA COMPLICATIONS. IT'S BETTER TO TAKE BUSES BETWEEN VILNIUS ↔ WARSAW (EASY, OVER-NIGHT) UNTIL NEW TRAIN LINE OPENS
BREST
NYAS-VIZH
[BARANAVICHI]
[PINSK]
UKRAINE
BELARUS
MAZYR
HOMEL (OMEL)
RUSSIA UKR.
UKR.
CHERNOBYL

For map of Minsk see p278

Belarus

After only five years of independence, Belarus voted itself out of existence again. It hoped to re-join Russia. But Russia didn't want it back. So Belarus (formally Byelorussia – White Russia) limps on into an uncertain future. Lukashenko, its authoritarian leader, still appears to dream of rebuilding the USSR. He calls for help from 'Brother' Russia, then provocatively locks up Russian journalists. He demands Western investment while proudly pooh-poohing any World Bank recommendation. To ensure friendships with the US Belarus expelled an American diplomat for watching an anti-government demonstration and drove out the Soros Foundation whose large charitable donations it wanted to tax.

In the shadow of Chernobyl, this former economic powerhouse of the USSR languishes in a tragically comic malaise apparently assuming that it will wake up one day and find that capitalism was just a bad dream. There's little to see; the whole area was utterly devastated during World War Two. But as a cultural souvenir of communist era mis-management, Belarus is something unique. Practically speaking, the main reasons to visit are the cheap overnight trains from Brest or Minsk to Moscow. Brest is conveniently placed on the Polish border and Minsk is a cheap bus hop from Vilnius, Lithuania.

❑ **W&M's country ratings – Belarus**

● **Expense $$** Transport and food are cheaper than in Russia, it's cheaper to buy 'Russian' souvenirs in Minsk than in Moscow. Hotels and restaurants are expensive.

● **Value for money ✔✔✔** OK, except for hotels which are desperately over priced for foreigners.

● **English spoken ✔✔** Rare, especially in the countryside.

● **Getting around ✔✔✔** Regular and inexpensive.

● **Woman alone ✔✔✔✔** Few special problems.

● **For vegetarians ✔✔** Like Russia.

PRACTICAL INFORMATION
Visas and formalities

Belarus tourist or 'entry' visas require an invitation. This is easily obtained in neighbouring Lithuania through **Violota Travel** (☎ 370 2 652238) Basanviciaus 15, Vilnius, or in Russia via the St Petersburg Youth Hostel. However, the Belarus embassy in Vilnius is very slow and chaotic. Transit visas are no longer available at the border or airport, except as a money making scam on the Lithuania-Poland railway line where the train sneaks through a few kilometres of Belarus and you're charged $30 for the privilege. Instead you must apply in advance and show an onward ticket (which undermines the idea of visiting Belarus to buy a cheap local rail/bus ticket). Transit visas are typically $20 and sometimes permit two entries. Fortunately, there's usually no need to get a Belarus visa at all. If you're heading for

Russia or Central Asia, the visas that you already have should allow you to transit the country for at least 24 hours (see Visa Shuffle, p557). We tested the system, successfully leaving Belarus and getting into Poland on a Kyrgyz visa. Entering **from** Poland in this way might cause more questions. Once you're in Belarus on a different country's visa, hotels may prove reluctant to let you stay (they're never that friendly anyway). So if you want to stay, you'll need to head for the Ministry of Foreign Affairs at 19 Lenina, Minsk. They can give you a visa on the spot for $60, though you may need to persuade a local citizen to come along with you and act as your 'sponsor'. You are supposed to register your stay with the police, though hotels will do this for you.

Money

A scampering bunny on the diminutive one rouble notes gave the currency its quaint nickname *zaichiki* (rabbit). However the monetary rabbit is now as extinct as its Chernobyl brethren as the rouble pushes on towards US$1=BR50,000. It's likely to spiral down ever further until someone has the guts to tell President Lukashenko to read an elementary economics textbook.

Travellers' cheques can be cashed at **Belvneshcombank** (Zaslavskaya St), **Belbusinessbank** in Minsk (Lenin 16; open Monday to Friday, 10am-1pm) and in some hotels. **Prior Bank** (Very Haruzai 31a, Minsk; open Monday to Friday, 9am-12.30pm) will give cash advances on Visa and MasterCard credit cards. An agreement with Russia envisaged that Belarus would eventually readopt the Russian rouble rather than introducing a new currency, the *taler*, but Russia is not enthusiastic.

Transport
● **Air Belavia Airlines** (☎ 227 6254), Karl Marksa 29, Minsk, sells tickets for travel within the CIS; for international tickets go to Chkalova 38, Minsk, (☎ 225 0231).

Accommodation
Minsk in Your Pocket (an indispensable guide) describes finding a hotel room in Minsk as a 'Kafka-esque nightmare'. The *Motel Minsky* (☎ 17-299 5140/32), 17km out of town on the road to Brest, is the most inviting and affordable with rooms for under $10 that don't require booking. The majority of city centre hotels either charge outrageous foreigner surcharges or don't take foreigners at all. Many demand pre-booking, though we were offered a $12 room at the very dingy but central *Hotel*

❏ **Essential information for travellers – Belarus**
● **Visas** Required by most. Tourist visas require an invitation. Visa shuffle works (see p557).
● **Currency** Belarus Rouble; $1=BR41,000 (steady inflation); (approximately BR7000 = 1 Russian Rouble.)
● **Time zone** 2 hours ahead of GMT (the same as the Baltic states, one hour behind Moscow); 3hrs ahead of GMT in the summer.
● **Special dangers** Fresh fruit and mushrooms in parts of the country are still considered to be contaminated with radioactivity from the Chernobyl disaster. Recently printed maps mark the contamination zones but travelling across these extensive regions is not in itself risky.
● **When to go** Summer is wet and warm, winters are snowy and freezing cold.
● **Traveller destinations** Minsk and Brest railway stations while in transit. Mir (impressive castle), Brest (site where the infamous Russo-German agreement was signed in 1918), Grodno (two 'castles' in the town centre), Vitebsk (the birthplace of Marc Chagal) though it lost all the signs of its 1000 year history during WW2.
● **Pulse of the country** Faint.

Svislatz. We eventually found a friendly African university student with a comfortable floor. Another traveller apparently found a homestay through an agency at Skaryny 93 (metro Park Calijuskincau). See p278 for map of Minsk.

Staying in touch

● **Mail** Mail from Belarus is cheap and, in our experience, fast (five days to the UK).

● **Phone** Local call boxes require telephone cards (bought from kiosks) which you can return after use for a partial refund. The phone system has been overhauled. Numbers are now seven digits: add a 2 in front of old six figure numbers.

International phone code: +375 (it used to be 7). The new city codes are Minsk: 17, Brest: 16, Homel: 23, Grodno: 15, Vitsebsk: 21. To get an international operator dial Minsk (☎ 233-2971).

Further information

The quarterly updated pamphlet *Minsk in your pocket* ($1) is available at top hotels (eg the Orbita, 39 Pushkinskaya, on the ring road) and book shops; it gives lots of up to date and practical help for the capital, and contains a good city map. If you can't find one call their office ☎ 17-243 0582. For a copy before you go, write to PO Box 52, 2000 Vilnius-C, Lithuania (e-mail viyp@ post.omnitel.net).

The business centre in room 350 of the Hotel Minsk was helpful with city enquiries and is conveniently close to the bus and railway stations.

Belintourist (the state tourism concern) is based at Hotel Jubileynaya (☎ 17-226984, fax 17-231143), 19 Masherov Ave, Minsk.

Belarus is included in Lonely Planet's *Russia* guide.

❏ **Geo-political information – Belarus**

Population: 10.5 million (1997), 10.1m (1989), 9.8m (1983).

Area: 207,000 sq km (20% still affected by the fallout from Chernobyl).

Capital: Minsk (1.7 million, 1995).

Other major cities: Homel (500,000), Mogliev, Vitsebsk (350,000), Brest, Grodno (300,000), Bobruysk (230,000), seven more cities over 100,000. Some Belarussians consider Vilnius (capital of Lithuania) as the 'Belarussian Jerusalem'.

GNP per capita: $2160 (1994).

Currency history: Belarus Rouble/US$1 – Feb 1998: BR41,100 Oct 1997: BR27,800, May 1996: BR12,400, Nov 1995: BR11,700, Dec 1994: BR10,600.

Major exports/economy: Once the industrial heartland of the USSR, now struggling to maintain industries while agriculture, though efficient, has been hard hit by the nuclear fallout from Chernobyl.

Ethnic mix: Belarussian (78%), Russian (13%), Polish (4%), Ukrainian (3%).

Official languages: Russian/Belarussian.

Religious mix: Estimated Orthodox Christian (70%), Roman Catholic (19%).

Landmarks of national history: 1812: Devastation by Napoleon who tried to create a Belarus state as a bargaining chip to swap with Russia for Lithuania. **25 Mar 1918:** Belarussian People's Republic declared. **1919:** The Byelorussian Soviet Socialist Republic founded but its western flank was lost to Poland in a 1920 war. **1922:** Founder member of the USSR. **After WWII:** The western flank was regained but 25% of the population were killed or deported during the German occupation and 9000 villages burnt. **Aug 1991:** Independence from the USSR. **1995:** Signed customs agreement with Russia; plans to develop a closer union.

Leader: President Alexander Lukashenko, elected July 1994.

Pressing political issues: Union with Russia, Chernobyl problems, economic mismanagement.

Web sites

An excellent online guide to Minsk is at www.inyourpocket.com/mnhome.htm.

www.belarustourist.minsk.by is the homepage of Belarustourist and has good information on obtaining visas.

www.belarus.net/index_1.htm has a lot of information on Belarus, though it is mostly geared towards business people.

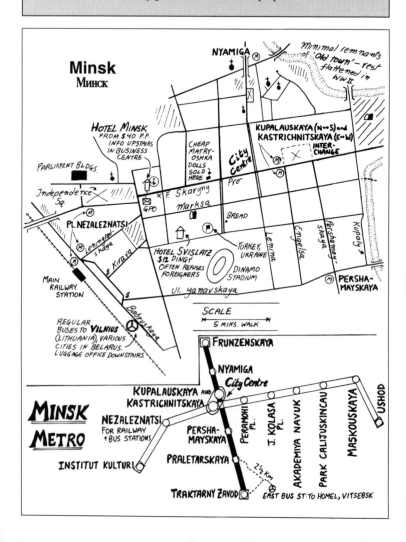

Ukraine

Ukraine, the rather empty breadbasket of the ex-Soviet Union, is an almost undiscovered travellers' gem. Ukrainian visas are difficult to get hold of but once you're in there's much more than Chernobyl fallout to see. Ukrainian cities are cosmopolitan and attractive with a great variety of architectural influences. There are great hikes, hidden half-forgotten cave cities in the Crimea, and a length of Black Sea coast backed by dramatic rocky escarpments. Kiev and especially Lvov (Lviv) offer you the chance to experience genteelly crumbling yet intensely cultured socialist cities with many historical subtexts.

PRACTICAL INFORMATION
Visas and formalities

● **Visa strategy** Visas are required by most Westerners and an invitation or tourist voucher is almost always needed. If you don't have friends or business contacts, an invitation may be procured in Moscow through visa support companies or agencies. **Ukrainian Russian Tourist Bureau** (☎ 493 2330), Boulevard Yana Rainitsa 5, Moscow (Metro: Skhodnenskaya), will provide an invitation for a five-day stay for $40. For a longer stay add $5 per unit of five days, up to 31 days ($65). The office is open Monday to Friday, 10am-6pm, and invitations are best arranged in person. Look in Moscow's Traveller Yellow Pages directory for details of other agencies.

Kobasaniuk Travel (fax 212-454-4005), 157 2nd Ave, New York City, USA, will also provide an invitation letter but since a crackdown in 1996 it has been very hard to get visa support in Western European capitals.

Once you have the invitation it still may take up to two weeks and $35 or the equivalent to issue a visa (though by paying double most embassies will issue one the next day). However visa applications can be processed in Minsk in one hour (in Moscow it usually takes 10 days): try Ul Kirova 17, Minsk (☎ 017-227 7004), open Monday to Friday, 9am-1pm, for the invitation. You can get the visa on arrival at the airports for $150 (if there happens to be a Ukrainian embassy/consulate in your home country) or $75 (if there isn't), but you'll still need an invitation or tour voucher.

One traveller reported getting a Ukrainian visa without an invitation in Australia. The other best hope is Przemysl in Poland where several hotels can conjure up a visa in less than 24 hours – total cost $70. Coming from the east, the Tashkent (Uzbekistan) consul will issue you a transit visa if you can show tickets (eg a Tashkent to Kharkov rail ticket), but – catch 22 –

❑ **W&M's country ratings – Ukraine**
● **Expense $$** Food and transport are cheap. Hotel accommodation is often expensive but you can find unofficial family-run B&Bs for $2-10, though prices are rising quite rapidly.
● **Value for money** ✔✔✔
● **Getting around** ✔✔✔ There are regular services on most routes though they are not especially frequent. Tickets can be hard to buy.
● **English spoken** ✔✔✔ Many people can speak some English though initially they may be too shy to try.

you can buy these tickets only with a visa! Two-day transit visas are sometimes issued at major border points but these are very expensive and anyhow you should not count on getting one.

● **Entry formalities** Ukraine is an unenthusiastic member of the CIS and its borders with Russia have passport checks. A Russian visa doesn't allow you to transit Ukraine and will be cancelled if you cross the Ukrainian frontier. Currency Declaration Forms are collected on departure to non-CIS countries (see p559).

Money

The first Ukrainian currency was the Karbovanets, known universally as the Kupon. Hyper-inflation took it to nearly K200,000=$1 before stabilising. However, the new *Hryvnia* (pronounced Greevnya) has remained within the target band between H1.7 and 1.9 to $1 throughout

---

❑ **Geo-political information – Ukraine**

Population: 50.6 million (1997), 51.4m (1989), 49.7m (1979).

Area: 603,700 sq km.

Capital: Kiev (2.6m, 1990).

Other major cities: Kharkov (1.6m); Dnepropetrovsk (1.2m); Donetsk, Odessa (1.1m); Lvov (800,000); Krivoi Rog (Kryvyi Rih) (700,000); Mariupol, Mikolayev (Mikolaiv), Luhansk (500,000); 21 other cities over 200,000.

GNP per capita: $1570 (1994).

Currency history: Hryvnia/US$1 – Feb 1998: H1.88, 1997: H1.7-1.9 (fixed band) , Karbovanets – July 1996: K179,250, Jan 1996: K186,500, Dec 1994: K104,100, Dec 1993: K30,900.

Major exports/economy: Coal, heavy industry. Major debtor (to Uzbekistan, Turkmenistan et al for gas). The effects of the Chernobyl nuclear disaster of 1986 continues to affect the economy.

Ethnic mix: Ukrainian (72.7%), Russian (22.1%), Byelorussian (1%), Jewish (1% but many have emigrated since the census, small communities of other East European nationalities, 50,000 Roma (Gypsies), 48,000 Crimean Tartars.

Official languages: Ukrainian. Many Russian speakers especially in the Crimea.

Religious mix: Predominantly Christian: Eastern Orthodox, four Ukrainian church denominations, some Greek Orthodox Catholics.

Landmarks of national history: **482AD**: Official founding date of Kiev. **9th-12th centuries**: 'Kievan Rus' became Christian and a major economic and cultural centre. **1667**: Divided between Poland and Russia. **1686**: Orthodox Church forced to take authority from Moscow. **1793**: Polish sections transferred to Russia. **1917**: Declared a People's Republic. **Feb 1918**: Occupied by Soviet forces. **Dec 1922**: Founder member of the USSR with national revival until crushed by Stalin. **1941**: German occupation. **1944**: German forces expelled from Lvov just before the beautiful old city could be dynamited. **1944**: Tartar population of Crimea deported en masse to central Asia – Stalin thought them collaborators. **Feb 1945**: The division of Europe after WWII was planned at summit meetings in Livadia palace, Yalta, by Stalin, Roosevelt, and Churchill. **1954**: Crimea given to Ukraine (formerly part of Russian Federation). **1986**: Chernobyl disaster. **1991**: Independence. **1994**: Crimea made a de facto declaration of independence. **March 1995**: Crimean presidency abolished. **April 1995**: Ukrainian President assumed direct control of Crimea.

Leader: President Leonid Kuchma.

Pressing political issues: Status of Crimea, parlous economy, power supply, Chernobyl safety and clear up, power of the presidency.

1997. This new found stability has undermined the 'national sport' of betting on the day's exchange rate and some of the once ubiquitous exchange booths have closed. It is less necessary now to carry US$ though homestay hosts still prefer greenbacks.

Several banks offer cash advances on credit cards. Travellers' cheques are cashed by Exibank, the Savings Bank of Ukraine, and others (2% commission).

Transport
● **Train** Long distance trains are as efficient and comfortable as in Russia, and potentially much cheaper, but only if you can get a ticket. Ticket offices in big stations are subject to long queues. 'Mafia' agents buy up large blocks of tickets, reselling them at a massive mark up (eg $30 for a $1 ticket). This scam is common in Lvov and Simferopol, and especially in Kiev where several travellers reported getting stuck, though if you're prepared to pay foreigner prices there's a special tourist counter in the upstairs waiting lounge. To get a local price ticket out of Lvov, you can avoid the chaos by taking a cheap one-hour ride on the *electrichka* (local train) to Mostitska on the Polish border. The daily overnight Mostitska-Kiev service is never full and there are no queues at the ticket office. For tickets ex-Simferopol, you could take the electrichka to Bakhchiserai (itself a fascinating place) where the quiet, computerised ticket office usually has berth allocations to a variety of cities on the mainline from Sevastopol. Alternatively, there's a helpful ticketing office in Yalta, even though Yalta has no railway station. If you're buying a ticket into Kiev it's worth booking an onward ticket at the same time – this saves trouble leaving Kiev and is cheaper than buying the two tickets separately.

● **Buses** Bus services cover the country but they are infrequent and there are almost no overnight services except on the cross border routes from Lvov to Poland. Note that on routes that cross out of the CIS, buses prove much cheaper than trains, while for domestic journeys the train is cheaper, especially in *platscart* class. Queues at bus-station ticket windows look daunting but move steadily. What is probably the world's longest trolley bus route runs between Yalta and Simferopol: the journey takes $3^{1}/_{2}$hrs over a pass and along the Crimean coast.

Accommodation
There is a severe lack of accommodation in Kiev and the cheapest hotel room is

❏ Kiev's nuclear families

I arrived too early in Kiev for a choice of accommodation touts at the railway station so I left my rucksack in left luggage and went off to the opera (*La Traviata* for 90 cents). When I returned, a woman called Galina was one of several touts with a grasp of English. Like the others, she was not impressed with my $5 offer for her room, which she assured me was on a desirable tram route. I agreed to wait and see if she could find some more clients but eventually, with her young daughter losing patience, she decided to accept my price. When I saw the little room, I was relieved not to be sharing.

Galina explained that she was a trained nuclear physicist. She translated documents from German and English and her husband programmed military computers. But pay was not what it was. Nowadays they liked to take lodgers to supplement their income. I settled amongst a library of books to be surprised later with a simple, tasty meal before retiring gratefully to bed. Next morning I awoke early and wandered into the kitchen for a glass of water. Mother and daughter awoke, slightly startled, from their blanket on the floor. As shocked as them, I realised that in fact I was occupying the only bed in the flat. Husband, it transpired, now lived at their dacha growing potatoes to ward off their starvation. Potatoes were more valuable than his expertise. Galina's monthly income was a mere $3 a month. 'But if you get $5 a night from me, why work all month for $3?', I asked perplexed. 'Oh. When times are hard, you must work even harder' she replied adamantly. Across Ukraine, and indeed the whole USSR, many people work on – noble or foolish I can't decide – because they always have. One day it will be better. Without these stoics, how would the country function?

US$35 for a single. Fortunately many city dwellers go to the station after work and stand around with little hand-written notices. They are not begging but offering homestays to visitors – $10-$20 a night is typical but bargaining works, especially later in the evening when the 'touts' are keen to go home to their children after a long day. We paid $5 each which included cooked meals.

In summer, Yalta and the Crimean coast remain very popular with rich Russian tourists. A splendid four-room ocean view apartment which cost us just $2 from a bus station tout in October, cost $25 in August. Seaside hotel prices also quadruple in summer. Homestays are harder to find in smaller towns where there are fewer visitors. Try asking those you stay with in Kiev or Yalta to recommend friends.

❏ Language

Ukrainian is written in Cyrillic script with a few special letters (see language appendix). Town names have Ukrainian and Russian variant spellings: we mostly use the Russian spellings where they are more familiar to most westerners, but increasingly the Ukrainian transliterations are becoming the standard, eg Lvov = Lviv, Kharkov = Kharkiv, Kiev = Kyiv.

Some phrases in Ukrainian (the language is similar to Russian, numbers and many greetings are the same):

How are you? – *Yakzhi vesh?*
Reply (good) – *Dobre/Yakzhi*
Thank you <u>very much</u> – *Dyak-uyu düzhe*

Staying in touch

● **Mail** Stamp prices seemed utterly random but extremely cheap. Stamps for a certain rate are marked with a letter rather than a cash value. Different post offices charged us different prices for the same denomination.

● **Phone** 24-hour foreign language operators are available: for French dial 8191, English 8192, and German 8193. In some cities, local calls from telephone boxes are free; at least until the boxes are modified to take tokens/cards.

International phone code: +380. Kiev: 044, Kharkov: 0572, Simferopol: 0652. Do not dial the zero when calling from abroad.

Further information

● **Books** *Ukraine Language and Travel Guide* by Linda Hodges and George Chumak (Hippocrene Publishers) takes the language seriously but is not a practical travel guide.

Ukraine gets lumped in with other countries in several recent guides including Lonely Planet's *Russia*, Let's Go's *Eastern Europe*, and Bradt's *Hiking Guide to Poland and Ukraine* – all of them are useful.

● **Maps** The local company Kartografia produces highly detailed $2.50 city maps of 15 Ukrainian towns as well as 1:200,000 scale maps of the country's 25 regions for $3 each. Some are in English but most are in Ukrainian Cyrillic script. Their map shop/office at 54 Popudrenko St, Kiev (☎ 552 8126) carries the full range. Although maps can often be found at kiosks or sold by street vendors (especially around Nezalezhnost Sq, Kiev), it's worth buying any map you might need as soon as you see it.

● **General** The **Association of Foreign Tourism** (☎ 212 5570), Yaroslaviv val 36, Kiev, never seem to answer the phone.

Web sites

Surprisingly, Ukraine has extensive travel information on the web. Two of the best sites are www.geocities.com/TheTropics/2550/guide_fr.html and www.usemb.kiev.ua/Ukraine; the latter with a text-only option for faster viewing.

Information specifically for Kharkov is at www.itl.net.ua/misc/kharkov.html and for the Crimea at www.elis.crimea.ua/CTS.html.

A collection of Ukrainian related links is at www.physics.mcgill.ca/WWW/oleh/ukr-page2.html.world at www.towd.com

Ukraine

KHARKOV – KEY METRO STOPS

Pl. Svobody

PIVDENNY VOKZAL

TSENTRAL RYNOK
RADYANSKA

ISTORYCHNY MUSEU

DERZHPRDM
→ to GEROYOV PRATSI

UNIVERSITET

Ul. Sumska
City centre

MARSHALA ZHUKOVA

→ PROLETARSKAYA

PL. GAGARIN
Bus to
↑ OSNOVA-SM

TURIST $20

KEY
•→ = DISTANCE & DIRECTION OF THE TOWN
Ⓐ→•= ... FROM BUS STA.
⌁ = DISTANCE WALK TO BORDER

ALUT-SHIV

SUMY
Ⓡ→23:23

RUSSIA

OCHTIRKA   KHARKOV (KHARKIV)

POLTIAVA   Ⓡ→20:58
🚉 3KM NE
→ PL. KRUHLA 3KM NW

RUSSIA
UKR.

LUHANSK (LUGANSK)

SHEVCHENKO

DNIPROPETROVSK

ZAPORIZHZHYA

DONETSK

TAGANROG

KRIVIROG (KRIVIYRIH)
Ⓡ→22:43

ROSTOV

NOVA KIACHOVKA

Kiev Time
ADD 1HR
SUB 1HR TRACT

MIKOLAEV

Sea of Azov

KRASNODAR

Moscow Time

TEMRIUK

ANAPA

RUSSIA

Crimea was a part of Russia till given as a present to Ukraine in the 1950's by Uncle Krushchev. The Russian speakers are none too chuffed and rumble about independence.

Crimea

SIMFEROPOL
YALTA   SOUTHERN CRIMEA

Black Sea

SOCHI

ADLER

YALTA
Tower blocks peer over a palm-treed promenade backed by Crimean crags. Accommodation touts meet trolleybuses. In Oct, we paid $2 for a three-room apartment ($25 in summer).

Town centre

Promenade

V. USEFUL RAIL BOOKING OFFICE

STEPS

Harbour

NO FERRIES TO RUSSIA OR GEORGIA. SUMMER HOPS & ALONG COAST + WEEKLY FERRY TO ISTANBUL ($150)

Popular SA

CASINO & OUTDOOR BAR

HOTEL YAZHUMA $40 ($11 OFF-SEASON)

Kiev (Київ)

Central metro and bus links

Twice as old as Moscow and almost twice as charming. Alive with music and culture, the big city is centred on a walkable area around Kreshchatyk Metro – grand commercial boulevard with interesting streets off either side.

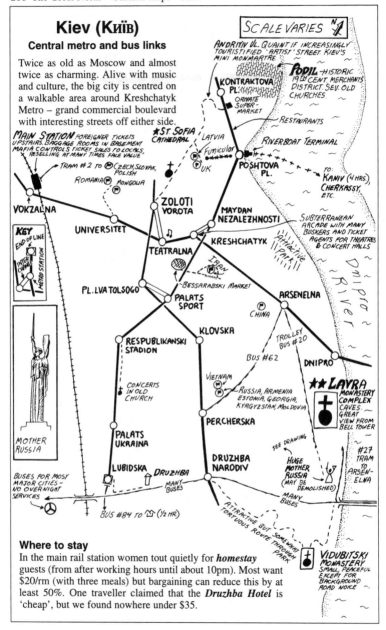

SCALE VARIES N

ANDRIIV UL. QUAINT IF INCREASINGLY TOURISTIFIED 'ARTIST' STREET. KIEV'S MINI MONMARTRE

PODIL – HISTORIC 19TH CENT. MERCHANTS DISTRICT. SEV. OLD CHURCHES.

KONTRAKTOVA PL.

ORNATE SUPER-MARKET

RESTAURANTS

RIVERBOAT TERMINAL

MAIN STATION FOREIGNER TICKETS UPSTAIRS. BAGGAGE ROOMS IN BASEMENT MAFIA CONTROLS TICKET SALES TO LOCALS, RESELLING AT MANY TIMES FACE VALUE.

TRAM #2 TO Ⓟ CZECH, SLOVAK, POLISH

ROMANIA Ⓟ MONGOLIA Ⓟ

★ ST. SOFIA CATHEDRAL

LATVIA

Ⓟ Funicular
Ⓟ UK

POSHTOVA PL.

TO: KANIV (4 HRS.), CHERKASSY, ETC.

VOKZALNA

ZOLOTI VOROTA

MAYDAN NEZALEZHNOSTI

KEY
END OF LINE
☐ INTERCHANGE
○ 1 METRO STATION

UNIVERSITET

TEATRALNA ♫

KRESHCHATYK

SUBTERRANEAN ARCADE WITH MANY BUSKERS AND TICKET AGENTS FOR THEATRES & CONCERT HALLS

Attractive Park

Dnipro River

IRAN

PL. LVA TOLSOGO

BESSARABSKI MARKET

PALATS SPORT

Ⓟ CHINA

ARSENELNA

KLOVSKA

TROLLEY BUS #20

DNIPRO

RESPUBLIKANSKI STADION

BUS #62

BUS #62

VIETNAM Ⓟ Ⓟ

RUSSIA, ARMENIA ESTONIA, GEORGIA, KYRGYZSTAN, MOLDOVA

★★ LAVRA
MONASTERY COMPLEX
CAVES. GREAT VIEW FROM BELL TOWER

MOTHER RUSSIA

CONCERTS IN OLD CHURCH

PERCHERSKA

SEE DRAWING

#27 TRAM TO ARSEN-ELNA

PALATS UKRAINA

HUGE MOTHER RUSSIA (MAY BE DEMOLISHED)

LUBIDSKA

DRUZHBA

DRUZHBA NARODIV

BUSES FOR MOST MAJOR CITIES – NO OVERNIGHT SERVICES

MANY BUSES

MANY BUSES

BUS #84 TO 🏠 (½ HR)

ATTRACTIVE BUT SOMEWHAT TORTUOUS ROUTE THROUGH PARK

VIDUBITSKI MONASTERY SMALL, PEACEFUL EXCEPT FOR BACKGROUND ROAD NOISE

Where to stay

In the main rail station women tout quietly for *homestay* guests (from after working hours until about 10pm). Most want $20/rm (with three meals) but bargaining can reduce this by at least 50%. One traveller claimed that the *Druzhba Hotel* is 'cheap', but we found nowhere under $35.

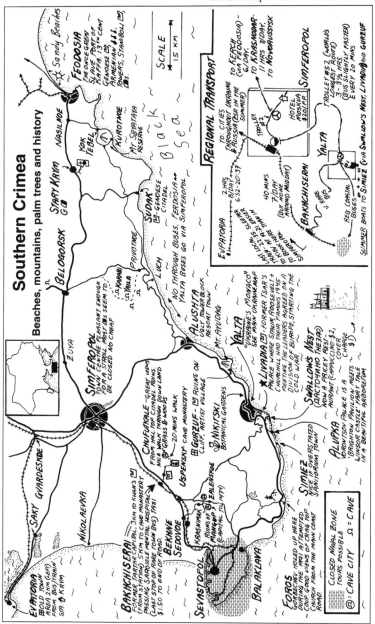

Southern Crimea
Beaches, mountains, palm trees and history

SCALE
15 KM

FEODOSIA THE ONCE GREAT SLAVE PORT OF KAFFA. 13TH CENT GENOESE, Armenian, Armenian TOWERS, STAMBOLI.

Sandy Beaches

NASLNOE

STARY KRYM

KUROTNOE

MT SOPAYAKA RESERVE

YOK TEBEL

BELOGORSK

Black Sea

SUDAR' — GENOESE CITADEL

PRIVOTNOE

LUCH

REGIONAL TRANSPORT

TO KERCH (VIA FEODOSIA) —

TO KRASNODAR, 11 HRS 3/DAY, TO NOVORUSSYSK

TO CITIES THROUGHOUT UKRAINE & RUSSIA (CSR IN THE SUMMER)

HOTEL MOSKVA $10/P.P.

TROLLEY #2

SIMFEROPOL

EUPATORIA 2 HRS 8/DAY 6:52-20:37

(AS IT IS EASIER, FASTER 23 A TRAIN (LOCAL 3+ SLEEPER))

40 MINS 7/DAY (BUT NONE AROUND MIDDAY)

BAKHCHISERAI

YALTA

TROLLEY #52 (WORLD'S LONGEST ROUTE) 3 - 3½ HRS (BUS SLIGHTLY FASTER) EVERY 20 MINS

TO KIEV FOR BOOK FOR SIMEIZ

REG COASTAL BUSES TO SIMEIZ

SUMMER BOATS TO SIMEIZ (VIA SWALLOW'S NEST, LIVADIA AND GURZUF)

ZUYA

SIMFEROPOL TOWN CENTRE PLEASANT ENOUGH — CENTRAL MOST DBS SEEM TO BE CLOSED OR CHEAP

NO THROUGH BUSES, FERDOSIA GO VIA SIMFEROPOL
YALTA BUSES GO VIA SIMFEROPOL

KARABI YAILA

ALUSHTA UGLY TOWER BLOCK RESORT TOWN

MT AYUDAG

YALTA "UKRAINE'S "MONACO" SEE MAIN UKRAINE MAP

CHUFUTKALE — GREAT VIEWS FROM HILL TOP CAVE RUINS. NICE WALK THROUGH DOWN LAND, GRASS & WOODS
20 MINS WALK

USPENSKY CAVE MONASTERY

GURZUF — RUINS ON ARTIST VILLAGE

NIKITSKI BOTANICAL GARDENS

LIVADIA — FORMER TSAR'S PALACE WHERE STALIN, ROOSEVELT + CHURCHILL HAD THEIR FAMOUS 1945 MEETING THE LEADERS AGREED ON A DIVISION OF EUROPE, STARTING THE COLD WAR.

SWALLOW'S NEST (ЛАСТОЧКИНО ГНЕЗДО) NOW A PRICEY REST-AURANT (CAPPUCCINO $2, COVER CHARGE $1)

ALUPKA VORONTSOV PALACE IS A "BRIGHTON PAVILION MEETS WINDSOR CASTLE" FAIRY TALE IN A BEAUTIFUL ARBORETUM

BAKHCHISERAI FORMER TARTAR CAPITAL. 3KM TO KHAN'S (FROM STATION) 5KM TO CAVE MONASTERY PASSING SAROSELE MENTAL HOSPITAL. $1.50 (LAST STOP OF SPARE (TOWN BUS) TARI TO END OF ROAD.

BEKHNE SEDOVOE

SIMEIZ NICE IF OVERSTATED SANITORIUM TOWN

KRASNIMAT

RUINS OF ZALENSHOE MANGUP (CAPITAL TIL 1475)

EVPATORIA OLD TOWN AND ЛТ (LEFT) FROM BUS TRAIN STA KRYM

SAKY GVARDISNDE

NIKOLAEVKA

SEVASTOPOL

BALAKLAVA

FOROS GORBACHEV HOLED UP HERE DURING THE APRIL ATTEMPTED COUP AGAINST HIM. CRYING 600 CHURCH FROM THE MAIN COAST ROAD.

CLOSED NAVAL ZONE
TOURS POSSIBLE

🅗 CAVE CITY   Ω = CAVE

Autonomous areas of Russia

AUTONOMOUS AREAS:
① MORDVA [SARANSK]
② CHUVASH [CHEDOKSAN]
③ MARI EL [YOSHKATOLA]
④ TATARISTAN [KAZAN]
⑤ UDMURT [IZHEVSK]
⑥ BASHKORTISTAN [UFA]

[= CAPITAL CITY]

⑦ ADEGEYA [MAYKOP]
⑧ KALMYKIA [ELISTA]
⑨ KARACHAY CHERKESS [CHERKESSK]
⑩ KABARDINO BALKARIA [NALCHYK]
⑪ N. OSSETIA [VLADIKAVKA]
⑫ INGUSHETIA [NAZRAN]
⑬ DAGESTAN [MAKHACHKALA]
⑭ CHECHNYA [GROZNY]

INDEPENDENT COUNTRIES ONCE PART OF THE USSR:
Ⓐ ESTONIA
Ⓑ LATVIA
Ⓒ LITHUANIA
Ⓓ BELARUS [TRYING TO JOIN RUSSIA]
Ⓔ MOLDOVA
Ⓕ GEORGIA
Ⓖ ARMENIA
Ⓗ AZERBAIJIAN
Ⓘ TATIKISTAN
Ⓙ KYRGYZSTAN

~~~~~~~~ BORDER OF RUSSIA
——— BORDER WITHIN RUSSIA
- - - - FORMER USSR NATION

COLOUR SECTION (following pages)

● **C1 Top**: Registan, Samarkand, Uzbekistan (©ME). **Btm left**: Masjid Imam, Isfahan, Iran. Asia's most dazzling blues (©ME). **Btm rt**: Hoşap Castle, near Van, Turkey (©ME).
● **C2 Top**: Kunming side street, Yunnan (©ME). **Bottom**: This Bactrian camel at Kashgar's Sunday market cost $100 in Turkmenistan (©ME).
● **C3 Top left**: Auto-rickshaw, India (©BT). **Top right**: *Linega* share taxi, Sule Pagoda, Rangoon, Burma (©WK). **Bottom**: Public bus, Vangvieng, Laos (©WK).
● **C4 Top left**: Off to Opal market, Xinjiang (©ME). **Top right**: Porter, Nepal (© Janet & John Anderson). **Bottom**: Trans-Mongolian train (©BT).
● **C5** Typical Yazd *khuche* (alley) and *badgir* (wind tower, see p75), Iran (©ME).
● **C6** Like most Burmese, this sugar-cane seller protects her face with *thanakha* bark powder (©WK). Used with foundation cream *thanakha* is almost invisible.
● **C7 Top**: Angkor Wat, Cambodia (© Christian Braun). **Btm**: Majishan, China (©DSJ).
● **C8** Elephant rides: a cheap, fun way to view wildlife in India/Nepal national parks (©BT).

WK=Wil Klass, ME=Mark Elliott, DSJ=Douglas Streatfeild-James, BT=Bryn Thomas

ПЕКИН—УЛАН-БАТОР—МОСКВА
北京—乌兰巴托—莫斯科
БЭЭЖИН—УЛААН-БААТАР—МОСКВА

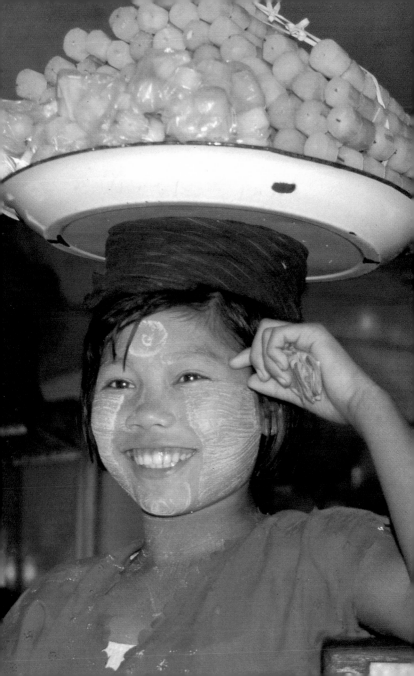

Russia

Moscow's Kremlin and St. Petersburg's waterfront palaces remain the most visited attractions in this vast country. Stereotypical Russian landscapes are of endless snowbound forests and of rolling meadows interspersed by ugly constructivist cities. These scenes are common enough, but tucked in Caucasian corners are also palm-lined beaches and snow-capped peaks. Many cities have been busily re-gilding their onion dome churches since 1991 and despite much architectural vandalism, the USSR has left a legacy of grand government buildings and museums in most major towns. Hiding behind the disincentives of foreigner pricing and continued Soviet-style service-with-a-shrug, lies an extremely hospitable culture. The Russian Federation is by no means pure Russian. Mountain Muslims, tundra Turks and Baikal Buddhists are part of a complex ethnic jigsaw held loosely together through a common history of tragedy and vodka.

Confusion still clouds many Western minds as to the exact difference between the Russian Federation and the ex-Soviet Union. If you're not sure, see p269-70. The situation is no simpler now. As well as Russia proper, today's Russian Federation consists of 21 smaller republics of varying degrees of waywardness. Only Chechnya has attempted a direct declaration of independence, though Tataristan has negotiated a very high degree of autonomy. Huge, mineral rich Sakha (Yakutia) acts much as though it is independent while denying any short term plans to break away. Throughout the federation the economic dislocation of capitalist transition remains painful but the locals are stoics. Churchill's 1939 assessment of Russia as 'A riddle wrapped in a mystery inside an enigma' remains as true as ever.

❑ **W&M's country ratings – Russia**

● **Expense $$$$** Prices in Moscow and St Petersburg are now equivalent to Western Europe for accommodation and restaurant meals. A wide range elsewhere but it's still considerably more expensive than other CIS states.

● **Value for money** ✔✔ Transportation is reasonable value. Accommodation may charge Western prices but without the quality. Restaurant food is rarely inspiring unless it's very expensive.

● **Getting around** ✔✔✔ Despite the huge size of the country, you can get almost anywhere once you've mastered the alphabet.

● **English spoken** ✔✔ Tourist hotels usually have English speaking staff if with heavy Dracula accents. A phrase book is highly recommended and is essential away from the main city centres.

● **Woman alone** ✔✔✔✔ Sexism exists as in most of the world but harassment is rare by the sober. Men are generally 'touchingly chivalrous'.

● **For vegetarians** ✔✔ *Ovashchi bez myasa* means 'vegetables without meat'. Good luck finding some.

❑ Essential information for travellers – Russia

● **Visa** Required. Several weeks planning is crucial unless you're excessively rich. Registration once in Russia is important.

● **Currency** Russian Rouble. US$1=6.02Rbls. (Three zeros were dropped at the start of 1998, so 6000Rbls became 6Rbls).

● **Time zones** 11 time zones. Moscow and most of European Russia is 3hrs ahead of GMT, (see map p299 for others)

● **Religious tone:** Little spiritual feel though the Russian Orthodox church is growing.

● **Health factors:** Tap water is drinkable in many cities, but St Petersburg is not one of them. No malaria risk. If hiking in the Siberian Taiga forests Feb-June, wear strong, long trousers tucked into thick socks. This is to avoid being bitten by ticks which might carry encephalitis, a paralysing and life-threatening disease.

● **Special dangers:** Chechnya remains unstable at the time of writing. The much touted 'mafia' are unlikely to do you any harm unless you foolishly forgot to pay them for a heroin consignment. Beware of groups of loitering 'gypsy' children in city squares who use the 'mob and rob' technique.

● **Typical traveller destinations:** Moscow, St. Petersburg, Lake Baikal.

● **Highlights** St Petersburg, Astrakhan, the Golden Ring Cities, the Caucasus.

● **When to go** The image of frigid winters really does apply to most of the country from November to April. The penetrating icy damp of St Petersburg is crueller than the much colder but dry air of Siberia. Sochi on the rainy Black Sea coast has the mildest winters and is a prime beach resort in the summer. Sky high August prices fall by the end of September as it's a little too cold to swim. The Caucasus peaks are permanently snow capped. Lower slopes are warm in the summer sunshine but clouds roll in rapidly, so cosy waterproofs are worth carrying at any time. May would be pleasant in Siberia if it weren't for the ticks (see Health factors). By late June the Siberian air is unpleasantly dense with mosquitoes and mid-summer can be surprisingly hot – up to 35°C. Autumn is ideal, though by October winter has opened the fridge door. Vladivostok gets iced in by mid-winter yet celebrates a beach-side jazz festival in September after heavy summer rains. Moscow and St Petersburg are very pleasant in the early summer, if occasionally stuffy.

● **Pulse of the country:** Vegetable plots of country dachas

● **Key tips:** Carry US$ in new (post 1990) bills: the old ones are very tough to exchange.

❑ Place names

Since 1991, many cities have reverted to their pre-revolutionary (1917) names. Some important examples are: Gorkii > Nizhni Novgorod (though we use Gorkii on our maps for its convenient brevity), Kalinin > Tver (unrelated to Kaliningrad which has **not** reverted to its Prussian name Königsburg), Kuybeshev > Samara, Leningrad > St. Petersburg (sometimes abbreviated to StP in this book), Ordzhonokidze > Vladikavkaz, Sverdlovsk > Ekaterinburg (often written Yekaterinburg), Ulyanovsk > Simbirsk, Ustinov > Izhvesk, Zagorsk > Sergiev Posad (Zagorsk still popularly used). Yakutia has been renamed the Sakha Republic but its capital Yakutsk ('Emerald') remains unchanged. Street names have changed beyond all recognition but often the old names are still used colloquially.

PRACTICAL INFORMATION
Visas and formalities

● **Visa strategy** To get a Russian visa you will need an invitation or pre-booked accommodation/tour (except for transit visas, see below). There is little way around this. For those without friends in Russia, there used to be many 'visa service' agencies who'd simply write the invitation letter for you in return for a small fee. Sadly most of these closed following a tightening of policy in 1995. All letters are now supposed to be cleared with OVIR in the Russian towns for which the visa is valid. However, you can still get valid invitations through the youth hostel in St Petersburg, the Travellers' Hostel in Moscow or by booking accommodation through certain homestay agents. The hostels charge about $60 for the letter and one night's accommodation, plus they'll help you with registration once you arrive. Fax them the dates you want your visa to be valid for, your passport details (name, nationality, passport number, date and place of issue, date of expiry, date and place of birth), and a credit card number. You may also need to fax a copy of the credit card itself to satisfy banking rules. They'll fax back an official invitation letter, usually within 24hrs. Take the letter to a Russian embassy or consulate with three photos and a photocopy of your passport. You'll be able to get a two-week or one-month visa despite having booked only one night's stay. However, the Russian embassies in Washington DC or London have recently been refusing to give visas at all based on such invitations. Choose any other consulate.

The visa is issued on a separate sheet of paper so the consul doesn't need to keep your passport during the visa issuing process. It costs much more to have the

---

❑ **Travel agents and visa help**
(see also Trans-Siberian contacts p12)

● Travellers Guest House, 50 Perejeslavskaya, 10th floor; Moscow. (☎ 971-4059, fax 280 7686. E-mail tgh@glas.apc.org) (see map inset)

● St. Petersburg International Hostel, 3rd Sovetskaya Ul. 28, St. Petersburg, 193036. (☎ 277-0569, fax 5102 or 329-8019. E-mail: ryh@ryh.spb.su) – see map.

● Sinbad Travel (☎ 327-8384, fax 329-8019. E-mail: sinbad@ryh.spb.su) (associated travel agent in same building).

● Russian Youth Hostels & Tourism 409 N Pacific Coast Highway, 106/3901 Redondo Beach, CA, 90277 USA. Slightly more expensive visa help than St PYH. (☎ 310-379-4316, fax 8420. E-mail: 71573.2010@compuserve.com.)

● White Nights (archaeological digs in Siberia) - 8323 Delmar Blvd, Suite 2E, St Louis, MO 63124. (USA ☎/fax (314) 991-5512. http://206.13.127.134/bus/wnights/Index.htm.)

● Mir Corporation (homestays $55/sing, $70/dble) 85 S Washington St., Suite 210; Seattle WA 98104. (☎ 206-624-7289, fax 7360, e-mail: mir@igc.apc.org.)

● HOFA homestays (St Petersburg), (e-mail alexei@hofak.stu.spb.su. ☎ 275 1992). (Contact in UK ☎ 01295 710648.)

● Russia Rail, http://www.russia-rail.com is very knowledgeable and helpful for all Russia needs. Can provide visas, organise accommodation and book rail tickets on all lines of the ex-USSR. Run by Athol Yates, author of guide books *Russia by Rail* and *Siberian BAM Railway Guide*. E-mail russia-rail@russia-rail.com

● Team Gorky Adventure Travel Company (runs trekking in Siberia and Altai region, biking trips around Moscow, rafting in Siberia) PO Box 93; Nizhny Novgorod, 603137. (☎ 651-999, fax 691-875, e-mail: adv@team-gorky.nnov.ru.)

● Visa Services (helps arrange new Russian visas once already in Russia) Bol. Bolyanka Ul 28/1; (Moscow ☎ 237 7522).

❏ Geo-political information – Russia

Population: 148 million (1997), 148.5 million (1991), 133.7m (1973).

Area: 17,075,000 sq. km (almost twice the size of the USA).

Capital: Moscow (9m).

Other major cities: StP (4.5m), Nizhny Novgorod, Novosibirsk, Ekaterinburg (1.4m), Samara (1.2m), Omsk, Chelyabinsk, Kazan, Perm, Ufa (1.1m), Volgagrad, Rostov (1m), Krasnoyarsk, Saratov, Voronezh (900,000), Izhevsk (formerly Ustinov), Tolyatti, Simbirsk, Yaroslavl, Irkutsk, Krasnodar, Barnaul, Novokuznyetsk, Orenburg (600,000) and 37 more over 300,000.

GNP per capita: 1994: $2650. Average monthly wage in Moscow $76, in Russia overall $69.

Currency history: Rouble/US$1 – Feb 1998: 6.02 'new' Roubles (three zeros dropped) Nov 1997: 5810, July 1996: 5117, Jan 1996: 4670, Dec 1994: 5610, Dec 1993: 1240, 1991: 0.58 (32 on the black market).

Major exports/economy: Heavy industry, mining, agriculture.

Ethnic mix: Russian (84%); Tatars (3.7%); Ukrainians (2.6%); Chauvash (1.3%); Bashkirs, Mordvins (1% each); Belorussian (0.7%); Udmurts, Chechens, Kazakhs, Mari (0.4% each). Germans and Jews formerly constituted about 0.6% each though both groups have seen mass migration since 1991.

Official languages: Russian plus several local languages.

Religious mix: Russian Orthodox est 35m, Roman Catholics 370,000, Sunni Muslim (mainly in Tataristan, Bashkortistan, and the north Caucasus – no figures), Jewish (650,000 remained in 1993 but still emigrating steadily), Buddhists (est 500,000 especially in Buryatia and Tuva plus the unlikely Mongol/Tibetan Kalmyks).

Landmarks of national history: **1136:** Novgorod declared independence from Kiev (earlier Russian empires had in fact been centred upon Ukraine) and prospered through the Mongol invasions. **1462-1505:** Ivan the Great of Muscovy (Moscow) welded Russian principalities into an empire. **1546:** Ivan the Terrible crowned himself the first 'Tsar', defeated the khanates of Kazan and Astrakhan. **1604:** Tomsk (Central Siberia) founded. **1709:** Peter the Great defeated Swedish invasion at Poltava. **1712:** St Petersburg became capital. **1774:** Black Sea coast annexed under Catherine the Great. **1812:** Napoleon marched into Moscow which burnt itself down leaving his troops stranded and starving as winter set in. All made for a great Tchaikovsky overture. **1853-6:** Crimean War – pre-emptive attacks on Russia by France and Britain deflected Russia from dismembering the feeble Ottoman empire. **1861:** Serfdom abolished. **1867:** Alaska sold to the USA. **1891:** Vladivostok founded, Trans-Siberian railway construction began. **1905:** Japan sank the Russian fleet, claimed southern Sakhalin Islands. **1917:** Revolution and counter-revolution overthrew Tzars and installed Bolshevik government under Lenin (dies 1924). **1922:** USSR formed. **1932-3:** Collectivisation of agriculture: six million died of starvation when farmers killed their animals rather than hand them over. Mass deportations. **1934-39** Stalin's purges (estimated seven million+ died). **1942:** Battle of Stalingrad: most of Volgagrad destroyed but the German advance was halted and Russia maintained control of its oil supply (Azerbaijan). **1944-5**: More deportations. **1953:** Stalin died. **1961:** Gagarin first man in space. **1991:** Collapse of USSR.

Leader: Boris Yeltsin – many regional leaders wield considerable local influence.

Pressing political issues: Continued instability in the Caucasus (especially Chechnya), economic inequality, falling living standards.

visa issued quickly eg $30 if you wait three weeks, $60 within a week, $150 issued next day. However, different consulates seem to apply different rules. Sleepy posts with few applicants are typically more pleasant. Consuls in Rangoon, Vientiane, Kathmandu, Osaka and Islamabad were especially helpful. One underworked consul in SE Asia reduced the price of my visa after a long friendly chat. Other embassies are so mobbed by applicants that you're lucky to get in the door at all. Baku, Beijing, Istanbul, Ankara, Almaty and Budapest seemed especially difficult.

To obtain a Russian visa for a period of stay of over one month you may be asked to show proof that you are HIV negative.

If you're only transitting through Russia, remember the Visa Shuffle (p557). Kyrgyz or Armenian visas are much easier to procure than Russian ones and allow you at least a three-day transit. The Russian consul in Bishkek assured us that we could stay three days **on top** of time spent travelling eg three days starting from **arrival** in Moscow on a train from Bishkek. In the event nobody checked, but keeping the rail tickets as proof of arrival date is advisable in case you're challenged.

If you book a package tour to Russia, your travel agency will provide you with vouchers confirming to the embassy that you've paid for hotel rooms for the duration of your stay. The Russian consulate in Krakow, Poland (11 Westerplatte St, open MWF 8.30am-12.30pm) is the only one we know of which allows you to use 'fake' vouchers called 'general service vouchers'. These otherwise worthless pieces of paper cost 50 zloty ($15) from the Orbis office in the Cracovia Hotel and make possible a seven day visa. For each subsequent day add 5z. Being so different from the system elsewhere, this probably won't last.
● **Transit visas** Transit visas are available at some embassies if you show a confirmed ticket out of (and often into) the country. Holders of Trans-Siberian tickets are usually granted 10-day transit visas even without the onward ticket. Holders of air tickets are usually given 72 or 48 hours.

A 72hr transit visa on arrival is available for a whopping $110 at Moscow's Sheremetyevo-2 airport, but only if you arrive between 7am and 8pm and have a confirmed plane ticket out of the country within that time.
● **Registration** You must register with OVIR within three days of arrival in Russia. Whoever sponsored your visa is meant to do this for you, so it helps to get an invitation letter from someone who is both co-operative and is located in a city where you're likely to find yourself at the beginning of your trip. The hostels in Moscow and StP are obliging. Registering late can result in an arbitrary, but usually smallish, fine. Failure to do so altogether is taken seriously especially if you leave by air. If you leave by land into another CIS state, there may not be any checks at all.
● **Visa extensions** Visa extensions were previously possible through MID but recently have become almost impossible. In Moscow there are numerous agents who offer help in procuring new visas. Look in the *Travellers' Yellow Pages* or other Moscow directories for listings.

Money

In Moscow and StP, there is a blossoming of ATM cash machines and throughout Russia at least 500 bank branches cash travellers' cheques or give credit card cash advances for varying commissions. Outside the main centres, however, US$ cash rules. New bills please. During 1998 'old' roubles remain valid (1000 old=1 new.)

Transportation

● **Train** A comfortable, sensible way to cover the vast distances involved. See the CIS transport section (p271) for details of the different classes. Foreigner pricing can mean a small extra fee, double price or a $20 surcharge depending on the station. But in Volgagrad, Astrakhan, and other less touristy cities we were sold tickets at local prices. Station policies change rapidly and prices seem to vary according to the direction you travel. Ticket windows still have a tendency to suddenly close on an angry line of hopefuls but queues are not as horrendous as they used to be. Almost all stations have computerised ticketing. A Cyrillic version of your name will appear on the ticket itself: a system designed to prevent ticket touts. Ticket clerks are meant to look at your passport but some simply ask your name. If you're trying to avoid paying foreigner supplements, watch the queues carefully for such clerks. Give them a heavily Russified pronunciation of your own name, the train number (from the departure timetable), the class you want to travel (*platkcart* is the best deal) and the day. *Sivodny* (today) or *zavtra* (tomorrow) are easier to splutter out than giving a date. After some rejections we avoided foreigner prices even in Moscow using this technique and were not fined the difference by the conductor (though other travellers have been). Make sure you know which of the

❏ Underground entertainment

Sveta Elchaninova is known as Moscow's 'Miss Punkstress', though you would never guess her punk credentials from her unobtrusive fashion sense. She is a remarkable woman, the mastermind of a series of music festivals and underground clubs catering to the increasingly marginalised 'ordinary youth' of the city. In money grabbing Moscow, most club venues have sold their souls to the $50 cover charge, businessman-meets-prostitute market. Sveta's clubs, by contrast, have been derelict cellars, painstakingly cleaned by the local punks. She runs a sort of music welfare program, entertaining the forgotten generation for a couple of dollars a gig. To Sveta, punk means energy and expression, philosophically closer to flower-power hippyism than wanton nihilism. It is an outlet for pubescent energy, which Sveta funnels towards positive ends by staging such extraordinary events as Moscow's 'Punks against fascism' rally. Her first ground breaking club was in the basement of a public building which was later sold to a bank in a spate of privatisation. The idea of punks squealing beneath their premises appealed even less to the bankers than it had to the reluctant city authorities and the club was to be evicted. The youngsters, only three of them over 18, barricaded themselves into the place, booby trapping the door so that a forced entrance would break open a gas main potentially killing all inside. An Armenian mafia group, brought in to rough the punks up, backed off when they learned that the greedy bank merely wanted to terrorise a group of kids for the sake of a mouldy cellar. In the dramatic stand-off, Sveta was eventually promised an alternative site for her club near the university (the Jerry Rubin club, see Moscow map). Similar problems continue to hound her. In the rarefied capitalism of today's Moscow anything less than 110% commercial is unlikely to survive for long.

Underground Russia: some leads

● Jerry Rubin Commune, Moscow (62 Leninski Pr. at time of writing. Check press as it keeps moving. Gigs and films, often free.)

● Tam Tam Club, St Petersburg (Adinatsetaya Linea St. Metro: Vasileostrovskaya)

● Underground music newspaper Ensk (short for Novosibirsk – N'sk – where it's produced) has a cult readership. Only available in Russian.

● Feb 1st, Moscow (Johnny Rotten's birthday; celebrated with Russia's only annual punk festival).

● Watch for the little known Samantha Smith record label. It's named after the 11yr old American schoolgirl famed in Russia for her letter to Gorbachev saying 'Please Mr Gorby, will you stop the Cold War'. She died shortly afterwards in a plane crash which the Soviet press blamed on the CIA.

town's stations your train leaves from. Local price tickets for imminent departure (within 48hrs) will be sold there. For advance purchase tickets there's often a special office. In Moscow you can telephone book rail tickets three to 30 days in advance on ☎ 266-8333. In person go to Griboedova 6, metro Turgenev. There's also an English- speaking ticket office selling tickets for all destinations above Moscow's Belaruskaya station though you'll pay a $20 foreigner surcharge.

Robberies on trains have been over dramatised (especially on the Helsinki-St P-Moscow route). Advice given by expats to ride the more expensive *kupe* class 'for your protection' seems counter-productive when travelling alone. We prefer the protective camaraderie of the open *platkcart* cars over the isolation of the individual *kupe* compartments where no-one can see what's happening to you should you find yourself in a company of rogues. On the other hand the lockable door can be a psychological comfort. All in all there is little reason to worry in any class especially if you smile, share food and make conversation with fellow passengers.

● **Bus** Less comfortable than trains but the only option in parts of the Caucasus and in rural backwaters. There are no foreigner surcharges, but tickets can be relatively pricey to start with.

● **Boat** Long distance river boats operate on many of the great rivers including the Volga, Lena and Amur. Predictably, local passenger ferries are much cheaper than tourist cruises. Launches are the only sensible way to get around Lake Baikal in summer. In the winter, however, most freshwater routes freeze: some become roads.

● **Hitching** In rural areas hitching is a second form of public transport. If you are declared to be a '*ghosty*' (guest) then paying would be inappropriate, but otherwise offer the same as the normal bus fare. Licence plate numbers indicate where a vehicle is registered and can be used to spot potential long distance truck rides.

● **Urban transport** Remains relatively efficient. The stylish metro systems require pre-purchased tokens. Buses, trams and trolley buses often still rely on people honestly punching *talony* (pre-purchased tickets bought in strips from kiosks or some drivers).

Accommodation

In hotels, a double rarely costs much more than a single, dormitories are extremely rare. Either way, hotels in most of Russia tend to be shabby yet incur ridiculous foreigner surcharges (double to six times local price). In Moscow/St P any accommodation is fiercely expensive to start with. Even if you can get local prices it is still rare to find any bed for less than $6-8, $20 in Moscow/St P. Many hotels remain the property of institutions or factory combines so are not set up to accept 'walk in' custom. This situation results in a growing B&B network with private individuals renting out flats or rooms in their homes. Prices by negotiation **start at** $7-10 per person. Rooms will be cleaner and more characterful than in hotels and you gain an interaction with local families. Meet potential hosts touting at stations or (more expensively) ask for *chasny kvatiera* (private flat) at *kvartirnoe* bureaux or in tourist, station or airline offices. You can pre-arrange homestays with English speaking families across Russia with a variety of organisations eg HOFA, Mir, Russia-Rail (see Travel agents, below) – the prices will be much higher (minimum about $30/night) but the agents can use your bookings to get your visa.

The cheapest options are the spartan *turbaza* or *alplaga* (summer only hut accommodation), railway or boat-terminal rest rooms or camping if you're self sufficient.

Food and drink

The food shortages of the early 1990s are long gone. Plentiful and classy as they've become in Moscow and StP, restaurants are now very much upscale affairs: an IMF loan approval is recommended before ordering in some establishments. The alter-

❑ Meeting the locals

● **The people** The word *nyet* (no) used to be the automatic response before the listener had even registered a question. Today a little more charm is starting to infiltrate but you may still sense a Soviet-style brusque unhelpfulness, especially amongst those who you might think are meant to help or serve you. But that is business. And *bizniz* is still a dirty, unbrotherly word.

At a deeper level Russians are unfailingly hospitable. An old maxim still holds true: 'a guest should not thank the host, the host should thank the guest'. The Russian character is big-hearted beneath a lugubrious cynicism. Russians love the 'large' personality. Spontaneity and a sense of humour will take you far. Toast before you drink and remember to have fun. If you don't like alcohol, learn.

At the height of the cold war, Russians were less fooled by the heavy handed Soviet propaganda than we were by more sophisticated 'free press' anti-Soviet paranoia. Even the most politically anti-Western '*stary-communist*' has long recognised the gulf between individuals and the provocative views of their governments. There's no problem discussing politics. However, WWII (The Great Patriotic War) is one subject that is still touchy. The trauma of 35 million deaths remains understandably strong and some Russians seem to view the war as having happened only yesterday. Playing down WWII, or making fun of it, can cause serious insult.

Making local friends is not quite as effortless as it was six years ago. The mystique of the Western world has dimmed and your mere presence as a foreigner doesn't have the same cache as it once did. In major centres, approaches are increasingly financially rather than friendship motivated. Many Moscow homestay families that five years ago loved to entertain their wards as true guests, are understandably burnt out and now see you as just another client. So to meet the 'real' people you'll need to take a small step away from the tourist hubs to colleges or suburban wastelands or to small villages where your mere presence may still cause interest, if not suspicion. For this approach you'll ideally need some Russian. Alternatively try a dip into the alternative culture (see box, p294).

● **Language** Russia is one country where a little effort to get a grasp of the language is a great investment. Without at least a dictionary and phrase book you may be really stranded in some places. Though speaking Russian well is very tough, getting a few basic words down will help enormously. The alphabet is not difficult though apparent similarities with Latin letters can cause confusion, see p561.

Some phrases in Russian – NB see also the language appendix on p560.

> Hello – *dobri den* (good day)
> How are you? – *z draz veets ya*
> Thank you <u>very much</u> – *spaseeba <u>bolshoi</u>*
> Beautiful – *krasivi*
> Delicious – *verkusna*
> How much is it? – *skolka stoit*
> May I? Is it OK? It's OK – *mozhna*
> Don't worry; good; all is well in the world – *narmal*
> In a little bit; not yet; after that; no hurry – *patom*

native is a *stolovaya*: a cheap and cheerless canteen, sometimes standing-room only dispensing cheap, cardboard flavoured open sandwiches (*buterbrod*) and bowls of unidentifiable but filling slop. In bigger cities, *stolovayas* have largely disappeared from the increasingly chic centres. This is good news for the discerning, but bad for the impecunious as the hot dog and Coca Cola stand replacements are rarely any healthier despite almost Western prices. Buy your own fresh food from markets (*ry-nuk*). Common Russian snacks include *bliny* (filled pancakes), *manti/pelmyeni* (a local style of ravioli), *pirozhki* (doughnut style deep fried turnovers filled with potato, vegetables or meat). If all else fails you can always dine on Snickers bars from ubiquitous kiosks.

Mineral water and *limonad* (unidentifiably flavoured fizzy drinks often made from pears) are still available cheaply in the old Soviet style returnable bottles from ironically named *gastronom* state grocery stores, though these too are being privatised. Kiosks prefer to sell you imported versions at five to 10 times the price. White slices of *sala* – pig fat are an unappetising but effective way to reduce the side effects of alcohol abuse.

Staying in touch
● **Telephone** To call out of Russia (and out of most other CIS countries) dial 8. Wait for a new tone then dial 10 before the country code. If you don't manage to direct dial, you can 'request' an international line by dialling 8-194.

International country code: 7. Moscow 095, St P 812, Nizhny Novgorod (Gorkii) 8312, Irkutsk 3952, Novosibirsk 3832. Note that several city codes start with a '0' which, unusually, should **not** be omitted when dialling from abroad (ie for Moscow dial 7-095). The telephone systems of certain cities have been augmented by efficient but more expensive private services. These towns can have more than one city code according to the root company.
● **Fax** Certain businesses use shared faxing services and thus when faxing to them

you will need to write their box number clearly in the top left hand corner. A computer transfer is then made from fax receiver to destination computer (or the paper is simply passed on). Delivery may not be instantaneous. Sending faxes from Moscow's central telephone office is reasonable ($2/page to Europe, $4 to US).
● **E-mail** Russian businesses are increasingly realising the need to get on-line. From Russia, you can use the cyber café in the St P Youth Hostel ($0.50 per e-mail message plus $3/hr for computer use).

Activities
● **Hiking and mountaineering** Europe's highest mountain (Elbruz) is in the Russian Caucasus. Kamchatka has some extremely dramatic volcanoes though communications difficulties can make this distant land very expensive. *Trekking in Russia and Central Asia* (Frith Maier, The Mountaineers) covers many lesser known areas with topographical sketches and hike descriptions. West Col produces trekking maps of Elbruz and the neighbouring mountains, available in Western bookshops. The central Dom Kniga in Novisibirsk (Pl Lenin) is a good bet for detailed trekking maps of Siberia.
● **Swimming** Though hardly famed for its golden sands, Russia does have a few fine beaches and Sochi (Black Sea) surprises many with its palm trees as well as with its high summer prices and nouveau riche/mafia clientele. Less probable still are the beaches some 50km south of Vladivostok in the far East.

Further information
● **Books** Lonely Planet's *Russia, Ukraine and Belarus* is the most comprehensive guide available and includes details of places like Tuva that are well off the normal tourist loops. Athol Yates' *Russia by Rail* (Bradt) is also extremely thorough, complete with timetables and clear concise survival information. Some travellers recommend Robert Greenall's *An Explorer's Guide to Russia* (Zephyr Press) though it ignores the east of the country. *Russia*

Survival Guide: Business and Travel by Paul E. Richardson (Russia Info Sources) is a fact-rich, regularly updated practical guide to living in Russia ($18.50 paperback from Moscow bookshops). In Moscow and StP it is easy to find detailed directories of companies, services and contacts (eg *Where in Moscow*, *Travellers' Yellow Pages* etc) and glossy what's on magazines. If you need specific pieces of information you can usually find it by browsing copies of these in the book stands of top city hotels. Try the hostels in St Petersburg and Moscow for buying onward guide books or doing book swaps with other travellers.

● **Maps** City maps of Moscow and St Petersburg are sold at almost every street corner or central metro station. Some include street finders, house numbers, metro maps, suburban train maps, bus lines, city centre insets, suburban maps etc but none has all of these so it may be worth buying a couple of different versions. City centre maps are available free from top hotels. Maps of other Russian cities can be harder to track down. Most of the populat-ed area is covered by very accurate 1:200,000 topographic maps which were originally restricted to military use but are now freely sold for 15Rbls a sheet. However, they are all in Cyrillic script and finding copies is not always easy. The best bet is Globus map shop, Moscow at 45 Volgogradsky Prospect, across the overpass from Tekstilshiki metro or Slavyanka (9 Ul Kuznetsky Most). Alternatively try the map producer's office in Novosibirsk at 80 Krasny Prospect, (☎ 205575, e-mail: sibgi @niiru.sib.ru). If you want to buy maps ahead, a good selection is available from Omni (PO Box 2096 Burlington, NC 27216 USA, e-mail custserve@omni-imap.com) or Jürgen Kestling (Geraer Weg 6, Hamburg-Wilhelmsburg, Germany).

● **Other information   Ministry of Foreign Affairs**, MID at metro Smolenskaya, Moscow. ☎ 244 2459.

Intourist, Central Bureau 16 Okhotny Road. ☎ (095) 203-6962.

OVIR (for registration in Moscow), 42 Chernyshevskogo (now Pokrovka) ☎ 207-0113. Open MWThF and some Sat mornings 9am-1pm, 3-5pm.

Web sites

The most up-to-date Russia, Belarus and Ukraine visa information is at www.russia-rail.com/travel/visas.htm; they also have info on Russia train travel.

www.russiatoday.com gives an unbiased view of current events in Russia (mostly political).

www.goski.com/russia.htm gives information on and links to skiing resources in the former USSR.

www.spb.su has information on St. Petersburg, including accommodation information, job listings, and a map of sites.

gomoscow.miningco.com has useful travel info on Moscow

There is a clickable map of Russia at www.ras.ru/map.html that links to at least a dozen cities.

ww.cs.toronto.edu/~mes/russia/travel.html links to travel travelogues about Russia trips, including several on the Trans-Siberian.

www.interknowledge.com/russia/rusguest.htm is the official site of the Russian tourist agency with basic information on the main tourist attractions.

www.geocities.com/WallStreet/1242/fareast.html has some basic travel information on the far east of Russia

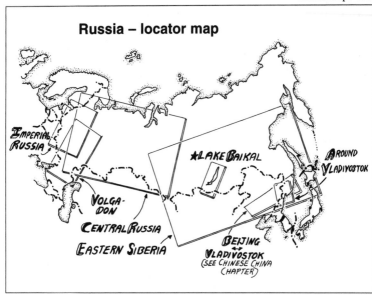

Russia – locator map

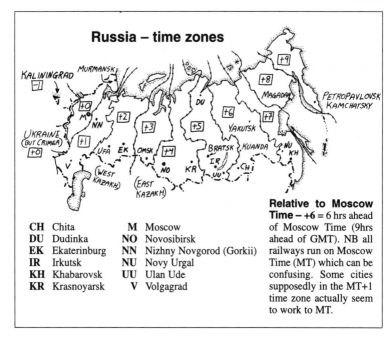

Russia – time zones

CH	Chita	**M**	Moscow
DU	Dudinka	**NO**	Novosibirsk
EK	Ekaterinburg	**NN**	Nizhny Novgorod (Gorkii)
IR	Irkutsk	**NU**	Novy Urgal
KH	Khabarovsk	**UU**	Ulan Ude
KR	Krasnoyarsk	**V**	Volgagrad

Relative to Moscow Time – +6 = 6 hrs ahead of Moscow Time (9hrs ahead of GMT). NB all railways run on Moscow Time (MT) which can be confusing. Some cities supposedly in the MT+1 time zone actually seem to work to MT.

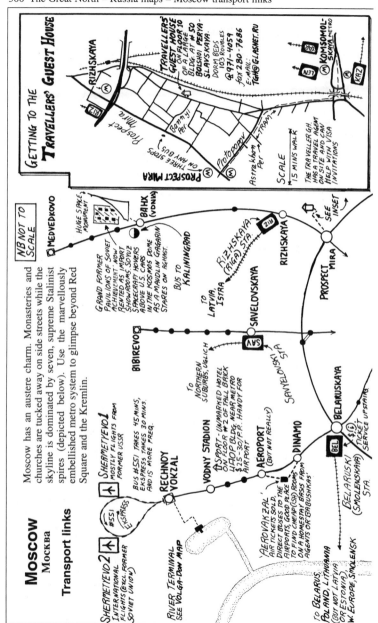

Moscow
Москва
Transport links

Moscow has an austere charm. Monasteries and churches are tucked away on side streets while the skyline is dominated by seven, supreme Stalinist spires (depicted below). Use the marvellously embellished metro system to glimpse beyond Red Square and the Kremlin.

SHEREMETIEVO 2
INTERNATIONAL FLIGHTS (EXCL. FORMER SOVIET UNION)

SHEREMETIEVO 1
MOSTLY FLIGHTS FROM FORMER USSR

RIVER TERMINAL
SEE VOLGA-DON MAP

#SSI
#SSI
EXPRESS

NB NOT TO SCALE

MEDVEDKOVO

HUGE SPACE MONUMENT

BAHX (VDNKh)

GRAND FORMER PAVILIONS OF SOVIET ACHIEVEMENT, NOW RENTED AS IMPORT SHOWROOMS. SOYUZ SPACECRAFT HOVERS ABOVE U.S. CARS IN THE KOSMOS DOME AS A MAUDLIN GAGARIN STARES ON ACROSS.

BIBIREVO

BUS #SSI TAKES 45 MINS, EXPRESS TAKES 30 MINS AND IS MORE FREQ.

To NORTHERN SUBURBS, Uglich

RIZHSKAYA (RIGA) STA.

ZIV

To LATVIA, Istra

BUS TO KALININGRAD

SAVELOVSKAYA

SAV

SAVELOVSKI STA.

RIZHSKAYA

SEE INSET

PROSPECT MIRA

RECHNOY VOKZAL

VODNY STADION

AEROPORT (BUT NOT REALLY)

TRSPORT - UNMARKED HOTEL ON FLOOR #2 OF TALL BRICK LHOP BLDG. NEAR METRO $25-30/P.P. HANDY FOR AIRPORT

DINAMO

'AEROVOKZAL' AIR TICKETS SOLD. DIRECT BUSES TO THE AIRPORTS, GOOD PLACE TO FIND CHEAP (ISH) ROOMS ON A HOMESTAY BASIS FROM AGENTS OR BABUSHKAS'

BELARUSKAYA

BEL

BELARUSKI (SMOLENSKAYA) STA.

$ £ TICKET SERVICE UPSTAIRS

To BELARUS, POLAND, LITHUANIA (BUT NOT LATVIA OR ESTONIA) W. EUROPE, SMOLENSK

GETTING TO THE TRAVELLERS' GUEST HOUSE

RIZHSKAYA

RIZ

TRAVELLERS' GUEST HOUSE ON A LARGE BLDG. AT #50 BOLSHOI PERYA- SLAVSKAYA.
DORM BEDS 105 ROUBLES
☎971-4059
Fax 280-7686
E-MAIL:
TGH@G-LASNET.RU

Prospect Mira

Banny Per.

Protopopov.

PROSPECT MIRA

Astrakhan Per. ON 3 SIDES ON ANY BUS

TRAM

KOMSOMOL-SKAYA METRO

YAR

LEN

KAZ

SCALE
15 MINS WALK

THE TRAVELLER GH HAS A TRAVEL AGENT ON SITE AND CAN HELP WITH VISA INVITATIONS

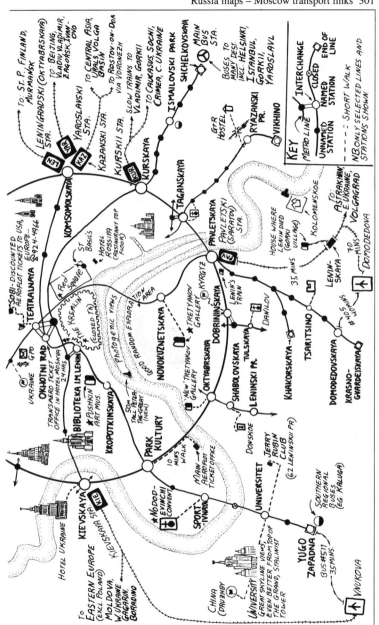

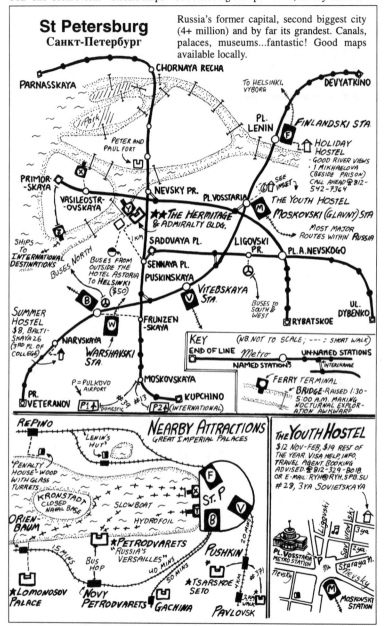

St Petersburg
Санкт-Петербург

Russia's former capital, second biggest city (4+ million) and by far its grandest. Canals, palaces, museums...fantastic! Good maps available locally.

CHORNAYA RECHA

PARNASSKAYA

To HELSINKI, VYBORG

DEVYATKINO

PL. LENIN

FINLANDSKI STA.

Park

PETER AND PAUL FORT

HOLIDAY HOSTEL
· GOOD RIVER VIEWS
· 1 MIKHAELOVA (BESIDE PRISON)
CALL AHEAD ☎ 812-542-7364

PRIMOR-SKAYA

SEE INSET

NEVSKY PR.

PL. VOSSTARIA

THE YOUTH HOSTEL

VASILEOSTR-OVSKAYA

★★ THE HERMITAGE & ADMIRALTY BLDG.

MOSKOVSKI (GLAVNY) STA.

MOST MAJOR ROUTES WITHIN RUSSIA

SHIPS TO INTERNATIONAL DESTINATIONS

SADOVAYA PL.

LIGOVSKI PR.

PL. A. NEVSKOGO

BUSES NORTH

BUSES FROM OUTSIDE THE HOTEL ASTORIA TO HELSINKI ($50)

SENNAYA PL.

PUSKINSKAYA

VITEBSKAYA STA.

BUSES TO SOUTH & WEST

UL. DYBENKO

FRUNZEN-SKAYA

RYBATSKOE

SUMMER HOSTEL
$8, BALTI-SKAYA 26 (3RD FL. OF COLLEGE)

NARVSKAYA

WARSHAVSKI STA.

KEY (NB. NOT TO SCALE; --- = SHORT WALK)

END OF LINE   Metro   UN-NAMED STATIONS
NAMED STATIONS   INTERCHANGE

FERRY TERMINAL

P = PULKOVO AIRPORT

MOSKOVSKAYA

PR. VETERANOV

P1 DOMESTIC   #13   P2 (INTERNATIONAL)

KUPCHINO

BRIDGE-Raised 1:30-5:00 A.M. MAKING NOCTURNAL EXPLORATION AWKWARD

NEARBY ATTRACTIONS
GREAT IMPERIAL PALACES

REPINO

LENIN'S HUT

"PENALTY HOUSE" WOOD WITH GLASS TURRETS

KRONSTADT CLOSED NAVAL BASE

SLOWBOAT

HYDROFOIL

F   ST. P   X   Y   V   B

ORIEN-BAUM

★ PETRODVARETS "RUSSIA'S VERSAILLES"

BUS HOP

PUSHKIN

15 MINS

20 MINS

40 MINS

50 MINS

★ LOMONOSOV PALACE

NOVY PETRODVARETS

GACHINA

★ TSARSKOE SETO

4 KM

#371

2 KM WALK

PAVLOVSK

THE YOUTH HOSTEL

$12 NOV-FEB, $19 REST OF THE YEAR. VISA HELP, INFO, TRAVEL AGENT, BOOKING ADVISED. ☎ 812-329-8018. OR E-MAIL: RYH@RYH.SPB.SU

#28, 3YA SOVIETSKAYA

PL. VOSSTARIA METRO STATION

Nevsky

Ligovsky   Suvorovsky   3ya   2ya   Staraya n.   Nevsky

MOSKOVSKI STATION

Imperial Russia

The area on this map, especially to the NE of Moscow, is great for random exploration. The map shows a simplified overview view to help with route planning. For more information, Athol Yates' *Russia by Rail* guide (Bradt Publications) is recommended. **Note:** Only certain local rail lines and a few connecting roads are shown. Most cross-country routes are omitted.

KEY
⌂ KREMLIN ⊡ SMALL TOWN
⌂ OPEN AIR MUSEUM
⚡ NOTE WORTHY CHURCH
🏛 MONASTERY/CONVENT
➤ END OF SUBURBAN SERVICE

(SUZ) ★SUZDAL ⊡➤ ⌂⊡⊡⊡⊡⊡⌂⌂ ⊡/⌂ TOURISTY

(PZ) ★PERESLAVI ZALESSKI ⊡⊡⊡ ⚡⌂⚡

(R.Y.) ROSTOV YAROSLAVSKI
⌂(WITH ⌂ INSIDE), ⚡⚡⚡⊡
MANY ⊡/⌂ IN NEIGHBOURING VILLAGES

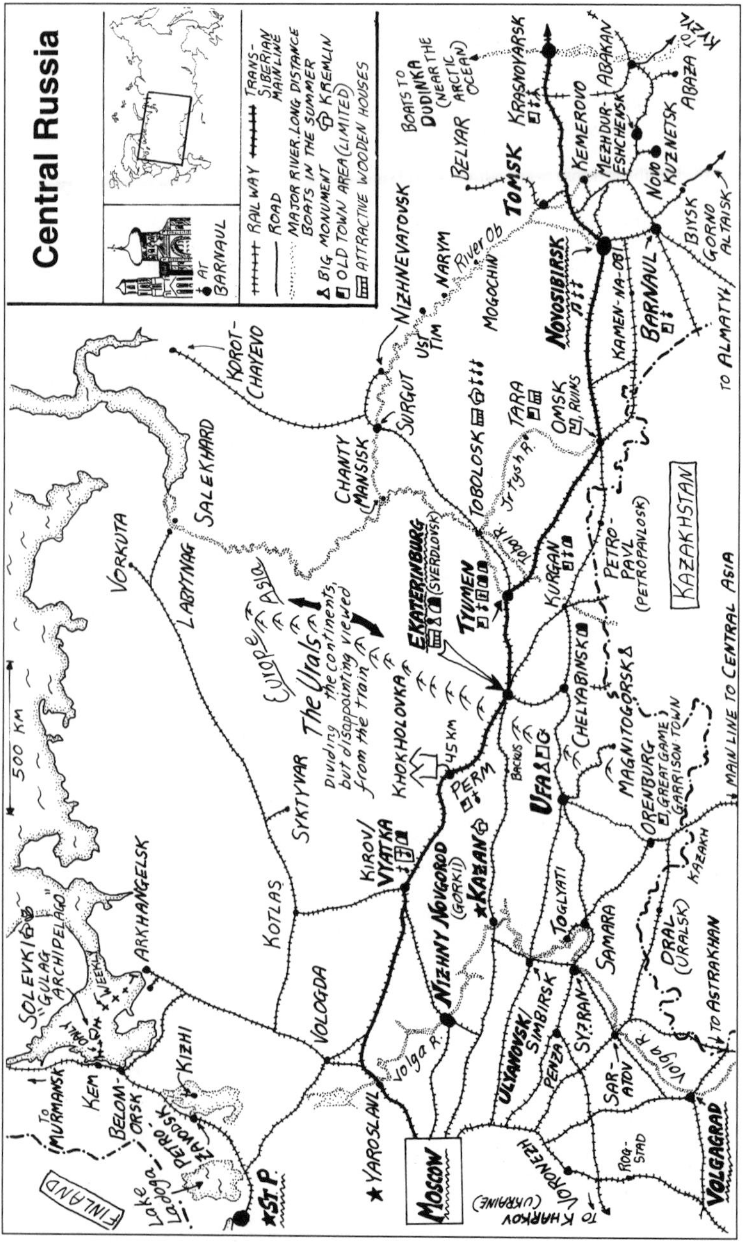

Central Russia

Legend:
- +++++ RAILWAY
- —— ROAD
- ++++++ TRANS-SIBERIAN MAIN LINE
- ······ MAJOR RIVER, LONG DISTANCE BOATS IN THE SUMMER
- ▲ BIG MONUMENT ⊕ KREMLIN
- ☐ OLD TOWN AREA (LIMITED)
- ⊞ ATTRACTIVE WOODEN HOUSES
- AT BARNAUL

FINLAND

TO MURMANSK
Lake Ladoga
Lake Onega
PETROZA-VODSK
KEM
BELOM-ORSK
KIZHI
SOLEVKI "GULAG ARCHIPELAGO"
VYEGA
ARKHANGELSK
VORKUTA
LABYTNAG
SALEKHARD
KOROT-CHAYEVO
NIZHNEVARTOVSK
Ust Tim
NARYM
Mogochin
River Ob
BELYAR
BOATS TO DUDINKA (NEAR THE ARCTIC OCEAN)
KRASNOYARSK
ABAKAN
ABAZA
KYZYL
KEMEROVO
MEZHDUR-ESHCHENSK
TOMSK
NOVO KUZNETSK
BIYSK
GORNO ALTAISK
BARNAUL
NOVOSIBIRSK
KAMEN-NA-OBI
TO ALMATY
CHANTY MANSISK
SURGUT
TOBOLOSK ⊞⊕⊞
TARA
OMSK ☐ RUINS
Irtysh R.
PETRO-PAVL (PETROPAVLOVSK)
KAZAKHSTAN
SYKTYVAR
Europe/Asia
The Urals
Dividing the continents, but of disappointing viewed from the train
KHOKHOLOVKA
45 KM
PERM
BACHKA
URALSG
TYUMEN
EKATERINBURG (SVERDLOVSK)
KURGAN
CHELYABINSK
MAGNITOGORSK
ORENBURG GREAT GAME GARRISON TOWN
KAZAKH
MAIN LINE TO CENTRAL ASIA
KIROV/VYATKA
KAZAN ⊕
NIZHNY NOVGOROD (GORKII)
TOGLYATI
SAMARA
URAL (URALSK)
Volga R.
VOLOGDA
KOTLAS
YAROSLAVL
ULYANOVSK/SIMBIRSK
PENZA
SYZRAN
SAR-ATOV
Road Stad
Volga R.
VOLGOGRAD
TO ASTRAKHAN
MOSCOW
VORONEZH
TO KHARKOV (UKRAINE)
ST. P.
500 KM

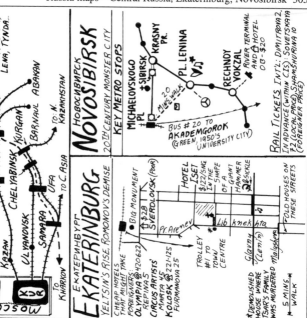

While none of the cities of central and eastern Russia is very attractive or interesting, most have imposing main streets, a pleasant river front, a few museums and areas of older wooden houses.

Possible stops on Trans-Siberian mainline

● **Kirov/Vyatka** Pleasant riverfront, Trifon Monastery, *Motel Kolos* $8/dorm.

● **Perm** Old town area around Perm 1 and river terminal, 5km by suburban train from main Perm 2 station. *Hotel Tsentranaya* $29/s River. $5 beds at *Komnata Otdikha* – enter from front of station.

● **Tyumen** Siberia's oldest city: Some old bldgs on S bank of Tura River. $5 beds at *Komnata Otdikha* – enter from front of station.

● **Krasnoyarsk** Hilltop church, old town area around cathedral. *Hotel Krasnoyarsk* best deal: $30. Bazaikha for chairlift to massive anthropomorphic rock pillars (bus #7 from Pl Predmostnaya, south of road bridge over river). 1hr by hydrofoil to Yenisey Dam.

● For **Yaroslavl and the Golden Ring cities** See Imperial Russia and Volga-Don maps.

Other Ural/Siberian towns

● **Kurgan** Old trading city. Head for Ul Klimova and riverside.

● **Ufa** Some old town mansions on slope behind demolished kremlin site (now the giant Friendship Monument on Pervmayskaya Sq.) and down Karl Marxa Ul. 19th century mosque on Tukaeva.

● **Tobolsk** Historic old town drowning in petro-chemical city haze. Smaller Tara upriver from Tobolsk said to have greater charm.

● **Tomsk** Once powerful river city, some attractive old wooden houses. Secret satellite towns site of 1993 nuclear accident.

● **Chelyabinsk** Mineral Museum, nearby nuclear accident zone.

● **Biysk** Bus to Gorno Altaisk (3hrs), whence buses to the remote Altai Mountains.

● **Abakan** 20km to Minusinsk. 85km to Shushenskoe, an 1870s reconstructed village where Lenin was exiled. Daily bus to Kyzyl, Tuva takes all day.

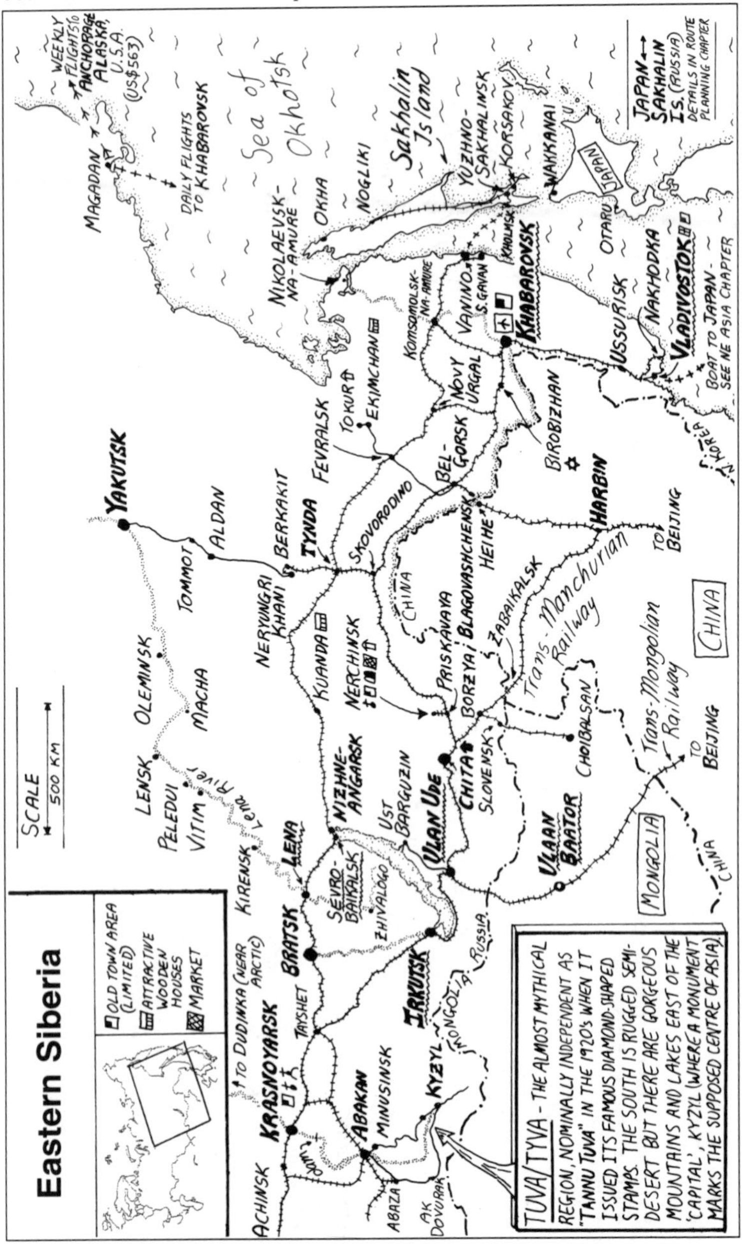
Eastern Siberia
OLD TOWN AREA (LIMITED)
ATTRACTIVE WOODEN HOUSES
MARKET
SCALE
500 KM
TUVA/TYVA - THE ALMOST MYTHICAL REGION, NOMINALLY INDEPENDENT AS "TANNU TUVA" IN THE 1920'S WHEN IT ISSUED ITS FAMOUS DIAMOND-SHAPED STAMPS. THE SOUTH IS RUGGED SEMI-DESERT BUT THERE ARE GORGEOUS MOUNTAINS AND LAKES EAST OF THE 'CAPITAL', KYZYL (WHERE A MONUMENT MARKS THE SUPPOSED CENTRE OF ASIA)
ACHINSK
KRASNOYARSK
TO DUDINKA (NEAR ARCTIC)
TAYSHET
ABAKAN
MINUSINSK
ABAZA
AK DOVURAK
KYZYL
IRKUTSK
BRATSK
KIRENSK
LENA
SEVERO-BAIKALSK
ZHIVALOGO
MONGOLIA
RUSSIA
ULAN UDE
UST BARGUZIN
NIZHNE-ANGARSK
VITIM
PELEDUI
LENSK
Lena River
OLEMINSK
MACHA
TOMMOT
ALDAN
YAKUTSK
NERYUNGRI
KHANI
BERKAKIT
TYNDA
KUANDA
NERCHINSK
CHITA
SLOVENSK
BORZYA
PRISKAVAYA
BLAGOVASHCHENSK
ZABAIKALSK
CHINA
SKOVORODINO
FEVRALSK
TO KURA
EKIMCHAN
BEL-GORSK
HEIHE
HARBIN
TO BEIJING
Trans-Manchurian Railway
Trans-Mongolian Railway
CHOIBALSAN
ULAAN BAATOR
MONGOLIA
CHINA
TO BEIJING
BIROBIZHAN
NOVY URGAL
KOMSOMOLSK-NA-AMURE
VANINO
S. GAVAN
KHABAROVSK
KHOLMSK
USSURISK
NAKHODKA
VLADIVOSTOK
BOAT TO JAPAN - SEE NE ASIA CHAPTER
KOREA
OTARU
JAPAN
WAKKANAI
KORSAKOV
YUZHNO-SAKHALINSK
Sakhalin Island
NOGLIKI
OKHA
NIKOLAEVSK-NA-AMURE
Sea of Okhotsk
MAGADAN
DAILY FLIGHTS TO KHABAROVSK
WEEKLY FLIGHTS TO ANCHORAGE ALASKA, U.S.A. (US$563)
JAPAN ↔ SAKHALIN IS. (RUSSIA) DETAILS IN ROUTE PLANNING CHAPTER

Possible stops on Trans-Siberian mainline

● **Irkutsk, Baikal** and **Ulan Ude** – see Lake Baikal area maps.
● **Chita** Military/industrial city. Bus No 4 to Open Air Museum of military vehicles. *Taiga Hotel,* (Ul Lenina 75) has dorms ($5).
● **Nerchinsk** Old gold mining town 10km up branch line from Priskavaya. Small but with old mansions, cathedral and old arcade.
● **Birobidzhan** Smallish capital of Jewish Autonomous region. Signs written in Hebrew though most Jews have departed for Israel. *Hostel Vostok* ($35/50 s/d); take bus No 5 east from stn.
● **Khabarovsk** and **Vladivostok** – see Russian Far East map.

Looping the Lena

This trip is largely within the autonomous Republic of Sakha. It has an embassy conveniently located in Almaty (Kazakhstan); theoretically you can be fined for not having a Sakha visa, or at least a Sakha town on your Russian visa.

BAM Railway

Inspired by communist zeal and cut by gulag prisoners, the remote Baikal Amur Magistral (BAM) line has been only fully operational since 1990. Many towns are small with areas of waste ground awaiting now indefinitely postponed expansion. But there's a high proportion of attractive wooden houses especially in Nizhneangarsk, Kuanda, Fevralskoe (200yr old village 6km from Fevralsk) and Ekimcham. Even tiny village halts have station hostels so it's easy to get a relatively intimate view of small town Siberia and its friendly locals (few English speakers). Athol Yates' *Siberian BAM Railway Guide* (also from Trailblazer) is indispensable, with excellent background information.

Possible stops on BAM Railway

● **Bratsk** Big new city. The train crosses its prime attraction, the 3.5km long dam. *Hotel Bratsk* $25+.
● **Sverobaikalsk** Good base for N Baikal (see Baikal map).
● **Lena** River terminal for Yakutsk ferries (see opposite).
● **Kuanda** Model town. BAM monument. $2 hotel.
● **Novaya Chara** BAM museum; improbable Chara sand dunes 6km NW; lovely Lake Zapod hike via Kyust Kemda; gulag expeditions. *Hotel Kodar* $30.
● **Khani** Picturesque valley; *hostel.*
● **Tynda** BAM museum. *Hotel Orbita* $16.
● **Chegdomyn** 17km N of Novy Urgal. N Korean miners in gulag conditions. N Korean embassy. *Hotel Bureya* $16.
● **Komsomolsk-na-Amure** Tank museum. *Hotel Brigantina* at river terminal (tram No 2 from station).
● **Vanino** Ferries to Sakhalin; hitch a boat to Japan?

Lake Baikal
Озеро Байкал

The world's deepest and oldest lake. Despite pollution the water remains pure enough to drink (except around Baikalsk and the Selenga Delta). Contains 20% of all the world's fresh water! The north and south are connected by boat only. The north is less touristy but more difficult to get around. The lake freezes Jan-March. Mosquitoes and ticks (in forests) in early summer. August is best. Great hikes are possible – many companies in Irkutsk are keen to help (eg the friendly Baikal Complex).

Long distance hydrofoils: (info Irk ☎ 342565). Irkutsk-Nizhneangarsk via Port Baikal and Svbk with request stops en route. $42. dep alternate days. Irkutsk-Bargazin via B. Listvianka, B. Pschannay, Khuzyr. $20. 10 hrs, dep 9am Mo' going N, Tue going S.

100 KM

KICHERA
NOVY UOYAN
2 LOCAL TRAINS to SVB
Холодная KHOLODNAYA 4HRS. WALK TO GULAG. DETAILS IN BAM BOOK
DZELINGA
Нижнеангарск NIZHNEANGARSK
Bam Railway
ZAMIKA
NEED OWN FOOD FOR HIKE & TENT FOR
SVB
AYA
NAMA
СЕВРОБАЙКАЛЬСК
SEVEROBAIKALSK (SVB) ● TOWN CENTRE
BAIKAL-SKOE
KHAKUSY 2657
$25 IN NICE COTTAGES WITH HOT H₂O (15 MINS. FROM TRAIN STA.)
TEMPLES & PRAYER FLAGS IN MTS.
Ⓐ MARITUI - GHOST TOWN
Ⓑ PORT BAIKAL ⊞
Ⓒ BOLSHOI LISTVYANKA
Ⓓ KHUZYR (ON OLKHON Is.)
DAVSHA NAT'L PARK HQ
KURUM-KAN
КУРУМ-КАН
Source of the Lena R.
⊞ BARGUZIN
ZORINO
ОНГУРЕН ⊞ ONGUREN
Mûle More (Little Sea)
Усть БАРГУЗИН UST BARGUZIN
☼ SAMARA LOCALS SWIM HERE
Seals
DAILY BUS TO ULAN UDE (8-9 HRS)
САХЮРТА SAKHYURTA
Ⓓ
GORYCHINSK
BAYANDAI
Lake Baikal (шир)
TURKA ТУРКА
Selenga Delta
ГРЕМЯЧИНК GREMYACHINSK
Усть ОРДЫНСКИЙ UST ORDINSKII
NESTEROVO НЕСТЕРОВО
IRKUTSK
to BRATSK
РАКЕТА TERMINAL
BUKHTA PESCHANNAYA
OIMUR
Trans-Siberian
KLUTUK
LONG DISTANCE HIKING PATHS BUT TREES SO DENSE THAT VIEWS ARE RARE
SHIGAEVO
BOLSHOI GOLOUSTNOYE
Rough road
ULAN UDE
Ⓐ Ⓑ
Ⓒ
БАБУШКИН BABUSHKIN (MYSOVAYA)
ИВОЛГИНСК ☼ IVOLGINSK ⊞
⊞ ⊞ ⊞ ARSHAN
Tunnels
☼ Novo-SELENGINSK BUDDHIST MONASTERY
SEAT OF RUSSIAN BUDDHISM. THE MAIN ★ MONASTERY REMAINS, BUT MOST BUILDINGS NEW. BUS #104 FROM ULAN UDE
TANKOI
108 KM TO MONDY
SLUDYANKA ⊞ BUS TO ARSHAN
Paper Mill don't drink water here
GUSINOE OZERO STATION
☼ JIDA ДЖИДА
BAIKALSK БАЙКАЛЬСК
IRKUTSK ↔ ULAN UDE TRAIN - 7½ - 8 HRS, 15/DAY, $16 PLATSCART
N. JOREI
ЗАКАМЕНСК ЗАКМЕНСК
МИХАЕЛОВКА MIKHAELOVKA
MONGOLIA

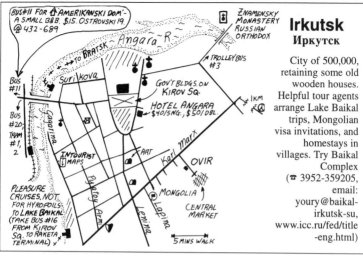

Irkutsk
Иркутск

City of 500,000, retaining some old wooden houses. Helpful tour agents arrange Lake Baikal trips, Mongolian visa invitations, and homestays in villages. Try Baikal Complex (☎ 3952-359205, email: youry@baikal-irkutsk-su, www.icc.ru/fed/title-eng.html)

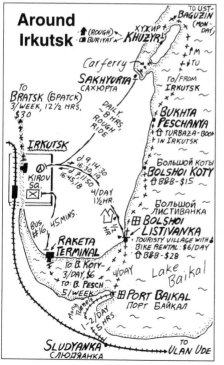

Ulan Ude
Улан Уде

Capital of Buddhist Buryatiya. Big town with too many drunks but a few interesting old buildings. Relatively cheap hotels make it a good base for day trips (Ivolginsk monastery). Daily train to Ulaan Baator $57 (flight $80).

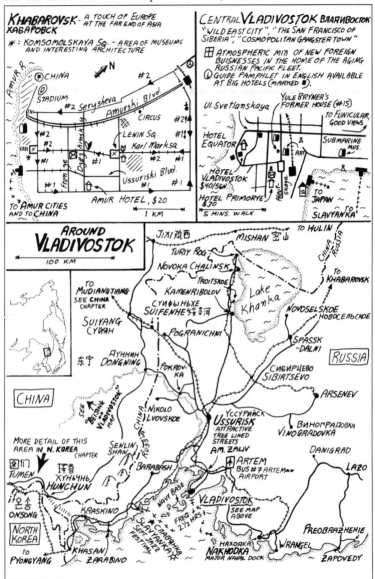

KHABAROVSK - A TOUCH OF EUROPE
ХАБАРОВСК   AT THE FAR END OF ASIA

✳ = KOMSOMOLSKAYA Sq. - AREA OF MUSEUMS
AND INTERESTING ARCHITECTURE

CHINA
STADIUM
Amur R.
#2 Serysheva
Amurski Blvd.
CIRCUS
#2
#2
#2
LENIN Sq.
#11
Karl Marksa
#2
#2
From 2e
Dezhinsky
#1
#1
#1
#1
Ussuriski Blvd.
#1
#1
#1
N
#2

TO AMUR CITIES
AND TO CHINA
AMUR HOTEL, $20
1 KM

CENTRAL **VLADIVOSTOK** ВЛАДИВОСТОК
"WILD EAST CITY", "THE SAN FRANCISCO OF
SIBERIA", "COSMOPOLITAN GANGSTER TOWN"

⊞ ATMOSPHERIC MIX OF NEW FOREIGN
BUISNESSES IN THE HOME OF THE AGING
RUSSIAN PACIFIC FLEET.
ⓘ GUIDE PAMPHLET IN ENGLISH AVAILABLE
AT BIG HOTELS (MARKED ■).

Ul. Svetlanskaya
YULE BRYNER'S
FORMER HOUSE (#15)
TO FUNICULAR,
GOOD VIEWS
HOTEL
EQUATOR
ART
SUBMARINE
MUS.
HOTEL
VLADIVOSTOK
$40/SGN
Aleutskaya
TO
JAPAN
HOTEL PRIMORYE
$30
TO
SLAVYANKA
5 MINS. WALK

**AROUND
VLADIVOSTOK**
100 KM

JIXI 鸡西
MISHAN 密山
TO HULIN
TURIY ROG
Novoka Chalinsk
TROITSKOE
KAMENRIBOLOV
СУИФЫНЬХЕ
SUIFENHE绥芬河
POGRANICHNI
Lake
Khanka
CHINA-RUSSIA
TO
KHABAROVSK
NOVOSELSKOE
НОВОСЕЛЬСКОЕ
SPASSK
-DALNI
RUSSIA
СИБИРЦЕВО
SIBIRTSEVO
ARSENEV
ВИНОГРАДОВКА
VINOGRADOVKA
DANIGRAD
LAZO

TO
MUDIANGJIANG
SEE CHINA
CHAPTER
SUIYANG
СУЙЯН
东宁
DONGNING
АУННИН
POKROVKA
NIKOLO
ILVOVSKOE
УССУРИЙСК
USSURISK
ATTRACTIVE
TREE LINED
STREETS
AM. ZALIV
ARTEM
BUS #7 ARTEM
AIRPORT

CHINA

MORE DETAIL OF THIS
AREA IN N. KOREA
CHAPTER
SENLIN
SHAN
坪春
TUMEN
ХУНЧНЬ
HUNCHUN
ONSONG
KRASKINO
BARABASH
NAVY BASE
VLADIVOSTOK
SEE MAP
ABOVE
FREQ
2½ HRS

NORTH
KOREA
TO
PYONGYANG
KHASAN
ZARABINO
SLAVYANKA
SEPT JAZZ
FESTIVAL
НАХОДКА
NAKHODKA
MAJOR NAVAL DOCK
WRANGEL
PREOBRAZHENIE
ЗАPOVEDY
ZAPOVEDY

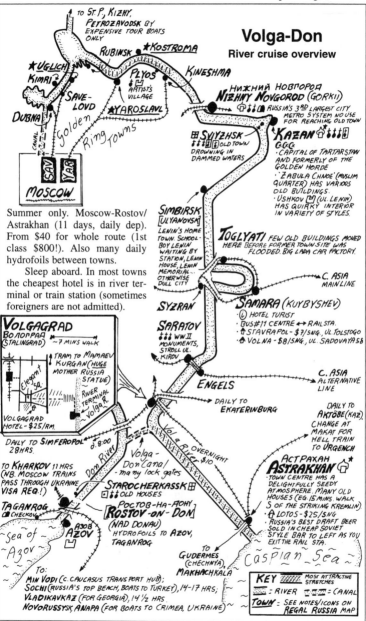

Volga-Don
River cruise overview

TO ST. P., KIZHY, PETROZAVODSK BY EXPENSIVE TOUR BOATS ONLY

RUBINSK ★KOSTROMA

★UGLICH KINESHMA

KIMRI

PLYOS ♛ ARTIST'S VILLAGE

SAVE-LOVD

★YAROSLAVL

DUBNA

Нижний Новгород
NIZHNY NOVGOROD (GORKII)
· RUSSIA'S 3RD LARGEST CITY. METRO SYSTEM NO USE FOR REACHING OLD TOWN

⊞ SVIYZHSK OLD TOWN DROWNING IN DAMMED WATERS

KAZAN
G.G.G.
· CAPITAL OF TARTARSTAN AND FORMERLY OF THE GOLDEN HORDE
· 'ZABULA CHNOE' (MUSLIM QUARTER) HAS VARIOUS OLD BUILDINGS.
· USHKOV ♛ (UL. LENIN) HAS QUIRKY INTERIOR IN VARIETY OF STYLES.

Golden Ring Towns

SAV YAR
MOSCOW
CANAL

Summer only. Moscow-Rostov/
Astrakhan (11 days, daily dep).
From \$40 for whole route (1st class \$800!). Also many daily hydrofoils between towns.

Sleep aboard. In most towns the cheapest hotel is in river terminal or train station (sometimes foreigners are not admitted).

SIMBIRSK (ULYANOVSK)
LENIN'S HOME TOWN. SCHOOL-BOY LENIN WAITING BY STATION, LENIN HOUSE, LENIN MEMORIAL... OTHERWISE DULL CITY

TOGLYATI FEW OLD BUILDINGS MOVED HERE BEFORE FORMER TOWN SITE WAS FLOODED. BIG LADA CAR FACTORY.

← C. ASIA MAIN LINE

SYZRAN

SARATOV WW II MONUMENTS, STROLL UL. KIROV

SAMARA (KUYBYSHEV)
ⓗ HOTEL TURIST
· BUS#11 CENTRE ↔ RAILSTA.
· ♛ STAVRAPOL - \$7/SNG, UL. TOLSTOGO
· ♨ VOLNA - \$8/SNG, UL. SADOVAYA 58

C. ASIA ALTERNATIVE LINE

ENGELS

DAILY TO EKATERINBURG

DAILY TO AKTÖBE (KAZ) CHANGE AT MAKAT FOR HELL TRAIN TO URGENCH

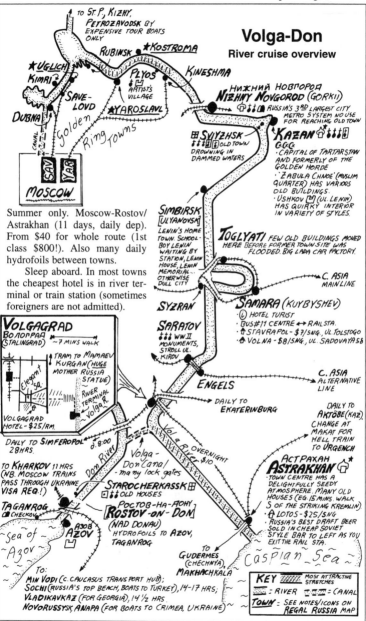

VOLGAGRAD
Волоград
(STALINGRAD)
~ 7 MINS WALK
→ TRAM TO MAMAEV KURGAN (HUGE MOTHER RUSSIA STATUE)
Elegant Sea
RIVER TERMINAL VOLGA R.
VOLGAGRAD HOTEL - \$25/RM.

DAILY TO SIMFEROPOL 28HRS.

TO KHARKOV 11 HRS (NB. MOSCOW TRAINS PASS THROUGH UKRAINE VISA REQ'!)

TAGANROG 🏛 CHECKOV

Sea of Azov

AZOV

Don River

Volga-Don Canal / many lock gates

Volga River

d. 8:00

OVERNIGHT \$10

STAROCHERKASSK ⊞ OLD HOUSES

Ростов-на-Дону
ROSTOV-ON-DON (NAD DONAU)
HYDROFOILS TO AZOV, TAGANROG

ACTPAXAH
ASTRAKHAN
· TOWN CENTRE HAS A DELIGHTFULLY SEEDY ATMOSPHERE. MANY OLD HOUSES (EG. 15 MINS. WALK S OF THE STRIKING KREMLIN)
· ♨ LOTOS - \$25/SNG
· RUSSIA'S BEST DRAFT BEER SOLD IN CHEAP SOVIET STYLE BAR TO LEFT AS YOU EXIT THE RAIL STA.

Caspian Sea

TO GUDERMES (CHECHNYA) MAKHACHKALA

To:
MIN VODI (C. CAUCASUS TRANSPORT HUB);
SOCHI (RUSSIA'S TOP BEACH, BOATS TO TURKEY), 14-17 HRS;
VLADIKAVKAZ (FOR GEORGIA), 14 ½ HRS.
NOVORUSSYSK, ANAPA (FOR BOATS TO CRIMEA, UKRAINE)

KEY
▨▨▨ MOST ATTRACTIVE STRETCHES
▨▨▨ = RIVER   ▨▨▨ = CANAL
TOWN = SEE NOTES/ICONS ON REGAL RUSSIA MAP

Mongolia

Peoples from all over Turkic west Asia and much of Russia can trace their ancestry back to one of the waves of nomad invasions which swept out of the Mongolian steppe. At its 13th century height, the Mongol empire was the greatest on earth, stretching from South East Asia to Finland. Today's independent Mongolia is much reduced in size and the majority of Mongols now live across the border in northern China. Since the USSR imploded in 1991, Mongolia has experienced something of a cultural revival. Though nominally independent since 1921, it had been completely Soviet-influenced and until seven years ago there was barely a *ger* (tent) to be seen around Ulaan Baator. Now the city is ringed with ger suburbs and horsemen roam free once more. The traditional Lamaist (Tibetan style) Buddhism is back in fashion. Much to China's annoyance the Dalai Lama has made two high profile visits.

Travel in Mongolia remains awkward. Distances are great, the population is sparse and transportation unreliable. Few people speak a word of any language you're likely to recognise and though the nomads can be delightfully hospitable, Ulaan Baator's bar-room brawls live up to the fierce, hard-drinking image that Genghis Khan made famous.

PRACTICAL INFORMATION
Visas and formalities
Tourist visas are available only to those on an approved 'tour'. Many daunted visitors are thus frightened into paying through the nose for short, expensive Trans-Siberian stopover packages. However, you only have to book a one-day tour to qualify for a full 14- or even 30-day visa. In the summer, Nomads Expeditions and the other agents listed below, charge $120 per person for the most basic itinerary: one night in a decent hotel, transfers from station or airport and a quick drive around Ulaan Baator. You can save 30% in the winter, but you have to pay 50% extra if you're travelling alone.

If the visa you're issued with is marked 'entry' rather than 'entry-exit', then you'll need an exit permit to leave Mongolia. This costs $20 from the Ministry of Foreign Affairs but your tour company should arrange it for you. If you're passing straight through and can

---

❑ **W&M's country ratings – Mongolia**
- **Expense $$$$** If you are self sufficient and don't join any tours it is much cheaper.
- **Value for money ✔✔** Tours aim to please but seem a little hollow.
- **Getting around ✔** Very difficult without your own horse.
- **English spoken ✔** A phrase book or guide is essential in most places.
- **Woman alone ✔✔✔** A female traveller reported: 'Mongolians are generally very friendly and I felt very much at ease with them.'
- **For vegetarians ✔✔** OK in Ulaan Baator but in rural areas mutton is unavoidable.

show your tickets in and out of the country, you can get a 48-hour transit visa without undue formality. The London embassy has been known to give transit visas by mail without demanding to see the tickets at all.

Tour agents who will help with visas if you book through them include: **Nomads Expeditions** (☎/fax 328146, e-mail: nomads@magicnet.mn), PO Box, 1008, Ulaan Baator 13, are a very helpful, independent travel company. They also have a US branch at 5 Independence Way, Suite 300, Princeton NY 08540, USA. **Boojum Expeditions** (US ☎ 406-587-0124, fax 406-585-3474, e-mail: Boojum@delphi .com), 14543 Kelly Canyon Road, Bozeman, MT 59715 USA, (runs horseback tours of Mongolia). **Blue Sea Travel**, 39-41 Hankow Rd, Kowloon, Hong Kong.

● **At the border** Though it doesn't fit with any of the official rules we met two travellers who had both managed to get a transit visa at the border for $60 – however er people living in Mongolia tell us that this is very rare and ill advised.

● **Registration** As in Russia, you are required to register your arrival within 10 days at the police station in Ulaan Baator (3rd floor). You will be fined on exit if you forget.

● **Visa extensions** Although a transit visa is theoretically not extendible, there can be extenuating circumstances: if you have a problem (such as illness) which might be convincing enough, get off your deathbed and warn the people at the police station before the visa expires. They will arrange the necessary forms; expect to pay a hefty

---

❑ **Geo-political information – Mongolia**

Population: 2.5 million (1997), 2.3m (1995), 2m (1989), 1.6m (1979).

Area: 1,566,000 sq km.

Capital: Ulaan Baator (620,000 in 1993).

Other major cities: Darham (67,000), Erdenet (58,000) no other town registered above 20,000.

GNP per capita: $340 (1994), $310 (1993), $473 (1988).

Currency history: Tugrik/US$1 – Feb 1998: T817, Oct 1997: T805, April 1996: T410, Feb 1994: T401, Dec 1993: T362, 28 May 1993: market flotation at T400, Sept 1992: T40.2, Oct 1990: T3.36.

Major exports/economy: 50% of exports are from the copper/molybdenum works at Erdenet. The main occupations are still agriculture and herding.

Ethnic mix: Khalkha (Halh) 79%, Kazakh 6%, Duörvöd 2.7%, Bayad 1.9%, Buryat 1.7% (ie approximately 35,000).

Official language: Khalkha Mongolian.

Religious mix: Lamaist Buddhism. Officially there are 2500 Christians – a catholic church was built in 1996.

Landmarks of national history: A wolf mated with a doe and produced the Mongol princes. **1206**: Genghis Khan went into overdrive. **1691**: Conquered by Manchuria. **1911**: Monarchy. **11 July 1921**: People's Republic declared by Damdiny Sühbataar. **1945**: Plebescite pro-independence, accepted by China. **1992**: Soviet forces withdrew. **30 June 1996**: Democratic Union Coalition party won the election (the first non-communists for 75 years) instituting draconian reforms.

Leaders: Since 20 June 1997 President Natsagiyn Bagabandi (former communist), Prime Minister Mendsayhany Enhsayhan (democrat).

Pressing political issues: Rejuvenation of Buddhist traditions, developing a relationship with the Dalai Lama as spiritual leader without angering China who sees him as a political figure. Unemployment.

fine as well as an extension fee.

● **Permits** Police permission is necessary to venture into many of the more remote countryside areas. Travellers report being fined for a lack of permit, even where they'd been told that permits weren't necessary. Ulaan Baator travel agencies can help you get a permit that lists the places where you intend to stop.

Money

Natsagdorj St in Ulaan Baator is the best area for changing cash (US$, Chinese yuan and Russian roubles) with minimal fuss and at slightly better than bank rates. Changing travellers' cheques in Ulaan Baator is no problem: the **Trade and Development Bank of Mongolia** charges a 2% commission to change US$ traveller cheques to US$ cash.

Cash advances without commission are possible at the **State Bank of Mongolia**.

Banks are open Monday to Friday, 10am-3pm.

Transport

● **Train** Tickets on the major rail line (the Trans-Mongolian) linking Moscow, via Irkutsk and Ulan Ude, to Beijing are much cheaper when purchased in sections to and from the border rather than buying the special through fares including border crossing. The trains tend to be very heavily booked. Since getting a visa extension is so awkward it's worth booking berths in advance, especially for the summer months.

● **Air** Foreigner pricing exists on **MIAT**, the Mongolian Airline. In the past, fuel shortages have made schedules erratic, though things have improved recently. Considering the vast emptiness of much of the terrain, flying does make sense.

● **Bus, truck and jeep** Bus travel is cheap but rough and crowded. Buses depart from in front of the Museum of Fine Arts in Ulaan Baator. For long rides (ie over 200km) transport is usually by truck though this can be even more uncomfortable than the bus. Hitching is possible but

---

❏ **Essential information for travellers – Mongolia**

● **Visa** Required. A two-day transit visa is given if you have an onward visa and a through train ticket. To get a tourist visa you generally need to have booked a tour. The usual fee is $25 and a visa is issued in three days.

● **Currency** Togrog (often still known by its Russian name, Tugrik), T1=100 mungu. US$1= T817.

● **Time zones** Ulaan Baator is 8 hours ahead of GMT (same as China and as the Irkutsk/Ulan Ude time zone, 5hrs ahead of Moscow). West Mongolia is 7hrs ahead of GMT and the far east of the country is 9hrs ahead.

● **Religious tone** Recent resurgence in Tibetan-style Buddhism.

● **Health factors** Tap and well water are supposedly drinkable but stream water should be purified or avoided. Drink plenty of water – the dry air makes it's easy to get dehydrated quickly, even in cold weather.

● **Special dangers** Drunks roaming rural as well as urban areas; bar room brawls.

● **Typical traveller destinations** Ulaan Baator and Terelj.

● **When to go** June and September are at the pleasant cusp between the great heat (especially in the Gobi) of the summer and the deep cold of winter; the cold is made worse by the strong winds that blow across the open landscape. Throughout the winter there are occasional blizzards. The limited rainfall comes mainly in the summer.

● **Pulse of the country** Naadam mid-summer festival; horsemen converge on Ulaan Baator and other centres for horse races, wrestling and archery contests.

slow and you should be self sufficient in case of lengthy waits. Some travellers opt to rent a jeep with a driver. The standard rate is a pricey T130 per kilometre (making a 150km trip split between four passengers about $10 each).

In Ulaan Baator there are many city buses or you can flag down a private car and negotiate a ride to wherever you want. There are relatively few official taxis.

Accommodation
In the main towns there are usually a few dingy, sometimes unmarked, hotels – ask locals where you could find a cheap room (*hyamd oroo*). Staying in a *ger* (the Mongolian version of a Kazakh yurt) sounds appealing but most tours take you to *gers* which have been set up especially for tourists. A night in a typical tourist camp will cost around $30. However, it's possible to venture out into the grasslands and find your own families to stay with.

Having your own tent would be an important fall back. Mongolian authorities warn against such freelance expeditions but those who have ventured as little as 70km from Ulaan Baator claim to have had thoroughly positive experiences (despite the drunkards). There are *ger* suburbs even at the edge of Ulaan Baator.

Food and drink
The food here is similar to that in central Asia; mutton and more mutton. *Lapsha* is the Mongolian version of *lagman* – noodle and mutton fat soup. *Boodog* is a feast where the whole sheep is roasted from the inside by being stuffed with red hot stones. *Airag* is fermented mare's milk (the equivalent of *koumys* in Kyrgyzstan).

Staying in touch
● **Phone/fax** It costs about $7-8 a minute to phone/fax the USA from Ulaan Baator. However, fax prices vary wildly from

---

❑ Meeting the locals
● **The people** The fearsome reputation earned by the armies of Genghis Khan is not entirely anachronistic if one sees a group of Mongols drinking. But in their pastoral home setting the tent dwelling semi-nomadic people are extremely friendly and hospitable, and amazed to see you. Meeting real locals like these is not hard but requires one to escape imposed tourist itineraries and accept the very intermittent transport limitations. Join a tour to get into the countryside then cut loose – follow a river and see who you meet.
● **Language** The traditional Mongolian script is a strikingly calligraphic one, the only alphabet consistently written vertically, top down. Though it has begun to make a comeback in the last few years, it is rarely used. The staff at one embassy admitted to finding the Mongolian script almost illegible. Usually, Mongolian is rendered in Cyrillic (Russian) script, which was introduced by the Moscow-backed government in 1944 to Russify the culture.
Some phrases in Mongolian:
        Greeting (How are you?) – *San ban oo*
        Reply (Fine, and you?) – *Sain ta sain bai-noo*
        Fine – *Sain bai-nah*
        Thank you – *Bai yar laa*
        Friend – *Naiz*
        How much is it? – *Eneh yamar unetee ve?*
        This food tastes <u>delicious</u> – *Eneh hool <u>amt-tai</u> baina*
        How far to the next town? – *Darah-geen sum hurtel hol oo?*
        Where can I rent/buy a horse? – *Hahn-ahs moree hulslej/hudaldan
                                          avch boloh ve?*
        I'm not Russian – *Ee bos bish*

place to place. The post office is reputed to be the most expensive. International country code: +976, Ulaan Baator: 1.

● **E-mail** Messages can be sent from the business centres at the Ulaan Baator Hotel (4th floor) and Bayan Gol Hotel.

● **Mail** The postal system works; it cost T264 to send a letter to Europe from Ulaan Baator and it arrived in 12 days.

Activities

● **Hiking/mountaineering** Organised hikes and some mountaineering is available through tourist agencies like Nomads and Juulchin. The cost for a one-week trek including three meals per day, a quality hotel in Ulaan Baator, all camping equipment or accommodation in a *ger* camp and English speaking guides would be about US$1000. **Mongol Altai Club**, PO Box 49-23, Ulaan Baator, can arrange permits for climbing in West Mongolia.

● **Work** The increasing number of Westerners teaching English without work permits was part of the reason for the recent visa clamp down. The wages are not stunning at $3-5/hour but you can swap lessons for accommodation or lessons in Mongolian.

Further information

● **Books** Lonely Planet is the only choice. Old editions suggest somewhat dangerously that there is a bus from Olgii to northeast Kazakhstan through Russia. From our research this is certainly not a possibility for Westerners, if it runs at all.

● **Maps** For about $6/map you can buy 1:500,000 TPC charts (11 sheets cover all Mongolia) though these, like Operational Navigational Charts (six sheets) are based solely on aerial data collection, resulting in many naming uncertainties and 'roads' which turn out to be rough tracks. The Russian military has produced excellent 1:200,000 topographical maps covering the country in 339 sheets. These are now commercially available, if only through very specialised map shops in the west (at around $2700 per set!). Within Mongolia they seem impossible to find and may still be considered to be militarily sensitive.

Many maps of China inadvertently include most of Mongolia.

● **Other Mongolia Travel Information Centres**: c/o Lernidee Reisen, Dudenstrasse 78, 10965 Berlin, Germany, (Germany ☎ 030 786 5056, fax 030-786 5596) and 80 Nonhyon Dong, Kangnam Ku, Seoul, South Korea (Korea ☎ 02-540-3928, fax 02-540 1118).

Juulchin (the main tourist corporation) has offices at: 5b Chingi Khan Ave, Ulaan Baator, Mongolia (☎ 328428, 322884, fax 320246); Arnold Zweig Str 2, 3R, 13189 Berlin, (Germany ☎ 030-471 8833, fax 030-478 2484) and Japan: Tokyo (☎ 03-5256 4801, fax 03-5256 0228), Osaka (☎ 06-441 0521, fax 06-445-7255).

Mongolian Tourism Corporation of America (US ☎ 908-274-0088), Princeton Corporate Plaza, 1 Deer Park Dr, Suite M, Monmouth Junction, NJ 08852, USA.

See also Visas and formalities section.

Web sites
Nothing on travel but excellent information on Mongolian history, economy and culture at the Mongolia Homepage:
http://www.bluemarble.net/~mitch/mong/cult.html

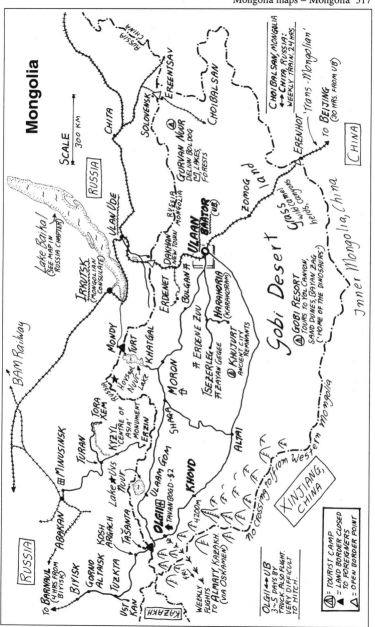

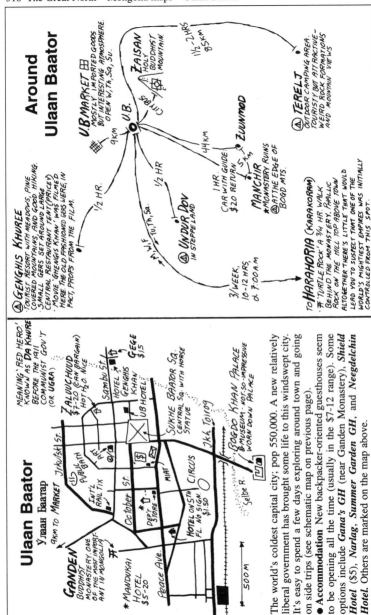

Around Ulaan Baator

GENGHIS KHUREE — TOURIST RESORT WITH MEADOWS, PINE COVERED MOUNTAINS, AND GOOD HIKING. SMALL GERS SET AROUND LARGE CENTRAL RESTAURANT TENT (PRICEY). MOVIE 'GENGHIS KHAN' WAS FILMED HERE. THE OLD FASHIONED GERS WERE, IN FACT, PROPS FROM THE FILM.

U.B. MARKET — MOSTLY IMPORTED GOODS BUT INTERESTING ATMOSPHERE. OPEN W, Th, Sa, Su.

ZAISAN — HOLY BUDDHIST MOUNTAIN

½-2 HRS / 85 KM

9 KM — U.B.

CITY BUS

½ HR

W, F — 10, Th, Sa.

UNDUR DOV — IN STEPPELAND

½ HR

44 KM — **ZUUNMOD**

1 HR CAR WITH GUIDE $20 RETURN

MANCHIR ★ MONASTERY RUINS @ AT THE EDGE OF BOGD MTS.

TERELT — △ OUTDOOR CAMPING AREA. TOURISTY BUT ATTRACTIVE — WEIRD ROCK FORMATIONS AND MOUNTAIN VIEWS

3/WEEK, 10-12 HRS, @ 7.00 AM

TO HARAHORIA (KARAKORAM) — ★ 'TURTLE ROCK' A ¾ HR WALK BEHIND THE MONASTERY. PHALLIC ROCK ON THE HILL TOP ABOVE TOWN ALTOGETHER THERE'S LITTLE THAT WOULD LEAD YOU TO SUSPECT THAT ONE OF THE WORLD'S MIGHTIEST EMPIRES WAS INITIALLY CONTROLLED FROM THIS SPOT.

Ulaan Baator
Улаан Баатар

9 KM TO MARKET

GANDEN — BUDDHIST MONASTERY. ONE OF THE MOST IMPORTANT IN W MONGOLIA

MEANING 'RED HERO' KNOWN AS **DA KHURE** BEFORE THE 1911 COMMUNIST GOV'T (OR UGRA)

Jirkutski St.

ZALUUCHUUD $7-20 (CAN BARGAIN) HOT H₂O. NICE

Sambu St.

GENGHIS KHAN HOTEL — UB HOTEL

GEGE $15

★ MANDUKAI HOTEL $5-20

Int'l Rail Tix

Public Bath

October St.

Dept. Store

MIAT

CIRCUS

Selbe R.

Jrka Toirog

SUKHE BAATOR SQ. — CENTRAL SQ. WITH HORSE

SUKHE BAATOR STATUE

BOGDO KHAN PALACE — & MUSEUM - NOT-SO-IMPRESSIVE WORN DOWN PALACE

HOTEL ON 5TH FL. NO SIGN. $1.50

Peace Ave.

500 M

The world's coldest capital city; pop 550,000. A new relatively liberal government has brought some life to this windswept city. It's easy to spend a few days exploring around town and going on side trips (see schematic map on previous page).

● **Accommodation** New backpacker-oriented guesthouses seem to be opening all the time (usually in the $7-12 range). Some options include *Gana's GH* (near Ganden Monastery), *Shield Hotel* ($5), *Narlag*, *Summer Garden GH*, and *Needgelchin Hotel*. Others are marked on the map above.

THE SUBCONTINENT

This section covers Pakistan, the Karakoram Highway which links Pakistan with China, India, the semi-independent Himalayan kingdom of Bhutan, Nepal, Bangladesh and Sri Lanka.

If it's your first visit to the Indian sub-continent, little can prepare you for the intense stimulation that you're about to experience. Nowhere in Asia is as immediately 'different' in terms of sights, atmosphere and culture. There's a chapter on each of the countries shown on the map below plus a special 'Karakoram Area' chapter reflecting the importance of the 'KKH' – the only reliable land route north or east.

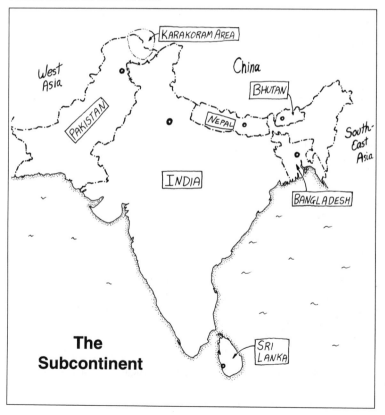

Pakistan

Pakistan's main attractions are the colourful market city of Peshawar and the jagged mountain scenery in the far north of the country. The hilly North West Frontier Province (NWFP) is home to the culturally unique Kalash and to the fierce, hospitable, chivalrous Pathans, who share a common ancestry with many Afghans. The south west is inhospitable desert, but Pakistan's heartland is the Indus river valley where some of the world's most ancient civilisations developed over 4500 years ago. The ruins of Moenjodaro are in this area.

Travel in Pakistan is cheap if not very comfortable, but it is complicated by political instability. Though the main routes to Iran, China and India are safe enough, much of the country is under little or no government control: see 'Dangers' on p328. On a personal level, the sexually repressive atmosphere often results in an annoying level of harassment for Western women (and indeed men).

Fortunately, the area along the Karakoram Highway to China, in addition to being the most spectacular area of Pakistan, is relatively relaxed and safe. Indeed it is so culturally and scenically different from the rest of Pakistan that we have given the Karakoram area its own chapter (p334).

The rest of Pakistan need not be avoided. There are many ruins to explore around the Grand Trunk Road and plenty of attractive highland valleys without going all the way to Gilgit. In the flat, agricultural centre it is fun to venture into rural areas; the villages may not be spectacular but the bemused locals always gave us a friendly reception. Like Alexander the Great you may find a visit to Pakistan relatively hard work, but it will certainly be a colourful and memorable experience.

❏ **W&M's country ratings – Pakistan**

● **Expense $$** Travel in the $5-10 per day range including transport is very possible.

● **Value for money** ✔✔✔ Accommodation is reasonable for the price; food is inexpensive.

● **Getting around** ✔✔✔ Crowded and uncomfortable but frequent; few cities have a single centralised bus station.

● **English spoken** ✔✔✔✔ A former British colony where many people think they speak English.

● **Woman alone** ✔ Expect to be the subject of constant curiosity and very unwanted attention. Pakistani women would never travel alone. Some cheaper hotels won't let a woman who is on her own have a room. Things are easier in the Karakoram area.

● **For vegetarians** ✔✔ Genuine Pakistani food is meat laden, but you can usually find some meatless options.

PRACTICAL INFORMATION
Visas and formalities

● **Visa strategy** Tourist visas are usually straightforward to obtain. The cost depends on your nationality and ranges from free (Swedes, Japanese) to $50 (British, Canadian). Visas are usually valid for four to six months and allow a three-month period of stay.

● **At the border** Technically visas are not issued on arrival (see the Karakoram section for a longshot exception). We met travellers who had been refused entry having foolishly arrived at Karachi and Islamabad airports without a visa.

● **Visa extensions** Extensions are available only in Islamabad. They take at least a full day to obtain – start at the **Foreigners' Registration Office**, and be prepared to visit at least two other offices.

Some travellers have received a one-week extension at the Foreigners' Registration Office in Gilgit (see Karakoram chapter).

Money

It's easy to change dollars and traveller cheques (for a slightly higher rate) in all major and many mid-sized cities. In large cities most hard currencies are exchangeable, commission-free credit card advances are possible at a few banks.

Banks are open Sunday to Thursday 9am-1pm, Saturday 9-11am.

❏ **Geo-political information – Pakistan**

Population: 132 million (1997), 122m (1992), 84m (1981), 65m (1972) (the figures exclude the remaining Afghan refugees).

Area: 880,000 sq km.

Capital: Islamabad (205,000).

Other major cities: Karachi (5.1m in 1981, now much bigger); Lahore (3m); Faisalabad (1.1m); Rawalpindi (800,000); Hyderabad (750,000); Multan, Gujranwala, Peshawar (500,000+); Sialkot, Sargodha, Quetta (300,000); Jhang, Bahawalpur (200,000).

GNP per capita: $440 (1993), $385 (1988).

Currency history: Rupee/US$1 – Feb 1998: Rs43.80, Oct 1997: Rs40.4, Dec 1995: Rs34.2, Dec 1994: Rs30.8, Dec 1993: Rs30.

Major exports/economy: Textile yarns, fabrics, clothing.

Official language: Urdu, yet only 7.6% speak it as their first language. Other languages: Punjabi (48.2%), Pushtu (13%), Sindi (12%), Saraiki (10%).

Religious mix: Muslim (97%), there's a small Christian community in Karachi.

Landmarks of national history: 3rd millennium ancient Indus Valley civilisation blossomed around Harappa and Moenjodaro. **1500BC**: Aryan invaders. **325BC**: Alexander the Great stormed by. **321BC**: Mauryan Empire founded. **1524**: First Mughal invasion. **1849**: The British took over the Punjab after the war with the Sikhs. **1916**: Jinnah's Lucknow Pact (Muslim support for Indian self rule). **June-Aug 1947**: Mayhem as Pakistan was sheared off India and the population had to decide whether to stay or move; Mojahir influx from Hindu India. **1948** and **1965**: Wars with India over Kashmir which was eventually divided between them. **1970**: Completion of Karakoram Highway to China. **1971**: East and West Pakistan split. **1977-1985**: Martial law. **1980s**: The Soviet invasion of Afghanistan led to Pakistan being swamped with refugees and guns.

Leaders: Farooq Leghari is President, but political power is wielded by Prime Minister Nawaz Sharif.

Pressing political issues: Continued squabbles with India over borders. Mojahir issue in Sind. See 'Dangers' (p328) for more details.

Transport

● **Bus** Older Bedford buses drip with bells and dangling ornaments, musical horns, fairy lights and pious slogans all painted in swirling technicolour. Sadly, colour is their only recommendation. Breakdowns are frequent (Karachi to Lahore took 40 hours instead of the advertised 18). The driving is erratic; our rainbow and chrome chara-bang squealed to a sudden halt on a hairpin ledge high above the Indus.

Local government tourist-board buses are an entirely different breed from the Bedford variety. The vehicles are much better quality and are reasonably reliable. Services operate between most large cities and tourist centres. Tickets are purchased at the tourist offices and are reasonably priced. In theory, students can get a discount but they must book ahead and fill out the proper form which the office might or might not have. Travel by minibus is not much more expensive and can also be booked in advance.

Urban buses and vans run set routes but can be very crowded.

● **Train** Pakistani trains have a reputation for being late but ours were always more

---

❏ The heavenly handshake

A Pakistani man who invited me for tea asked the standard list of questions: he wanted to know where I was from, what my job was, my age, if I was married. I recited my brief biography before asking him the same questions. He was from a small town, a business student, 25 years old, and he wasn't married but he did have a girlfriend. I asked how long he had known his girlfriend. And, with that question, the entire tone of conversation changed, and his story began...

He had met her at a market. They didn't exchange any words but, as he said, 'She gave me a look'. I was sceptical, but he assured me, 'There is only one look, and it only means one thing.' Through some friends he was able to discover where this woman-of-the-look lived. Then, secretly, they began writing letters to each other. He pulled one of the letters out of his sports coat pocket to show me. It read like a teenager's letter to his first crush – full of honest feelings and sappy similes. He carefully placed it back in a bundle wrapped with a gift handkerchief into which she had sewn his name. 'The most important thing I own,' he said.

I couldn't resist asking: had they kissed? 'No,' he sighed. And then, he added with a smile, 'But we did shake hands.' Apparently, after eight months of writing letters he had broached the possibility of a handshake. It took a month to weigh the merits and pitfalls, and another month to arrange how their hands might meet in secret. 'Her brothers would kill me if they knew,' he said giving no indication of an overstatement. 'After I am a business man, I can ask her family for marriage. But now, no one can know.' He described how, at the appointed time, he had climbed over the fence of her parents' house waited 'for hours' for a hand to emerge from her window. And finally it did.

I struggled for the right response, but all I could manage was: 'So, uh...was it a good handshake?'

'Oh! The best!' he said, 'Do you know that Lionel Ritchie song 'Hold out your hand and I'll be there?' That song was written for us!'

I wondered what he thought of Western culture, in which men and women can shake hands without even knowing each other's names. Before I had a chance to find out, he asked me how courtship works at home. 'I hear in America that you can ask a woman for tea and that is OK. Is this true?' 'In America,' I told him, 'relationships are...confusing.'

or less on time. Trains are somewhat more comfortable and predictable than buses on most long distance services (though not so between Quetta and Iran where the trains often get bogged down in shifting sands). Sleeper berths usually sell out long in advance, but once aboard you can some-times upgrade your ticket to take unfilled spaces. In the cheapest class, there are sleeping places above the seats; theoretically you can use them for a Rs50 supplement but staking such a claim proved very difficult in the crowded reality and anyhow they are miserable. Night trains in winter

---

❏ **Essential information for travellers – Pakistan**
(See also Karakoram section, p334).

● **Visa** Required by most and usually easy to obtain; a three-month period of stay is allowed.

● **Currency** Rupee. US$1=Rs43.8 (Travellers cheques Rs44.5).

● **Time zone** 5 hours ahead of GMT ($\frac{1}{2}$hr ahead of Afghanistan, $\frac{1}{2}$hr behind India, $1\frac{1}{2}$hrs ahead of Iran in winter, $\frac{1}{2}$hr in summer).

● **Religious tone** Islam – with strong fundamentalist influences.

● **Health factors** Malaria is a risk at altitudes below 2000 metres. The tap water is unsafe to drink.

● **Special dangers** The areas which are out of government control (see p328).

● **Social conventions** Travellers often think Pakistan is less Muslim than Iran. In fact, most of the religious assumptions are the same. So, while Pakistani women might not legally be required to cover up, most do. Western women would be advised to do likewise. The simple addition of a *dupatta* (light scarf draped around the shoulders and head) will cut the high hassle factor a little; wearing the traditional, highly comfortable *shalwar-kamiz* could cut it considerably. Both are cheap and readily available throughout Pakistan. Male versions of the *shalwar-kamiz* are also comfortably cool and sensible and much more appropriate than shorts and sleeveless shirts which may offend.

Between men, most interactions of any length are begun with a handshake or embrace; the Pakistani handshake is not the strong Western-style one but more the 'dead fish' variety.

● **Typical traveller destinations** Lahore, Moenjodaro, Peshawar, transit through Islamabad.

● **Highlights** Peshawar (old area), the Kagan and Swat valleys.

● **When to go** The best time to visit the lowlands is from late October to February – expect pleasant, mostly dry days, though nights might require a decent sweater. Sometime in March the heat sets in, with Sibi and Sukkur being famously unpleasant, and from late June the monsoon rains bring humidity. Most of this rain falls in the hills – Karachi gets all the humidity without much cooling rain.

The other northern valleys are cool in the summer; as a result half the Punjab seems to descend upon Murree and the surrounding hill resorts. Though August may bring monsoon rains and road blocks on some valley roads, the area remains popular and hotel prices can be three times higher than in winter when upper Swat and the higher passes may get cut off by snow.

● **Pulse of the country** Karachi (economic), Islamabad (political), Lahore (cultural).

● **Key tips** Western women are not legally required to conform to the Islamic dress code, but doing so will reduce hassle and gain respect.

Keep abreast of the security situation in the places you intend to visit.

can be cold – bring warm clothes and a blanket. Between Lahore-Pindi-Peshawar consider taking buses as the trains become like sardine cans.

Getting a ticket may require you to visit several counters (you first have to get a seat reservation, then pay for the ticket, and finally return for the reservation slip). Different destinations and classes of trains have different ticket windows.

A 25% tourist discount (50% with a student card) is possible in bigger towns – with a lot of hassle. The quest for the discount begins at the office of the **Divisional Superintendent of Trains**, but the office is rarely in an obvious location. The fortunate might obtain the discount after a bureaucratic half hour. In Karachi we were shuffled between several offices and the procedure took us all day. Student discounts in Lahore take two to three hours to obtain; the process is easier in Quetta.

● **Air**   Flights between Karachi and Islamabad/Lahore have been recently opened to private competition. There are so many flights on these routes that there is no reason to purchase a ticket in advance.

Domestic flights are much cheaper in Pakistan than bought abroad. Thus, on long-haul flights it is usually cheaper to fly into Karachi and buy a separate Karachi-Islamabad/Lahore ticket (there are several offices directly outside the main doors), than to buy an add-on ticket in your home country.

From Islamabad there are cheap if sporadic (weather vulnerable) flights to Gilgit, Chitral and Skardu (see Karakoram section, p334).

The international departure tax (Rs500 or 700) is paid when the ticket is purchased; check whether the quoted price includes the tax.

Accommodation

In almost every Pakistani town you can find a room for under Rs70, and certainly under Rs100. In large cities, most cheap options are clustered together, often around the main train station and/or around the main bazaar (which is often named Sadar Bazaar). Since cheap accommodation is easy to find we have made little reference to it on the schematic maps, except where specific details seem especially useful. Prices in the Swat and Kagan valleys and around Murree rise drastically in summer.

Some of the most rustic spots have official lodges owned by the Forestry Department, the Communication and Works Dept of North West Frontier Province, and various other government and provincial authorities which need to be booked in advance from departmental offices in major cities.

Food and drink

Pakistani food is similar to Indian – it also makes heavy use of yoghurt, lentils and curry – but tends to have more meat. Common dishes are: *sag gosht* (spinach and lamb curry), and *brain masala biryani* (rice with spices, meat and yoghurt).

❑ Festivals

Event	Place	Usual time	What happens
Sibi Festival	Sibi, Balochistan	Last week of February	Traditional sports and handicraft exhibits.
Sind Horse and Cattle Fair	Jacobabad, Sind	Last week of February	Similar to above but also with horses and cattle.
Mela Chiraghan	Lahore (outside Shalimar Gardens	Last week of March	Week-long festival of lamps.
Jashan-e-Shikarpur	Shikarpur, Sind	First week in April	Handicrafts and local sports.
Lok Mela	Islamabad	First week of October	Five-day folk festival.

Mughal food such as *shish kebab* (grilled meat on skewers) is a specialty of Lahore.

The most common drink is *chai* (sweet milk tea). In some areas, especially around Peshawar, you can also find *kawa* (a type of green tea).

Cheaper places rarely have menus but where there is one it is often in English.

Non-Muslim tourists can obtain permits to buy alcohol though the rules vary in different areas: enquire at top hotels or at regional customs and excise offices.

Staying in touch

Mail to Europe and the US took about one week; most letters we sent arrived. The two parcels we sent sea mail to the USA (Rs500/10kg) arrived in four months. One hadn't been opened, the other had. It had lost two shirts and a pair of *shalwar-karmiz*

trousers, but had somehow gained a book, a packet of photographs and some letters! 'Edith' is welcome to contact us for her things back.

There are **American Express** offices in: **Islamabad**: Ali Plaza, 1-E, Blue Area (☎ 51-212425), **Karachi**: Shaheen Commercial Complex, Dr Ziauddin Ahmed Rd (☎ 21-2630260), **Lahore**: 112 Rafi Mansions, Shahrah-E-Quaid-E-Azam (☎ 42-6279230), **Rawalpindi**: Rahim Plaza, Muree Rd (☎ 51-566001/2/3/4/5). All the offices are open Sunday to Thursday 9am-4.45pm, Saturday 9am-12.45pm. There is also an office in Faisalabad.

International country code: +92. Karachi: 21, Lahore: 42, Rawalpindi and Islamabad: 51, Peshawar: 521, Quetta: 81, Gilgit: 572.

❏ **Meeting the locals**

● **Language** Urdu, the national language, is practically identical to Hindi, though it is written in Arabic script (see p59). The majority of Pakistanis have a regional language, notably Sindi or Punjabi, as their mother tongue.

Some Muslim phrases:

Greeting (Arabic) – *salam alekum* (as in Iran, if you are not Muslim, people may greet you with the more secular *salam*)

Reply – *elekum a salam* (or *salam*)

Thank you – *shukria*

● **Some topics for conversation**: Cricket, and especially the marriage of Imran Khan, Pakistan's top star and budding fundamentalist Muslim politician, to Jemima, the daughter of Jewish-British business tycoon, James Goldsmith.

Pakistani music, of which most are extremely proud (despite possible contradictions with the Islamic stricture against dancing). Noor Jahan, Ahmad Rushdie and Mehdi Hasan are popular.

Politics – Pakistanis are very well informed about their government and like to discuss it. Be aware that political strife causes suffering to many people, especially in Karachi. Some restaurants and buses have Urdu signs, 'Please prevent political debate.' Be sensitive.

Many Pakistani men want to talk about women and sex; their views range from sweet to alarming (see box p322).

Note: Men who travel on their own in Pakistan can expect forthright gay propositions. The logic goes something like this: 'I am thinking that in your country homosexuality is legal. I am having no woman, you are having no woman, so let's be enjoying together!' It is particularly important to ascertain your host's attitude before accepting hospitality, especially in small farmsteads where there may be only one shared bed per sex.

Shopping

Quetta and Peshawar have very colourful and photogenic markets. Afghan carpets are good value in Peshawar if you're competent at bargaining. Although a similar carpet might be cheaper in Turkmenistan, Pakistani export restrictions are much easier. However, that doesn't mean you can send home that jaunty fake Kalashnikov that you bought in Darra Adem Khel.

Further information

● **Books** The two best Pakistan guide books are Isobel Shaw's *Pakistan Handbook* (Moon) and the Lonely Planet *Pakistan Travel Survival Kit*. Neither is sold in India and they appear relatively rarely in the book havens of Kathmandu or Bangkok. Within Pakistan try the **Book Centre** (☎ 65234), 32 Haider Rd, Rawalpindi. In Iran, your best hope is doing a book swap with another backpacker at the Tourist House in Bam.

Old editions of Trade & Travel/Footprint's *South Asia Handbook* can be found in second-hand bookstalls in Kathmandu and (occasionally) in India. Pre-1993 versions included an excellent section on Pakistan.

See the Karakoram Chapter for books dealing specifically with the northern region.

● **Maps** Beware that most Pakistani-made maps of the country will show borders that are more optimistic than real. At the time of writing, Srinagar and Jammu are under Indian control and the roads that appear to go there are more likely to lead you to an international incident.

● **Information offices** There are 23 **Pakistan Tourist Development Corporation** (PTDC) offices in Pakistan, including ones at Karachi, Lahore and Islamabad airports. Each office has at least a small selection of free maps and useful local information. Theoretically there is also one in Taftan at the Iran border but if (like us) you miss it there is another convenient and friendly office in the Muslim Hotel, Quetta (see map p333, ☎ 081-79519). The PTDC office in **Islamabad** (☎ 51-811001, fax 51-824173) is at House No 2, Street 61, F-7/4, and in **Rawalpindi** (☎ 51-565449) at Hotel Flashman, The Mall. There are also offices in **Abbottabad** (☎ 05921-4946) Jinnah Road; **Karachi City** (☎ 021-5681293); **Lahore** (☎ 042-6306528) Faletti's Hotel, room No 3; Moenjodaro (☎ 0741-60906); **Peshawar** (☎ 0521-279781) Dean's Hotel.

Web sites

Few web sites specific to Pakistan have useful travel information. The Pakistan section of an all-Asia site would probably be more useful, especially the Lonely Planet site. Nevertheless, you could try:

www.alephx.org/karachi has a guide to Karachi, meant mostly for expats.

Pakistan's only online magazine is at www.saher.com; it has a special section for travel stories.

Links to ex-pat oriented guides to Lahore, Islamabad, Peshawar, and Multan are at 204.250.12.11/one7/travel.html.

A Pakistani student has pictures of his country at www.inform.umd.edu/StudentOrg/psa/Pakistan.

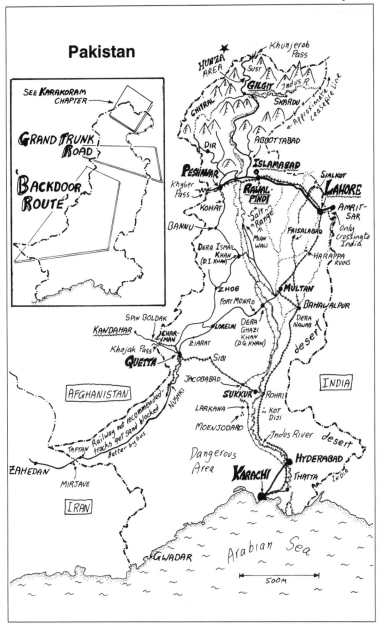

PAKISTAN – DANGERS

Though it should not deter your trip to Pakistan as a whole, be aware that there are several areas of instability in the country:

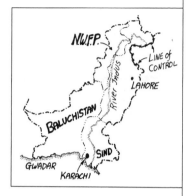

Line of Control
● **Problem**   Sensitive border/ceasefire line in Kashmir.

● **Historical background**   When British India was being partitioned in 1947, princely states could choose which new nation to join. Jammu Kashmir is a largely Muslim hotpot of isolated mountain kingdoms, but the Maharajah decided to join Hindu India when he saw that independence was impossible. The local population revolted. India and Pakistan went to war, each hoping to grab Kashmir for itself but the 1949 ceasefire ended in de facto partition which continues to cause severe tensions.

● **Travel implications**:   The issue has caused full-scale war in the past, so every incursion seems to get over publicised. In most cases the worst that actually happens is that some of the treks around Skardu become out of bounds. There is no need to avoid the northern region; incidents of Kashmiri terrorist groups taking Western hostages have been solely on the Indian side, though there are some hiking areas where you should venture only with a guide.

Baluchistan
● **Problem**   The loose government control away from the main cities, particularly in the Makran (south west) area. Bandits are notorious along roads heading north east from Quetta.

● **Historical background**   The historic khanate of Kalat that controlled much of Baluchistan, like Kashmir, tried to hold out for independence rather than join India or Pakistan in 1947 (though other Baluchi tribal chiefs acceded to Pakistan). This was the end, at least publicly, of an independence movement, but the central government's heavy handed attempts to get rid of the residual power of tribal chiefs in the late 1970s sparked an atmosphere of violence which persists to some extent even now.

● **Travel implications**   The Quetta-Taftan road and the railway are considered safe. The dangers in other areas are mostly apocryphal as few venture to find out. Travellers who have crossed northern Baluchistan, hitching trucks or taking buses along the infamous 'robbers road', have reported very friendly, colourful people. The dangers remain tangible, however, and great caution is advised.

Karachi and the Sind
● **Problem**   Intense communal violence. Extortion rackets, tit for tat killings, violent deaths, assassinations and police reprisal violence. All of which are exacerbated by the drug traffickers operating in the area.

● **Historical Background**   Though very complex, a pivotal cause of the discontent that fuelled the outbreaks of violence is the perceived unfair system of allotting government jobs. And in Pakistan, most jobs are government jobs. An outwardly well-intentioned law designed to prevent rural areas becoming ever more under developed, was introduced by former prime minister Bhutto (father of Benazir Bhutto). The aim was to give a quota of jobs to each area of the Sind and make Sindi the language of local government. But Karachi and the surrounding area has a large population of Mojahirs: Urdu-speaking descendants of the Muslim Indians who left India for Pakistan in 1947. The Mojahirs are typically seen as better educated and they feel that the quota system, as well as the language condition, is fixed against them. Sindis, on the other hand, clearly fear any erosion of their job opportunities. Distrust amongst the communities was smoothed under the Zia administration (which gave some encouragement to Mojahirs), but re-emerged when Benazir Bhutto came to power; the Bhuttos were rural Sindis. The Mojahir Qaumi Movement (MQM), a major opposition party in Karachi, has been painted by some as a terrorist front. The truth is very hard to gauge, but the communities have slowly sunk deeper into a violent mistrust.

● **Travel implications** Karachi airport (where most international flights arrive and leave) is safe enough for changing planes though it's best to jump straight onto a cheap internal flight to Lahore or Islamabad rather than hang around. In town, danger areas are hard to predict with some murders even reported in the classy Clifton suburbs. Although foreigners are rarely targeted specifically, two US consular officials were gunned down in March 1995. The consulate has since closed as it is considered too unsafe to maintain operations. Much of the Sind is considered to be similarly unsafe, and the areas round the Moenjodaro Ruins and Sukkur are notorious for banditry.

North West Frontier Province
● **Problem** The area is thought of as lawless. More fairly it has its own rather arbitrary legal system which operates independently from that of Pakistan's national law. It's not as dangerous as the Sind despite the hype.

● **Historical background** Much of the province is Pathan (Pushtun), so the people are ethnically the same as the majority of Afghans, millions more of whom arrived as refugees from the Soviet invasion of Afghanistan. A high level of autonomy was the price for maintaining any kind of viable hold during the British era and this autonomy remains today.

● **Travel implications** Certain so-called Tribal Areas are often off-limits to foreigners. Permits to visit certain such areas can be time consuming or impossible to arrange. Guns abound and are treated like toys – the greatest danger comes from the lack of safety catches: bumpy roads can set off a carelessly carried Kalashnikov à la *Pulp Fiction*. Otherwise few travellers have reported any unpleasant incidents. Peshawar, Chitral and the main tourist destinations are safe. Police-dodging by travellers trying to get to the gunsmiths' town of Darra Adem Khel seems to be something of a game.

Lahore
Unlike Karachi, Lahore is not a violent place. However, be careful where you stay. For years there have been repeated reports of theft and rip-offs in the cheap hotels in the streets around the station. These are not exaggerated. The YWCA and the Salvation Army hostel (if it re-opens) are the safest cheap options.

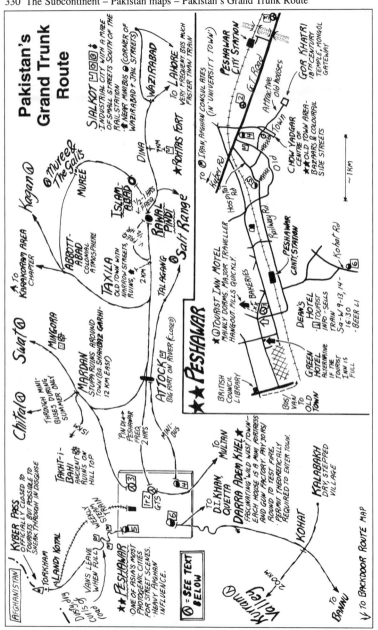

Pakistan's Grand Trunk Route

LAHORE PAKISTAN'S CULTURAL HEART AND 2ⁿᴰ LARGEST CITY

GOOD VIEWS FROM MINAR PAKISTAN TOWER

Badshahi Mosque

'KIM'S GUN' AND ★ MUSEUM

Old ★ City

Railway Stn

The Mall

Abbey

FREE MAPS

BEWARE THEFTS AND RIP-OFFS ARE COMMON AT THE CHEAP HOTELS IN THE STATION AREA

YWCA BEST IN TOWN 125rs/DBL.

SALVATION ARMY HOSTEL CLOSED IN '95

SCALE
~1KM
NB-ONLY MAIN ROADS SHOWN

Hill towns, valleys and soaring mountains

You don't have to go all the way up the KKH to enjoy cool mountain air and dramatic panoramas, though the lower valleys are packed with local tourists. Accommodation in areas below marked ## tend to have heavily inflated summer prices (Rs200+) till late September.

● **Chitral** Base to visit the steep, partly wooded Kalash Valleys (Bumberat, Rumbur, Birir) where the locals are said to be descendants of Alexander the Great's wayward troops. The women wear distinctive black costumes decked with cowries and lead their menfolk (many of whom seem to be stoned senseless) in unique whirling dances held at hard to find moonlight locations (follow a friendly local). There are also much less evocative tourist dance displays (for a fee). Look out for unburied coffins, and note (but don't enter) the *bashilini* (menstruation huts) in which women are incarcerated monthly. The valleys are 3-4 hrs walk from Ayun, which is 15km S of Chitral town. Chitral to Peshawar by daily flight or 12hrs by summer only road via Dir (bazaar, palace). Jeeps up to 2/week to Gilgit or head to Buni/Mastuj and trek to Teru (rest house) or Phandar (hostel/lake) whence jeeps more frequent.

● **Muree and the Gali's ##** A string of forested hill towns. Touristy Muree's modest appeal is overwhelmed by throngs of locals escaping the heat of the Punjab cities. (Cart Rd for cheapest rooms). Two hours and several *gali* hill towns beyond is Ayubia, itself a group of *gali* hamlets set in a pleasant national park area of forested mountains (cable car from Gora Daka, hikes). Nathiagali is nicer still.

● **Kagan Valley ##** Dramatic alpine scenery, Saiful Muluk Lake (rest house) 3hrs walk from Naran. Route from Naran rejoining the KKH is spectacular but there's no public transport.

● **Kurram Valley** 200km west of Kohat, lovely views of snow-capped Zafed Koh mountains en route to attractive Parachinar (via Thal).

● **Salt Range** Dry, aesthetically less appealing mountains, dotted with forgotten pre-Islamic temples, eg at Amb, Malot, Sassi da Kallara. Two crumbling walls are the minimal post-Genghis Khan remains of Nandna, a once great city of erudition where 11th century academic Beruni had calculated the circumference of an earth that Europeans still though flat.

● **Swat Valley ##** Semi-independent till 1969. Many ruins around Mingora include large citadel and remains of Ora at Udegram. Fort ruins en route to Kalam. Skiing at Malam Jaba. Hiking further north great but seek advice re local dangers. (dull village in gorgeous valley).

To the India-Pakistan border

The daily Lahore-Amritsar train service takes at least 4hrs as the whole train must clear customs. It's quicker to take buses to/from each border (frequent services Lahore-Wagah and Atari-Amritsar). Much quicker than either, a taxi will do the whole trip in as little as an hour. The border is open 10am to 3pm and there's a *PTDC motel* in Wagah should you get stuck.

Getting around Islamabad–'Pindi: Some useful van (Toyota&Ford) routes: #1— 'Pindi GPO, 'Pindi Station, Murree Rd near the Popular Inn, Islamabad's Aabpara Market, G-6, F-6, Marriott Hotel; #3, 120—Aabpara Market, Bari Imam; #105—Aabpara, G-7. S Bedford buses follow van route #1 but turn left at F-6 (i.e. to F-7). Small Suzuki vans follow route #1 from 'Pindi as far as Aabpara market; they also run between the airport and 'Pindi GPO (ask for 'Saddar Bazaar').

RAWALPINDI ('PINDI)

ISLAMABAD'S SISTER CITY.
MOST TRAVELLERS STAY HERE RATHER
THAN ISLAMABAD—THERE IS MORE
CHEAP ACCOMMODATION AND ATMOSPHERE.

Islamabad

Islamabad has little of tourist interest—the only reason to come here is to obtain a visa or run other errands. Be warned that this hot, spread out city is the least pedestrian-friendly capital in Asia. A series of vans and Bedford mini buses carry passengers between points on the main roads, but they don't often venture into the side streets where most embassies are. Fortunately, the street-layout is logical—the city's major avenues form a grid with each block area divided into four sub-zones. Numbered 'streets' run N-S within a sub-zone, numbered 'roads' run E-W. Our map shows the main areas travellers deal with.

Area	Name	What's There
F-6	Super	Good Bookstores, many banks, western fast food.
F-7	Jinah	The best bookstores, souvenir shopping.
F-8	Ayub	10 mins walk to the Kazakh Embassy (4th road, enter from 1st street).
G-6	Melody	Main GPO (w/ poste restante), a good bakery, luxury hotels with food buffets. Fabric & tailors at the Aabpara Market.
G-7	Sitara	A few hotels with rooms in the 150-200rs. range.
	Blue Area	Airline offices and travel agents.

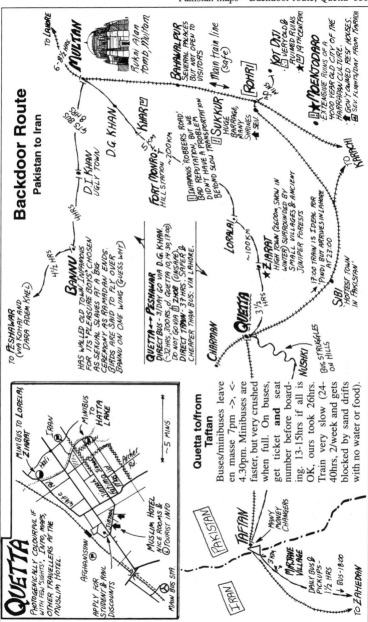

Backdoor Route
Pakistan to Iran

TO LAHORE

6 - 8½ HRS

MULTAN
Ruhni Alan tomb, Multan

TO PESHAWAR
(VIA KOHAT AND DARRA ADEM KHEL)

4½ HRS

BANNU
HAS WALLED OLD TOWN. INFAMOUS FOR ITS PLEASURE BOYS, CHOSEN AS SEXUAL SLAVES AT A BIG CEREMONY AS RAMADAN ENDS. BIRDS ARE SAID TO FLY OVER BANNU ON ONE WING (GUESS WHY)

4 HRS

D.I. KHAN
UGLY TOWN

D.G. KHAN

FTS BUS
8 HRS

KHAR

5 HRS
BUS → 200KM

BAHAWALPUR
SEVERAL PALACES BUT NOT OPEN TO VISITORS

Main train line (safe)

ROHRI

KOT DJI
□ VERY OLD B RUINED RUINS
★ 19TH CENT. FORT

MOENTODARO
EXTENSIVE RUINS OF A 4000 YEAR OLD CITY OF THE HARRAPIAN CULTURE.
□ GOVT OWNED REST HOUSES.
□ SEX. FLIGHTS/DAY FROM KARACHI.

SUKKUR
HUGE BARRAGE, MANY SHRINES

TO KARACHI

FORT MONRO
HILL STATION ↑
T → 200KM

□ INFAMOUS 'ROBBERS ROAD'. BAD REPUTATION, BUT WE DIDN'T HAVE A PROBLEM BEYOND SLOW TRANSPORTATION

LORALAI

~ 100KM

QUETTA ↔ PESHAWAR
DIRECT BUS - 3/DAY GO VIA D.G. KHAN.
(~32HRS, 300RS, d. QUETTA 10, 14, 19 (17.00)
DO NOT GO VIA □ ZHOB (UNSAFE)
DIRECT TRAIN - 37 HRS. SAFER & CHEAPER THAN BUS: VIA LAHORE.

★ ZIARAT
HIGH TOWN (2600M, SNOW IN WINTER) SURROUNDED BY SMALL VILLAGES & ANCIENT JUNIPER FORESTS.

17.00 TRAIN IS IDEAL FOR 'PINDY BUT ARRIVES LINE AT 23.00

SIBI
'HOTTEST TOWN IN PAKISTAN'

CHARMAN

QUETTA

3½ HRS

NUSHKI
BUS STRUGGLES ON HILLS

Quetta to/from Taftan

Buses/minibuses leave en masse 7pm →, ← 4.30pm. Minibuses are faster, but very crushed when full. On buses, get ticket **and** seat number before boarding. 13-15hrs if all is OK, ours took 26hrs. Train very slow (24-40hrs, 2/week and gets blocked by sand drifts with no water or food).

QUETTA
PHOTOGENICALLY COLOURFUL IF WITH FEW SIGHTS. INFO, MAPS, OTHER TRAVELLERS AT THE MUSLIM HOTEL.

MINIBUS TO LORELAI,
ZIARAT

Iran
Hali

MINIBUS TO HATTA LAKE

~ 5 MINS.

Jinnah Rd
Archer Rd
LANE

AFGHANISTAN

APPLY FOR STUDENT & RAIL DISCOUNTS

MAIN BUS STN.

MUSLIM HOTEL
NICE ROOMS & ☺ TOURIST INFO

PAKISTAN

TAFTAN
MANY MONEY CHANGERS

3 KM

MIRJAVE VILLAGE

DAILY BUS & PICKUPS -
1½ HRS
BUS -18.00

IRAN

TO ZAHEDAN

Karakoram

The 'Karakoram Highway' (KKH) is a double misnomer. For the road doesn't cross the Karakoram Pass (now in Indian-controlled Kashmir). Neither is it a smoothly paved highway divided into lanes. But it is a road, and an extremely useful one – it's the only reliable land route between China and the subcontinent.

The isolated, spectacularly mountainous Karakoram area through which the road winds is culturally and scenically different from the rest of Pakistan. It was a patchwork of independent kingdoms and principalities until last century and even today most valleys retain their own culture and language. Few locals think of themselves as Pakistani and the area remains Pakistan's most religiously diverse region. Shamanistic sentiments still survive – many children wear make up around their eyes to ward off evil spirits. The Kalash valleys near Chitral have a unique and colourful culture all of their own and are known for their all-night dances, their black, bead-embroidered women's costumes, and (to Pakistanis) their shameless hedonism. Local Islam takes several forms, tempered by centuries of now faded Buddhist culture. Forty per cent of the local population are of the tolerant Ismaili Muslim tradition. Women travellers usually notice considerably less hassle in Ismaili areas; these tend to be concentrated near and to the west of the highway. Further east you'll find a somewhat more argumentative, male-centred form of Shia Islam. Bisham is a particularly conservative area and you're unlikely to see many women wandering alone there.

Steep mountains and deep, sharp valleys make travel slow but awe inspiring. Of all the many magical valleys, Hunza is an understandable favourite. It's not a town but a cluster of small villages and a couple of ruined fortresses. Amid glades of apricot trees, Hunza clings to the dusty slopes in the awesome shadow of towering Mt Rakaposhi. Karimabad, the main village, has sprouted a few hotels too many, but remains small. Its situation makes it an idyllic base to explore this most spectacular land.

❑ **W&M's country ratings – Karakoram Area**
- **Expense $$** With a little effort it is possible to get by on $5-7/day.
- **Value for money** ✔✔✔✔ Accommodation and food are basic...but look at that view.
- **Getting around** ✔✔✔ There are many buses and vans (though most transport leaves in the morning); the limited number of roads means it is difficult to get lost. For more remote areas you'll have to walk.
- **Woman alone** ✔✔ More laid back than in the rest of Pakistan.
- **For vegetarians** ✔✔✔✔ Usually multiple vegetarian options.

PRACTICAL INFORMATION
Visas/formalities as for Pakistan

● **At the border** For the desperate only. We met people who had crossed from China on the Karakoram Highway without a Pakistan visa. However, the only reason the Pakistanis would let them in is because the Chinese wouldn't take them back. These travellers were given a temporary entry permit allowing passage to Islamabad where the permit had to be converted to a visa. This visa cost more than it would have done at an embassy and the two week (strictly non-extendible) validity of the visa was largely filled by the application procedure, leaving little time for any sightseeing. Those who have been through the process stress that this really is a last resort. Sometimes the Chinese refuse to let you out if they notice your lack of Pakistan visa.

● **Permits** The majority of trekking in Pakistan doesn't require permission or fees. However, if you are planning a trek above 6000m or you're venturing into sensitive border areas (ie near the line of control with India or Wakhan Corridor) you will probably need a permit. Inquire at **Islamabad's Ministry of Tourism**, 13-T/U College Rd, Commercial Area, Markaz F-7. Expect to wait at least two weeks for the permit, if they answer. Budget for an extra Rs65,000 fee if you plan to climb K2 (a bargain compared with the $60,000 Everest permit price).

Transport

● **Vans and buses** These ply the Karakoram and the Skardu-Gilgit road. Most depart early (ie 5-6 am) and leave less frequently as the morning progresses. Theoretically, it is possible to stand on the side of the road and flag down transportation, but much of it (the vans especially) tend to fill quickly.

● **Jeeps** Rougher roads are served by cargo jeeps. The baggage is arranged with ropes so that the area of carrying space is maximised, allowing as many as a dozen passengers to ride in the open air. Don't carry anything too fragile to sit on, and be prepared for changeable weather; even in

---

❑ Essential information for travellers – Karakoram Area

● **Health factors** No malaria risk since the area is too high. Around Hunza the water, boiled or not, swirls with mica particles which should be left to settle but are not in themselves dangerous. Beware of altitude sickness.

● **Typical traveller destinations** Gilgit, Karimabad (Hunza), Kunjerab Pass, Kalash Valleys.

● **Highlights** All of the above. Also trekking, remote lakes and villages.

● **When to go** You won't have to worry about rain in the Karakoram area – there isn't much. But if you are going at any other time than between June and August (the high season) you might have to worry about the cold. During spring (late March-May), and autumn (September-November) it is warm in the sun, but cool in the shade, and nights are freezing. During mid-winter it is bearable out in the sunshine, but the air temperature is cold all day long.

Around mid-October the leaves change colour in the Hunza valley. Beautiful!

● **Pulse of the country** Drying apricots on flat-roofed hovels in mountain villages.

● **Key tips** There is nowhere in Xinjiang or Western China to get a visa. Almaty, Tashkent, and Beijing are the nearest embassies if you're entering from the north. It is possible to cross to/from China year round, though in the winter you might have to wait for a day or two while they clear snow; the through buses stop running but you can take a land cruiser.

● **Languages** Burashki around Hunza, Kowar in Chitral, Balti around Skardu, Kalasha in the Kalash Valleys.

mid-summer we had to endure a brief, cold thunderstorm on the Gilgit-Chitral 'road'.

A jeep with driver can be rented in the northern areas for Rs800 to Rs1300 a day, depending on a complicated formula involving the distance you intend to travel, the number of people, and, of course, your bargaining power. We recommend inspecting the jeep and meeting the driver before agreeing to anything.

● **Air** The Islamabad-Gilgit flight is one of the most spectacular in the world and at $23 one way for the hour's flight you can't beat the price. In theory there are three flights per day; however the entire valley must be cloud-free before the plane will take off. On a good day, the first two flights leave, on a bad day they are all grounded. The flights are so unpredictable that Pakistan Airlines (PIA) will only sell you a standby ticket. The day before the flight you are required to check with the PIA office to see if you have a seat. The numerous flight cancellations, the heavy demand and the size of the plane (often seats have to be left empty for weight reasons) mean there is a good chance you won't be able to get on.

The standard trick for getting on a full flight is going to the PTDC office and getting a specially reserved 'tourist seat'. This works occasionally but is far from certain. For those who want to avoid the 15-hour bus to/from Rawalpindi and are frustrated at being continuously told to come back to the PIA office the next day, we have two suggestions: **1)** Show up at the airport with your standby ticket. We managed to get on a flight which the PIA office said was full (although that was in October, and not during the high season). **2)** Fly to Skardu which is a hair-raisingly beautiful seven-hour bus ride from Gilgit (though the town itself isn't so nice). Skardu airport is bigger (and so is the plane serving it) though there are fewer flights.

● **Hitching** Traffic tends to be light and overcrowded so hitching is not easy. Of the two longer rides that we hitched (both in jeeps), one was free and the other cost considerably more than the bus. Both resulted in tea and hospitality.

Accommodation

Almost any village on a road will have a cheap guest house; exceptions are noted on the map. In the warmest and busiest time of year (July-September), a tent can assure you of a place to stay (some guesthouses will let you pitch a tent in their courtyard for a nominal fee). Guesthouses are stocked with blankets but if you don't have your own sleeping bag you will probably have to sleep in all your clothes in winter.

You can sleep in the dramatic *Eagle's Nest* overlooking Hunza by arrangement with the owner of the Hisar Inn, Altit.

Sometimes, even after a day or two in the wilderness, you can come across shepherds' huts or a government lodge beside some isolated mountain lake. However, longer hikes pass through areas inhabited

---

❏ Events and festivals in the Karakoram area

Event	Place	Usual time	What happens
Nauroze	Gilgit	21-23 March	Famous for polo games. Also football, volleyball, hockey matches and folk dancing.
Joshi (or Chilimjusht)	Kalash Valleys	14-15 May	Celebrates the arrival of spring. Folk dances and music
Shandur Polo Tournament	Shandur Pass	24-28 July	Polo (see below).
Utchal	Chitral	15-16 July	Harvest festival, celebrated by Kalash people.
Phool	Kalash Valleys	20-25 Sep	Festival of grapes and walnuts.
Chowas	Kalash Valleys	18-21 Oct	Celebrates first snow fall.

only by sheep and yeti so you'll really need a tent to go trekking. There's nowhere to rent camping equipment in the region.

Food and drink

Apricot soup is a speciality of the Hunza area and is believed to be a reason why the natives of that valley have one of the highest life expectancy rates in the world.

Arak is deservedly illegal; it's 70% alcohol and the rest is probably methanol as it is said to make habitual drinkers go blind. Hunza wine's technical illegality is less deserved. There are two kinds; mulberry and grape based. Neither bears much resemblance to Bordeaux; both are sweet and pricey. But somehow furtive attempts to find a supplier are part of the delight.

Staying in touch

Gilgit is the most reliable place to send or receive mail and almost the only place to make telephone calls.

Activities

● **Trekking** The Karakoram area is not set up for spontaneous organised trekking in the way Nepal is. There are no tea-houses, no well marked routes and fewer travellers, all of which make a trek into the Karakoram hinterlands a real adventure. The easiest, but most expensive, way to do a trek is to go through a trekking company. It is possible to organise treks individually by hiring your own porters and equipment, and stocking up with your own food before leaving, but even this option is likely to cost you $40-50 a day. Perhaps the best, long trek is the three-week Hushe-Sigar route to the K2 base camp. If you want to get out into the mountains there are many one and two-day walks. The Ultar glacier walk from Karimabad is especially recommended; it's possible to do in one long day or you can spend the night in shepherds' huts halfway. Some walking possibilities are marked on the maps, though a specialised guidebook is recommended for any trekking, if only for the maps.

The travellers' notebook at the Hisar Inn, Altit has many trekking suggestions.

Trekking agencies worth trying include: **Concordia Tours and Trekking Service** (☎ 051-220338, fax 051-220849), 35 Chughtai Plaza, First Mezz, West Blue Area, Islamabad; **Hindukush Trails** (☎ 051-821576, fax 051-215031), House No 37, Street 28, F-6/1, Islamabad; **Pamir Tours** (☎ 572-3939, fax 572-2525), PO Box 545, Airport Road, Gilgit.

● **Polo** The people of the Karakoram will tell you that polo originated there; in fact, it is more likely that it was brought from Tibet by the Mongols (*polo* means 'ball' in Tibetan). Today, though, polo is *the* sport of the Karakoram. Gilgit, Chitral, Skardu, and the Shandur Pass have the major polo grounds (the one at Shandur is reputed to be the highest in the world). Periodic tournaments are held throughout the year.

● **Whitewater rafting** Gilgit is the centre for rafting agencies; half-day trips cost $25. Open rivers for rafting are the Indus (Jaglot to Thakor), Kunhar (Naran to Kaghan), Chitral (Dir to Batkhela), and Hunza (Aliabad to Gilgit).

Further information

● **Books and maps** If you're just passing through, there's basic Karakoram information in Lonely Planet's *China, Pakistan,* and *Central Asia* guides and in Cadogan's *Central Asia* book. All of these are available at the un-named bookshop in Karimabad (Hunza), diagonally across from the Tourist Complaints Office. More detailed regional guides are John King's *Karakoram Highway* (Lonely Planet) and Isobel Shore's *Pakistan Trekking Handbook*. Both have useful maps. Four 1:200,000 trekking maps of the region are published by West Col (UK). The PTDC free map of the area is not very accurate.

If you have no maps or guides whatever, it's easy enough to glean information from other travellers in Karimabad. The Hisar Inn in nearby Altit has a travellers' tip book with many local suggestions for visits and day hikes and the owner is helpful and knowledgeable. Interesting background reading includes Patrick French's *Younghusband* biography.

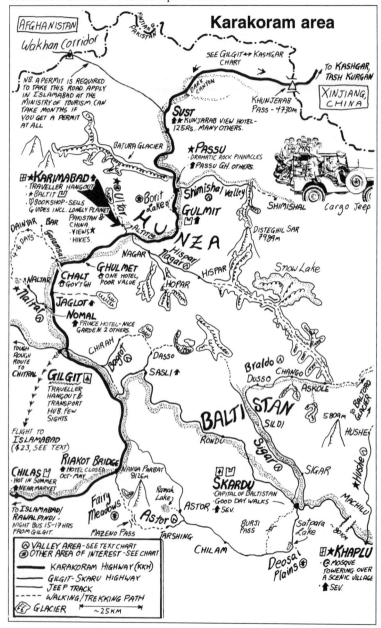

Karakoram area

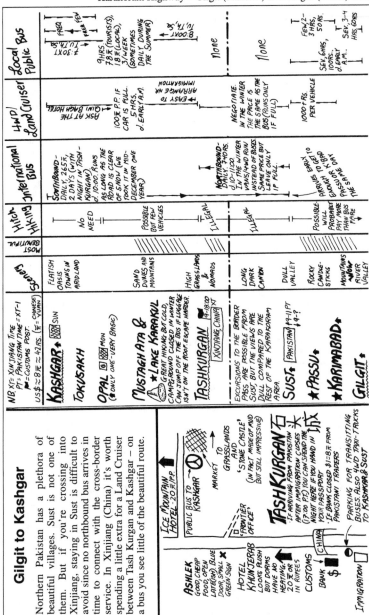

Gilgit to Kashgar

Northern Pakistan has a plethora of beautiful villages. Sust is not one of them. But if you're crossing into Xinjiang, staying in Sust is difficult to avoid since no northbound bus arrives in time to connect with the cross-border service. In Xinjiang (China) it's worth spending a little extra for a Land Cruiser between Tash Kurgan and Kashgar – on a bus you see little of the beautiful route.

NB: XT = XINJIANG TIME = XT-1
PT = PAKISTAN TIME = XT-1
M = CUSTOMS POST.
US$ ≈ 8元 ≈ 42 RS. (元 = CHINESE YUAN)

	Scenery	Most Beautiful	Hitch Hiking	International Bus	4WD Land Cruiser	Local Public Bus
KASHGAR ☀ SUN	FLATISH OASIS TOWNS IN ARID LAND			SOUTHBOUND – DAILY, 2 DAYS (WITH NIGHT IN TASH-KURGAN) d. 10.00. RUNS AS LONG AS THE ROAD IS CLEAR OF SNOW (WE TOOK IT IN MID-DECEMBER ONE YEAR)	ASK AT THE QINI BAGH HOTEL	FREE FEW / FREE FEW / FREE / TU.TH.SA. 1元:30 XT 9 HRS. 78元 (TOURISTS), 18元 (LOCAL), 3/WEEK (SOMETIMES DAILY DURING THE SUMMER)
TOKUSAKH			NO NEED			
OPAL ◑ MON (● ONLY ONE – VERY BASIC)						
MUSTAGH ATA & ★LAKE KARAKUL ≈1800 GREAT HIKING BUT COLD. CAMPGROUND CLOSED IN WINTER CAN JUMP OFF THE BUS IF LUGGAGE ISN'T ON THE ROOF. ESCAPE HARDER.	SAND DUNES AND MOUNTAINS		POSSIBLE BUT FEW VEHICLES		100元 P.P. IF CAR IS FULL. d. EARLY A.M.	
TASHKURGAN XINJIANG CHINA XT	HIGH GRASSLANDS & NOMADS		ILLEGAL	NORTHBOUND– DAILY, 9 HRS. d. 10-11.00. IN THE WINTER VANS/4WD RUN INSTEAD OF BUSES. SAME PRICE BUT LEAVE ONLY IF FULL.	EASY TO ARRANGE NR IMMIGRATION 5 HRS. d. EARLY A.M.	none
EXCURSIONS TO THE BORDER PASS ARE POSSIBLE FROM SUST, BUT THE VIEWS ARE DULL COMPARED TO THE REST OF THE KARAKORAM	LONG DARK CANYON		ILLEGAL	ARRIVES EARLY ENOUGH K'BAD PASSUR DAY	NEGOTIATE. IN THE WINTER THE PRICE IS THE SAME AS THE BUS (RUNS ONLY IF FULL)	none
SUST PAKISTAN 元4-11 PT 元4-?	DULL VALLEY		POSSIBLE – WILL PROBABLY PAY MORE THAN BUS FARE		1000+RS. PER VEHICLE	FEW 2-3 HRS, SO.R.
★PASSU	ROCKY CANDLE-STICKS					SEV. 6 HRS, 100 RS. d. EARLY A.M.
★KARIMABAD	MOUNTAINS NOW RIVER VALLEY					SEV. 3-4 HRS. GO R.S.
GILGIT ★						

ICE MOUNTAIN HOTEL 20元/P.P.

PUBLIC BUS TO KASHGAR →

MARKET → GRASSLANDS AND 'STONE CASTLE' (IN FACT MADE OF MUD BUT STILL IMPRESSIVE)

"FRONTIER OFFICE"

TASHKURGAN 喀 什

· IF ARRIVING FROM PAKISTAN AFTER IMMIGRATION CLOSES (17.00 PT) YOU CAN SPEND THE NIGHT HERE IF YOU HAND IN YOUR PASSPORT
· IF BANK CLOSED $1=8元 FROM PAKISTANI TRADERS

PARKING FOR TRANSITING BUSES. ALSO 4WD TAXI-TRUCKS TO KASHGAR & SUST

ASHLEK GOOD, CHEAP FOOD, OPEN LATE(ISH) BLUE DOOR SMALL GREEN SIGN ✗

HOTEL KHUNJERAB LOOKS PLUSH BUT DORMS HAVE NO HEATING. 20元 OR IN RUPEES

CUSTOMS 💲

CHINA

BANK 💲

IMMIGRATION

Selected valleys and other areas off the Karakoram Highway

Valley or area	What's there	Transport	Accommodation away from KKH	Equipment/ requirements
Shim-shal Valley	Glaciers. Steep mountain walks. Yak farming lands.	Pasu to Shimishal 70km. We found no public transport; hired jeeps can go part way if road OK.	Three new guest houses in Shimishal.	A jeep if going for day/night (hire in Passu). Area beyond Shimishal is restricted – treks require local guide.
Borit Lake	A Gulmit-Passu hike passing Borit Lake and three vast glaciers (not visible from KKH). Between Borit Lake and KKH is a long suspension bridge.	Passu and Gulmit are both on the KKH and have frequent transport. Borit Lake is a 4-5hr walk from Gulmit, 2-3 hrs from Passu.	A guesthouse and campground at Borit Lake. It is possible to walk Gulmit-Passu in a long day, but more relaxing to stay here.	No tent needed if staying at Borit Lake. A map is useful but guest houses in Passu have info and friendly locals show travellers the way.
Ultar Glacier	Ultar glacier and dry mountain landscape. Meadows with shepherd huts lay conveniently half-way between Karimabad and the glacier.	Wagons go direct Karimabad-Gilgit early a.m. Many vans go to/past the Karimabad turnoff, from which K'bad is a 40 min walk or easy hitch. Ultar glacier is a 1-2 day walk.	No guesthouses but many good campsites. The shepherds reportedly allow travellers to stay in their huts, but they were not to be found when we went in October.	A tent is needed to walk all the way to the Ultar Glacier. Without a tent, it is still worth hiking as far as the shepherd huts and returning to K'bad the same day.
Nagar/ Hispar Valley	Glaciers. Pastures and farming away from the road.	Jeep to/from Gilgit for Rs1200. One wagon/day Gilgit-Hopar.	Very basic guest house and tent pitching area in Hopar.	Nothing if staying in Hopar.
★ **Naltar Valley**	Forest in south part of valley, alpine scenery in north. Pudra Lake 3-4 hrs walk from Naltar.	A seat on Gilgit-Nomal jeeps for around Rs70. Also occasional buses.	Government Guest House in Naltar (pre-book in Gilgit).	Guide suggested for Nomal-Chalt walk, though locals helpful in giving directions.
Sigar/ Braldo Valleys	Many glaciers and lakes.	Several jeeps/day run Skardu-Sigar (1hr). A few go all the way to Askole.	Dusso and Sigar have government guest-houses (pre-book in Skardu).	Guides, porters and some mountaineering experience for Hispar-Askole glacier walk.

Valley or area	What's there	Transport	Accommodation away from KKH	Equipment/ requirements
Bagrot Valley	Dry and rugged with excellent glacier views. Good for walking. Few tourists despite proximity to Gilgit.	Cargo jeeps run Gilgit- Chirah (3-4 hrs.) There are also supposed to be buses but we didn't find any.	The 'Inspection Bungalow' in Chirah (pre-book in Gilgit).	A guide is strongly recommended if walking beyond Chirah (ie to Dusso/Sasli).
Deosai Plains	Satpara Lake is famous for its fishing. Beyond the lake, the Deosai Plains are barren, snowy and windy.	Jeeps freq run Skardu-Satpara Lake, but it is more pleasant to walk (c2½ hrs). Jeeps rarely go as far as Chilam.	Satpara Lake has a cheap guesthouse. No accommodation beyond.	Nothing for the walk to Satpara. A guide for the technical trek via the Burji Pass (arrange in Skardu).
★ **Hushe Valley**	Snow-capped peaks, especially the photogenic Mt Mashbran.	Jeeps run Khaplu-Hushe surprisingly frequently (2½ hrs). Some jeeps run Skardu-Hushe via Khaplu (6½ hrs, dep early am).	Hushe has several cheap guesthouses.	Nothing for day walks. A good map and/or guide for longer treks. Guides can be arranged in Hushe.
★ **Astor Valley**	Some green fields surrounded by towering peaks. Lake Ramah is a 3hr walk through pine forests from Astor.	Gilgit-Astor jeeps cRs70. 4WD Jaglot-Astor vans cRs50. Astor-Tarshing jeeps Rs100-300. Tarshing-Astor. Rs3000 for hired jeep from Gilgit.	Three cheap GHs in Astor. A spectacularly situated gov't RH near Ramah Lake (book in Gilgit). Basic seasonal hotel in Tarshing.	No guide or tent for walking to Ramah Lake (with pre-booked hotel room). Guides recommended for other treks.
Fairy Meadows	Sound-of-Music-esque plateau. Sadly, many travellers find the locals unfriendly.	Charter jeeps from Gilgit are possible but expensive. Best to take a bus (2-3hrs, Rs40) to Riakot Bridge and walk 2-3 hrs.	A campground at the meadows rents tents and sleeping bags (for a steep Rs150).	Nothing during summer when campground is open. The hike to Tarshing requires guide and trekking experience.

GILGIT ~5MINS→
THE LARGEST TOWN OF THE KARAKORAM AREA. IT'S A GOOD PLACE TO STOCK UP ON SUPPLIES AND GET INFORMATION FROM OTHER TRAVELLERS. NICE HIKES IN SURROUNDING VILLAGES.

TO CHITRAL
POLO FIELD
ARMY BARRACKS
GOV'T BUSES
COMPANIES SELLING BUS TICKETS TO ISLAMABAD
Babar
HUNZA INN
Airport Road
P.I.A.
~1KM TO AIRPORT
VANS TO SUST KARIMABAD
NAPWD NORTHERN AREA PUBLIC WORKS DEPT. TO BOOK GOV'T GHS (SEE CHART)
★MADINA GH TRAVELLER HANG-OUT. MESSAGE BOARD & COURTYARD CAFÉ

India

India. There's nowhere quite like it. It's really more a continent than a country with everything from the high Himalaya to the deserts of Rajasthan, wonderful backwater trips in Kerala to some of Asia's best dive sites (the Andamans).

There are more sights to see than you could hope to see, but it's the mere being there that is most memorable. For many travellers India is both the high point and the low point of a trip to Asia. Nowhere in the world is so simultaneously fascinating and frustrating, beautiful and repulsive, civilised yet offensive, charming and repulsive. You'll love and hate it.

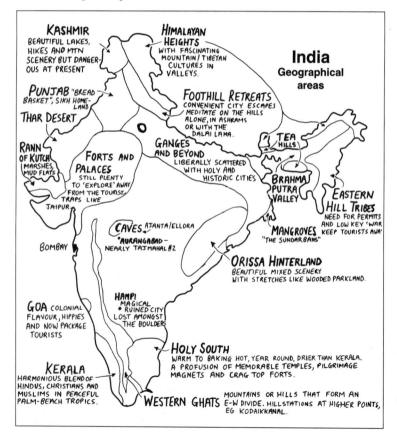

PRACTICAL INFORMATION
Visa and formalities

● **Visa strategy** It's worth applying in your home country, where feasible, as otherwise visa applications are referred back to the embassy in your home nation anyway, and you have to both wait and pay for the fax/telex charges. Supposedly your background will be checked, though in reality it seems to be more of an annoying formality. Visa costs vary greatly with nationality.

● **Extensions** The only visas that can be extended are 6-month tourist visas. Note that 6-month visas run from **date of issue** not from the date you enter the country. Extensions 16 days to three months cost around Rs700.

● **Permits** Restricted Area Permits are required for the following states in India. **Sikkim** (15 days – get it in Siliguri at the SNT bus stand). **Andaman Islands** (30 days, issued at the airport if flying in, if coming by boat you need to get it in advance from the Foreigners' Registration Offices (FRO) in Madras or Calcutta). **North East Region** (no permits now needed for Assam, Tripura or Meghalaya but you still need one for Manipur; permits are also required for Arunachal Pradesh, Mizoram and Nagaland but your chances of getting one are greater if you're on a tour, or if you have an invitation to stay from someone. In theory permits should give you 10 days but they are not easy to get, Nagaland in particular.

Money

Thomas Cook travellers' cheques are a good brand to carry in India as they have numerous branches and you won't pay a commission charge. Amex will reconvert up to $500 if you have an Amex card and a plane/bus ticket out of the country within 48 hours.

Having money sent to India is now much easier than in years past. Money can be wired to Western Union almost instantly and, best of all (!), the person who sends the money also pays the wire charge (usually $30, but it depends on the country).

Credit cards are quite widely used in India now and cash advances on a MasterCard or Visa card easy to arrange.

Transport

● **Air** There are 25% discounts available for foreign passengers aged 12-30. If you are going to fly on a couple of internal routes, look into the relative cost of getting a multi-stop pass instead, which can sometimes prove cheaper. These cost $300 for a week's unlimited travel in one of four sectors (north, south, east or west). An all-India pass costs $500 for two weeks or $750 for three weeks.

● **Bus** Typically, buses in India are extremely uncomfortable, and move really slowly. They're also very cheap. Take care if you sit on the roof (exhilarating if you're travelling in the mountains) as passengers are occasionally knocked off by low branches.

❑ **W&M's country ratings – India**

● **Expense $** As little as $6/day on rock-bottom budget possible in most of India – major cities, especially Bombay, are more

● **Value for money** ✔✔✔✔ Transport excellent value; hotels good though takes shopping around.

● **English spoken** ✔✔✔✔ A legacy of the colonial era.

● **Getting around** ✔✔✔✔ While transport goes everywhere, there's often more than one bus/train station but locals generally helpful.

● **Woman alone** ✔✔ Constant over-attention and occasional groping. Shout '*besharam*' ('pervert') and consider hitting out! Little real physical threat according to our correspondents.

● **For vegetarians** ✔✔✔✔✔ Plenty of choice, especially in South. Jains and some Hindus are vegetarian. Hindus and Sikhs eat no beef.

● **Train** British rule left India criss crossed with railways in all but the most mountainous of regions. Trains remain the most comfortable and reliable way to travel around the country. Timetables are commonly available, but can be confusing to use. Buy a copy of *Trains at a Glance* (Rs15), available at station book shops. It lists the main trains in the country. There's also the more comprehensive but frequently unavailable *Indian Bradshaw* which lists all trains in India.

India used to be known for its steam trains but most have now been retired, the

---

❏ Geo-political information – India

Population: 967 million (1997), 935m (1993), 575m 1973.

Area: 2,973,000 sq km.

Capital: New Delhi (7.2 million).

Other major cities: Bombay (9.9 million), Calcutta (4.4m), Madras (3.8m), Bangalore (3.3m), Hyderabad (3.1m), Ahmedabad (3m), Kanpur (1.9m), Nagpur, Pune, Lucknow (1.6m), Surat, Jaipur (1.5m), Indore, Bhopal, Baroda, Ludiana, Kalyan (1m+). If including the surrounding conurbations Cochin, Coimbatore, Madurai, Patna, Varanasi and Visakhapatnam all pass 1m, while Greater Bombay is 12.6m.

GNP per capita: $310 (1994), $300 (1988).

Currency history: Rupee/US$1 – Feb 1998: Rs38.3, July 1996: 35.4, Jan 1996: 35.77, July 1995: 31.36, Jan 1995: 31.40, Jan 1994: 31.37, Dec 1991: 25.8, 1986: 13.1, 1976: 9.0.

Major exports/economy: Cotton fabrics, tea, jute, coffee, spices, cashew nuts, gems, engineering, garments. 70% agricultural. Reforms since 1991 deregulating the economy have attracted $10 billion in investment.

Official language: Hindi (spoken by 20%), English ('associate language'), 17 other languages are recognised in the constitution.

Religious mix: Hindu (80%), 11% Muslim, Christian (4% – more than half Catholic), Sikh (2%), Buddhist (0.7%), Jain (0.5% ie 3.2m), Zoroastrian (120,000).

Landmarks of national history: **1500-1200BC**: The Vedas, the Hindu sacred scriptures were written. **1500-200BC**: Aryan invaders gained control of northern India. Dravidians pushed south. **232BC**: Death of Ashoka led to collapse of Mauryan Empire. **850AD**: Cholas came to power in Southern India. **1527-1757**: Mughal period – six great emperors including Shah Jahan who built the Taj Mahal in memory of his wife. **1612**: The British established the first of many trading posts in Gujarat. **1857**: Indian Mutiny (northern India only), **1915**: Mohandas Gandhi returned from S Africa and started non-cooperation, non-violence movement for independence. **1919**: Massacre at Amritsar. **14 Aug 1947**: Independence, Jawaharlal Nehru became India's first prime minister, thousands killed as Muslims moved to Pakistan and Hindus and Sikhs to India. **30 Jan 1948**: Gandhi assassinated by a Hindu fanatic. **1966**: Indira Gandhi (Nehru's daughter) became first female prime minister. **31 Oct 1984**: Assassinated by her Sikh bodyguards, succeeded by her son Rajiv. **21 May 1991**: Rajiv also assassinated, by a terrorist bomb.

Leaders: President Shankar Dayal Sharma, but political power normally wielded by Prime Minister. At the time of writing (February 1998) general election in progress.

Pressing political issues: Hung parliaments. Independence movement/terrorist actions in Kashmir. Border disputes with Pakistan. Continued refusal to sign nuclear non-proliferation treaty causes some tension with USA.

'toy train' that climbs to Darjeeling being an exception. For the last few years the country has been overhauling the rail system and converting most metre gauge and narrow gauge lines to broad gauge. There's a brand new line running down the west coast from Bombay through Goa to Mangalore – the Konkan Railway – which opened in 1997. Theoretically this should make getting to Goa much easier but the line is subject to closure as hastily built embankments collapse onto the track in the monsoon season.

Forget the Indrail Pass. It's a waste of

❑ Essential information for travellers – India

● **Visa** Required by all, easy to obtain in your home country, easy but takes time from abroad. Six-month multi-entry is possible but not from all embassies. Prices vary with issuing office and nationality.

● **Currency** Indian Rupee (=100paise). US$1=Rs38.3.

● **Time zone** $5\frac{1}{2}$ hours ahead of GMT (2hrs ahead of Iran, 1hr ahead of Afghanistan and Pakistan, 1hr behind Sri Lanka, $\frac{1}{2}$ hr behind Bangladesh, $\frac{1}{4}$ hr behind Nepal).

● **Religious tone** The majority are Hindus but most of the world's religions are represented here bringing tensions in many areas. Sensitivity is important.

● **Health factors** Malaria is a risk at altitudes below 2000 metres – much of the country. Home of Delhi Belly – the tap water is unsafe to drink.

● **Special dangers** Avoid Kashmir. Sensory overload.

● **Social conventions** Sikhs use 'Singh' at the end of their name, though not all 'Singh's are Sikhs.

India is not friendly to left-handers. Use right hand for greeting and eating (and everything else public).

The head wobble, which would either indicate 'I don't know' or a muscle problem in the West, means 'yes' in India.

Some Hindus and Sikhs don't allow leather inside temples. .

● **Typical traveller destinations** Tourist Triangle (Agra, Delhi, Jaipur), Hippy Trail (Goa, Pushkar, Manali), Varanasi, Hampi, Kerala.

● **Highlights** Numerous. In addition to the places mentioned in typical traveller destinations above: the temples of Khajuraho, the Taj Mahal (of course), the Andaman Islands, Kanha National Park (Madhya Pradesh), Madhu (Madhya Pradesh), Ladakh, camel safaris from Jaisalmer, Pondicherry.

● **When to go** For the north, late October to early March is best. The size of the country means there is no one ideal time. February to May is generally hot (particularly in southern India); the monsoon season starts in the south in June and affects most of the country until October. November to February are the busiest tourist months though in the far north it gets very cold.

● **Pulse of the country** Varanasi (India is too large and diverse to be captured in a single place—but Varanasi comes closest).

● **Key tips** Take a deep breath, stay calm. Get a multiple entry visa so you can 'escape' to Nepal for a 'rest'

There are too many brilliant sites to attempt too see them all. More than anywhere, India is a place where slowing your pace will pay dividends, and you'll get to see Indians who are not just after your rupees when they ask your 'good name'. Try taking a meditative spiritual retreat in one of the many ashrams, or monasteries.

Keep abreast of the security situation in the places you intend to visit.

money. For short journeys it's no problem travelling 2nd class unreserved. For overnight journeys it's best to have a reserved 2nd class berth.

● **Boat** The most popular boating trips for foreigners in India are the journeys made through the backwaters of Kerala. There's a catamaran service between Bombay and Goa but it's not cheap (from Rs1050). You're better off going by train.

● **Hitching** Not easy and since public transport is so cheap you wouldn't need to hitch except perhaps on some mountain routes. Most drivers, particularly truck drivers, may expect some kind of payment.

● **Bicycle** You can rent bikes almost anywhere for Rs3-5 per hour.

● **Motorbike** The Enfield India is an old British design dating back almost 50 years. It's still produced at the factory just outside Madras. You can rent one of these heavy 350cc or 500cc machines for around Rs300 per day. Smaller bikes (Honda 100 scooters) cost less than this and are easier to ride. If you want to buy your own Enfield it'll cost you around Rs60,000.

❏ Festivals in India

Because of its immense size and diversity, India has a greater selection of festivals and special occasions than almost any other country. Some which occur on a regular basis include:

Event	Place	Usual time	What happens
Kite Festival	Ahmedabad	~13 Jan	3 days of kite flying; markets.
Desert Festival	Jaisalmer, Raj.	~13 Feb	Touristy but interesting camel sports, folk dancing
Khajuraho Festival	Khajuraho.	~12 Mar	6 days of dancers from all over India
Pooram	Trichur, Kerala	3rd wk Apr	Elephants carrying priest and figures of the deities parade to celebrate coming monsoon.
Hemis Festival	Hemis, Ladakh	June	3 day Buddhist festival at cliff-side monastery.
Rath Yatra	Puri, Orissa	June-July	A week of Hindu ceremonies draws over/million devotees. The god Jagannath is pulled through the streets on an enormous chariot.
Onam Festival	Alleppey	2nd Sat in Aug	Water events takes place all over Kerala to celebrate the harvests. Snake Boat Race in Alleppey is the most popular.
Dussehra	Kulu, H.P.*	October	Hindu celebration of Rama's victory over Ravanna. Dancing and a parade. The Kulu Valley version includes a large market.
Camel Fair	Pushkar, Raj.	Oct-Nov	Touristy camel market. Interesting, but most people prefer Pushkar when the fair's not on.

* Our recommendation for the best place to be for Dussehra, although it's celebrated elsewhere in India.

Accommodation

Indians travel a lot for business and pilgrimage, so almost everywhere you go is likely to have a good range of cheaper places. Round the bus station and railway station is always a good place to look, although it's best to walk a few streets back to the quieter, cheaper places. In tourist areas, there are likely to be dormitory rooms for less than US$1 per bed. Some can be distinctly grotty: talk to fellow travellers, of whom there are many, to get recent recommendations.

You can even stay at railway stations. Most have 'retiring rooms' and the charge for a dorm bed can be as little as Rs30. If you need a break from the heat, they usually also have a few air-con rooms that can be good value. There are even retiring rooms at certain airports which can be a bargain compared with the usual high prices charged at airport hotels.

Some temples and monastery complexes welcome guests for a donation, (the Golden Temple at Amritsar, for example). Off the beaten track, villages with no hotels are fortunately the very places you're most likely to rediscover the great Indian hospitality.

If you're high-rolling, you can stay in old palaces in Rajasthan (for less than an average five-star hotel in Europe – although prices of these places have risen considerably in the last few years). More affordable are the *havelis* (old merchants' houses in Rajasthan).

Cheap hotel doors have latches that padlock closed. Bring your own lock for added security.

Food and drink

Indian food is probably already familiar, especially to Brits. In India you may find it more spicy than you're used to in restaurants at home, and street snacks can really burn. Things spice up even more as you head south where the cuisine is distinctly different and includes the marvellous *masala dosa* – a huge crispy rice pancake filled with curried vegetables. Note that 'curry' is a term invented by the British for any 'native', cumin influenced food rather than a term in general use within local cuisine.

Shopping

There's an infinite variety here but bargain, bargain, bargain – never accept the first price! Most of the tourist areas are now packed with Kashmiri traders plying their attractive papier maché wares and carpets.

When the heavy sales pitch gets too much, and you just want to browse unpestered, visit one of the state emporiums – each state sells its own handicrafts through a number of branches in the main cities. The Cottage Emporium in New Delhi is not the cheapest place to buy clothes and handicrafts, but it has a huge selection from all over India.

Staying in touch

● **Mail and fax** Post restante is reliable in India and it's also cheaper to send home packages from India than from Nepal, and safer than from Bangladesh. (For example, airmail to France: 8kg Rs2500, 10kg Rs3000; seamail to the USA/UK: 5kg Rs917/901, 10kg Rs1561/1181). Packages must be sewn in a white cloth, with the seams sealed in wax. Have this done by one of the vendors near the PO entrance.

Faxing from India is usually simple, with lots of places offering the service.

● **Phone** Example telephone rates from a guest house: to Europe, Oceana, Asia (ex Nepal): Rs75/min; to North America: Rs100/min, to Nepal Rs60/min.

International country code: +91. New Delhi: 11, Agra: 562, Bombay: 222, Calcutta: 33, Goa: 832, Varanasi: 542, Udaipur: 294.

Further information

● **Maps** Good maps (when available) at Survey of India office in New Delhi. See the New Delhi map for details.

● **Information offices** As well as the Government of India tourism offices to be found in all major cities, there are also state tourism departments, which also have offices. Neither is of great use to the traveller, though. If you want to know a bus or train time it's much better to ask a shopkeeper or at the station itself.

● **Books** When travellers in India talk about 'the book' they mean the Lonely Planet *India* guide. It is popular for a reason—it is an excellent book, full of maps and info even on some of the more obscure places. The best reason not to get one is that everyone else has one. Alternatives include the Rough Guide, which has more detail than Lonely Planet but covers fewer places. Footprint's *India Handbook* is preferred by most bikers, as it describes many of the road conditions. It is, for better or worse, very objective. Its route format makes it occasionally difficult to use, though it is thoroughly indexed. The Cadogan guide is also in a route format, and has very extensive transportation information.

Used guidebooks, and certainly new ones, to Nepal, Thailand, Bangladesh and China are available in major cities and tourist centres. Though there is no law forbidden the sale of guidebooks on Pakistan, one bookseller told us it would 'cause great trouble' if he did. Books for larger regions that include Pakistan (eg. Lonely Planet's *West Asia*) are sometimes sold.

For general books about India the reading list is endless. One good thing is that almost everything you'd want to read is available in India at prices far lower than in the West. Old favourites include *A Passage to India* by EM Forster, and Paul Scott's atmospheric recreation of the last days of the British Raj – *The Raj Quartet*. Vikram Seth's *A Suitable Boy* is another blockbuster that will help even the longest train journey speed by. *City of Djinns* by William Dalrymple is a highly readable book about Delhi and the year the author spent there.

● **Contacts** American Express has offices in Calcutta (21 Old Court House St; PO Box 2311; 700001, ☎ 2488 570), Goa (c/o Menezes Air Travel; Tua De Ourem; PO Box 12 and 13; 403011, ☎ 43261), New Delhi (Wenger House; A Block; Connaught Place; 110001,☎ 332 4119, fax 332-3879).

Ashoka Tour & Travels (☎ 332-5035) 305, 3rd floor, New Delhi House, Barakhamba Road New Delhi, runs several tours, including a New Delhi day tour and Bhutan tour.

If you're interested in doing voluntary work, it's best to contact a charity before you come to India. You could also try the Joint Assistance Centre (☎ 8924-51122) 20/14 Urban Bank St, Yellamanchili, 531055, Andhra Pradesh.

For Hindi language courses, Landour Language School (☎/fax 0135-63917) Landour, Mussoorie, UP 248179 has been recommended.

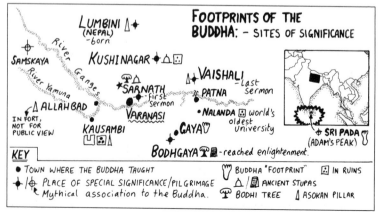

❑ Meeting the locals

● Language

There's no single Indian language but over 1500 different languages and dialects spoken in the country. Eighteen of these are officially recognised, and among them Hindi is the most important, and spoken by about a fifth of the population. It's really the language of the north, though. More people speak Telugu and Tamil, the main languages of the south. As a legacy of the time the British spent here, English is also widely spoken.

Some Hindi phrases:

Greeting – *Namaste* (to Hindu), *salam alekum* (Muslim), *sut sree ahkal* (Sikh)

How are you? – *Aap kaiseh haan*

Thank you – *Danybaad*

How much is it? -*Kitnee paisa*

On my last day here I'll do my shopping – *Akeeree deen kahring-geh* (good way to get rid of touts/salesmen)

You look like a donkey with that moustache (humorous insult, good way to embarrass lecherous men...and often true.)

Ap mooch meh gadeh lag teh hai

Peace, chill, take it easy — *Shanti*

● Script

VOWELS   Form #1 → at start of syllable. #2 → after consonant.

	A	Ā	E	Ē	I	Ī	I	Ī	O	Ō	U	Ū	ə	Ə̄
#1	ऋ	ऋा	ए	ऐ	ऋ	ऋ	इ	ई	ओ	औ	उ	ऊ	ऌ	ॡ
#2	ा	ँ	ँ	ि	ी	f	ी	ो	ौ	ु	ू	ृ	ॄ	

CONSONANTS — I.E, A CONSONANT IS ASSUMED TO BE FOLLOWED BY "A" UNLESS THERE'S ANOTHER VOWEL MARKER.

B	Bh	Ch	Chh	D	Ḍ	Dh	Ḍh	F/Ph	G	Gh	H	Ḥ	J
ब	भ	च	छ	द	ड	ध	ढ	फ	ग	घ	ह	:	ज

Jh	K	Kh	L	M	Ṃ	N	Ṇ	Ṅ	Ny	P	R	S	Ṣ	Tch
झ	क	ख	ल	म	•	न	ण	ङ	ञ	प	र	श	ष	

RARELY USED

T	Ṭ	Th	Ṭh	V	Y
त	ट	थ	ठ	व	य

● Some topics for conversation:
Politics. Cricket – you'll need to know the names of every member of your country's team, though. Movies – famous actors: female: Madhuri Dinth; male: Anil Kapoor, Sharuk Khan.

Hinduism

Hinduism is the result of a fusion of two ancient cultures from along the Indus River – the indigenous Dasa and the Aryan that invaded them around 1800BCE. The Aryans were a fair skinned, Greek and Persian influenced people; they were nomadic and left few remains of their culture. The Dasa were dark skinned, Eastern influenced, and, judging from the ruins of their cities at Mohenjodaro/Harappa (Pakistan) they had developed a civilised society at least 4000 years ago. From the combined cultural melting pot of customs, stories and religious notions grew the seeds of Hinduism and a new language: Sanskrit.

By the time writing developed 300 years later, the Dasa and Aryan traditions were already intermingled. Their joint songs; ideas and magic spells collectively known as the *Vedas* (from the Sanskrit for 'knowledge') form the four oldest surviving Indo-Aryan books: perhaps the oldest repository of written information in the world, and still a source of inspiration to many Hindus. Over the next 1000 years a written mythology developed, resulting in the multi-armed wild-looking gods Westerners usually associate with Hinduism. Hindu classics, such as the *Ramayana* and *Mahabharata*, recount the fruity earthbound romps of these gods, along with a colourful cast of evil demons, heroic and/or egotistical semi-deities and the odd human character. Gods can take various forms; they are born, have birthdays, spouses, children and can even die.

While the written texts of Hinduism are greatly respected by all Hindus for their age and wisdom, they are not holy books in the tradition of the Bible or the Koran. Hinduism has no founder, no single prophet, and no creed. The very term 'Hinduism' (the religion of Hindustan – ie India) is a 17th century invention of ever-generalising Westerners. It remains a very diverse religion: many gods have had eras of greater or lesser popularity and certain gods are particularly celebrated in certain regions. Most individuals have their personal favourite god to whom they

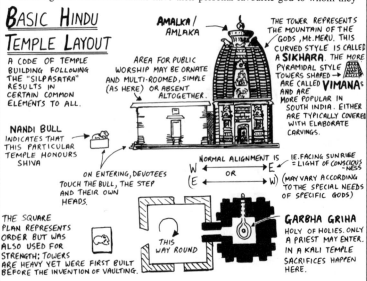

BASIC HINDU TEMPLE LAYOUT

A CODE OF TEMPLE BUILDING FOLLOWING THE "SILPASATRA" RESULTS IN CERTAIN COMMON ELEMENTS TO ALL.

AMALKA / AMLAKA

AREA FOR PUBLIC WORSHIP MAY BE ORNATE AND MULTI-ROOMED, SIMPLE (AS HERE) OR ABSENT ALTOGETHER.

THE TOWER REPRESENTS THE MOUNTAIN OF THE GODS, Mt. MERU. THIS CURVED STYLE IS CALLED A **SIKHARA**. THE MORE PYRAMIDAL STYLE TOWERS SHAPED → ARE CALLED **VIMANA**s AND ARE MORE POPULAR IN SOUTH INDIA. EITHER ARE TYPICALLY COVERED WITH ELABORATE CARVINGS.

NANDI BULL INDICATES THAT THIS PARTICULAR TEMPLE HONOURS SHIVA

ON ENTERING, DEVOTEES TOUCH THE BULL, THE STEP AND THEIR OWN HEADS.

NORMAL ALIGNMENT IS
W ←——→ E
OR
(E ←——→ W)

IE. FACING SUNRISE = LIGHT OF CONSCIOUS-NESS (MAY VARY ACCORDING TO THE SPECIAL NEEDS OF SPECIFIC GODS)

THE SQUARE PLAN REPRESENTS ORDER BUT WAS ALSO USED FOR STRENGTH; TOWERS ARE HEAVY YET WERE FIRST BUILT BEFORE THE INVENTION OF VAULTING.

THIS WAY ROUND

GARBHA GRIHA HOLY OF HOLIES. ONLY A PRIEST MAY ENTER. IN A KALI TEMPLE SACRIFICES HAPPEN HERE.

give special allegiance as well as others for more specific spiritual or superstitious needs. Krishna and Ganesh are specially well loved.

Yet despite their abundance, gods are not at the centre of Hinduism. It is possible to be Hindu yet have no belief in god whatever. The only religious tenet unifying all Hindus is that of *darshana*. Darshana is 'insight' or 'truth' or 'life force' and the search for it is the thing in Hinduism. At a fundamental level, the multiple deities are understood to be but a part of a single divine one-ness. Humans are caught in a pitiless cycle of re-births. While darshana can improve your starting point in the next life, it can not help you in this one (as it can in Buddhism). Most Hindus also believe in the holiness of nature. Certain places, mountains, rivers and phallic rocks are more holy than others. The Ganges is the holiest river and it is the wish of many Hindus to enter their next life from a cremation on its banks in the holiest of all cities: Varanasi. Most Hindus regard vegetarianism as laudable, though relatively few practice it. However, beef is out. The Vedas call cows *aghnya*: that which does not deserve to be killed, and these four-legged symbols of Mother Earth roam streets and beaches with impunity. Killing a cow, even by accident, is a serious crime.

Popular gods   When they are themselves, the Big Three: **Brahma** (Creator) **Vishnu** (Preserver) and **Shiva** (Destroyer) usually appear as four-armed males. Brahma, who may also have four heads and ride a swan chariot (swans symbolise knowledge), is relatively rarely depicted, though his consort Saraswati (goddess of music and arts) features in many schools. The vast majority of temples, however, honour specific forms of either Vishnu or Shiva.

Vishnu may be spied sleeping upon a seven headed snake or carrying a spiral *chakra* weapon. His consort, **Lakshmi**, is the goddess of good fortune and wealth. She often holds lotuses in two of her four arms. Vishnu himself has 10 different incarnations. Most notable are: #7 **Rama**, representing truth and morality (oft depicted holding a long-bow and/or grouped with wife Sita and brother Laxman). #8 **Krishna** (a charming, flute playing charioteer/playboy) – the most popular form as he offers a direct possibility of salvation to his devotees. The **Buddha** has been adopted as #9. When #10 (**Kalki**) rides in on his horse then the world will end.

Shiva, posing with sons and wife (**Parvati**) represent harmonious family life. But another of Shiva's consorts is bloodthirsty **Kali**, (depicted holding a sickle and severed head). Tantric sects worship Kali through sacrifices, secretive sexual practices and arcane uses of skulls and corpses. Shiva himself, appearing as **Bhairav**, wears a necklace of skulls and can only be appeased with offerings of meat and alcohol. Bhairav's consort is the 8 armed, tiger riding goddess **Durga**. Shiva's most recognisable forms are as **Nataraj** (4 armed Lord of the Dance in an arc of flames) and his manifestation as a lingam (phallus).

Ganesh, with his elephant head and body of a sumo wrestler, is the god of wisdom and prosperity. He's the son of Shiva and Parvati and brings luck in day to day affairs (many Hindus keep a picture of him in their wallets). His 'vehicle' is a very under-sized rat.

Gar is an elephant god and Lord of the Forests. **Gahr**, who takes the form of a crocodile, is Lord of the Rivers. **Garuda**, is the giant eagle ridden by Vishnu.

Hanuman is the monkey king, famously loyal to Rama. His army rescued Sita from the evil ten-headed demon Ravana in Sri Lanka, and inspired the wicked witch's monkey army in *The Wizard of Oz*.

Nandi is Shiva's bull, to be seen at any Shiva temple. Touch his testicles for fertility. **Narashima** is the lion headed fourth form of Vishnu. He's often seen attacking the stomach of a demon.

Web sites

Because there are so many sites on India, knowing where the good India links are is almost more helpful. Try www.travel.com under countries, India, hulk.bu.edu/misc/india/tourism.html and members.tripod.com/~ireddy/india.html.

The most informative single site on India is at www.allindia.com; most tourist information at this site is given under the cities heading.

www.goa-interactive.com has a lot of Goa-specific information

www.welcometoindia.com/home.html has extensive travel information, though mostly for up-scale tourists.

www.andhratoday.com/festival/festi.htm has a description of the major country-wide festivals in India and www.indiagov.org/culture/festival/calendar.htm has the current dates.

www.rajasthanweb.com/festival/ has the dates and descriptions of Rajasthani festivals.

On the lighter side, check out the 10 rules for making a Hindi movie at www.mahesh.com/india/films/top-10-rules.html.

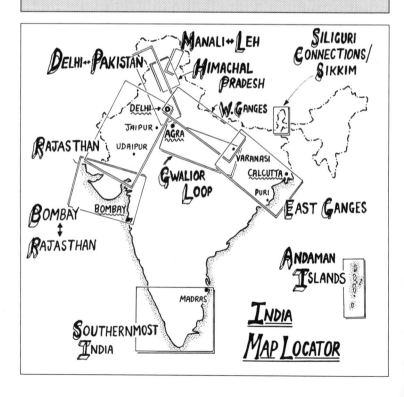

Holy sites in India and beyond

Hinduism's semi-official 'Holy Places' and 'Abodes' (listed below) are not necessarily the most interesting places, nor by any means the only towns to draw pilgrims. Any choice of 'best' temple is very subjective. Included on the map opposite is our personal selection (see also regional schematic maps).

● **The seven Hindu Holy Places** **Ayodhya** (the sacred spot housed a Mogul era mosque, whose destruction caused recent riots), **Dwarka** (also an 'Abode'), **Hardwar, Kanchipuram ★** (dozens of temples many over 1200 yrs old), **Mathura** (birthplace of Krishna), **Ujjain**, **Varanasi ★** (the most holy; photogenic ghats, maze of old-town streets; many wish to be cremated here).

● **The four Hindu Abodes** **Badrinath** (Vishnu), **Dwarka** (Krishna, five-storey Dvarkanath temple, Krishna isle), **Puri** (Jagannath★), **Ramesvaram** (where Hanuman rescued Sita and killed Ravana; massive temple with Hanuman statue).

● **Hindu curiosities** **Amarnath** (Shiva's ice penis varies in size with the season. In a cave, some five days' hike amid thousands of pilgrims at August full moon. The last section is barefoot on a glacier). Kalighat temple, **Calcutta** (ceremonies once included human sacrifices; blood, now mainly from goats, still flows). **Chengannur** (small Parvati temple where the goddess statue is said to menstruate). Rat temple, **Deshnok** (rats in surreal numbers scurry all over the building and are fed). **Hampi ★** (Vishnu's carved chariot in atmospheric ruins of bolder-strewn ancient city. **Pavagadh ★** (near Champaner; dramatic fortress and de-Hinduised temple on the lump of mountain that Hanuman dropped here on the way back from the Himalaya. **Tirumalai** (near Tirupati) Its seven hills represent the heads of serpent god Adidesha. The Sri Venkatesvara temple is India's richest.

● **Buddhist and Jain special sites and curiosities** Sheesh Mahan Jain temple, **Indore** (outwardly inconspicuous but has a dazzling mirrored interior). Swayambunath, **Kathmandu ★** (stupa atop a steep stairway, swings with fearless gangs of monkeys). **Sravanabelagola ★** (Prince Bahubali realised the futility of earthly success and became a pacifist, naked Jain saint. A 1000-year old, 50ft statue on a rocky hill reflects this. Many pilgrims). **Ajanta** and **Ellora** Caves (the best known of many richly decorated Buddhist caves).

● **Islamic sites** The Muslim 'Mogul' empire built many superb mosques (eg at **Delhi, Fatehpur Sikri, Hyderabad**), as well as palaces and tombs of which the Taj Mahal (**Agra**) is justifiably the most celebrated. Other Muslim era attractions include **Gaur** and **Mandu** (deserted 15th-century city ruins), and **Gulbarga**.

● **Ashrams** Hindu based meditation, study and retreat

Place	Guru	Reputation
Pune	Bagwan Sri Rajneesh	Gained notoriety as much for his many Rolls Royces as for the 'meditation by orgy' technique of his Oregon community. Pricey.
Shirdi	Sai Baba	Became rich, but did he really raise the dead?
Ahmadabad	Gandhi	No longer functions, now a museum.
Auroville	Sri Aurobindo	Tantric leaning with yoga, stresses early Vedas
Rishikesh★	many	Calm, rural place to 'sample' an Ashram.
Tirvannamalai★	Ramana Maharishi	At foot of rocky hill, another Shiva home.

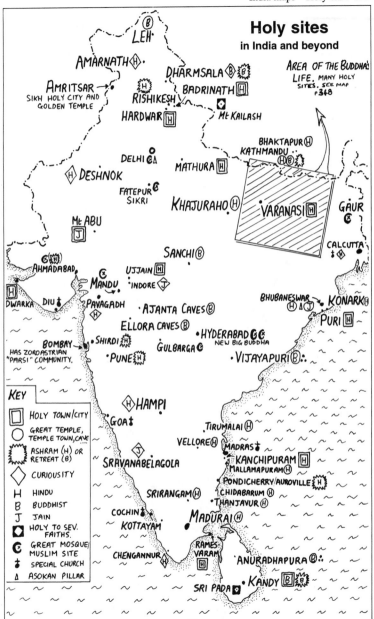

Holy sites
in India and beyond

LEH (B)

AMARNATH (H)

AMRITSAR →
SIKH HOLY CITY AND
GOLDEN TEMPLE

DHARMSALA (B) (B)

BADRINATH (H)

RISHIKESH (H)

HARDWAR (H)

Mt KAILASH (◆)

AREA OF THE BUDDHA'S
LIFE. MANY HOLY
SITES. SEE MAP
p 348

BHAKTAPUR (H)
KATHMANDU (H)(B)

DELHI (C)(△)

MATHURA (H)

DESHNOK (H)

FATEPUR (C)
SIKRI

KHAJURAHO (H)

VARANASI (H)

GAUR (C)

Mt ABU (J)

SANCHI (B)

CALCUTTA ♰ (H)

AHMADABAD (C)(H)

UJJAIN (H)

MANDU (C)

INDORE (◇)

DWARKA (H)

DIU ♰

PAVAGADH (H)

AJANTA CAVES (B)

ELLORA CAVES (B)

HYDERABAD (C)(C)
NEW BIG BUDDHA

BHUBANESWAR
(H) (△)(J)

KONARK (H)

PURI (H)

BOMBAY •
HAS ZOROASTRIAN
"PARSI" COMMUNITY.

SHIRDI (H)

PUNE (H)

GULBARGA (C)

VIJAYAPURI (B)

KEY

▢	HOLY TOWN/CITY
◯	GREAT TEMPLE, TEMPLE TOWN, CAVE
⬡	ASHRAM (H) OR RETREAT (B)
◇	CURIOUSITY
H	HINDU
B	BUDDHIST
J	JAIN
◈	HOLY TO SEV. FAITHS.
C	GREAT MOSQUE/ MUSLIM SITE
♰	SPECIAL CHURCH
△	ASOKAN PILLAR

HAMPI (H)

GOA ♰

TIRUMALAI (H)

VELLORE (H)

MADRAS ♰

SRAVANABELAGOLA (◇)

KANCHIPURAM (H)
MALLAMAPURAM (H)

PONDICHERRY/AUROVILLE (H)

SRIRANGAM (H)

CHIDABARUM (H)

THANJAVUR (H)

COCHIN ♰

KOTTAYAM

MADURAI (H)

CHENGANNUR (◇)

RAMES-
VARAM (H)

ANURADHAPURA (B)

KANDY (B)(B)

SRI PADA (◈)

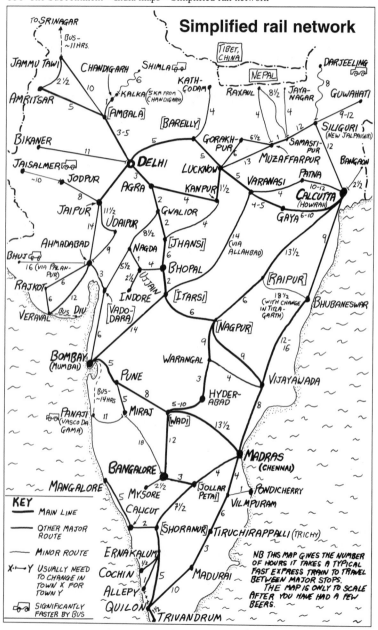

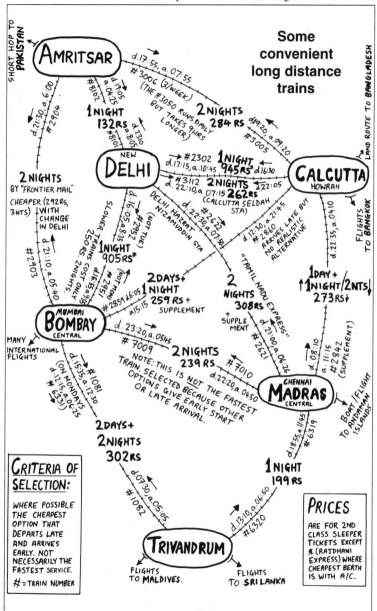

Some
convenient
long distance
trains

SHORT HOP TO PAKISTAN

LAND ROUTE TO BANGLADESH

AMRITSAR

d.17:55, a.07:55
#3006 (3/WEEK)
(THE #3050 RUNS DAILY BUT TAKES 9HRS LONGER)
2 NIGHTS
284 RS

d.19:05, a.04:25
#8102

d.21:30, a.6:00
#2904

1 NIGHT
132 RS

d.23:10, a.8:05
#8101

NEW DELHI

d.19:20, a.09:20
#3005

CALCUTTA
HOWRAH

→ #2302 1 NIGHT
d.17:15, a.10:45 945 RS* d.16:30

→ #3112 2 NIGHTS
d.22:10, a.07:15 262 RS
(CALCUTTA SELDAH STA)

d.22:05

2 NIGHTS
BY "FRONTIER MAIL"
CHEAPER (292RS, 3NTS) WITH CHANGE IN DELHI

SLOWER TRAINS 250RS, 2NIGHTS. COST ONLY #2616

d.16:05, a.8:35
#2951 1 NIGHT
905 RS*
(NOT MON)

DELHI HAZRAT NIZAMUDDIN STA
(NOT TUE)
#2622

d.22:30, a.07:50

d.12:30, a.21:45
#2860
ARRIVES LATE BUT NO REALISTIC ALTERNATIVE

FLIGHTS TO BANGKOK

d.22:35, a.0410

d.21:10, a.05:40
#2903

2 DAYS+
1 NIGHT
259 RS +
SUPPLEMENT
d.15:15
#2859 d.16:05

2 NIGHTS
308 RS
+ SUPPLE-MENT

1 DAY +
↑1 NIGHT/2NTS↓
273 RS+

d.08:10
a.11:15
#2842
(SUPPLEMENT)

MUMBAI
BOMBAY
CENTRAL

d.23:20, a.05:45
#7009 2 NIGHTS
239 RS #7010
NOTE: THIS IS NOT THE FASTEST TRAIN. SELECTED BECAUSE OTHER OPTIONS GIVE EARLY START OR LATE ARRIVAL.
d.22:20, a.0450

"TAMIL NADU EXPRESS"
d.21:00, a.06:26
#2621

MANY INTERNATIONAL FLIGHTS

d.15:35, a.12:30
#1081
(ON MONDAYS
d.12:15, a.06:25
#1051)

CHENNAI
MADRAS
CENTRAL

BOAT/FLIGHT TO ANDAMAN ISLANDS

2 DAYS+
2 NIGHTS
302 RS

d.07:30, a.05:05
#1082

d.18:55, a.11:45
#6319

1 NIGHT
199 RS

d.13:10, a.06:50
#6320

TRIVANDRUM

FLIGHTS TO MALDIVES.

FLIGHTS TO SRI LANKA

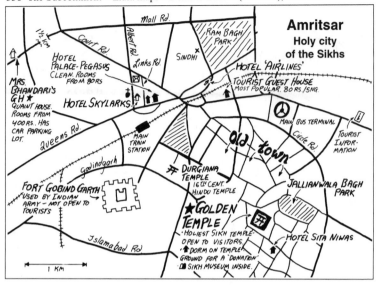

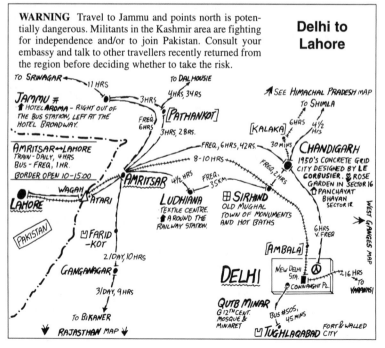

Delhi is really two cities. **New Delhi** is the commercial and political section stretching south of Jawaharla Nehru Road. **Old Delhi** contains the Red Fort, the Jama Masjid and atmospheric side streets. *Delhi Diary* (from news stalls) lists current events and has a city map.

● **Airport transport** The Ex-Servicemen's Air Link (EATS) runs a bus to/from Connaught Place (Rs25, 45 mins, dep every 30 mins, 4am-11pm). Flights tend to depart at awkward times (1-5am). If you arrive late at night, wait for the first EATS bus; taxis from the airport are notorious for scams. You can't check into cheap hotels before dawn.

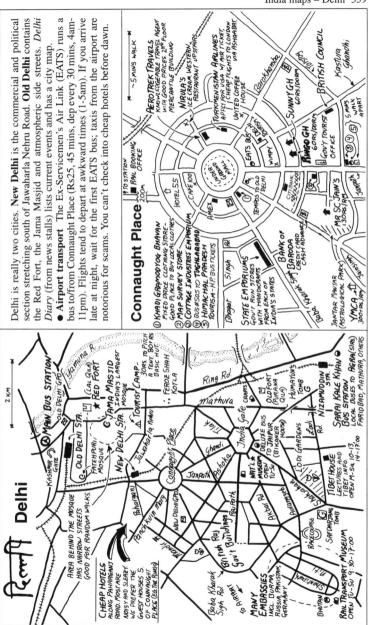

Connaught Place

① KHADI GRAMODYOG BHAVAN
FIXED PRICE CLOTHING STORE-
GOOD PLACE TO BUY LOCAL CLOTHES.
② MAP SURVEY STORE
③ COTTAGE INDUSTRIES EMPORIUM
④ BUS/ADS TO TUGHLAABAD
⑤ HIMACHAL PRADESH
TOURISM - H.P. BUS TICKETS

STATE EMPORIUMS
GOV'T RUN STORES
WITH HANDICRAFTS
FROM EACH OF
INDIA'S STATES

BANK OF
BARODA
CREDIT CARD
CASH ADVANCE

AEROTREK TRAVELS
KNOWLEDGEABLE TRAVEL AGENT
WITH GOOD PRICES. 1ST FLOOR
MERCANTILE BUILDING

NIRULA'S
ICE CREAM, WESTERN
RESTAURANT UPSTAIRS

TURKMENISTAN AIRLINES
FOR VISA W/ AIR TICKET.
APPLY CHEAP FLIGHTS TO LONDON
UNITED COFFEE VIA ASHGABAT.
HOUSE

BRITISH COUNCIL

Kasturba Gandhi

RINGO GH
GOV'T TOURIST
OFFICE

SUNNY GH
GORS/DORM

WIMPY

EATS BUS

CAFE 100

HOTEL 55

RAIL BOOKING
OFFICE

TO STATION
200m

UNDER
GROUND
WALK

TEMPO'S TO OLD
DELHI

CITIBANK

CUTIBANK
ATM

AMEX

MR SC JAIN'S
30hrs IRM

Janpath

~ 5 MINS WALK

Barakhamba

Rasvisi

~ 5 MINS WALK

5 MINS
WALK
APART

Singh Rd

Bhagat

Singh Rd

YMCA
300rs/rm, IRM

JANTAR MANTAR
(ASTROLOGICAL PARK)

Baba ... Army

Delhi
रिल्ली

2 KM

AREA BEHIND THE MOSQUE
HAS NARROW STREETS
GOOD FOR RANDOM WALKS.

Yamuna R.

MAIN BUS STATION
OLD DELHI GPO

KASHMIR
GATE

OLD DELHI STA.

(LAL QILA)
RED FORT

JAMA MASJID
INDIA'S LARGEST
MOSQUE

FATEHPURI
MOSQUE

NEW DELHI STA.

Jawaharlal Nehru

TOURIST CAMP-
30rs. TO PITCH
A TENT. BOTERS
BASIC HUT.

FEROZ SHAH
KOTLA

Ring Rd.

Mathura

CHEAP HOTELS
ALONG PAHARGANJ
ROAD. MOST ARE
NOISY AND SLEAZY.
WE PREFER THE
GUEST HOUSES S.
OF CONNAUGHT
PLACE (E.G. THE RINGO)

Connaught
Place

Janpath

Panchkuin Marg

Baba Kharak
Singh Rd.

TO AIRPORT

MANY
EMBASSIES
INCL. BURMA,
RUSSIA, PAKISTAN,
GERMANY

BHUTAN

Mandir

Rahanganj

New Delhi GPO

British Raj
Gov't Buildings

Ashoka

RACECOURSE

SAFDARJANG
TOMB

RAIL TRANSPORT MUSEUM
OPEN TU-SU 9:30-17:00

Rafi

Akbar Rd

Aurangzeb

NAT'L
MUSEUM
OPEN
TU-SU

LODI GARDENS

Lodi
Rd.

TIBET HOUSE
LECTURES AND
TIBET INFO.
OPEN M-Sa 10-13,
14-17:00

India
Gate

Gandhi

Tilak

CRAFTS

OLD FORT
(PURANA
QILA)

HUMAYUN'S
TOMB

NIZAMUDDIN
STA.

SARAI KALE KHAN
BUS STATION
LOCAL BUSES TO AGRA (SIRS),
FARIDABAD, MATHURA, OTHERS

DELUXE BUS
TO JAIPUR
(BIKANER
HOUSE)

LOCAL BUSES TO AGRA (SIRS)

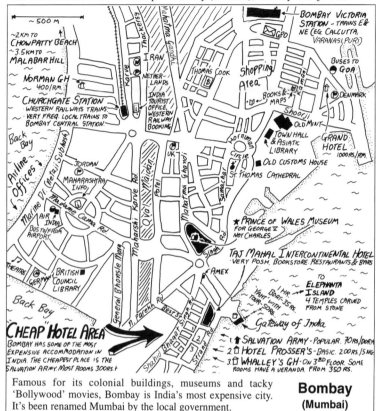

Famous for its colonial buildings, museums and tacky 'Bollywood' movies, Bombay is India's most expensive city. It's been renamed Mumbai by the local government.

Bombay (Mumbai)

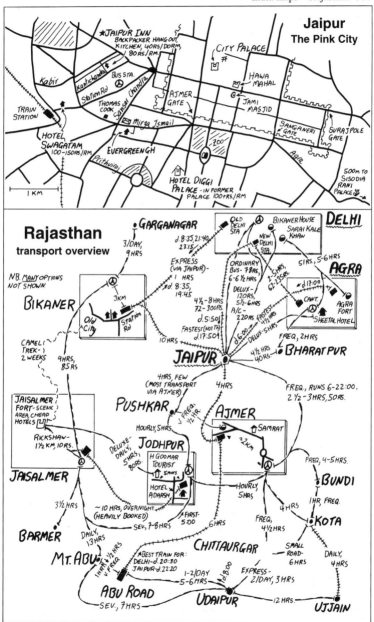

Jaipur
The Pink City

★ JAIPUR INN
BACKPACKER HANGOUT,
KITCHEN, 40RS/DORM,
80RS/RM

CITY PALACE

HAWA MAHAL

Kabir

Kantichandra

BUS STA.

Station Rd

Thomas Cook

Saksn Chandra

AJMER GATE

JAMI MASJID

TRAIN STATION

Mirza Ismail

SAMGANERI GATE

SURAJPOLE GATE

HOTEL SWAGATAM
100-150RS/RM

EVERGREENGH

ZOO

Prithvini

Agra

500m to SISODIA RANI PALACE

HOTEL DIGGI PALACE -IN FORMER PALACE. 100+RS/RM

1 KM

Rajasthan
transport overview

NB. MANY OPTIONS NOT SHOWN.

GARGANAGAR

3/DAY, 9 HRS

OLD DELHI STA.

BIKANER HOUSE
SARAI KALE KHAN

DELHI

NEW DELHI STA.

d. 8.35, 21.40 23.15

EXPRESS (VIA JAIPUR) - 1 HRS
d. 8.35, 19.45

5 1RS, 5-6 HRS

AGRA

ORDINARY BUS - 78RS, 6-6½ HRS

2-5 HRS, 67.235RS

BIKANER

Old City

3 KM

Station Rd

4½-8 HRS 72-300RS

d. 5.50}
FASTEST(MOTH)
d. 17.50}

10 HRS

DELUX - 120RS, 5½-6 HRS

A/C - 220 RS

d. 17.00

CANT.

AGRA FORT

SHEETAL HOTEL

FASTEST 1½ HRS

d. 6.00

DELUX - 5 HRS

CAMEL (TREK) 2 WEEKS

9 HRS, 8.5 RS

JAIPUR

4½ HRS 40RS.

FREQ, 2 HRS

BHARATPUR

JAISALMER FORT-SCENIC AREA, CHEAP HOTELS

4 HRS, FEW (MOST TRANSPORT VIA AJMER)

4 HRS

FREQ., RUNS 6-22:00, 2½-3HRS, 50RS.

RICKSHAW- 1½ KM, 10 RS.

PUSHKAR

v. FREQ. ½ HR.

AJMER

SAMRAT

~2 KM

JAISALMER

DELUXE- DAILY- 5 HRS, 80RS

HOURLY, 5 HRS

JODHPUR

H GOOMAR TOURIST
5 MINS

FREQ, 4-5 HRS.

BUNDI

3½ HRS

BARMER

DAILY, 13 HRS

MT. ABU

HOTEL ADARSH

~ 10 HRS, OVERNIGHT (HEAVILY BOOKED)

SEV, 7-8 HRS

★FIRST- 5:00

6 HRS

HOURLY, 5 HRS

FREQ, 4½ HRS

SMALL ROAD- 6 HRS

1 HR, FREQ.

KOTA

DAILY, 4 HRS

1HR½HRS v. FREQ

★BEST TRAIN FOR: DELHI-d. 20:30 JAIPUR-d. 22:20

CHITTAURGAR

ABU ROAD

SEV, 7 HRS

1-2/DAY 5-6 HRS

d. 18.00

UDAIPUR

EXPRESS- 2/DAY, 3 HRS

12 HRS.

UJJAIN

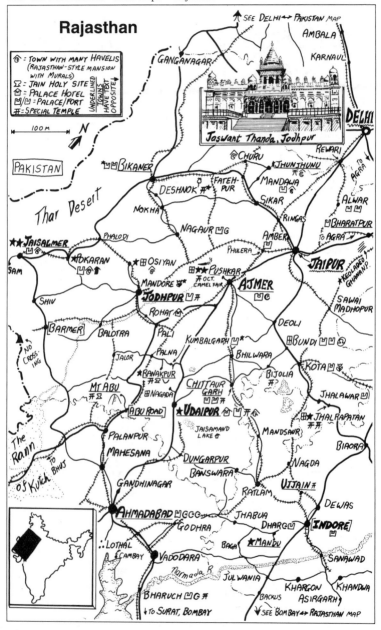

Rajasthan

☖ = TOWN WITH MANY HAVELIS (RAJASTHAN-STYLE MANSION WITH MURALS)
⚖ = JAIN HOLY SITE
☖ = PALACE HOTEL
⊞/⊟ = PALACE/FORT
⌗ = SPECIAL TEMPLE

UNDERLINED TOWNS HAVE TEXT OPPOSITE

100 M   N

PAKISTAN

SEE DELHI ↔ PAKISTAN MAP

AMBALA

KARNAUL

GANGANAGAR

Jaswant Thanda, Jodhpur

DELHI

REWARI

⌗☖ CHURU

⊞⊟ BIKANER

DESHNOK

FATEH-PUR

JHUNTHUNU

MANDAWA

ALWAR ⊞⊟

SIKAR

NOKHA

RINGAS

Thar Desert

PHALODI

NAGAUR ⊞G

AMBER

BHARATPUR

to AGRA

★★ JAISALMER
⊟☖

★⊞ OSIYAN
⊟☖

PHULERA

JAIPUR

★☖ POKARAN
⊟☖

⊞★★ PUSHKAR

KEOLADEO GHANA N.P.

SAM

MANDORE ⌗

⌗ OCT. CAMEL FAIR

AJMER ⊟☖

SHIV

JODHPUR ⊟⌗

SAWAI MADHOPUR

ROHAT

DEOLI

BARMER

BALOTRA

PALI

KUMBALGARH ⊟★

⊞ BUNDI ⊟☖

JALOR

PALNA

BHILWARA

KOTA ⊟⚖

NO CROSSING

MT ABU
⌗⚖

★ RANAKPUR
⌗⚖

BIJOLIA

★⊞ NAGADA

CHITTAUR GARH
⊟⊟⌗

⌗★

JHALAWAR ⊟

ABU ROAD

★ UDAIPUR ⊟ ⊟ ⌗☖

⊞★ JHALRAPATAN
⌗⌗

The Rann

PALANPUR

JAISAMAND LAKE ☖

MANDSAUR

BIAORA

MAHESANA

DUNGARPUR

NAGDA

of Kutch Bhuj

GANDHINAGAR

BANSWARA

UJJAIN ⌗

RATLAM

DEWAS

AHMADABAD ⊟GGG⌗

JHABUA

DHARG⊟

INDORE ⊟

GODHRA

BAGH

★ MANDU

LOTHAL

CAMBAY

VADODARA

SANAWAD

Narmada R.

KHARGON ASIRGARH

KHANDWA

BHARUCH ⊟G⌗

JULWANIA

BACKUS

↓ to SURAT, BOMBAY

↓ SEE BOMBAY ↔ RAJASTHAN MAP

● **Ahmadabad** Many mosques in a huge polluted city. *A-One Guest House* (across from train station, Rs70/basic single). Several hotels in the old city opposite Sidi Saiyad's Mosque.

● **Ajmer** Hop-off for Pushkar. Akbar's Palace and Sher Shan's mosque. *King Edward Rest House* (opp station, Rs70).

● **Bharatpur Tourist Lodge** (by Mathura Gate, Rs40/sgl) has good info on Keoladeo Ghana NP, world-heritage bird sanctuary. Best time: Oct to Feb.

● **Bikaner** Desert city with a large fort. Atmospheric old town area. Hotels near the station.

● **Chittaurgarh** 5km fortress wall ruins on hill above town. Hotels (inc *Hotel Chetak*) near the station.

● **Deshnok** Bizarre Karni Mata, a temple crawling with rats. *Yatri Niwas* (Rs40/dorm, Rs120/sgl). Hourly bus from Bikaner (45mins, Rs10).

● **Dungarpur** Modernish city. A ruined old town is 3km away.

● **Jaipur** See city map. Walled old city within a huge metropolis. Many old buildings, including the City Palace and Hawa Mahal (Palace of the Winds). Very popular with tourists, more for its proximity to Delhi than its atmosphere. Given limited time, we'd prefer to explore other towns in Rajasthan.

● **Jaisalmer** The ultimate desert citadel – most of the town's population still lives within it. Sleep on top of the citadel's walls at the *Deepak Rest House* (Rs15). Several other guesthouses are inside (inc *Hotel Laxmi Niwas*). Watch sunsets from the Brahmin Cemetery. Camel treks cost Rs200-300/day including your own camel, guide and food. R/t camel treks, to desert villages and the sand dunes near Sam, last 1-7 days. Longer treks go as far as Bikaner and Jaipur. We suggest a 2-3-day return trek for the optimum ratio of enchanting experience to sore bottom.

● **Jhunjhunu** Capital of the Shekhawati region, famous for old homes and architecture. Many guest houses near bus stn.

● **Jodhpur** A large city with a relative-ly atmospheric old area. Meherangarh Fort. *Govind Hotel* (opp post office).

● **Kumbalgarh** Huge hill-top fort. No cheap accommodation.

● **Mandu** (Across the Rajasthan border in MP). Well preserved ruins of 15th century Afghan Mughal fort and royal enclave overlook a simple village. Hotels have limited space, so arrive early or call ahead. *Traveller's Lodge* (Rs250/dbl.; book through MP Tourism 0731-383888). *Tourist Rest House* (Rs30/rm) but often full.

● **Mt Abu** Hill station reached via Abu Road (frequent buses from 6am, 1hr), honeymoon haven, and laid back Jain pilgrimage site. Hotel rooms from Rs120, high season, from Rs80 low season. *Hotel Panghat* (on the lake).

● **Pushkar** Huge camel fair held every autumn. The rest of the year it is a laid back Hindu holy town, appreciated as much for the ban on motorised vehicles in the centre as for the beautiful lake. 400 temples within a few hours walk. Hotels along the lake. Travellers' scene.

● **Ranakpur** Large Jain temple (open to non-Jains 12-5pm). Several hotels, or stay in the temple for a donation.

● **Udaipur** Grand city of palaces set around Lake Pichola. Many scenic old side streets. Several former palaces used as hotels. The most plush is the *Lake Palace Hotel* in the middle of Udaipur's main lake (rooms from $150, ☎ 52-7961). Cheaper palace hotels, such as the *Jagat Niwas* (on the lake beneath the city palace, rooms from Rs150, ☎ 52-3891) and *Rang Niwa* (on Lake Palace road, Rs30/dorm, Rs175/rm) are exceptional values. Many more average backpaker haunts, inc *Lake Ghat GH* (near Jagdish Temple).

● **Ujjain** (Across the Rajasthan border in MP). One of the seven holy Hindu cities, but lacks atmosphere except during the annual festival beginning on the full moon of the Hindu month of Chaitra (around March). Hotels, such as the *Vikram* (Rs80/rm.), are opposite the station.

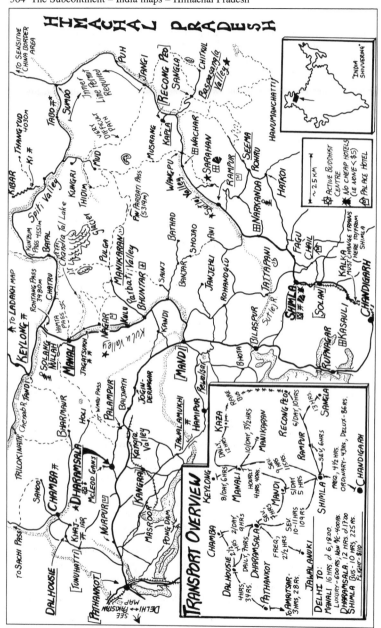

Himachal Pradesh – the beautiful mountain state

● **Baspasangla Valley** Scenic villages. Cheap accommodation in Sangla and Chitkul. Cannot go beyond Chitkul without an Inner Line permit.

● **Chail** The palace of this former summer capital is now a *hotel* (Rs500/rm).

● **Dharamsala** Home of the Dalai Lama and capital of the Government of Tibet in Exile. *Rising Moon Hotel* (Rs50/dorm). Most of the traveller hangouts and Tibetan cultural happenings are in McLeod Ganj. One of the best bases for day walks (guest houses have information). Meditation courses. Many guest houses.

● **Dalhousie** Very spread out hill station at 2036m. *Youth Hostel* (Rs20/dorm for non-members).

● **Jawalamuki** Low-lying (500m) Hindu pilgrimage site with a temple and eternal flame. *Hotel Jawalaji* (Rs300/dbl, Rs45/dorm).

● **Kalpa** Said to be the winter home of the Hindu deity, Siva. Rest house. One hour walk from Recong Peo.

● **Keylong** Many interesting temples and day walks. Many cheap hotels, including the *Tourist Bungalow* (Rs45/dorm) and the *Gyespa Hotel* (in the bazaar).

● **Kulu Valley** Former kingdom. Orchards, wooden temples, beautiful women, trekking. Manali not Kulu town is the traveller hub.

● **Manali** The backpacker and hippie hangout of Himachal Pradesh. A good place to get info and arrange treks, through not the nicest town in the region. Old Manali is more scenic and has many cheap guest houses, eg *Veer Paying GH* (Rs50-80/sgl). Vashisht, 3km NE, has hot springs and some accommodation.

● **Mandi** Sivarati Festival (Feb/March). *Raj Mahal* hotel (garden, Rs100/rm). 750m.

● **Manikaran** Hot springs. Sikh & Hindu temples. *Padha Family House* (hot bath, Rs100/rm).

● **Narkanda** Skiing late Dec-March. Rent skis Rs150/day.

● **Palampur** Good base for walks in hills and around tea plantations. *Silver Oaks Motel* (out of town).

● **Rampur** Market town and transport centre for the region. *Padam Palace* opposite the main bus stand.

● **Rewalsar Lake** Pilgrimage site for Buddhists, Hindus and Sikhs. *Tourist Inn* (Rs45/dorm).

● **Sarahan** Typical hilltown architecture. The Bhimakali Temple here is made of two wooden pagodas (possible to spend the night). *Hotel Srikhand* (Rs45/dorm, Rs150/dbl).

● **Seema** Stay in *log cabins* (book in Shimla).

● **Shimla** The capital of HP. Summer capital of all India during Walk to the Jakhu (monkey) temple. Prices high in season: cheapest accommodation at the *YMCA* (200rs/rm). Many day trips to surrounding villages and temples, including: Sankat Mochan (view of Shimla, 7km away.

● **Solang Nullah** Skiing. Rent skis 150rs./day. *Friendship Hotel* (150rs./dbl).

● **Sutjil Valley** Five-day walk between Sarahan and Wangpu has *guest houses* along the way.

Ladakh

Ladakh is a highland desert, a mesmerising land of Buddhist monasteries and rugged mountains culturally tied to Tibet. Leh, the capital, is worth a visit in its own right. It has a mini-Potala, several gompas, and many possibilities for day-excursions into the surrounding hills. However, the opportunity to go trekking may be the best reason to make the long trip to Leh. Unlike the 'teahouse' treks of Nepal, you'll need advanced planning and guides. Expect to pay $20+/day for treks organised by Leh agencies. Alternatively, arrange a trek yourself and pay $5-9/day to rent (mediocre quality) equipment in Leh and share the cost of the guides and pack animals with a group (guest house bulletin boards have messages from people looking for trekking partners). For complete information on route options and arranging a trek see *Leh & Trekking in Ladakh* by Charlie Loram (Trailblazer Publications).

● **When to go & getting there** The main trekking season is from mid-June until late Oct, with Sep being best. The Manali-Leh Road is open summer months only. There are many crowded but cheap local buses along the route, and a daily Himachal Tourism direct bus (2 days, Rs700 + Rs300 for optional accommodation or sleep in bus). Flights year round from Delhi ($86, Indian Airlines, direct or via Jammu). Beware of altitude sickness for the first few days after arrival in Leh.

Manali-Leh Road
World's 2nd highest bus route

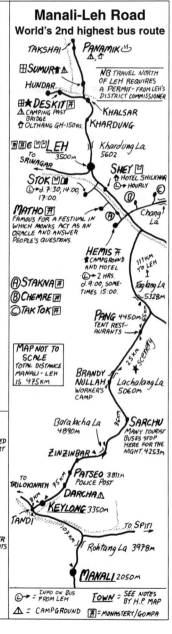

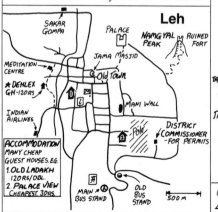

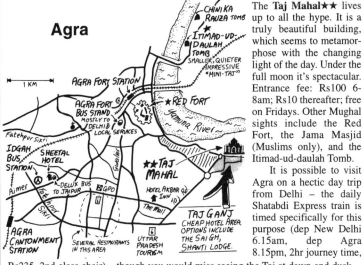

Agra

1 KM

CHINI KA RAUZA TOMB
ITIMAD-UD-DAULAH TOMB
SMALLER, QUIETER IMPRESSIVE "MINI-TAJ"

AGRA FORT STATION

AGRA FORT BUS STAND
MOSTLY TO DELHI & LOCAL SERVICES

★ RED FORT

Jamuna River

Fatehpur Sikri

IDGAH BUS STATION
SHEETAL HOTEL
Ajmer
DELUX BUS TO JAIPUR
GPO
★★ TAJ MAHAL
HOTEL AKBAR INN
The Mall

AGRA CANTONMENT STATION
SEVERAL RESTAURANTS IN THIS AREA
UTTAR PRADESH TOURISM

TAJ GANJ
CHEAP HOTEL AREA. OPTIONS INCLUDE THE SAI GH, SHANTI LODGE.

The **Taj Mahal**★★ lives up to all the hype. It is a truly beautiful building, which seems to metamorphose with the changing light of the day. Under the full moon it's spectacular. Entrance fee: Rs100 6-8am; Rs10 thereafter; free on Fridays. Other Mughal sights include the Red Fort, the Jama Masjid (Muslims only), and the Itimad-ud-daulah Tomb.

It is possible to visit Agra on a hectic day trip from Delhi – the daily Shatabdi Express train is timed specifically for this purpose (dep New Delhi 6.15am, dep Agra 8.15pm, 2hr journey time, Rs235, 2nd class chair) – though you would miss seeing the Taj at dawn and dusk.

Outside the town is **Fatehpur Sikri**, the city begun by the great Mughal ruler, Akbar, and then mysteriously abandoned. The mosque is still in use. Get there by taxi tours: 45 mins, cRs300 return.

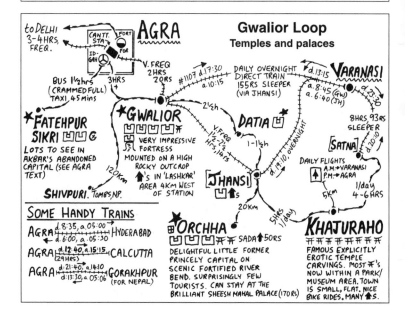

Gwalior Loop
Temples and palaces

AGRA
to DELHI 3-4 HRS, FREQ.
CANTT. STA
FORT
ID-GAH

V. FREQ. 2 HRS 20RS
BUS 1½hrs (CRAMMED FULL) TAXI, 45 mins
3HRS

#1107 d.17:30 a.10:15

DAILY OVERNIGHT DIRECT TRAIN 155RS SLEEPER (VIA JHANSI)

d.13:15
★ VARANASI
a.8:45 (GW) a.6:40 (JH)
a.23:30

★ FATEHPUR SIKRI
LOTS TO SEE IN AKBAR'S ABANDONED CAPITAL (SEE AGRA TEXT)

★ GWALIOR
VERY IMPRESSIVE FORTRESS MOUNTED ON A HIGH ROCKY OUTCROP
♠'s IN 'LASHKAR' AREA 4KM WEST OF STATION

2½h

★ DATIA

V. FREQ. 1½-2½ HRS, 14RS

1-1½h

8HRS, 93RS SLEEPER
SATNA
a.12:10

120km
SHIVPURI. TOMBS, NP.

JHANSI
20Km

d.19:10, overnight

DAILY FLIGHTS
A.M.→VARANASI
P.M.→AGRA
1/day 4-6 HRS
5Km

SOME HANDY TRAINS

AGRA d.8:35, a.05:00 → HYDERABAD ← d.6:00, a.05:30

AGRA d.12:40 → a.15:15 → CALCUTTA (29HRS)

AGRA d.21:40, a.14:10 → GORAKHPUR d.13:30, a.05:06 (FOR NEPAL)

★ ORCHHA
SADA ♠ 50RS
DELIGHTFUL LITTLE FORMER PRINCELY CAPITAL ON SCENIC FORTIFIED RIVER BEND. SURPRISINGLY FEW TOURISTS. CAN STAY AT THE BRILLIANT SHEESH MAHAL PALACE (170RS)

5HRS 1/day

KHAJURAHO
FAMOUS EXPLICITLY EROTIC TEMPLE CARVINGS. MOST ♯'S NOW WITHIN A PARK/ MUSEUM AREA. TOWN IS SMALL, FLAT, NICE BIKE RIDES. MANY ♠S.

West Ganges River Plain (North India)

To the far north of Uttar Pradesh are the ★**Garhwal** and **Kumaon** districts – touristy mountain regions which Hinduism holds holy. Destinations include **Kedernath** (Hindu temples towered over by snow-capped peaks; 10 hrs from Rishikesh) and **Yamunotri** (source of Yamuna, Hinduism's second holiest river; 6hr walk from Hanumanchatti). Many trekking opportunities. Further info in Rishikesh or (as with rest of India) from the excellent Lonely Planet *India* guide.

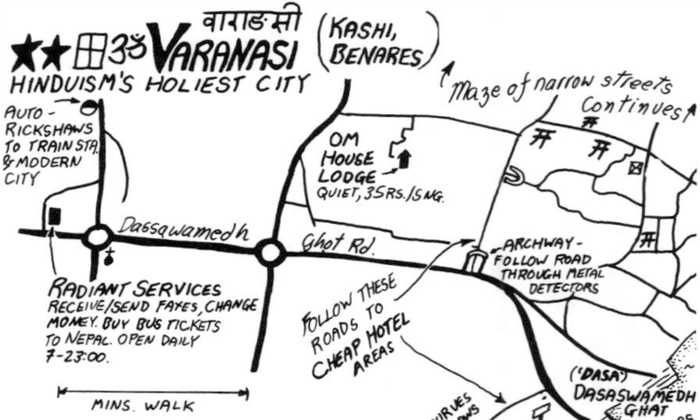

Legend:
⊞ = SIGNIFICANT TEMPLE
☸ = ACTIVE BUDDIST SITE
ॐ = HINDU HOLY SITE

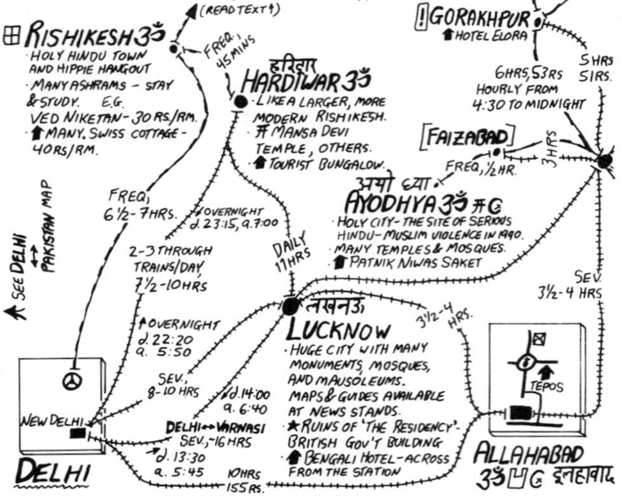

★ ⊞ ॐ वाराणसी **VARANASI** (KASHI, BENARES)
HINDUISM'S HOLIEST CITY

Soak up the atmosphere of the ghats and temples in the narrow streets along the Ganges. Row boat tours cost Rs5-15. The main burning ghat is north of Dasaswamedh, another is Chauki Ghat, south of Dasa.

● **Accommodation** Walk by river or along main streets and you'll see signs for cheap hotels (prices Rs30/dorm, Rs100/dbl). Try: *Vishnu GH* (Pandey Ghat S of Dasa; message board, sitting area, river view; Rs70/sgl, Rs120/triple). Cheapest: *Om Lodge* (follow road N; Rs10/dorm, Rs25/sgl).

● **Transport** Cycle rickshaws cost Rs10-15 to centre from the bus terminal, train stn, or last stop of airport bus. Ask for Golden Temple or Dasaswamedh Ghat.

Map labels (Varanasi):
- Maze of narrow streets ... continues
- ARCHWAY - FOLLOW ROAD THROUGH METAL DETECTORS
- (DASA) DASASWAMEDH GHAT
- SMALL GANGES
- SMALL TEMPLE 'MAA SHITLA TEMPLE'
- Ghat Rd.
- OM HOUSE LODGE QUIET, 3SRS/SNG
- FOLLOW THESE ROADS FOR CHEAP HOTELS
- ROW GIRLS OUT TOURS
- Dasaswamedh
- ... MINS WALK
- RADIANT SERVICES RECEIVE/SEND FAXES, CHANGE MONEY, BUY BUS TICKETS TO NEPAL. OPEN DAILY 7-2300.
- AUTO-RICKSHAWS TO TRAIN STN & MODERN CITY

Map labels (region):
- To SUNAULI, NEPAL / To PATNA
- ⊞ GORAKHPUR — Hotel Elora
- 5 HRS S/RS. — 6HRS, 53RS HOURLY FROM 4.30 TO MIDNIGHT — FREQ, 3HRS — 3HRS — SEV. 3½-4 HRS
- [FAIZABAD] — FREQ, 1/2HR
- अयोध्या **AYODHYA** ⊞G - HOLY CITY: FIRST SITE OF SEROUS HINDU-MUSLIM VIOLENCE IN 1990 MANY TEMPLES & MOSQUES — PATNIK NIWAS SAKET
- नगरी **LUCKNOW** - HUGE CITY WITH MANY MONUMENTS, MOSQUES, AND MAUSOLEUMS. MAPS & GUIDES AVAILABLE AT NEWS STANDS. ★RUINS OF 'THE RESIDENCY' BRITISH GOV'T BUILDING — Bengal Hotel - ACROSS FROM THE STATION — 3½-4 HRS
- ॐ इलाहाबाद **ALLAHABAD** 33 L/G — TEPOS
- हरिद्वार **HARIDWAR** 33 - LIKE A LARGER, MORE MODERN RISHIKESH. ⊞ MANSA DEVI TEMPLE, OTHERS. TOURIST BUNGALOW
- ऋषिकेश **RISHIKESH** 33 - HOLY HINDU TOWN AND HIPPIE HANGOUT - MANY ASHRAMS - STAY & STUDY. E.G. VED NIKETAN - 30 RS/RM. MANY, SWISS COTTAGE - 40RS/RM. (REPDT TEXT?)
- **DELHI** / NEW DELHI
- SEE DELHI / PAKISTAN MAP
- FREQ, 6½-7HRS. — OVERNIGHT Q 23.15, Q.7.00 — 2-3 THROUGH TRAINS/DAY 7½-10HRS — DAILY 11HRS — DELHI→VARANASI SEV.16HRS — OVERNIGHT 14:00 Q. 6.40 — SEV. 10HRS ISTRS. — 10HRS Q.5.45 — SEV. 8-10 HRS Q.5.50 — Q 22.20 — OVERNIGHT Q.13.30

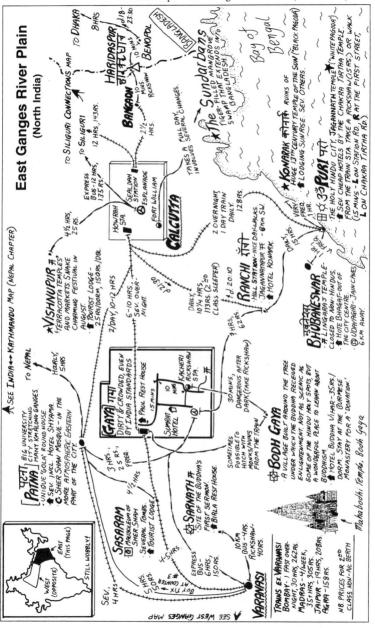

East Ganges River Plain
(North India)

↑ SEE INDIA→KATHMANDU MAP (NEPAL CHAPTER)

TO DHAKA

↑8 HRS

TO DHAKA

HARIDASPUR हरिदासपुर
10 MINS RICKSHAW
BENOPOL
→18-23:30

BANGAON बनगाँव
2½ HRS.

To SILIGURI CONNECTIONS MAP

To Siliguri

12 HRS, 143 RS.

The Sundarbans
TIGER-FILLED MANGROVE SWAMP THAT EXTENDS INTO BANGLADESH.

Bay of Bengal

TAKES A FULL DAY, INVOLVES SEVERAL CHANGES.

EXPRESS BUS-12 HRS, 135 RS.

SEALDAH STATION
ESPLANADE

KONARK कोणार्क RUINS OF HUGE 13TH CENTURY TEMPLE OF THE SUN ('BLACK PAGODA')
● LODGING SUNRISE. SEV. OTHERS.

FORT WILLIAM

CALCUTTA

4½ HRS, 25 RS.

HOWRAH STA.

2 OVERNIGHT, 1 DAY TRAIN
DAILY
128 RS.

VISHNUPUR ## 'TERRACOTTA TEMPLES' AND MARKETS. SNAKE CHARMING FESTIVAL IN AUGUST.
● SEV. INCL. TOURIST LODGE - 2.5 R/DORM, 15 RS./DBL.

॰॰ PURI पुरी
THE HOLY HINDU CITY. JAGANNATH TEMPLE ('WHITE PAGODA')
● SEV. CHEAP HOTELS BY THE CHAKRA TIRTHA TEMPLE, FROM THE TRAIN STA. TAKE A RICKSHAW (3 RS.) OR WALK (15 MINS - LON STATION RD, R AT THE FIRST STREET, LON CHAKRA TIRTHA RD.)

VERY FREQ. 1 HR.

2/DAY, 10-12 HRS
6-10 HRS, SEV. OVER-NIGHT.

DAILY, 10¼ HRS, 113 RS. (2 2ND CLASS SLEEPER)

DAILY ←21:30

RANCHI राँची
HILL STATION - NICE DAY-WALKS.
● JAGANNATHPUR ## - 8 KM SW.
● HOTEL KONARK.

←21:20:10

BHUBANESWAR भुवनेश्वर
LINGARAJ TEMPLE - CLOSED TO NON-HINDUS.
● HOTE BHAGAT-OUT OF THE CITY CENTRE.
● UDAYAGIRI: JAIN CAVES 6 KM AWAY.

DAN-5, 15 HRS

10¾ HRS, 62 RS.

7 HRS, 62 RS.

PATNA पटना, BIG UNIVERSITY CITY STRETCHING ALONG GANGES.
● MANY KM ALONG GANGES
● SEV. INCL. HOTEL SHYAMA.
● C. SHER SHAH MOSQUE - IN THE MORE ATMOSPHERIC EASTERN PART OF THE CITY.

To NEPAL
HOURLY, 5 HRS.

GAYA गया DIRTY & CROWDED, EVEN BY INDIA STANDARDS.
● PAUL REST HOUSE
KACHERI RICKSHAW STA.
10 MINS
15 MINS

● SUMRAT HOTEL

30 MINS, DANGEROUS AFTER DARK (TAKE RICKSHAW)

3 HRS, 2.5 RS, FREE.

SOMETIMES POSSIBLE TO HITCH WITH MONKS/NUNS FROM THE TRAIN.

SASARAM सासाराम
▣ MAUSOLEUM OF SHER SHAH, SEVERAL TOMBS.
● TOURIST LODGE

SARNATH सारनाथ ## SITE OF THE BUDDHA'S FIRST SERMON.
● BIRLA RESTHOUSE

4½ HRS.

☸ Bodh Gaya
- A VILLAGE BUILT AROUND THE TREE UNDER WHICH THE BUDDHA RECEIVED ENLIGHTENMENT. NOT AS SCENIC AS SOME OF THE HINDU HOLY SPOTS, BUT A WONDERFUL PLACE TO LEARN ABOUT BUDDHISM.
● HOTEL BUDDHA VIHAR - 3 5RS.
● DORM. STAY AT THE BURMESE MONASTERY FOR A DONATION.

4 HRS.

10 KM BUS-4 HRS. RICKSHAW 4 HRS.

Mahabodhi Temple, Bodh Gaya

SEV., 4 HRS.

VARANASI

EXPRESS BUS- 6 HRS, 15 RS.

WEST (OPPOSITE)
EAST (THIS PAGE)

STILL WOBBLY!

← SEE WEST GANGES MAP

TRAINS EX VARANASI
BOMBAY - 1 FAST OVER-NIGHT, 30 HRS, 262 RS.
MADRAS - 41 WEEK, 35+ HRS, 305 RS.
JAIPUR - 19 HRS, 205 RS.
AGRA - 158 RS.

SEV., 4 HRS.

BUY TIX AT COUNTER #3

NB PRICES FOR 2ND CLASS NON-AC BERTH

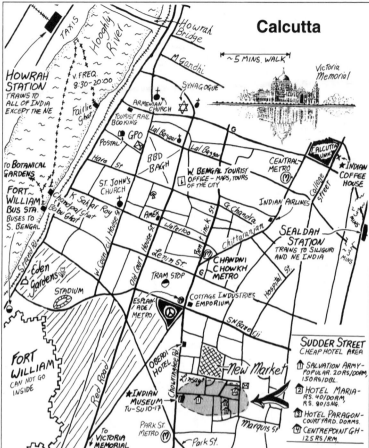

Calcutta is the hub of India's artistic and cultural wheel. If Bombay is India's Los Angeles, and Delhi is its Washington DC, then Calcutta is its New York (with friendlier residents). It is a dense urban metropolis swilling in chaos, making it the bane of some travellers for the same reason we love it. Good areas of the city for random exploration include the university district, the area between Howrah Bridge and BBD Bagh, and the Bengali market area of Gariahat (c3km SE of this map). Many buildings, including the Victoria Memorial and the nearby St Paul's Church, remain from when Calcutta served as the capital of British India. There are numerous art exhibitions, poetry readings and plays (many in English). *Calcutta This Fortnight* (available for free at tourist offices and some luxury hotels) lists current offerings.

● **Transport** The one line metro is open 8.15am-8.30pm Mon-Sat, 3-8.30pm Sun. Useful buses include #5, 6 (Howrah Stn, Sudder St), and #8 (Howrah Stn, Esplanade Metro Gariahat). An Indian Airlines bus runs between the airport and Sudder Street.

Andaman Islands

A remote string of sparsely populated tropical islands closer to Burma than to India. Sand beaches and palm trees abound, although your movement is restricted by the Indian Navy (which uses some islands as a major base).

● **Getting there** A boat for Port Blair departs from Madras and Calcutta every 10 days (3-4 days depending on the tide; Rs830/bunk; basic meals available). Buy tickets in Madras at the Dir of Shipping (by harbour on North Beach Rd. Despite horror stories about the boat, no one we met who took it had any problems. Flights $125 o/w and fill quickly.

● **Permits and restrictions** Permits required. Obtain one 1) when you apply for your Indian visa, 2) at a Foreigner Registration Office in Madras, Calcutta, Delhi or Bombay, or 3) on arrival at the airport (not ferry port) at Port Blair. Permits allow 30-day stay from your stated entry date (you can enter after that date but lose those days).

● **Diving** A five day scuba diving course costs $350. Rent a snorkel and mask in Port Blair for Rs50/day.

● **Transport** Ferries connect islands. South Andaman has many bus routes, but most only run a few times a day. Scooter rental possible.

● **Places to visit** (transport info is from Port Blair). **Chiriya Tapu:** Good beach, snorkeling. Bus 1hr, 4/day. **Havelock Is:** Classic beaches and coral. The beaches and villages are numbered. The Port Blair ferry arrives at village #1. The island's commercial centre is at #3 (bus from #1) where you can buy basic supplies and rent bicycles (Rs30/day) and motorcycles (Rs100-150/day). Beach #5 has a Rs300/rm *hotel*. Beach #7 has a *tented camp* popular with backpackers (Rs100/2 person tent; or pitch your own). Bring supplies, although water and basic food is available.

```
        LANDFALL IS.
  ⊢25KM         ○   ROSS IS
        PAGET        #2
        IS. ○
NORTH              SMITH IS.
ANDAMAN          DIGLIPUR
                    ⊢
            a
       AUSTEN
INTER-         SOUTH IS
VIEWS        MAYABUNDER

MIDDLE   RANGAT
ANDAMAN    ⊢
                LONG IS. ⊢
BHARATANG IS.
              OUTRAM IS.
SPIKE IS. ○
SOUTH
ANDA-              LAWRENCE
MAN                IS.
            MADHU-    HAVELOCK
            BAN      IS. ⊢
       MT HARRIET   NEIL IS.
         Ross IS. #1
      PORT BLAIR ⊢
 WANDOOR
          CORBYN'S COVE
       CHIRIYA TAPU
JOLLY
BUOY    RUTLAND IS.
IS.      CINQUE IS.

↓ TO NICOBAR ISLANDS
  (FOREIGNERS NOT ALLOWED)

⊢ = FOREIGNERS ALLOWED TO SPEND THE
    NIGHT (WITH GENERAL ANDAMANS
    PERMIT)
  = THEORETICALLY ONLY DAY TRIPS
    ALLOWED.
```

Bus transport limited. **Long Is:** One village. Beaches, camp with permission obtained in Port Blair. A bicycle (brought from Port Blair) is useful. Ferry-2/week. **Neil Is:** One basic *guest house*. Ferry 3hrs. **Port Blair:** The Andaman capital. A good place to obtain info (the tourist office is helpful and has free maps) and rent scooters, but there's little reason to stay around. The traveller hangout is the *Jagannath Guest House* (clean, luggage storage, rooms from Rs50). **Smith Is:** Remote getaway. Bring your own supplies, though a store (a 3hr walk up the E coast, then 1km inland) sells potatoes, candles, biscuits and rice (that's a complete list). Ferry from Diglipur. **Wandoor Marine Park** has coral reefs and diving. Boats go to the park and to Red Skin (Rs50) and Jolly Buoy (Rs75). Bus 1hr, d 7.30, 8.30.

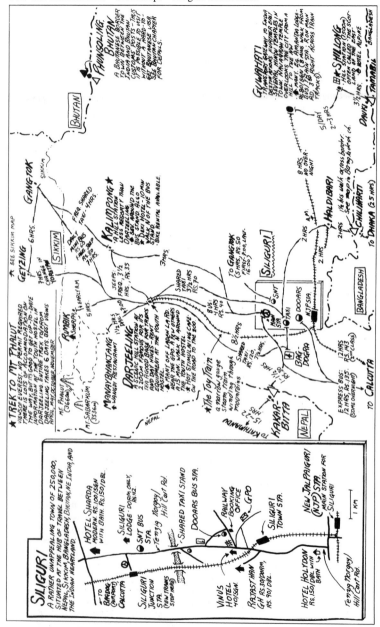

★ TREK TO MT PHALUT
VIEWS OF EVEREST. NO PERMIT REQUIRED. THERE IS LOTS OF ACCOMMODATION ON THE WAY, BUT IT'S GOOD TO GET UP-TO-DATE INFORMATION AT THE TOURIST HOSTEL IN DARJEELING. ENTIRE ROUTE TREK FROM DARJEELING TAKES 6 DAYS. BEST VIEWS APRIL, MAY/OCTOBER, NOVEMBER.

PHONGSOLING BHUTAN.
A BHUTANESE BORDER TOWN BETWEEN THE INDIAN AND BHUTANESE DOOARS. POSSIBLE TO VISIT WITHOUT A PERMIT, BUT IT'S A HARD TO SEE BHUTANESE. VISIT BHUTANESE CHAMBER FOR DETAILS.

BHUTAN

GUWAHATI
TRANSPORT GATEWAY TO SASHI DESTINATIONS FURTHER EAST (SILCHAR, IMPHAL, TOURAGATI). NICE CITY TO VISIT. OVERLOOKS THE BRAHMAPUTRA HILL TO THE NW... MANY... Eg. NAVAGRAH LODGE... BUS. 3RD RIGHT ACROSS TRACKS)

★ SHILLONG
HILL STATION (1500m) OFTEN CALLED "THE SCOTLAND OF THE EAST"... HOTEL ALPINE.

GEYZING GANGTOK
SEE SIKKIM MAP
SIKKIM

KALIMPONG
A HILL STATION, LESS "RESORTY" THAN DARJEELING. JEEPS AROUND THE BUS STAND. ALSO DEKI HOTEL - 10 MIN WALK OUT OF THE BUS STAND.
- BIKE RENTAL AVAILABLE.

GANGTOK
SIKKIM

MANAYBHANTANG
★ WANGDI RESTAURANT

DARJEELING
A SCENIC HILL STATION IN 2 AGOOD BASIS FOR TREKS AND DAY HIKES - RENT EQUIPMENT AT THE YOUTH
★ MANY OFF LADHI LA RD NEAR THE GPO A FEW OTHERS ALSO... ★ THE YOUTH HOSTEL IS HIGH AT STIMULATING CAFE ON THE ROAD TO THE ZOO.

RUMBIK
★ SHERPA
YEMIYAM

MT PHALUT (3636m)
MT SABAKHUM (3556m)

NEPAL

★ The Toy Train
a narrow gauge STEAM RAIL TRIP WINDING THROUGH MOUNTAINS

SILIGURI

HALDIBARI

CHILWARI
TO DHAKA (2½ HRS)

BANGLADESH

KAKAR BITTA
NEPAL

To Kathmandu

BAG-DOGRA

TO CALCUTTA

SILIGURI
A RATHER UNAPPEALING TOWN OF 250,000, SITUATED AT THE HUB OF TOWEL BETWEEN NEPAL, SIKKIM, BANGLADESH, BHUTAN, NE INDIA AND THE INDIAN HEARTLAND.

HOTEL SHARDA
MODERN. RS.100/SGN WITH BATH. RS.150/DBL.

SILIGURI LODGE - DORM ONLY, RS.52.

SMT BUS STA.

SHARED TAXI STAND

DOOARS BUS STA.

RAILWAY BOOKING OFFICE

GPO

SILIGURI TOWN STA.

NEW JALPAIGURI (NJP) STA.
MAIN STATION FOR SILIGURI

TO BIRPARA (WHARF) CALCUTTA

SILIGURI JUNCTION STA.
(NEW TRAINS STOP HERE)

VINUS HOTEL 40/SGN

RATRAST'HAN GH RS.30/DORM, RS.90/DBL.

HOTEL HOLYDON RS.150/DBL. WITH BATH

Tenzig Norgay Hill Cart Rd.

1 KM

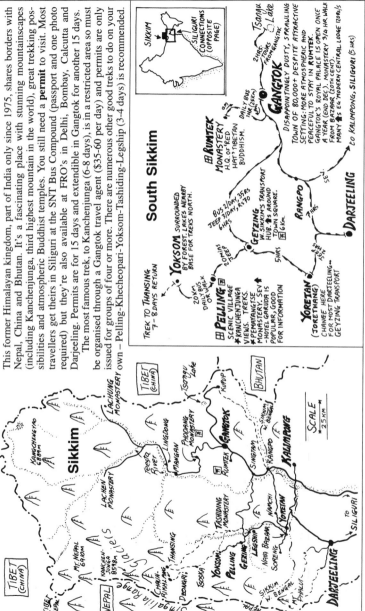

This former Himalayan kingdom, part of India only since 1975, shares borders with Nepal, China and Bhutan. It's a fascinating place with stunning mountainscapes (including Kanchenjunga, third highest mountain in the world), great trekking possibilities and atmospheric Buddhist temples. You still need a **permit** to visit. Most travellers get theirs in Siliguri at the SNT Bus Compound (passport and one photo required) but they're also available at FRO's in Delhi, Bombay, Calcutta and Darjeeling. Permits are for 15 days and extendible at Gangtok for another 15 days.

The most famous trek, to Kanchenjunga (6-8 days), is in a restricted area so must be organised through a Gangtok travel agent ($35-60 per day) and permits are only issued for groups of four or more. There are numerous other good treks to do on your own – Pelling-Khecheopari-Yoksom-Tashiding-Legship (3-4 days) is recommended.

South Sikkim

GANGTOK
DISAPPOINTINGLY DUSTY, SPRAWLING TOWN OF 80,000+ DESPITE ATTRACTIVE SETTING: MORE ATMOSPHERIC AND PEACEFUL TO STAY IN RUMTEK. GANGTOK'S ROYAL PALACE IS OPEN ONCE A YEAR (END DEC.). MONASTERY 3/4 HR WALK FROM BAZAAR (20th CENT.). MANY 5's E4 MODERN CENTRAL LODGE 120R,/s

RUMTEK MONASTERY
H.Q. OF RED HAT TIBETAN BUDDHISM.

DAILY BUS 1HR (24km)

TO KALIMPONG, SILIGURI (5 HRS)

YOKSOM SURROUNDED BY FOREST, LAKES NEARBY. BASE FOR TREKS NORTH.

TREK TO THANSING 7-8 DAYS RETURN

PELLING SCENIC VILLAGE ★KANCHENJUNGA VIEWS. TREKS.
20KM DAILY BUS OR WALK
90mins JEEP

PEMAYANGTSE MONASTERY, 5KM – HOTEL GARUDA IS POPULAR, GOOD FOR INFORMATION

GEYZING
N. SIKKIM'S TRANSPORT HUB. JEEP 3/DAY, R.70 BUS 2/DAY, 3.5RS 6HRS. TOWN SQUARE.
E 6 KM

RANGPO

DARJEELING

YORETAN (TORETHANG)
CHANGE HERE FOR MOST DARJEELING– GEYZING TRANSPORT
5HRS

2HRS

SE

5HRS 5HRS SUN

TIBET (CHINA)

Sikkim

KANGCHENYAO 6889m

MT. NEPAL 6909m

LACHUNG MONASTERY

TIBET (CHINA)

Tsangu Lake

KUPUP

BHUTAN

LINGDONG

LINGTAM

MANGAN

Teesta River

PHODONG MONASTERY

●GANGTOK

RUMTEK

SINGTAM

RANGPO

N. SIKKIM W. BENGAL

TIBET NEPAL

MT. NEPAL 6598m KANCHEN–JUNGA 8598m

Himalayas

CHURNG RINKHLUNG

THANSING

DZONGRI

YOKSOM

PELLING

TASHIDING MONASTERY

GEYZING

LEGSHIP

NAYA BAZAAR

NAMCHI

YORETAM

SINGRAM

KALIMPONG

TO SILIGURI

EGSKA

SENGIC SCENIC

SIKKIM W. BENGAL

NEPAL

MT. BENGAL

PHALUT

DARJEELING

NEPAL

Simalila Range

SCALE
25 KM

SILIGURI CONNECTIONS COMPOSITE PAGE
SIKKIM

Southernmost India Highlights

(NB. VISIT DEC-FEB)

KEY

- Castle/Fort
- Colonial Era Fort
- Fort/Temple on Hill or Crag.
- Maintains Some Colonial Feel.
- Area of Interesting Villages
- Famous Ashram
- Hindu Holy City
- Temple Town
- Package Tourists

100 Km

MANGALORE

SRAVANABELAGOLA Extraordinary 10th Cent. Statue of Naked Prince/Saint Bahubali, 17m Tall.

BANGALORE Huge, Pleasantly Green City.

SRIRANGAPATNAM (SERINGAPATAM) Small Fortified Town on an Island in River Kaveri.

MYSORE Several Lovely Palaces, Two Are Now Hotels

CANNANORE

MADRAS St. Thome, Mylapore

to Port Blair (Andamans)

KANCHIPURAM 33

MAMALAPURAM Massive Rock Carvings

PONDICHERRY French Enclave 1673-1954 Visit Auroville.

CHIDAMBARAM Nataraj

GINGI Massive!

KUMBAKONUM ~ Darasurum 5km

VELLORE Jalkantesvara

SOMNATHPUR Village

TIRUVANNAMALAI Southern Home of Shiva.

TRUVELLARAI Village

NAMAKAL

SRIRANGAM

TRICHY (Truchchirapalli)

DINDIGUL

PUDOKKOTTAI

THANJAVUR Brihadisvara

MADURAI Medieval Atmosphere Around the Minakshi

RAMESVARAM Rameslinga

✗ Ferry to Sri Lanka Remains Suspended

SRI LANKA REMOVED!

TELICHERRY

CALICUT/Kozhikode The Historic International Spice Trading Centre.

to Lakshadweep Isles

MEGALITH VILLAGES E.G. PORKALAM

TRICHUR

COCHIN

KERALA BACKWATER CRUISES Beautiful Waterways Ferries Gliding Between Green Palm Tousled Villages, Though Alleppey – Quilon (8hrs) Is A Bit Too Long.

ERNAKULAM

Ooty Kotagiri, and Coonoor hill stations

KODAIKKANAL Cool Hill Stn.

KOTTAYAM 5km to Vallia Palli 13th Century Nestorian Church

ALLEPPEY CHEAP

QUILON

KUTTALAM WATERFALLS (100m High, Near TENKASI)

PADMANHAPURAM

TRIVANDRUM "NAPIER" Attractive, Relaxed City. Flights to Sri Lanka, Maldives.

KOVALUM

KANNIKYAKUMARI, Southernmost Point. Gandhi's Ashes.

Bhutan

Bhutan's ancient culture is a rich blend of superstition, Buddhist traditions and reverence for nature. In this century, however, Bhutan has found the outside world closing in and its culture, once sheltered by mountain isolation, now needs laws to protect it. Televisions are banned and the Bhutanese are required to live in Bhutanese-style houses and wear the national dress (a multi-coloured robe and bamboo hat) though you'll see the occasional daring t-shirt and base-

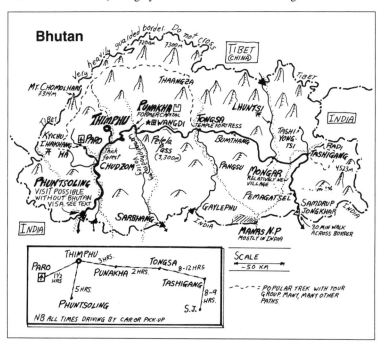

□ **W&M's country ratings – Bhutan**
● **Expense $$$$$** Because it's a tour or nothing.
● **Value for money ✔✔✔✔** Tours are usually professional, all-inclusive and comfortable (though not the luxury the price suggests).
● **English spoken ✔✔✔** There are surprising numbers of English speakers in Thimpu and the Paro Valley but virtually none in rural areas. Ask in advance if your guide speaks English – some don't.

ball cap. Bhutan is a closed country. Tourist visas are granted only to those on government approved tours. While there is no longer a limit to how many tourists are allowed into Bhutan, artificially high prices kept all but 4000 from making the trip in 1995. Aid workers, too, have a difficult time getting into Bhutan – aid projects are often rejected by the Bhutanese government.

Bhutan's efforts at cultural protection make life difficult for Nepali immigrants who settled there, some many generations ago. A recent census found that Nepalis outnumbered Bhutanese. In response, the nervous feudal government quickly legislated to make ethnic Nepalis within its borders, non-citizens. Many were deported and still languish in refugee camps. The rest were required to conform to the same cultural decrees as the Bhutanese, and speak Drugpa, not Nepali. Bhutanese culture is closely related to Tibetan though the locals are likely to claim that there are few similarities. Drugpa, the national language, is to Tibetan as Portuguese is to Spanish. Bhutanese Buddhism is very similar to the Lamaist style in Tibet.

Bhutan's cultural strong-arming has undoubtedly achieved its aims. The culture is alive with the vibrancy and depth it has had for centuries and the environment is pristine and protected – all of which creates contradictions in the minds of travellers who'd love to see Bhutan stay free from other tourists while simultaneously wishing to visit themselves. Those who have splurged on a tour have found the experience a highlight of their Asian experience.

PRACTICAL INFORMATION
Booking a tour
Tours are expensive: typically $120/day for an organised trek, $200/day for a group of five or more staying in hotels, $230 for individuals. The cost no longer depends on the season and does not include transport to and from Bhutan – an expensive addition; most agencies insist that tourists fly at least one way on Druk Air (Bhutan's national airline). Druk flies from: Bangkok, Delhi, Dhaka, Calcutta and Kathmandu.

Darjeeling, Calcutta and especially Kathmandu are the best places to arrange tours. Many agencies have photo albums to help you choose your itinerary. Most agents outside Asia require three months' notice to arrange the necessary paperwork; in Kathmandu it can take as little as four

---

❑ **Geo-political information – Bhutan**
Population: 1.8 million (1997), 1.3m (1983).
Area: 47,000 sq km.
Capital: Thimpu (officially 17,000 in 1993 but private estimates put the population at 35,000. Perhaps ethnic Nepalis aren't counted in the official tally.)
Other major cities: None. 85% of the population is classified as rural.
GNP per capita: $400 estimate (1994).
Major exports/economy: Cardamon (world's top exporter). The country is largely self-sufficient in food. It receives small, regular payments from India as compensation for lands annexed during the British period.
Ethnic mix: Officially: Bhutanese (70%), Nepali (30%). The reverse proportions are probably true.
Leader: Dragon King (Druk Gyalpo) Jigime Singye Wangchuk, absolute feudal monarch, chairman of Council of Ministers. India has control of foreign policy in exchange for military protection (from China).

❑ **Essential information for travellers – Bhutan**
● **Visa** Required. Travellers to Bhutan can only obtain a visa (at the airport, $20) if they are on a tour. The only possible exception is if you are a devout Buddhist who wishes to study religion. See also Bhutan without a visa suggestions below.
● **Currency** Ngultrum. US$1=Ng38.3 (pegged to the Indian Rupee at 1:1).
● **Time zone** 6 hours ahead of GMT (same as Bangladesh, 1/4hr ahead of Nepal, 1/2hr ahead of India).
● **Religious tone** Buddhism, the state religion, pervades the entire country.
● **When to go** Ideally in November. June to October is monsoon season.
● **Key tips** Do not sneak illegally into Bhutan. It is a closed country, the laws are strict, and the police force is well trained. People who have tried crossing illegally have ended up in prison or disappeared.

days. Some tour agencies to consider:
● **Bhutan Travel** (US and Canada toll free ☎ 1-800-950-9908, ☎ 212-838-6382 from outside the US, fax 212-750-1269), 120 56th St E, New York, NY 10022, USA, has a very large variety of tours, including treks, festivals and bird watching; the company also runs tours for individuals.
● **InnerAsia Expeditions** (☎ 1-800-777-8183), 2627 E Lombard St, San Francisco, CA 94123, USA.
● **Asian Light Travels** (☎/fax 977-1-420-444), PO Box 8948, Kathmandu, Nepal, can arrange visa paperwork in four days.
● **Mandala Trekking** (☎ 1-228600, fax 1-227600), Kantipath, GPO Box 4563, Kathmandu, Nepal, are very experienced and charge standard prices.
● **Ashoka Tour & Travels** (☎ 332-5035), 305, 3rd Fl, New Delhi House, Barakhamba Rd, New Delhi, offer 4-day tours not including air fare for $161/day.
● **Lhomen Tours & Trekking Co** (☎/fax 00975-24148), PO Box 341, Thimpu, are recommended; average cost is $200/day.

Visiting Bhutan without a visa:
There are two ways in which you can do this legally:
1) **Phuntsoling** If you have a double/multiple entry Indian visa you can cross out of India into Phunstsoling. It's in Bhutan, but the Bhutanese customs post is on the far side of town, so you're free to walk through. Though the town is more Indian influenced than the rest of Bhutan, it is still a different world from India proper. People

seem more relaxed, the stores accept both Indian rupees and ngultrum and you can send postcards with colourful Bhutanese stamps. The Queen of Bhutan has her personal gompa on a nearby hill top, though visiting it is of dubious legality. Once you reach the immigration post, ask innocently if it's possible to get a visa on arrival. It isn't. You'll be asked to walk back to India.

Note that if you have only a single entry Indian visa, Indian officials will not let you out of India.
2) **Manas National Park, Assam** This is an Indian national park, a small part of which extends into Bhutan. It's sometimes closed owing to militant activity.

Further information
The Bhutan Tourism Corporation (☎ 22647), GPO Box 159, Thimpu.
America-Bhutan Council, 423 East Ojai Ave, Suite 107-108, Ojai, CA 93023, USA.

Odyssey's *Bhutan* guide is informative. A 1:250,000 'travel map' is sporadically available in Kathmandu and in map shops in the West. *Kuensel*, the Bhutanese newspaper is available in Kathmandu.

❑ **Language**
Some words in Drugpa:
Common greeting – *guzuzampola*
Thank you – *kadrinche*
Friend – *chah-ro*
The food is delicious – *jeh go sheem tok toh too*
Nice yak – *yah leh hem do*

Nepal

Nepal is one of the most memorable places on the globe. The majesty of its mountains is laid at your feet through a network of long distance trekking paths whose popularity keeps them well serviced with shelter and food. The little rectangular kingdom exudes historic atmosphere in towns which, although they have suffered the ravages of pollution and modernisation, retain a very rich cultural vein. There are exhilarating rafting rivers which deposit you on lowland plains near jungle reserves in which you can see rhinos, elephants and river dolphins. All this comes with the added bonus of low prices (if somewhat more than India) and helpful, smiling (if not always efficient) people.

Kathmandu, the old focus of the hippy trail, is today more than ever the travellers' Mecca par excellence. If there is a god of travellers, he created Kathmandu as his official merchandising centre: attractive handmade clothes, used trekking supplies to rent or buy, beautiful cards and postcards, and a remarkable range of books both new and second hand. Some travellers advise you to get out quickly before the great live music bars and selection of delicious Western-approximation foods tempt you to stay much longer than you'd planned.

Tourism is Nepal's top foreign currency earner (just ahead of carpets) and tourists throng Thamel, Pokhara and the popular treks. Yet away from these areas much of the country still remains roadless and charmingly cut off from the main stream of the twentieth century. 'You have everything from the Iron Age to Cyberspace', was how one Indian visitor accurately summed up the country.

❏ **W&M's country ratings – Nepal**

● **Expense $** Kathmandu is a little pricier than India and with so many temptations it's hard to stick to budget. In the villages, however, necessities are extremely cheap.

● **Value for money** ✔✔✔✔ Accommodation and food are particularly good value. Buses are cheap but uncomfortable.

● **Getting around** ✔✔✔ Few roads, but those that exist have buses. Otherwise walk.

● **English spoken** ✔✔✔✔ English is almost lingua franca along the well-trodden tourist routes. However, very little is understood in the small villages of the Terai and the less-visited mountain villages.

● **Woman alone** ✔✔✔✔ A chance to relax after the hassles of India, though late at night Kathmandu hisses somewhat disconcertingly with the soto voce suggestions of sex-starved rickshaw wallahs and hashish peddlers.

● **For vegetarians** ✔✔✔✔✔ Excellent selection in tourist centres. Menus in the mountains are tough for carnivores.

❑ **Essential information for travellers – Nepal**

● **Visa** Required but effortlessly available on arrival (by air or land). It costs $25 for a one-month stay; and this is easily extended. Trekking permits cost extra and must be arranged within Nepal.

● **Currency** Nepali Rupee; US$1=Rs62.5 (bank); Rs64-65 (black market from carpet shops).

● **Time zone** 5¾hours ahead of GMT (¼hr ahead of India; ¼hr behind Bangladesh; 1¼hrs behind Thailand, 2¼hrs behind Tibet).

● **Religious tone** Hindu with Buddhist leanings and a strong Tibetan Buddhist sub-community give Nepal a strong spiritual feel – temples and prayer flags everywhere.

● **Health factors** Beware of altitude sickness. Malaria risk in the southern lowlands only. Water should be boiled and filtered. Leeches can be annoying if walking in the summer months but are not dangerous – no problem at all in the trekking season.

● **Special dangers** None, but you may eat, drink and spend more than you planned.

● **Social conventions** Walk around a Buddhist gompa/stupa in a clockwise direction.

● **Typical traveller destinations** Annapurna trek, Everest trek, Royal Chitwan National Park, Kathmandu Valley, Bhaktapur.

● **Highlights** Any mountain trek (literally takes your breath away); Royal Bardia National Park; the great food, live music and hang-outs in Kathmandu and Pokhara; white water rafting; *tongba* halls in the back streets of Boudnath.

● **When to go** Summer is not a good time to visit the mountain kingdom. Monsoon rains last from June to September, there is flooding in the Terai and clouds obscure the mountains. October is ideal for whitewater rafting due to the monsoon run-offs, though there is a river for most seasons.

The peak trekking period is November/December; it's not too cold and the clouds have cleared. Prices drop in January and February; this is considered the low season as many of the major trekking passes are covered in heavy snow. Though some teahouses close, it's still possible to trek at this time if you're prepared for the cold nights and a higher chance of cloud cover. The sky may clear again at the end of February but snow remains on many treks. Rhododendron forests make lower altitude trekking (eg in Helambu) delightful in March/April.

By the end of April it gets humid and increasingly hot as a precursor to the monsoons, though Kathmandu is still a welcome change from sweltering India, especially in the evening breezes.

● **Pulse of the country** Durbar Square of any small town.

● **Key tip** Plan more time for a trek than you think you really need – as well as being more pleasant, moving slowly gives you time to acclimatise to the altitude; the fittest (and therefore fastest) hikers are the most likely to get altitude sickness. Visit the Himalayan Rescue Association (HRA) in Kathmandu before trekking for knowledgeable advice and independent tips.

● **Festivals** Losar (Tibetan New Year) happens three days after the February new moon – it's a big event at Boudnath so arrive early and watch out for the dancing monks. Dasain is a very important festival – everything closes down for up to 10 days in October so that families can reunite to celebrate Rama's victory over Ravana. And there are dozens more.

PRACTICAL INFORMATION
Visas and formalities

● **Visa strategy** Visas are available at borders (including from Tibet) for the same price, and with less delay than at embassies. Costs have been reduced since 1994 and now a 60-day multiple entry visa costs US$60; 30-day single entry $25, double entry $40; 15-day single entry $15. At Kathmandu airport you can sometimes pay in other currencies. The enterprising officers simply convert it for you and pocket a small profit. Using US$ cash is thus marginally cheaper.

● **Visa extensions** Extensions allow a total stay of up to 120 days in one calendar year (including the original visa period) and are now automatically given on request. Yes, this does mean you could actually stay eight months by arriving in early September because on 1 January your accumulated total stay reverts to zero.

Extensions cost $1/day and the simple procedure is completed the same day (closed Saturdays) – go to the Immigration Office in Kathmandu or Pokhara. A fifth month is possible but not automatic; you may be required to show a plane ticket home and to visit the Home Ministry for an interview. Prepare a reason why you want to stay.

● Visa extensions no longer require you to show exchange receipts (previously you had to prove $20 a day exchanged).

● You can apply repeatedly for extensions in small units if you are uncertain as to how long you'll stay.

● If your visa has already expired when you go to get an extension you'll have to pay $2/day (instead of the normal $1) for each expired day.

● Trekking permits no longer double as visa extensions as they bizarrely once did.

● If you leave the day after your visa

❑ Geo-political information – Nepal

Population: 22.6 million, (1997), 20.4m (1995), 18m (1991), 14m (1980).

Area: 136,000 sq km.

Capital: Kathmandu.

Other major cities: Biratnagar.

GNP per capita: $200 (1993), $159 (1988).

Currency history: Rupee/US$1 — Feb 1998: Rs62.5, Oct 1997: Rs58.5, April 1996: Rs58.2, Dec 1995: Rs54.3, Dec 1994: Rs49.4 (official rates).

Major exports/economy: Carpets, garments, tourism, paper making. 55% of GDP is agricultural, employing 93% of the population.

Official language: Nepali (58.4%). Others include Maithili (11%), Bhojpuri (8%), Magar (3%), Awadhi (1.5%). Tibetan is spoken by pilgrims and there are Tibetan language bookshops in Kathmandu.

Religious mix: 89% Hindu, 5.3% Tibetan Buddhist, 2.5% Muslim. 50,000 Christians.

Landmarks of national history: 1482: Yaksa Malla divided the kingdom into three principalities based in Patan, Kathmandu and Bakhtapur. **1769:** Gorkha ruler conquered the whole valley. **1951:** Restoration of King's powers following the toppling of the 'Prime-Minister-for-life' system favouring the Rana family. **1959:** First constitution. **1990:** Violent protests, constitutional crisis and the beginning of the 'democracy experiment'. **1991:** First refugees from Bhutan arrived (still in camps in Japa district). **1993:** 3500 people killed in heavy floods.

Leaders: King Birendra is popular. Frequently changing political leadership less so. Prime minister Sher Bahadur Deuba (NCP).

Pressing political issues: Ethnic Nepali refugees from Bhutan languishing in camps, water supply problems in the Kathmandu valley, balancing politically between huge neighbours, India's control of trade.

expires the transgression will be overlooked, but cheating doesn't make sense. One traveller who tried to leave having forged an extra five days by changing the date in his visa, got a week in jail after he was beaten by guards and caught typhoid.

● **Permits** Permits are required for trekking in most areas to which there is no road (much of the country). These can cost from $5 to $500/week. See Trekking section, p383. There are also many national parks and wildlife sanctuaries to which entry will cost Rs650 for periods of time that vary between parks.

Money

The black market is commonplace in Kathmandu and Pokhara – carpet shop salesmen will beckon you to 'change' as you walk by (tell them you are perfect the way you are). Changing US$ cash on the black market will give you about 6% more rupees than at the bank, though the market rate varies according to an obscure formula reliant on the price of gold in Hong Kong. Though such transactions are not strictly legal, neither are they a cloak and dagger affair and most dealers won't rip you off beyond offering poorer than necessary rates. Walk-away bargaining works well (most will bump their opening rate up a full rupee). Pounds sterling and Deutschmarks can also be exchanged on the black market, though the rates are not as favourable as for dollars.

Some carpet shops and hotels will cash travellers' cheques at rates similar to the banks but without the queues or commission (which can be 2% or higher, with a Rs100-125 minimum). Cash advances are an excellent way to obtain money – credit card companies usually give rates equivalent to the higher travellers cheque rate and Kathmandu banks don't charge any commission. There are banks in some trekking centres but these will not give cash advances. Money changed officially (keep receipts) may be reconverted into any currency at Kathmandu airport, or at the Indian border into Indian Rupees only. Reconversion at banks is not possible.

Transport

With so many mountains, there are still many areas of the country that can be reached only on foot. As the government extends roads to each of the provincial centres, the bus network grows.

● **Air** Internal flights can be a dramatically beautiful way to reduce the time spent on a trek. Planes reach many inaccessible places – such as Lukla where the runway clings to the mountainside and the plane has to turn sideways to stop it slipping away while passengers embark. Flying at the end of a trek is usually more sensible than flying to the start because the inward trek points you towards the views of approaching mountains. Also because going suddenly from low to high is the cause of altitude sickness.

● **Bus** The Kathmandu-Pokhara road is good, but most others are very rough and slow. Seats at the back of the bus are designed to turn stomachs into post-digestive food mixers and it may be worth booking ahead or waiting a day to ensure you have one of the front 10 seats.

● **Train** Nepal's only line is a short stretch heading south east from Janakpur; services in overcrowded mini-steam trains operate twice a day. Agents in Kathmandu can pre-book berths on Indian train connections for you; this is not done by computer but by physically sending a contact person across the border who will later meet you with the tickets, so mark-ups are understandable.

● **Taxis and rickshaws** The vehicles with black number-plates are the cheapest taxis: about Rs15 for a five-minute ride, once you've battled to have the driver turn on the meter. Auto-rickshaws charge about a third less than a taxi but the saving isn't really worth the exposure to the choking fumes of Kathmandu's traffic. Fares on cycle-rickshaws are highly negotiable.

● **Bicycle/motorbike** Motorbike rental from around Rs350/day is recommended for the Kathmandu valley. Legally the driver must wear a helmet, but not so the family of passengers! The lack of a licence is not necessarily an impediment to rental.

Taiwanese mountain bikes can be rented for Rs70-100 per day, old Chinese Flying Pigeons are around Rs30. For reaching outer Kathmandu bicycles may be faster than buses.

Accommodation

Hotels send touts to the international airport and one is mobbed on arrival with offers of free rides. It is tempting to assume that all these aggressive heavy sellers are going to cheat you. However, we had free rides and to our amazement were charged the agreed Rs120 per room; they also made no complaint when we decided to move out the next day.

Cheap places are available in all Nepali towns and at restaurants in some villages where there is no hotel. In the off-season there is intense competition between backpacker hotels and you can bargain the already cheap rooms to as little as one third of the asking price if you think that's morally acceptable.

Along the most popular trekking routes, so called 'tea houses' are really very basic hostels. They rarely cost more than Rs40/night, but you'll need a sleeping bag to keep warm.

Food and drink

Real Nepali food is *dal bhat*, a soupy lentil curry with rice, traditionally eaten at 10am and before bed at around 8pm; there's no such thing as lunchtime. One Nepali friend admitted that without at least a little dal bhat every day he couldn't feel satisfied. Like most Nepalis he swears that the flavours of every dal bhat are different. True as that may be, many trekkers can't help looking forward to returning to the endless variety of cooking styles, cake shops and bakeries in Kathmandu. Tibetan *momos* and *thukpa* are commonly available (see p248).

As in India, sweet milky tea is a favoured drink, though until recently it was considered a luxury in villages. If you're served coffee by a family this is a show of great generosity as coffee remains very pricey for locals. There are several street stands in Kathmandu where good chocolate-less cappuccinos can be enjoyed for Rs8, compared with Rs25 for a poor second best in Thamel restaurants. *Tongba* (pronounced tum-ba) is a typical Sherpa/Tibetan concoction offering unbeatable value for the alcoholic at only one sixth of the price of a beer. You'll be presented with a *dungro* (wooden churn decorated with brass girds) filled with fermented millet grains. Add boiling water, and after a few minutes, drink the hot liquid through a bamboo straw that filters out the seeds. Searching for tongba can lead you into some wonderfully dingy and atmospheric local bars though when the place is busy and all the dungros are used up, the tongba comes less attractively in a plastic jug with an aluminium straw. Custom dictates that you stir only on the third refill. *Chhard* is a pre-prepared version of tongba; since it is made with cold water it offers a greater opportunity for stomach problems. *Chhang* is a milky wine-strength drink which warms tired porters at the mountain trailside equivalent of truckstops, while *rakshi (roxy)* is the local moonshine.

Staying in touch

● **Mail** The postal system is sporadic – we received one letter from Europe in four days, yet others took three weeks. Most outgoing letters arrived eventually, though the mail system is not 100% trustworthy. Several shops, bookstores and 'business centres' will sell stamps and take your mail to be franked at the post office. We tested several in the Thamel area and all seemed reliable.

Outgoing parcels will need to be wrapped and sewn into cotton, and checked by customs at the GPO. Packing agents will arrange everything for an extra Rs1000 on top of the postage (eg Rs2643 for 10kg).

Mail is received reliably at the **American Express** office (fax 226153) c/o Yeti Travels, Hotel Mayalu, Jamal Tole, Durbar Marg, PO Box 76, Kathmandu.

● **Phone** International calls cost Rs165 per

minute to Europe or the US from offices round Kathmandu, Pokhara and even in some mountain villages. Charges are per minute not per second. Bring your own stopwatch! International country code: +977. Kathmandu: 1, Nepalganj: 81, Pokhara: 61.

● **Fax** Sending faxes is easy from various private offices (Rs170 per minute to Europe or North America). The price is charged in minute-minimum units, which is annoying as most pages take just over a minute to send and hence cost Rs340 for one sheet.

● **E-mail** As a sign of how much has changed on this planet in recent years, several private telephone offices in Kathmandu now offer an e-mail sending service. We found the cheapest rates at **Global Communications** in the Thamel area – Rs60 per kilobyte (about 12 typed lines of text). Global was also the only place we found where you could **receive** e-mail (Rs20 per kb – so long messages will be expensive). Their address is: GLOCOM@globpc.wlink.com.np.

Trekking

Nowhere in the world offers such spectacular trekking or is as well set up to make it easy for you. Good maps, trekking guides (relevant to the route you'll walk) and all the equipment you'll need are available cheaply in Kathmandu; you can rent or buy – new or second hand. It's easy to employ porters and guides (though get recommendations before hiring), and on the most popular treks you'll find teahouses with basic beds and sometimes surprisingly good meals right the way along. Mid-October to mid-December is the ideal time for many treks; but since it is the high season some treks are a little over busy.

● **Information** Before going trekking a visit to the **Himalayan Rescue Assoc (HRA)**, 1st floor, Tilicho Hotel, PO Box 4944, Thamel, is advised. The office is in the alley round the corner from the Immigration Office. They have travellers' report books with up-to-date tales written by other trekkers on many of the routes you may be considering. They have Western volunteer doctors posted at

---

❏ **Kathmandu by night**

At 10pm Kathmandu pulls down the shutters on its live music cafés, Mexican restaurants and chocolate-cake shops. Guest houses lock their gates (so learn where the doorbell is!) and rickshaws jostle to persuade straggling tourists to take a ride home. It's the drivers' last chance to recoup the Rs80 half-day hire fee, before curling up in the colourful chariot to sleep like a contorted foetus. If you want a beer after 10.30pm the only official options are the casinos (Hotel de l'Annapurna is the nearest to Thamel) where Indian low rollers chain smoke over bottles of Challenger Whiskey.

Behind the shutters, however, party life goes on a little longer. Disproving yet again that all the street folk are avaricious beggars, a rickshaw wallah led us without charge to a tiny hatchway. 'You can get a beer in here', he assured us. Up a dark set of stairs and across a hallway sat a small group of Nepalis slamming playing cards onto the table with unnecessary vigour. The beer was warm but not expensive and we settled down with our instant friends. 'Would you like to meet the man with two heads?' asked one. It was not lewd double entendre, and one of the players was quick to whip off his hat. On the crown of his scalp, rising hairless like a fleshy hillock his second head was a perfectly central goitre. We were invited to feel the lump which he and his friends described as his blessing; a wonderful exercise in positive thinking. Just as rickshaws double as beds for the drivers, so building sites crawl with builders' families and many a restaurant sleeps its chefs. These lads, workers at the 'closed' bar, literally had no home to go to and long flowed the beer.

❏ Trekking in Nepal
Which trek?

Variety of cultures	Annapurna Circuit, Ganesh Himal, Helambu, Jomson, Mustang.
Mountain scenery	Annapurna Base Camp (ABC), Ganesh Himal, Manaslu, Rolwaling.
Variety of scenery	Annapurna Circuit, Helambu, Langtang, Pokhara to Jomsom.
Nature	Helambu (Rhododendrons in April), Kanchenjunga approaches.
Teahouse trek (no tent needed)	ABC, Annapurna Circuit, Everest Base Camp, Helambu, Jomson.
Technically difficult	Link sections eg between Langtang and Tarke Ghyang, Rolwaling.
Guide needed	Dolpo, Ganesh Himal, Humla/Kailash, Kanchenjunga Base Camp, Mustang, Rolwaling.
Good in the summer	Upper and Lower Dolpo, Humla/Kailash.
Circular treks	Annapurna Circuit, Helambu, many other trek sections can be linked.
Walk in, fly out	Suggested for Everest base camp (Lukla), Humla (Simikot).
Easy access	ABC (Pokhara), Helambu (start just ¾hr taxi ride from Kathmandu).
Busiest treks	ABC, Annapurna Circuit, Everest base camp, Pokhara to Jomsom.

Which permit?

Trekking permits are a legal requirement if you plan to stay anywhere to which there is no road link. Permits have become much easier to apply for. If you go to the Immigration Office before 1pm, you'll be able to collect the permit the same afternoon before 4pm. Fees are paid in rupees calculated at that day's exchange rate, from prices listed in US dollars.

The Immigration Office in Pokhara issues permits for Annapurna area treks, for other permits apply in Kathmandu (which can also issue permits for Annapurna). Permits aren't needed for day hikes from Pokhara or treks in the Kathmandu valley.

Trekking area	Permit cost
Other than those below:	$5/week. Treks lasting over four weeks $10/week.
Kanchenjunga and Lower Dolpo	$10/week.
Manaslu	$90/week, $95 September to November.
Humla	$90 first week then $15/day.
Mustang and Upper Dolpo	$700 for 10-day permit + $70/day thereafter.

NB The Mustang and most other expensive treks also require you to employ a Liaison Officer which adds to the costs still further. If you enter one of the national park areas (as you probably will) there is an extra $10 conservation fee.

Manang and Pheriche during the March to May and October to December seasons, and receive up-to-date weather reports by radio. There is a small library and free advice on safety with talks on altitude sickness during the main seasons. You're advised to register your planned routes with them; they pass information to your embassy in case of mishaps. You don't need to de-register but might consider returning after a trek to add to the report books to help other trekkers.

Kathmandu Environmental Education Project (KEEP) (fax 411533. e-mail: GRT@greatpc.mos.com.np), PO Box 9178, Tridevi Marg (around the corner from the HRA) also offers free trekking advice and gives leaflets on how to reduce the environmental impact of your trek. It seems less busy than the HRA and the staff are extremely knowledgeable and helpful. In the UK you can contact KEEP at 3 Bangor Rd, Hollywood, Co Down, Northern Ireland, BT18 0NT.

Other activities
● **Buddhist guidance and meditation**
Though Nepal is a majority Hindu nation, there is a large Buddhist population and influence. Many Tibetan Buddhists have settled here since the Chinese annexation of Tibet. There are numerous possibilities for retreats, seminars, lectures and study with various Buddhist masters. Boudnath near Kathmandu is a Tibetan pilgrimage centre. Some suggestions for English speaking lamas and retreat centres in the Kathmandu valley: **Chuökyi Nyima Rinpoche** has a monastery at Boudnath with an extensive Buddhist library. Talks are held regularly on Saturday mornings, but he will meet interested visitors on other mornings by appointment (☎ 470933). **Thrangu Rinpoche** gives formal teachings at a monastery just north of the Bodnath stupa (☎ 472024). **Nepal Vipassana Centre**: 12-day Theravada meditation retreats begin on the 1st and 14th of each month. Kathmandu office (☎

❏ **Nepal's national parks**
Nepal is not just mountains. There are also excellent wildlife watching opportunities in the many national parks. The three most popular are:

Park	To see	Accommodation	Costs
Bardia	Tigers, dolphins elephants, jungle	Cheapest Rs200 for bungalow	Park fee Rs650/3 days Guides Rs200/day

To get there it's 16 hours to Ambassa then 1-1¾hrs to cover the last 10km: buses leave at 11am, 2, 3, 4 and 5pm. The jungle is more beautiful than at Chitwan. Elephant rides are the same price.

Park	To see	Accommodation	Costs
Chitwan	Rhinos, jungle, river life	Rs60 huts	Park fee Rs650/2 days Guides Rs200/4hrs

Chitwan is 6 hours from Pokhara, 4-5hrs from Kathmandu to Taldi Bazaar then 15 minutes to the river. Touts with jeeps meet the buses and take you the rest of the way or you can arrive by raft. Comparatively commercialised but still appealing, lots of choice, canoe trips are possible on the river.

Park	To see	Accommodation	Costs
Koshi Tapu	Flat wetland countryside, rich in bird life	The only place is a tiny restaurant in Koshi Barrage	Park fee Rs650/2 days Guide Rs100 for two hours

The main bus route from Kathmandu to Biratnagar passes through Koshi Barrage. If the restaurant's accommodation is full, people with sleeping bags can sleep on the floor. Note that there's almost as much bird life outside the park as within.

225490). **Pullahari Monastery**: the hilltop retreat of the late Jamgon Kongtrul Rinpoche. Twenty minutes walk east of Kopan. Hosts individual and group retreats (☎ 471112). **Himalayan Yogic Institute**: regular workshops on Mahayana Buddhism, residential courses at Kopan hilltop monastery. They also arrange massage, yoga and other courses. (☎ 413094).
● **Yoga** Many courses are available.

❑ **Meeting the locals**

● **The people** If a Gurkha draws his *kukri* (curved sabre-like hand knife) it is said that he must draw blood before it is re-sheathed. The Limbu people are big hearted types, but don't get them angry. A two-inch deep wound inflicted is considered to be a joke in reasonable taste! This may be true but what an unfairly brutal representation of the average Nepali this introduction would give. For nowhere else in the sub-continent can you be assured of so many smiles, such a delightfully friendly rainbow of cultures, such helpful if quaintly inefficient service, and such a relative lack of hassle. Many of Kathmandu's pestering 'Hello-Sir-Chess-set-Tiger-Balm' salesmen are not Nepali at all but opportunistic Indians.

● **Language** Gaining a basic grasp of Nepali is easier than doing the same in Hindi, though to understand deeply you'd have to grapple with 11 extra tenses. Since English is commonly spoken and written, the first priority is to understand the way in which words are romanised. An 'h' is used to show a breathy, 'aspirated' consonant, so that 't' and 'th' sound similar; the latter having a greater exhalation. There is no 'th' as in 'thank' sound. Indeed Nepalis find the 'sh' sound in English hard to pronounce. By the same rule 'chh' is a heavily aspirated 'ch'. An 'a' is pronounced like the 'u' in cut, 'o' like the 'oo' in look. A letter 'y' slipped between a consonant and vowel may be silent (eg Kyanjin sounds like Kanjin).

Written Nepali uses the same alphabet as Hindi – Devengari (see p349).

Nepali numbers (same as Hindi) are used on the largely redundant coins, and on calendars. Restaurant menus and shops generally use Western numbers.

Addressing people using *dai* (big brother), *bhai* (little brother) *didi* (big sister) or *bahini* (little sister) according to your relative ages and position will win you respect. *Timi* should be used for kids, *ou/mampaka* for a joke with good friends.

  Some phrases in Nepali:

        Hello – *namaste*
        Thank you – *danyabad*
        <u>Very</u> good/beautiful – *deri ramro chha*
        Delicious – (deri) *mito chha*
        How much is it? – *kati paisa parchha?* (paisa being the subdivision of the rupee, but still used in this sense)
        Really? – *Sachi?*
        I don't need it (to get rid of salesmen) – *Chan dai na*

Chalcha is a word that means 'Oh, it'll do'. The prevalence of a 'Chalcha state of mind' makes Nepal delightfully laid back, though some economists lament that it's a major reason why Nepal doesn't get richer quicker.

● **Some conversation starters** Democracy, or its evils – 1990 was the dawn of democracy in Nepal but it was followed by rioting amongst teenagers for whom democracy was equated with the liberty to do what you like. The resulting anarchy led many people to question the benefits of democracy altogether.

Nepotism – How does one get a government job?

Birthdays – Does your Nepali acquaintance know his/hers? In which calendar? Who could and couldn't check into a place called Joshi Hotel?

● **Music** Great sitar/tabla concerts are held at the **National Music Ashram** (2nd floor of unmarked house) at 6pm on Sundays, Wednesdays and Fridays (Rs200). The fliers distributed in Thamel restaurants have a map showing how to get there – you may still get a private performance as it is a little hard to find. The musicians can help you get a good bargain on a sitar in Kathmandu shops if you want to buy one.

● **Massage** Massage courses similar in style to Northern Thai massage are available in Kathmandu. Five to 10-day courses cost Rs3500/7000 at the **Himalayan Yogic Institute** (☎ 413094).

● **Work** Typical pay for English teachers in private language institutes is around Rs200/hour. **Insight Nepal** (☎ 1-418954, fax 1-416144), PO Box 6760, Kathmandu, runs teaching and volunteer programs for high school graduates. The three to four-month programme costs $600.

Further information

There are several useful libraries: at KEEP (also at HRA) for trekking, at the British Council (Kanti Path) for background, reference works and periodicals, and at the Bookworm Café in the Pilgrim's Hotel, Thamel, for a wide range of travel guides to other countries.

● **Maps** Nepa trekking maps seem to offer the best detail/price ratio of the many brands available: from Rs125. The tourist information office on New Rd at the north end of Freak Street, Kathmandu, is helpful and has free city maps. These are also free

❏ **Lines of spiritual power**
Kathmandu is full of holes. Find one, and you could theoretically look all the way through the city. Good spirits it was (and still is) believed, travel in straight lines. Where a building blocks an astral highway, of which there is a complex web, small holes are deliberately made in the walls to allow the spirits free passage.

in the airport, at some hotels, and even some bookshops.

● **Books** Given the reasonable prices and great selection of guide books (Trailblazer, Lonely Planet, Rough Guide, Moon) available in Pokhara and Kathmandu, it's best to buy on arrival rather than in Bangkok, Delhi or at home. We're not paid extra to admit that Trailblazer's Nepal Trekking Guides (*Annapurna*, *Everest*, and *Langtang, Helambu & Gosainkund*) are both genuinely popular and perhaps the best available. Second-hand guides are also commonly sold. Notably hard to find is the Cadogan *Central Asia* guide, though Peter Hopkirk's various romping Central Asian histories are ubiquitous.

There is an almost endless selection of background reading on Nepal and Tibet on sale in Kathmandu and Pokhara and books are cheaper here than in Western countries. Pilgrim's Bookshop in Thamel, though not the cheapest, has a very wide selection.

Web sites
Nepal is one of those countries that draws a lot of interest on the web. www.catmando.com/nepal.htm and www.uni-mainz.de/~baadj000/nepal.htm have two of the best collections of links and is the best place to start your surfing.

www.travel-nepal.com has a Nepal chat and links to several commercial sites.

south-asia.com/dotn/index.html has the usual government tourist info on Nepal.

kocsis.mswin.net has basic descriptions and how-to information on the Annapurna, Langtang and Everest treks.

www.visitnepal.com provides a sort of online travel guide.

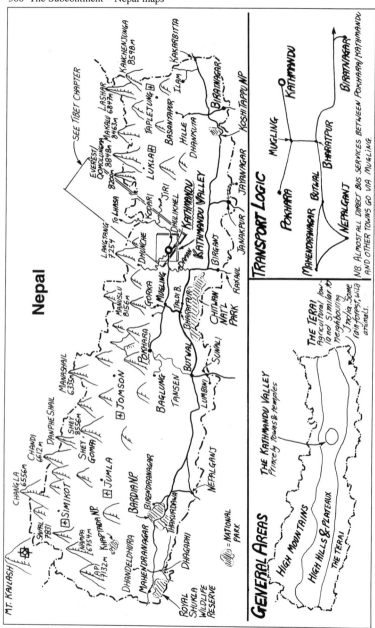

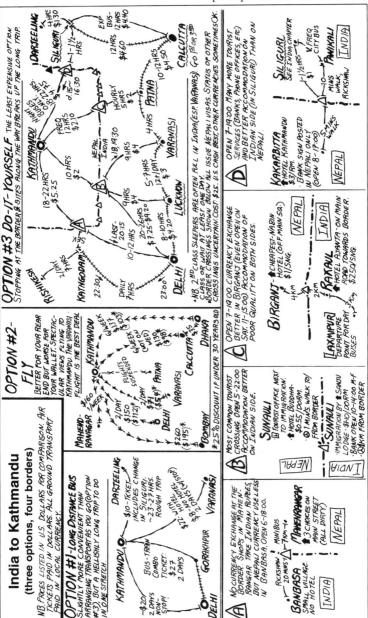

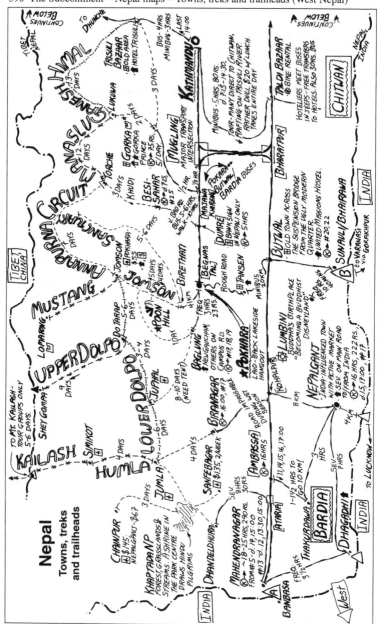

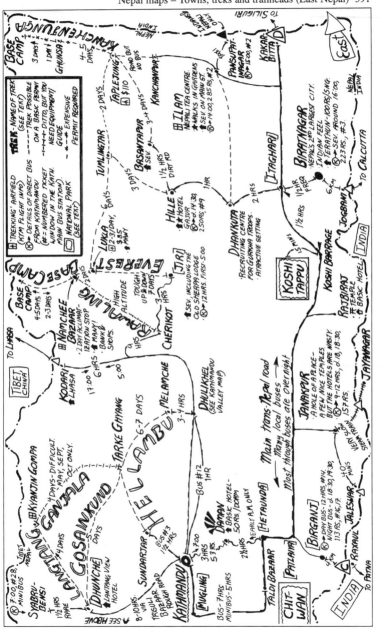

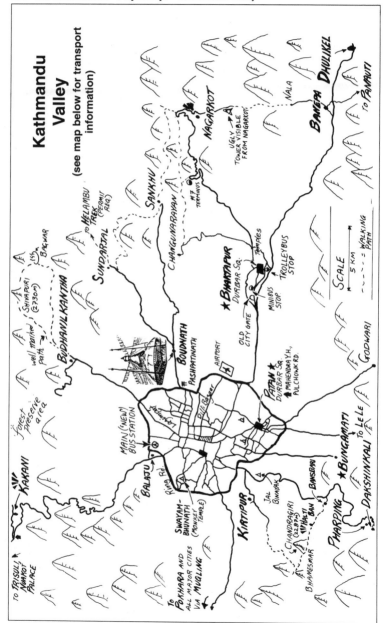

Kathmandu Valley
(see map below for transport information)

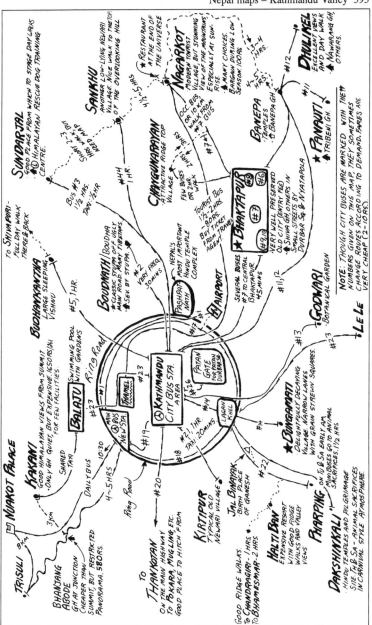

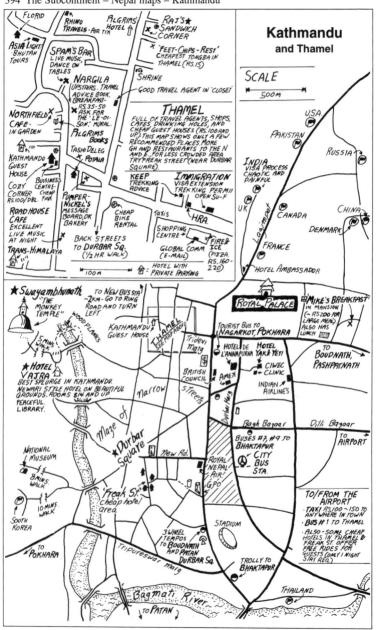

Kathmandu
and Thamel

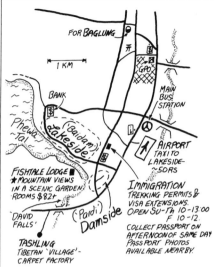

Pokhara

Gateway to the popular Annapurna trekking region, this laid-
back hangout has superb mountain
views. Swim in the lake, laze
around or rent bikes/motorcycles
for trips into the surrounding hills.

● **Accommodation** Typical room
prices are Rs150/dbl, but can be as
low as Rs60. Damside is peaceful
but has no view of the main lake.
Lakeside has more guest houses
and more services but also more
crowds. For the best of both
worlds we prefer the private
homes renting rooms in the green
back streets up from the main
Lakeside road (5-15 mins walk).
Or go by boat to the far side of the
lake, roll out your sleeping bag,
and sleep under the stars.

❏ Himalayan views without the effort

Trekking gives you some stupendous mountain views like those from the top of
Thorong La or Poon Hill (both on the Annapurna Circuit). But if you can't or
won't put on your hiking boots, there's still many an impressive Himalayan
panorama within easy reach. Right in Pokhara the backdrop is stunning. And all
the following viewpoints are accessible with minimal walking from a road.
Approximate transport times from Kathmandu are given. Note that it is worth
staying overnight to see the views at sunrise when the air is clearest.

● **Nagarkot** (90 minutes from Kathmandu by tour bus or via Bakhtapur).
Very wide panorama with few obstructing hills. There are dozens of reasonably
priced hilltop lodges to choose from. However, the village itself is not very atmospheric and there's always a bus load of other tourists.

● **Kakani** (under one hour by motorbike, a nice but tiring uphill bicycle ride).
Sweeping views of Manaslu and Ganesh Himal plus back into the Kathmandu
Valley. Fewer white peaks than are visible from Nagarkot, very few tourists, and
only one guest house (over $20) on the top and one other 3km below.

● **Dhulikel** (one hour, No 12 bus). Wide panorama from a viewpoint a short walk
above town. Dhulikel is itself on a rather busy main road, but there's a choice of
cheap and atmospheric accommodation.

● **Halti Ban** (50 mins by motor bike, or 2km up a steep track off No 22 bus route).
An awesome panorama of the whole mountain range with the Kathmandu Valley
in the foreground. However, the view is often very hazy and the peaks are more
distant than when seen from Nagarkot. Expensive hotel but camping is possible.

● **Daman** (3hrs by bus). Magnificent but very distant panorama.

● **Other options:** $90 for an out-and-back mountain viewing flight. If the view is
too cloudy the plane won't leave and you get your money back. There are also hot-
air balloon rides ($195) or helicopter charters (too noisy, $700 for four people).

Bangladesh

Bangladesh has an innocent charm and, if you look for it, an abstract, understated beauty. The flat land is a patchwork of greens and earthy hues sewn together by intricate networks of rivers bobbing with slow moving boats. But, compared with the architectural wonders of India, Bangladesh's few historical

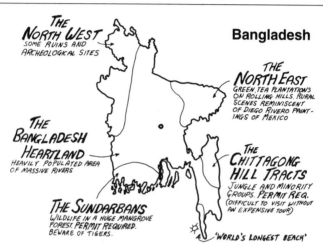

NB Even the most important architectural sites (Paharpur, Bagerhat, Dhaka's Lalbagh Fort) are less visually dramatic than more average sites in India. To enjoy Bangladesh, it's best to simply wander in random areas, move slowly on boats or buses, meet and talk to people.

❏ **W&M's country ratings – Bangladesh**
● **Expense $$** Bargain hard in Dhaka and Cox's Bazaar, elsewhere you can be more relaxed.
● **Value for money** ✔✔ Cheap, but you get what you pay for.
● **Getting around** ✔✔ Transport goes almost everywhere but there are many big rivers to cross, often by slow ferry. Bus signs are in Bengali. The unsurfaced roads become impassable in the wet season.
● **English spoken** ✔✔✔ Almost everywhere you'll find heavily accented speakers asking your 'good name'. English is common in Dhaka.
● **Woman alone** ✔✔ Possible but not relaxing.
● **For vegetarians** ✔✔✔ Veg options are usually available and are cheap.

sites are of limited interest. The towns are undistinguished and there are no high mountains to cool the sweaty brow. As a result, the country is barely touched by tourism.

Bangladesh is well known for its disastrous floods. That these seem to get ever worse and more frequent is not necessarily down to a vengeful Allah. Deforestation in the Himalaya means that headwaters dash unimpeded towards the sea, so floods hit faster than before. In the meantime the Bangladeshi population keeps growing, driving more and more people to seek a place to live. Attempts to settle the less flood-prone hill tracts have already soured relations with the Chakmas and other hill tribal groups who now teeter on the verge of insurrection. The impenetrable Sundarban mangrove forests are a valuable protected area and a little too full of tigers to make an appealing home. So, in the end, populations continue to crowd onto and cultivate the highest risk areas. Ironically, in the dry season, drought is also a possibility especially when India diverts away too much water from the upper rivers. None of this is helped

---

❏ Geo-political information – Bangladesh

Population: 125 million (1997), 115m (1993), 105m (1991), 74m (1973).

Area: 134,000 sq km.

Capital: Dhaka (6.5 million, 1991).

Other major cities: Chittagong (1.6 million), Khulna (600,000), Rajshahi (300,000), Rangpur 220,000).

GNP per capita: $230 (1994), $160 (1987).

Currency history: Takka/US$1 – Feb 1998: TK45.3, Oct 1997: TK43.6, June 96: TK41.2, Jan 96: TK40.2, 1991: TK38.5, 1986: TK30.4, 1976: TK15.3.

Major exports/economy: Jute (Bangladesh has a Ministry of Jute). Bangladeshis working abroad also send back significant funds. $2 billion is received in aid.

Ethnic mix: Bengali (98%), also Chakma and other Hill Tribes plus some Biharis.

Official languages: Bangla (Bengali).

Religious mix: Islam. 88% Muslim, 10% Hindu, a small but noticeable Buddhist community in the Hill Tracts.

Landmarks of national history: **1608**: Dhaka founded as the seat of the Moghul viceroy of Bengal. **1797**: Bengal formed the first major chunk of India to fall under direct British rule. **1906**: Dhaka hosted emerging anti-colonial Muslim League. **16 Aug 1946**: Muslim Direct Action day. **Aug 1947**: Birth of Pakistan (Bangladesh then being East Pakistan). **Nov 1970**: Cyclone and tidal wave killed 200,000. **26 Mar 1971**: Bangladesh declared effective independence igniting war between Pakistani army and Awami league supporters. **Dec 1971**: India invaded forcing Pakistani surrender, Bangladesh gained independence.

Leaders: President A R Biswas. Political power wielded by the prime minister, currently Shaikh Hasina Wajed who took over from Begum Khaleda Zia in 1997 after months of destabilising bickering. Both women are widows of former leaders.

Pressing political issues: Water rights with India, ecological worries (lower dry season water levels in the rivers mean higher salinity in the delta and threatens the mangrove forests of the Sundarbans), ethnic tensions in Chittagong Hill Tracts, domestic political squabbling.

by the fractious bickering of the politicians or the *hartals* (general strikes) which they engineer as levers of personal power.

Even when things are going well, 'normal' life is hardly easy. It's hard not to be moved by the smiling perseverance of the jute cutters who stand chest deep in water to harvest a crop destined to be no more than rough sacking. An official pamphlet looking at national development since independence candidly admits that planned policy and hard work 'so far haven't worked'. So the nation is 'hoping for luck'. Such quaint naiveté sums up this perversely loveable nation.

❑ **Essential information for travellers – Bangladesh**

● **Visa** Required for most nationalities. A two-week visa is granted on arrival at Dhaka airport, or a longer one if you obtain it from an embassy in advance. Visas can be extended.

● **Currency** Takka. US$1=TK45.3; TK40 (in some hotels).

● **Time zone** 6 hours ahead of GMT (½hr ahead of India; ½hr behind Burma; 1hr behind Thailand; ¼hr ahead of Nepal).

● **Religious tone** A large majority of Bangladeshis are Muslims who are reasonably devout but not as fanatical as those in Pakistan. Ramadan is respected by many people but food remains on sale during the day, at least in major cities.

● **Health factors** Malarial risk, bad water, hygiene problems.

● **Special dangers** Civil disturbances are common during election times and during *hartals* (general strikes) which also paralyse transportation. To our knowledge, foreigners have never specifically been the target of violence and rarely the target of antagonism, but it is important to stay alert.

● **Social conventions** Be aware of Islamic etiquette
. Women should wear long sleeves and cover their legs, though a veil or even headscarf is not essential. Swimwear is theoretically acceptable on the beaches in the south east, but don't be surprised if you attract an audience anywhere near habitation.

● **Typical traveller destinations** Tourists are not a common sight but Cox's Bazaar draws local holiday makers.

● **Highlights** 'Rocket service' boats, the Sundarbans, the hill tribes of the Chittagong Tracts.

● **When to go** Bangladesh suffers many climatic calamities; April brings growing heat and humidity, and May can see destructive cyclones. Droughts at this time are frequently followed by severe monsoons and flooding. The monsoon season is approximately June to September but is very variable. The winters are pleasantly cool with clear skies. A light sweater is useful at night.

● **Pulse of the country** The rickshaw jams around Dhaka's Gulistan bus station.

● **Key tips** Be aware of the political situation. If you have to go anywhere on a day that a general strike is called do so as early in the morning as possible – strikes usually start at 8am. Inter-city transport departing before the official start of the strike usually still runs.

If your bag is stored on the top of a bus, get off as quickly as possible after arriving – bags seem to be thrown down instantaneously and have a way of wandering off if you aren't there to claim them.

PRACTICAL INFORMATION
Visa and formalities
● **Visa strategy** There's a special visa-free rule for a forced stopover – see Stopover box below. Two-week visas are available on arrival at Dhaka airport but not at the land borders; note that Irish citizens do not need a visa. Typical costs vary greatly according to nationality eg Japanese and Polish visas are free, Portuguese $9, German $13, Swiss $18, Australian and US $21, Danish $22, New Zealanders $23,

---

❏ The Bangladesh stopover

If you fly Bangladesh Biman (the national airline) and have to wait more than eight hours in Dhaka for a connecting flight you will be provided with a hotel room, meals, and visa exempt transfers to and from the airport. The qualifying hours are counted from your actual arrival time to your planned departure. If, as seems suspiciously common, the plane crawls in an hour or two late, clipping your stopover time to seven hours, you'll lose your chance to visit the city visa free. Instead, you will receive a free glass of Coca Cola and one sandwich.

To make use of a Biman free stopover **do not** pass through Immigration until you have reported to the transit lounge on the top floor of the airport – otherwise you'll be charged for a visa and will lose the freebies. At the transit lounge, they will hold your passport until you have finished check-in for your onward flight. Though passportless you remain free to wander the streets of Dhaka. Remember that you will be unable to cash travellers' cheques without your passport so carry a little hard currency to exchange for Takkas.

Biman tickets tend to be very reasonably priced (when they lose your luggage you'll understand why). On some routes an imaginative travel agent can deliberately choose flights with poor connections to allow you that brief free taste of Bangladesh. However Biman will only pay until the next available flight and departures have a habit of changing at short notice, so nothing is certain. If you choose to stopover rather than appearing forced to do so, you will not only pay your own visa and hotel bills but there will be an extra stopover fee, ranging from $50-$200, added to the price of the ticket.

The free pick up for transit passengers supposedly takes you to, and collects you from, your hotel. We waited almost three hours for the bus from the airport. On returning, the bus left our hotel as promised. But another couple reported that their bus didn't come at all. Staff at the hotel assured them it was coming but it never did, and only thanks to a last minute taxi dash did they make it before their plane and pre-checked baggage left without them.

Most stopover travellers find themselves at the Sundarban Hotel wondering how to make the most of a few hours in the city. If you don't want to risk setting off alone for Lalbagh Fort and Chowk Bazaar an easy option is to cross the double road to the corner by the five-star Sonargaon Hotel (which, incidentally, has the best toilet in Bangladesh). Look lost here and in seconds potential guides appear offering their services at an opening price of around TK100 an hour (very bargainable). 'Without a guide you see nothing interesting' they exaggerate. But though the teeming streets themselves are fascinating, it is true that a guide really helps to whisk you into the more scenic parts of town. The guide may or may not be an autorickshaw or rickshaw driver. It's better if he isn't (although you'll have to pay extra for transport) because if/when you hit a traffic jam you can get out and walk. Anyhow, walking in the old city is sensible in the cool of winter. During the monsoon season leaving the airport at all may be foolish.

Spanish $24, French $41, Canadian $55 and British $60. Most embassies give visas allowing a one month period of stay but some in Europe and North America give three months.

If you plan to enter by air but leave by land a special permit is necessary from Dhaka. The office that issues these permits has moved to 17 Segunbagicha and is open Monday to Friday, 9am-2.30pm.

● **Visa extensions** These are issued only in Dhaka. A two-week extension will be given readily, up to a month is possible but will require some explanation. The Immigration Department is on Topkana Rd.

● **Permits** Permits are still required to visit some areas, including the two with most tourist potential – The Sundarbans and the Chittagong Hill Tracts.

The Sundarbans are more conveniently visited as part of a tour (otherwise you'll have to rent a whole boat for yourself and may not find helpful guides), and the agent should arrange the necessary permits on your behalf. If you insist on going independently the **Divisional Forest Office** (☎ 41-20665), Circuit House Rd, Khulna has been known to grant permits to the persistent.

Visiting the Chittagong Hill Tracts requires a permit too; this is checked on the Chittagong-Rangamati road. The permit is normally procured in Dhaka (taking a couple of weeks!), though one traveller got a permit very quickly through the Parjatan motel near the railway station in Chittagong, having booked a TK200 room in the motel's Rangamati guest house. At the time of research, travellers were only being admitted on expensive tours, supposedly due to an upsurge of insurgency activity by the *Shanti Bahini* (literally Army of Peace). Check current conditions.

Money

Travellers cheques can be changed at Dhaka banks or at the American Express office but your passport is required. Outside Dhaka we experienced difficulties cashing travellers cheques.

Banks are open Saturday to Wednesday 9am-1pm, Thursday 9-11.30am. Airport banks are open longer – we changed US$ cash on arrival at 3am.

Note that there is no black market and that takkas are called *tiks* by some locals.

Transport

● **Bus** There are bus services to most parts of Bangladesh but the many wide rivers mean the buses sometimes have to queue for long periods to get on board ferries – consider buying tickets only to the river crossings, then looking for other buses ahead in the queue.

Local services cram in as many people as possible while Deluxe ones offer greater comfort and a guaranteed seat. Deluxe buses are not supposed to stop and pick up more passengers; if you want to get on or off midway you will have to find one of its slowing down points and jump on while it is still moving. The conductor will help drag your bags aboard.

There are different bus terminals in Dhaka for different divisions (see map notes). Times and schedules to the Western Divisions will change drastically once the Jamuna Bridge is completed.

● **Train** There are two gauges of railway, so no train can use the whole rail network. In addition, since no bridge spans the Padma or, as yet, the Jamuna rivers (which are 5km wide at points) all services between Dhaka and the West must head first for the crossing points at Junagath Ganj or Dewan Ganj, for a ferry connection. Hence they are considerably slower and less predictable than services to and from the east.

There are local (slow), mail and express (semi-fast) and inter-city (fast) trains. The speed varies greatly between these services.

Students qualify for a 50% discount.

● **Air** The international departure tax is TK300.

Biman Airlines operate a bus service to/from the Golden Gate and Zakaria hotels (8am-10pm); this takes around 40 minutes if the traffic and weather are good.

An autorickshaw from the airport into the city should cost TK50 after strenuous bargaining. The journey takes $^3/_4$hr in perfect conditions; over two hours if there are jams or if it's the monsoon season.

● **Boat** River transport is vitally important and in the wet season there is no better way to get around. Fields become lakes and hollowed palm trunk canoes replace bicycles as the main form of rural transport. In the dry (winter) season many of the mighty rivers are very low – river steamers can not operate upstream and the river crossing ferries take longer as they have to weave between islets (on which they occasionally get stranded). The year-round Dhaka-Khulna 'Rocket Service' is in fact a Mississippi-style paddleboat that potters rather than rockets, but is rather romantic and gives a great taste of delta life. Book a few days ahead to get a second class berth. First class costs more than flying (to Jessore plus bus connection).

Ecological problems (silting, water diversion etc) have reduced the number of navigable waterways in recent years with some rivers drying up entirely in the dry season – thus disrupting river transport.

● **Rickshaws** Cycle-powered rickshaws with their gaudily painted adornments of Bollywood film stars or Islamic images (or both) are much better for sightseeing than the cramped auto rickshaws. They are cheap (TK10 right across town but be prepared to bargain) yet are thought to provide as much as 20% of Dhaka's economy (if you include rickshaw makers and repairers as well as the drivers themselves).

❑ **Meeting the locals**

● **The people** I was wandering aimlessly through some back streets in Dhaka hoping, fruitlessly as it transpired, that the mouldering concrete architecture might transform itself into something more attractive in the narrower alleys. Instead, the open sewers pulled closer together and the rickshaws passed each other with even fewer nanometres to spare. And as the alleys twisted and turned I soon realised I was lost.

'What your country?' a voice cried out from the half dark of a candle-lit tailors' shop (this block was having its regular black-out). 'Why are you here?' Tourists are rare enough in Bangladesh that one hears this question everywhere. But this time it was a sensible query. Before I could answer, a group had formed around me sharing disconnected sentences about their pride in the Bangladesh teak industry, how good it was to be Muslim, and the disgrace it is that Britain is so heartless at refusing visas. I swapped addresses with three completely unknown and barely seen disembodied smiles as the group escorted me toward a major road, and demanded the honour of buying me tea and cake before allowing me to wander on.

● **Language** The national language, Bangla, is interchangeable with the Bengali spoken across the Indian border. Hotels are generally marked in English, but otherwise most signs are in local script; this looks similar to but is different from Hindi's *Devenagri*. In the Chittagong Hill Tracts a collection of tribal languages are spoken. See p561 for Bengali/Bangla numbers.

Some phrases in Bengali/Bangla:

        Greeting (hello) – *jonaf*
        Reply – *jonaf*
        Greeting (literally: hey, listen!) – *é shonen*
        Welcome – *swa-ga-tam*
        Reply – *danyabad* (thank you)
        Delicious – *shad/darun*
        How much is it? – *dam koto*

● **Other** Taxis are pricier and get quickly caught in traffic jams, but at least you can stay dry. Minibuses are good for crossing town on major streets, as are the decrepit Leyland double decker buses.

Accommodation

Cheap accommodation (TK50-150) is available in all larger towns and cities. The cheapest hotels in Dhaka's old city seemed reluctant to take foreigners citing the lack of a registration book, sufficient facilities or, in one case the bizarre argument: 'Foreigner is always a guest here, so how can we be taking responsibility he safety'. We didn't understand either.

In villages, at archaeological sites, and in the tea gardens of the north east, the only accommodation available may be in government or departmental resthouses. These are only officially allowed to accommodate members of the public with the prior written permission of the controlling department so you need to plan your route ahead. If you're allowed in, resthouses generally cost around TK150 a night and are very comfortable. The Dept of Archaeology ones have some particularly pleasant locations; letters requesting permission to stay should be sent to the **Department of Archaeology**, 22/1 Babur Road, Mohammedpur, Dhaka. Permissory notes state the exact dates for which a stay is authorised, though arriving a few days late (by bicycle) we managed to persuade a couple of them to let us in. Travellers report mixed success at being allowed to stay at resthouses for which they have made no prior arrangements, so don't be too hopeful.

The long beach strip around Cox's Bazaar is not really set up for Western tourists and lacks the beach bungalows of Thailand or Goa. There always seem to be people around which makes finding a secluded camping spot difficult. Hotels for local tourists are set back from the beach somewhat due to the cyclones and monsoon storms that might otherwise blow them away.

Food and drink

The food is similar to that in India though there is less variety. Samosas and other spicy street snacks cost from TK1. *Hilsa* is a popular type of fish which is usually served smoked.

Cha (sweet, milky tea) is ubiquitous and costs only TK2 a cup; it is often accompanied by a tempting glass of water which you drink at your peril. Locally made soft drinks are widely available. Alcohol, though not banned, is relatively difficult to find despite the range of bottles available at Dhaka airport's duty free store.

Staying in touch

Mail from Bangladesh is much less reliable if it's sent from outside Dhaka. The **American Express** office (☎ 2-326820), c/o Vantage Tours and Travel, Hotel Sonargaon, Karwan Bazaar, PO Box 2112, Dhaka, can receive mail.

Dhaka has many IDD 'telephone offices' some of which actually have phones. Typical rates: $8 per three minute call to Europe, $9 per three minutes to the US.

International country code: +880. Dhaka code: 2, Khulna: 41.

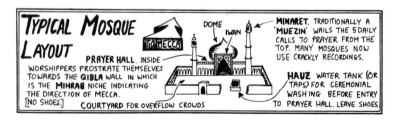

TYPICAL MOSQUE LAYOUT

DOME
IWAN
TO MECCA
PRAYER HALL. INSIDE WORSHIPPERS PROSTRATE THEMSELVES TOWARDS THE **QIBLA** WALL IN WHICH IS THE **MIHRAB** NICHE INDICATING THE DIRECTION OF MECCA. [NO SHOES.]
COURTYARD FOR OVERFLOW CROWDS

MINARET. TRADITIONALLY A 'MUEZIN' WAILS THE 5 DAILY CALLS TO PRAYER FROM THE TOP. MANY MOSQUES NOW USE CRACKLY RECORDINGS.

HAUZ WATER TANK (OR TAPS) FOR CEREMONIAL WASHING BEFORE ENTRY TO PRAYER HALL. LEAVE SHOES!

Activities

● **Cycling** Bangladesh is excellent for exploring by bicycle. The people are friendly, if inquisitive, there are places to stay at regular intervals, and major roads are not too busy (except the Sylhet and Cox's Bazaar to Dhaka routes). Many locals use bikes too. There is no charge for carrying a bicycle on most buses, though you may be charged a handling fee if you can't hoist it onto the roof yourself.

● **Volunteering** The **Bangladesh Workcamp Association** (fax 2-863797) 289/2 Work Camps Rd, North Shahjahanpur, Dhaka 17, runs seven to ten day volunteering projects which usually draw a mix of people from around the world. The cost is $100 directly through the Bangladesh Workcamp Association (though they are hard to get in touch with), but usually more through your local workcamp association.

Further information

● **Books** There are plenty of background works on Bangladesh's history and culture available from a string of bookshops on the north side of New Elephant Road, Dhaka, a block south and west of the Sheraton Hotel. Guide books are more of a problem. Lonely Planet's indispensable *Bangladesh* guide is now into a third edition, though the second edition remains surprisingly accurate. However, neither is easy to find in Bangladesh; try the bookshop in the Sonargaon Hotel. Used copies occasionally turn up in Bangkok and Kathmandu book exchange shops.

● **Maps** Within Dhaka (formerly Dacca), road names are confusing and rarely marked. People more often use landmarks or the names of areas. Maps tend to disagree on road names and where one becomes another (eg Mitford Road in the old town is sometimes called Waterworks Road and becomes Posta Rd near the Lalbagh Fort). Fulbaria Rd, which leads to to Gulistan (or Fulbaria) city bus station, is marked on some maps as Zahir Raihan Rd. The so-called Circular Rd isn't (though it curves a bit). Some roads have dual (old and new) numbering systems.

Parjatan (Bangladesh Tourist Corporation) offices (see below) sell passable maps of Dhaka and of Bangladesh for TK10 each. The former are much better than the TK50 Graphosman Dhaka maps from the Sundarban hotel's Stop and Shop store. The best map (though it's hard to follow in the old city) is published by The Mappa. It shows the embassy area in great detail and is available for TK100 at the Sonargaon Hotel or for TK60 from The Mappa, 2nd Floor, 112 Green Rd, Dhaka. They're also bringing out guide maps for Chittagong, Cox's Bazaar and Sylhet as well as a Bangladesh atlas. The Nelles map of Bangladesh is more detailed than the cheap Parjatan one, but some roads are misleading. Many towns are missing from both.

● **Information offices** **Parjatan** (Bangladesh Tourist Corporation) has offices at Dhaka airport, at the Dhaka Sheraton (☎ 2-509479) and in several rural centres. The staff are helpful enough but are keen to find you a tour. The main office in Dhaka (☎/fax 2-317836/817855) is at 233 Airport Rd, Tejgaon. Phone numbers for other offices are: Cox's Bazaar (☎ 341-4246/4258), Bogra (☎ 51-6753), Chittagong (☎ 31-209845), Rangamati (☎ 351-3126), Rangapur (☎ 521-3681), Rajshahi (☎ 721-5492), Sylhet (☎ 821-2426).

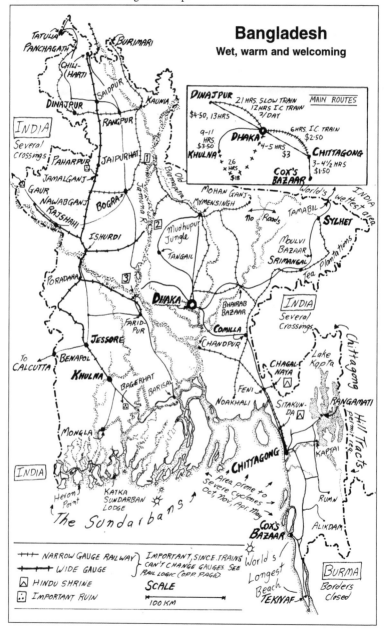

Bangladesh
Wet, warm and welcoming

MAIN ROUTES

DINAJPUR — 21 HRS. SLOW TRAIN / 12 HRS. I.C. TRAIN 2/DAY — $4·50, 13HRS — DHAKA — 6HRS. I.C. TRAIN $2·50 — CHITTAGONG

9-11 HRS $3·50 — KHULNA — 4-5 HRS $3 — 26 HRS $18 — COX'S BAZAAR — 3-4½ HRS $1·50

India, World's wettest area

Tatulia, Panchagath, Burimari, Chili-(Harti), Dinajpur, Saidpur, Kaunia, Rangpur, India Several crossings, Paharpur, Jaipurhat [1], Old Brahmaputra, Jamalganj, Gaur, Nawabganj, Rajshahi, Bogra, Ishurdi, Mohan Ganj, Mymensingh, No Roads, Tamabil, Sylhet, Poradaha, [2], Mudhupur Jungle, Tangail, Moulvi Bazaar, Srimangal, Tea plantations, [3], Dhaka, Bhairab Bazaar, Comilla, India Several Crossings, Farid-pur, Jessore, Chandpur, To Calcutta, Benapol, Khulna, Bagerhat, Barisal, Chagal-Naya, Feni, Noakhali, Sitakun-da, Lake Kapta, Rangamati, Kaptai, Mongla, India, Heron Point, Katka Sundarban Lodge, The Sundarbans, Area prone to severe cyclones Oct, Nov, Apr, May, Chittagong, World's Longest Beach, Cox's Bazaar, Teknaf, Rumi, Alikdam, Burma Borders Closed, Chittagong Hill Tracts permits

+++ NARROW GAUGE RAILWAY
+—+ WIDE GAUGE
⌂ HINDU SHRINE
⊡ IMPORTANT RUIN

IMPORTANT, SINCE TRAINS CAN'T CHANGE GAUGES, SEE RAIL LOGIC (OPP. PAGE).

SCALE
100 KM

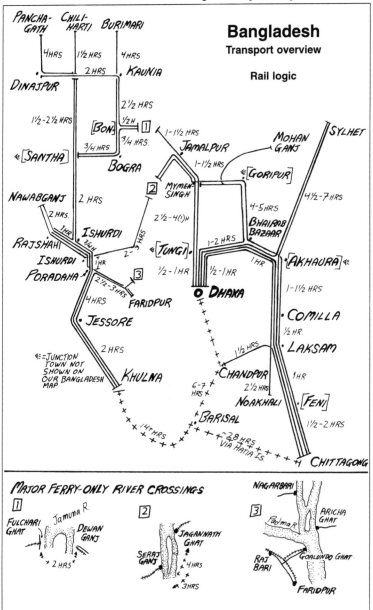

Bangladesh
Transport overview

Rail logic

PANCHA-GATH   CHILI-HARTI   BURIMARI

4 HRS   1½ HRS   4 HRS

2 HRS   KAUNIA

DINAJPUR

2½ HRS

1½-2½ HRS   BON   ½ H   1

SANTHA   ¾ HRS   ¾ HRS.   1-1½ HRS   JAMALPUR   MOHAN GANJ   SYLHET

BOGRA   1-1½ HRS   GORIPUR

NAWABGANJ   2 HRS   2   MYMEN SINGH   4-5 HRS   BHAIRAB BAZAAR   4½-7 HRS

2 HRS   2½-4(!)H

1HR   ISHURDI   2-3 HRS   1-2 HRS   AKHAURA

RAJSHAHI   ¾H   TUNGI

ISHURDI   1HR   ½-1 HR   1 HR

PORADAHA   2½-3HRS   3   ½-1 HR   1-1½ HRS

4 HRS   FARIDPUR   O DHAKA

JESSORE   COMILLA

2 HRS   ½ HR.

⇐=JUNCTION
TOWN NOT
SHOWN ON
OUR BANGLADESH
MAP   1½ HRS   LAKSAM

KHULNA   CHANDPUR   1 HR

6-7 HRS   2½ HRS   NOAKHALI   FENI

BARISAL   ~28 HRS   1½-2 HRS

14 HRS   VIA HATIA IS.   CHITTAGONG

MAJOR FERRY-ONLY RIVER CROSSINGS

1

FULCHARI GHAT   Jamuna R.   DEWAN GANJ

2 HRS

2

JAGANNATH GHAT

SERAJ GANJ   4 HRS

3 HRS

3

NAGARBARI   ARICHA GHAT

Padma R.

RAJ BARI   GOALUNDO GHAT

FARIDPUR

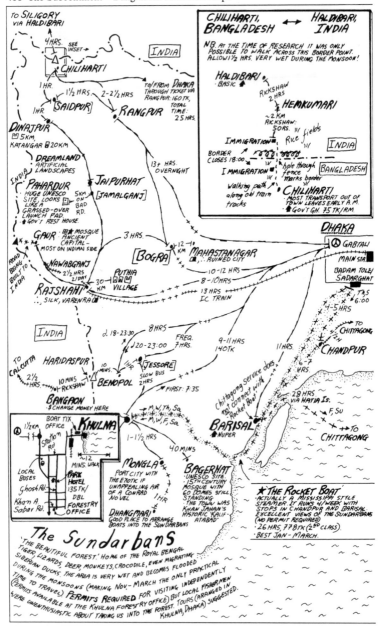

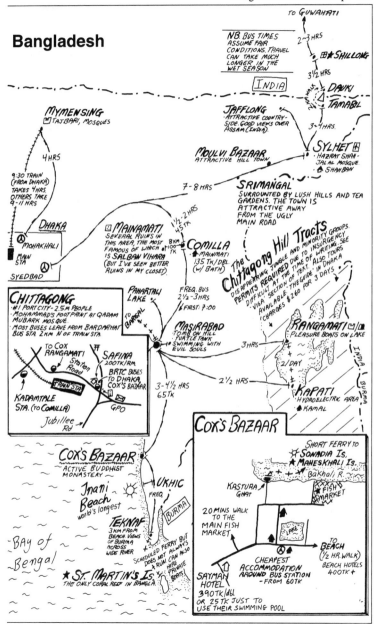

Bangladesh

NB. BUS TIMES ASSUME FAIR CONDITIONS. TRAVEL CAN TAKE MUCH LONGER IN THE WET SEASON

INDIA

TO GUWAHATI

2-3 HRS

⊞ ★ SHILLONG

3½ HRS

DAUKI
△ TAMABL

MYMENSING
☐ TAJBARI, MOSQUES

4 HRS

9:30 TRAIN (FROM DHAKA) TAKES 4 HRS, OTHERS TAKE 9-11 HRS

JAFFLONG
ATTRACTIVE COUNTRY-SIDE. GOOD VIEWS OVER ASSAM (INDIA).

3-4 HRS.

MOULVI BAZAAR
ATTRACTIVE HILL TOWN

7-8 HRS

SYLHET ⊞
HAZRAT SHAH-JALAL MOSQUE.
△ SHAHBAN

SRIMANGAL
SURROUNDED BY LUSH HILLS AND TEA GARDENS. THE TOWN IS ATTRACTIVE AWAY FROM THE UGLY MAIN ROAD

DHAKA
○ MOHAKHALI
MAIN STA.
△
SYEDBAD

MAINAMATI
SEVERAL RUINS IN THIS AREA, THE MOST FAMOUS OF WHICH IS SALBAN VIHARA (BUT I'VE SEEN BETTER RUINS IN MY CLOSET).

½-2 HRS
45 TK

8KM
₹100
TO

COMILLA
MAINMATI
135 TK/DBL.
(W/ BATH)

The **Chittagong Hill Tracts**
DISAPPEARING JUNGLE AND MINORITY GROUPS. PERMITS REQUIRED DUE TO INSURGENCY. DIFFICULT AT THE TIME OF WRITING, SEE VISA, SECTION OF TEXT. ALSO TOURS AVAILABLE. 'THE GUIDE' IN DHAKA CHARGES $260 FOR 3 DAYS.

FREQ. BUS
2½-3 HRS
FIRST: 7:00

PANARTALI LAKE
TO BARCAL

MASIRABAD
TOMB ON HILL
TURTLE TANK
SWIMMING WITH EVIL SOULS

3 HRS

2/DAY

RANGAMATI ☐/○
PLEASURE BOATS ON LAKE

2½ HRS

KAPATI
HYDROELECTRIC AREA
○ KAMAL

INDIA | BURMA

CHITTAGONG
#1 PORT CITY - 2.5M PEOPLE
MOHAMMAD'S FOOT PRINT AT QADAM MUBARK MOSQUE.
MOST BUSES LEAVE FROM BARDARHAT BUS STA. 2 KM N OF TRAIN STA.

To Cox RANGAMATI
Station Road
🚩 **SAFINA**
200TK/RM.
BRTC BUSES TO DHAKA, COX'S BAZAAR
✉ GPO
TRAIN STA
KADAMTALE STA. (TO COMILLA)
Jubilee Rd

3-4½ HRS
65 TK

COX'S BAZAAR
ACTIVE BUDDHIST MONASTERY

~ Inani Beach
world's longest

TEKNAF
3 KM FROM BEACH VIEWS OF BURMA ACROSS WIDE RIVER

UKHIC
FREQ
BURMA

SCHEDULED FERRY BUT DOES NOT ALWAYS RUN. CAN ALSO HIRE PRIVATE BOATS

Bay of Bengal

★ **ST. MARTIN'S IS.**
THE ONLY CORAL REEF IN BANGLA.

COX'S BAZAAR

SHORT FERRY TO
☀ SONADIA IS.
★ MANESKHALI IS.
Bakhali R.
FISH MARKET
KASTURA GHAT

20 MINS WALK TO THE MAIN FISH MARKET

LAKE

TO **BEACH**
(½ HR. WALK)
BEACH HOTELS
400TK +

CHEAPEST ACCOMMODATION AROUND BUS STATION - FROM 60TK

SAYMAN HOTEL
390TK/DBL
OR 25TK JUST TO USE THEIR SWIMMING POOL

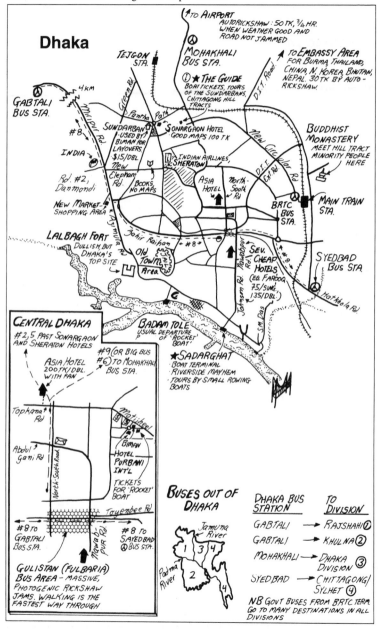

Dhaka

↑ TO AIRPORT
AUTORICKSHAW: 50 TK, ¾ HR.
WHEN WEATHER GOOD AND
ROAD NOT JAMMED

TEJGON STA.

MOHAKHALI BUS STA.

ⓘ ★ THE GUIDE
BOAT TICKETS, TOURS
OF THE SUNDARBANS,
CHITTAGONG HILL
TRACTS

↑ TO EMBASSY AREA
FOR BURMA, THAILAND,
CHINA, N. KOREA, BHUTAN,
NEPAL. 30 TK BY AUTO-
RICKSHAW.

GABTALI BUS STA.

4 KM

Mirpur Rd

Greenra.

Pantha Path

D.I.T. Road.

New Circular Rd.

D.I.T. Ext Rd.

BUDDHIST MONASTERY
MEET HILL TRACT
MINORITY PEOPLE
HERE

#8

SUNDARBAN
-USED BY
BIMAN FOR
LAYOVERS.
$15/DBL

SONARGAON HOTEL
GOOD MAPS 100 TK

INDIA

New Elephant Rd.

Rd. #2, Danmondi

INDIAN AIRLINES,
SHERATON

BOOKS
NO MAPS

ASIA HOTEL

NORTH-SOUTH RD.

BRTC BUS STA.

MAIN TRAIN STA.

NEW MARKET-SHOPPING AREA

Aymura

Jahir Raihan

LALBAGH FORT
DULLISH, BUT
DHAKA'S
TOP SITE

OLD TOWN Area

#8

SEV. CHEAP HOTELS
(EG. FAROOQ
75/SING,
135/DBL)

Mohadpur Rd.

Johnson Rd.

S.M. Das

SYEDBAD BUS STA.

Hot Khola Rd.

CENTRAL DHAKA
#2,5 PAST SONARGAON
AND SHERATON HOTELS

ASIA HOTEL
200 TK/DBL
WITH FAN

#9 (OR BIG BUS
#6) TO MOHAKHALI
BUS STA.

Topkhana Rd.

Motijheel

Abdul Gani Rd

BIMAN

HOTEL PURBANI INT'L

North-South Road

TICKETS
FOR 'ROCKET'
BOAT

Tayembee Rd.

← #8 TO
GABTALI
BUS STA.

Nawabpur Rd.

#8 TO
SAYEDBAD
BUS STA.

GULISTAN (FULBARIA)
BUS AREA - MASSIVE,
PHOTOGENIC RICKSHAW
JAMS. WALKING IS THE
FASTEST WAY THROUGH

BADAM TOLE
USUAL DEPARTURE
P OF 'ROCKET'
BOAT

★ SADARGHAT
BOAT TERMINAL
RIVERSIDE MAYHEM
TOURS BY SMALL ROWING
BOATS

BUSES OUT OF DHAKA

Jamuna River

Padma River

1 3 4
2
4

DHAKA BUS STATION	TO DIVISION
GABTALI →	RAJSHAHI ①
GABTALI →	KHULNA ②
MOHAKHALI →	DHAKA DIVISION ③
SYEDBAD →	CHITTAGONG/ SYLHET ④

NB GOVT BUSES FROM BRTC TERM.
GO TO MANY DESTINATIONS IN ALL
DIVISIONS

Sri Lanka

Sri Lanka, the teardrop cried by India, has a coast carpeted in palm trees, misty hills of green tea plantations, ancient Buddhist cave monasteries and some extraordinarily-carved rock forts. In a single day you can buy sapphires in a

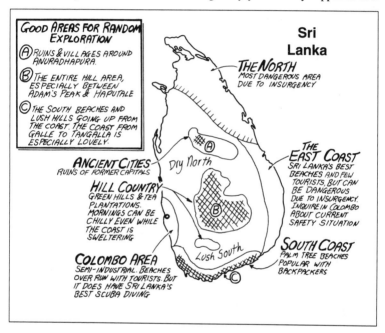

GOOD AREAS FOR RANDOM EXPLORATION

(A) RUINS & VILLAGES AROUND ANURADHAPURA.

(B) THE ENTIRE HILL AREA, ESPECIALLY BETWEEN ADAM'S PEAK & HAPUTALE

(C) THE SOUTH BEACHES AND LUSH HILLS GOING UP FROM THE COAST. THE COAST FROM GALLE TO TANGALLA IS ESPECIALLY LOVELY.

Sri Lanka

THE NORTH MOST DANGEROUS AREA DUE TO INSURGENCY

ANCIENT CITIES RUINS OF FORMER CAPITALS

Dry North

THE EAST COAST SRI LANKA'S BEST BEACHES AND FEW TOURISTS, BUT CAN BE DANGEROUS DUE TO INSURGENCY. INQUIRE IN COLOMBO ABOUT CURRENT SAFETY SITUATION

HILL COUNTRY GREEN HILLS & TEA PLANTATIONS. MORNINGS CAN BE CHILLY EVEN WHILE THE COAST IS SWELTERING

Lush South

SOUTH COAST PALM TREE BEACHES POPULAR WITH BACKPACKERS

COLOMBO AREA SEMI-INDUSTRIAL. BEACHES OVER RUN WITH TOURISTS. BUT IT DOES HAVE SRI LANKA'S BEST SCUBA DIVING

❏ **W&M's country ratings – Sri Lanka**
● **Expense $$** You can easily exist on less than $10/day especially during the low season (May to Sep). Traveller centres are often cheaper than other places.
● **Value for money** ✔✔✔ Even inexpensive hotel rooms don't usually crawl with insects.
● **Getting around** ✔✔✔ Buses are very frequent, though non-express services are painfully slow. Hitchhiking is easy.
● **English spoken** ✔✔✔ Similar to India.
● **Woman alone** ✔✔✔ A Buddhist country which is much more laid back than India, despite the annoying touts.
● **For vegetarians** ✔✔✔✔ Welcome to vegetarian nirvana.

walled colonial citadel, sweat on a beach with traditional stilt fishermen and walk across moorland to the World's End.

Apart from the astoundingly persistent touts in some tourist areas, travel here feels more relaxed than in India. Maybe it is the soothing sea breezes or the culture. Southern Sri Lanka is the centre of Therevada Buddhism and other Therevada countries (such as Thailand and Burma) look to it for religious guidance. So it seems odd that this spiritual land should play host to a seemingly interminable civil war. Yet conflicts between the Tamil north and Sinhalese south have continued sporadically for a thousand years; the island had been divided into separate kingdoms several times before British colonialisation. After independence in 1956, Sinhalese replaced English as the national language – this outraged the Tamil community who were thus expected to learn a globally 'useless' tongue. Following a massacre of Colombo Tamils in 1983 the discontent turned violent and the Tamil Tigers (Liberation Tigers of Tamil Eelam) set out to wrest control of a Tamil homeland. For several years the northern Jafna peninsula remained out of government control and though the army retook Jafna in 1996, its control of the city remains tenuous. All roads to Jafna pass through areas sympathetic to the Tamil Tigers who

---

❏ Geo-political information – Sri Lanka

Population: 18.7 million (1997), 18.4m (1995), 14.9m (1981), 12.9m (1971).

Area: 64,740 sq km.

Capital: Colombo (615,000, 1990). Seat of government Sri Jayawardenepura Kotte.

Other major cities: Dehiwal-Mount Lavinia (200,000); Moratuwa (170,000); Jafna (130,000); Kotte, Kandy (100,000).

GNP per capita: $640 (1994).

Currency history: Rupee/US$1 – Feb 1998: Rs61.6, Oct 1997: Rs59.3, July 1996: Rs55.3, Jan 1996: Rs53.5, Jan 1995: Rs49.7, Jan 1994: Rs49.2.

Major exports/economy: Tea (25% of export earnings – the world's main exporter), gems, rubber.

Ethnic mix: Sinhalese (74%), Tamil (16%), Sri Lankan 'Moors' (7%), Burghas (mixed blood Eurasians) and Veddahs (aboriginals) in very small numbers.

Official language: Sinhala. Tamil is a national (but not official) language.

Religious mix: Buddhist (68%), Hindu (15%), Muslim (8%), Christian (8%) [estimates].

Landmarks of national history: Abode of Adam and Eve after their ejection from paradise. **6th century BC**: Vijaya established as first Sinhalese king. **3rd century AD**: Buddhism introduced, branch of Bodhi tree planted at Anaradhapura. **12th century AD**: Lanka's Golden Age. **1505**: Portuguese build fort at Colombo. **1658**: Became Dutch possession. **1802**: British colony. **4 Feb 1948**: Dominion status (as Ceylon). **1951**: Declaration of Sinhala as national language sowed seeds of Tamil discontent. **22 May 1972**: Independence. **1983**: State of emergency due to terrorist attacks. **Dec 1995**: Government forces captured Jafna from LTTE. **Oct 1997**: Huge bomb blast rocked Colombo.

Leader: President (Ms) Chandrika Bandaranaike Kumaratunga.

Pressing political issues: Continued Tamil grievances. Civil war rumbles on despite army advances.

have simply relocated to the east coast and north central areas that they still control. With no imminent sign of any peaceful solution to the underlying conflict, in October 1997 a Colombo hotel and shopping complex was ripped apart in the worst bomb blast for a decade. This was followed in January 1998 by an explosion at the Temple of the Tooth, despite heavy security around this famous temple. Such attacks are, however, exceptional in the normally peaceful south of the island where the lure of idyllic beaches, wild elephants and dreamy hill towns remains largely untarnished.

❑ **Essential information for travellers – Sri Lanka**

● **Visa** Not required by most nationalities for a 30-day stay. A further 30-day extension is possible.

● **Currency** Sri Lanka Rupee. US$1=Rs59.3. Travellers cheques get a better exchange rate than cash. Credit card advances in Colombo are commission free.

● **Time zone** 6 hours ahead of GMT ($\frac{1}{2}$hr ahead of India).

● **Religious tone** The Buddhist feel is strongest in the centre and south. There are also Muslim and Hindu communities.

● **Health factors** Moderate malaria risk. It's not wise to drink the water.

● **Special dangers** Bombings have rarely injured tourists. The areas of fighting shift but they are consistently fairly well removed from the main places of interest (ie north and east of Anuradhapura). Some travellers have visited the east coast without difficulties, though many locals warn against it.

● **Typical traveller destinations** Kandy, Hikkaduwa beach, Anuradhapura, Ratnapura (to be ripped off by gem salesmen).

● **Highlights** Galle, Polonnaruwa, Sigiriya, wild elephants and birds at Bundala National Park, motorbike rides through the tea plantations, Nuwara Eliya's Hill Club, pilgrims at Adam's Peak, the moors at Horton Plains. Meditation retreats.

● **When to go** The coast is hot year round. Monsoon rains hit the north coast from early October to mid-December but the rest of the year is dry and much of the north and east is surprisingly arid. Rain is less predictable in the south west but the main monsoon here is from early June till mid-October.

The southern beaches are most popular from December to April (Hikkaduwa is particularly packed around Christmas), but even during the monsoon rain often falls for just a few hours in the afternoons, leaving the mornings sunny and bright.

The hill country gets the monsoon seasons of both the northern and southern coasts combined. And here it might rain for days. January to June is the best time to visit. Dry days are short sleeve warm, damp days are chilly, and nights can be rather cold.

● **Pulse of the country** Anuradhapura (spiritually – the Buddhist ruins), Kandy (culturally and historically).

● **Key tips** Colombo, the capital of this charming country, is not an attraction and there is no need to visit it. The international airport, though often referred to as Colombo, is in fact at Katunayake, 35km north of the city. If you are departing on a morning flight it is easier and more atmospheric to stay in Negombo, an unspectacular but passable beach resort just 6km further north. (Cheap accommodation is available along Lewis Place.) There are also direct (morning) buses from the airport to Kandy. Even if you do go into Colombo a rapid escape is easy with frequent bus services to all parts of the island from the central bus station (last services around 5pm).

● **Adam's Peak (Sri Pada)** The summit shrine is sacred to several faiths for its footprint of Adam/Buddha/Siva. More appealing are the throngs of pilgrims (Dec-May) and the mountain's celebrated perfect triangular shadow (look the wrong way at dawn). The climb is steep but clearly visible even in the moonlight, approx 3hrs from Dalhousie which is reached by bus from Hatton. Accommodation at Maskeliya, Dalhousie or at a monastery 1hr into the ascent.

● **Anuradapura** 2000-yr-old sacred Bo tree still stands in this 4th-9th century capital, now a fascinating, widely spread collection of ruins.

● **Arugam Bay (!)** Sri Lanka's surfing centre, also wreck dives, seabirds. Rent beach huts.

● **Batticaloa (!)** Listen for 'singing fish' on the Lagoon Bridge, summer evenings.

● **Bundala** Shallow lakes draw flocks of wading birds and the odd wild elephant.

● **Colombo** Unexciting capital. Pettah district for markets, bus station (on Olcott Mawatha). Tourist information/maps 78 Stuart Place, Galle Rd.

● **Galle** Very evocative Portuguese fortified citadel on sea-swept peninsula, old bldgs, stilt fishermen, sapphires cheaper here than in more traditional gem centres but you need to know your gems or you'll land up with a piece of coloured glass.

● **Haputale** Lacking any specific sights, this hillside village becomes atmospherically engulfed in mists most evenings and was a personal favourite base for excursions into the wonderful tea gardens. Nice views when clear. A motorbike is useful – they can be rented in Hikkaduwa.

● **Hikkaduwa** Sri Lanka's Kuta Beach, package tourists, drug scene, discos but good for finding rental motorbikes, tourist trinkets, quality rooms at bargain prices in the off season.

● **Horton Plains** Moorland hikes ending at World's End (GH) where the plateau plummets a vertical kilometre. Quiet, cool, often too misty to see the view.

● **Jafna (!!)** Turmoil-wracked second city. Big, Dutch fortress, Dutch church and King's House colonial mansion. Very unsafe.

● **Kaloya** For jeep tours into the Wilipatu national park (famous for its leopards).

● **Kandy** Attractive, larger town once an independent kingdom. Centred on lake. Temple of The Tooth (bombed in January 1998). Lovely botanical gardens at Peradeniya (5km) used for movie locations. Perahera festival (July/August) superb. The touts are very annoying and persistent. Many temples and meditation retreats in surrounding hills. Katugastota for elephant baths (4km, touristy).

● **Matara** Remains of Dutch fortifications in small, atmospheric town. Big, bad taste Buddhas at Weherehena temple and at Wewurukanalla temple, near Dickwella.

● **Matale** Smaller, typical town site of Rama's mythical battle with Ravana. Many working elephants in surrounding villages.

● **Negombo** Pleasant town with package tourist beach. Lewis Pl for cheap GHs.

● **Nuwara Eliya** (Nürelia) Over-rated hill town with some 18/19th century homes and the brilliantly Raj redolent *Hill Club* with elephant foot umbrella stands, Churchill photos, men-only smoking room etc (dress up, tie essential for dinner).

● **Polonnaruwa** 11/12th century capital, lake, ruins, palaces, dagobas, Buddhas.

● **Sigiriya** 20 frescoes survive half way up the precarious climb to lion paws and ancient palace/citadel remnants atop a huge rock outcrop. *GH*. Bus>>Dambulla

● **Unawatuna** More relaxed beach hang out than Hikkaduwa.

(!) Potentially dangerous owing to insurgency.   (!!) Particularly dangerous. Avoid.

PRACTICAL INFORMATION
Transport
● **Air** The only way in or out is by air – the ferry which used to link Sri Lanka to India has not run for several years. Air Lanka flies to several south Indian cities, eg Trivandrum for $35 and usually allows Sri Lankan stop-overs on discounted tickets between Europe and Bangkok or Hong Kong. See also Key Tips.

● **Bus and train** During the first bus ride we took in Sri Lanka, the vehicle's windscreen fell out during a torrential downpour. The driver simply borrowed my sun glasses and drove faster while the passengers fled to the back of the bus and put up their umbrellas. Other rides proved less eventful, though services on smaller roads can be rather full. On main routes, buses are faster and much more frequent than trains. The only overnight rail service is the mail train from Kandy that takes 8hrs to wind its way just 170km to Badulla.

● **Motorbikes** These can be cheaply rented in Hikkaduwa without the inconvenient necessity of showing of a licence. Motorbikes are an ideal way to explore the south coast, though remember to take a waterproof jacket and warm clothes for rides up into the hills.

● **Hitch hiking** This proved surprisingly effective.

Accommodation
Accommodation is very cheap (around $5) in most of Sri Lanka but not everywhere. Certain towns and villages mysteriously seem to have no budget options whatsoever. Both times we found ourselves stranded in such a place, however, more interesting options turned up – once in a monastery and once with a family. If you're prepared to sleep on the floor with Buddhist acolytes and monks, you may do so in many a temple for a small donation. There are also several monasteries around Kandy offering meditation retreats, yoga and beautiful views for a few dollars per day including spartan accommodation and vegetarian meals.

The towns in which we know of no cheap accommodation are: Beruwela (an upmarket beach resort), Dikwella, Dondra (there's not even expensive accommodation here), Kondra, Horton Plains Park (but there are many camping sites), Kurunegala, Mihintale (though a day trip from Anuradhapura is possible). Nuwara Eliya has a limited range of budget choices.

Food and drink
If you like curries, you'll love Sri Lanka. Breakfast is curry with bread, lunch is curry with rice. In the evening you can have lunch all over again or eat your curry with *hoppers* (crispy rice flower and coconut milk hemispheres into which an optional egg may have been half cooked). Order a curry in many simple restaurants and what you actually get is a selection of contrasting concoctions dolloped onto a plate or banana leaf, along with some yoghurt.

Staying in touch
The GPO in Colombo has a Poste Restante service. International calls can be made there or at the telegraph office in Duke St.

International country code +94. There are no city codes.

Further information
There's a tourist information centre at the airport and at 78 Stuart Place, Galle Rd, Colombo (☎ 437059), Monday to Friday 8.30am-4.15pm, Saturday and Sunday 8am-12.30pm. The tourist board also has information offices in Frankfurt, Paris, London, Tokyo and Bangkok; elsewhere you can get basic maps and pamphlets from Air Lanka offices. One of their free country maps manages to cram a remarkable amount of detail onto a single A4 sheet.

For more detail, the Sri Lanka survey department produces excellent topographical maps, covering the country in four 1:250,000 sheets, sold from their sales office on York St in central Colombo.

SOUTH-EAST ASIA

It's hardly surprising that this is one of the most popular regions for travellers in Asia. Whether you're looking for deserted beaches or five-star resorts, jungle adventures or a hassle-free stopover; there's something for everyone here. This chapter includes Indonesia, Singapore, Malaysia (with Brunei), Thailand, Burma (Myanmar), Vietnam, Cambodia, Laos and the Philippines.

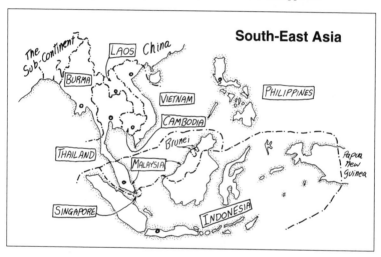

South-East Asia

STUPA/PAGODA DESIGNS

SANCHI, INDIA   TIBETAN, NEPAL   6TH, JAPAN   "CHEDI", LAOS   YUNNAN/BURMA

Indonesia

The most populous nation in South-East Asia, Indonesia's rapidly growing population is unevenly sprinkled on the biggest one thousand of a 13,667 island volcano-popping archipelago which stretches over 6000km, further than from Moscow to Madrid, or Seattle to Savannah.

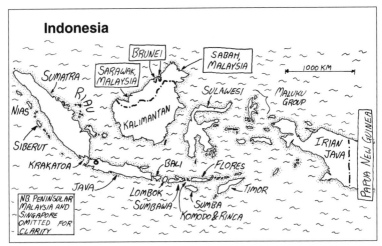

❏ **W&M's country ratings – Indonesia**

The ratings vary greatly between the many islands in this huge archipelago.

● **Expense $$$** Kalimantan and Irian Jaya tend to be more expensive than the more populated regions; since transport is limited you may have to take internal flights.

● **Value for money** ✔✔✔✔ Cheap and cheerful.

● **Getting around** ✔✔-✔✔✔✔✔ This depends on the region; it's very easy in Java and Bali but very patchy in Kalimantan and Irian Jaya where there are few roads.

● **English spoken** ✔-✔✔✔✔✔ You can always find someone who speaks English in Bali or Java, but in the more isolated regions Bahasa Indonesia is essential; it's easy to master.

● **Woman alone** ✔✔ Women report a noticeable difference between the Muslim and non-Muslim areas. Mild harassment is common but it rarely gets physical – saying you're married may help.

● **For vegetarians** ✔✔✔✔ You'll have few problems, especially if you eat fish and seafood.

Indonesia is a natural paradise of intense greens; emerald rice terraces, ancient rainforests, and lush roadside foliage weighed down with hibiscus flowers and bougainvillea. The claim is of a land 'so fertile that a stick will sprout' – a poetic exaggeration we thought until we saw a Flores fencepost that had indeed grown leaves. The country is rich in history with Hindu, Buddhist, and most recently Islamic influences coming together over a melting pot of diverse animist cultures. The combination has produced some architectural splendours, particularly in Java and Bali.

Less attractively, Indonesia is also a rapidly industrialising country; the capital Jakarta is a pit worth avoiding and the clearfelling of forests that we saw in Kalimantan is shocking. There is a lot of land to spoil, but the sooner you go the more that will remain for you to savour.

❏ **Geo-political information – Indonesia**

Population: 209 million (1997), 198m (1995), 179m (1990), 135m (1975).

Area: 1,812,000 sq km.

Capital: Jakarta (8.2 million, 1990).

Other major cities: Surabaya (2.4m), Bandung (2m), Medan (1.7m) Semarang (1.3m), Palembang (1.1m), Ujang Pandang (900,000), Malang, Padang (600,000) and 21 other cities with over 100,000.

GNP per capita: $880 (1994), $475 (1988).

Currency history: Rupiah/US$1 – Feb 1998: Rp7300, Oct 1997: Rp2905, July 1995: Rp2227, Jan 1994: Rp2100, Jan 1991: Rp2102, 1985: Rp1125.

Major exports/economy: 80% of earnings from oil/gas, though still a major producer of spices (nutmeg, cloves, pepper) and copra (from coconuts). Self sufficient in rice. Despite its diversifying economy Indonesia received over $5 million in aid in 1994/5. Massive stock market and currency crash in 1997.

Ethnic mix: Reflected in the many languages.

Official languages: Bahasa Indonesia. Though most of the population can speak Bahasa Indonesia, only 15% claim it as a mother tongue. There are 583 other languages including Javanese (38.2%), Sundanese (14.9%), Madurase (4.2%) and around two million speakers each of Batak, Micaoc, Buginese, Banjarese and Balinese. Chinese was included in the 17% of 'others' in the 1990 census.

Religious mix: Muslim (87%), Christian (10%), Hindu (Bali), Buddhist.

Landmarks of national history: **7th century**: Palembang became the Buddhist centre of the Srivijaya empire. **800AD**: Borobudur and other Buddhist temples were constructed. **1292-1398**: The Majapahit empire created an Indonesian identity. **1520s**: Portuguese and Spanish raced to the spice islands (Moluccas). **16th century**: Islam spread through seaborne commerce while Dutch colonialism took root. **1619**: Genocide of Banda Islanders by the Dutch to protect their nutmeg trade. **1908**: Balinese royal family killed by Dutch soldiers. **1942-5**: Japanese occupation. **1949**: Independence from Holland after a protracted war. **1965**: Suharto coup and anti-communist witchhunt/massacres. **1969**: Dutch New Guinea annexed as Irian Jaya (referendum cancelled). **1975**: Invasion of Portuguese East Timor.

Leader: President Suharto, in power since March 1967.

Pressing political issues: The status of East Timor (former Portuguese colony), nepotism (most famously in the motor industry – president's sons gain favourable positions); the economic collapse.

PRACTICAL INFORMATION
Visas and formalities

Most nationalities can travel to Indonesia without a visa if they enter and exit through certain specified 'visa waiver' gateways. The list of these gateways has expanded in recent years to include almost every sensible entry/exit point, although it still does **not** include land or air crossings from Papua New Guinea nor the boat from Sabah (East Malaysia). Jungle hikes to/from Sarawak will also need full visas but the Kuching-Pontiniak road is now included in the waiver, except when closed altogether as happened during the 1997 political protests. Theoretically you must be in possession of an onward or return ticket when you arrive in Indonesia. Our tickets were checked at Kupang airport, though this seems to be rare. Those arriving by boat (eg from Singapore) are almost never asked. To be safe, buy a full price Medan-Penang ticket from any Garuda office. It is fully refundable within the next year, though you may have to return it to the original issuing office.

● **Visa extensions** When we visited, extensions to the two-month visa-free stay proved quite impossible despite numerous attempts. However, at the time of writing the tourist bureau tells us that a further two month extension should now be possible.

Money

The US dollar is the most accepted currency but all major currencies, as well as travellers' cheques, are accepted in Bali, Java and the other main cities. Credit card cash advances are possible in Java, Bali etc but they are not available in Nusa Tenggara, east of Martaram (Lombok).

Banks are open Monday to Friday, 8am-3pm. A few banks are open on Saturdays, 8-11am.

It can be difficult to change money at all in remote areas, especially at weekends.

Transport

● **Air** Garuda Indonesia, the national flag carrier, operates on both international and domestic routes. Domestically it serves 33 cities including all the provincial capitals. Merpati Nusantara Airlines is the second national carrier and flies to about 110 destinations in Indonesia and has some border crossing flights to Australia (Darwin), Brunei Darussalam and East Malaysia (Kuching). Bouraq's internal flights are typically slightly cheaper than Garuda's. In remoter areas tiny seven-seater planes flown by missionaries drop supplies into remote valleys. If there's space you can sometimes hitch a lift. You pay just for the fuel that your extra weight requires but this still isn't a very cheap way to travel.

International departure tax: $5. The cost of the domestic tax varies but the average is $2. Getting to and from Jakarta's Sukarno Hatta International airport by taxi costs approximately $8 (plus a $2 toll road fee); by bus $2, every 30 minutes.

❏ **100% Golkar**
Amidst vast ethnic and religious divisions, a binding force within Indonesian culture is *mufakat* (consensus). Developed as a necessity in the context of densely populated Javanese villages, mufakat is reached through *musyawarah* (consultation) and *gotong royong* (mutual assistance). One high profile manifestation of consensus is the *Panca Sila* (five principles) of the Republic; nationalism, humanitarianism, religious plurality, justice and 'guided democracy'. In the latter all opposition political parties are expected to pledge fundamental support for the Golkar government (which gets to appoint the majority of politicians anyway). The role of the opposition is thus to give constructive advice (and by its mere existence, to keep the Western powers happy). When you see a village sign announcing that it voted '100% Golkar' remember that this is not proof of oppression; more a collective pride in reaching a true, recordable consensus.

● **Train** Train services are available only in Java and in parts of Sumatra. Several trains run between Jakarta and Surabaya. The most comfortable are the air-conditioned *Bima* sleeper train and the *Mutiara* which both travel at night. The Bima passes through Yogyakarta and Solo while the Mutiara takes the northern route through Semarang. The *Senja Utama* is an express service to Yogyakarta and Solo and it has reclining seats but no air-conditioning. The *Parahyangan* offers four services a day

---

❏ **Essential information for travellers – Indonesia**

● **Visa** A two-month visa-free stay is possible if you enter at certain specified places. An onward ticket is theoretically required.

● **Currency** Rupiah. US$1=Rp7300.

● **Time zone** Sumatra, Java, west and central Kalimantan are 7 hours ahead of GMT (same as Thailand); east and south Kalimantan, Timor, Sulawesi, Bali and Nusa Tenggara are 8hrs ahead (same as Malaysia); Maluku and Irian Jaya are 9hrs ahead (same as Japan).

● **Religious tone** A relaxed Muslim feel from Sumatra to Sumbawa; a unique form of Hinduism heavily mixed with local culture is found in Bali. Christian areas such as Flores and others, particularly central Sulawesi, retain a strong animist feel. Irian Jaya, like neighbouring Papua New Guinea, is home to tribes with various fascinating beliefs.

● **Health factors** Malaria risk. Drinking the water is not encouraged.

● **Special dangers** The kidnappings in Irian Jaya in 1995 seem to have been isolated incidents; the political demonstrations in July 1996 turned nasty; the forest fires in autumn 1997 choked the Sumatra and Borneo skies and caused at least one serious air crash.

● **Social conventions** Cover your mouth when yawning or using a toothpick. Showers are rare in Indonesian bathrooms; use the scoop to pour water over you. Don't use the *mandi* tub as a bath. Tipping is not expected.

Much of the country is Muslim so conservative dress is important – no shorts, bare shoulders, etc except in beach areas.

● **Typical traveller destinations** Bali, Lombok, Bukkitingi and Lake Toba.

● **Highlights** Tanah Torajah, Nusa Tenggara, Komodo dragons at Rinca rather than Komodo, Borobudur – and many more.

● **When to go** Straddling the equator, coastal Indonesia is always hot though mountain tops can be surprisingly cold at night and the peaks of central Irian Jaya have some of the world's more unexpected permanent snows. The seasonal variation is between wet and dry. Even the 'dry' is damp and humid. The wet season starts later the further east you head: Sumatra (September to March), Java (October to April), Bali, Lombok and Nusa Tenggara (November to May) though the Moluccas don't fit the pattern – the wet season there is from April to August. The rainy season brings dramatic downpours. As these typically only last for a couple of hours each afternoon there is no reason to avoid a visit, except perhaps in the more remote islands where mud roads become impassable (eg West Flores).

● **Pulse of the country** Yogyakarta (Java), Ubud (Balinese cultural centre).

● **Key tips** Learn the language – it's so easy. If you can't get a visa extension, consider seeing the country in two loops; two months simply isn't enough to get a feel of more than a small portion.

● **Festivals** In such a huge, multi-cultural nation, there are an almost uncountable number of festivals; a free, annually updated *Calendar of Events* booklet available from tourist offices around the world lists almost 300.

between Jakarta and Bandung, taking about three hours. Prices vary enormously between classes and the different trains.

● **Bus** Bus services are increasingly comprehensive even on immensely long journeys such as Bali-Banda Aceh, travelling night and day. Buses on Bali, Java and Sumatra are generally air-conditioned and have reclining seats as well as TV with video programmes. Kalimantan and Irian Jaya have few roads and none that penetrate deep into the interior. Western Flores, parts of Sulawesi and other rural areas have poor roads and slow, bone-rattling bus services which cruise the town centres touting for business before going to fill up with petrol and finally limping off. Earplugs and/or a broadened mind towards the worst twangs of 1970s pop music are often necessary.

● **Bemo** These are covered pick-up trucks with bench-seats in the back; they're designed for 10 small passengers but are usually even more crowded and uncomfortable. They offer a cheap form of transport and are used as a minibus system within towns.

● **Boat PELNI**, the state-owned shipping company, has modern ships serving the main ports from Banda Aceh on the west of the country to Sorong in Irian Jaya on the east. The ships are air-conditioned and were built to accommodate 1000 to 1500 passengers in four classes. First class cabins have attached bathrooms and TV. Economy class accommodation (raised mats on a large communal floor) is much cheaper and perfectly acceptable except when the boat is overloaded. Meals (typically fish-head soup) are included but blink and you'll miss them.

Most ships work on two-week loop schedules so getting a current timetable is important, especially for the out of the way ports in Maluku and Irian Jaya. Timetables are available at any PELNI office around Indonesia or from Jalan Pintu Air #1, Jakarta, but are hard to find abroad.

There are many small private boats on which you can negotiate a passage but the process is hit and miss. We waited a week

in Palu (Sulawesi) looking for a ride to Kalimantan. Going from Banjarmarsin to Surabaya, on the other hand, proved easy – we left the same evening. NB The seas are far too rough to make such crossings enjoyable if you lack sea legs.

● **Motorcycles** Motorcycles can be rented for about US$6-8/day, weekly rates work out slightly cheaper. Insurance is usually covered in the rate. Getting a temporary motorbike licence is easy but can take a day. There's a fee to pay.

● **Other** Taxis are available, though meters are commonplace only in Jakarta, Bandung, Semarang and Surabaya.

A *bajaj* is a miniature tricycle seating two passengers rather tightly with its driver in the front. These are gradually replacing *becak*s (bicycle rickshaws). Typical pre-bargained *becak* fares are between US$ 0.40 and 0.60.

A *suzuki* is a bemo-style shared taxi. There are also *colts* (say 'coll') and jeepney-esque *opalets*. *Dokar*s are horsedrawn buggies which are seen in Sumbawa and parts of Java (eg Bogor, Yogyakarta, Solo and Surabaya); bargain to US$0.60/0.80 per kilometre. Bicycles can often be rented (average $1.50/day). An *ojek* is a motorbike hired with its rider.

Accommodation

The ubiquitous *wisma* and *losmen* are cheap guest houses offering a shared *mandi* (bucket shower) and adequate beds for $2-5 – expect to pay a little more in Kalimantan. The price rarely reflects the quality of a cheap place; a beautiful, clean beachside bungalow might cost the same as a flea pit shack in a dreary town. *Penginapan* are even more basic. 'Hotels' are likely to be more expensive.

In very small villages if there is no formal hotel, seek out the *kepal desa* (village chief) and introduce yourself – in Bahasa Indonesia (or the local language if you're really clever). He will conjure up a family (probably his own) for you to stay with. We were initially sceptical about this but the four times we tried it, it worked unbelievably well – perhaps because the villages were so very remote. We never even had to ask for accommodation. Though an offer of payment might be refused when offered verbally, it is appropriate to leave a sum equivalent to a basic losmen charge. Carry a few envelopes so that you can do so tactfully.

Food and drink

The staple food in most of Indonesia is rice. Spices are often used liberally and fish, chicken and coconut are common ingredients. *Nasi goreng* (fried rice), *bami goreng* (fried noodles) and *gado gado* (spicy peanut and tempeh salad) are found virtually everywhere.

If you eat meat you'll probably prefer flesh (*daging*) to innards (*babat*). However, in the rural areas of Nusa Tenggara the only food available in the evening was boiled rice and a diminutive dried fish. In Sumatra particularly, watch out for the searingly hot Padang-style food that burns its own ring of fire. The tandoori red appearance is a giveaway. The cheapest places to eat are *warung* (street stalls).

Drinks are standard from region to region – tea is king. There are, however, several breweries which produce local beer (beer is available even in Islamic areas.)

Staying in touch

● **Mail** The letters we posted arrived reliably, the quickest taking only five days.

American Express offices including those in Medan, Padang, Surabaya, Ujung Pandang will keep mail for you, as will the branches of **Pacto Ltd Tours & Travel** in Yogyakarta: c/o Hotel Ambarrukmo Palace (☎ 562906), Jalan Laksda Adjsucipto, PO Box 1050, Yogyakarta 5501; Bali: Jl Raya Ngurah Rai, Sanur, PO Box 52, Denpasar (☎ 436101) and Jakarta: Exchange House Building (☎ 521 6238), Kav 3, Jl HR Rasuna Said Blok X-1, Jakarta 10330.

● **Phone** International telephone code: +62. City codes: Jakarta: 21, Yogyakarta: 274, Medan: 61, Bali: 22, Surabaya: 31.

Activities

● **Hiking** Indonesia has many fabulous treks though for many a guide is essential.

❏ **Meeting the locals**

● **The people** A very complex mixture of ethnic and religious groups. The Javanese are the most populous and enforce a political dominance. People are typically friendly, sometimes too much so, but in tourist areas there can be an air of money grabbing and pestering; cries of 'Hello Mister' haunt travellers of either sex throughout the eastern islands.

● **Language** Bahasa Indonesia is a cinch – it's perhaps the world's easiest language. Just pick up a *kamus* (dictionary) and translate word for word what you want to say; it may not be stylish but it works. There is no difficult grammar, no weird script, and the pronunciation is very straightforward (note that 'c' is always pronounced 'ch' and 'e' is 'eh'). Plurals are formed by saying a word twice; orang (man), orang orang (men) though this is usually written orang2.

People often ask 'Where are you going?' This is not the Spanish Inquisition, they are just making pleasant conversation. Answer *jalan jalan* – just wandering about.

Some words in Bahasa Indonesia (like Malay, slightly simplified):

Thank you very much	– *Terima kasih banyak*
Good morning	– *Selamat pagi*
Good afternoon/evening	– *Selamat sor-eh*
Goodnight	– *Selamat malam*
How are you	– *Apa kabar*
Response	– *Kabar baik*
Sorry	– *Ma-af*
It's delicious	– *Enak saja*

There are likely to be some discomforts – knee-high mud in Siberut, leeches in the Borneo jungles etc. Sulawesi is marvellous trekking country with a well-used donkey track still used as a supply road (there are no vehicles) between Palu and Tentena where some Bada valley villages have megaliths. A grasp of Indonesian, or a dictionary, is essential as you have to stay in people's homes along the way. Also in Sulawesi, Tanah Torajah offers endless day walks amongst the stylish boat-shaped grain stores, grave cliffs and impressive rice terraces. Dayak tribesmen can take you on pig hunts or medicine-gathering walks into the deep Borneo jungles (eg from Data Dawai). Our trip involved paddling and punting up canopied tributaries while the guide shot at hornbills with his blowpipe, then walking for hours through leech-infested forest. We camped on a hunter's raised wooden platform, covered by a tarpaulin, and surrounded by the echoes of a jungle night. Bring anti-mosquito protection. Guides can be hired for between $12 and $20 a day, depending on the services provided.

Volcano climbs are deservedly popular. Leave early in the morning for Mt Bromo or Kelimutu (with its three-coloured crater lakes) in order to see the sunrise from the top. Mt Rinjani is a tougher climb taking 3-4 days to or from Sapit (Lombok); guides are advised.

● **Scuba Diving** The best sites are in north-west Bali (eg Malalayang Beach), and near Manado in Sulawesi. There are also several sites in the Moluccas. The reefs at Maumere in Flores have been damaged by typhoons.

● **Surfing** Surf beaches in Bali include Nusa Dua and Sanur (October to March), Kuta (summer), Ulu Watu (for experts); and in Java, Pelabuhan Rata (two hours from Bogor) and Batu Keras, west of Pangandaran (for beginners).

Further information

● **Books and maps** The best place to buy maps of Indonesia is in Singapore or in Western countries. Bill Dalton's *Indonesia Handbook* (Moon Publications) is our favourite practical travel guide with a genuine appreciation for the country. The Lonely Planet guide is as solid as ever and *Culture Shock! Indonesia* is also excellent.

Women's Voices (Longman Australia, 1995) is a collection of stories by Indonesian woman writers but it is difficult to find outside Indonesia and Australia. *Travelling to Bali: 400 Years of Journeys* compiled by Adrian Vickers (Oxford in Asia, 1994) is a collection of travel prose from the 16th century to the 1980s. *A Nation In Waiting: Indonesia in the 1990s* by Adam Schwarz (Allen and Unwin, 1994) is an excellent summary of current events written by a writer for the Far Eastern Economic Review. Another good read is *The Head-Hunters of Borneo* by Carl Bock (OUP, 1986).

● **Information offices** Glossy pamphlets and booklets are available free from Indonesian Tourist Promotion Offices in Frankfurt, London, Los Angeles, Singapore, Taipei and Tokyo.

In each of the 27 provincial centres there are government tourist offices (DIPARDA) which have local maps. The **Central Department of Tourism** (☎ 21-383 8236, fax 21-386 7589), 17-19 Merdeka Barat, Jakarta (PO Box 1409) is helpful in answering direct questions.

Web sites

www.indonesiatoday.com has an overview of destinations.

Peter M. Geiser's Online Sumatra Travel Guide is at www-students.unisg.ch/~pgeiser/sumatra/index.htm.

A good collection of Indonesia links is at mawar.inn.bppt.go.id.

Indonesia – Island by Island A-Z

Bali

Lush mountains, glorious but tourist-saturated beaches (Kuta is cheaper than Sanur). Unique Hindu based culture with more temples and shrines than houses. Many traveller services but touts and vendors can get annoying. Local motorbike licences are available on passing a rudimentary test, bike rental is cheap.

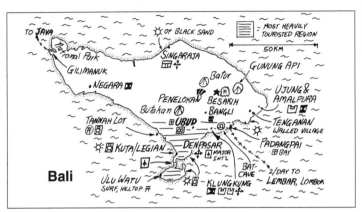

Biak

Air transport hub for N Irian Jaya. Flights to USA. Bosnik (former capital) 25km, beach.

Flores

Delightful, slow moving garden island, Nominally Christian villages full of over-friendly 'Hello Mister' kids. Komodo dragons roam the western tip as well as Komodo/Rinca islands.

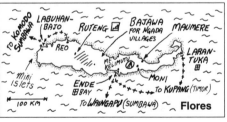

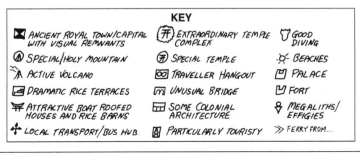

KEY

🗺 ANCIENT ROYAL TOWN/CAPITAL WITH VISUAL REMNANTS	🏯 EXTRAORDINARY TEMPLE COMPLEX	♡ GOOD DIVING
Ⓝ SPECIAL/HOLY MOUNTAIN	⊕ SPECIAL TEMPLE	☼ BEACHES
🌋 ACTIVE VOLCANO	∞ TRAVELLER HANGOUT	♙ PALACE
🌾 DRAMATIC RICE TERRACES	⋒ UNUSUAL BRIDGE	♜ FORT
🚢 ATTRACTIVE BOAT ROOFED HOUSES AND RICE BARNS	⊞ SOME COLONIAL ARCHITECTURE	⚱ MEGALITHS/ EFFIGIES
✚ LOCAL TRANSPORT/BUS HUB.	🅱 PARTICULARLY TOURISTY	≫ FERRY FROM....

Irian Jaya
The west half of New Guinea. Impenetrable jungle, snow topped mountains, undiscovered Stone Age tribes. Expensive and tough to get around without flying. Pastoral Balem Valley (fly to Wamena) is the Kathmandu Valley of IJ with some tourism, many hikes eg to Wolo, Akima for the famous smoked mummy. Paniai Lakes sound fantastic (fly into Enarotali). Sibil Valley for stone-built villages, wildly adorned locals. >> Crossing to Papua New Guinea is only possible by air and only with a full Indonesian visa (not on the two-month visa waiver scheme).

Java
In the fertile spaces between its fizzing volcanoes, Java houses more than half the Indonesian population, the capital (Jakarta), major cultural and industrial cities plus the fabulous ancient temple complexes of Borobadur and Prambanan.

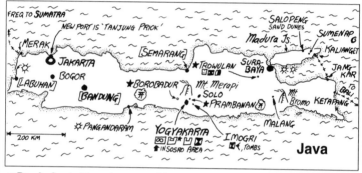

● **Borobadur★** The universe as a 9th century Buddhist metaphor in carved stone. One of the greatest sites in Asia though some find it too solid and square to impress.
● **Jakarta** Various Soviet-esque monuments. Kota area for old Batavia houses, Sunda Kelapa port and watchtower. Merdeka Sq for a fort, national museum, and huge mosque. Jalan Jaksa for cheap hotels.
● **Mt Bromo** Spectacular views, lava 'sand sea' fills awesome volcanic crater. Climb via Problinggo/Ngadisari/Cemoro Lawang or Blimbing/Tumpang/Ngadas.
● **Prambanan★** Spectacular remains of 9-10th century Hindu temple complexes. Great exploration potential across several km. 17-20km from Yogyakarta.
● **Trowulan★** Scattered ruins of 14th century city around small village – wonderful place to explore. Stay in Mojokerto for atmospheric old houses (10km).

Kalimantan
Vast tracts of mostly flat jungle, heavily logged in parts. Few towns are linked by roads. Hopper flights into the interior are typically cheaper and more frequent than longboats. Note that the inland Dayak culture is being rapidly eroded especially near airstrips: walk and paddle through leech-infested forest to find remaining longhouse villages (with a guide). Visit Banjarmarsin for canals, floating markets, massive hats but 'Venice of the East' is an exaggeration.

Krakatoa
Its massive 1883 volcanic explosion killed 40,000 with tidal waves, shook clocks in Europe and blotted out the sun with ash. Today's hissing remains are fleetingly visible from Padang-Jakarta boats. For a better view charter boats from Labuhan (Java) (at least 10hrs return).

Komodo and Rinca

The Komodo dragon, the world's largest lizard, is visible for a fee and a goat in Komodo, or with luck in Rinca/far-western Flores. >>Labuhanbajo (Flores) or Sape (Sumbawa) 2/week. Or hire a boat.

Lombok

Some traditional villages in the far south and on the foothills of holy Mt Rinjani. The great beaches at Senggigi and the Gili Islands are an increasingly popular escape for package tourists daring to go beyond Kuta in Bali. Bus hub is Sweta. >>3/day Labuhan Lombok to Poto Tano (Sumbawa); 2/day Lembar-Bali (6hrs).

Madura

See Java map. Summer bull races. Bypassed by tourists despite good beaches.

Maluku (Moluccas)

The original Spice Islands and spur to colonialism are now quiet desert island backwaters dotted with Dutch fortress ruins and picturesque volcanoes. Only a small selection of the easier (but still awkward) to reach islands are depicted here.

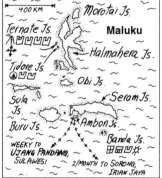

● **Ambon** Rhododendrons, cloves, fortress ruins, Maluku's modest ferry/air hub. >>Sulawesi, Irian Jaya.

● **Banda Island** Scene of Dutch perpetrated genocide. Bandaneira town is attractive with old villas and forts.

● **Halmahera** Jungles hide war wreckage, eg around Kao Bay (beaches).>>Ternate.

● **Seram** Wet, forested. Birdlife and no tourists. Great exploration opportunities.>>Ambon.

● **Ternate/Tidore** Tiny isles, once powerful sultanates. Ternate>>Sulawesi.

Nias

Some stilt villages of traditional 'boat' houses in south. Surf at Lagundi beach.>>Sibolga (Sumatra)

Nusa Tenggara

Collective name for the string of islands from Lombok east (but not East Timor).

Siberut

Rewarding but time-consuming canoe boat expeditions into roadless forest villages, best undertaken with a guide/permit; arrange in Padang or Bukittingi (Sumatra).

Sulawesi (Celebes)

Culturally varied (Muslim S, Animist C, Protestant N) and geo-

graphically appealing with a jungle/mountain heart. Tanah Toraja is a region of fabulous rice terraced hills dotted with scenic 'boat' house villages where Christianity has animist safeguards (funeral sacrifices, voodoo-style *tau-tau* memorial figures in carved cliff niches). Rather touristy unless you hike a good way beyond Rantepao, the traveller hub. The walk is an easy five-day stroll between Gimpu (bemo from Palu) and quaint Tentena (outrigger boats across lake to Pendolo). Follows donkey tracks through lovely flower filled, roadless villages and the megaliths of the Bada valley. Can send your bags ahead by *bemo*. Sweltering Ujang Pandang (formerly Makassar) harbours many elegant Bugis schooners; cheap hotels around the fort.

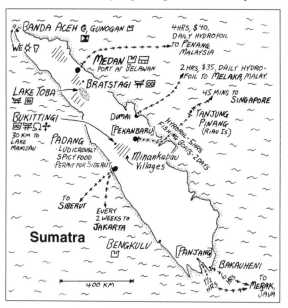

Sumatra

Some tracts of jungle and mangrove still survive the onset of the oil business and make the east coast tough to travel through. Backpackers gravitate to the north where villages around Samosir Island (on Lake Toba – boat from Prapat) retain some attractive traditional architecture while fortunately ditching cannibalism. Ambarita is Toba's traveller centre. Brastagi also draws visitors for jungle exploration trips. There are beach bungalows from Rs7000 on We Island (great snorkelling/dives).

Sumba

Mainly flat and barren. Famous for cattleman festivals – like mini tribal wars – eg at Lamboya (Feb), Wanokaka (Mar) other villages (Mar-Apr); bring betel nuts. Rende, Pau and other villages have big stone tombs. Waingapu (main town) >> Ende (Flores), Bima (Sumbawa).

Sumbawa

Beautiful, rugged largely Muslim island. Palaces in Sumbawa Besar and Bima, traditional villages around Donggo. Sape (attractive port, many horse carts)>>Komodo (2/week); Poto Tano >>Lombok (3/day); Bima>>Ende (Flores), Ujang Pandang (Sulawesi) (2/month).

Timor

Lopo beehive shaped huts in hill villages around Soe. Disputed East Timor (ex-Portuguese colony occupied by Indonesia since 1975) is open to tourists again: Baukau has colonial charm; lovely beaches; Dili-Maubise road said to be spectacular. Kupang's 2/wk flight to Darwin (Merpati Airlines) is cheapest way to Australia.

Singapore

Clean, safe, efficient, modern, convenient, helpful and orderly. Maybe too orderly. Singapore has none of that 'Asian mayhem' which adds the atmosphere and the hassle to travel elsewhere on the continent. It's a truly international city – you might think you were in America except that the people look richer and smarter. Come here to re-charge your batteries with the great selection of food, and forget about dropping litter (S$1000 fine), chewing gum, jay walking and, of course, drugs.

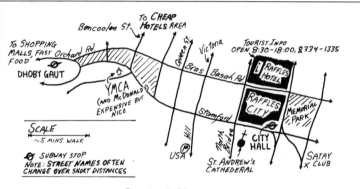

Central Singapore

Alternatives to shopping: temple hopping; Tiger Balm Gardens ('so bad it's good'); visit the zoo (recommended by people who like zoos); walk around Arab Street, Chinatown, Little India; tour touristy Sentosa Island (ferries from World Trade Centre); check for special happenings in *Singapore This Week*.

❏ **W&M's country ratings – Singapore**
● **Expense $$$$** Slightly less than the USA and a real shock coming from Indonesia.
● **Value for money** ✔✔✔ Food is good value but the budget accommodation is terrible.
● **Getting around** ✔✔✔✔✔ Public transport is extremely efficient.
● **English spoken** ✔✔✔✔✔ English is an official language, spoken along with Chinese, Malay, Tamil.
● **Woman alone** ✔✔✔✔✔ Trouble-free, like everything else in Singapore.
● **For vegetarians** ✔✔✔✔ A wide variety of food available for all tastes.

❑ Essential information for travellers – Singapore
● **Visa** A visa free two-week stay is plenty for most. Immigration requires an onward ticket or sufficient funds, but officials rarely check.
● **Currency** Singapore dollar. US$1=S$1.72.
● **Time zone** 8 hours ahead of GMT (1hr ahead of Thailand, Java, Sumatra; same as Malaysia, Borneo).
● **Health factors** The tap water is clean and malaria has been eradicated.
● **Typical traveller destinations** Restaurants and shopping malls.
● **Highlights** The food, Ubin Island (to get close to a traditional Singapore feel).
● **When to go** It's always hot and humid and short rainstorms are common, especially from November to January. The weather makes little difference to a city that largely consists of air-conditioned shopping malls.

PRACTICAL INFORMATION
Visas and formalities
See box above.

Money
Exchanging travellers' cheques is easy and you get a better rate than for cash; travellers' cheques are also accepted in some stores. There are plenty of ATMs, and credit card advances are straightforward and commission free.

Accommodation
Unless you're happy to spend the night on a park bench, the cheapest accommodation options in Singapore are its appropriately named crash pads (prices average around S$8). The park bench might be more comfortable: a stay in a crash pad often involves sleeping on the floor in crowded rooms, hallways or (in at least one case) the bathtub. Most crash pads and cheap guest houses are around the Dhoby Ghaut

❑ Geo-political information – Singapore
Population: 3.4 million (1997), 2.8m (1995), 2.7m (1990), 2.5m (1984).
Area: 610 sq km.
GNP per capita: $23,300 (1994).
Currency history: S$/US$1 – Feb 1998: S$1.72, Oct 1997: S$1.51, July 1996: S$1.41, Jan 1996: S$1.41, Jan 1995: S$1.46, Jan 1994: S$1.61.
Major exports/economy: Financial services, oil refining, manufacturing, ship repair, tourism.
Ethnic mix: Chinese (77.6%), Malay (14.1%), Indian (7.1%).
Official languages: English. 37% speak Chinese dialects as a first language. Malay and Tamil are also spoken.
Religious mix: Buddhist (1.2m), Muslim (340,000), Christian (280,000), Hindu (80,000), Sikh (9000).
Landmarks of national history: **1819**: Leased from the Sultan of Johore by Stanford Raffles. **1867**: With Malacca (now in Malaysia) and Penang became the Straits Settlements British crown colony. **1942**: Invaded by Japan (defence bungled by Churchill, Australasian casualties). **1959**: Self government. **1963-65**: Part of Malayan Federation. **1965**: Independence.
Leaders: President Ong Teng Chong in power since 1993. The Prime Minister is appointed by the president; currently Goh Chok Tong.
Pressing political issues: Financial controls following the Barings Bank affair (British trader Nick Leeson was jailed for 6½years having lost $1.4 billion on derivatives deals in 1996).

Mass Rapid Transit (MRT) station and on nearby Bencoolen St – particularly between No 27 (7th floor) and No 173 (2nd, 5th and 6th floors). Some are unmarked.

Other cheap accommodation areas are around Little India (singles are under S$20 at *Nan Yong Hotel*, 1/1A Robert's Lane), in Chinatown (Outram Park MRT) and on Geylang Rd (try the tiny *Kung Tai Hotel* at No 465A – Aljunied MRT).

For those who can clear the psychological hurdle of spending almost S$23 for a dorm bed in Asia, the *YMCA* is an excellent choice. With a weight room, swimming pool and kitchens, it is perhaps the nicest YMCA in the world. It is also often full. Book well in advance (☎ 336 6000, fax 337 3140) or show up early and hope.

Transport
Fares for the extensive bus and subway (MRT) systems (open 6am-midnight) depend on distance but average S$0.80. A **Singapore Explorer Ticket** allows unlimited travel on both and comes with a free map: $7 for one day, $15 for three. Singapore Tourist Promotion Board

(STPB) publishes the useful pamphlet *See Singapore by Bus*.

International airport tax: S$15 – this can be paid in advance at airline offices, upmarket hotels and larger travel agents.

Staying in touch
● **Mail American Express** (☎ 235 5789), 304 Orchard Road, #1-6 Luck Plaza, Singapore 0923, keep mail. Sending parcels is very reliable.

● **Phone** The cheapest place for international calls is the GPO (near Anderson Bridge, about one kilometre from Raffles Hotel, ¾km from Raffles MRT). Place international calls by dialling 104 (109 for Malaysia).

International country code: +65. There are no city codes.

Further information
● **Maps and books** A guidebook is unnecessary as STPB offers excellent information on everything in Singapore – bus maps, transportation schedules and mini-guides to different areas.

New guidebooks for other countries can be bought in one of Singapore's many

---

❏ **Food and drink in Singapore**
A few places for culinary indulgence:

Place	Where	When	What
The Long Bar	Raffles Hotel (see map)	11am-1am	Singapore Sling. They are cheaper in other bars, but Raffles is where they were invented.
Bencoolen St Market	Bencoolen St (see map)	8am-10pm	A bit of everything
Orchard Rd	(see map)	Various	All sorts of restaurant chains. Denny's for 'real American breakfasts'.
Satay Club	(see map)	2pm-1am	Peanut satay
People's Park Centre	by Pearl's Centre Mall	9am-7pm	Mostly Chinese food
Zhjiao Centre	Serangoon and Hastings Rd	7am-9pm	Indian food
Cuppage Rd market	opposite Somerset MRT	7am-8pm	Strange (and pricey) dishes
UDMC Seafood Centre	near East Coast Park		Seafood (surprise!)

book shops (there are several on Orchard, Stanford roads). For used guides to Malaysia and Indonesia try **Evernew Books** (see map).

● **Information offices** STPB's head office is at Raffles City Tower #36-04, 250 North Bridge Road (☎ 339-6622, fax 339-9423). It also has an office on the ground floor of Tourism Court, off Cuscaden Road at 1 Orchard Spring Lane (☎ 738 3889/9), which is open daily 8.30am-6pm and inside the Raffles Hotel Arcade at 328 North Bridge Road (toll-free ☎ 1-800-334 1335) which is open daily 8.30am-8pm. STPB also operates a free 24-hour automated tourist information line (☎ 1-800-831-3311).

STPB offices abroad also provide stacks of free brochures, and useful maps on request.

Web sites

An overview of sites, festivals and practical information is at www.regit.com/regi-tour/spore/regitour.htm.

The official Singapore Online Guide is at www.travel.com.sg/sog.

www.sg has an extensive list of links.

Malaysia

Peninsular Malaysia is less exotic than Thailand, less developed than Singapore, and more expensive than Indonesia. Stuck in the middle, somewhat lacking an image, it's often overlooked by travellers who're just passing through. Yet there is an appealing cultural mix, a rainbow of ethnicities and cuisines and the country itself is actually a confederation of nine separate sultanates, each with its own character and royal palace. Chinese Buddhist shrines and Hindu temples rub shoulders with stylish new mosques. Jungles steam on the outskirts of gleaming modern cities which are dotted with the colonial relics of 300 years as the region's main trading centre. Even the Borneo provinces of Sarawak and Sabah are part of a full scale drive towards forging a dynamic, modern society whose clearest emblems are the world's tallest twin towers (Petronas in Kuala Lumpur) and the recently started project to create the first purpose-built techno/cyber-city.

PRACTICAL INFORMATION
Visas and formalities
● **At the border** Hippie types are officially banned from Malaysia. The process by which authorities determine exactly who is one remains a state secret but it's advisable to be reasonably tidy for border crossings.

Money
All major currencies can be changed into Ringgit. Credit card advances are commission free. Banks are open Monday to Friday 9am-3pm, Saturday 9.30-11.30am.

Transport
● **Bus** Malaysia's bus system is extensive and efficient. There are three basic types: non-airconditioned state, non-airconditioned interstate and airconditioned express. The difficulty in taking a bus is not so much in finding one going your way (unless you are going between two particularly obscure towns) but finding one that doesn't stop too often en route – the time it takes to traverse identical routes with different companies can vary by 50%. Airconditioned express buses are faster, but not as consistently so as one might hope.

Most non-airconditioned state buses allow passengers to get on and off anywhere along their route – this is very handy for spontaneous exploration. If there's no bus, hitchhiking is relatively easy.

❑ **W&M's country ratings – Malaysia**
● **Expense** $$$ It's becoming more expensive but cheap accommodation and food are still easily found.
● **Value for money** ✔✔✔ Good.
● **Getting around** ✔✔✔✔ Efficient and extensive bus and train services.
● **English spoken** ✔✔✔ Widely spoken, English is compulsory in schools.
● **Woman alone** ✔✔✔ Similar to Thailand, though the north east coast is more fundamentalist Muslim.
● **For vegetarians** ✔✔✔ The wide variety of food means there is something for everyone.

● **Train** Students are entitled to a 50% discount; the fare then is comparable to that for the bus.

A **KTM** (Keretapi Tahah Melayu – Malay for Malayan Railway Network) Tourist Railpass offers unlimited 2nd class train travel (excluding berth charges) in Malaysia and Singapore. The 10-day pass costs US$55, which means you would have to traverse the entire country twice for the pass to pay for itself. The 30-day pass costs US$120. They must be purchased outside the country.

● **Air** International departure tax: M$20 (except to Brunei and Singapore: M$5).

● **Taxis** In large cities the fare is M$1 for the first kilometre and 30sen for each subsequent half kilometre: there is also a 20-30% airconditioning charge. At night drivers prefer to fix a price for the destination.

Accommodation

You can find a bed almost everywhere, even if it is only in a dorm, for under M$15 (often around M$6). In some tourist areas, touts come to the bus/train station with photos of the guesthouse they represent and maps of how to get there.

A good waterproof tent is recommended for jungle camping. You are supposed to obtain permission from the Forestry Department before setting up make-shift

---

❑ **Geo-political information – Malaysia**

Population: 20.3 million (1997), 17.6m (1991), 13.5m (1980).

Area: 328,500 sq km.

Capital: Kuala Lumpur (1.2m).

Other major cities: Ipoh (400,000), Johore Bahru (330,000), Malacca, Petaling Jaya, Tawai, Kelang, Kuala Trengganu, Sandakan, Kota Bahru, Georgetown (Penang), Kota Kinabalu, Kuantan, Taiping, Seremban (all over 180,000)

GNP per capita: $3520 (1994), $2040 (1988).

Currency history: Ringgit (or Malaysian dollar)/US$1 – Feb 1998: M$4.29, June 1996: M$2.49, Feb 1996: M$2.56, 1991: M$2.75, 1981: M$2.25.

Major exports/economy: The world's leading producer of palm oil and the third largest producer of rubber having been overtaken by Thailand and Indonesia in 1993. A growing industrial base.

Ethnic mix: (1991 when the total population was 17.6m) Malay 11.3m, Chinese 4.8m, Indians 1.4m, 0.1m for indigenous tribes in east Malaysia.

Official languages: English, Malay.

Religious mix: Islam (mostly Malay) 53%, Buddhist (mostly Chinese) 19%, large Hindu (Indian) and Christian (mixed) minorities, animist groups in Sabah/Sarawak.

Landmarks of national history: **1511**: The Portuguese took Malacca. **1641**: Dutch took over. **1795**: Start of British rule. **1838**: James Brooke arrived in Sarawak later to become the White Rajah. **1888**: Britain extended rule over Sabah (and Brunei). **April 1946**: Malayan Union formed. **31 Aug 1957**: Independence of Malaya. **1950s and 1960s**: Communist insurgency campaign from southern Thailand. **16 Sept 1963**: Malaysia formed from Malaya plus Sarawak and British North Borneo (Sabah). **Aug 1965**: Singapore left the union. **1970**: Anti-Chinese riots. **1987**: Amnesty finally ended the communist insurgency.

Leaders: Figurehead Sultan/King is elected from amongst the nine hereditary rulers of the Peninsular Malay States. Currently Jafar Abul Rahman. However, political clout is wielded by the Prime Minister, Mahathir Mohammad.

Pressing political issues: Maintaining dynamic economic growth, repatriation of Vietnamese boat people, ecological concerns over the rapid logging in Sarawak/Sabah. South-East Asian economic crash.

camping sites in parks. There are plenty of campgrounds.

Many beaches have A-frame style huts, similar to those in Thailand. Rooms in government resthouses can be rented in most hill stations.

Food and drink

The food in Malaysia is as diverse as its people: Indian, Chinese, Thai and Western fast food are especially widely available.

Malaysian food consists of a large variety of spices with some food (often rice) added for seasoning. Authentic Malay food can be slightly hard to find – family establishments on the east coast are the best places to try: *satay* (barbecued meat with peanut sauce) and *gado gado* (cold vegetable salad). There is a tantalising variety of tropical fruit.

Staying in touch

● **Mail** The mail system is efficient – letters reach Europe or North America in just over a week. Major cities have Poste Restante services which are more reliable than those in Thailand. **American Express** can also hold your mail. It has offices c/o Mayflower Acme Tours (☎ 248-6700), Angkasa Raya Bldg, Jalan Ampang 50450, Kuala Lumpur, and in 17 other Malaysian cities.

● **Phone** Dial 108 for the operator to place an international calls.

International country code: +60. Kuala Lumpur: 03, Penang: 04.

Activities

● **Beaches** Malaysia has many great beaches. The more developed west coast is touristy in winter. The wilder, more attrac-

---

❑ **Essential information for travellers – Malaysia**

● **Visa** Most nationalities are allowed a three-month visa free stay.

● **Currency** Ringgit (or Malaysian Dollar) (M$1=100sen or cents). US$1=M$4.29. The prices quoted are pre-crash ie US$1=M$2.60.

● **Time zone** 8 hours ahead of GMT (same as Singapore; 1hr ahead of Thailand and Indonesia).

● **Religious tone** The official religion is Islam but many others are freely practised – particularly Buddhism (the Chinese) and Hinduism (Indians).

● **Pulse of the country** East coast, from Kuantan north.

● **Health factors** Tap water is technically safe but avoid it if your stomach isn't used to Asia. The malaria risk is moderate.

● **Special Dangers** 200g of marijuana means you are trafficking drugs – this means the death penalty.

● **Typical traveller destinations** Penang, Cameron Highlands, Langkawi Island, Tioman Island.

● **Highlights** Rain forest parks, Bukit Larut government rest house, Pulau Perhentian Kecil (an idyllic island), Niah Caves (Sarawak).

● **When to go** Sailors knew Malaysia as 'the land where the winds meet' and when they meet they like blowing up mischief. The monsoons in Peninsula Malaysia are supposed to come from late May to October on the west coast, and from early November to March on the east. But the monsoons are, apparently, unaware of this: we enjoyed a week in late November on east coast beaches with no more than a single shower. On our December west coast trip in another year, it rained constantly in Malacca but was beautiful in Penang. The standard advice is: if it is raining on one coast, try the other.

November to January is more consistently wet in Taman Negara (national park) so it's a miserable time to visit the park. Regardless of the rain, days are usually hot and nights pleasantly warm. The highlands are, of course, cooler. Borneo is wettest October to February.

❏ **Meeting the locals**

● **The people** Malaysia is one of the world's most multi-racial societies. Despite some tension between the politically powerful Malay majority (about 60%), the wealthy Chinese middle classes and the marginalised Borneo forest tribes, the country remains a showcase of multi-culturalism. Malaysia has a similarly complex religious tapestry. The Muslim majority follow a fairly low key form of Islam but it's polite to avoid wearing shorts and sleeveless shirts in more conservative areas.

● **Language** Bahasa (Malay) is the official language and one of the world's easiest. It is worth trying to learn some Bahasa – especially if you're heading to Indonesia where the language is very similar. But wherever you go you'll find English speakers. Like Indonesian, Bahasa uses the Western alphabet.

Some phrases in Malay:

Thank You – *terima kasih*
Excuse me – *maafkan saya*
Good-bye – *selamat tinggal*
How are you? – *Apa khabar?*

---

tive east coast is more likely to be sunny in summer. There's everything from isolated, idyllic nothing-to-do huts on the Perhentian Isles to the backpacker beaches of Tioman Island to the Club Med and resort hotels of Kuantan.

● **Jungle exploration ideas** 'Jungle Train' – Great forest views effortlessly glimpsed from the train window. **Taman Negara** – Huge jungle park. A sense of adventure at a reasonably affordable cost. It's best to pre-book accommodation through **MTIC** (☎ 244 3929), 109 Jalan Ampang, KL. **Endau Rompin Park** – Remote and spectacular but expensive and awkward to reach. **Borneo Jungles** – There has been very extensive logging and the longhouse lifestyle has been abandoned by many locals. Nonetheless, Sarawak still contains some remote, majestic forests. It's expensive to reach by river or air, but worth the effort.

Further information

● **Books** Tourist offices and other travellers can provide all the basic information you need as you go along, so surviving without a guide book is quite possible. There are many English language bookshops but Georgetown (Penang) is the best place to look for secondhand guides.

● **Maps and information offices** Tourism Malaysia offices are an excellent source of free information. The main **Tourism Malaysia** office in Kuala Lumpur is at: Menara Dato' Onn, Putra World Trade Centre, 45 Jalan Tun Ismail, 50480 Kuala Lumpur, (☎ 02-293-5188). There are also offices in Penang, Langkawi Island (in the airport, in Kuha town and at the Jetty Point Complex), Perak Is (in Lumut), Kedah and Johore Bahu (in Tanjung Puteri Tour Bus Complex). Tourist offices are also easy to find outside the country: eg Bangkok: (Silom Rd), Singapore (Johore Causeway).

Web sites

tourism.gov.my is the homepage of the tourism promotion board.

www.jaring.my/msia/back/main2.html has basic travel information, the most useful of which is on upcoming festivals.

www.kc.com.my/borneo is the homepage for Borneo Online; their 'places of interest' gives a nice overview of destinations but their 'useful information' isn't.

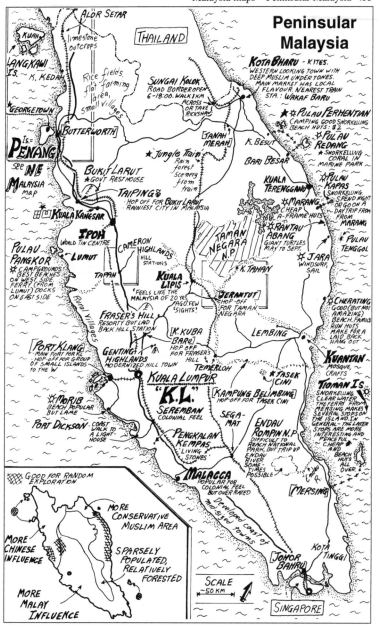

Peninsular Malaysia

KUAH

LANGKAWI IS. ~ K. KEDAH

ALOR SETAR

limestone outcrops

THAILAND

GEORGETOWN

Rice fields flat farming area, small villages

SUNGAI KOLOK
Road border open
6-18:00. WALK 1KM
ACROSS OR TAKE
RICKSHAW

KOTA BHARU – KITES.
WESTERN LOOKING TOWN WITH
DEEP MUSLIM UNDER TONES.
MAIN MARKET HAS LOCAL
FLAVOUR. NEAREST TRAIN
STA.: WAKAF BARU

BUTTERWORTH

PENANG Is. = N.E.
SEE MALAYSIA map

JANAH MERAN

★ Jungle Train
Rain forest scenery from train

K. BESUT

BARI BESAR

★ PULAU PERHENTIAN
CAMPING GOOD SNORKELLING
BEACH HUTS: $2

★ PULAU REDANG
~ SNORKELLING CORAL IN MARINE PARK

BUKIT LARUT
★ GOVT RESTHOUSE

TAIPING ★ ◎
HOP-OFF FOR BUKIT LARUT
RAINIEST CITY IN MALAYSIA

KUALA KANGSAR

KUALA TERENGGANU

☆ PULAU KAPAS ~
SNORKELLING
SPEND NIGHT
OR GO ON A
DAY TRIP FROM
MARANG

IPOH
WORLD TIN CENTRE

LUMUT

CAMERON HIGHLANDS
HILL STATIONS

★ MARANG
CHEAP
A-FRAME HUTS

PULAU PANGKOR
☆ CAMPGROUNDS
BEST BEACHES
ON WEST SIDE.
FERRY (FROM
LUMUT) DOCKS
ON EAST SIDE

TAPAH

TAMAN NEGARA N.P.

★ RANTAU ABANG
GIANT TURTLES
MAY TO SEPT.

☆ JARA
WINDSURF, SAIL

KUALA LIPIS
"FEELS LIKE THE
MALAYSIA OF 20 YRS.
AGO. FEW
SIGHTS!"

K. TAHAN

River villages

FRASER'S HILL
RESORT-Y BUT LAID
BACK HILL STATION

[K. KUBA BARU]

JERANTUT
HOP-OFF
FOR TAMAN
NEGARA

LEMBING

★ PULAU TENGGOL

★ CHERATING
GOOD (BUT NOT
AMAZING) BEACH. FAMILY
RUN HUTS
MAKE FOR A
LAID BACK
HANG OUT

PORT KLANG
MAIN PORT FOR
HOP-OFF FOR GROUP
OF SMALL ISLANDS
TO THE W

GENTING HIGHLANDS
MODERNIZED HILL TOWN

[K. KUBA BARU]
HOP OFF
FOR FRASER'S
HILL

TEMERLOH

KUANTAN
MOSQUE,
CRAFTS

KUALA LUMPUR
"K.L."
SEREMBAN
COLONIAL FEEL

★ TASEK CINI

TIOMAN IS.
☆ SNORKELLING.
CLEAR WATER
THE FERRY FROM
MERSING MAKES
SEVERAL STOPS ON
THE ISLAND. IN
GENERAL - THE LATER
STOPS ARE MORE
INTERESTING AND
PEACEFUL. CHEAP
AND
BEACH
HUTS
ALL
OVER.

☆ MORIB
BEACH POPULAR
BUT LAME

KAMPUNG BELIMBING
HOP-OFF FOR TASEK CINI

PORT DICKSON - COAST
WALK TO A
LIGHTHOUSE

SEGA-MAT

ENDAU ROMPIN N.P.
DIFFICULT TO
REACH NATIONAL
PARK, BUT TRIP UP
ENDAU
RIVER
SOME-
TIMES
POSSIBLE

PENGKALAN KEMPAS
LIVING STONES

MALACCA
POPULAR FOR
COLONIAL FEEL
BUT OVER RATED

Developed coast of mid-sized towns

MERSING

▨ GOOD FOR RANDOM
EXPLORATION

MORE CONSERVATIVE
MUSLIM AREA

KOTA TINGGI

MORE CHINESE
INFLUENCE

SPARSELY
POPULATED,
RELATIVELY
FORESTED

JOHOR BAHRU

SCALE
~ 50 KM

MORE MALAY
INFLUENCE

SINGAPORE

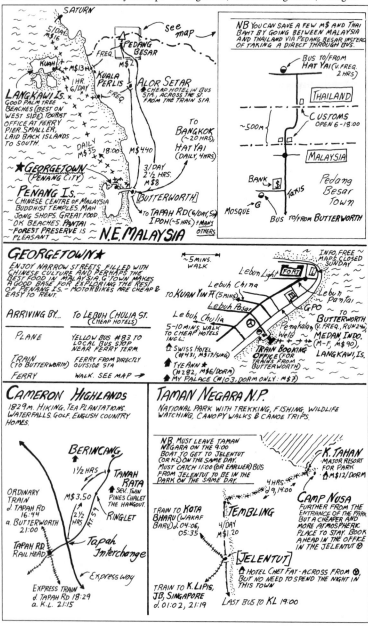

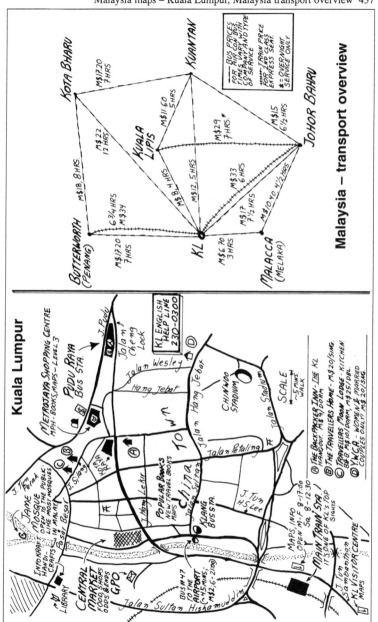

Malaysia – transport overview

Kuala Lumpur

BORNEO DIVISIONS

SABAH (MALAYSIA)
BRUNEI
SARAWAK (MALAYSIA)
KALIMANTAN (INDONESIA)

East Malaysia
Sarawak and Sabah,
North Borneo

200 Km

KUDAT

★ **Mt. KINABALU**
4011m. HIGHEST IN
S.E. ASIA. GREAT
2 DAY WALK TO TOP.
HUTS EN ROUTE.

KOTA KINABALU ("KK") INDONESIAN CONSULATE

3 HRS

PORING

SANDAKAN

6-7 HRS

SEPILOK: ORANG-UTANS

3 HRS

MENUMBOK
2 HRS

LABUAN Is. DUTY FREE ISLE ½ HR OFFSHORE

BEAUFORT
2 HRS

MADAI CAVES

LAHAD DATU

2½ HRS

★ **NIAH CAVES**
HUGE CAVES FULL OF
BATS + BIRDS, SOURCE
OF BIRDSNEST SOUP.
4 KM BY BOAT/TAXI/WALK
FROM BATU NIAH
↑ PARK HOSTEL

MIRI
BATU NIAH
2 HRS

LAWAS
BRUNEI

*BARIO ⊞ TREKS

TAWAU
NUNAKAN
TARAKAN

NEED AN
INDONESIAN
VISA TO
ENTER OR
LEAVE
TO TAWAU

BINTULU
OIL TOWN

Ω·M·M

GUNUNG MULU
N.P. WORLD'S
BIGGEST CAVE.
(GUNUNG API TREKS,
STONE FOREST-ROCKY
PINNACLES.
RATHER EXPENSIVE
TO VISIT (FLIGHTS,
GUIDE, PERMIT...)

4 HRS
SIBU

4 HRS SPEED BOAT

KAPIT ⛰
PERMITS FOR
UPRIVER TRAVEL

INCL. 4 HRS CHANGE OF BOAT

9-10 HRS VISA WAIVER OK

KUCHING
COLONIAL ARCHITECTURE, CATS,
■ ▲ ⓘ NEAR FERRY TO ⛰,
↑ "B+B" (JALAN TABUAN)

INDONESIA

No Road

PONTIAK

$35 FLIGHTS TO MIRI

BRUNEI DARUSSALAM

INCREASINGLY ISLAMIC MINI INDEPENDENT NATION
RULED BY THE WORLD'S RICHEST MAN. VISAS ARE
REQUIRED BY AUSSIES + KIWIS - NOT AVAILABLE AT
BORDERS. CROSSING THE COUNTRY IN A SINGLE DAY
IS TOUGH GIVEN SEVERAL FERRY CROSSINGS.

LABUAN

ONLY ONE CHEAP HOSTEL IN
B.S.B. ("BANDAR"): PUSAT BELIA'
ON JALAN S. KIANGGEH, $10.
OTHERS $40+. THE CITY
IS VERY MODERN WITH
SOME GRAND NEW
BUILDINGS.

BERAKAS
JERUDONG
FREE THEME PARK
OPEN AT NIGHT

MUARA

PUNANG

to Sabah via Merapok

SERIA OIL
TOWN, "BILLIONTH
BARREL"
MONUMENT

TUTONG

B.S.B.

LAWAS

No Road

KUALA
BELAIT

LAMUNIN

LABU

BANGAR

MIRI

LUMUT

LIMBANG
FLY TO MIRI
VIA GUNUNG
MULU
$70

AMO

MALAYSIA

SARAWAK, MALAYSIA

FLIGHTS
TO LABUAN
AVOID
BRUNEI
ALTOGETHER
FOR ABOUT
$35

KUALA
BALAI

TEMADA

LABI

WATER FALLS

LONG HOUSES

ULU TEMBURONG N.P.
FOREST CANNOPY
WALK WAYS

to Kuching (Good road)

MARUDI

RAIN FOREST

MALAYSIA

50 Km

ROYAL PALACE, BANDAR SERI BAGAWAN (B.S.B.)

Thailand

Thailand is a great place for a holiday – a holiday from a long trip or from the office grindstone. Transport is frequent, cheap and relatively efficient and Tourist Authority of Thailand (TAT) offices provide plenty of free information. Everything is so easy, in fact, that we have kept this chapter relatively short. Don't be put off by the few over-developed resorts (Pattaya, Phuket). Thailand is packed with forested mountains, national parks, lazy Mekong views, paradise beaches with simple (and cheap) huts, and plenty of chances to relax.

PRACTICAL INFORMATION
Visas and formalities

Most Westerners can stay for 30 days without a visa. For longer stays, a two-month visa is readily granted at Thai embassies (usually US$15); up to two one-month extensions are allowed. Apply at Soi Suanphlu, Sathon Tai Rd, Bangkok or the Immigration Office in any other provincial capital (B500 per extension). If you need just a day or two extra, it's cheaper to pay the small overstay 'fine' at the airport or border. Scandinavians, South Koreans and New Zealanders get three months stay without a visa.

Technically you are supposed to be in possession of 'sufficient funds' and a return or onward ticket when entering Thailand. However, in reality this is almost never enforced, even when arriving on a one way ticket.

Money

The usual commission for travellers' cheques is B14. All major currencies are exchangeable in large cities. Credit card advances are common and commission free. ATMs are available in Bangkok and increasingly elsewhere as well.

Transport

● **Bus** Thailand has an extensive and efficient long-distance bus system which makes it easier to cross the country than to cross Bangkok. Buses leave on time, are rarely full and usually pre-assign seat numbers. The price of a ticket varies substantially according to the quality of bus. Top of the scale are 24-seat, air conditioned, VIP buses which some travellers liken to flying first class. Tickets for these services often include one night's accommodation in your destination city. The cheapest ser-

---

❏ **W&M's country ratings – Thailand**
● **Expense $$$** Most individual items are inexpensive, but the constant temptations can make money go dangerously fast.
● **Value for money** ✔✔✔ Food and transport are excellent value for money, but cheap accommodation is basic.
● **Getting around** ✔✔✔✔ Very easy! Trains should be booked one day in advance.
● **English spoken** ✔✔✔ Almost everywhere.
● **Woman alone** ✔✔✔✔ Solo women travellers are common.
● **For vegetarians** ✔✔✔ A little more difficult if you don't eat seafood, but there are always tasty options.

vices are on older, non air-conditioned buses or (on a few routes) illegal smuggling buses whose operators are more interested in you taking up a seat than they are in taking your money. Kao San Rd travel agents who sell smuggling-bus tickets wisely require you to sign a form abdicating them of all responsibility. However, the worst we have heard of these illegal buses is that they sometimes drop you off a long way out of town.

● **Trains** Book early as tickets are often sold out one day before departure; otherwise trains are very convenient. We found the cheaper upper berths (supplement: B100 non A/C, B250 A/C) every bit as comfortable as the lower ones (B150/B320).

● **Motorbikes** Renting motorbikes is easy in any large city or tourist area. The average cost is $7-10 per day and a licence is not usually asked for.

● **Hitchhiking** Hitching is good once you get out of the large cities. Rides are usually free, but offering the equivalent of the bus fare would be a polite gesture.

Accommodation

Any town of any size will have a cheap place to stay (ie B150/single or less, sometimes much less). Dorms, when available are typically B50.

On small tropical islands (Ko Phi Phi, Ko Samet, etc) the best and cheapest accommodation (and often the beaches) are on the opposite end of the island from where the boat drops you off.

It is advisable to inspect rooms carefully before renting one; check for peepholes and alternate ways in. We suggest staying in guest houses where you can use your own padlock on the door.

Camping or government-run accommodation are often the only choices within

---

❏ **Geo-political information – Thailand**
Population: 59.4 million (1997), 58.8m (1995), 54.5m (1990).
Area: 511,000 sq km.
Capital: Bangkok (5.8 million, 1990).
Other major cities: Nakhon Ratchasima (280,000), Songkha, Nanthaburi, Khon kaen (200,000+); Chiang Mai, Nakhon Suuran (150,000+).
GNP per capita: $2210 (1994).
Currency history: Baht/US$1 – Feb 1998: B47.1, 1997: B36.7, July 1996: B25.41, Dec 1995: B25.19, Dec 1994: B25.10, Oct 1993: B25.33.
Major exports/economy: Textiles, electronic goods, rubber, gems, cassava, sugar, rice.
Ethnic mix: Thai (74%), Chinese (14%), Khmer, Mon and many other smaller groups.
Official language: Thai. Many speakers of Min (Chinese languages and a wide variety of hill tribe tongues.
Religious mix: Buddhist (95%), Muslim (4%).
Landmarks of national history: **1220**: Sukhothai founded. **1350s**: Ayutthaya became dominant. **1569**: Burmese occupation ended by Prince Naresuan (Thai Hero) in 1587. **1767**: Ayutthaya sacked by Burmese. **1688**: Law minimised contacts with foreigners (in attempt to prevent colonial takeover) – lasted 150 years. **1782**: Capital moved to Bangkok. **1867**: Swapped Cambodia for continued independence from France. **1893**: Gave away Laos too. **1896**: UK and France recognised Thailand as a neutral buffer state. **1932**: Revolution transformed absolute to constitutional monarchy. **1939**: Changed name from Siam.
Leaders: King Bhumibol, Prime Minister Gen Chaovalit Yongchaiyut.
Pressing political issues: Prostitution and AIDS. Bangkok's urban planning nightmare. The banking sector collapse in 1997.

national parks: advance booking through the **Royal Forestry Department** (☎ 02-579 0529), National Parks Division, Phaholyothin Rd, Bangkhen, Bangkok, may be necessary and is recommended.

A tent allows a greater choice of do-it-yourself treks in the mountains.

Food and drink

Muesli to McDonald's to Muslim mutton concoctions, Thailand's cities and tourist areas provide for every culinary whim. Backpacker cafés offer a vast range of transcontinental traveller favourites to cheaply satisfy even the most xenophobic palate. But if you can cope with its jangling chilli heat, there's little to match the rich spectrum of Thai flavours. Lime, lemon grass, and coconut milk add zest to dozens of unique dishes, best sampled initially from smaller restaurants where everything is pre-prepared and clearly displayed so you can see what you're getting.

Ask if it's *phet*. Any dish can be spicy, but if it's *phet* it may blow out your sinuses.

Pad tai is a common dish of rice noodles and other assorted ingredients which every restaurant seems to interpret differently. Among a myriad of other meals are *tom yam* (spicy lemongrass soup), *mat sa man mang sawi rat* a vegetable curry, and *som tam* (an often spicey unripe papaya salad). On a menu *plaa* is fish, *plaa meuk* is squid, *pet* is duck and *kai* (chicken) is confusingly similar to *khai* (egg).

Mekong rice-whisky and the surprisingly expensive Singha beer are the sources of many an unnecessary headache.

Staying in touch

● **Mail** Letters and cards take an average of nine days to/from Europe and the USA. Letter rates are B16 to Europe, B20 to USA and Oceania.
● **Phone** International calls are relatively inexpensive: the access code is 001.

❏ Essential information for travellers – Thailand

● **Visa** At least 30-days visa free for most Western nationalities.
● **Currency** Baht. US$1=B47.1. The exchange rate dropped dramatically in late 1997 after years of stability so prices in Baht will be higher than quoted.
● **Time zone** 7 hours ahead of GMT (same as Indochina; 1hr behind Malaysia and China; ½hr ahead of Burma).
● **Religious tone** 97% Theravada Buddhist. Every Buddhist male becomes a monk at some point in his life. Temples are found everywhere.
● **Health factors** Malaria exists but is not a widespread problem. The tap water is unsafe to drink.
● **Special dangers** Flooding in the rainy season.
● **Pulse of the country** The night time roadside food stalls.
● **Typical traveller destinations** Bangkok, the mountains (particularly Chiang Mai), the southern beaches (especially Krabi, Samui and Phuket).
● **Highlights** Renting motorbikes and going for random rides.
● **When to go** Thailand is hot and humid most of the time. High season is October to February; during these months it's very warm and relatively dry in Bangkok and cool at night in the mountains, though a modest sweater is sufficient. March to May is sweltering and sticky, with temperatures over 35°C for weeks at a time. Summer is the rainy season; the uncertain weather keeps the southern beaches refreshingly free of tourists till the end of September. Clouds gather in the afternoons but mornings can be clear and sunny.
● **Key tips** Obtain a visa beforehand if you might want to stay more than one month. Stay in rooms that you can secure with your own padlock. Bangkok (along with Penang, Malaysia) offers the cheapest airfares in South East Asia.
● **Festivals** TAT produces a complete listing.

Collect calls are possible as are direct dial calls to most countries. International country code: +66. Bangkok: 02, Chiang Mai: 053, Phuket: 076, Hat Yai: 074.

Shopping

Thailand is the type of place where everything seems to be for sale – much of it fake: student and press ID cards, music cassettes ($2), 'Bennetton' clothing, 'Rolexx' watches, 'Ray Bun' sunglasses.

Clothes are the best bargain – from executive suits to t-shirts, Thailand has cheaper offerings than most other countries in South-East Asia. Bangkok has a selection of handicrafts from all over Thailand, but we found shopping at the Chiang Mai night market more enjoyable.

Activities

● **Hiking/trekking** Some travellers, especially those coming from Nepal, are disap-

---

❑ Accommodation

In the following cities, accommodation is a little more difficult to find or there is one guest house we know of that is particularly recommended. The accommodation listed is less than B150, unless otherwise marked.

City	Name of hotel	Notes
Bangkok and Chiang Mai		[see maps]
Chiang Rai	*Ya GH*	15 mins walk from the bus station – north up Phahonyothin Rd, left on Banphaprakan).
Chiang Khan	*Nong Sam*	Between Soi 12 and 13.
Chiang Khong	*Tamila GH*	On the riverbank.
Hat Yai	*Kim Hua*	129/10 Nuphat-Uthit Rd. Several other cheap places can be found within a few blocks on the same road.
Hua Hin	*Damrong*	B100.
Kanchanburi	*River Guest House*	
Lop Buri	*Asia Hotel*	In the old city.
Nakhon Si Thammarat	*Si Thong*	Cheap accommodation across from the train station.
Nan	*Nan GH*	10 minutes walk from the bus station.
Nong Khai	*Mut Mee*	Peaceful spot on the Mekong; self-service drinks; bookstore; (motor)bikes rented on site.
Pattaya	*Der Herbergh*	B150/dbl. Pattaya hotels are overpriced, but there are several cheap options on 2nd (main) road, between Sois 9 and 13.
Phetchaburi	*Chom Kow Hotel*	East side of Chomrut Bridge.
Phitsanulok	*Youth Hostel*	38 Sanam Bin Rd.
Phrae	*Dao Phin GH*	
Ranong	*Asia Hotel*	
Songkhla	*Sawaddi*	B80-160. Nakhon Nai Rd.
Surat Thani	*Rat Thai*	B130/single in the bus station. Other cheap options are found across from the railway station, or along Talad Kaset St.
Trat (see map in Cambodia chapter)	*Foremost GH*	Good information on Cambodia and Vietnam. Cheap. 49 Thon Charoen Rd.
Ubon Ratchathani	*River Moon GH*	120 metres from the railway station.

pointed with treks in Thailand. There is almost certainly better trekking elsewhere if you want mountain walking with great views, but Thailand does have a lot to offer if you like hill tribes and semi-forested agricultural landscapes.

The north-west area of Thailand has the best trekking – Chiang Mai and Chiang Rai are the major centres though more personal (and often less expensive) treks can be arranged from smaller towns (marked on the map, p448). Most people go on treks with tour groups but it is possible to trek independently if you have a good map, plan a bit, and take your own tent and food.

Hiking and walking trails also criss cross the rest of Thailand. Most of Thailand's national parks offer hikes of some sort. Phuket has a jungle trail though we found it disappointing. Inquire at TAT.

● **Water sports** The average cost for a four-day open water scuba diving course is US$240. The best time for scuba diving is between March and October. A few of Thailand's dive sites are listed below. Tourist resorts, such as most of Phuket,

---

❑ **Meeting the locals**

● **The people** Thailand is a Buddhist country and normal Buddhist conventions apply. Thais are laidback people who are also very forgiving of foreigners' foibles – visitors are traditionally viewed as being sent from God. Nonetheless consistent faux pas (such as wearing shorts in monasteries) have made tourists, especially backpackers, appear rude and uncaring of the local traditions. If the reason you are in Thailand is to get to know the country, you will have an uphill struggle proving your sincerity. Those who do make it are uniformly delighted by the gentle and hospitable culture they find.

Thais take their royal family seriously; offending the King (even indirectly or jokingly) will not go down well and could theoretically land you in jail.

The *wei*, the Thai greeting of holding hands prayer-like at the chest, can mean 'really good to see you', 'good bye', 'sincere thanks', or be a sign of respect. It is polite to gesture back a *wei* when gestured to, or give a pre-emptive *wei* yourself.

● **Some phrases in Thai**:

Welcome/Hello – *sah-bai-dee*
Thank you – *khorp-kun-kahp* (male speaking); *khorp-kun kah* (female).
Excuse me – *khor thot*
How much – *tow rie*
Very expensive – *pan pai*
Never mind (or 'It's OK') – *mai pen rai*
Very delicious – *ah-roy marg*
Not too spicy, please – *kor mai phet*

● **Simplified Thai script**

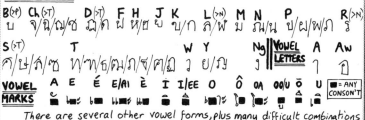

CONSONANTS

There are several other vowel forms, plus many difficult combinations

Pattaya and Chumphon, have windsurfers and jet skis for hire and also offer water skiing. See map (p449) for beaches.

● **Work** Any native English speaker marginally enthusiastic about teaching their language should be able to find a job in Thailand. The pay, averaging $6-10 an hour, isn't likely to make you rich but it covers living expenses and you might be able to save something. Bangkok seems the best place to arrange a job – many schools there have branches all around Thailand. *The Bangkok Post* has a few advertisements (we counted five in one day) but talking with other teachers is the best way to find contacts and get a feel for the current teaching situation. Many teachers live in the Apple Guest Houses in the Kao San area.

Otherwise the best jobs should be applied for before arrival. One college graduate we met got a job selling paint for $2000/month (with an apartment and car) – though he sent off 60 letters from Australia before getting an offer. A few qualified travellers have found jobs at diving schools. Many tourist cafés hire travellers on the spot as waiters/bar staff though the pay is only enough to tempt the very desperate or the very bored: food, drink (not alcohol) and B100 for 8 hours' work. Bangkok's Big Blue I Bar hires go-

go dancers by the day. The pay is inversely proportional to the number of clothes worn: B140 in costume, B170 topless, and B250 wearing slightly less.

Further information

● **Books** There are more guides specific to Thailand than any other country in Asia, which is ironic as Thailand is easier to travel in than almost any other country in Asia. For background and cultural information we recommend *Culture Shock! Thailand*. New and used guidebooks are easy to find in Thailand.

General books about Thailand are also easy to find locally. One which was recommended to us is *Monks and Magic* by BJ Terwiel (White Lotus, 1994): it's about a Buddhist community in central Thailand.

The Kao San area of Bangkok has an excellent but increasingly pricey selection of used guidebooks.

The Silom and Patpong areas of Bangkok have the largest selection of bookstores for new books. White Lotus Books (☎ 662-311 2177, fax 662-311 4575), 11/2 Soi 58 Sukhumbit Rd, has many books about Thailand and South East Asia. It also has a mail order catalogue. Guidebooks sold in the departure lounge in Bangkok airport are at least double the regular price.

❏ Some dive sites in Thailand

Dive Site	What's there	Notes
Chumphon	Standard underwater marine life	Dive sites over an hour away by boat.
Ko Dok Mai	Coral, caves, wall dives	90km east of Phuket
Ko Phi Phi	Fish, coral but no amazing drop offs	Good place to learn.
Ko Tao	8km of coral reef	Tours from Ko Samui and Chumphon. Especially good for learning.
Pattaya	Shallow dives (18-27m), shipwrecks	Large selection of diving companies.
Similan Isles	Coral, advanced diving, tunnels and caves	Live-aboard 5-day boat tours from $450
Shark Point	Leopard sharks and sting rays	90km east of Phuket.

● **Maps** TAT offers a free map of Thailand but one with more detail is worth paying for. The Nelles map is excellent and widely available in Thailand. A Bangkok map showing bus routes is indispensable.

● **Information offices** TAT has excellent free information though you'll often need to ask specifically for the brochures and maps you need. Their most useful publications are the Bangkok and Chiang Mai maps and the bus and train timetables (ask for north and south).

The main TAT office (☎ 02-226-0062, fax 224-6221) 372 Bamrung Muang Rd, Bangkok 10100, is open daily from 8.30am-4.30pm). There are also offices at Bangkok airport and in Chiang Mai, Hat Yai, Kanchanaburi, Nakhon Ratchasima, Pattaya, Phitsanulok, Phuket, and Surat Thani – and in many Western capitals.

Web sites

www.ait.ac.th/Asia/travel.html is your best starting place for getting information about Thailand; links are arranged by province and category

www.tat.or.th is the surprisingly useful tourist information page; it includes the dates of upcoming festivals.

www.nectec.or.th has the self-described 'Big Picture' of Thailand; check out the information under the 'Virtual Thailand' area which includes answers to frequently asked questions at www.nectec.or.th/soc.culture.thai/travel.html.

For motorbiking information, try to Golden Triangle Rider homepage at www.geocities.com/MotorCity/5354.

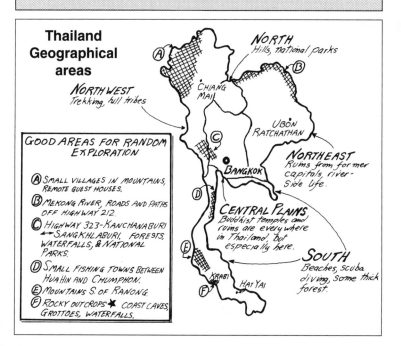

Thailand Geographical areas

NORTH
Hills, national parks

NORTHWEST
Trekking, hill tribes

CHIANG MAI

UBON RATCHATHAN

NORTHEAST
Rums from former capitals, river-side life.

BANGKOK

CENTRAL PLAINS
Buddhist temples and rums are everywhere in Thailand, but especially here.

SOUTH
Beaches, scuba diving, some thick forest.

KRABI   HAT YAI

GOOD AREAS FOR RANDOM EXPLORATION

(A) SMALL VILLAGES IN MOUNTAINS, REMOTE GUEST HOUSES.

(B) MEKONG RIVER, ROADS AND PATHS OFF HIGHWAY 212.

(C) HIGHWAY 323-KANCHANABURI ←SANGKHLABURI, FORESTS, WATERFALLS, & NATIONAL PARKS.

(D) SMALL FISHING TOWNS BETWEEN HUA HIN AND CHUMPHON.

(E) MOUNTAINS S. OF RANONG.

(F) ROCKY OUTCROPS ✱ COAST CAVES, GROTTOES, WATERFALLS.

Bangkok

Some areas
● **Silom** Famed sex-shows on Patpong Road(s). Top-end hotels, travel agents, airline offices, many new book stores.
● **Siam** Mix of modern malls, street stalls and fast food shops. Young persons' hangout. Cafés, movie theatres, book stores, British Council library.
● **Chinatown** Difficult to describe as scenic, but has character and has changed much more slowly than the rest of Bangkok. Busy, dirty streets contrast with quiet drink-spots in alleyways.

Accommodation
Most cheap options are in the Khao San Road area (see box). Other possibilities:
● **1)** Various Thewet area *guesthouses*. Dorm ~B50, rooms ~B100/single.
● **2)** *Bangkok Youth Hostel*. Open 24 hours; dorms B50 (also singles/doubles); can apply for required YH card on grounds. 25/2 Phitsanulok Rd. Bus: 16, 72, 99, 3, 53, 56, 12, 43.
● **3)** *River View GH*. Great location near River City and Sheraton. Does, in fact, have a view of the river (best rooms, by far, on the top floor, river side). B100-200. 768 Soi Phanurangsi, Songwat. Boat: Si Phraya pier; bus: 1,16,36,93.
● **4)** *TT Guesthouse*. Clean well-run place on edge of Chinatown. No dorms, single B140; 6-7min walk from train station--cross Rama IV Rd. and walk down Mahanakhon Rd. Signs show you the way. 516-518 Soi Sawang, Si Phraya Rd.
● **5)** *Oriental Hotel*. A/c, hot water, decent coffee; often ranked as the best hotel in the world but has no dorms. We suggest their deluxe suite (B88,000). Boats: Oriental Hotel pier.

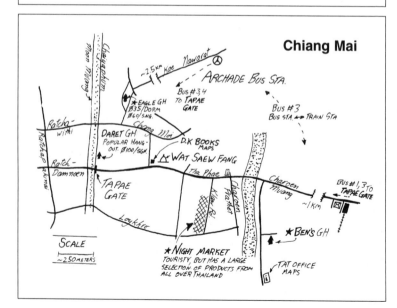

Chiang Mai

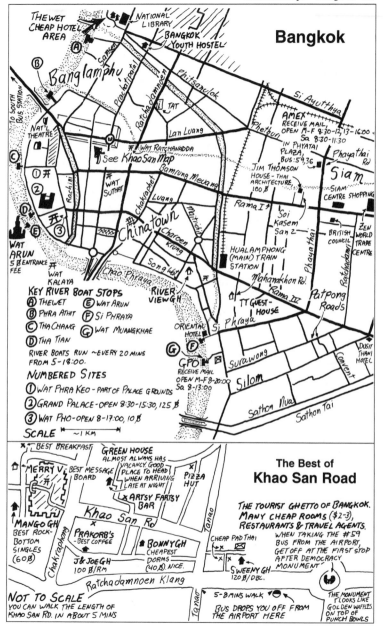

Thailand ไทย

LAOS

CAMBODIA
Crossing by road very dangerous possible but not legal but possible. See Cambodia chapter.

BURMA
No crossing by land at the past time of writing. In the past it was possible to make day trips across the border at Mae Sai. Crossing at Mae Sot or at Three Pagoda Pass are likely to open to foreign tourists shortly.

TACHILEK
MAI SAI ["GOLDEN TRIANGLE" NOW A DISAPPOINTING TOURIST TRAP]
BAN HOUAYXAY
MAE SALONG
THATON
MAE SALAK
SOPPONG
CHIANG KHONG
Mekong River
CHIANG RAI
PAI
NAN
The loving framing of N. of Thailand
HUAY MALAN
HUAY MAE MALAI
MAE HONG SON
Good staying point for 2-3 day treks but NOT for jeep tent
250M?
MAE AN
MAE
CHIANG MAI
LAMPANG
WAT PHRATHAT
PHRAE
WAT PHRATHAT
NAN

VIENTIANE
See map of crossing in the Laos chapter
NONG KHAI
Staging point for Laos trips. See Laos chapter for map
CHIANG KHAN
Wooden houses, Laos back feel
Hwy 212 public bus all along Hwy 212
Hwy 211
PHU KRADUNG NP
Hiking mid-October to mid-July
PHU KRADUNG town
in hills

SUKHOTHAI
SI SATCHANALAI
old Mahanat ruins
MAE SOT
Heavily armed smuggling town
UM PHANG
1980M
Mae Nam Ping
in central plains

THAT PHANOM
Thai pilgrimage centre, temples, Lao influence
SAVANNAKHET, LAOS
Mekong River
NAKHON PHANOM
SAKHON NAKHON
MUKDAHAN
PHA THEN NP (caves & waterfalls)
BAN CHIANG
See oldest old ruins. Oldest found bronze in the world. Heritage site
UDON THANI
not-off for
KALASIM
UBON RATCHATHANI
PAKSE, LAOS
SURIN
SI SA KET
PHANOM RUNG
PHIMAI
Khmer ruins similar in style to Angkor Wat
KHON KAEN
ROI ET
BURI RAM
NAKHON RATCHASIMA
PRASAT PREAH VIHEAR CAMBODIA
Ruins technically in Cambodia (but controlled by Thais). No visa needed.

PHITSANULOK
A photogenic Buddha statue Phra Si Rattha Mahathat
LOP BURI
Monkeys
BANGKOK
AYUTTHAYA
Buddhist ruins in central plains

KANCHANABURI
River Kwai, Allied war cemetery. Touching inscriptions on tombstones.
SANGKHLABURI
Three Pagoda Pass
BURMA
Hwy 323

Andaman Sea
Gulf of Thailand
RANGOON

SCALE varies
100km - 60 MILES

☐ = GOOD PLACE TO ARRANGE TREKS.
☒ MINI ISLES
🏠 = CHEAP (UNDER $5 NIGHT) HUTS ON THE BEACH. EASY TO FIND
⛊ = MAJOR TEMPLE RUINS
ⴲ = MAJOR SCUBA DIVING CENTRE
ᛒ ☐= 10-BIG BUDDHAS

NB. THIS IS A HIGHLIGHTS MAP. SOME TOWNS ARE SHIFTED SOMEWHAT FROM THEIR GEOGRAPHICAL POSITION TO ALLOW SPACE FOR TEXT.

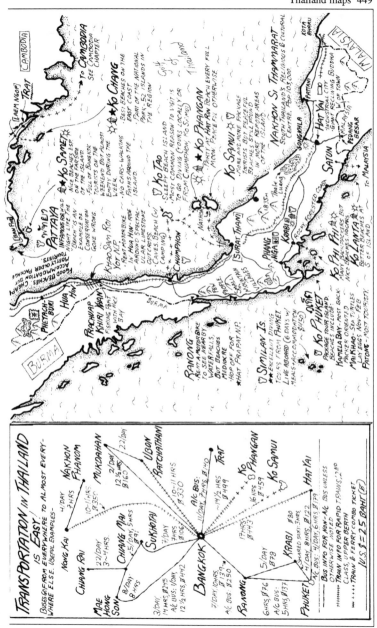

TRANSPORTATION IN THAILAND IS EASY!

BUSES GO FROM EVERYWHERE TO ALMOST EVERY-WHERE ELSE. USEFUL EXAMPLES:-

NONG KAI — 4/DAY 7 HRS. ₿350
NAKHON PHANOM — 10-11 HRS. ₿350
MUKDAHAN — 2/DAY 12½ HRS. ₿160 / 22/DAY
UBON RATCHATHANI — 10-11 HRS. ₿330
CHIANG RAI — 22/DAY 3~4 HRS.
CHIANG MAI — 2/DAY 5 HRS. ₿91
MAE HONG SON — 8/DAY 8 HRS.
SUKHOTAI — 7/DAY 7 HRS. ₿96
A/C BUS: 5/DAY ₿142 12½ HRS. ₿142
TRAT — A/C BUS: 4/DAY 7 HRS. ₿140
KO PHANGAN — A/C BUS: 11/DAY 14½ HRS. ₿499
KO SAMUI — 17 HRS. ₿443 / 16 HRS. ₿459
HAT YAI — A/C BUS: 4/DAY 6 HRS. ₿199
KRABI — ₿80 / SHARED TAXI 3 HRS. ₿122
PHUKET — 3/DAY 14 HRS. ₿245 / A/C BUS ₿250
A/C BUS: 5 HRS. ₿137 / 12½ HRS. ₿142
RANONG — 5/DAY ₿79
BANGKOK — 7/DAY 10 HRS. ₿137 / A/C BUS ₿250 / 4/DAY 8 HRS. ₿199

BUS INFO FOR NON-A/C BUS UNLESS OTHERWISE NOTED.
+++ TRAIN INFO FOR RAPID TRAINS, 2ND CLASS, UPPER BERTH
+++++ TRAIN & FERRY COMBO TICKET

U.S. $ = 25 BAHT (₿)

CAMBODIA

To CAMBODIA SEE CAMBODIA CHAPTER

TRAT — [DAEM KHOP]
☆ [BAN PHE]
★☆ KO SAMET — INFAMOUS FOR WILD NIGHTLIFE, NICE BEACHES ESP. ON THE FAR SIDE OF THE ISLAND — FULL OF BANGKOK TOURISTS ON THE WEEKEND BUT ALMOST EMPTY DURING THE WEEK

★☆ KO CHANG — BEST BEACHES ON THE EAST COAST — PART OF THE NATIONAL PARK - 52 ISLANDS IN THE REGION

☆★ PATTAYA — ACCOMMODATION CHEAP, MOSTLY OLDER GUY TOURISTS, AN EXAMPLE OF CONSERVATION GONE WRONG, LIKE THE BEACH IS AN EXAMPLE OF DEVELOPMENT GONE WRONG

GOOD BEACHES CHEAP

CHUMPON
KHAO SAM ROI YOT N.P. — RENT MOTORBIKE IN HUA HIN - RIDE AROUND SPECTACULAR LIMESTONE CLIFFS, CAVES, BEACH (CAMPING)

PRACHUAP KHIRI KHAN — FISHING BOAT TRIP WITH RICE BAY

HUA HIN

PHETCHA BURI

BURMA

BURMA

RANONG — RENT A MOTORBIKE TO SEE NEARBY WATERFALLS, BUT BEACHES MEDIOCRE — HOP OFF FOR ★ HAT PRAI PAT N.P.

SIMILAN IS. ★★ EXCELLENT DIVING — TOURS FROM PHUKET — LIVE ABOARD (6 DAYS w/ MEALS, ACCOMMODATION $250)

☆ KO TAO — SLEEPY BEACH ISLAND — MOST COMMON REASON TO VISIT IS TO GO DIVING (TOURS LOCALLY OR FROM CHUMPON, KO SAMUI)

★ KO PHANGAN — TRAIT AT HAT RIN BEACH EVERY FULL MOON. PEACEFUL OTHERWISE

☆ KO SAMUI — MORE AND MORE PACKAGE TOURISTS BUT PEACEFUL BEACHES STILL FOUND IN MORE REMOTE AREAS OF THE ISLAND

NATHON
Thale Luang
(1,835m)

SURAT THANI

PHANG NGA — SEA-KAYAK THROUGH MANGROVE CAVES

KO PHI PHI — MANY BACKPACKERS BUT NICE BEACHES, WORKS

KO LANTA — BETTER BEACHES AT S. OF ISLAND

KO PHUKET — PACKAGE TOUR ISLAND. BEACHES INCLUDE KAMELA BAY - MOST BACK PACKER ORIENTED, MAI KHAO - SEA TURTLES LAY EGGS, NOV-FEB, PATONG - MOST TOURISTY.

KOMBI

DENSELY FORESTED CORE

NAKHON S. THAMMARAT — SOUTH THAILAND'S RELIGIOUS & CULTURAL CENTRE. POP. 103,000. GIANT RECLINING BUDDHA

SONGKHLA
HAT YAI — INDUSTRIAL CITY

SATUN

PATTANI
[MALAY MUSLIM] MAJORITY OF TOWN

To MALAYSIA
PADANG BESAR
KOTA BHARU

MALAYSIA
Thailand
Gulf

Burma
(Myanmar)

Burma's gentle cultures, infectious smiles and rich history should make it one of Asia's most fascinating destinations. The awesome ruined city of Pagan, the great palace at Mandalay, and the golden pagodas which tower above the encroaching jungle ooze with atmosphere and echo with faded glory.

But faded it is. The country is a loose union of disparate regions, much of the nation only very tenuously under central control. Most borders and border areas are closed. Democratic elections in 1990 were won by 'the Lady' (opposition leader Daw Aung San Suu Kyi) but quashed by the self-named State Law and Order Restoration Council (SLORC – 'Slor-awk') with the complicity of the armed forces (Tatmadaw). Renamed Myanmar by its military dictators, Burma is reckoned to be one of the world's worst abusers of human rights. Whole towns have been wiped out at the government's whim and thousands of people are press-ganged into forced labour units. Some of the tourist infrastructure has been built by such slaves.

SLORC's 'General Number One' Ne Win is known locally as 'the Old Man'. Burma's English language newspaper *The New Light Of Myanmar* tries to humanise him with constant photos of handshakes and hospital openings. But popular support remains with the Lady. She was unable to collect her 1991 Nobel peace prize thanks to continued house arrest, but this was finally relaxed in 1995. At the time of writing one can once again hear her speak outside her Rangoon home though meetings are prevented by the government from time to time.

Given the repressive regime, posters in Bangkok suggest that you 'shouldn't visit Burma until democracy does'. The idea is to deprive SLORC of the hard currency that tourism brings. Visiting does, however, give locals a sense that they're not forgotten by the world outside and if you follow these sugges-

---

❏ **W&M's country ratings – Burma**

● **Expense $$** With some effort, it is possible to do a four-week trip on the $300 that you have to exchange.

● **Value for money ✔✔✔** Trains (because of tourist pricing) and hotels in Rangoon are expensive; private bus companies offer excellent value.

● **Getting around ✔✔** Excellent between main tourist centres, very difficult or non-existent to outlying areas.

● **English spoken ✔✔✔** Burma was once a British colony so it's not difficult to find someone who can speak English, even in rural areas.

● **Woman alone ✔✔✔✔** Similar to Thailand.

● **For vegetarians ✔✔✔** Good news: usually one vegetarian option. Bad news: usually not more. Seafood common on coast.

tions you can minimise how much of your cash gets into SLORC coffers:
- Avoid taking trains. Foreigner pricing funds SLORC plus many of the rail lines were built and repaired using forced labour.
- Stay in non-government hotels where possible. Most of the best cheap ones are private anyway.
- Avoid changing money at the airport. (See Money p453).

❑ Essential information for travellers – Burma

- **Visa** Required. Expect to pay about $18 but visas cost more in some embassies outside Asia. They are usually issued within 24 hours and allow a four-week stay. A two-week extension is possible in Rangoon.
- **Currency** Kyat. US$1=120Ky at the black market rate, 5.44Ky bank rate at time of research; also Foreign Exchange Certificates: US$1=FEC1. It is mandatory to exchange US$300 (cash or travellers' cheques) for FECs on arrival.
- **Time zone** 6½ hours ahead of GMT, ½hr behind Thailand, 1hr ahead of India, 1½ hrs behind China).
- **Religious tone** Deeply Buddhist country coping with less than spiritual military government.
- **Health factors** Don't drink the tap water. There's a real risk of malaria throughout most of the country and some of cholera.
- **Special dangers** Insurgency in some outlying areas (rebel groups don't seem to target foreigners).
- **Social conventions** The standard Buddhist conventions apply in Burma (eg walk around pagodas in a clockwise direction). Long skirts or trousers are appropriate for visits to all monasteries and temples; some won't let you on their grounds if you're wearing shorts. Shoes must be removed before walking around.
- **Typical traveller destinations** Rangoon, Mandalay, Pagan, Inle Lake.
- **Highlights** Swedagon Pagoda, hearing Aung San Suu Kyi speak, river boat trips, getting off the tourist trail.
- **When to go** March to May is the hot season and it's really hot! Hill stations are more bearable but, on the whole, the only saving grace for spring-time travel is the *Thingyan* New Year festival in April during which you'll be splashed with too much water (and be having too much fun) to feel hot.

After May the monsoons begin, bringing lower temperatures but higher humidity. The rain isn't too bad in Mandalay and the north, but Sittwe is a giant rainstorm, and the Gulf of Martaban region isn't much better. Many roads get washed out, especially on the west coast.

Around late September the monsoons begin to fade away, though not always in a hurry – it rained a bit every day during our mid-November stay in Pagan (Bagan). The coolest time is between October and February. Rangoon (Yangon) is pleasantly warm during these months, but you'll need a sweater at night in the interior of the country, and perhaps a jacket at higher altitudes.

- **Pulse of the country** Swedagon Pagoda in Rangoon.
- **Key tips** Old guidebooks (ie 1970s) are often better than recent editions. Overland entry is possible from China with an escort (see Permits). A knowledge of Burmese architecture prevents Pagoda saturation coming on too quickly. Buddhist-related postcards from outside Burma make valued gifts. One postcard of Wat Po we forgot to mail from Bangkok is now the central altar piece in a café in the Kimpoo base camp beneath the Golden Rock.

❏ **Geo-political information – Burma**

Population: 46 million (1997), 35m (1983), 30m (1975).

Area: 658,000 sq km.

Capital: Rangoon, 4 million.

Other major cities: Mandalay (550,000), Moulmein (220,000), Bassein, Bago (150,000), Taunggyi, Sittwe, Manywa (100,000).

GNP per capita: $725 estimate (1994). Realistic figures put average wages at 1500Ky a month.

Currency history: Kyat/U$1 – Sep 1997: 6.2Ky (official rate), Jan 1997: 5.4Ky, 1994: 5.9Ky, 1991: 6.3Ky, 1986: 7.3Ky. The black market rate is a lot higher.

Major exports/economy: Gemstones, timber, agriculture.

Ethnic mix: Complex: Burmese, Mon, Karen (11%), Shan (5%), Chin, Kachin (3%), Chinese (1.2%).

Official languages: Burmese (also spoken are Chin, Kachin, Karen, Kayah, Mon and others).

Religious mix: Buddhist (85%), Muslim (4%), Hindu (4%).

Landmarks of national history: **849**: Pagan founded. **1287**: Mongol invasion. **1826**, **1852** and **1885**: Wars with British India resulted in progressive annexation of the Burmese kingdoms. **1857**: Capital of upper Burma moved to Mandalay from Amarapura. **1890**: Shan States became British. **1948**: Independence. **27 May 1990**: Election ignored by SLORC (State Law and Order Restoration Council) – the ruling military Junta. **1991**: Nobel Peace Prize for Aung San Suu Kyi.

Leader: Generals Than Shwe and Ne Win.

Pressing political issues: International outcries against human rights abuses, fudged democracy. Drafting of a new constitution which the SLORC abolished in 1974; a new constitution has been planned since 1993. Democracy groups in 1996 announced plans to formulate an alternative constitution, which the SLORC made a criminal offence (punishable by 20 years in jail) a few days later.

PRACTICAL INFORMATION
Visa and formalities

● **Visa strategy** All tourist visas allow a one month period of stay, though at the time of writing there were rumours this would be extended to three months. Extensions (for two weeks) are currently being granted only in Rangoon and cost $36. Go to the **Myanmar Tour and Travels** (MTT) office in Rangoon (☎ 1-75328, fax 1-82535, 77-91 Sule Pagoda Rd) for the necessary forms; they'll tell you where you have to go next. Some travellers have obtained extensions within a few hours, but allow two days. The fine for overstaying your original visa is $3 per day overstayed during the first three months, $5/day thereafter.

Those with a contact in Burma can obtain a three-month business visa, with the possibility of a three-month extension.

● **Permits and off-limit areas** The rules regarding where tourists can and can't go seem to be constantly changing, even MTT didn't know exactly.

In general the possession of a train or plane (but not bus) ticket seems to qualify as a sort of official permission to visit a city (though not necessarily the rural areas that surround it). Border areas, especially the border with India and the long thin tentacle of land stretching south along the Thai border, are typically the most sensitive and the police will turn you back if they find you there. It seems to be enough to plead ignorance (honestly in most cases) and diplomats in Rangoon have never heard of a traveller being detained – or fined – for entering restricted zones. To travel legally through these areas (eg to

❑ Old and new names

Pointing out (correctly enough) that many place names were colonial anachronisms, the SLORC set about renaming towns, rivers and states. Burma itself is now officially the Union of Myanmar. Most locals, however, dislike the new names, and several Burmese democracy groups suggest people continue using the old ones as a sort of anti-government protest. In this book we've used the form that seems most generally accepted. Everyone knows the old names, so their use shouldn't cause much confusion.

Town names

Old	New	Old	New
Akyab	Sittwe	Moulmein	Mawlamyine
Amherst	Kyaikkami	Pagan	Bagan
Ava	Inwa	Prome	Pyay
Bago	Pegu	Rangoon	Yangon
Bassein	Pathein	Sandoway	Thandwe
Maymyo	Pyin U Lwin	Syriam	Tanyin

State names

Old	New
Arakan	Rakhine
Karen	Kayin

River names

Old	New
Irrawaddy	Ayeyarwady
Talween	Thanlwin

enter or exit Burma overland) you'll need to employ an official escort. Inquire at a local MTT office or at the Department of Immigration. This will be possible only in areas under government control.

Money

The Kyat (Ky) pronounced 'chat' is the money locals use in their day-to-day transactions. For years its value has been artificially set between 5Ky and 7Ky to the US$. At this rate, Burma would be very pricey. Fortunately an illegal but very widespread black market offers an enormously better deal; around 120Ky=$1 and rising rapidly. At these rates, travel in Burma is very cheap. Too cheap for the government which has thus invented Foreign Exchange Certificates (FECs). An FEC is basically a US dollar which can only be used in Burma. On arrival, you're supposed to exchange US$300 (or equivalent in £ sterling) for 300FECs. More would be just fine. The idea is that everyone will be forced to spend at least $300 during their stay in Burma. However, the system breaks down quickly – the black

market will happily buy back your FECs for either kyat or US$. And anywhere which takes FECs also takes dollars, often giving dollar change when breaking a bigger FEC bill.

Thus, changing the $300 on arrival need not represent any loss to you. However, it does put hard currency into the dirty pockets of SLORC (see introduction). As a political gesture many travellers try to avoid it. From our plane, one couple acting as though deep in conversation, managed to walk straight past the exchange desk. Another bribed the official $10 for the right to exchange only $100.

Once past the airport hurdle, you'll need to buy some kyat (although, we suggest keeping at least $100 in dollars/FEC). Some travellers have managed to fund almost their entire trip in kyat. However, airport taxes; train and air tickets; hotels in Rangoon, Moulmein and Mandalay; and upmarket restaurants/bars (mostly in Rangoon) will only accept hard currency/FEC. Cheap backpacker hotels will usually quote a rate in FEC, but will often accept kyat if you are persistent about it.

Finding somewhere to buy 'black market' kyat is not a cloak and dagger affair. When, as an experiment, we tried changing a few dollars at the official rate in a bank, the teller motioned us to meet him around the corner. He told us that the bank rate was bad and personally offered to give us a better one! Restaurants, jewellery stores and market stalls usually give good rates and are least likely to cheat you. Taxi drivers give poorer rates, especially at the airport. Changing money with strangers on the street is never recommended. As well as the usual scams, you may be palmed off with 15Ky, 25Ky and 75Ky bills. These were declared worthless overnight in 1988. Another common trick is to hand you a confusing array of 45Ky and 90Ky notes which are too awkward to add up quickly.

Black market rates are very volatile and vary from place to place. On our last visit, the best rates were available in Ruli, China where US$1 bought 125-127Ky. The Rangoon rate for dollars was 120-123Ky, while FEC were sold for 118-120. The slight advantage of dollars over FECs reverses around New Year as money pours into Burma – gifts from relatives abroad. Locals, who are not legally allowed to possess hard currency, eagerly exchange their dollars for FECs driving up the relative value of the FEC. NB The rates change constantly, so by the time you read this the exact figures could have doubled. However the relative rates are fairly stable.

Banks are open Monday to Friday, 10am-2pm, and many will change US$ travellers' cheques for FECs. The **Foreign Exchange Bank** in Rangoon gives US$ credit card cash advances but charges 6%

❏ The Swedagon Pagoda

The greater a site is the more it inspires awe, wonder and a sense of mystery. But, at a point, a site becomes so great that it elicits exactly the opposite effect – one of confusion, of being overwhelmed and made to feel small. The Swedagon Pagoda in Rangoon is something like this.

Guidebooks exalt the Swedagon's physical features – the base of the pagoda has a perimeter of 1420ft (426m); the tip of the stupa alone has 5448 diamonds and 2317 rubies – and its ancient history (it was established around 500BC by King Okkalapa and expanded to today's size in the 13th century). There is a modern history too, of the Swedagon as the central gathering point for anti-government resistance, first to the colonists and then to the current military junta. There are stories based on fact – like the one of the Portuguese traders who stole a 30-ton bell from the pagoda grounds only to lose it in the Bago River (it has never been found). And there are stories which are more the stuff of legends – the pagoda, it is said, was originally built to house relics of the Buddha, including eight magical hairs which the Buddha personally gave to two Burmese trading brothers. According to one monk I spoke to here, however, the pagoda houses only seven hairs; the eighth is in a pagoda across town. 'Your book must get this right!' the monk implored me.

I spent an afternoon at the pagoda listening to the chimes tinkering in the wind and the shuffle of bare feet on marble. I looked at people pouring water over statues at one of eight planetary stations – one for each day of the week (Wednesday is broken into two). I am driven crazy by tourists wearing shorts running up to monks with video cameras (rather like a Burmese person in a *loungiy* running onto the altar during a Christmas mass, I think to myself). The architecture, the positioning of the stupas and monuments, it all seems so random, yet I know there is a logic to it all; and I know that even this logic would not explain what the Swedagon Pagoda is, why it is that this building can have such a direct effect on the soul.

commission. Some shops and restaurants also take plastic but make quite certain that you'll be billed in a hard currency before you charge anything to your card. One traveller returned home from Burma to a big shock: his 3000Ky purchase that would have cost $25 in black market cash, was billed at US$551.41.

Transport

● **Linega** *Linega* (literally 'line bus') are pick ups or small trucks with makeshift seats in the back. They run between two points (which could be across town or across Burma) dropping off and picking up passengers on the way. Linega won't leave until they have a pre-set number of passengers. This number depends on the vehicle, but will always far exceed the number of people you would think could possibly fit. Indeed, the last passengers are left clinging to a side railing or a few precious inches of the bumper.

Some linega drivers don't like taking foreigners – 'You move around too much,' one told me. An assurance that you'll behave is usually enough and will win you respect if you can keep it. Alternatively for about 50% more you can sit in a real seat in the front with the driver. As a foreigner it is possible you'll be charged about 50% more anyway. This is pure pragmatism; you take up about 50% more space.

● **Buses** The government has recently allowed private 'express' buses to compete on major routes. The best of them, such as Leo and Rainbow, offer a level of luxury that seems out of place for Burma. A pleasant, tape- recorded message welcomed us aboard one Leo bus; it wished us a 'physically and spiritually comfortable journey'. The ticket price included restaurant stops for dinner, breakfast and a midnight snack. Free bottled drinking water was provided en route and, to compensate for the lack of air conditioning, a legion of women had been employed to fan customers by hand. Dinner turned out to be somewhat of a cabaret, though the strangled renderings of Madonna's *Material World* did not quite fit our definition of 'spiritual comfort'.

Only on the highly competitive Rangoon-Mandalay route can you expect such levels of service. As yet, express buses serve relatively few routes and some companies (eg Pagan Express) are notorious for breakdowns. Nonetheless, express buses remain much more reliable then the alternative; public 'local' buses. These are cheap, (200Ky for an eight hour ride) but slower and only marginally more comfortable than linega.

● **Train** Trains are comfortable but slow. At many stations, tickets are sold at an inflated tourist rate. Tickets from Mandalay and Rangoon are doubly expensive as foreigners may only buy first class tickets. However, in the Gulf of Martaban prices are reasonable and travelling by train in this region is particularly sensible as there are no express buses. In an area that's 'off limits', travelling by train makes sense as your ticket can qualify as a quasi-official permit to pass through (see Permits, above).

● **Air** Flying is the only way to travel to some places in the rainy season eg Akyab (Sittwe). You can fly to towns you can't get

---

❏ **Superstitions or facts of life?**
People born on a Wednesday or Saturday make the best couples, according to a superstition which pervades Burmese culture. Eight is the lucky number of the opposition, thus the 8th of the 8th month, 1988 was chosen as the beginning of a pro-democracy strike, and it started at eight minutes past 8am. Ne Win's lucky number is nine, hence the 90Ky and 45Ky bills (both being divisible by nine and having digits which add up to nine). Being a former British colony, the Burmese used to drive on the left hand side of the road; until, the story has it, Ne Win was told that his right side was his lucky side and ordered everyone to change. You can still see many cars with the steering wheel on the 'wrong' side.

permission to travel to by land eg Ye. The international departure tax is $6.

● **Boat** Boat travel gives a magical insight into Burmese life, but can be very slow – Rangoon to Mandalay (ie upstream) takes about two weeks. The most popular boat trip with tourists is downstream from Mandalay to Pagan. A twice-weekly express boat is $11 and takes 10hrs. The daily local boat costs 200Ky but takes nearly two days, stopping overnight. There are many shorter boat hops, especially in the Irrawaddy (Ayeyarwady) Delta.

● **Other** In most cities of tourist interest it is possible to rent bicycles although we didn't find anywhere to do so in Rangoon. Taxis are inexpensive; 70Ky for a 10-minute ride, c200Ky for an hour's hire.

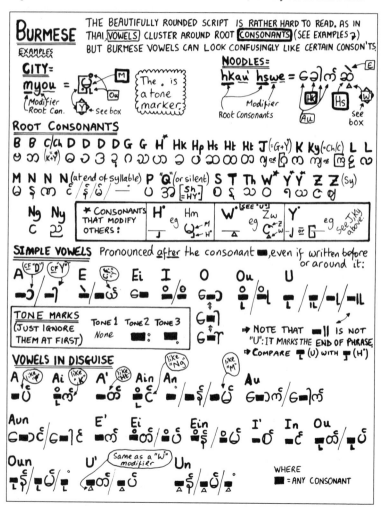

Accommodation

At the time of research, bargaining for accommodation was the order of the day. Not all travellers received as much of a discount as the two we met at Rangoon's Future Hotel who paid $4 for a $35 room, but everyone managed to bring the price down somewhat.

In general, a basic room (bed, communal hole-in-the-floor toilets, mosquito net) costs between 200Ky and 300Ky. Nicer rooms with a fan, shower (sometimes hot), and screened windows are usually between 300Ky and 600Ky. Most hotels, especially those used to receiving tourists, include breakfast in the price. It is useful to make clear that breakfast is included with the room before bargaining – otherwise you might find an unexpected charge on your bill. Apart from when you are in Rangoon, you should be able to negotiate a room price in kyat. Accommodation in Rangoon is the most expensive in Burma – the cheapest room there is $7.

Note that the room prices quoted on the map are those we or other travellers have managed to bargain, not the price offered. How much you pay will depend on the season, the time of day you show up (prices are cheaper at night), and how long you plan to stay.

Food and drink

Burmese food is a not always successful marriage between Indian and Chinese cuisine. The standard breakfast meal is

---

❏ Meeting the locals

● **The people** Rules regulating communication with foreigners in Burma have eased in recent years. The Burmese seem naturally friendly and many are now approaching travellers and starting conversations. In government controlled areas people are very hesitant to talk about the junta – they could get into trouble over anti-government statements and shouldn't be pushed too hard on the topic. In areas not under government control, people will make their opinions known. An introduction might begin 'I am a Karen rebel, my name is.......'

Many Burmese students learn how to write English without learning how to speak it; a pen and paper can open language barriers.

● **Language** Many tribal groups within Burma have their own language, but Burmese is the official one. Spoken Burmese is a tonal language though it seems easier to make yourself understood than in some other tonal languages, such as Chinese or Vietnamese. The written script consists of curved shapes with rough right angles added for dramatic effect (see opposite). While spoken Burmese has its origin in Central Asia, the script comes from South India and is similar to the Sinhalese writing found today in Sri Lanka.

Roman numbers are widely understood and usually used in shops. Burmese numbers, however, are more often used for local transport (eg bus numbers and time tables). (See p561).

Some phrases in Burmese:
    Hello – *mingala ba*
    Thank you – *khezu kinbare*
    Don't have/not possible – *mishibu*
    (A nice way to turn some one down) – *ahnah-bareh*
    It tastes good – *sak-kounde*

Some famous people to bring up in conservation: Zaw Win Hiut is a well known male singer who sings a type of rock and roll; Kyaw Hein is Burma's most famous actor – you're unlikely to find someone who doesn't like him; Than Toe Aung, Burma's best soccer player, is also an engineering student.

mohinga (rice noodles with fish gravy). *Mohinga* is sold in street stalls and restaurants from 5am until about 9.30am. There are also roving hawkers selling the stuff – you can spot them carrying their equipment around. Tounggyi, Moulmein (Mawlamyine) and Mandalay are major *mohinga* centres. The dish comes with different garnishes in the different regions.

A standard dinner might be *ngapi* (rice with fish paste). The Burmese will be surprised if you ask for it and after you smell it you might wish you hadn't. Other common dishes include: *amehnat* (roast beef cooked with sugar, onions and garlic), *myinkuayuet* (a side dish of leaves with roots, salad, ground nuts and garlic), *bangoki* (fried cauliflower), and *gobido* (fried vegetables with eggs, potatoes or beans). For dessert, you can try *sawin-ma-kin*.

Indian and Chinese restaurants are also common. The Chinese establishments especially are more expensive than the Burmese places and seem more geared towards large parties than individuals. If you wanted duck in one Chinese restaurant we visited, for example, you could only order a whole one (400Ky). Western food is available but hard to find; one Rangoon street stall we saw served *dick macs*.

Chinese tea is the standard beverage and it usually comes free with a meal. Coffee and Indian-style tea are also common. Both are served so sweet many of the Burmese seem to have a problem drinking them as well. Ordering your drink *jah-neh-neh* (with less sugar) might help. Tap water is very unhealthy in Burma but bottled water is available everywhere: 45Ky for a big bottle, 25Ky for a small one.

Staying in touch

● **Mail** Using black market kyat, the postal services are perhaps the cheapest in Asia – 5Ky per letter (to Europe or North America), 3Ky per postcard. Sending mail is surprisingly efficient, especially from Rangoon. We were advised to make all mail look as worthless as possible and even urged to sign the front of our postcards to keep someone from ripping off the picture (to be pasted on another piece of cardboard and re-sold)! That said, all of our mail arrived safely in Europe and the US within 10 days or less.

The **American Express** office (☎ 75361), 148 Sule Pagoda Road, Rangoon, is reliable for holding mail.

❑ **Festivals**

Burma is a country of festivals. Many are specific to local areas so there's always one going on somewhere. The most popular or nationally known include:

Month	What happens	Best place to see it
Feb	Htamane harvest festival; eat traditional rice meals.	Rural villages
April	Thingyan water spraying mayhem for Burmese new year. Lasts 3-4 days.	Downtown Rangoon
May	Pouring water on the roots of bodhi trees.	Small local temples around Bago/Gulf of Martaban
June	Mt Popa festival	Mt Popa near Pagan
Sept	Boat racing	Inle Lake or Royal Lake, Rgn
Oct	End of Buddhist 'Lent' celebrated with a festival of light; lamps and candles illuminate pagodas signifying Buddha's return to earth. Many weddings.	Nationwide, especially at the holiest sites: Swedagon and Kyaikto
Nov	Kahtein festivals. Weaving contests between unmarried women to create the best ceremonial robes for monks.	Nationwide
Dec	Nat festivals, to placate the local spirits.	Various, eg Pagan

● **Telephone** International telephone calls are very cheap from Mandalay, but are difficult to place elsewhere. Rates to Europe and North America are 255Ky for three minutes (minimum time) from a calling office, 500-600Ky from a hotel.

International country code: +95. Rangoon: 1, Mandalay: 2, Prome: 53.

Activities

● **Hiking** The most popular hiking area is around Inle Lake (guides can be found locally).

● **Buddhism** Buddhist meditation courses are available. Visas can be extended beyond six weeks for those who want to study Buddhism.

The **Vipassana Centre** (☎ 1-39290), Burma Dhamna Joti, Nga Htat Gyi, Pagoda Rd, Bahon Township, Rangoon, runs 10 or 11-day retreats twice a month.

Panditarama, 80-A Thanlyin Road, Shwegondine PO, Bahan, Rangoon, offers Vipassana meditation. Long retreats are possible and they will help get a visa. The main teacher is Sayadaw U Pandita.

● **Language** It is possible to study Burmese through several schools in Rangoon (look in the phone book or ask MTT); one school told us they can 'very likely' help with extending visas.

● **Martial arts** Classes are held regularly at the Rangoon YMCA; Tuesday, Thursday and Saturday, 3.30-5.30pm.

Further information

● **Books** For trips off the beaten track, the best guidebooks by far are those from the 1960s and 1970s. They can be easily bought in the book selling area of Rangoon (see map). The advantage of these old books is that they cover the whole country – including areas now either officially closed or recently opened. In many cases the town plans haven't changed much since the 1960s anyway.

At the time of writing, there were no good up-to-date guidebooks on Burma – the country was simply changing too quickly. The Burma section of the *Thailand Handbook* (Footprint) seemed to be the one preferred by travellers. The Lonely Planet book has several good maps but received mixed reviews – it is available in Rangoon. Bradt's *Burma* guidebook has less practical information than the previous two, but has good, traveller-relevant history sections.

Several books have been written about current political happenings. *Freedom From Fear* by Aung San Suu Kyi (Penguin, 1991) is an excellent read, as is Bertil Lintner's *Outrage* (White Lotus, 1990) which details the 1988 democracy uprising, and Edith Mirante's *Burmese Looking Glass: A Human Rights Adventure and a Jungle Revolution* (Grove, 1993). For a colonial account of Burma, a classic read is *Burmese Days* by George Orwell (Penguin). Orwell's book includes descriptions of places and people which read as if they were written yesterday. All are widely available in Bangkok.

We found nowhere in Burma to buy guidebooks for onward travel.

● **Maps** The nearest cities selling good Latin-script maps of Burma are Bangkok, Kathmandu and Singapore. Nowhere in Burma sells one, though book stores and Rangoon road-side vendors sell maps in the Burmese script which are very helpful for deciphering bus signs.

● **Information offices** MTT's offices in Mandalay, Pagan and Rangoon are good places to go for all sorts of information and city maps. Their map of Mandalay is very reasonable and their Rangoon map is OK, though the scale is out around Inya (not Inle) Lake. More recent and of better quality is the Ministry of Forestry's Rangoon map but it's difficult to find. Try the Inwa Bookstore and the shops around 37th St.

Web sites
Lonely Planet's page on the ever changing situation in Burma is the most useful:
http://www.lonelyplanet.com.au/dest/sea/myan.html

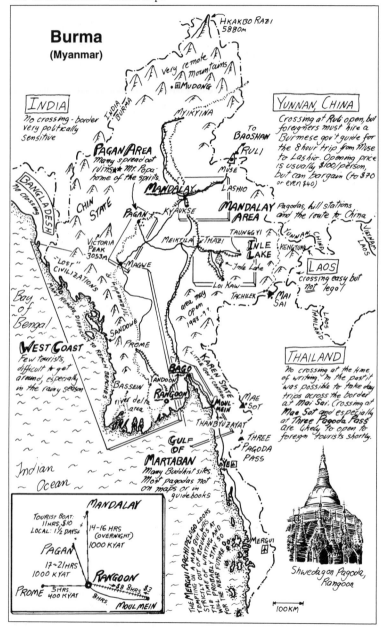

Shwedagon Pagoda, Rangoon

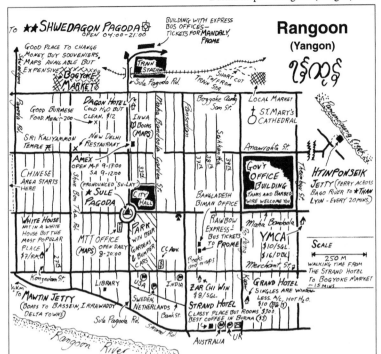

Rangoon (Yangon) map with labels including:

To ★★SHWEDAGON PAGODA☼ OPEN 04:00–21:00

BUILDING WITH EXPRESS BUS OFFICES – TICKETS FOR MANDALAY, PROME

Rangoon (Yangon)

GOOD PLACE TO CHANGE MONEY, BUY SOUVENIRS, MAPS AVAILABLE BUT EXPENSIVE

BOGYOKE MARKET

TRAIN STATION

Sule Pagoda Rd.

SHORT CUT TO/FROM TRAIN STA.

LOCAL MARKET

ST. MARY'S CATHEDRAL

Bogyoke Aung San St.

DAGON HOTEL COLD H₂O BUT CLEAN. $12 ✕

GOOD BURMESE FOOD. MEAL-200 ✕

INWA Books (MAPS)

NEW DELHI RESTAURANT

SRI KALIYAMMON TEMPLE

Maha Bandola Garden St.

Pansodan

Seikkantha

Anawrahta St.

AMEX OPEN M-F 9-17:00 SA 9-12:00 (PRONOUNCED SU-LAY)

CHINESE AREA STARTS HERE

37½ 38½ 39½

★ SULE PAGODA

CITY HALL

GOV'T OFFICE BUILDING TANKS AND BARBED WIRE WELCOME YOU

HTINPONSEIK JETTY (FERRY ACROSS BAGO RIVER TO ★THAN LYIN - EVERY 20 MINS)

WHITE HOUSE NOT IN A WHITE HOUSE BUT THE MOST POPULAR PLACE $7/RM.

MTT OFFICE (MAPS) OPEN DAILY 8-20:00

PARK WITH BEER GARDENS & BUMPER CARS

CC Adv.

BANGLADESH BIMAN OFFICE

RAINBOW EXPRESS - BUS TICKETS TO PROME

Maha Bandola

YMCA $10/SGL $16/DBL

Merchant St.

SCALE 250 M WALKING TIME FROM THE STRAND HOTEL TO BOGYOKE MARKET - 15 MINS

Konzedan St.

LIBRARY

USA

INDIA

Books and maps

GRAND HOTEL

To MAWTIN JETTY (BOATS TO BASSEIN, IRRAWADDY DELTA TOWNS)

SWEDEN, NETHERLANDS

Bank St.

Sule Pagoda Rd.

Strand Rd.

ZAR CHI WIN $8/SGL

STRAND HOTEL CLASSY PLACE BUT ROOMS $300 BEST COFFEE IN BURMA ($3)

GRAND HOTEL SINGLES ARE WINDOW-LESS. A/C, HOT H₂O. $10

AUSTRALIA UK

Rangoon River

Some things to see
● The Shwedagon Pagoda★ is the highlight,but there are many others such as Chauk Hat Gyi (north of Royal Lake). Most pagodas are marked on MTT's map.
● The park around Royal Lake.
● Syriam town A beer and Hindu centre 45 mins by ferry from Htinbonseik Jetty. Giant catfish at the Kyaikpun Pagoda, 30 mins south of Syriam by bus.
● Daw Aung San Suu Kyi★ At the time of research, the junta was permitting her to give speeches Saturday and Sunday in front of her house (54 University Ave). Starts at 4pm, be there by 3pm.

Accommodation
See map above for central listings. Other places include *Motherland Inn* (out of town, but free transport; $5 B&B) and *Westend* (a little out of town, $8-10/rm).

Transport
● **Getting to/from the airport** Taxi **to** the airport: around 200 kyat. Taxi **from** the airport: $1 (drivers hope to change dollars at a poor rate and/or get commission from your hotel). Shared taxi to/from the long distance bus station: 5 kyat.
● **Useful buses** (from Sule Pagoda; often marked only with Burmese numbers)

9, 51	Long distance bus station (near the airport)
33, 36	Mawtin Jetty
44, 45	Inya Lake
45	Shwedagon Pagoda

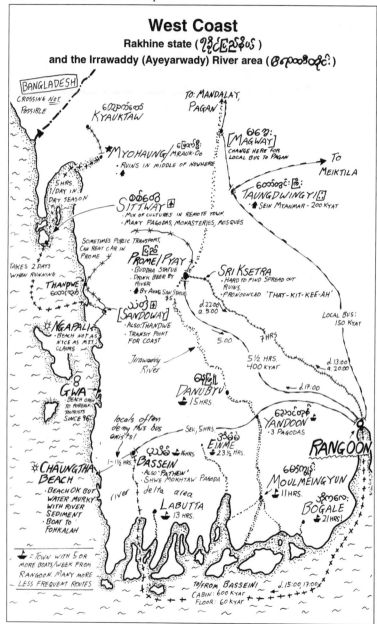

West Coast
Rakhine state (ရှိုင်းပြည်နယ်)
and the Irrawaddy (Ayeyarwady) River area (ဧရာဝတီတိုင်း)

BANGLADESH
CROSSING NOT POSSIBLE

မြောက်ဦး
KYAUKTAW

TO: MANDALAY, PAGAN

မြောက်ဦး
MYOHAUNG/MRAUK-OO
• RUINS IN MIDDLE OF NOWHERE

မကွေး
[MAGWAY]
CHANGE HERE FOR LOCAL BUS TO PAGAN

TO MEIKTILA

5 HRS. 1/DAY IN DRY SEASON

စစ်တွေ
SITTWAY
• MIX OF CULTURES IN REMOTE TOWN.
• MANY PAGODAS, MONASTERIES, MOSQUES

တောင်တွင်းကြီး
TAUNGDWINGYI
• SEIN MYANMAR - 200 KYAT

TAKES 2 DAYS WHEN RUNNING

SOMETIMES PUBLIC TRANSPORT. CAN RENT CAR IN PROME

ပြည်
PROME/PYAY
• BUDDHA STATUE
• DRINK BEER BY RIVER
• BY AUNG SAN STATUE

SRI KSETRA
• HARD TO FIND SPREAD OUT RUINS.
• PRONOUNCED 'THAT-KIT-KEE-AH'

THANDWE
သံတွဲ

 သံတွဲ
[SANDOWAY]
• ALSO: THANDWE
• TRANSIT POINT FOR COAST

NGAPALI
• BEACH NOT AS NICE AS M.T.T CLAIMS

d.22.00
a.5.00

5.00

7 HRS

LOCAL BUS: 150 KYAT

Irrawaddy River

5 1/2 HRS. 400 KYAT

d.13.00 a.20.00

GWA
• BEACH OPEN TO FOREIGN TOURISTS SINCE '96

ဓနုဖြူ
DANUBYU
15 HRS.

d.17.00

locals often deny this bus exists!

SEV. 5 HRS.

 အောင်တံခွန်
YANDOON
• 3 PAGODAS

RANGOON

CHAUNGTHA BEACH
~ BEACH OK BUT WATER MURKY WITH RIVER SEDIMENT
• BOAT TO FONKALAH

ပုသိမ် 16 HRS.
BASSEIN
• ALSO 'PATHEIN'
• SHWE MOKHTAW PAGODA

အိမ်မဲ
EINME
23 1/2 HRS.

river   delta   area

LABUTTA
13 HRS.

မော်လမြိုင်
MOULMEINGYUN
11 HRS.

ဘိုကလေး
BOGALE
21 HRS!

1-1 1/2 HRS.

= TOWN WITH 5 OR MORE BOATS/WEEK FROM RANGOON. MANY MORE LESS FREQUENT ROUTES

TO/FROM BASSEIN
CABIN: 600 KYAT
FLOOR: 60 KYAT

d.15.00 17.00

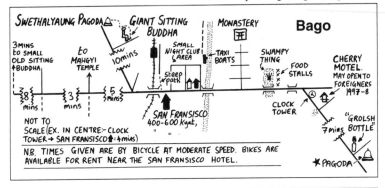

Pagan (Bagan)

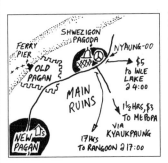

Pagan★, one of the world's greatest cities before the Mongols destroyed it, survives today as a great tourist attraction. Guides and books on the area are available locally but Pagan's 5000+ ruins are not displayed in a look-at-me fashion. Instead they're left for people to find on their own. Travellers don't need much imagination to feel like they are the first ones to the pagodas since Kublai Khan.

● **Accommodation** In Old Pagan (walk to/from ferry pier), there's the *Co-operative* (the only cheapie in the area). Today, the old area is only a ghost-town after the government forced all the town's residents to move out as punishment for being anti-junta. In New Pagan (2km walk from ferry pier) there are several cheap choices which are quiet and close to largest concentrations of ruins. In Nyaung-Oo, *Luck 7 GH* ($4/pp with breakfast) is close to the market, bus station and the pagoda.

● **Transport** For **Inle Lake** buses depart very early in the morning. MTT bus will drop you anywhere on Kalaw-Taunggyi road. For **Prome** buses take five to six hrs; change in Magwe. The express bus to **Rangoon** (1000 kyat) leaves at 5pm. For **Mandalay** it's one long day (sometimes more) on linega. There's also the ferry (1½ days), and a tourist ferry on Sunday. For **Mt Popa** see below.

Mt Popa★
The mountain home of the spirits is well worth a visit but no place to spend the night. Taxis between Mt Popa and Pagan take 1½ hrs an cost 300-400 kyat. Buses (100 kyat) go via Kyaukpadang and leave mostly in the morning from Pagan; last bus back from Mt Popa is at 6pm.

North of Pagan
The Chin state was out of bounds at the time of writing. We met one group who had been turned back at Singu. Pakokka is the gateway to the Chin state.

Mandalay area

To MUSE & YUNNAN, CHINA
8~9 HRS FROM LASHIO. GOVT ESCORT REQ'D - STANDARD PRICE IS $100 BUT CAN BE BARGAINED TO $70~40. ASK AT MTT

LASHIO
GOOD MARKET
NEW ASIA. 600 KYAT/DBL (V/SHOWER). 500/DBL L/RO SHOWER), 300/SHVR. OFTEN FULL.

CHECK POST

150 ★ KYAT

HSIPAW △ ("TEE-POH")
NEAR TV TRANSMITTER
Aung Tha Pyay - 100 KYAT

8 HRS.
200 KM.

KYAUKME
VERY RUINED

LASHIO ↔ MANDALAY
BUS RUNS 3 TIMES A DAY (~12 HRS, 250 KYAT) IN THEORY FOREIGNERS CAN ONLY TRAVEL BY ROAD AS FAR AS HSIPAW. IF STOPPED TAKE THE TRAIN INSTEAD.

MAYMYO (PYIN-U-LWIN)
OLD BRITISH HILL STATION
CANDACRAIG- CLASSIC COLONIAL HOTEL W/ HORRIBLE FOOD & EXPENSIVE ROOMS. HAVE A COFFEE.
400 KYAT
AMISAKAN WATERFALL

FREQ. VATOO RUNS

CAN TAKE 5 HRS. EXPENSIVE

Mogok
JADE SELLING CENTRE
NO BUS TO MANDALAY

(NO FOUND NO BUS)

To MYITKYINA
REMOTE ATMOSPHERE
MARKET
● TEMPLE

Foreigners may *not* take the bus to/from Myit-Kyina. Enforced!! →

DAILY 7:00
DAILY d 15:00 a 18:00 (NEXT DAY!) SEAT $27
SU/TU/W/F d 19:30 a 18:00
SEAT $30, SLEEPER $60

To MYITKYINA
REMOTE ATMOSPHERE
DAILY 7:00
DAILY d 15:00 a 18:00
SU/TU/W/F d 19:30 a 18:00
SEAT $30, SLEEPER $60

ROAD TRANSPORT- MANDALAY TO:
RANGOON- 1000 KYAT ON EXPRESS BUS (eg. FROM LEO EXPRESS OFFICE)
PAGAN- 300 KYAT ON BUS. d 9, 16:00
160 KYAT ON LIMEGA. CAN TAKE UP TO 2 DAYS.
TAUNGGYI- FREQ. 350~400 KYAT
MEIKTILA- BUS d 7, 9, 16:00

MANDALAY HILL

★ ROYAL HOTEL $6

★ BIKE RENTAL. 150 KYAT/DAY

ROYAL PALACE

SCALE
~5 MINS WALK

26TH

78 TH

TO MTT (IN MANDALAY HOTEL)

500

GPO
80 TH

82 ND

84 TH

GARDEN & NYLON HOTELS $6

ZEGYO MKT.

29TH

35TH

GAWEIN JETTY

LEO EXPRESS

LINEGA: 2 HRS 50 KYAT

KYAUKSE
DIRTY, 180 KYAT

TO THAZI $3
RANGOON $35

AMARAPURA
PAGODAS, LAKES
CAN ALSO TAKE TUK-TUK (15~20 MINS FROM DOWNTOWN)

MANDALAY

AVA
MAHA AUNG MYE BONZAN MONASTERY
ANCIENT CITY WALLS
. 1 HR FROM MANDALAY

★ **MINGUN**
. A BUDDHIST KING STARTED BUILDING THE WORLD'S LARGEST PAGODA HERE....THEY RAN OUT OF MONEY
. HOME OF THE WORLD'S LARGEST *UNCRACKED* BELL. A GOOD SLEDGEHAMMER BLOW WOULD MAKE IT THE SECOND LARGEST CRACKED BELL (AFTER THE ONE IN MOSCOW).

FERRY TO MINGUN
RUNS 7-16:00. 15 KYAT.
1 HR.

⊞ △ **SAGAING** ("SAH-KAI")
. PAGODAS, PAGODAS IN AND AROUND TOWN.
. BUS STOPS AT THE MARKET 4 KM OUTSIDE OF TOWN.

To PAGAN
TOURIST BOAT- $10, 11 HRS, d 7. a 5:30. BUY TIX FROM MTT.
LOCAL BOAT- DAILY. STOPS FOR THE NIGHT IN PAKOKKU

FREQ. 2 HRS.
RUNS 7-16:00

To MONYWA ⊕ △
. HUGE RECLINING BUDDHA.
. ACROSS THE RIVER IS AN OLD PAGODA NOW INHABITED BY MONKEYS.

3½ HRS

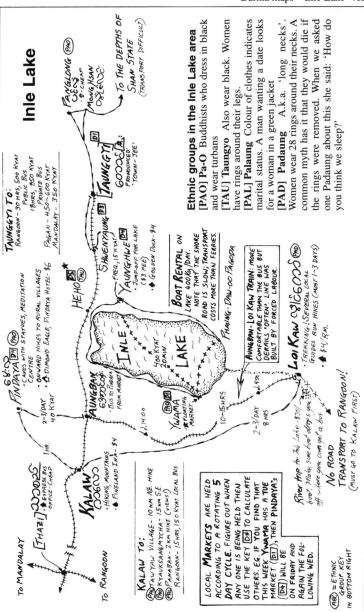

Inle Lake

TO MANDALAY

TO RANGOON

[THAZI] သာစီ
• EXPRESS BUS
OFFICE-CHEAP

KALAW ကလော
• HIKING, MOUNTAINS
• PINELAND INN-$4

KALAW TO:
(PAO) TAW YAW VILLAGE - 10KM NE. HIKE
(PAO) KYAUKSAMAYCHA - 15 KM S.E.
(PAD) PANABAN - 2 KM HIKE (VIEWS)
RANGOON- 15HRS, I50 KYAT LOCAL BUS

LOCAL **MARKETS** ARE HELD
ACCORDING TO A ROTATING **5**
DAY CYCLE. FIGURE OUT WHEN
ANY ONE IS BEING HELD THEN
USE THE KEY (D4) TO CALCULATE
OTHERS. EG, IF YOU FIND THAT
THIS WEEK YWAMA HAS A TUE
MARKET (D1), THEN PINDAYA'S
(D4) WILL BE
ON FRIDAY AND
AGAIN THE FOL-
LOWING WED.

(ABC) = ETHNIC
GROUP KEY
IN BOTTOM RIGHT

ပင်းတယ FINDAYA (D4) (PAO)
• CAVES WITH STATUES, MEDITATION
  CENTRE
• ONWARD HIKES TO RURAL VILLAGES
• DIMOND EAGLE, PINDAYA HOTEL-$6

2-3/DAY
40 KYAT

1HR.

AUNGBAN ၆၀၆၀ E02
BUS TO PINDARA
FROM MARKET

1, 1:40,00

ဟဲဟိုး HEHO (TAU) ★ ⊠

SHWENYAUNG (PAO) D1

ယောင်ရွှေ YAUNGHWE (D1)
• JUMP-OFF FOR LAKE
  ($3 FEE)
◆ FREG, IS KYAT?
◆ GOLDEN DUCK- $4

BOAT RENTAL ON
LAKE 400Kk/DAY.
NOTE THAT THE SHORE
ROAD IS SLOW; TRANSPORT
COSTS MORE THAN FERRIES.

PHAUNG-DAW-00 PAGODA

INLE
×   ×
×   LAKE ×
×   ×
400 KYAT ×
20MIN ×

AUNGBAN-LOI KAW TRAIN: MORE
COMFORTABLE THAN THE BUS BUT
DERAILS 'OFTEN'. LINE WAS
BUILT BY FORCED LABOUR.

YWAMA ၆၃၀၀ E02 (D1)
★ FLOATING
  MARKET

No ROAD
TRANSPORT TO RANGOON!
(MUST GO TO KALAW FIRST)

River trip to the Lake -$20/
boat. Make sure tour stops you
off where you can get a bus

2-3/DAY
8 HRS

400

10-15HRS

LoiKAW (PAO) လွိုင်ကော်
• TREKKING, SEVERAL LOCAL
  GUIDES RUN HIKES (MOST 1-3 DAYS)
◆ $4/RM.

TAUNGGYI TO:
RANGOON - 30 HRS, 500 KYAT
        PUBLIC BUS
18HRS, 950 KYAT
        PRIVATE BUS
PAGAN - 450-600 KYAT
MANDALAY - 350 KYAT

တောင်ကြီး [TAUNGGYI] (D1) ⊠
၆၀၀၀ (R) PRONOUNCED:
        'TOWN-JEE'

ပင်းလုံ PANGLONG (PAO)
(DE) • CHEAP

MONG HSAN OE LEUDE

TO THE DEPTHS OF
SHAN STATE
(TRANSPORT DIFFICULT)

Ethnic groups in the Inle Lake area

[PAO] Pa-O Buddhists who dress in black and wear turbans

[TAU] Taungyo Also wear black. Women have rings around their legs.

[PAL] Palaung Colour of clothes indicates marital status. A man wanting a date looks for a woman in a green jacket

[PAD] Padaung A.k.a. 'long necks'. Women wear 28 rings around their necks. A common myth has it that they would die if the rings were removed. When we asked one Padaung about this she said: 'How do you think we sleep?'

Gulf of Martaban area

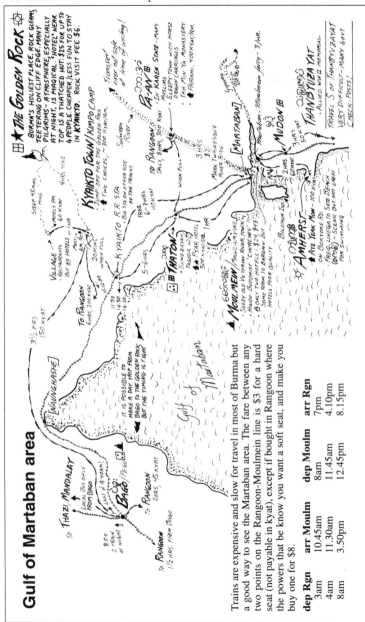

☆ THE GOLDEN ROCK ⟡
BURMA'S HOLIEST PLACE. ROCK GLEAMS TEETERING ON CLIFF EDGE. MANY PILGRIMS - ATMOSPHERIC, ESPECIALLY AT NIGHT, IS MAGICAL. HOTEL NEAR TOP IS A THATCHED HUT. $25 FOR UPTO 4 PEOPLE, CHEAPER (LESS FUN) TO STAY IN KYAIKTO. ROCK VISIT FEE $6.

STEEP 45 MINS HIKE

4 HRS HIKE

VILLAGE
- RESTAURANTS
- HOTELS
MISTY AM, OK
• MONEY PM, 60 KYAT ~ 1HR

KYAIKTO TOWN/KIMPO CAMP
- JUMP-OFF FOR THE GOLDEN ROCK
- TWO CHOICES, ~ 300 KYAT/RM.

KYAIKTO RR STA.
- BUS STA ON OTHER SIDE OF THE TRACKS

FREQ.
6-7HRS
KYAIKTO

[WAUNGHSHE]

To RANGOON
6 HRS, 200 KYAT

20 MINS
WHEN FULL

11:50
14:50
↓12:00
↓ 16:20

5-6 HRS

☵ THATON ⊡
★ SHWEZAYAN
PAGODA 250
★ PYAR HOTEL
300 KYAT/DBL, 1 HR

Salween River

To RANGOON
DAILY, 8HRS,
30 KYAT

3 HRS
$3

A-AN ✶ ⊞
- IN KAREN STATE - MANY MUSLIMS
- SLEEPY TOWN WITH HORSE DRAWN CARRIAGES
- TAH MWI YA MONASTERY
- PARAMI, 400 KYAT/RM.

Transport
INTO NOT SAFE
↑ AT HOME OF WRITING!

[MARTABAN]
Martaban-Moulmein ferry - 3/HR.

MARK TWAINESQUE RIVER RIDE

WHEN FULL

MUDON ⊞

3HRS
30 KYAT

THANBYUZAYAT
ALLIED WWII MEMORIAL.
TRAVEL S. OF THANBYUZAYAT VERY DIFFICULT - MANY GOVT CHECK-POSTS!

MOULMEIN/MAWLAMYINE
660 ⊡ ⊞
- SEEDY OLD VICTORIAN RIVER TOWN
- HINDU, BUDDHIST CHURCHES
• ONLY TWO HOTELS: $24, $48
SOME ROOM TO BARGAIN BUT
HOTELS POOR QUALITY

AMHERST
★ ATE TEAK MON- 100 KYAT
ON BONYOKE RD.
FREQ. LINEGA TO SETE BEACH
(30KM) - SCENIC BUT NOT GREAT
FOR SWIMMING

BILUKUN IS.

2 HRS
$2

THANBIN ⊞
CONVENT

Gulf of Martaban

IT IS POSSIBLE TO MAKE A DAY TRIP FROM BAGO TO THE GOLDEN ROCK BUT THE TIMING IS TIGHT.

To THAZI, MANDALAY
LOCAL BUS ONLY FROM BAGO
LAST AT 9.40AM!

3HRS
150 KYAT

BAGO ☰⊞ ⊡
To RANGOON
2HRS, 45 KYAT

8:00
2 TRAIN
AT NIGHT

To RANGOON
1½ HRS. FROM BAGO

9.00
2 TRAIN AT NIGHT

Trains are expensive and slow for travel in most of Burma but a good way to see the Martaban area. The fare between any two points on the Rangoon-Moulmein line is $3 for a hard seat (not payable in kyat), except if bought in Rangoon where the powers that be know you want a soft seat, and make you buy one for $8.

dep Rgn	arr Moulm	dep Moulm	arr Rgn
3am	10.45am	8am	7pm
4am	11.30am	11.45am	4.10pm
8am	3.50pm	12.45pm	8.15pm

Vietnam

During the American war (or Vietnam war as we know it) the Hanoi Hilton was Vietnam's most infamous prison. In 1995 it was being torn down to be replaced by a 22-storey shopping complex. A former American prisoner of war turned businessman visited the demolition site looking for a souvenir of his captivity. He explained his quest to a construction worker at the gate. The opportunistic labourer picked up a loose brick and snapped: 'Five dollars'.

Welcome to the new Vietnam. Following nearly two decades of boycotts, the foreigners are back, this time as business people and tourists. New buildings are springing up as foreign investment pours in. And the locals are quick to spot ways to make a quick buck. Sometimes, it seems that nobody, from the construction worker up, cares about anything else. One can't blame them. Vietnam is one of the poorest countries in Asia. A college professor makes only $40 a month and to survive must extort bribes from students. Similarly, patients bribe doctors for operations. And everyone bribes the police for everything – and for nothing. 'We give money so they be our friends,' said one shopkeeper noting that 'bad fortune' falls on those who do not pay.

Tourists sometimes feel they are a constant target for beggars, shoe-shine boys, postcard sellers, and overcharging everywhere. It's enough to make you jump on the next plane, bus, or cyclo out of Vietnam. But give it time. With a smile and a little patience you can usually break through the money barrier to the charm of the people on the other side. Return frequently to the same places – repeat business is respected. Every day during a week in Nha Trang, we rented bicycles from the same lady. The first day we haggled. On the fifth day she decided not to charge at all. Elsewhere guest house staff, who were cold at first, waved us off with Vietnamese candies and shots of brandy after a two-week stay. With persistence you can find a Vietnam to savour. If you don't have time, try a little creativity: the Hanoi Hilton businessman returned to the construction site late one night, sneaked inside, and got his souvenir brick. For free.

❏ **W&M's country ratings – Vietnam**
- **Expense $$$** Less than $12/day is possible if you bargain heavily and fight against foreigner pricing.
- **Value for money** ✔✔ Standards vary greatly within the price ranges.
- **Getting around** ✔✔✔✔ There is an array of transport options. The tourist buses are convenient.
- **English spoken** ✔✔ Some in Saigon, but little along the standard tourist routes. A knowledge of French is useful.
- **Woman alone** ✔✔✔ Shouldn't be a problem.
- **For vegetarians** ✔✔ Meat seems to sneak into most local dishes (especially in the north); vegetarian meals can easily be found in travellers' cafés.

❑ Essential information for travellers – Vietnam

● **Visa** Required. The average cost is $50 and the visa must state the correct border points if you are entering by land.

● **Currency** Dong. US$1= D12,280. Cash gets a better exchange rate and is easier to convert than travellers' cheques.

● **Time zone** 7 hours ahead of GMT (same as Thailand, Laos, Cambodia; 1hr behind China).

● **Health factors** Drinking tap water is not recommended; mineral water is readily available. There's a malaria risk in the Mekong Delta.

● **Special dangers** Beware of unexploded mines and bombs along the Laos border area.

● **Social conventions** Crossing your index and middle fingers (a sign of good luck in the West) is a rude gesture in Vietnam. The Vietnamese often cross their arms when listening intensely.

Age is respected in Vietnam – direct eye contact with older people (ie grandparental age) is considered rude.

The person who invites another to a meal pays the bill.

● **Typical traveller destinations** Saigon, Cu Chi tunnels, Dalat, Hue, Hanoi, Halong Bay and the Mekong Delta villages.

● **Highlights** Sapa and the highlands beyond, Hoi An, Hanoi's old city.

● **When to go** The climate differs between the southern, central, northern and highland areas.

Saigon and the south has the most predictable climate. It is always hot and rain usually falls in heavy afternoon spurts, particularly from July to January. The Mekong Delta receives even more rain – flooding is possible during September and October. December is the best month to visit the south.

The central area is usually best in February and March but varies greatly from year to year. It is wet from May to January though October is usually the only month which sees constant rain. Flooding – a common feature – makes minor roads impassable and pleasant walking impossible.

Hanoi and Halong Bay, in the north, have the most pleasant temperatures in October and November – clear skies, short sleeve days, long sleeve nights. December to February is cooler (some days will require a sweater) and, more importantly, cloudy. Halong Bay, which is so magnificent in the sunshine, looks rather ordinary on an overcast day. In March the heat sets in and then, in May, the monsoons. The mountainous areas receive less rain and more moderate temperatures.

Dalat offers a nice respite from Saigon year round. In December, in fact, Dalat can be chilly, and the northern mountains can be downright freezing.

● **Pulse of the country** The streets of old Hanoi where conical hatted merchants dangle a mass of goods from their *gwang ganh* poles.

● **Key tips** Unlike some other far eastern countries, exact street addresses are meaningful and thus are worth noting.

● **Festivals** Unless you have close friends in Vietnam, *Tet* (Vietnamese New Year) is not a good time to go. During the four days of *Tet*, which takes place in February or March according to the lunar calendar, most shops and moneychangers are closed and few buses run. Tourist hotels are very rarely used by Vietnamese, so you shouldn't have a problem finding a place to stay (though some guest houses will still try to charge double).

PRACTICAL INFORMATION
Visas and formalities

● **Visa strategy** Visas for Vietnam typically cost between US$50 and $65, take about one week to process, and allow a one-month period of stay (but see below). Since the application process is straightforward, the Vietnamese authorities had to contrive another way to complicate your life. They decided that you can enter and leave Vietnam only through the border points stated on your visa.

Trying to leave through a land border not listed on your visa will probably result in a fine (usually $20-25) but might be overlooked. Trying to enter Vietnam at a different land entry point is a more serious matter – you will probably be able to pay a fine or bribe to be allowed in (usually $40-

100 but this will depend on your bargaining skills). However, you might be turned back all together.

Some Vietnamese embassies are willing to list several land entry/exit points on your visa (eg Vientiane, Laos), some aren't willing to list any (eg Bangkok) and some will list them only if you pay an extra charge (eg Hong Kong).

Vietnamtourism (☎ 04-257245, fax 04-252707), 54 Nguyen Du, Hanoi, and (☎ 08-299868, fax 08-299868), 128A Pasteur, Saigon 1, Ho Chi Minh City, will add visa exit points. This takes four days and costs $18.

● **Extensions and longer visas** Visa extensions are theoretically impossible though in recent years some have been granted. Travellers have inconsistently

---

❏ **Geo-political information – Vietnam**

Population: 75.1 million (1997), 74.5m (1995), 52.7m (1979).

Area: 325,400 sq km.

Capital: Hanoi (3 million, 1990).

Other major cities: Ho Chi Minh City (over 4m); Haiphong (1.5m); Danang (400,000), Cantho, Nha Trang, Hue, Nam Dinh, Long Xuyen, Qui Nhon (over 200,000); Thai Nguyen, Vung Tau, Hong Gai, Cam Pha, Viet Tri (over 100,000)

GNP per capita: $190 (1994).

Currency history: Dong/US$1 – Feb 1998: D12,280, Sep 1997: D11,600, Dec 1995: D11,010, Dec 1994: D11,079, Dec 1993: D10,820.

Major exports/economy: Coffee, oil, seafood.

Ethnic mix: 90+% Vietnamese, 3% Chinese (though many fled after the 1979 war – the census details are old!).

Official language: Vietnamese.

Religious mix: Various forms of Buddhism, CaoDai (3%), Christian (7%).

Landmarks of national history: 111BC: Conquered by Chinese emperor WuTi. **939AD**: Ngo Quyen defeated the Chinese. **1044**: Capital moved to Hanoi. **1371**: Hanoi stormed by Champa army. **1471**: Champa conquered and absorbed. **1802**: Vietnam united after period of north-south division. **1847**: Missionaries expelled. **1858**: French invasion began at Danang. **1867**: French colony declared in the Saigon Delta (called Cochin China) **1883**: The French took Hue, the imperial capital, and declared the northern protectorate of Annam and Tonkin. **July 1954**: Division into north and south following Dien Bien Phu battle where the French were defeated. **1965**: US intervention began. **Jan 1973**: Ceasefire. **1975**: Saigon fell, 200,000 people fled. **1979**: Border war with China and invasion of Cambodia to oust Pol Pot. **3 Feb 1994**: US embargo lifted.

Leaders: President: General Le Duc Anh. Council of Ministers headed by General Vo Van Kiet.

Pressing political issues: Spratly Islands dispute, public morals campaign.

❏ Vietnam land entry/exit points

Border crossing	Why you might want it listed on your visa
Moc Bai	For the bus between Saigon and Phnom Penh, Cambodia.
Lao Bao	To/from Laos.
Dong Dang	For China on through trains Hanoi-Nanning-Beijing.
Huu Nghi	For the same border, if you want to cross by road (a cheaper option).
Laõ Cai	For the train line between Hanoi and Kunming, China (though you can cross on foot).
Móng Cái	For the coastal border point – Halong Bay-China.

obtained extensions in Hue (two weeks for $15 in one case, $20 in another – but this was only possible within three days of the visa's expiry), Dalat (one month, $45) and Vinh (two weeks, $12 or $15). It is unclear whether these extensions were official or the work of corrupt bureaucrats and thus not genuinely valid.

If you think you'd like to stay more than a month and don't want to risk being refused an extension you can try getting a longer visa to begin with. One traveller was granted a three-month visa in Geneva by claiming (truthfully in fact) that she was visiting friends. She needed no official letters of invitation, though other embassies require such papers. If you're planning more than one visit to Vietnam, Vietnamtourism can arrange 'visa approval': $90 for a three-month stay, $120 for six months. The fee is for the approval only, so you'll pay again when you take the letter to a pre-selected Vietnamese embassy to get the visa stamped in.

Money

US$ cash can be exchanged almost anywhere: banks, guesthouses and most jewelry shops will change cash at similar rates. Changing money with people who approach you on the street is not recommended – there is nothing to be gained and you risk being cheated. Rates are better in larger cities than in rural areas. US$ cash can be used interchangeably with Vietnamese dong in many situations in large towns (though only dong is strictly

legal tender). Travellers' cheques of various currencies can be exchanged at select banks in Hanoi, Hue and Saigon. In other cities, US dollar traveller cheques are exchangeable in at least one bank in bigger towns. Commission ranges from 0% to 2.5% – Vietcom Bank seems to offer the best deals. At border towns you'll need US$ cash.

Credit card cash advances are available in major cities. Visa card incurs a 4% commission, MasterCard and JCB were commission free.

Bargaining in dollars but paying in dong can sometimes save you around 20% (especially in the south) as some people let you round the exchange rate down to D10,000.

Bank hours vary: most are open Monday to Friday 8-11.30am, some are also open in the afternoon.

Transport

● **Bus** Vietnam has an extensive network of buses, though getting to rural destinations can involve several changes. Express buses stop only at designated bus stations and have priority over local buses at ferry crossings. Long distance buses often depart between 4 and 6am, with the better quality ones leaving first.

The standard fare for Vietnamese on a local bus is D10,000 for every 100km. However some bus drivers/bus stations try charging foreigners up to 400% more, especially in the south. Usually (though not always) vigorous bargaining will bring down the quoted price.

There are also special tourist buses and minibuses, tickets for which are sold at and around backpacker hangouts. Tourist buses serve the major routes and are faster and more comfortable than express buses; they usually cost only slightly more than an express bus with full foreigner mark up. Note that some tourist buses stop at grossly expensive restaurants with suspiciously unpriced menus, so take some food with you.

The $35 open ticket for Sinh Café's bus services in southern Vietnam is highly recommended. The ticket allows you to hop on and off buses between Saigon and Hue with stopovers in Dalat, Nha Trang and Hoi An. A bus runs each leg daily in both directions. Sinh has branches in each town for onward bookings (buses are rarely completely full). Each leg takes most of a day as there are side tours and photo breaks en route.

● **Train** The twice-weekly 'Reunification Express' can now cover the 1700km of single track railway between Saigon and Hanoi in 36 hours. The two daily services take either 40 or 44 hours. Trains would be similar in cost to the bus if it weren't for the roughly 300% foreigner surcharge. Station hopping may suit the impecunious – take a bus to a non-touristy town up or down the line and hope they don't charge you the foreigner rate.

Classes on the train are very similar to other Asian countries: hard and soft seat, hard and soft berth, and deluxe. Soft seat is comfortable – generally more so than the bus – but tickets sell quickly as they are very popular with Vietnamese. Hard sleeper fares include a blanket and pillow; your compartment attendant will provide these as long as you show your ticket. Prices are lower for the upper berths but they are more cramped than the middle and lower ones and they get terribly hot in summer.

● **Air** Flights incur a heavy foreigner surcharge: eg Hanoi to Nha Trang costs $130. International departure tax is $7.

● **Motorcycle** Motorbikes can be rented in most tourist centres and are particularly recommended for the Mekong Delta and the hill-tribe villages in the north. A 100cc Honda Dream typically costs $6-9 a day with lower rates negotiable for rentals of more than two days. Fuel costs between D3400 a litre (cities) and D5200 (remote areas) and is usually sold at street-side stalls in cans and plastic bottles.

It is also very possible to buy a motorbike for your time in Vietnam – check noticeboards in Hanoi or Ho Chi Minh City traveller cafés. The Russian-made Minsk is the most popular model; it's not noted for reliability but it's still better than its cousin, the Boshok. We saw advertisements in Hanoi for a 125cc Minsk for $200 to $250. Motorcycles over 150cc are available but incur a special import duty and are thus significantly more expensive. Motorbike prices in Saigon tend to be 10-15% higher than in Hanoi. When buying a motorbike it is important to get the regis-

---

❑ **Man bites dog**

The Vietnamese do, indeed, eat dog meat *(thit cay)*. It is considered a delicacy and is eaten mostly by men because, as one male Vietnamese explained to us 'Dog meat you must eat slowly with wine, so women don't like. Women like to eat quickly.' A Vietnamese woman had a more plausible explanation: 'It tastes bad'– though dark-haired dogs are supposed to taste better than light.

From the 15th to the end of the lunar month is the most fortuitous time to delight in canine cuisine. At the start of the month eating dog meat is bad luck and many *thit cay* places are closed. A good place to feast is north of Hanoi's Ho Tay lake. It used to be full of Russians, when Russians had money. Today, touts work to herd the remaining customers into their establishments. A selection of cuts with noodles can be had for D20,000. And, if you don't finish, you can always ask the waiter to put the rest in a....!

tration card with the motorcycle licence plate and engine number on it – whoever has this card owns the motorcycle. You theoretically also need a driver's licence to buy or rent any motorbike over 100cc, though these never seem to be asked for. You should also, as it said on one motorcycle rental contract, 'be able to be driver to avoid being accident.'

● **Bicycle** These can easily be bought or rented (D7000 per day's hire) in all tourist areas and large cities.

● **Hitchhiking** Most hitchhikers report great success. The hitching symbol consists of waving your entire arm up and down with your palm face down. Misunderstandings can be avoided by determining beforehand if your driver expects to be paid; an amount comparable to the bus fare is reasonable. There may be local hitchers to compete with.

● **Boat** The Mekong Delta region has an extensive network of river crossing ferries and long-distance boats. Many of the long-distance boats leave infrequently (eg one a week or three a month) but it is rarely a problem to find a boat that is at least going in your direction. For river crossings, touts will usually grab you before you have a chance to search for a boatman.

A boat trip is the only way to fully appreciate the glory of Halong Bay – conveniently the boat from Haiphong to Hong Gai takes you through some of the best scenery.

Ships ply the length of the Vietnamese coast and are worth considering if you have the patience and the sea legs.

● **Cyclos** The ubiquitous three-wheeled cyclo is a back-to-front rickshaw. Driving a cyclo is more profitable than teaching, especially for English speakers who can make money from affluent tourists. Saigon rates are about D5000 for a 10-minute ride or from US$1 an hour – double what locals pay. Motorcyclists (or *xe om* – Vietnamese for 'hugging vehicle') also offer rides and charge only slightly higher rates.

Accommodation

Larger cities and tourist centres have a variety of budget hotels, often in the same area. Rates vary a lot between cities: from around $12/double in Hanoi to $2/double in Cantho. The quality of room varies greatly too, even within the same price range – especially in towns where a cartel system appears to have fixed a standard rate. Towns and larger villages usually have at least one cheap option though there may not be a sign. Ask for a *khach san* (hotel) or *nha khach* (guest house). Tourists are rare in villages without a guest house, but if you do turn up the locals will probably arrange a place somewhere, possibly on the floor of the local school.

Food and drink

It is often possible to guess what you are ordering even if you don't know the form

---

❑ **Vietnam war sites**

The Vietnam War consumed the entire country so in some ways everywhere in Vietnam is connected to the war. The following is a list of places where the war is the overriding reason for a visit:

Place	What's there and why it's famous
Dien Bien Phu	Last stand of the French forces.
Quang Ngai	For visits to My Lai, site of the infamous massacre which further increased anti-war sentiments in the US.
Khe Sanh	A former French combat base; salesmen hawk rusty dog tags
Between Saigon and Cantho	The flag of South Vietnam is still faintly visible under the paint on one of the bridges you'll pass.
Demilitarised Zone (DMZ)	The demilitarized area which divided the north from the south until 1975. Tours show you a few ditches.

it will take – the names of most dishes tell you the main ingredients they contain. Common ingredients include rice (*com*), fish (*ca*), squid (*muc*), chillies (*ot*), vegetables (*rau*), crab (*cua*), pork (*heo*), beef (*bo*), chicken (*ga*), and potatoes (*khoai* [*tay*]). *Pho*, a noodle soup, is often served for breakfast: *pho ga* is noodle soup with chicken. Try stuffed crepes (*bang xeo*). Dishes vary greatly between the regions.

Tea and beer are popular drinks. The days of communism and trade embargoes were also good coffee days for Vietnam. Today, most of the good coffee is exported to France. Most tourist cafés serve a reasonable percolator coffee but local establishments are likely to serve instant coffee from Thailand if you don't specifically ask for *feen café*.

Staying in touch

● **Mail** D7000 for a letter to Europe, D9000 to North America; an expensive but fairly reliably service. Expect mail to take between one and three weeks. Insist on seeing your stamps franked, even if the postal workers claims that it isn't necessary.

● **Phone** Making international calls is expensive – the average cost of a three-minute call to Europe from a post office is about $11 (from a guest house it's about

---

❏ Meeting the locals

● **The people** Almost every Vietnamese adult can, and often will, share stories of bravery and fortitude from the decades of strife their country endured in the years of war. The suffering, destruction and death America and France caused in this sliver of south-east Asia is unfathomable, and yet their nationals usually get a better reception than others. The forgiving attitude of the local people is, in itself, a reason to make the trip, especially if you have a personal connection. To be an American whose father was a pilot in the Vietnam War and now to be sitting in a café in Hanoi being smiled at and brought free cups of tea by an old woman who lost every single member of her family to US bombing was truly heartening. 'We take care of each other now,' the old woman said.

Because the rules affecting tourists seem relatively lax it is easy to overlook the discreet pressure on local people from a government which remains quietly oppressive. While discussion of the war and political issues of the past is fairly open, former South Vietnamese soldiers (especially those of high rank) still suffer some discrimination – discussion of political topics with them should be broached sensitively.

● **Language** Spoken Vietnamese has many regional dialects and six accent tones which makes it a difficult language to pick up. The letters 'r', 'g', and 'z' are all pronounced like an English 'z' in the north (the sound becomes more like the English transliteration as you head south).

Some phrases in Vietnamese (transliterated as it sounded to us; official Vietnamese in parentheses):

> Hello – *Sin chao [xin chao]*
> How are you? – *An ko kwé hong? [Anh có khoe khong]*
> Fine – *Toi khoe [Doi kwé]*
> And you? – *Kon ban?*
> Thank you <u>very much</u> – *Kam-on <u>zat new</u> [cam on <u>rat nhieu</u>]*
> No worries – *Kam bu ji [Kam pu chia]*
> Delicious – *Ngon lam*
> How much is it? – *Za bao new? [Gia bao nhieu?]*
> Expensive – *Zoat kwa [Dat qua]*

$21). Placing calls is easy however, and connections seem to be remarkably good. If you know someone with a videophone, you can talk to and see them from the Saigon post office. Some post offices and guest houses charge for a minimum of three minutes, some charge by the minute (rounding up of course), and some will charge by the fraction of minutes so it is worth shopping around.

International country code: +84. Hanoi: 04; Ho Chi Minh City: 08.

Further information
● **Books** Basic travel information and book swaps can be found through traveller cafés. Many have noticeboards, and the backpacker sitting beside you has probably just been where you want to go. Other travellers are usually pleased to help once you get past the 'it's in the book' attitude: the underlying assumption is that you're carrying the Lonely Planet *Vietnam* book. There is quite a lot of choice for other Indochina guide books, though many are in French.

❏ **Tours in Vietnam**
Foreigner pricing on public transport has created a niche for 'Café Tours'. For little more than you'd spend travelling by crushed full death-trap local buses, you get a place on a passable tourist minibus. Many tours include accommodation and food at rates you'd find hard to get as an individual. Thus if you want a hassle-free time, picking one of the better tours might not be a bad idea, though not all tours offer the same benefits. Our analysis:

Tour of...	From	Cost
Mekong Delta	Various Saigon cafés	$7/one day; $32/three days

This tour solves the problem of organising river transport (which can be annoying in the Delta), but prevents you from staying in places as long as you like. Inquire about the possibility of going with one tour and returning with another.

Cu Chi Tunnels	Saigon cafés and hotels	$5/one day tour

Going on your own would cost about the same but would be a bit of a pain as the sites are spread out. The big advantage of the tour is the guide (make sure he/she speaks English well).

Demilitarised Zone	Hue cafés and hotels	$15/one day tour

The former Demilitarised Zone is basically just hills and trees; the tour guide is essential in helping you appreciate their significance.

Sapa hill tribes	Hanoi cafés and hotels	$50/four days

Guides are available in Sapa which makes it easy to go by yourself. There is little, if any, economic advantage to this tour. And the train is more comfortable than the long, bumpy minibus ride.

Halong Bay	Hanoi cafés and hotels	$25 for two days

Transport is less convenient to arrange on your own and taking a tour may be cheaper. But if the view is misty you don't have the freedom to wait it out and try again the next day. Anyhow you typically arrive by minibus not by boat.

Halong sailboat	Green Bamboo, Hanoi	$40 for three days

Sailing around Halong Bay by junkboat would be very expensive on your own. The tour is not so nice if there is little wind as the boat can't get out of the immediate harbour area. The combination sailboat/motor boat tour is the safer option.

NB The cost of a tour varies according to the number of people, the tour company and, of course, the length of the tour.

Vietnam: For Travellers By Travellers (Stuart McDonald and Danielle Karalus) has an appealing personal style and handy hitchhiking notes though it's difficult to find outside of Australia where it is published by Tales From The Other Side. Barbara Cohen's *Eurasia Guide* is popular with visitors on business and returning veterans. Rough Guide has a new *Vietnam* guide.

All the street sellers seem to have the same selection of cheap photocopied books: Lonely Planet's *Vietnamese Phrasebook* ($1), Graham Greene's *The Quiet American* ($3) and *The Sorrow of War*. Bookstores and street stalls (try near the main post office in any town) also sell coffee table picture books and various background works.

If you're heading for China (but not to Hong Kong) it is worth playing safe and getting a China guide before you arrive in Vietnam. However, there is a fair chance of swapping guide books in Hanoi, Sapa or Saigon guest houses or cafés. We noted one Lonely Planet *China* guide in the Green Bamboo book swap when we were in Hanoi. Few new guides were available.

● **Maps** In Hanoi, Saigon and Hue, a roaming map-seller will find you before you have a chance to find maps of Vietnam or city maps. However, the best selection of maps is sold from an unassuming stall at 61 Trang Tien St, beside the Bodega Café in Hanoi. It stocks a great selection of highly detailed French-era maps – though clearly out of date, these are particularly useful for motorbike explorations of the north. As they are not on show, you'll have to ask specifically.

Activities

● **Scuba diving** The easiest place to dive is around Nha Trang. Equipment hire and double boat dive cost from $50 and the coral beds are nice if not pristine. There are said to be much better sites around Phu Quoc Island (off the Cambodian coast) though there are no facilities as yet. Best of all would be the Spratley Islands if you could ever get there.

CAO DAI CATHEDRAL NEAR TAY NINH

Web sites

Peter M. Geiser's constantly updated Vietnam Internet Travel Guide is at www-students.unisg.ch/~pgeiser/vietnam/vietnam.htm.

Travelogues include a 1994 bicycle trip at www.mindspring.com/~jrolls/cv1.html (also in German), a 1995 3 week trip to the major tourist destinations at russell.webtravel.org/avpa,

grunt.space.swri.edu/visit.htm has Vietnam photos, travel reports, and list of recommended books, among other information.

Vietnamtourism, at www.erols.com/dreese/, issues Vietnam visas in Washington DC.

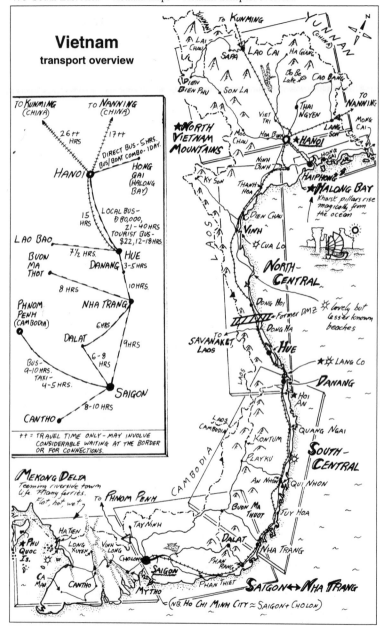

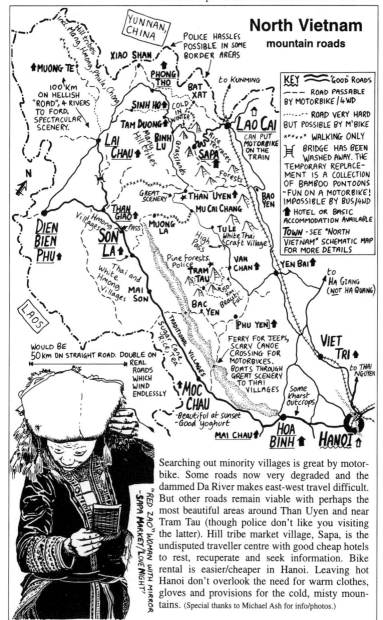

North Vietnam
mountain roads

YUNNAN, CHINA

POLICE HASSLES POSSIBLE IN SOME BORDER AREAS

KEY
- ～～ 'GOOD' ROADS
- – – – ROAD PASSABLE BY MOTORBIKE/4WD
- ······· ROAD VERY HARD BUT POSSIBLE BY M'BIKE
- ×××××× WALKING ONLY
- 🚲 BRIDGE HAS BEEN WASHED AWAY. THE TEMPORARY REPLACEMENT IS A COLLECTION OF BAMBOO PONTOONS - FUN ON A MOTORBIKE! IMPOSSIBLE BY BUS/4WD
- ⬆ HOTEL OR BASIC ACCOMMODATION AVAILABLE
- **TOWN** - SEE "NORTH VIETNAM" SCHEMATIC MAP FOR MORE DETAILS

Hill Tribes Many Hmong, Phula, Giong

⬆MUONG TE

XIAO SHAN

PHONG THO

to KUNMING

BAT XAT

100 KM ON HELLISH "ROAD", 4 RIVERS TO FORD. SPECTACULAR SCENERY

SINH HO

COLD IN WINTER

TAM DUONG

LAO CAI

CAN PUT MOTORBIKE ON THE TRAIN

LAI CHAU⬆

BINH LU

Many Hill Tribes

SAPA⬆

Rice Terraces

N

THAN GIAO⬆

GREAT SCENERY

×××××× THAN UYEN⬆

Grasslands

Forest

BAO YEN

DIEN BIEN PHU⬆

Hmong Villages

SON LA⬆

PASS

MUONG LA

MU CAI CHANG

High Pass

TU LE White Thai Craft Village

VAN CHAN⬆

YEN BAI

to HA GIANG (NOT HA QUANG)

Thai and White Hmong Villages

MAI SON

Pine forests. Police

TRAM TAU

Also beauti- ful

BAC YEN

PHU YEN⬆

VIET TRI⬆

to THAI NGUYEN

LAOS

WOULD BE 50 KM ON STRAIGHT ROAD. DOUBLE ON REAL ROADS WHICH WIND ENDLESSLY

TRADITIONAL SUGAR CANE/TEA VILLAGES

MOC CHAU
- Beautiful at sunset
- Good yoghurt

FERRY FOR JEEPS, SCARY CANOE CROSSING FOR MOTORBIKES. BOATS THROUGH GREAT SCENERY TO THAI VILLAGES

Some Kharst outcrops

Some Kharst outcrops

MAI CHAU⬆

HOA BINH⬆

HANOI⬆

"RED ZAO" WOMAN WITH MIRROR - SAPA MARKET/LOVE MARKET

Searching out minority villages is great by motorbike. Some roads now very degraded and the dammed Da River makes east-west travel difficult. But other roads remain viable with perhaps the most beautiful areas around Than Uyen and near Tram Tau (though police don't like you visiting the latter). Hill tribe market village, Sapa, is the undisputed traveller centre with good cheap hotels to rest, recuperate and seek information. Bike rental is easier/cheaper in Hanoi. Leaving hot Hanoi don't overlook the need for warm clothes, gloves and provisions for the cold, misty mountains. (Special thanks to Michael Ash for info/photos.)

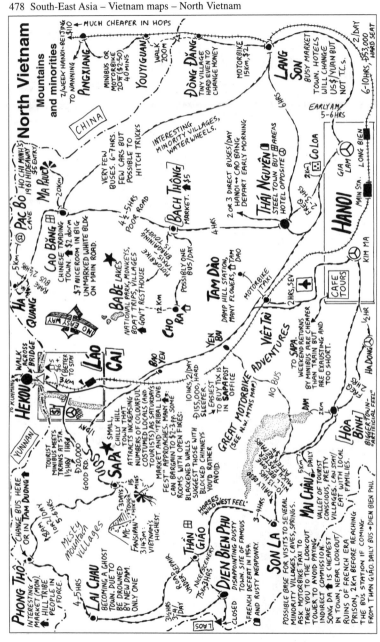

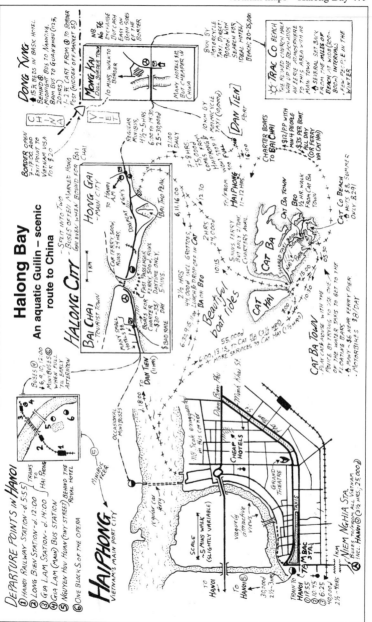

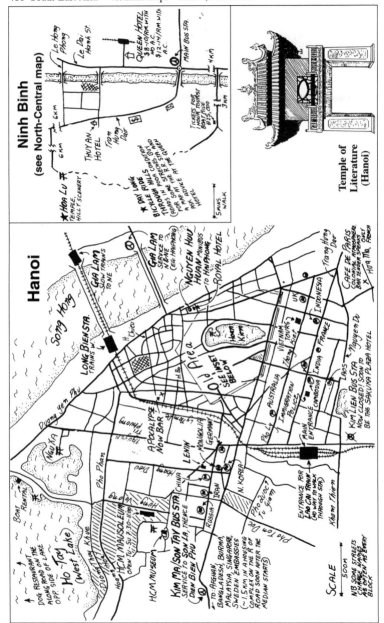

Ninh Binh
(see North-Central map)

QUEEN HOTEL $8-10/RM WITH NO A.C. $12-14/RM WITH A.C.

Le Hong Phong

Le Dai Hanh St.

MAIN BUS STA.

4KM

THUY AN HOTEL

Tran Hung Dao

6KM 6KM

TICKETS FOR 1 HOUR TOURIST BOAT RIDE 25,000

3KM

HOA LU, TEMPLE, HILL SCENERY

★ DAY LONG BICYCLE HILLS CONDITION THRO'N POOR SCENERY AND (ROAD) SOME THE R OF THE QUEEN A MAP/ADVICE AT THE ASK AT HOTEL

5 MINS. WALK

Temple of Literature (Hanoi)

Hanoi

Song Hong

GA LAM SON TRAINS TO NE

GIA LAM SERVICE TO (EG. HAIPHONG)

NGUYEN HUU HUAN MINIBUS TO HAIPHONG

ROYAL HOTEL

Trang Hung Dao

CAFE DE PARIS COLONIAL ATMOSPHERE BAR TENDER SPEAKS ONLY FRENCH

HOA MA

LONG BIEN STA. TRAINS W.

H. Chieu

Old Area

SEE INSET BELOW

Hoan Kiem

UK

VIETNAM Tay Ho TRAVEL TOUR6

INDONESIA

Duong Yen Phu

Pho Phan

Phuong

APOCALYPSE NOW BAR

Le Thanh

MONGOLIA

GERMANY

Hoang Dieu

INDIA FRANCE

LAOS

Nguyen Du

Bao Ly

AUSTRALIA

IMMIGRATION POLICE

CAMBODIA

KIM LIEN BUS STA. NOW CLOSED, SOON TO BE THE SAKURA PLAZA HOTEL

MAIN ENTRANCE

Nguyen Khe

Ho Tay (West Lake)

BOAT RENTAL

HCM MAUSOLEUM OPEN TU-SU 7.30-11.00

HCM MUSEUM

Pho Duc

LEVIN

CHINA

RUSSIA

TRAN

N. KOREA

Pho Duc, To Gram

ENTRANCE FOR LAO CAI TRAIN (NO WAY TO WALK THROUGH STA.)

Kham Thien

KIM MA/SON TAY BUS STA. (DIEN BIEN PHU) SERVICE TO SON LA, THENCE

—TO: AFGHAN, BANGLADESH, BURMA, MALAYSIA, SINGAPORE, SWEDEN EMBASSIES (~1.5 KM IN A HOUSING COMPLEX ON THE R OF ROAD SOON AFTER THE MEDIAN STARTS)

SCALE

500M

NB SOME STREETS CHANGE NAMES AS OFTEN AS EVERY BLOCK

Hanoi – Hoan Kiem Lake

The old area of Hanoi extends to the north and west of Hoan Kiem Lake. The streets were originally named after the types of shops located on them. Today, each street still specialises in one type of merchandise, though what that speciality is has changed:

Street Name	Original speciality	What's sold there today
Hang Tre	Bamboo	Steel rods
Hang Khoai	Potatoes	Rice makers
Ngo Tram	Sculpture	Alcohol
Thuoc Bac	Herbal tea	Ironmongery
Hang Bac	Jewellery	Tombstones
Hang Ruoi	Worms	Bags

Accommodation

There are also dozens of hotels in this area with doubles in the $10-15 range; cheap recommended options are marked on the map. The **Queen**, **Real Darling**, and **Green Bamboo** cafés are traveller hangouts that offer dorms for $5- 6/bed.

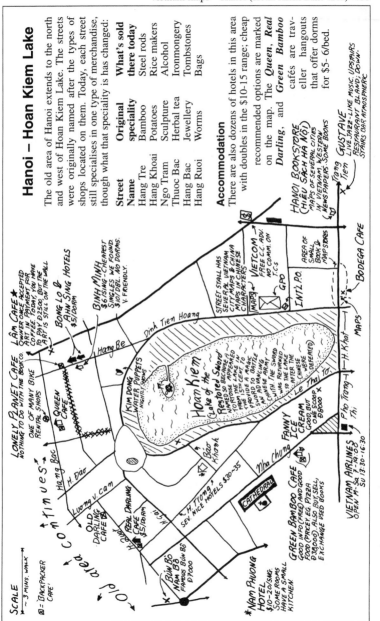

SCALE
~ 3 MINS. WALK
⊞ = BACKPACKER CAFÉ

"O l d ... c o n t i n u e s ... a r e a"

LONELY PLANET CAFE ★
NOTHING TO DO WITH THE BOOK CO.
ONE OF MANY BIKE RENTAL SHOPS

LÂM CAFE ★
OWNER ONCE ACCEPTED ART IN PAYMENT FOR COFFEE. TODAY, YOU HAVE TO PAY D3,500, BUT THE ART IS STILL ON THE WALL

BONG LO & ANH SING HOTELS
$5/DORM

BINH MINH
$6/SING – CHEAPEST SINGLES WE FOUND
$10/ DBL. NO DORMS
V. FRIENDLY.

QUEEN CAFE

Hang Bac

Hang Be

H. Dao

Luong V. Cam

OLD DARLING CAFE ⊞

REAL DARLING CAFE ⊞
$5/DORM

H. Gai

BUN BO NAM BO
FAMOUS BUN BO
D7000

★ NAM PHUONG HOTEL
$10–20/SING; SOME ROOMS HAVE A SMALL KITCHEN

GREEN BAMBOO CAFE
GOOD INFO (FREE) AND GOOD FOOD (PRICEY EG. PIZZA D35,000). ALSO BUY, SELL, EXCHANGE USED BOOKS

Dinh Tien Hoang

Hoan Kiem (Lake of the Restored Sword)
NAMED SO BECAUSE A TORTOISE APPEARED FROM THE LAKE TO PROVIDE A MAGIC SWORD TO AN ADVANCING VIETNAMESE ARMY. WITH THE SWORD, THEY WERE RETURNED TO THE LAKE AFTER THE CHINESE WERE DEFEATED

KIM DONG WATER PUPPETS
NIGHTLY SHOWS

Bao Khanh

Le Thai To

FANNY ICE CREAM
GOOD, BUT PRICEY. ONE SCOOP D8000

Nha chung

H. Trong
SEV. NICE HOTELS $30–35

Pho Trong Thi

H. Khat

MAPS

CATHEDRAL

VIETNAM AIRLINES
OPEN M–SA 8AM–8.00 SU 13.30–16.30

STREET STALL HAS SEVERAL VIETNAM CITY MAPS & CHINA MAPS IN CHINESE CHARACTERS

MAPS

VIETCOM
FREE C.C. ADV.
NO COMM. ON T.C.S

GPO

INT'L PO.

AREA OF SMALL BOOK & MAP STORES

HANOI BOOKSTORE (HIEU SACH HA NOI)
MAPS OF SEVERAL CITIES IN VIETNAM, WESTERN NEWSPAPERS, SOME BOOKS

Trang Tien

TRANG GUSTAVE
LIVE JAZZ-LIKE MUSIC. UPSTAIRS RESTAURANT. BLAND, DOWN-STAIRS OUR ATMOSPHERIC

BODEGA CAFE

GREEN BAMBOO CAFE

North-Central Vietnam

VINH
DULL, TRANSIT TOWN.
~5 MINS WALK~ Duong Le Loi

Duong Phan Boi Chau
Nguyen Si Sach
$ THANH LICH $8/RM
Duong Le Hong Phong
Duong Dinh Cong Trang
MAIN BUS STA.
Tran Hung Dao
SAN BINH DAN $4.50/SING

TO HANOI
BUS: 4 HRS
MINIBUS: 2½ HRS
TO HAIPHONG

NINH BINH
· HOA LU ⊞ · ANCIENT CAPITAL 4KM NW
· HOP-OFF FOR ★ CUC PHUONG N.P.-FOREST, GROTTOS. GOOD TO EXPLORE BY MOTORBIKE. GH IN PARK

TRAIN TO HUE (13 HRS)

[THANH HOA]
⊕THANH HOA HOTEL $10/RM.

3 HRS

6½H

☆SAM SON
NICE BEACH POPULAR WITH VIETNAMESE

[DIEN CHAU]

LAOS

☆Point Ron

KHE SANH
FORMER COMBAT BASE ON THE HCM TRAIL (ALMOST IN-VISIBLE TODAY). NEED PERMIT AND GOV'T GUIDE. CRATERS IN THE AREA FROM LOCALS DIGGING UP SCRAP METAL, NOT FROM BOMBS.

VINH
15KM
4 HRS

[PHUC SON]
ONE OF SEV. HOP-OFFS FOR POINT RON BEACHES

TO SAVANNAKHET

LAO BAO
30 MINS
2 KM. MOTORCYCLE TAXI: Đ5000

KIM LIEN
HCM BIRTH-PLACE, ⊞

3½ HRS

3~4/DAY Đ25,000 4 HRS

DONG HOI
HOP-OFF FOR PHONG NHA CAVES
· ON MAIN ST. NEXT TO GPO (EG. HOA BINH)

⊞ ★ **HUE** ONCE HAD A 'FORBIDDEN CITY' TO RIVAL BEIJING'S, UNTIL IT WAS BOMBED TO RUBBLE-MASSIVE CITY WALLS AND SECTIONS OF THE PALACE REMAIN. OVERGROWN TOMBS AND PAGODAS IN SURROUNDING COUNTRY-SIDE (EG. ★ MINH MANG TOMB 11KM S). ENTRY FEES ADD UP AT $5/EACH.

DONG HA
HOP-OFF FOR D.M.Z. TOURS
⊕ HAI LY GH-$6/SING

AN HOA BUS STA.
· 1KM N OF RIVER TO ALL MAJOR DESTINATIONS NORTH OF HUE

★ The Citadel
The Imperial Palace & Old Hue

MAIN GATE
PEOPLE'S GATE

DONG BA LOCAL BUSES

Large moat

~Perfume~R.~

TO LAO BAO & LAOS

DAILY DIRECT BUS

3½ HRS

THUAN AN☆
BEACH SET IN SCENIC LAGOON
Đ5000

Le Loi Rd.

MORIN $6/SING
EXP. BUS TO SAIGON

★ THANH THUY (#46 LE LOI) ATMOSPHERIC

HUE
SEE MAP

#2 HOTEL
MAIN HANG-OUT. $7/SING.

MINMOSA $8/RM. WITH A.C.

★ #3 CAFE
①. HANG-OUT.
⊕ BIKES & MOTORBIKE FOR RENT

⊕ AU CUU BUS STA.
· 1KM S OF LE LOI RD.
· TO MAJOR DESTINATIONS SOUTH OF HUE

BUS: 6 HRS Đ22,000
MINIBUS: 5 HRS Đ30,500

TO DA NANG

~10 MINS WALK~

HUE IS WONDERFUL TO EXPLORE BY BICYCLE. MAPS ARE SOLD AROUND TOWN (I.E. AT THE TRAIN STA.) AND IN HANOI AND HO CHI MINH CITY

↓ SEE SOUTH-CENTRAL VIETNAM MAP

HUE TO: HANOI - LOCAL: Đ30,000, 21-40H
TOURIST: $22, 12~18 HRS
NINH BINH - 17~19, Đ60,000
VINH - 12 HRS., Đ45,000
KONTUM - 14 HRS., Đ48,000

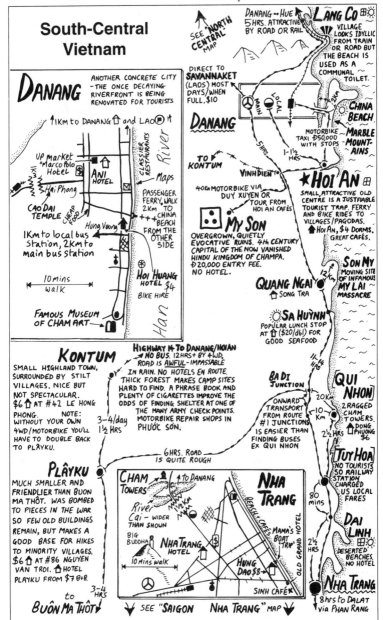

South-Central Vietnam

SEE "NORTH CENTRAL" MAP

DANANG ↔ HUE 5 HRS. ATTRACTIVE BY ROAD OR RAIL

LANG CO
VILLAGE LOOKS IDYLLIC FROM TRAIN OR ROAD BUT THE BEACH IS USED AS A COMMUNAL TOILET.

DANANG

ANOTHER CONCRETE CITY - THE ONCE DECAYING RIVERFRONT IS BEING RENOVATED FOR TOURISTS

DIRECT TO **SAVANNAKET** (LAOS) MOST DAYS/WHEN FULL. $10

DANANG

MAIN / LOCAL

CHINA BEACH

MOTORBIKE TAXI Đ50000 WITH STOPS

MARBLE MOUNTAINS

TO KONTUM

5 HRS

1-1½ HRS

↑ 1KM to DANANG ⌂ and LAO ⊕

UP market "Marco Polo" Hotel

ANI HOTEL

CLOSIER RESTAURANTS

River

Maps

Hai Phong

CHEAP FOOD

CAO DAI TEMPLE

PASSENGER FERRY. WALK 2KM TO +++ CHINA BEACH FROM THE OTHER SIDE

Hung Vuong

HOI HUANG HOTEL $4 BIKE HIRE

Han

1KM to local bus Station, 2KM to main bus station

⊢ 10 mins walk ⊣

FAMOUS MUSEUM OF CHAM ART →

VINH DIEN

40km MOTORBIKE VIA DUY XUYEN OR TOUR FROM HOI AN CAFÉS

MY SON
OVERGROWN, QUIETLY EVOCATIVE RUINS. 4TH CENTURY CAPITAL OF THE NOW VANISHED HINDU KINGDOM OF CHAMPA. Đ 20,000 ENTRY FEE. NO HOTEL.

★ **HOI AN**
SMALL, ATTRACTIVE OLD CENTRE IS A JUSTIFIABLE TOURIST TRAP, FERRY AND BIKE RIDES TO VILLAGES/PAGODAS.
↑ HOI AN, $4 DORMS. GREAT CAFÉS.

12

SON MY
MOVING SITE OF INFAMOUS MY LAI MASSACRE

QUANG NGAI
⌂ SONG TRA

☼ **SA HUỲNH**
POPULAR LUNCH STOP AT ⌂ ($20/dbl) FOR GOOD SEAFOOD

1-1½ HRS

KONTUM

SMALL HIGHLAND TOWN, SURROUNDED BY STILT VILLAGES. NICE BUT NOT SPECTACULAR. $6 ⌂ AT #42 LE HONG PHONG. NOTE: WITHOUT YOUR OWN 4WD/MOTORBIKE YOU'LL HAVE TO DOUBLE BACK TO PLÀYKU.

HIGHWAY 14 TO DANANG/HOIAN
→ NO BUS. 12 HRS+ BY 4WD. ROAD IS AWFUL-IMPASSABLE IN RAIN. NO HOTELS EN ROUTE. THICK FOREST MAKES CAMP SITES HARD TO FIND. A PHRASE BOOK AND PLENTY OF CIGARETTES IMPROVE THE ODDS OF FINDING SHELTER AT ONE OF THE MANY ARMY CHECK POINTS. MOTORBIKE REPAIR SHOPS IN PHƯỚC SƠN.

BA DI JUNCTION

ONWARD TRANSPORT FROM ROUTE #1 JUNCTIONS IS EASIER THAN FINDING BUSES EX QUI NHON

20km

10 Km

QUI NHON
2 RAGGED CHAM TOWERS
↑ DONG PHUONG $6
2½ HRS

3-4/day 1½ HRS

6 HRS. ROAD IS QUITE ROUGH

TUY HOA
NO TOURISTS SO RAILWAY STATION CHARGED US LOCAL FARES

PLÀYKU

MUCH SMALLER AND FRIENDLIER THAN BUON MA THÔT. WAS BOMBED TO PIECES IN THE WAR SO FEW OLD BUILDINGS REMAIN, BUT MAKE A GOOD BASE FOR HIKES TO MINORITY VILLAGES. $6 ⌂ AT #86 NGUYEN VAN TROI. ⌂ HOTEL PLÀYKU FROM $7 B+B.

CHAM TOWERS
↑ to DANANG

River Cai – WIDER THAN SHOWN

BIG BUDDHA

NHA TRANG

BEACH CAFÉS

Nha Trang HOTEL $

⊢ 10 mins walk ⊣

MAMA'S BOAT TRIP

OLD GRAND HOTEL

HUNG DAO $8 →

SINH CAFÉ

80 mins

DAI LINH
DESERTED BEACHES NO HOTEL

2½ HRS

3-4 HRS

to **BUÔN MA THÔT** ↓

↓ SEE "SAIGON NHA TRANG" MAP ↓

NHA TRANG
8 hrs to DALAT via PHAN RANG

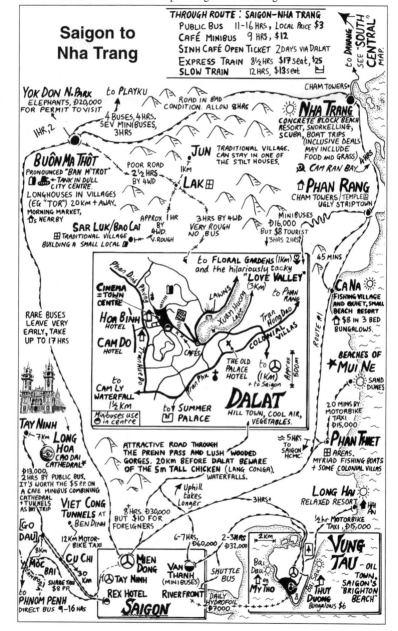

Saigon to Nha Trang

THROUGH ROUTE : SAIGON–NHA TRANG
- PUBLIC BUS 11–16 HRS, LOCAL PRICE $3
- CAFÉ MINIBUS 9 HRS, $12
- SINH CAFÉ OPEN TICKET 2 DAYS VIA DALAT
- EXPRESS TRAIN 8½ HRS $17 seat, $25
- SLOW TRAIN 12 HRS, $13 seat

to DANANG SEE "SOUTH" CENTRAL MAP.

CHAM TOWERS

YOK DON N. PARK
ELEPHANTS, Đ20,000
FOR PERMIT TO VISIT

to PLAYKU

ROAD IN BAD CONDITION. ALLOW 8 HRS.

NHA TRANG
CONCRETE BLOCK BEACH RESORT, SNORKELLING, SCUBA, BOAT TRIPS (INCLUSIVE DEALS MAY INCLUDE FOOD AND GRASS)

CAM RAN BAY

1 HR, 2

4 BUSES, 4 HRS. SEV MINIBUSES, 3 HRS.

BUÔN MA THÔT
PRONOUNCED "BAN M'TROT"
TANK IN DULL CITY CENTRE.
LONGHOUSES IN VILLAGES (EG "TOR") 20 KM + AWAY.
MORNING MARKET, NEARBY

JUN TRADITIONAL VILLAGE. CAN STAY IN ONE OF THE STILT HOUSES.

1 KM

POOR ROAD 2½ HRS BY 4WD

LAK

3 HRS BY 4WD VERY ROUGH NO BUS

PHAN RANG
CHAM TOWERS/ TEMPLE
UGLY STRIPTOWN

MINIBUSES Đ16,000 BUT $8 TOURIST 3HRS 2HRS?

SAR LUK/BAO CAI
TRADITIONAL VILLAGE BUILDING A SMALL LOCAL

APPROX 1 HR BY 4WD. V. ROUGH

45 MINS

to FLORAL GARDENS (1KM) and the hilariously tacky **"LOVE VALLEY"** (3KM)

CA NA
FISHING VILLAGE AND QUIET, SMALL BEACH RESORT
$8 IN 3 BED BUNGALOWS.

RARE BUSES LEAVE VERY EARLY, TAKE UP TO 17 HRS

CINEMA = TOWN CENTRE

Phan Dinh Phung

LAWNS

to PHAN RANG

HOA BINH HOTEL

Xuan Huong Lake

Tran Hung Dao

COLONIAL VILLAS

BEACHES OF MUI NE

SAND DUNES

CAM DO HOTEL

CAFÉS

THE OLD PALACE HOTEL

to (1KM) + to SAIGON

Approx 500m

Tran Hung Dao

Tran Phu

to **CAM LY WATERFALL** 1½ KM

to SUMMER PALACE

DALAT
HILL TOWN, COOL AIR, VEGETABLES.

20 MINS BY MOTORBIKE TAXI Đ15,000

PHAN THIET
AREAS.
MYRIAD FISHING BOATS + SOME COLONIAL VILLAS

Minibuses use in centre

TAY NINH

7 KM **LONG HOA CAO DAI CATHEDRAL**
Đ13,000, 2 HRS BY PUBLIC BUS. IT'S WORTH THE $5 P.P. ON A CAFÉ MINIBUS COMBINING CATHEDRAL + TUNNELS AS DAY TRIP

ATTRACTIVE ROAD THROUGH THE PRENN PASS AND LUSH WOODED GORGES. 20 KM BEFORE DALAT BEWARE OF THE 5m TALL CHICKEN (LANG CONGA). WATERFALLS.

≈ 5 HRS TO SAIGON! HCMC.

Uphill takes longer

LONG HAI
RELAXED RESORT

HAI AN

VIET CONG TUNNELS AT BEN DINH

8 HRS, Đ30,000 BUT $10 FOR FOREIGNERS

3 HRS+

½ hr MOTORBIKE TAXI Đ15,000

GO DAU

12 KM MOTORBIKE TAXI

6–7 HRS, Đ60,000

2–3 HRS Đ32,000

2 KM

Bai Dau eg My Tho

VUNG TAU – OIL TOWN, SAIGON'S "BRIGHTON" BEACH

8 KM

CU CHI

30 KM

MIEN DONG

VAN THANH (MINIBUSES)

SHUTTLE BUS

MOC BAI

SHARE TAXI $8 PP

to **PHNOM PENH**
DIRECT BUS 9–16 HRS

TAY NINH

REX HOTEL

SAIGON

RIVERFRONT

DAILY HYDROFOIL Đ7000

THUY DUONG Bungalows $6

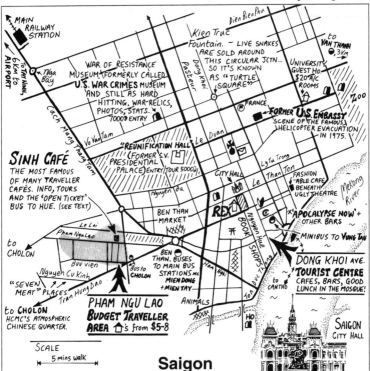

Saigon

Saigon (the area shown above) combined with Cho Lon form Ho Chi Minh City. This bustling place is Vietnam's economic engine and at the leading edge of its changes. If Hanoi is like a grandfather's house, dusty but full of interesting bits and pieces, then Saigon City is like a college student's flat – open, active, and full of life. HCM City is used as a transit point by most travellers but it's a city that grows on those who stay for more than a few days.

Transport

Buses from Cambodia terminate at Phnom Penh Garage (115 Nguyen Hue, near Rex Hotel). Buses from N of HCM use Mien Dong Bus Stn. Local buses (eg. from Vung Tau) operate out of Van Thanh Stn. Cho Lon Tay Bus Stn is for buses from Mytho and (maybe) Ben Tre.

To/from all bus stations there is a city bus to Ben Than Market. From all bus stations (except Mien Tay) it's $1 or less by motorbike taxi to the Pham Ngu Lao 'traveller ghetto'. From the airport costs $5+ by taxi, or you could walk five minutes to the main road and take a $1 motorbike taxi.

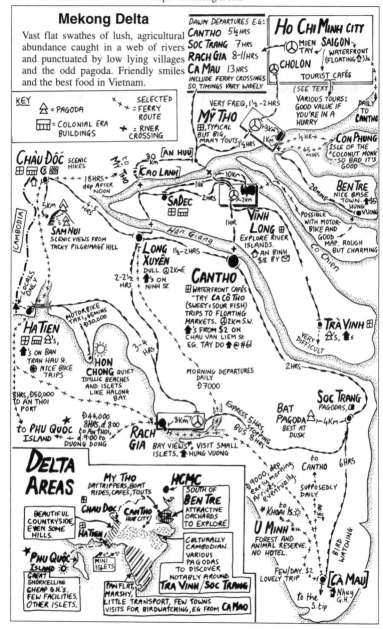

Mekong Delta

Vast flat swathes of lush, agricultural abundance caught in a web of rivers and punctuated by low lying villages and the odd pagoda. Friendly smiles and the best food in Vietnam.

DAWN DEPARTURES E.G:
CANTHO 5½ HRS
SOC TRANG 7 HRS
RACH GIA 8-11 HRS
CA MAU 13 HRS
INCLUDE FERRY CROSSINGS SO TIMINGS VARY WIDELY

HO CHI MINH CITY
MIEN SAIGON
TAY WATERFRONT (FLOATING)
CHOLON TOURIST CAFÉS
(SEE TEXT)
VARIOUS TOURS: GOOD VALUE IF YOU'RE IN A HURRY
DAILY TO CANTHO

KEY
⌂ = PAGODA
⊞ = COLONIAL ERA BUILDINGS
×⁺×⁺× = SELECTED = FERRY ROUTE
+ = RIVER CROSSING

VERY FREQ, 1½-2 HRS
MỸ THO
⊞, TYPICAL BUT BIG, MANY TOUTS
3 KM
1 KM
½ HR +
1½ HRS
CON PHUNG ISLE OF THE "COCONUT MONK" - SO BAD IT'S GOOD
45 - 65 MINS

CHÂU ĐỐC SCENIC HIKES
⊞ ⌂ ▦
18 HRS + dep AFTER NOON
5KM
4.5 HRS
[AN HUU]
[CAO LANH]
SADEC
⊞ ⌂
30 HRS
10 km
1HR
2 KM
2 HRS
1HR

BEN TRE NICE BASE TOWN. HUNG VUONG #45
20 MINS
POSSIBLE WITH MOTOR-BIKE AND GOOD MAP. ROUGH BUT CHARMING
Cổ Chien

CAMBODIA

SAM NUI SCENIC VIEWS FROM TACKY PILGRIMAGE HILL

LONG XUYÊN DULL. @2 KM E.
⌂'s ON NINH St.
1½-2 HRS
2-2½ HRS

VĨNH LONG ⊞ EXPLORE RIVER ISLANDS.
⌂ AN BINH $8 BY ✉

Han Giang

CANTHO
⊞ WATERFRONT CAFÉS TRY CA CÔ THO (SWEET + SOUR FISH) TRIPS TO FLOATING MARKETS. @2 KM S.W.
⌂'s FROM $2 ON CHAU VAN LIEM St EG. TAY DO ⌂ @ #61

TRÀ VINH ⊞
⌂'s, ⌂'s
VERY DIFFICULT

HA TIEN ⊞ ▦ ⌂'s,
⌂'s ON BAN TRAN HAU St. ❀ NICE BIKE TRIPS
MOTORBIKE TAXI, 45 MINS Đ30,000
LOCALS ONLY

HON CHONG QUIET IDYLLIC BEACHES AND ISLETS LIKE HALONG BAY.

MORNING DEPARTURES DAILY Đ7000
3-4 HRS

LONELY TRIP
2 HRS

SOC TRANG PAGODAS, ⊞
4 KM
BAT PAGODA ⌂ BEST AT DUSK

8 HRS, Đ50,000 TO AN THOI PORT
Đ44,000 8 HRS, Đ 8:00 TO AN THOI, Đ 9:00 to DUONG DONG

to PHU QUOC ISLAND

RACH GIA
8 KM
BAY VIEWS. VISIT SMALL ISLETS. ⌂ HUNG VUONG

EXPRESS 5 HRS, STOPPING BUS 8 HRS

Đ9000, dep early morning. Arrives eventually.
to CANTHO
6 HRS
SUPPOSEDLY DAILY
to KHOAI IS.
BIRD WATCHING

DELTA AREAS

MY THO DAYTRIPPERS, BOAT RIDES, CAFÉS, TOUTS
HCMC
SOUTH OF BEN TRE ATTRACTIVE ORCHARDS TO EXPLORE

CHÂU ĐỐC
CANTHO HUE CITY
HA TIEN
BEAUTIFUL COUNTRYSIDE EVEN SOME HILLS.
MINI ISLETS
CULTURALLY CAMBODIAN. VARIOUS PAGODAS TO DISCOVER NOTABLY AROUND TRA VINH / SOC TRANG

★ PHU QUOC ISLAND ❂
GREAT SNORKELLING CHEAP G.H.'s. FEW FACILITIES. OTHER ISLETS.

FAN FLAT, MARSHY, LITTLE TRANSPORT, FEW TOWNS VISITS FOR BIRDWATCHING, EG FROM CA MAO

U MINH FOREST AND ANIMAL RESERVE. NO HOTEL.
FEW/DAY. $2
to the S. tip

BIRD WATCHING

[CÀ MAU]
⌂ Nhuy G.H.

Mekong Delta transportation

'Café' tours rush from town to riverside town for a very reasonable price. However, as there's nothing that really rates as a sight, you may feel happier retiring to a random town that takes your fancy and getting to know it. Any larger town will have its riverside cameos and cafés and getting around is fairly easy.

Public buses seem to go from everywhere to everywhere else except from where you happen to be. If so, head onto the main highway (usually 2-3km from town centres) and flag one down. Beware that roads tend to flood in summer. More relaxing/frustrating depending on your schedule are the inter-town ferries. Waterways outnumber roads and very slow boats go almost anywhere – if there appears to be no service you're probably at the wrong pier. Some docks are well out of town. Take food for the journey and be prepared to arrive whenever.

Chartering a boat is worthwhile as a way to cruise the backwaters at your own pace, and can be very cheaply done if you find an unofficial boatman. Police want all foreigners to use official (pricey) tourist craft claiming (often justifiably) that local boats are unsafe. So don't be overly alarmed if the 'boat' you've hired initially turns out to be a motorbike whisking you off to a secluded jetty beyond official view. My Tho is most accustomed to tourists and there are (too) many boat touts ready to help you. In Ben Tre things are more relaxed and the waterways are more scenic. Bargain carefully.

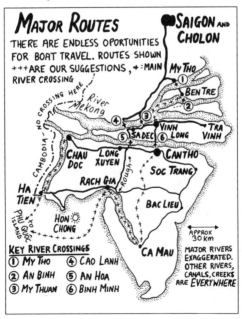

Where does the boat to .... leave from? = *O dau don tau be di ....?*

Cambodia

Most travellers venture into Cambodia to see Angkor Wat. With its massive arches, overgrown stone carvings and temples half-suffocated by contorted trees, Angkor certainly ranks among the most impressive sites in the continent. But there are other temple complexes in Cambodia, too, as well as pristine beaches, mountain hikes, tropical jungles, and an ancient culture which was once amongst the most influential in Asia. But with political instability and a civil war still smouldering, care-free exploration is currently impossible.

Cambodia has experienced various periods of instability since its independence from France in 1953. The decision of Cambodian Prince Sihanouk to side with Hanoi late in the Vietnam War brought bombing by the Americans. A coup forced the prince to flee the country. And another civil war brought the Khmer Rouge to power, thus beginning the cruellest period of Cambodia history.

Pol Pot's Khmer Rouge believed fervently in the seemingly self-contradictory goal of a 'modernised, totally agrarian society'. They murdered those who had contact with the West, those who had an education, those who might have had an education because they wore glasses, anyone with a possible connection to royalty or wealth. And, of course, anyone who resisted them. In under four years a fifth of the population had died or fled, cities had been depopulated, money had been abolished and many cultural monuments had been deliberately defaced. Those who were not killed were sent as slave labour to communal farms, as depicted in the powerful movie *The Killing Fields*. There is a 'Killing Fields' museum of remembrance near Choeng Ek, 10km outside of Phnom Penh.

The Khmer Rouge terror was finally ended in 1978/9 as a result of Vietnam's invasion. The Khmer Rouge were forced into the hills and Vietnam established its own puppet government, eventually led by a Cambodian named Hun Sen. Strangely, the international outcry to the Vietnamese occupation was greater than that to the Khmer Rouge atrocities and Vietnam was pressured into withdrawing from Cambodia in 1989. A year later the United Nations

---

❏ **W&M's country ratings – Cambodia**
● **Expense $$$** Budget for high miscellaneous costs (eg the $15-60 entry charge for Angkor Wat).
● **Value for money ✔✔✔** Typical for a developing Asian country.
● **Getting around ✔✔** Safety problems limit travel on many routes.
● **English spoken ✔✔** Little in rural areas but OK in Phnom Penh and Siem Reap.
● **Woman alone ✔✔✔✔** The dangers are similar for men and women.
● **For vegetarians ✔✔✔** It's usually possible to find at least one meat-free dish.

moved in for a transitional period, which was the most peaceful in Cambodia since independence. In 1993, democracy was established under a new constitution, Prince Sihanouk returned as a ceremonial monarch, international aid money began pouring in. Elections were called – it seemed as if all would finally be well in Cambodia.

Unfortunately, since the 1993 election and the subsequent withdraw of UN troops, safety and stability have suffered. The Khmer Rouge boycotted the elections and continued fighting, especially in the north and north-western areas, financed by illegal timbering and kidnappings (a Western tourist was said to be worth $50,000). The election was won by Prince Ranariddh, son of (the now King) Sihanouk. Ranariddh, took 45% of the vote but was forced to share the power with Hun Sen (33%) thanks to the latter's tremendous power with the bureaucrats and army. The co-prime ministers engaged in a continuing power struggle while corruption became rife, underpaid soldiers took to robbery, and drug runners turned Cambodia into the main trans-shipment point for Burmese heroin. In 1997, Hun Sen violently took control of the government, and Price Ranariddh was forced to flee the country. Western nations protested against the coup by withdrawing most economic aid, causing the country to fall further into poverty.

❏ **Geo-political information – Cambodia**
Population: 11 million (1997), 10.3m (1993), 5.7m (1962).
Area: 181,000 sq km.
Capital: Phnom Penh (900,000 in 1991).
Other major cities: Battambang, Siem Riep, Sihanoukville (75,000).
GNP per capita: $700 (1994), average monthly income US$18.
Currency history: Riel/US$1 – Feb 1998: R3585, Oct 1997: R3200, Dec 1995: R2300, Dec 1994: R2600, Sept 1994: R2800, 1993: R2400, 1992: R2800, 1991: R500, 1988: R159. Money was abolished altogether in 1978 under Pol Pot.
Major exports/economy: Formerly rice but the economy is still tottering after the civil war. Khmer Rouge controlled areas are being rapidly deforested and timber products etc smuggled into Thailand.
Ethnic mix: Khmer (93%), Vietnamese (4%), and Chinese (3%).
Official language: Khmer.
Religious mix: Buddhist (95% pre-1976 when Therevada Buddhism was the state religion). Christianity was legalised in 1990 but estimates put the number of believers at only 20,000.
Landmarks of national history: **10-14th centuries**: Khmer Empire (great regional power). **1431**: Angkor sacked by Thai army. **1863**: French colonial protectorate declared. **1949**: Independence within the French Union. **1955**: Kingdom established. **1970**: The kingdom was overthrown (in 1975) after the civil war, by the Khmer Rouge. It is estimated that over a million were killed as the entire population was moved out of cities into Pol Pot's communist agrarian experiment. **1978/9**: The Khmer Rouge was ousted from power by the Vietnamese invasion. **1992**: UNTAC oversaw the restoration of the constitutional monarchy.
Leader: Hun Sen, sole Prime Minister since September 1997.
Pressing political issues: Continuing Khmer Rouge insurgency, land-mine clearance, shattered economy, smuggling of resources and illegal forestry.

As Cambodia now enters a period under a new (or returned) dictator, it has had to come to terms with an old one. Pol Pot, the murderous Khmer Rouge leader, was betrayed by his own men and turned into Cambodia authorities in 1997. He emerged from years in the jungle half-dead with malaria. After a brief communal trial, he was spared the death sentence and put under house arrest. In his first (and probably last) news interview he timidly denied personal responsibility for the genocide of his reign.

All of this leaves travellers wondering how safe it is to visit Cambodia. The answer depends on where you want to go (see Dangers box). Even during the coup in September 1997, no tourists were injured in Angkor or Phnom Penh. However, the area around the Thai border remains very dangerous. One foolhardy British cyclist pedalled right through the most perilous zone from Batdambang and made it to the Poipet border, scared but alive. Others have been less lucky. Once you arrive in Phnom Penh read the newspapers, visit your embassy (though they'll overstate the risks) and, best of all, talk to other travellers and especially aid workers. The notice board in Phnom Penh's Capitol Guest house is helpful. Wherever you go in Cambodia, keep alert. Soldiers are ubiquitous, and if you suddenly find yourself in an area without any, beware. If children refuse to join you on a walk in a rural area, it probably means there are land mines.

Thousands of travellers visit Cambodia without problems. Enjoy the country, but please be careful.

❏ **Essential information for tourists – Cambodia**

● **Visa** Required. Tourist visas allow a one-month stay ($20) and are generally issued in two to three days. They are also available on arrival at Phnom Penh airport. Extensions (for up to three months) are possible through the Ministry of National Security. NB No visas are issued on arrival at land borders.

● **Currency** Riel. US$1=R3585. Bring US$ cash – notes of various denominations are helpful.

● **Time zone** 7 hours ahead of GMT (the same as the rest of Indochina).

● **Religious tone** A deeply Buddhist country.

● **Special dangers** Khmer Rouge rebels operate in many parts of the country; watch out for land mines, ambushes and extortion from underpaid soldiers.

● **Health factors** Malaria is a problem in many regions.

● **Social conventions** Cambodia is largely a Buddhist country and the standard conventions apply.

● **Typical traveller destinations** Phnom Penh, Angkor Wat.

● **Highlights** Angkor Wat.

● **When to go** The temperature in most of Cambodia remains a constant 34°C to 39°C year around. October to April is the driest time. May to September is called the wet season, though only in the Cardamon Mountains are you likely to find heavy day-long downpours – most wet season rain confines itself to an afternoon shower.

● **Key tips** Determine the current safety situation. Transport on all but the most major routes stops around 3pm. Travelling in the morning is safer and easier. Use the safety chart opposite and talk to other travellers.

PRACTICAL INFORMATION
Visas and formalities
Getting a visa is easy – see Essential Information box.

Transport
● **Bus** The bus system is not extensive due to the lawlessness in rural areas but travel is inexpensive; taking a bus is more a matter of determining road safety than the fare.

● **Train** Trains are easy targets for the Khmer Rouge who have a habit of blowing up the tracks.

● **Air** Domestic flights operate out of Phnom Penh to Batdambang, Kaoh Kong, Sihanoukville, Siem Reap, and Stung Treng. They are relatively safe and moderately priced though the cost of the tickets doesn't always reflect the distance flown: Pnomh Penh-Siem Reap, 230km, $45; Pnomh Penh-Sihanoukville, 180km, $70. Baggage allowance is a paltry 10kg. Domestic airport tax $4. International $8.

● **Boat** Speedboats are considered to be the safest form of ground transport. The boat between Phnom Penh and Siem Reap is especially popular. It is possible to save around $10 by taking a shared taxi to Kampong Chhnang and catching the speedboat from the police checkpoint there. Since this isn't an official stop, you can bargain for the cost of the ticket – most travellers pay R30-35,000. There are also speedboats on portions of the Mekong.

Slow boats are very slow, especially during the dry season; in November-December of dry years slow boats might not run at all.

● **Motorbike** This is a popular means of exploring eastern and southern Cambodia. Motorbikes can easily be rented in Phnom Penh but it's important to be extra diligent about checking the current safety situation before heading too far afield.

● **Bicycle** Angkor Wat is a brilliant place to explore by bicycle. The problem is you can't rent bikes there. It is likely that tour operators and/or taxi drivers somehow pre-

---

❏ Safety in Cambodia
The safety situation in Cambodia is usually discussed by highway. This table gives an overview of the approximate levels of risk as of November 1997 but it's important to check the latest reports locally before setting out on any of the roads.

Highway	Route section	Safety condition
Hwy 1	Pnomh Penh-Vietnam border	Consistently safe.
Hwy 2	Pnomh Penh-Takeo	Safe. Road in good condition.
Hwy 2	Takeo-Vietnam border	Many smugglers and bandits. The border is closed here.
Hwy 3	Pnomh Penh-Kampot	The road itself is safe. Nearby rural areas are not.
Hwy 4	Pnomh Penh-Sihanoukville	Safe-ish since mid-1995, after years of acute danger.
Hwy 5	Pnomh Penh-Kampong Chhnang	Usually safe
Hwy 5	K Chhnang-Batdambang	Very variable but improving
Hwy 5	Batdambang-Sisophon	Very unsafe.
Hwy 6	Hwy 7 jctn-Siem Reap	Variable but typically dangerous.
Hwy 6	Siem Reap-Poipet	The most dangerous road in Cambodia
Hwy 7	Udong-Stung Treng	The Kampong Cham-Kratie stretch is unstable.
Hwy 7	Stung Treng-Lao border	'Relatively' safe since 1995.
Hwy 19	Stung Treng-Lumpat jctn	Mostly safe.
Hwy 19	Lumpat-Vietnam border	More dangerous as you head east.

❑ Shoot for the stars

After years of war and strife, guns have become an unfortunate fixture of Cambodian culture. Many men today carry a gun, partly for self protection and partly as a status symbol. And several have let the power a pistol yields go to their heads. So much so that while it is raining, people in Cambodia will shoot at the clouds to make it stop. Before a solar eclipse in 1995, newspapers ran advertisements asking people not shoot at the sky. When the eclipse came, expatriates in Cambodia were surprised at how little gun fire they heard. 'If there is one thing Cambodians are good at,' we overheard one say, 'it is at following orders.'

---

vent guest houses in Siem Reap from renting them. However bicycles can be easily rented in Phnom Penh and transported to Siem Reap by boat.

Money

Cambodia might have the *riel* but the US dollar is the de facto currency. Dollars are accepted (and preferred) everywhere. Indeed, for many larger purchases (ie over $8) you will be required to pay in dollars. Some cheap hotels (around $5) demand greenbacks, too.

There is no black market so if you pay for a R1000 item with a $1 bill, you will get R2500 change.

Thai Baht (cash) are easily exchangeable for riel throughout Cambodia, and can be used in some stores in Batdambang.

Travellers' cheques are difficult to change and commission is always charged. The two Phnom Penh banks which will oblige are **Foreign Trade Bank of Cambodia**, 24 Norodom Boulevard, and **Bangkok Bank** which is next door. They also offer Visa credit card cash advances.

Staying in touch

● **Mail** American Express (☎ 23-26648), c/o Diethelm Travel, No 8 Lenin Blvd, Phnom Penh, will hold mail.
● **Phone** International country code: +855. Phnom Penh: 23.

Activities

● **Hiking** The only area likely to be safe from both land mines and the Khmer Rouge is north-eastern and central Ratanakiri Province.
● **Work** At the time of writing, Phnom Penh was desperate for English teachers. One traveller was hired at $8/hour even though he was only staying for a week. Experienced teachers who were willing to stay for a few months were making $16-20/hour.

❑ Meeting the locals

● **The people** Cambodians are generally much more anti-Vietnam than anti-Khmer Rouge. Running around Phnom Penh yelling 'Up with Pol Pot!' might not bring you more than a few dirty looks; walking around silently with a Ho Chi Minh t-shirt could bring you some threats.
● **Language** The script is a modern variant of the 1700-year old Khmer writing. The alphabet has more letters than any other.
  Some phrases in Cambodian:
         Hello – *chum-reep su-or*
         How's it going? – *sok sabay ta?*
         Thank you – *or koun*
         This food is good – *mohope nis ch-gang*
         Is the road to _____ safe? – *tei plov tov _____ sroul ta?*
         Cheap hotel room – *hotel thork* ('hotel' is commonly used)

Further information

● **Maps and books** New maps and guidebooks of all sorts are available in Phnom Penh at Bert's Books. However, a trip to Phnom Penh and Angkor is easy enough without a guidebook – a background book (such as Passport's *Angkor*) may be more useful. Both Lonely Planet and Nelles have guides specifically on Cambodia. Cambodia is also included in most South East Asian guides (such as Let's Go's) and Indochina guides (such as Moon's and Bradt's). Most Western map companies include Cambodia on a map with Vietnam and Laos. One exception is the International Travel Map company whose Cambodia-only map is excellent.

The best/most accessible city map of Phnom Penh is in every issue of the Phnom Penh Post newspaper.

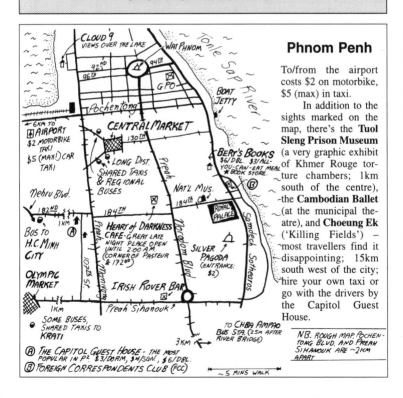

Phnom Penh

To/from the airport costs $2 on motorbike, $5 (max) in taxi.

In addition to the sights marked on the map, there's the **Tuol Sleng Prison Museum** (a very graphic exhibit of Khmer Rouge torture chambers; 1km south of the centre), the **Cambodian Ballet** (at the municipal theatre), and **Choeung Ek** ('Killing Fields') – most travellers find it disappointing; 15km south west of the city; hire your own taxi or go with the drivers by the Capitol Guest House.

NB. ROUGH MAP. POCHENTONG BLVD. AND PREAH SIHANOUK ARE ~2KM APART

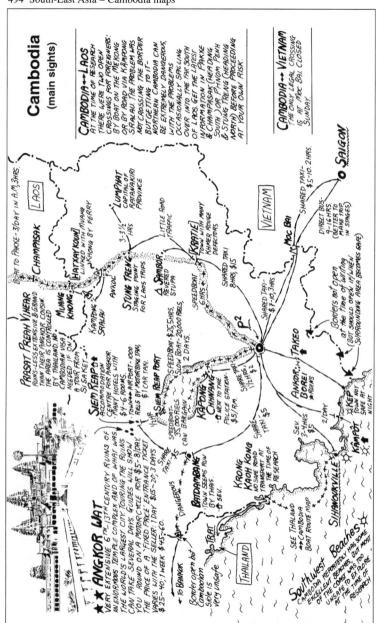

Cambodia
(main sights)

CAMBODIA ↔ LAOS
AT THE TIME OF RESEARCH THERE WERE TWO OPEN CROSSINGS FOR FOREIGNERS BY BOAT ON THE MEKONG OR BY ROAD VIA KÂMPONG SRALAU. THE PROBLEM WAS NOT CROSSING THE BORDER BUT GETTING TO IT — NORTHERN CAMBODIA CAN BE EXTREMELY DANGEROUS, WITH THE PROBLEMS OCCASIONALLY SPILLING OVER INTO THE FAR SOUTH OF LAOS. GET THE LATEST INFORMATION IN PAKSE & CHAMPASAK (HEADING SOUTH) OR PHNOM PENH & STUNG TRENG (HEADING NORTH) BEFORE PROCEEDING AT YOUR OWN RISK.

CAMBODIA ↔ VIETNAM
THE ONLY LEGAL CROSSING IS AT MOC BAI. CLOSED SUNDAY.

BOAT TO PAKSE - 3/DAY IN A.M, 3 HRS.

LAOS

CHAMPASAK

MUANG KHONG

[HATXAYKOUN] LINKED WITH MUANG KHONG BY FERRY

★ LUMPHAT CAPITAL OF RATANAKIRI PROVINCE

3-3½ HRS

PRASAT PREAH VIHEAR RUINS-LESS EXTENSIVE & GRAND THAN THEIR ANGKOR COUSIN. THE AREA IS CONTROLLED BY THAILAND. NO CAMBODIAN VISA NEEDED IF ON A TOUR FROM SI SAKET.

KÂMPONG SRALAU

AVKOL

STUNG TRENG STAGING POINT FOR LAOS TRIPS

SAMBOR REVERED STUPA

LITTLE ROAD TRAFFIC

[KRATIE] TOWN WITH MANY KHMER ROUGE DEFECTORS

SHARED TAXI $15

SPEEDBOAT 6 HRS

VIETNAM

SAIGON

MOC BAI

SHARED TAXI - $5-10, 2 HRS.

SHARED TAXI - $7-10, 3 HRS.

DIRECT BUS - 9-16 HRS (BETTER TO MAKE TRIP IN STAGES)

SHARED TAXI - $7-10, 3 HRS

P?

★ ANGKOR WAT
VERY EXTENSIVE 6TH-13TH CENTURY RUINS OF A ENORMOUS TEMPLE COMPLEX AND OF WHAT WAS THE WORLD'S LARGEST CITY. TOURING THE RUINS CAN TAKE SEVERAL DAYS. GUIDES WILL SHOW YOU ROUND ON A MOTORBIKE FOR $5-8/DAY. THE PRICE OF A 'FIXED PRICE' ENTRANCE TICKET VARIES WITH THE SELLER: 1 DAY $15-20, 3 DAYS $25-40, 1 WEEK $45-60.

SIEM REAP
ACCOMMODATION CENTRE FOR ANGKOR. MANY HOTELS WITH $4-6 ROOMS. TOWN → AIRPORT - 1000 RIELS BY AIRPORT TAXI. $1 CAR TAXI.

→ SIEM REAP PORT

SPEEDBOAT $25, 5 HRS. SLOW BOAT - 20,000 RIELS, 2 DAYS.

SPEEDBOAT - 35,000 RIELS, CAN BARGAIN.

½ HR

SHARE TAXI 11 HR, $2

KÂMPONG CHHNANG
○ NEXT TO THE POLICE STATION $5/ RM.

ANGKOR BOREI RUINS

TAKEO

BORDER'S NOT OPEN AT THE TIME OF WRITING (BUT SHOULD OPEN SOON) SURROUNDING AREA BECOMES SAFE.

KEP TOWN NOT SAFE AT NIGHT

KAMPOT

SHARE TAXI $5

SEV. 3-4 HRS $5

2/DAY

BATTAMBANG
TOWN SEEMS RUN BY THAIS.

→ TO BANGK.

DANGEROUS
SEV.

○ TRAT

BORDER OPEN BUT CAMBODIAN SIDE IS VERY UNSAFE.

KRONG KAOH KONG
NO SAFE ROAD TRANSPORT AT THE TIME OF THE RESEARCH.

SEE THAILAND - CAMBODIA BOAT ROUTE MAP

THAILAND

SIHANOUKVILLE

Southwest Beaches
CAMBODIA REPORTEDLY HAS SOME EXCELLENT BEACHES, BUT MOST OF THE COAST WAS TOO UNSAFE TO EXPLORE AT THE TIME OF RESEARCH.

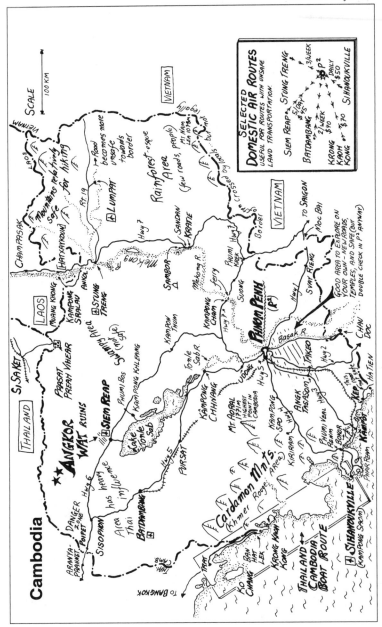

Thailand-Cambodia boat route

WARNING: At the time of writing Thailand does not consider the boat route to/from Cambodia as a legal border crossing. You will not get stamped in or out of Thailand. Some travellers entering Thailand this way have managed to convince immigration in Bangkok to stamp them in, but only after considerable time (two to seven days) and money ($20 to $300!). In the future Thailand may officially recognise this crossing if Cambodia becomes more stable. Get the latest information at the Foremost GH (Trat) or Sam's Hostel (Sihanoukville).

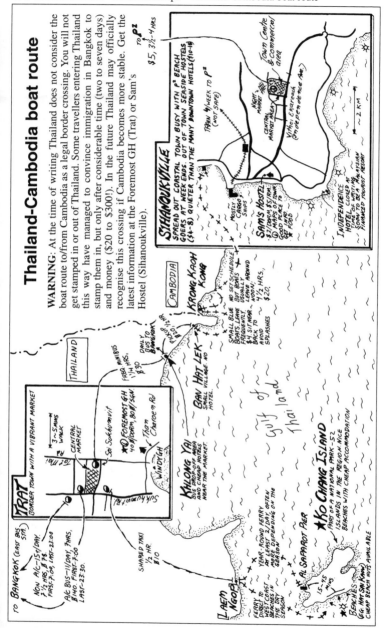

Laos
Lao Peoples' Democratic Republic (PDR)

There are few countries in Asia that have so few tourist 'sights' and yet so much appeal. There are no 'Great Walls', no magnificent monuments, no picture postcard beaches – even the temples which litter neighbouring Thailand are scarcer here – but there is a sense of having stepped back in time. Every morning at dawn the giving of alms to silent, saffron robed monks continues, even if imported chocolate bars are now included with the sticky rice and fruit offerings. Sleepy mountains hug sleepy mountain villages, hidden caves and lush river views murmur timeless charms and local people disarm travellers with an infectious serenity. Laos retains a few bureaucratic souvenirs from a communist era that hasn't formally ended, but Lenin is safely locked up in the Vientiane Revolutionary Museum. Meanwhile people go about their lives, happy to smile and chat when you approach them, but leaving you undisturbed if you choose to spend your day watching the Mekong flow by.

The country of Laos is a cartographer's lie. Though possessing boundaries and a currency, half of the people in Laos are not Lao but one of over 68 other ethnic groups. The national language itself is a hillbilly form of Thai (or so the people in Bangkok say) and is spoken by more people in north Thailand than in Laos. *Sa-bai-dee*, the Laotian greeting, used in Vientiane is simply not understood in some mountain villages.

The government leading this mirage country came to power in a 1975 coup which ousted the royal family; it has since embarked on the formidable task of forging some national unity. Laos is one of five countries which retains the nebulous classification 'communist' (along with Vietnam, Cuba, North Korea and China). But the Lao government has never been strongly driven by ideology. While there are plenty of hammers and sickles around Lao cities, the largest of them seem to be sponsored by Pepsi. The government doesn't appear

---

❏ **W&M's country ratings – Laos**
- **Expense $$** Less than $10/day is possible if you can split the cost of a double room with someone.
- **Value for money ✔✔✔** Vientiane hotels are expensive. Food is cheap and delicious.
- **Getting around ✔** Buses serve few routes, though pickups and trucks serve others. Everything breaks down.
- **English spoken ✔** People are starting to learn English, but very few at the moment speak it. A phrase book is very handy and French is useful occasionally.
- **Woman alone ✔✔✔✔** No particular problem.
- **For vegetarians ✔✔✔** If you can explain you are a *satavapet* (vegetarian) most places can serve meatless local dishes.

to exercise much direct control yet one senses a subtle feeling of secrecy which pervades all Laos. The entire country, from politics to the transport network, runs on rumours.

❑ **Essential information for travellers – Laos**

● **Visa** Required. A tourist agency sponsor is often needed for a tourist visa; once issued they are valid for two weeks. As we go to press reports suggest visas are now available for $50 at Vientiane airport or the Friendship Bridge. You'll need US$ cash.

● **Currency** Kip. US$1=K2444, Thai Baht (B1=K52) doubles as a second currency. It is much easier to exchange cash than travellers' cheques.

● **Time zone** 7 hours ahead of GMT (same as Thailand and Indochina; 1hr behind China).

● **Religious tone** A deep Buddhist undertone beneath a largely secular surface. Also animist and hill tribe faiths.

● **Health factors** Cholera is prevalent. There's also a moderate, drug resistant malaria risk outside Vientiane.

● **Special dangers** The Louang Prabang-Vientiane road; unexploded bombs in the Plain of Jars and Ho Chi Minh trail areas; wild dogs at night in Pakxe.

● **Social conventions** Although Laotians are not as easily offended as some other Asian cultures, the basic Buddhist conventions should be observed. The *nap*, the traditional Lao greeting – palms placed together prayer-like at chest level (identical to the Thai *wei*) – should be returned when given. A family-run guest house is best treated like a private home which means removing your shoes and behaving more like a guest than a paying customer.

● **Typical traveller destinations** Of the few travellers in Laos, most go to Louang Prabang. Many transit Vientiane.

● **Highlights** Louang Prabang, Nam Ou river boat trips, the small hill towns in the north (especially Muang Sing).

● **When to go** The coolest, driest season is November to January. Days are comfortable in short sleeves. At lower elevations a light sweater is the most you'll need at night, though in the hills it can get surprisingly cold and foggy. March and April are the hottest months; Vientiane can reach a sweaty 40°C. The monsoon season is from May to October. The rain itself is sporadic and pleasant but its effect is to turn most of the country's unpaved roads into impassable quagmires. River levels rise dramatically.

● **Pulse of the country** Louang Prabang (especially at dawn) and the slow boats to get there.

● **Key tips** Rivers flow north-south – southbound river trips are consequently considerably faster than northbound ones.

Plane tickets can be purchased in dollars but work out about 15% cheaper if you pay in kip.

Only tourist and business visas can be extended and only in Vientiane – plan accordingly. There is no problem overstaying your visa by a few days. Simply pay a token fine on departure (up to $5 a day).

● **Special occasions** Lao New Year (*Pi Mai*) is in April – celebrations last for three days. A parade is held on the afternoon of the first day and people throw water at each other (and at you) throughout the festival.

PRACTICAL INFORMATION
Visas and formalities

● **Visa strategy**   You have a choice of obtaining a business, tourist, or transit visa to get into Laos. Visas often do not state the period of stay when initially stamped into your passport so you might be tempted to believe you can stay forever. Sadly, this is not the case.

Business visas allow for an extendible one-month stay. You don't need to be a real businessman to get one, but you do need a letter of sponsorship. Agencies in Bangkok provide the letter (which you never see) and visa for around $100.

Tourist visas allow for a 15-day stay and typically cost between $40 and $70.

Most tourist visas have a Lao company acting as 'sponsor', a technicality that needs concern you only when it comes to extending the visa. Both tourist and business visas can take several days to issue.

Transit visas cannot be reliably extended. They allow a seven-day stay but cost only $20-30 and are issued in 24 hours. Officially a transit visa limits you to the quickest and most logical route through the country. In reality nobody seems to check. The exception is if you fly into Vientiane. The airport registration in your passport means that you won't be able to buy an internal plane ticket to anywhere else in Laos as you're supposed to have left straight across the Friendship bridge to

---

❏ **Geo-political information – Laos**

Population: 5.1 million (1997), 4.9m (1993), 3.6m (1985).
Area: 237,000 sq km.
Capital: Vientiane (442,000 in 1990).
Other major cities: Savannakhet, Pakxe, Louang Prabang.
GNP per capita: $320 (1994), $160 (1988).
Currency history: Kip/US$1 – Feb 1998: K2444, Oct 1997: K1300, 1996: K910-950, 1994: K720, 1992: K712, 1991: K701, 1990: K709.
Major exports/economy: Electrical power to Thailand. Opium.
Ethnic mix: Extremely complex. Lao, Thai, Mon, Khmer, Hmong, Mien.
Official languages: Lao (spoken by 65%).
Religious mix: Buddhist (Therevada).
Landmarks of national history: **1353-71**: First Lao nation called Lane Xang (land of a million elephants) developed under Fa Ngum with the capital at Louang Prabang until the mid-16th century. **1571-4**: Burmese invasion caused collapse. **1713**: Country split into Champusak (south) and Vietnamese controlled mini-kingdoms of Louang Prabang and Vientiane. **1778**: Thai invasion, kings ruled on within Thai empire. **1886-7**: French forces bullied Thailand into withdrawing and declared a French protectorate in 1893. **March 1945**: Laos declared independent by the Japanese occupation force. **1946**: The French returned but recognised the autonomy of Laos under King of Louang Prabang. **1949**: Independence within the French Union. **Late 1950s**: UK, France and USSR backed different Lao factions to USA and Thailand in repeated power struggles. **1962**: Country divided into two north-south strips with communist Pathet-Lao/Viet Minh forces controlling the east – an overspill of the Vietnam war. **1965-73**: USAF massive bombing campaign against Pathet Lao made Laos the 'most bombed nation in history'. **1973**: Vietnam ceasefire. **1975**: Laos fell to Pathet Lao, People's Democratic Republic declared. Widespread exodus of former elite and middle classes to Australia etc.
Leader: President Nouhak Phoumsavan in power since Nov 1992.
Pressing political issues: Degree to which the country should open itself to business and tourism.

Thailand. If you leave Vientiane by road, there's unlikely to be anyone to stop you, though there's a small chance of a $3.50 fine per day spent outside Vientiane. Feign ignorance.

The best places to obtain Lao visas are Rangoon and Canberra (Australia) because these embassies happen to issue visas with no fixed sponsor (see Extensions, below). Quick, but pricey, tourist visas are available in the Thai border towns of Chiang Kong ($70, two hours) and Nong Khai ($100, next day). The consulate in Kunming issues transit visas only.

● **Registration** Laos is currently in transition between the old set of rules which required travellers to seek permission before visiting a place, and a new set which are still being made up. In theory, travellers are supposed to get their departure card stamped in each place they visit. Failure to do so is meant to result in a $3.50/day fine. In reality, only officials in Louang Prabang seem to be strict about this requirement and even there a few minutes of arguing is often enough to avoid the fine. The stamp costs K100 for tourist or transit visa holders, K1000 for business visas.

● **Extensions** Tourist and business visas are extendible, but only in Vientiane and only when your current visa is within a few

---

❏ The road from Vientiane to Louang Prabang

'Is there a bus from Vientiane to Louang Prabang?' we asked a few locals:

'There's one bus a day at 7.30am.'
'There might be a bus on some days at 1.30pm.'
'There's a bus every two days.'
'There's a bus every now and then.'
'There is no bus so you have to hitch on trucks.'
'Many buses go but very few come back.'
'You should not go by this road because you will be shot.'

This latter claim is not quite as melodramatic as it may sound. The stretch of rough road between Kasi and Sala Pac Thu has become notorious for 'rebel' ambushes. We know definitively of two French tourists who were injured in late 1995 when their bus was shot at from the mountains. Four Lao passengers died in the attack. Other similar rumours are hard to substantiate.

The cause of the instability along this route is as uncertain as the schedule of buses which might ply it. Some insist that the armed groups are mere bandits. Others say they're rebels fighting half heartedly for the return of the pre-1975 regime – not to seriously challenge the current government but to keep money flowing in from anti-communist Laotians abroad. Others claim, with a straight face, that Lao Aviation pays the stooges to scare tourists into flying to Louang Prabang (twice a day, K37,500).

Dangerous or not, there are buses between Vientiane and Louang Prabang. Sometimes. Waiting time ranges from a few hours to a week (the average is about two days). When it finally comes, the bus may be escorted by armoured vehicles. Heading north, the place to wait is Kasi where the town's only hotel is on the main road. Bus and truck drivers often stop in its restaurant for some food and a lot of *lao-lao*. Hitching the trucks is in fact safer than taking the bus as trucks cover the dangerous stretch of road faster, in convoy and after dark. This is apparently better because, as one driver told us, optimistically, 'the rebels are sleeping'. Or perhaps they've had even more *lao-lao*.

If you want to steer clear of the road you could take a Mekong river boat, but only when the water level is right. Even then it will take some three to seven days.

days of expiring. Thus, if you want to spend a significant time in Laos but aren't planning on being in Vientiane during the second week of your stay (when a tourist visa would expire) it might be worth splashing out on a one month business visa. If you're only going to be a few days late, it's possible to pay a $5 fine at the border for each day you've overstayed. This is often cheaper as well as more convenient than getting an extension.

The official cost of visa extensions is $1 per extra day. However, you're normally required to get the extension through a representative of your original sponsoring agency. You're at their mercy and they'll typically charge you $5/extra day. However, if your original visa was 'unsponsored' eg issued in Rangoon, you are free to shop around for cheaper sponsors. The best deal seems to be $3/day with **Lao National Tourist** (☎ 216671, fax 212013), 8/2 Lane Xang Ave, Vientiane, (Monday to Friday, 8am-12noon, 1-5pm.

The rules state that transit visas cannot be extended. But this is Laos. While we were refused twice, we met other travellers who managed an extra week for a $10/extra day fee. Though this was an achievement, it would have been cheaper to simply overstay and pay the $5/day fine at the border.

Money

In towns along the Thai border, Thai baht can be used as easily as kip. US dollars cash can easily be exchanged – informally at some market stalls, hotels or jewelry stores, and officially at exchange booths. Other currencies (marks, pounds, yen etc) can be exchanged only in Vientiane. Beware of Thai banks which insist that you exchange to baht before exchanging to kip (this means double commission for them).

Travellers' cheques can also be exchanged in Louang Prabang and Vientiane. The commission structure varies: 2% is typical, there's a $2 minimum at Thai banks, or pay K500 per cheque at **Vientiane Commercial Bank** with better rates and only 0.125% commission.

Exchange booths charge 2% with no minimum. Credit card advances are possible in Vientiane only; a flat charge of $5 is payable.

Banks are open Monday to Saturday; 8.30am-1.30pm and 2-3pm (March to October); 8am-12pm and 1.30-4.30pm (October to March).

Transport

Public transport in Laos is slow and sporadic, when it works at all. Lower your clock-bound expectations.

● **Bus** The majority of routes, in the very limited network, radiate from the Vientiane area. Public buses leave at pre-determined times (even when they aren't full) and are very cheap (roughly $0.30 per hour's ride). The few new private services are less predictable and slightly more expensive. The last local services usually leave around 5.30 pm. Most long-distance buses leave in the early morning.

Even on the major Vientiane-Savannakhet road we heard about a bus that turned back due to bad road conditions, so estimated times should be seen as very broad approximations.

● **Pick-ups** Rough roads and a sparse population make pick-up trucks a sensible alternative to rural buses. Target schedules of a sort exist but vehicles leave when full – mostly in the early mornings from near a town's market. Useful items to have on pick-up journeys include sunglasses, a mask or bandanna (to prevent the inhalation of the dry season dust) and a warm pullover (especially on misty mornings and in case the driving continues after sunset). The pick-up's makeshift roof will not prevent you getting wet if it rains. Sturdy waterproof bags are also useful to protect your bags.

To enjoy the scenery at your own pace, you can often charter the same pick-ups for about ten times the standard one way fare.

● **Truck** Goods find their way to rural villages by truck and if you want you can too. All types of trucks charge the same fares but fuel trucks are typically faster than others. Trucks often gather in the morning at a petrol station near the main highway; enquire locally. The average price for a four hour journey is $3-4.

● **Boat** Locals usually prefer to travel by boat than by road. Boats are more comfortable, despite getting occasionally sprayed with water when shooting the rapids, but they are slow – especially when they travel upstream – and are prone to break down.

Some river transport in Laos is on scheduled boats, though much of it is on cargo services. If you are told there is no boat going to your destination this often means that there is no scheduled boat. Ask at the piers and, eventually, you should find a boat going your way. If you can't, it may be due to low water, high water or special conditions in a particular section of the river. Rather than giving up and being squashed into a truck, try hitching or taking a pick-up to a riverside village beyond the obstruction and finding a boat from there.

Scheduled boats usually stop for the night at villages with guesthouses. Cargo boats dock wherever they happen to be when it gets dark; you might be stuck on the boat. A sleeping bag and/or warm clothes are thus recommended, especially in the cool season. It is also wise to have enough water and food for your trip.

● **Speedboats** When boarding a speedboat, you'll be given a helmet to wear; you'll understand why when it takes off. Squealing like chainsaw mosquitoes, these low slung, narrow canoes surf the turbulent Mekong gravy with reckless abandon; torpedo taxis might be a more suitable name. Like pick-ups, few speedboats work to a fixed schedule.

The most regular speedboat service is on the Mekong between Houay Xai and Pakbeng (Thai $12 per person) and between Pakbeng and Louang Prabang (also $12). Renting a speedboat is expensive from Louang Prabang due to price fixing cartels. However, speedboats ply up the Song-Ou/Nam Ou (approx $10, two hours) and down the Mekong as far south as Vientiane (during the dry season) or Savannakhet (during the wet). It will cost

around $200 (for a boat holding up to six people) and take two days to Vientiane. It would be cheaper (and easier on your ear drums) to get a slow boat halfway (eg to Paklay) and hire a speedboat from there ($20/person, four hours).

● **Air** **Lao Aviation** is the only domestic carrier. The first time we walked into one of their offices there was no one around to help us. But there was a sign reading, 'You are perpetually welcomed by Lao Aviation'. It's more likely that you will be perpetually late.

Fares are reasonable (Louang Prabang-Vientiane takes 35 minutes and costs $40 if paid in kip, or $46 if paid in dollars). However, tickets aren't sold, nor is the schedule finalised, until the day before the flight. Flights are rarely full – whatever the airline office tells you – and tickets can be bought at the airport for the same cost and much less hassle than at the Lao Aviation office.

A great way to loop around Laos without doubling back is to take a flight from Vientiane to (Louang) Namtha. This gets you quickly into the hill tribe area of the north and you could then come downstream via Nang Kio on the Nam Ou river to Louang Prabang.

International departure tax is $5 payable in kip.

● **Other** Other varieties of local transport options include *samalors* (three-wheeled bicycle taxi), *jumbos* (the front is like a motorbike and the back like a small pick-up), *tuk-tuks* and taxis.

The lack of traffic makes renting a bicycle ($2/day) or motorbike ($10/day) a great alternative.

Accommodation

Foreigners often pay 20-50% more than locals for an identical room. Louang Prabang and Vientiane have the largest choice of accommodation, ranging from $6 for a spartan room to $12 for a slightly nicer place; attractive pensions cost $15 and up. In smaller towns, accommodation costs around $2.50-5 (double) and is usually more basic: expect fairly dirty rooms, cold communal showers and sometimes a fan. Most guest houses charge by the room, irrespective of the number of occupants.

Smaller villages aren't likely to have a guest house, but most have a 'café' which doubles as a sleeping area at night. K1000 is typical for a place on the floor. Ask for a *hangindu* (literally 'sleep, eat, drink place'). Villagers are exceedingly friendly.

Chinese-run hotels are likely to have dorms ($1 for a bed). Lao-run ones rarely do.

Food and drink
Lao food is similar to Thai minus most of the seafood.

The national dish is *fue* – a soup of vermicelli and meat which is often served with leaves which one tears up and adds as a condiment. Other dishes include *phakdak padek* (fish and sticky rice) and *khao poun* (cold rice vermicelli) which is a favourite at weddings. The Lao word for beef is *moo*!

Laotian rice, *khao*, is almost sticky enough to double as glue in an emergency.

Laotians, however, have a different alternate use for their khao – they ferment it. The result is *lao lao*, the unofficial national drink (indeed, the name means 'Lao alcohol'), an 80° proof potent demon. There is also *vin lao*, a wine made with black rice and lemon. Locally brewed Beerlao is increasingly popular, and much cheaper on draft than in bottles (one litre of cold draft for $0.80).

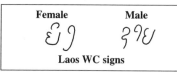

Female	Male
ຍ ງ	ຊ �нал ຍ

Laos WC signs

Staying in touch
● **Mail** It's cheaper and arguably more reliable to send packages from Vientiane than from Thailand.

American Express (fax 21-217151), c/o Diethelm Travel, Settathrath, Namphu Square, PO Box 2657, Vientiane, Lao PDR can hold mail but they don't exchange travellers' cheques.

❏ Meeting the locals
● **The people** Laotians are not great music lovers – one bus we were on played a tape of Air Supply and Rod Stewart medleys, if that is any indication. Popular Lao singers are Mrs Phuvieng and Mr Bao Ghean.

The Vientiane Monument (Pratuxai) is a popular gathering place for students, especially on Sundays.
● **Language** Outwardly the Lao script looks similar to Thai. Numbers are usually written in Western style but toilets (especially in rural areas) are often marked only by the Lao characters.

Some phrases in Lao:
    Hello – *Sah-bai-dee*
    Thank you (very much) – *Hawp-jai (le-lai)*
    How much? (in kip) – *Tao-dai (keep)?*
    Where are you going? – *Pai Sai?*
    Do you have ___? – *Mee ___ bao?*
    It tastes good – *Hong Ngam/See-bee-lai.*

Lao script

LAO CONSONANTS VOWEL MARKERS ARE COMPLEX AND SIMILAR TO THAI.

B	Ch	D	F	J	K	Kh	L	L	M	N	Ng	Ny	P	Ph	Rd	S	T	Th	Th	X
ບ	ຊ	ດ	ຟ	ຈ	ກ	ຂ	ລ	ຣ	ມ	ນ	ຫຍ	ຢ	ປ	ພ	ດ	ສ	ຫ	ຕ	ຖ	ຊ

● **Phone** Making international calls is easy from Vientiane, possible in Louang Prabang, and very difficult elsewhere. Direct dial rates at the public phone office from Vientiane to USA and Italy are: $3.30/min; Canada, UK, Germany: $2.80/min; France, Sweden: $1.50/min; Australia: $1.10/min. Dial 170 for an international operator.

International country code: +856.

Activities
● **Hiking** There are no organised trekking trails but it's easy for the adventurous to head into the hills. A tent and enough food for your trip are recommended, though there's a good chance that locals will put you up for the night.

● **Work** Laos is not a haven for jobseekers but teaching English in Vientiane can be surprisingly lucrative – wages average about $14/hour. However, a glut of teachers makes it hard to get more than a few hours work per week. Jobs are occasionally advertised in the *Vientiane Times* and on the door of the Phimphone Supermarket (see Vientiane city map).

Further information
● **Books** Lonely Planet's *Laos* guide is now into a welcomed second edition. Laos is also covered by several more generalised Indo-China guide books (especially in French), and by Footprint's *Thailand Handbook*. Vientiane has a limited selection of new and used books for onward destinations. You have about 50-50 odds on finding a guide to China; guides to Thailand and Vietnam are more widely available but the bookstore near the Mut Mee guest house in Nong Kai (across the border in Thailand) has a better selection than any in Laos.

Other books on Laos are difficult to find though Asia Books in Bangkok has a decent selection. An in-depth book on modern Laos is *Laos and Its Culture* by Perala Ratwan, a former ambassador. Less up-to-date is *Travels in Laos* by Lefevre (White Lotus Press) chronicling the travels of a Frenchman in the late 1800s.

● **Maps** City maps of Vientiane, Louang Prabang, Savannakhet, Thakhet and Pakxe can be found with a little searching in tourist shops and agencies in the respective cities. *Discover Laos*, often available free from Lao embassies, is a vaguely useful magazine with a Vientiane city map pull-out in the centre.

Poor maps of the entire country are fairly common in Louang Prabang and Vientiane but good ones are much harder to find. The best foreign-produced map we saw is published by Nelles and was readily available in Bangkok, and often in Vientiane's Rainbow Books. Lonely Planet publish a *Laos Travel Atlas*. A map of Yunnan's Cross-Border Communications (cheap in Kunming) gives fair detail for north and central Laos, though it uses a confusing pinyin romanisation of names. Vietnam also produces passable maps of Laos. The unpredictable transliteration of Laotian place names makes getting around more of a challenge; Saravane and Salavan do at least look similar, but if you were in Nang Kio, Nuangkio or Muang Keo and inquired about a boat to Ngoy you might be surprised to discover you were already there.

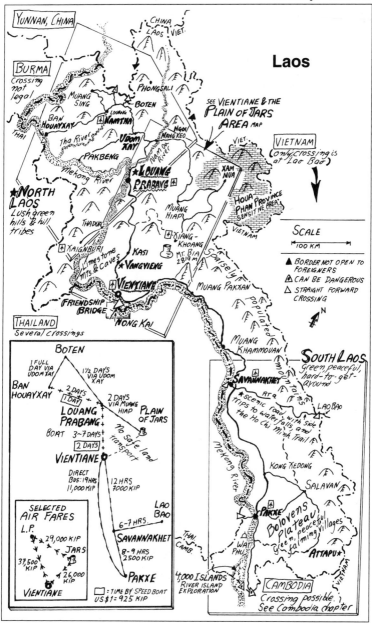

Laos

YUNNAN, CHINA

BURMA
Crossing not legal

SEE VIENTIANE & the PLAIN OF JARS AREA map

VIETNAM
(only crossing is at Lao Bao)

PHONGSALI

MUANG SING
BOTEN

BAN HOUAYXAY

▲ LUANG NAMTHA

THAI

Tha River

UDOM XAY

PAKBENG

Mekong River

NGOI NANG KEO

Nam Ou River

VIET.

XAM NUA

★ LUANG PRABANG

★ NORTH LAOS
Lush green hills & hill tribes

THADUA

HOUA PHAN PROVINCE SENSITIVE AREA

★ XAIGNBURI

Lime stone mts & Caves

KASI

MUANG HIAP

XIANG-KHOANG

Mt. BIA 2819 m

VIETNAM

SCALE
|←100 KM→|

▲ BORDER NOT OPEN TO FOREIGNERS
⚠ CAN BE DANGEROUS
△ STRAIGHT FORWARD CROSSING

N↑

★ VANGVIENG

★ VIENTIANE

FRIENDSHIP BRIDGE

NONG KAI

THAILAND
Several crossings

MUANG PAKXAN

Sparsely populated

MUANG KHAMMOUAN

SOUTH LAOS
Green, peaceful, hard-to-get-around

▲ SAVANNAKHET

★ scenic road with side trips to waterfalls and the Ho Chi Minh Trail!

Mekong River

LAO BAO

KONG XEDONG

SALAVAN

▲ PAKXE

Bolovens Plateau green, peaceful farming villages

WAT PHU

ATTAPU ★

4,000 ISLANDS RIVER ISLAND EXPLORATION

THAI. CAMB.

CAMBODIA
Crossing possible. See Cambodia chapter

BOTEN

1 FULL DAY VIA UDOM XAY

1½ DAYS VIA UDOM XAY

BAN HOUAYXAY

2 DAYS
[1 DAY]

2 DAYS VIA MUANG HIAP

PLAIN OF JARS

LOUANG PRABANG

No Safe land transport

BOAT 3~7 DAYS

[2 DAYS]

VIENTIANE

DIRECT BUS 19 HRS 11,000 KIP

12 HRS 7000 KIP

LAO BAO

6-7 HRS.

SAVANNAKHET

8-9 HRS 2500 KIP

PAKXE

□ = TIME BY SPEED BOAT
US $1 = 925 KIP

SELECTED AIR FARES L.P.

29,000 KIP

JARS

37,500 KIP

26,000 KIP

VIENTIANE

Central Vientiane

● **Accommodation** Relatively pricey. [1] *PhantavongGH* $6/dbl. Fills up fast. [2] *MIC* $8/dbl. Rooms nicer than outside of building suggests. [3] *Hua Guo GH.* $8/s. Poor value; always has space.

● **Transport** Rented **motorbikes** from several tourist agencies & guest houses around Nam Phu fountain. 100cc bike: $10–12/day, $6/half day. **Samlor:** sample fare: Morning Market– That Luang: 400 kip.

● **What to see** Selection of **wats** includes: That Luang, Wat Phra Keo, Wat Sisaket. **Beerlao brewery** On road to F'ship Bridge. Travellers fight for t-shirts. (20km)

● **'Ethnic theme park'** Disneyland meets mountain village. Nr brewery.

● **Buddha Park (Xiang Khuay)** 25km downstream on Mekong (E of Friendship Bridge). Strange fusion of Buddhism and Hinduism; companion to park in Nong Kai, Thailand.

ANOUSAVARI AREA

SQ WITH YOUNGE MONUMENT — LOOKS LIKE ARC DE TRIOMPHE WITH LAO BITS

Parade Grounds

★ THAT LUANG ("THE GREAT STUPA") INTERESTING EXPLORATION AROUND SIDE STREETS.

VIETNAM
INDIA
THAILAND
MALAYSIA

LOCAL STUDENTS SOMETIMES GATHER AT THE BASE OF THE MONUMENT (ESP SUNDAY AFTERNOONS)

1 KM

TO THE ANOUSAVARI AREA — SEE INSET

NATIONAL TOURISM AUTHORITY — M-F 8-12, 13-17:00

⑧ BUS STATION

THAILAND FRIENDSHIP BRIDGE

SCALE ⊢ 200M

TAXIS TO THAILAND FRIENDSHIP BRIDGE

MORNING MARKET OPEN 6-18:00 (AND THEREFORE NOT REALLY A 'MORNING MARKET')

Ⓐ ON TIME TRAVEL DESK — CAN RENT MOTORBIKES ($10/DAY) AND BUY TRAIN TICKETS EX-NONG KHAI, THAILAND (+ DAY ADV NOTICE REQ, CHEAPER IN THAILAND)

Ⓑ RAINTREE BOOKS — BOOKS. MAPS.

Ⓒ LOPERA — EXCELLENT PIZZA 5000 KIP. POL ROBER CHAMPAGNE 100,000 KIP

Say Lom
Sao Si

GPO
POSTE RESTANTE WINDOW #3

WAT SISAKET

Saam Seen Thai

Setthathirat

★ LANE II — BEST SPLURGE $25/SING, $40/DBL.

IMMIGRATION OFFICE

Makeol St

TO SOUTH EMBASSY AREA (3km) FRIENDSHIP BRIDGE — SEE MAPS OPP.

USA Ⓐ

EKLAMO METROINE $5-6

OPEN 8-22:00

WAT PHRA KEO

PRESIDENT HOUSE

PHIMPHONE MARKET — GREAT COOKIES. MAPS. JOB ADS ON MESSAGE BOARD.

A/C ROOM $10

NAM PHU — Fountain — EXPAT HANGOUTS

Ⓒ

AIR CON $20 KIP. SAME THING. GOOD.

AMEX DIETHELM TRAVEL

LIBRARY

LAO AVIATION

Fa Ngum Road

The Mekong River

Lao Aviation ⊕

SYRI G.H. $15/TRIPLE

REVOLUTIONARY MUSEUM

RARE OPENING LOOK IN

SCANDINAVIAN BAKERY COFFEE 900 KIP. CAKE $2

Manthatourat Rd

① ②

MAPS

JUST FOR FUN' VEG. RESTAURANT

MIXAI CAFÉ ✕ — COLD DRAFT BEER WHILE WATCHING SUNSET OVER THE MEKONG

VANNASINH GH $10/sng, $12/DBL. CLASSY!

CHEAP EATS AREA →

WIN WEST — EXPAT HANGOUT

△ WAT INPENG

RUSSIAN CULTURAL CENTRE — M-F 9-12, 15-20:00 Sa 15-20:00

IMPORT-EXPORT STORE

△ WAT ONG

Thong Khan Khom

PHORNTIPGH $3/RM.

WAT CHAN

TAIPAN HOTEL $25

WAT MINH

Minh Thaiwong Rd

✕ FOOD STALLS

Vientiane – south (embassy area)

TO CENTRAL VIENTIANE (3km)

NICE MOTORBIKE/BICYCLE RIDE TO MAIN BUS STA. & MORNING MARKET

BURMA M-F 8-12,14-1700

THIEN THONG $20/DBL

Sign

DAVONE CONSTRUCTION CO. (HANDY LANDMARK)

SAUNA WAT

GERMANY

WAT

Sri Amorphan

SCALE/KEY
~10 MINS WALK
= UNPAVED RD

CHINA Mon-Fri 9-11:30

FOOT PATH

TENNIS COURT

GATE FOR CONSULAR SECTION. 9-12 M,TW, Th,F,F,

CAMBODIA

BUS #14 FROM THE VIENTIANE BUS STA. (STAND) VI OR VII GOES ALONG MAIN RD. EMBASSY SIDE STREETS BEST NAVIGATED BY RENTED BICYCLE OR MOTORBIKE

VANHMALA G.H.

MONGOLIA

WAT

NORTH KOREA

RUSSIA

TATTY WAT

BUS DEPOT

POLAND

JAPAN

MUONG LAO CHINESE HOTEL $25*

AEROFLOT

MEKONG RIVER RESTAURANT river views

TO THA DUA, FRIENDSHIP BRIDGE BUDDHA PARK

Mekong River

Friendship Bridge

LAOS

TO BUDDHA PARK THA DUA TOWN

CHANGE MONEY HERE – GOOD RATES, NO PLACE ON THAI SIDE OF THE BORDER

CUSTOMS

MINI-FERRY — FOR LOCALS — ONLY

TO NONG KAI CENTRE

Nong Kai, Thailand

TRAIN STA.

FRIENDSHIP BRIDGE OPEN 8-18:00

15 MINS WALK (MAY NOT WALK)

BUS ACROSS BRIDGE

CUSTOMS CHARGES B40 EXTRA ON SUN AFTER 16:30

TUK-TUK TO/FROM TRAIN STA. B10 NONG KAI CENTRE B12
★ MUT MEE GH B10

Friendship Bridge

BUS TO THA DUA

BUS TO VIENTIANE (EVERY 45 MINS)

TO ETHNIC THEME PARK (1km) VIENTIANE (21 km)

CUSTOMS

Mekong River

25-30 MINS WALK

X X X SHOPS

dirt road

THAILAND

Vientiane to/from Friendship Bridge

Taxi: asking 3000kip per person. *Tuktuk*: asking 2000 kip per person (bargain to 2500kip for two people). Bus: #14. 300kip. Every 45 mins Monday to Saturday. Very few on Sunday. None after 5pm.

Nong Kai railway station to/from Friendship Bridge

If arriving on the overnight train from Bangkok, you'll have to wait for Customs to open – either take a *tuktuk* (asking 50baht, bargain to B10) or walk the pleasant 40 mins and arrive on time.

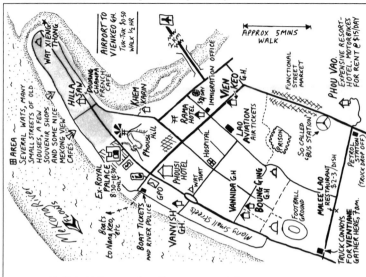

Louang Prabang

It has not been the capital of Laos since 1975 but little Louang Prabang is still the cultural centre. Thirty two of the 66 wats which existed before French colonialisation still stand, all of them are well kept and have numerous monks. Very scenic walks around wats (Wat Xieng Thong is our favourite). At around 4am the monks start beating drums and cymbals in the drum tower at Wat Ho Siang and Wat That, then they collect alms.

Accommodation

Vanvish GH is a small family-run place. No sign, look for the yellow house with a green gate. $9-10 including breakfast.

Boung Ging GH Nice hangout. Hot water only comes in a trickle (but this is more than in most places). $6/room. Bike rental: $2/day.

Vannida GH $7/room. No extra for the wildlife in the room.

Viengkeo Great porch. No hot water. $6/room.

Rama Modern. $8/room.

Khem Karin River view. $12/room.

Hilla Saw Hotel Stay in an old royal mansion. $45/room, $55/suite. Very stylish. Reserve in adv. (☎ 242267, fax in Vientiane (856) 21414223). If you can't afford to stay, stop by for a coffee ($1) but not for the food.

Short trips around Louang Pradang

Day and half-day trips include:

● **Ban Phnom** Silk weaving village 2.5km from town.
● **Suang Si Falls** Scenic ride. Hire a tuk-tuk.
● **Pak-ou Caves** Underwhelming caves, but beautiful boat ride to get there.

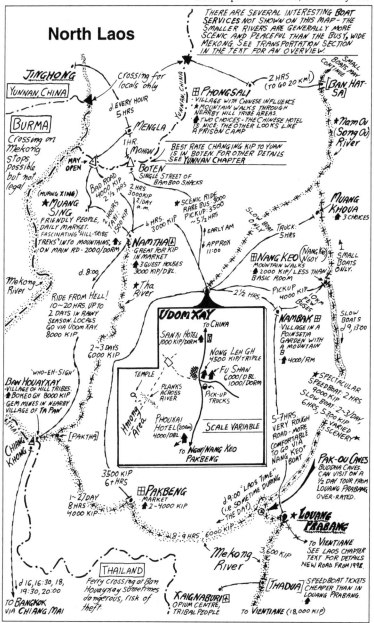

North Laos

THERE ARE SEVERAL INTERESTING BOAT SERVICES NOT SHOWN ON THIS MAP - THE SMALLER RIVERS ARE GENERALLY MORE SCENIC AND PEACEFUL THAN THE BUSY, WIDE MEKONG. SEE TRANSPORTATION SECTION IN THE TEXT FOR AN OVERVIEW.

JINGHONG

YUNNAN, CHINA

BURMA

Crossing on Mekong stops possible but not legal

Crossing for locals only

d. every hour 5 HRS

MENGLA

MAY OPEN

1 HR.

(MOHAN)

BOTEN
SINGLE STREET OF BAMBOO SHACKS

BEST RATE CHANGING KIP TO YUAN IS IN BOTEN. FOR OTHER DETAILS SEE YUNNAN CHAPTER

2 HRS (TO GO 20 KM!)

BAN HAT-SA

⊞ PHONGSALI
· VILLAGE WITH CHINESE INFLUENCE
★ MOUNTAIN WALKS THROUGH NEARBY HILL TRIBE AREAS.
· TWO CHOICES - THE CHINESE HOTEL IS NICE, THE OTHER LOOKS LIKE A PRISON CAMP

★ Nam Ou (Song Ou) River

(MUANG XING)

★ MUANG SING
FRIENDLY PEOPLE, DAILY MARKET. FASCINATING HILL-TRIBE TREKS INTO MOUNTAINS, ⌂'s ON MAIN RD - 2000/DORM

BAD ROAD 4000 KIP 2½ HRS

2 HRS 3000KIP 2/DAY a.m.

2 HOURS TAXI 500 KIP

4 HRS. 3000 KIP

★ SCENIC RIDE RARE BUS 3000 PICKUP 3500 ~5½ HRS

↑ EARLY AM

↓ APPROX 11:00

SLOW BOAT ONLY

TRUCK: 5 HRS

MUANG KHOUA
⌂ 3 CHOICES

Mekong River

NAMTHA ⊞
· GREAT FOR KIP IN MARKET
⌂ 3 GUEST HOUSES 3000 KIP/DBL

d. 8:00

★ Tha River

Tha River

⊞ Nang Keo
· MOUNTAIN WALKS
⌂ 2000 KIP/LESS THAN BASIC ROOM

(NANG KEO) (NGOY)

SMALL BOATS ONLY.

RIDE FROM HELL! 10~20 HRS. UP TO 2 DAYS IN RAINY SEASON. LOCALS GO VIA UDOM XAY. 8000 KIP

2½ HRS.

PICKUP 4000 KIP FEW BUSES

SLOW BOATS d. 9, 13:00

Udom Xay
San xi Hotel 1000 KIP/DORM

to China

2~3 DAYS 6000 KIP

'WHO-EH-SIGH'

BAN HOUAYXAY
· VILLAGE OF HILL TRIBES
⌂ BOKEO GH 8000 KIP
· GEM MINES IN NEARBY VILLAGE OF TA PAN

TEMPLE

PLANKS ACROSS RIVER

Nong Leh GH 4500 KIP/TRIPLE

Fu Shan 6000/DBL 1000/DORM

PICK-UP TRUCKS

NAMBAK ⊞
· VILLAGE IN A POINSETIA GARDEN WITH A MOUNTAIN B
⌂ 4000/RM

★ SPECTACULAR SPEEDBOAT 2 HRS 9000 KIP SLOW BOAT 2~3/DAY 6 HRS, 5300 KIP ★ VARIED SCENERY ★

[PAKTHA]

CHIANG KHONG

Hmong Area

Phouxai Hotel (200m) 4000/DBL

SCALE VARIABLE

to Ngoy/Nang Keo PAKBENG

5-7HRS. VERY ROUGH ROAD - MORE COMFORTABLE TO GO VIA NANG KEO' BOAT

PAK-OU CAVES
BUDDHA CAVES. CAN VISIT ON A ½ DAY TOUR FROM LOUANG PRABANG. OVER-RATED.

3500 KIP 6 + HRS

1~2/DAY 8 HRS 4000 KIP

⊞ PAKBENG
· MARKET
⌂ 2~4000 KIP

d. 9:00 "LAOS TIME" (i.e SOMETIME DURING THE DAY)

★ LOUANG PRABANG

→ To VIENTIANE SEE LAOS CHAPTER TEXT FOR DETAILS NEW ROAD FROM 1998.

[THADUA]
SPEEDBOAT TICKETS CHEAPER THAN IN LOUANG PRABANG.

d 16, 16:30, 18, 19:30, 20:00

TO BANGKOK via CHIANG MAI

THAILAND
Ferry crossing at Ban Houayxay sometimes dangerous, risk of theft.

8 - 9 HRS 6000 KIP

Mekong River

3,600 KIP

XAIGNABURI ⌂
OPIUM CENTRE, TRIBAL PEOPLE

to VIENTIANE (18,000 KIP)

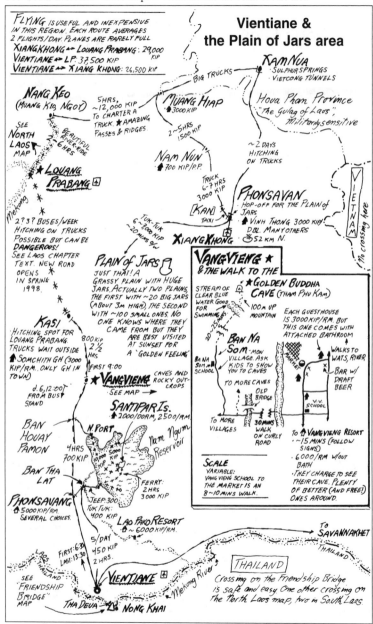

The Philippines

The 7100 Philippine islands are dotted with great beaches, dramatic volcanoes and Spanish colonial remnants. Lively locals ride gaudy jeepneys in the cities, while the mountains are still inhabited by fascinating hill tribes. A lack of regular boat services to neighbouring countries keeps the islands off the main trans-Asia route. However, reaching the Philippines need not be expensive thanks to free stopovers in Manila (and sometimes Cebu) which are possible on many discounted regional and trans-Pacific airline tickets.

PRACTICAL INFORMATION
Visas and formalities
See 'Essential information for travellers' (opposite).

Money
Exchange rates are better for cash (especially for high denomination US$ notes) than traveller cheques. The black market offers little extra and the risk of loss from the many scams is high. Cash advances are possible but any use of credit cards typically incurs a 7% surcharge. About 300 ATMs are on the Cirrus system.

Transport
● **Buses and Jeepneys** These shuttle along almost every road but using them is complicated due to the multiplicity of companies and the fact that the names on the route boards may not state the city to which you think you want to go: ie buses to Manila may be marked with the name of the area within Manila (Mabini, Taft, Harrison, Baclaran etc) where the bus will terminate rather than 'Manila' itself. It's worth taking a bit of time getting to know where Manila jeepneys go. For the Imelda Marcos shoe collection take the Quiapo-St Miguel line.

At Manila's Aquino airport the information office informed us that taxis or an expensive bus into the city were the only options. In fact, if you walk five minutes out of the airport you'll come to a major road. Take any passing jeepney (heading to your right as you emerge from the airport) which will drop you at Baclaran. From here you can walk 200 market-crowded metres to another jeepney for Mabini or

---

❏ W&M's country ratings – Philippines
● **Expense $$$** Similar to Thailand or Malaysia. Accommodation is slightly more expensive, but scuba diving is cheaper.
● **Value for money ✔✔✔** You get what you pay for.
● **Ease of transport ✔✔✔✔** Boats are frequent though not necessarily safe, Jeepneys are also very frequent and convenient – once you work out where they go.
● **English spoken ✔✔✔✔** English is the business language and much of the populous has at least a smattering of the language, though accents can be impossibly thick. Some Spanish is spoken.
● **Woman alone ✔✔✔** A few minor hassles reported.
● **For vegetarians ✔✔** For an island nation meat is surprisingly more popular than fish.

take the MetroRail which has its terminus there. Returning to the airport take Sucat-bound jeepneys from Baclaran.

● **Ferry** Since the islands are relatively close together there are frequent and cheap (if not especially seaworthy) shipping services all over the country. Also most islands are served by occasional direct boars from Manila.

● **Other** Trains are freight only in most of the country, though the Metrorail in Manila is handy. Domestic airfares are reasonable.

Accommodation

Youth hostels rarely require any kind of membership and simply denote dorm room availability. Hotel and guest house doubles cost little more than singles. The *Malate*

Pensione (1771 Adriatico, Manila) is a good place for meeting travellers (especially at breakfast in the downstairs restaurant); alternatively try any pension/hostel on Mabini or del Pilar streets.

As in Indonesia, the mayor or village chief of small, out of the way places may be able to help find you a place to stay when there is no hotel.

Food and drink

Many cheaper restaurants present food buffet style which makes choosing much simpler. In case you have to ask, any meal cooked *adobo*-style is real Filipino food, *pancit* are noodles and *kanu* is rice. Eating *balut* (a boiled egg with a fully formed foetus) is thought to be 'manhood enhancing'.

❏ Essential information for travellers – Philippines

● **Visa** A three-week visa free stay is possible for most nationalities. An extension allowing a total stay of two months costs approximately $20: apply in Manila, Angeles or Cebu.

● **Currency** Peso. US$1=P42.5.

● **Time zone** 8 hours ahead of GMT (same as Malaysia and Bali).

● **Religious tone** Strongly Catholic, the only predominantly Christian country in Asia. Especially interesting at Easter.

● **Health factors** The tap water in cities is theoretically drinkable. The malaria risk is worst in Mindanao, Sulu Archipelago and Palawan.

● **Special dangers** Smugglers/pirates in the Sulu Sea. In the southern island of Mindanao the Muslim separatist movement, the Moro Liberation Front (MLF), has agreed a ceasefire with the government, but some terrorist activity has continued courtesy of a small splinter group called the Moro Islamic Liberation Front (MILF). Tourist druggings and muggings in Baguio seem especially notorious.

● **Typical traveller destinations** Manila (including the bizarre Hobbit House dwarfs), Puerto Galera, Boracay, and Banaue.

● **Highlights** Vigan, Banaue, Boracay, Manila's Smokey Mountain rubbish dump city (though it's now being removed – take a jeepney for Gasak or Navotas and ask).

● **When to go** The climate varies considerably between the islands. In the west, monsoon rains fall in summer and the long dry season lasts from October to May. On the east coast, however, the heaviest downpours are in the winter months though it can rain at anytime. The country is likely to be hot and humid at any time unless you head for the mountains (rich Filipinos leave Manila en masse for Baguio in the summer).

● **Pulse of the country** Open-air Christian evangelical meetings.

● **Key tips** In Baguio and around Manila leave your valuables behind when exploring so that you don't need to fear and can happily take up invitations from the genuinely hospitable locals. Many hostels have lockers.

St Miguel Beer is drunk in great quantities and costs little more than soft drinks. Ask for wine and see what you get!

Staying in touch
● **Mail** This is relatively efficient. Poste restante worked OK in Manila and is said to be available at the GPO of any major town. Filipino post offices are more familiar with the American term 'General Delivery'.

● **Phone** International country code: +63. Manila: 2, Cebu City: 32, Davao: 82, Masbate: 56.

Activities
● **Scuba diving/swimming** Popular year round though the high season is from April to June. Diving is relatively inexpensive (the cheapest we found was only $13 for a boat dive including equipment), but much of the coral has been damaged by dynamite fishing. There are some stunning beaches, Boracay being, quite justifiably, the most famous but it's becoming increasingly touristy.

● **Hiking** The mountains and rice terraces of north Luzon are a worthwhile alternative to the over-commercialised hill tribe treks of northern Thailand.

Further information
Tourist information offices including the one at Manila's Aquino airport offer basic maps and help. Maps of the country are available in the stores in the Ermita (tourist) district of Manila, and from petrol stations.

There's a good library on the third floor of the grandiose modern **Cultural Centre of Manila** (Roxas Blvd) which is open 9am-6pm, Tuesday to Friday: membership costs P20 a day or P100 for a year.

❏ Geo-political information – Philippines
Population: 76.1 million (1997), 60.6m (1990).

Area: 300,000 sq km.

Capital: Manila 1.6m (but Metro Manila also includes Quezon City – 1.7m, Calocan – 700,000, Pasay – 300,000 and many more townships in a huge conurbation).

Other major cities: Davao (850,000), Cebu (600,000), Zamboanga (450,000), Bacolod (370,000), 10 more cities have over 100,000.

GNP per capita: $960 (1994).

Currency history: Peso/US$1 — Feb 1998: P42.5, Oct 1997: P33.2, July 1996: P26.20, Jan 1996: P26.23, Jan 1995: P24.44, Dec 1993: P27.65.

Exports/economy: The main source of foreign exchange is the remittances from Filipino workers abroad. Exports: pineapples, sugar cane, bananas, coconuts.

Ethnic mix/Languages: There are 988 languages: Tagalog (27.9%), Cebuano (24.3%), Ilocano (9.8%), Ilongo (9.3%), Bicol (5.8%).

Religious mix: 82.9% Roman Catholic, 8% other Christian, 4.6% Muslim (mainly in Mindanao).

Landmarks of national history: **1521**: Magellan claimed the islands for Spain. **1762**: Manila briefly occupied by Britain. **1872**: Independence struggle began against Spanish rule. **1898**: Independence declared but regardless of this the USA bought the territory from Spain. **1942**: Japanese invasion. **July 1946**: Independence. **1965**: Marcos became president. **1983**: Assassination of Benino Aquino (opposition leader returning from exile). **Feb 1986**: Marcos fled, Aquino's widow (Corazon) was declared president. **1992**: Was succeeded by Ramos.

Leader: President Fidel Ramos.

Pressing political issues: Continued insurgency in Mindanao, economic liberalisation, Metro Manila power supply.

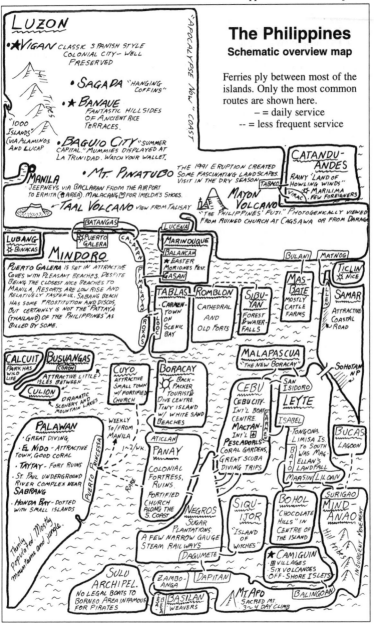

LUZON

- ★ **VIGAN** CLASSIC SPANISH STYLE COLONIAL CITY - WELL PRESERVED
- **SAGADA** "HANGING COFFINS"
- ★ **BANAUE** FANTASTIC HILLSIDES OF ANCIENT RICE TERRACES.
- **BAGUIO CITY** "SUMMER CAPITAL." MUMMIES DISPLAYED AT LA TRINIDAD. WATCH YOUR WALLET.
- **MT. PINATUBO** THE 1991 ERUPTION CREATED SOME FASCINATING LANDSCAPES. VISIT IN THE DRY SEASON.

"1000 ISLANDS" (VIA ALAMINOS AND LUCAP)

"APOCALYPSE NOW" COAST

MANILA JEEPNEYS VIA BACLARAN FROM THE AIRPORT TO ERMITA (☆ AREA). MALACANG ⬚ FOR IMELDA'S SHOES.

TAAL VOLCANO VIEW FROM TALISAY

The Philippines
Schematic overview map

Ferries ply between most of the islands. Only the most common routes are shown here.
– = daily service
-- = less frequent service

MAYON VOLCANO "THE PHILIPPINES' FUJI." PHOTOGENICALLY VIEWED FROM RUINED CHURCH AT CAGSAWA OR FROM DARAGA

CATANDU-ANDES RAINY "LAND OF HOWLING WINDS" ★ **MARILIMA** FEW FOREIGNERS
TABACO
VIRAC

BATANGAS
LUCENA
CALAPAN

LUBANG ★ BINACAS

★ PUERTO GALERA

MINDORO
PUERTO GALERA IS SET IN ATTRACTIVE COVES WITH PLEASANT BEACHES. DESPITE BEING THE CLOSEST NICE BEACHES TO MANILA, RESORTS ARE LOW RISE AND RELATIVELY TASTEFUL. SABANG BEACH HAS SOME PROSTITUTION AND DISCOS, BUT CERTAINLY IS NOT THE "PATTAYA (THAILAND) OF THE PHILIPPINES" AS BILLED BY SOME.

MARINDUQUE
BALANCAM
★ EASTER MORIONES FEST.
GASAN

TABLAS
CARMEN TOWN ON SCENIC BAY

ROMBLON CATHEDRAL AND OLD FORTS

BULAN
MATNOG

MAS-BATE MOSTLY CATTLE FARMS

SIBU-YAN FOREST & WATER-FALLS

TICLIN ★ NICE

SAMAR ATTRACTIVE COASTAL ROAD

CALCUIT PARK HAS WILDLIFE

BUSUANGAS CORON ATTRACTIVE LITTLE ISLES BETWEEN CULION

DRAMATIC SCENERY AND MOUNTAIN LAKES

CUYO ATTRACTIVE LITTLE TOWN W/ FORTIFIED CHURCH

BORACAY ★ BACK-PACKER TOURIST DIVE CENTRE TINY ISLAND W/ WHITE SAND BEACHES

MALAPASCUA "THE NEW BORACAY"

SOHOTAN NP

PALAWAN
- GREAT DIVING.
- **EL NIDO** - ATTRACTIVE TOWN, GOOD CORAL
- **TAYTAY** - FORT RUINS
- **ST. PAUL** UNDERGROUND RIVER COMPLEX NEAR SABRANG
- **HONDA BAY** - DOTTED WITH SMALL ISLANDS

THINLY POPULATED. MOSTLY MOUNTAINS AND JUNGLE.

PUERTO PRINCESSA

WEEKLY TO/FROM MANILA
1-2/WK.

ATICLAN

PANAY COLONIAL FORTRESS, RUINS. FORTIFIED CHURCH ALONG THE S. COAST

CEBU **CEBU CITY** INT'L BOAT CENTRE **MACTAN** INT'L ★ **PESCADORS** CORAL GARDENS, GREAT SCUBA DIVING TRIPS

SAN ISIDORO

LEYTE ISABEL

TONGONA. LIMISA IS. TO SOUTH WAS MAGELLAN'S LANDFALL MAASIN LILOAN

BUCAS LAGOON

NEGROS SUGAR PLANTATIONS A FEW NARROW GAUGE STEAM RAILWAYS
DAGUMETE

SIQUI-JOR "ISLAND OF WITCHES"

BOHOL "CHOCOLATE HILLS" IN CENTRE OF THE ISLAND

SURIGAO
MIND-ANAO

INSURGENT MOVEMENT

★ **CAMIGUIN**
- ⊞ VILLAGES
- SIX VOLCANOES OFF-SHORE ISLETS

SULU ARCHIPEL. NO LEGAL BOATS TO BORNEO AREA INFAMOUS FOR PIRATES

ZAMBO-ANGA

DAPITAN

BASILAN WEAVERS

MT. APO SACRED MT. 3 - 4 DAY CLIMB

BALINGOAN

❏ Meeting the locals

● **The people** Walking to Manila's surreal Chinese graveyard-city (where the dead have postboxes just in case), I was hailed by a swaying gang of drunken Filipino men who thrust a beer into my hand and demanded I sit and join the wedding festivities of a neighbour. I was most reluctant. Reports abound of travellers being drugged and robbed by apparently friendly locals. But I was carrying only a little loose change so I promised to return after looking round the graves. When I really did return they were delighted (and even drunker). They had apparently invited dozens of passing foreigners but all had shuffled past embarrassed, scared off by the rumours. Yet surely 'everyone knows Philippines is famous beyond anything for its hospitality' said Fidel, perplexed. Drink after dance after drink we became great friends, and we parted with a flurry of hugs, photos and address swapping. I stumbled off into the now dark streets, stopping and stooping into a little shop for some rice. The smiling owners, crouched below a low wooden ceiling, gave me a discount and a jolly conversation in English. 'But aren't you afraid to be here after dark?' 'Should I be?' 'Well, no. Not really. It's just that every tourist seems to think they should be'.

● **Some phrases in Tagalog/Filipino**:
Greeting – *Mabuhay*
How are you? – *Kumusta*
Thank you – *Salamat*
Delicious – *Masarap*
How much is it? – *Magkano?*

Web sites
City net Philippines has a travel related index at
http://www.city.net/countries/philippines/

NORTH-EAST ASIA

The countries in this section, fascinating as they are, don't attract many backpackers since none of them really ranks as a budget destination.

Japan and Taiwan are pointedly expensive, South Korea is a little less so following the recent currency collapse and North Korea is artificially exorbitant as you can only visit on a tour.

Most of the travellers who do come tend to drop in on free stop-overs available on flights via Taipei, Seoul, Tokyo and less frequently Kansai (Osaka). However, it's quite possible to arrive by boat. There's a fairly substantial ferry network linking China, Korea and Japan with some connections to Taiwan and Russia. Details of all the services that are presently operating are on pp14-15.

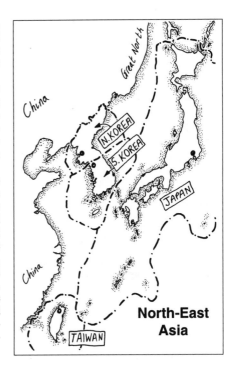

North-East Asia

Japan

In other Asian countries one sometimes feels as if the people would rush to become Western if only they could afford it. Rich Japan outwardly seems to have done just this, but look closely and you'll find: modern cities with rice paddies in the middle; baseball where the managers respect the umpires; vending machines which sell beer, batteries, rice, hamburgers and even (occasionally) used schoolgirls' underwear. Whatever idea Japan absorbs, be it curry or culture or car design, is reformed in a uniquely Japanese mould. For the visi-

❏ **Geo-political information – Japan**

Population: 125.7 million (1997), 125.1m (1993), 123.6m (1990).

Area: 376,500 sq km.

Capital: Tokyo (7.8 million, 1995).

Other major cities: Yokohama (3.2m); Osaka (2.5m); Nagoya (2.1m); Sapporo (1.7m); Kobe (1.5m); Kyoto (1.4m); Fukuoka, Kawasaki (1.2m); Hiroshima (1.1m); Kitakyushu (1m though actually a conglomerate of smaller cities); Sendai (900,000); Chiba, Sakai (800,000); Kumamoto, Okayama (700,000). There are 50 more cities with over 300,000.

GNP per capita: $34,600 (1994), $23,600 (1988).

Currency history: Yen/US$1 – Feb 1998: ¥125, 1997: ¥120, July 1996: ¥110.1, Jan 1996: ¥104.7, July 1995: ¥87.15, Jan 1995: ¥100.18, Jan 1994: ¥111.8, Jan 1993: ¥125.2, Jan 1991: ¥135.2.

Major exports/economy: Vehicles (world leader – 10.5m produced in 1994), diverse manufacturing. 60% self sufficient in food. A major fishing nation.

Ethnic mix: The term Japanese has been coined to include the disparate groups fused together by the shogunate as well as the Ryukyu (Okinawan) Islanders despite their distinct heritage. The Korean minority (1%) is refused Japanese nationality despite residence of several generations. The tiny populations of aboriginal Ainu have been assimilated and are outnumbered by migrant workers from Western countries, the Philippines (mainly women) and Iran (men).

Official languages: Japanese.

Religious mix: As many subscribe to more than one philosophical school, figures are hard to assess. Shinto and Buddhism are seen as fulfilling different roles but are not mutually exclusive. A majority of the population subscribe to both. Soka Gakkai (8.1m) and Rissho Koseikai (6.7m) are offshoots of Buddhism. Kofuku no Kagaku (8.3m) holds businessman-prophet Ryoho Okawa to be an incarnation of Buddha. There are about one million Christians.

Landmarks of national history: **1st and 2nd centuries AD**: Unification of over 100 small states. **604AD**: Constitution formulated. **607**: Horyuji temple (Nara) founded – it's now the oldest wooden building in the world. **710**: Nara became the capital. **794**: Capital moved to Heian (near Kyoto), state and religion (Buddhism) were separated. **1192**: Samurai-led Shogunate rule began with the capital at Kamakura. **1867**: Following the arrival of US Black Ships Japan was forced to open to trade and the Shogunate dissolved. **1905**: Japan defeated Russia in the Tsushima Straits naval battle and went on to colonise Korea and much of China. **7 Sept 1941**: Attack on Pearl Harbor. **6 and 9 Aug 1945**: Atomic bombing of Hiroshima and Nagasaki. **1952**: Post-war independence regained after allied administration. The economy boomed partly because Japan was the supply centre for the Korean war. **1972**: US handed back Okinawa.

Leaders: Emperor Akihito (succeeded 7 Jan 1989 the date from which Japan's calendar thus reverts to zero), is a constitutional monarch. Prime Minister Ryutaro Hashimoto. No one politician holds great individual power.

Pressing political issues: Defending domestic rice production from cheap imports. Corruption in business. Loss of job security. Lack of faith in the government. Whaling. Kurile Islands territorial dispute with Russia. Burakumin underclass prejudice. Ditto towards Korean Japanese.

tor, what results is a visual and cultural landscape at once familiar and yet foreign. Capitalism meets Zen and stops for a beer. A fast-paced lifestyle is lived with a slow-paced animist spirit. School children rehearse their campfire songs before they go camping, while drunken daddy draws polite applause for a slurred off-key rendition of Elvis Presley's *Rub Me Tender* in a bar. Japan is quietly humourous, often confusing and always fascinating.

Japan's obvious drawback is the potential expense of travel there. A coffee might cost US$8 (though $3.50 is more usual – or $1 in cans from a vending machine). Before going to Japan it is important to accept that your budget will be stretched, though the recent fall in the yen has made a visit here much better value. Costs can be minimised by hitchhiking, staying with those you meet or camping, and drinking free Japanese tea instead of coffee. You need not break the bank but you should splash out on a *ryokan* at least once. Japan may be expensive but no other rich country is so hospitable to foreign travellers.

PRACTICAL INFORMATION
Visas and formalities
● **Visa strategy** Australians and South Africans require a visa. These are free but a photo, an air ticket out of the country and proof of funds are required. It will take between three days and one week for a visa to be issued. If you aren't applying in your home country, you are usually required to write a letter explaining why. All other Westerners enter visa free for 90 days.

Work visas can be obtained only with a sponsor and only outside Japan. Many people leave on short visa-procurement vacations to Korea once a job has been found.

• **Arrival** Look respectable and carry plenty of money and a return/onward plane ticket. Immigration officers can refuse entry to those who they suspect plan to work illegally (even if they already have a tourist visa). If you speak Japanese pretend you don't; officers who don't speak English are less keen to trouble non-Japanese speakers.

Money
Japan is a cash orientated society. Even though an increasing number of stores take credit cards, most Japanese walk around with at least US$500 in their wallets.

Travellers' cheques can be cashed in most banks (look for a sign saying Authorised Foreign Exchange Bank) but the process can take half an hour and some banks will exchange them only between certain hours. Banks are open Monday to Friday, generally from 9am-3pm. Most

---

❏ **W&M's country ratings – Japan**
● **Expense $$$$$** Eating out is reasonable by Western standards if you have the cheapest option (around ¥500). There is no cheap accommodation.
● **Value for money ✔✔** The high quality is surpassed by even higher prices. Japanese consumer goods are paradoxically cheaper outside Japan.
● **Getting around ✔✔✔** Transport is super efficient, but in rural areas destinations are marked only in Japanese.
● **English spoken ✔✔✔** Six years of English study at school are mandatory yet few are able to hold a conversation and the others are too shy to try.
● **Woman alone ✔✔✔✔** Japan is very safe; underwear on washing lines is less secure.
● **For vegetarians ✔✔** Meat is common, life can be difficult for vegetarians who don't eat fish.

banks have ATMs; these are usually in a separate area inside the bank and are open from about 8am-7pm during the week and also at some branches at the weekend. However, very few ATMs are on an international system (such as Cirrus or Plus).

❏ **Essential information for travellers**

● **Visa** Most Europeans, Canadians, Americans, Israelis and New Zealanders are allowed to stay for 90 days without a visa. Australians and South Africans require a visa.

● **Currency** Yen. $1=¥125.

● **Time zone** 9 hours ahead of GMT (same as Korea, 1hr ahead of China).

● **Religious tone** Temples are everywhere and many families maintain shrines to ancestors in their home but the spiritual feel is not obvious.

● **Health factors** Tap water is safe and there's no malaria risk.

● **Special dangers** Spending too much money, growing too trusting of others (this is more of a problem when you leave!).

● **Social conventions** At a meal or party, delight your hosts by pouring beer or *saké* into their glasses not your own. They'll pour for you in return. Before you drink for the first time hold your glass up and say *kampai* (cheers).

Never use soap in a bath tub; wash using the shower or bowls (filled with water) and then rinse. Get into the bath only to relax. Don't pull the plug as others will use the same water.

Japanese life is a game of musical shoes. Leave your footwear at the front door, politely pointing them away from the door (to suggest that you're not going to stay long). Indoor slippers will be provided. These should be worn, but not in a *tatami* (straw mat) room where you should walk barefoot, and certainly not in the toilet. The *gaijin* (foreigner's) tendency to walk into a lavatory without putting on the special toilet slippers is a favourite Japanese joke, bettered only by wearing the toilet slippers into the main house.

● **Typical traveller destinations** Tokyo, Kyoto, Nara, Mt Fuji.

● **Highlights** Cherry blossom viewing parties, remote islands (such as Yakushima and those off Nagasaki-ken), the Eiheiji temple complex at dusk, Yoshino, Himeji Castle, Koya-san, Sapporo Snow Festival, Kerama Island (Okinawa) for scuba diving. Staying in *ryokans*.

● **When to go** Many Japanese are proud of their country's four distinct seasons – a quality some think is unique to Japan. Autumn and spring are the best times to visit, especially the months of April and May when the skies are clear and the temperatures mild. Winters on the north coast and in Hokkaido are very cold and there's plenty of snow. In southern Honshu and Kyushu snow is rare except on mountain tops, but a lack of central heating means family homes often feel colder than in the north. Summers are the worst time to visit; June is the rainy season, July and August are unpleasantly hot and humid, except in Hokkaido, and typhoons are common in September. Clear blue skies return with magnificent autumn colours in October/November.

● **Pulse of the country** Karaoke bars after an *enkai* (a party).

● **Key tips** Make use of the excellent TICs (Tourist Information Centres) and especially the toll-free Japan Travel Phone (see Further Information).

● **Festivals** Japan has a plethora of colourful festivals, many trawling at the animist roots of ancient Japanese culture. Tourist information offices can provide pamphlets outlining many of these.

Transport

● **Hitching** 'In Japan nobody hitchy haiku. So I musto stoppu for you. Or you will waito long time.' This attitude means you're likely to get a ride in five minutes; the collective desire to take care of you as a lost foreigner also results in gifts and meals and the occasional invitation to stay, drink and sing karaoke. The challenge of hitching in Japan is trying to prevent this excessive kindness. This can be hard when you don't speak Japanese as very few dri-

---

❏ Hitching tips

Hitchhiking is one of the best ways to meet the Japanese, but be aware that not all drivers understand entirely what you're doing. Some kind but infuriating souls drive off the motorway and take you to the nearest railway station, never fathoming that the horrendous cost of the ticket is the reason why you are hitching. Others feel responsible for you and make ridiculous detours to get you where

you want to go. One family who had intended to drive half an hour to a village up the road, chauffeured us five hours to our destination, unwilling to leave us to our uncertain roadside fate. Some general tips:

● Using the thumb is fine.

● Before you set off, look up the kanji characters for your destination. Make a sign using the basic design shown. (Direction of .... please).

● As in Europe, the best long distance hitching is from motorway service areas (*sarbisu aria*). Certain *haiway basu* (buses) from city centre bus terminals can drop you at such areas. However fares tend to be quite high. Alternatively, the ever-helpful travel phone (see Further Information) can often tell you the city bus number necessary to get you to a motorway slip road/junction.

● Once in a service area, if you're having trouble getting a ride and don't speak enough Japanese to ask drivers directly, here's a technique that often works. Sit on the steps of the restaurant, laboriously (re)copying your hitching sign. Cardboard is almost always available and you can usually borrow a chunky pen at the gift shop. In our experience, sympathetic drivers often stand and watch you writing. Gently ask '*sumimasen...*' (excuse me) and say the name of the place you want to go in a questioning tone. Make eye contact and smile unthreateningly. Even if they're not going your way, your audience may start asking other drivers on your behalf.

● For very long hitches, ask/write signs for intermediate towns. Drivers often don't think you'd be satisfied with a ride that stops half way. Assure them that it's fine.

● Good highway maps are available free at some service area information points, but are expensive in shops at the same areas. Before getting into the car, show the map to the driver and agree on which service area he/she will set you down. Watch carefully as this approaches; he/she is liable to overshoot, perhaps out of eagerness to take you further.

● In our experience, hitching is best in Kyushu and west Japan. The concrete spaghetti around Kyoto/Osaka and Tokyo makes driving extremely confusing, let alone hitch-hiking.

vers speak much of anything else; even those who understand you may reply in Japanese. See Hitching Tips box on p521.

Several Western women who travelled on their own have told us of hassle free hitching, but it is certainly not 100% safe.

● **Train** *Shinkansen* (bullet trains) fly along at over 200kmph but only on a few specially built lines and there's a very expensive supplement to pay. A cheaper, but still considerable, supplement applies to the fancifully personalised *tokkyu* (limited express) trains which are less than half the speed of the shinkansen but still way faster than the snail-paced *kyuko* (express) and *futsu* (normal) services. All services are punctual, except in the typhoon season.

In unreserved carriages, ticket collectors often rely on the honesty of those without tickets to identify themselves – which makes ticket dodging possible if you get on and off at small unmanned stations. *Shinkansen* tickets are always checked carefully.

Almost all the overnight trains are sleeper car only and these incur a supplement of ¥5150 (for a bunk in a four-berth cabin) on an already expensive ticket. The seat-only overnight exceptions are a handful of services in Hokkaido, and the completely unadvertised 'Ladies' car' – a half carriage of comfortable reclinable seats attached at present to only two daily sleeper trains on the Fukuoka-Kyoto service (reservations are essential, ¥500 extra). Men may use these seats despite the name.

Japan Rail (JR) has a variety of passes: some permit travel on JR West or JR East services only. The general JR pass is a go-anywhere card that, for the equivalent of ¥28,300, allows you a week's travel on any JR train (or bus) except the Nozomi (the fastest grade of Shinkansen); two (¥45,100) and three-week (¥57,700) passes are also available. Reservations are free and certainly recommended but the pass does not cover the sleeper supplement on overnight trains.

The pass cannot be bought in Japan; you have to buy a voucher from designated travel agents abroad (friends can do this for you and post it on). The voucher has to be converted to a pass in Japan, within three months of purchase. This can be done at major rail stations (or at the airport on arrival); only at this stage do you need to specify the exact dates for your pass. The pass is great value if you plan long distance journeys, particularly on the shinkansen.

Note that JR is the main, but by no means only, rail network – in the Kansai area (Osaka/Kyoto) particularly some of the more attractive destinations are on non-JR lines, ie not covered by the pass.

● **Boat** Long distance ferries are good value if you have plenty of time. There's no charge for sleeper berths in the bottom class (you sleep on a mat). Discounts (between 10 and 20%) are often possible if you have an international student card.

Ferries (and flights) out of Japan are generally much more expensive than those inbound, so a return or onward ticket is worth considering. See pp14-15 for international ferry connections, p523 for local.

● **Bus** Highway buses are cheaper than limited express trains. Overnight services between major cities often have videos (with earphones), toilets (slippers provided) and free hot beverages.

Accommodation

Sleeping in Japan is a major expense. Youth hostels generally cost around ¥3000; some require you to bring an IYHA card. All cities and most towns have business hotels (from ¥5000 for a single, no meals). However Japan has some interesting and rather unique options that require at least some consideration:

● **Ryokan and minshuku** Especially in rural areas and older cities, you can stay in a traditional Japanese Inn *(ryokan)*. Many establishments are in characterful, old, wooden homes. You sleep on a *futon* (mattress) on the *tatami* (straw mat) floor and Japanese meals (dinner and breakfast) are included in the price (typically ¥10,000 per person but some can be as much as ¥30,000). Meals will probably be served in your room.

Japan's best overnight boat hops

The routes shown here are a small selection (best value, most useful, most regular) of the **many** ferry possibilities. Unless otherwise marked there is at least one overnight service on each route shown (Fukuoka-Fukue and Hiroshima-Beppu are only overnight in the direction shown, returning by day). Prices quoted are for deck space. Blankets are provided and conditions are usually comfortable – an excellent way to save money on hotel accommodation. For about ¥2500 extra you can upgrade to a B cabin bed. Some companies give 10-20% discounts for students with ISIC cards. For more details on times, prices, and routes call the English help-line toll free ☎ 0120-800444/222.

NB Not to scale. Main island spacing exaggerated.

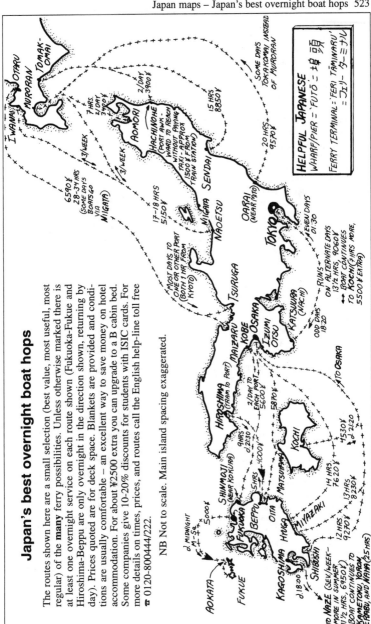

A *minshuku* is essentially the same as a *ryokan* though cheaper (¥5000 to ¥10,000 per person, but occasionally you can negotiate a room- only deal for around ¥3000). Minshuku are even more likely to be in a private home. Meals are usually served in a dining room. You may be expected to get your own futon ready and put it away in the morning – you'll find it in the big cupboard with sliding doors. *Yokui* (sleeping robes) may also be provided. It is acceptable to walk round in your *yokui* without appearing undressed.

Whether you choose a ryokan or minshuku, the owner is going to be nervous that you might do something appalling like using soap in the communal bath or walking with shoes on the *tatami* mats. (Where foreigners have previously screwed up, you may be told politely that the place is full or more bluntly that it's Japanese only.) Put the owner at ease by taking off your shoes at the door, donning slippers and doing plenty of bowing. Japan's tourist information has a free booklet on *ryokan/minshuku* behaviour.

It is also possible to stay in a working temple (¥3000, or ¥5000 with meals – almost always vegetarian). You can choose to be woken for pre-breakfast meditation sessions. Temples are often surrounded by idyllic Japanese gardens. Temple towns include Koyasan and Yoshino (see Kansai area map).

● **Capsule hotels** If you're alone in a big city, the best deals (¥2600-3500) are the unique *kapsuru hoteru*. Unfortunately these are usually for men only; they were designed for the many businessmen who get so drunk they miss the last train home. They are necessarily close to the main entertainment centres and are open all night. Guests sleep, literally, in capsules. Horizontal pods are stacked one atop another and have enough space inside to sit up and watch the fitted TV. Some have the opening on the end, mortuary-like, whilst others have a side opening which allows you to roll out of bed and out of your room at the same time. However, you need enter the capsule only when you're ready to

sleep as there are sauna rooms, jacuzzis, TV lounges and a cheap restaurant or two within most such complexes.

When you arrive you'll swap your shoes for slippers and you'll then be handed a key. This unlocks a long thin locker (designed for your clothes, suit and briefcase – backpacks will have to be handed to the confused clerk). In the locker you'll find a towel, a pair of boxer shorts and a *yokui* (sleeping robe) into which you change for the majority of your stay. Soap, razors and toothbrushes are free.

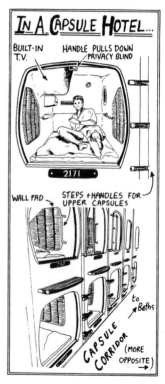

● **Love hotels** A love hotel is not a brothel. Though designed for carnal liaisons, you are expected to bring your own partner. In this country of paper thin walls some locals claim that these places are for spouses seeking a moment's privacy. Between 10pm and 10am most love hotels are less busy and offer a special all-night rate; a bargain at around ¥4000 for two people (more in Tokyo). Broader minded establishments don't charge extra for more than two in a room. The disadvantage is that you couldn't use it as a base; there is nowhere to leave bags, and booking is not possible even for the next evening.

The discreet lengths to which such places go to keep guests incognito (curtains to hide your parked car etc) suggest that secrets are the norm. Choose your room from a photo board in the lobby (if the display is lit the room is available) and collect the key from a tiny hatch. There's no need for eye contact! Head for your room, but don't be surprised if you're locked in. Since the rate is normally charged per hour, you have to phone down and tell the front desk to stop the clock when you're leaving. The door will then unlock automatically.

• **Staying with people** The best way to understand any culture is to stay in local homes. Though it can get very tiring when you don't speak the language, people are hugely hospitable and it is worth making the effort. SERVAS has many Japanese members who are keen to host foreign counterparts but you need to have joined well before you want to travel. For more information contact JNTO (see p529).

If you're stuck without contacts in a rural backwater you could try heading for the local school or town hall (ask for the *kyoiku inkai* – Board of Education). Ask for the local Assistant English Teacher (AET). Almost every town has a foreign teacher who knows the area well and may be able to help you find a cheap place.

If you're planning to stay for a while accommodation in cities can be found at *gaijin* (foreigner) houses; rents are as low as ¥36,000 a month, but this means sleeping on the floor and sharing a room.

• **Help with bookings** If you're on a brief stop-over, it may be worth pre-arranging accommodation to make the most of your stay. Cheap accommodation including 15

Tokyo hotels under ¥5000 can be pre-booked through Welcome Inn (fax 03-3211 9009, e-mail: wirc@jnto.go.jp). It's a non-profitmaking arm of the tourist information service and relies on booking in good faith; the service may stop altogether if there are too many no-shows. You'll need to give them a week's notice, more in peak seasons. A brochure of the possibilities is available through Japan National Tourist Organisation (JNTO) offices in most Western capitals. A similar service is available at Narita and Kansai airports.

Food and drink

In many restaurants you can find a daily *teishoku* (set menu) meal with miso soup, rice and a main dish for ¥5-600. Steaming bowls of *ramen* and *soba* noodles are available for about the same price, though these can be as cheap as ¥190 in service stations or city centre semi-automated restaurants (put the money in a machine, get a ticket for your chosen noodle style and topping then present it at the counter). Other cheapies are *katsu-donburi/oyako donburi* (fried breaded pork/chicken and egg on rice), *kare raisu* (supposedly curry rice)/*katsu kare* (the same but with a fried breaded pork cutlet on top) and *sara udon paré paré* a mixed vegetable and seafood dish which is served on crispy noodles. Plastic models of each dish or meal, usually with prices, are displayed in the window making ordering very easy; it is perfectly acceptable to beckon the waitress outside and point to what you want!

Sashimi (sliced raw fish, thought by many Westerners to be *sushi*) is a great delicacy but is expensive (from ¥1000 for a small selection) and far from filling. The subtle flavours are brought out by dipping the fish in soy sauce into which you have mixed the alarmingly green *wasabi* (Japanese horseradish). *Sushi*'s distinguishing feature is not the fish but the lightly vinegared rice. There are dozens of varieties: *maki zushi* is rolled in dried seaweed with various fillings; vegetarians might try *kapamaki sushi* (with cucumber); *nigiri zushi,* the most respected version of

❏ Meeting the locals

● **The people** Having taught us to bow, an expat explained: 'You don't really have a true Japanese friend until you've been drunk and naked with them' – not necessarily at the same time. An *onsen*, where the naked part is performed by soaking together in volcanic or artificially heated pools, is an experience not to be missed. Many Japanese become highly emotional after the first half thimbleful of *saké* (but never violent). Drunkenness is no shame and it is not uncommon to see a night's *saké* consumption eloping with a businessman's dinner down the vomit-streaked platforms of a Tokyo subway.

● **Language** Unlike other East Asian languages, Japanese is not tonal and is quite easy to pronounce. There are helpfully many loan words taken from English and other Western languages. However, these are not always easy to recognise as they've been pronunciationally battered to fit the Japanese spelling system. This is limited to 47 modifiable syllables. Several sounds just can not be transliterated: L is approximated to R, and V to B so that 'I love you' becomes 'I rub you'. The syllable Si is substituted by 'Shi' turning a Tokyo 'city lover' into a 'shitty rubber'.

Other fun anomalies make Coffee into 'Kohi', Spaghetti 'Supaget'tei' and stretch Jeans to 'Jipantsu' (from Jean Pants). All such words are written in angular katakana – differentiating them from pedigree Japanese which is written in a combination of kanji Chinese characters (see pp206-7) with hiragana syllables added to indicate which of many possible meanings and sounds the Kanji is taking.

Note that if written small, the letter 'Tsu' is silent and has the effect of adding a short gap – doubling the preceding letter.

THE SYLLABLES

	A	I	U	E	O	
ア/あ	イ/い	ウ/う	エ/え	オ/お	
カ/か Ka	キ/き Ki	ク/く Ku	ケ/け Ke	コ/こ Ko	Add " for Ga, Gi... eg ゲ = Ge
サ/さ Sa	シ/し Shi	ス/す Su	セ/せ Se	ソ/そ So	Add " for Za, Ji, Zu... eg ゾ = Zo
タ/た Ta	チ/ち Chi	ツ/つ Tsu	テ/て Te	ト/と To	Add " For Da... eg ド = Do
ナ/な Na	ニ/に Ni	ヌ/ぬ Nu	ネ/ね Ne	ノ/の No	ン/ん N At end of a word
ハ/は Ha	ヒ/ひ Hi	フ/ふ Fu	ヘ/へ He	ホ/ほ Ho	Add " for Ba, Bi... Add ° for Pa, Pi...
マ/ま Ma	ミ/み Mi	ム/む Mu	メ/め Me	モ/も Mo	
ヤ/や Ya		ユ/ゆ Yu		ヨ/よ Yo	⊛ ya, yu, yo
ラ/ら Ra	リ/り Ri	ル/る Ru	レ/れ Re	ロ/ろ Ro	Also used to write "L" syllables.
ワ/わ Wa				ヲ/を Wo/o	

ジ/じ = Ji

⊛ CAN BE COMBINED WITH ...i SYLLABLES eg キャ = Kya, ニュ = Nyu, チョ = Cho, ビョ = Byo, シャ = Sha etc..

Katakana and Hiragana

Some phrases in Japanese:

Greeting (first meeting) – *Hajimemashite*
Greeting (early morning) – *Ohaiyo gozaimasu*
Greeting (during the day) – *Konnichi wa*
Greeting (during the evening) – *Komban wa*
How are you? – *Ogenki desu-ka?* Reply (I'm fine) – *Genki desu*
Thank you/thank you very much – *Arigato* or *domo arigato/domo arigato gozaimasu*
Delicious – *Oishii* (while eating), *Oishikata* (when you've finished)
Friend – *Tomodachi* How much is it? *Ikura desu ka?*

sushi, is basically sashimi on a blob of rice with a dab of *wasabi* lurking beneath. Poor man's sushi, *o-nigiri*, are triangular rice balls sold with a sheet of wrap-it-yourself seaweed at 24-hour stores for ¥80-120. The tuna filled ones are delicious and filling, but watch out for outwardly identical *ume boshi* (sour plum) or *natto* filled versions. *Natto* (fermented soyabeans) is the nearest you'll come to eating spiders' webs.

Fugu (blowfish) is an exorbitant delicacy which gives an adrenaline rather than gastronomic thrill; it is fatally poisonous if wrongly prepared. Fortunately, restaurants serving this dangerous dish have specially licensed chefs who, to keep their honour, must kill themselves if one of their customers die from eating their *fugu*.

Many larger supermarkets offer samples of food – both savoury and sweet. If you visit a few of these you could scavenge a free meal.

Pocari Sweat, a very refreshing rehydration drink, is not as unappetising as the name suggests. It is consumed less by athletes (as the advertisements would suggest) than by those with *saké* hangovers.

Staying in touch

● **Mail** Sending anything by mail is expensive (international letters cost ¥170) but the service is one of the most reliable in the world.

Mail can be received in **American Express** offices in **Tokyo**: Shinjuku Gomeikan Building 1 Fl, 3-3-9 Shinjuku, Shinjuku-ku, Tokyo 160 (☎ 03-3352 1555), **Kyoto**: 52 Daikoku-cho, Sanjo Sagaru, Kawaramachi dori, Nakagoyo-ku, Kyoto 604 (☎ 075-212 3677, **Fukuoka**: 1-3 Shimokawabata-cho, Hakata-ku, Fukuoka 812, (☎ 092-272 2111). Other offices which will keep mail are in Nagoya, Okinawa City, Osaka and Sapporo.

● **Phone** International telephone calls can be made from card phones, but only those with a gold plate on the front; the other call boxes are for domestic calls only. There are several international telephone companies – dial access code 0051 rather than 001 for slightly cheaper calls.

International country code: +81. Tokyo: 3, Kyoto: 92, Nagoya: 52, Osaka: 6, Fukuoka: 92, Sapporo: 11.

Activities

● **Hiking** Japan, though well known for its industry, has more forest cover than almost any other Asian nation and there are many attractive hikes – though you rarely escape humanity for very long. One of the most interesting treks sets out from Yoshino (south of Nara) and follows an ancient pilgrimage route via Omine-san to Kumano in Wakayama ken. However, it is said that women walking this route will anger the god of the mountain. There are some great short hikes in the Japanese Alps – many are included in *Hiking in Japan* by Paul Hunt (Kodansha).

● **Scuba Diving** Despite the high cost of living, Japan is one of the world's cheapest places to learn scuba diving. In Okinawa, instructors use cheap compressed air, petrol and equipment subsidised by the American military bases so they can charge as little as $100-150 for an open

---

❏ **Tips for prospective English teachers**

● Drop subtle hints while hitchhiking. You will probably be asked what you are doing in Japan; if you say 'I'm a teacher' you may just be asked to give lessons.
● Make Japanese friends along the way across Asia who can help you once you arrive and possibly put you up. There are many very cosmopolitan young Japanese travellers on the road these days.
● Try heading for a smaller city or a town well away from Osaka or Tokyo where there will be fewer foreign teachers and where you'll arouse more interest by your mere presence. Foreigner communities in such cities (eg Kumamoto, Kagoshima) tend to be friendly and helpful, but there is still plenty of competition.

water course (land entry dives). Even though the water is clear, the coral has been abused by the large number of novices. Once qualified, much better diving is available in the glorious Kerama Islands but for this you'll pay Japanese prices of some $120 per double dive!

• **Swimming** Miyazaki-ken (Kyushu) has a 50km stretch of beach, much of it commercialised, which is popular with surfers. Okinawa has some beautiful coves but the main island has also been heavily despoiled by hotel development. Takahama on the far coast of Fukue Island, a three hour ferry ride from Nagasaki, has our vote for Japan's most attractive swimming beach, though Iriomote Island (most of the way to Taiwan) is idyllic.

Officially the jellyfish season begins on 15 August. Though it's hardly credible that one day could bring a threatening plague of stingers, you'll suddenly find you have the beaches to yourself (except in Okinawa) as locals are nervous to swim after that date.

• **Work** Working in Japan is not likely to be a gold mine unless you can get a cheap or free place to live and/or are prepared to stay for a while. Competition from other foreigners combined with the closure of many language schools has driven down average earnings for English teachers to about ¥2500/hour. This still sounds good but at first it can be hard just getting enough work to cover your rent (typically ¥60,000/month for a rabbit hutch in a provincial city and much more in central Tokyo), plus a one off payment of three months deposit and a month's worth of non-returnable 'key money'.

To teach English as a foreign language in Japan, a degree (however irrelevant) is essential; having a TEFL certificate as well is preferable. Legally speaking, you are required to find a legitimate employer to sponsor your visa, then leave the country (commonly to Korea) to collect this visa. It is not possible to change visa type within the country so it is easier and initially more profitable to try and arrange a job before arriving. Paul Abramson's *Japan Study*

and Teaching Guide (Tokyo Central, ¥1000) offers regularly updated listings of language schools which are worth approaching for jobs. **AEON** (US ☎ 310-550-0940), 9301 Wilshire Blvd #202, Beverly Hills, CA 90210, USA, has an extensive selection of language schools throughout Japan as does **Nova Group** (US ☎ 617-542-5027), 2 Oliver St, Suite 7, Boston, MA 02110, USA, though it is smaller. Once in Japan you could check advertisements in the many English language newspapers and magazines, as well as local TICs.

Terra Brockman's useful *Job Hunter's Guide to Japan* is published by Kodansha.

Further information

• **Books** Of the many guidebooks available, Kodansha's *Gateway to Japan* is our clear favourite. It gives a deeply sympathetic view of the country in a way that helps you to see the country's hidden charms through the facade of concrete and fear of expense. For once, the Lonely Planet guide is not recommended as its premise of budget travel is somehow incompatible with enjoying Japan and its 'nowhere cheap here, let's move on' attitude leaves you wondering why you came. The earlier Lonely Planet book by Ian McQueen is now published by Kodansha as *Japan: a budget travel guide*. A hilariously insightful, tongue in cheek cultural introduction is the *Bluffer's Guide to Japan* (Ravette Books, London, £2.50) which will teach you more about Japan than any book five times the size, price or seriousness. Sadly this is not available in Japan, but bigger bookshops in Japanese cities do usually have American humourist Dave Barry's witty and caustically accurate *Dave Barry does Japan* plus a selection of drier cultural and language books.

Japanese novels are typically slow moving and very studied but extremely evocative. An excellent first choice is Nobel prize winner Yasunari Kawabata's *Thousand Cranes*. Many Japanese read *manga* (comic books) more than novels, but being in Japanese it's hard to understand their weird, sometimes perverted or gruesome plots. A fascinating English language magazine called *Mangajin* helps by using *manga* as a medium for Japanese language learning giving many everyday insights into Japanese thinking.

Big city bookshops usually stock Fodor and Lonely Planet guides, Kinokuniya in Tokyo and elsewhere has Moon guides. Other series are more difficult to find. Prices are typically 70% higher than the marked US$ prices.

● **Maps** Free maps of Japan are available through travel information offices in major cities (and at larger JR railway stations where they are given to those exchanging Japan Rail Pass vouchers). These are all right for travel between major centres but for free regional and city maps in English ask at local TICs. Regional maps in Japanese are available free at most motorway service areas; they are very useful for hitching as all the rest areas are marked (ask someone to help translate the names). If you're staying for a while in one area consider buying an extremely detailed regional atlas which marks every hamlet and tiny track; Japan is divided into ten such atlases which cost ¥980 each from most bookshops – though they are in Japanese only.

● **Information services** The exceptionally helpful, toll-free Japan Travel Phone gives travel and tourist information and the operators speak excellent English. The service operates daily between 9am and 5pm. For northern Japan (including Tokyo) call ☎ 0088-224800, and for southern Japan (including Osaka and Kyoto) call ☎ 0120-444800. If you use a public phone (green or grey) you must insert a ¥10 coin or telephone card; this will be returned when you hang up.

JNTO's main information office will answer specific e-mail questions in a few days on jnto@jnto.go.jp, or contact one of the helpful international offices who will happily bundle you up with brochures and excellent maps. There are also JNTO offices in Chicago, Los Angeles, New York, San Francisco, Toronto, Paris, Geneva, London (jntolon@dircon.co.uk), Frankfurt (info@jntofra.rhein-main.com), Hong Kong, Bangkok, Seoul, Sydney.

Peace monument (Nagasaki)

Web sites
Japanese Information:
Great background and practical travel information
http://www.ntt.jp/japan/index.html

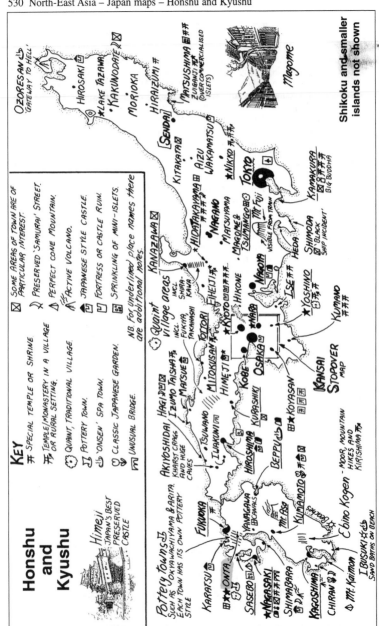

Honshu and Kyushu

Himeji
JAPAN'S BEST PRESERVED CASTLE

KEY

丼 SPECIAL TEMPLE OR SHRINE
⚗ TEMPLE/MONASTERY IN A VILLAGE OR RURAL SETTING.
✿ QUAINT, TRADITIONAL VILLAGE.
Ⅱ POTTERY TOWN.
♨ 'ONSEN' SPA TOWN.
♥ CLASSIC JAPANESE GARDEN.
⋈ UNUSUAL BRIDGE.

⊠ SOME AREAS OF TOWN ARE OF PARTICULAR INTEREST.
🗡 PRESERVED 'SAMURAI' STREET.
△ PERFECT CONE MOUNTAIN.
🌋 ACTIVE VOLCANO.
🏯 JAPANESE STYLE CASTLE.
🏰 FORTRESS OR CASTLE RUIN.
🏝 SPRINKLING OF MINI-ISLETS.

NB. FOR UNDERLINED PLACE NAMES THERE ARE ADDITIONAL NOTES.

✿ QUAINT VILLAGE AREAS INCL. SHIRA-KAWA.

OZORESAN ♨ 'GATEWAY TO HELL'
HIROSAKI 🏯
★LAKE TAZAWA
•KAKUNODATE 🗡⊠
MORIOKA
HIRAIZUMI 丼
MATSUSHIMA 🏝丼丼 ZUIGANJI 丼 (OVER COMMERCIALISED) (ISLETS)
Magome
[SENDAI] ⊠
KITAKATA
AIZU WAKAMATSU 🏯⊠
NIKKO 丼丼丼
KAMAKURA ⊠🏝丼丼 BIG BUDDHA
Tokyo 🏥
HIDATAKAYAMA 🏯⊠
NAGANO
MATSUMOTO
MAGOME & TSUMAGO 🗡✿ VISIBLE FROM TRAIN
SHIMODA ⊠ 'BLACK SHIP INCIDENT'
HEDA ♨
Mt FUJI △
KANAZAWA ⊠ ♥
HIKONE 🏰
EIHEIJI 丼⚗
KYOTO 丼丼🏯♥⊠⋈
NARA 丼丼★
OSAKA
KOBE
KURASHIKI 🏯⊠
HIMEJI 🏯★
MATSUE 🏰
MITOKUSAN 丼⚗★
TOTTORI ✿★
IZUMO TAISHA 丼丼
HAGI 🗡⊠ Ⅱ
AKIYOSHIDAI KARST CRAGS AND HUGE CAVES
TSUWANO ✿
IWAKUNI ⋈
HIROSHIMA 🏯⊠
BEPPU ♨⚗
KOYASAN 丼★⚗
ISE 丼丼
★YOSHINO 丼丼丼
KUMANO 丼丼丼

KANSAI STOPOVER MAP

Pottery towns Ⅱ
SUCH AS OKAWACHIYAMA & ARITA - EACH TOWN HAS ITS OWN POTTERY STYLE

KARATSU 🏯
田★OMTA 🏰♨
SASEBO 🏝Ⅱ丼
★NAGASAKI 🏯丼丼⊠
YANAGAWA ⋈⊠⋈⋈
SHIMABARA
FUKUOKA 丼
YAMAGAWA △ Mt Aso 🌋
KUMAMOTO ♨丼🏯⊠
Ebino Kogen - MOOR, MOUNTAIN HIKES AND KIRISHIMA 丼丼
KAGOSHIMA ♥🌋
CHIRAN ✿🗡
△ Mt. Kaimon
IBUSUKI ♨♨♨ SAND BATHS ON BEACH

Shikoku and smaller islands not shown

- **Aso** The world's biggest volcanic crater, so big it's effectively invisible. Great hikes from Naka-dake and Kuju. Holiday crowds. ☎ 0967-340804.
- **Beppu** Sex museum, mud baths, sand baths, hells. *Minshuku Kokage* nr station, ¥4000pp ☎ 0977-231753. Classier hot spring resort at Yufuin (30km).
- **Fukuoka** (station Hakata). Big, modern city. Shofuku-ji Japan's oldest Zen temple (metro Gion). Expats boogie Sat nights at *Club Bollox* (Tenjin). Large indoor ski slope.
- **Fuji** Photogenic viewed from afar. Dull, bleak and very commercialised to climb ('like climbing an ashtray'). It's 4-6hrs climb from Kawaguchi-ko (officially July and Aug only; *huts* and drinks en route; cold on top).
- **Hida Takayama** Kyoto's country cousin, dozens of temples and a great open-air village museum. *YH* in Tensho-ji temple ☎ 0577-326345.
- **Hiroshima** Vibrant modern city – only the famous shell of the city hall and the powerful peace museum hint at the 1945 nuke. Big castle. *Mikawa Ryokan* ¥4000, ☎ 082-261 2719.
- **Ise** The grand shrine of Shintoism set in delightful, extensive gardens but only the lavishly dressed priests may enter the inner sanctuary. Brilliant old *Hoshide Ryokan* only ¥4000 single, ¥9900 double ☎ 0596-282377.
- **Kagoshima** The city is constantly showered with ash from Sakura-jima volcano across the bay (ferries). *Nakazono Ryokan* ¥4000, ☎ 099-226 5125.
- **Kanazawa** Myoryuji 'Ninja' temple with secret passages.
- **Kobe** Pleasant city despite earthquake damage. Ikuta shrine. Kitano-cho area for older houses, temples. *YH* ☎ 078 707 2133.
- **Kumamoto** Large, humid university city. The huge rebuilt castle is brilliant at cherry blossom time. Honmyo-ji temple and ★*tea-house*. Expats drink at the *Rock Balloon* pub downtown near a men-only *capsule hotel* with 20 baths, jacuzzis and steam rooms included for ¥3000. *Kajita Minshuku* nr Shinmachi bus stop, ¥4000, ☎ 096-353 1546
- **Kurashiki** Big city whose solid, renovated old town streets are an over-rated tourist draw. 2*YHs*, ☎ 86 422 7355, 479 9280.
- **Kyoto** ★ Great ancient capital. See Kansai and Kyoto maps.
- **Magome** and **Tsumago** Well preserved museum villages on the ancient post-road, attractive if tourist infested. ★Lovely walk between them.
- **Mitok san** Small shrine set on stilts into the cliff face is reached by an attractive scramble up mossy mountain paths. Hitch from Miyasa or Kurayoshi.
- **Nagano** Search for the key of paradise in the pitch black chamber beneath Zenkoji temple floor. Ski centre (1998 Winter Olympics). Many delightful excursions into the dramatic Japanese Alps. *Kyojo-in* is a YH.
- **Nagoya** Nice ★castle but otherwise a big industrial city. Aichi art gallery at metro Sakae.
- **Nara** Even more ancient than Kyoto. Town is walkably small with deer park, lovely temples and the huge, thousand year old bronze Buddha. *YH*.
- **Nikko** Dazzling temple town in woodland setting. Short hitch-hike to waterfall, mountain and lakeside walks. *Turtle Inn* ¥4-5000 ☎ 0288-533168.
- **Nagasaki** Despite the atomic bomb, one of the most attractive large Japanese cities; many stairways and winding streets. Peace park/museum, Dutch houses and views at Glover Gardens, Gaudiesque church, eat Castella cake. *YH* ☎ 0958-235032.
- **Onta** Trickling streams and water wheels pounding clay add to the charm of this idyllic, untouristy pottery village. One *ryokan* ¥5000+/pp.
- **Osaka** Metropolis. National Bunraku puppet theatre. Castle.
- **Sasebo** US naval base. Nearby '99 Islands' are gorgeous – view from Ainoura port or from the azalea park (Tsutsuji koen) above Kosaza/Shikamachi villages. Huis Ten Bosch (10 mins south by train) is an unbelievable recreated 18-19th century Dutch city (entry ¥5500, peep through the fence for free).
- **Tottori** Tourists in suits ride camels on Saharan sand dunes!

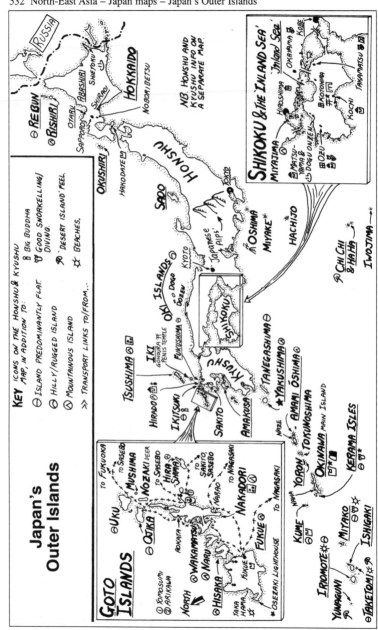

Japan's Outer Islands

KEY
ICONS ON THE HONSHU & KYUSHU MAP, IN ADDITION TO:

- Ⓞ ISLAND PREDOMINANTLY FLAT.
- Ⓞ HILLY/RUGGED ISLAND
- Ⓐ MOUNTAINOUS ISLAND
- >> TRANSPORT LINKS TO/FROM...
- 🍔 BIG BUDDHA
- 🐠 GOOD SNORKELLING/DIVING.
- 🏝 DESERT ISLAND' FEEL.
- ☆ BEACHES.

NB HONSHU AND KYUSHU INFO ON A SEPARATE MAP.

GOTO ISLANDS
- Ⓞ TONOSUMI
- Ⓞ ARIKAWA
- Ⓞ UKU
- Ⓞ OJIKA
- MUSHIMA   DEER
- NOZAKI
- Ⓞ HIRA SHIMA
- AOKATA
- TO FUKUOKA
- TO SASEBO
- TO SASEBO
- TO SAKITO SASEBO
- NARAO
- TO NAGASAKI
- NAKADORI Ⓐ
- Ⓞ WAKAMATSU
- Ⓞ NARU
- NORTH
- Ⓞ HISAKA
- TAKA HAMA ☆
- FUKUE Ⓞ
- FUKUE
- * OSEZAKI LIGHTHOUSE
- TO NAGASAKI

SHIKOKU & THE INLAND SEA 'Inland Sea'
- MIYAJIMA
- HIROSHIMA
- OKAYAMA Ⓞ
- KOBE
- YOKOHAMA Ⓞ
- TAKAMATSU Ⓞ
- MATSU-YAMA & DOGO ONSEN
- Ⓞ OZU
- SHIKOKU
- KOCHI Ⓞ

Main map labels
- RUSSIA
- SHIRETOKO
- Ⓞ REBUN
- Ⓞ RISHIRI
- ABASHIRI
- SHARI
- HOKKAIDO
- OTARU
- SAPPORO
- NOBORIBETSU
- OKUSHIRI Ⓞ
- HAKODATE
- HONSHU
- SADO
- ÔME
- JAPANESE ALPS
- KYOTO
- OKI ISLANDS Ⓞ
  - Ⓞ DOGO
  - DOZEN
- FUKUSHIMA Ⓞ
- IKI Ⓞ 🍔
  - GONOURA PENIS TEMPLE
- TSUSHIMA Ⓞ 🍔
- HIRADO Ⓞ 🍔
- IKITSUKI Ⓞ 🍔
- SAKITO
- AMAKUSA
- KYUSHU
- Ⓡ OSHIMA ☆
- MIYAKE
- HACHIJO
- 🏝 CHI CHI & HAHA
- IWOJIMA
- TANEGASHIMA Ⓞ
- ★ YAKUSHIMA Ⓞ
- AMAMI ÔSHIMA Ⓞ
  - NAZE
- 🏝 TOKUNOSHIMA
- YORON ☆
- OKINAWA MAIN ISLAND
  - NAHA
- KUME Ⓞ🐠
- KERAMA ISLES Ⓞ🐠☆
- 🏝 MIYAKO Ⓞ🐠☆
- ISHIGAKI Ⓞ☆🐠
- IRIOMOTE ☆🐠
- YUNAGUNI 🐠
- Ⓞ TAKETOMI ☆🐠

● **Amami Oshima** Scenic mountains/bays. Naze harbour (main port) picturesque at night. Beaches: Kinnao and Utabaru.

● **Chi Chi** Desert island 29hrs by weekly boat from Tokyo. *YH* ¥4300 ☎ 04998-22641 in port, *Hotel Ship* ¥5000, many **min-shukus** from ¥6000. Bike rental ¥1500/day. **Ha Ha Island** is 2hrs further. *Mayama Ryokan* ¥6000 ☎ 04998-32157. Iwojima (WWII battle site) uninhabited.

● **Fukushima** Behind village school is hut of Western pioneer Abe Smith. NB don't confuse with Fukushima City, Honshu.

● **Goto Islands** Most villages have cheap **ryokans. Ojika**: cattle farming, small, unique 'cow shrine'. **Fukue** 19th century castle building now used as the town library (nr ferry), lovely Takahama beach and dramatic Ose Zaki headland/lighthouse. **Hirashima** Isolated, no tourists. Wind-eroded sandstone formations on western cliffs, quaint hamlets, attractive port. **Hisakajima** Legendary home of Japan's most beautiful women. **Mushima** Populated by the inbred offspring of a ship-wrecked Portuguese and his concubines. **Nozaki** now deserted.

● **Hokkaido** Areas of agricultural land punctuated by large volcano-dotted national parks where you can sit in steam baths surrounded by snow. **Abashiri** Sea freezes late Feb, excursions by ice breaker (¥5500). **Hakodate** Pentagonal European style fortress, cable-car. *Pension Hakodatemura* ¥5800pp, ☎ 0138-228105. **Otaru** Big port, old semi-Russian style bldgs and many Russians. **Sapporo** Snow Festival (first week of Feb) awesome ice sculptures. Modern Art gallery. Ninniku (Garlic) restaurants. Nightlife. Skiing. **Shiraoi** Poignant Ainu village museum.

● **Iki** Dolphin Park. Nishikibama beach (one of Japan's best outside of Okinawa, camping). >>Fukuoka (Hakata), Tsushima.

● **Inland Sea** Pleasant views from quaint Tomo no Ura, Onomichi or from the many ferries that weave between the isles. **Miyajima Island**, famed for its classic 'wading' Tori gate & temple complexes, nice but touristy.

● **Ishigaki** Miyara Donchi (unique Okinawan mansion). *YH* ☎ 09808-23157.

● **Iriomote** Star sand, beaches, sugarcane, diving. *YH* (☎ 56255). >>Ishigaki.

● **Kerama Isles** (corals, scuba diving. Camping and passable hikes on especially on **Zamami**. Accommodation + dive deals, ¥9900+ on **Aku** >> Naha

● **Miyako** Sunagahama beach. *YH* ☎ 09807-37700.

● **Kume** Castle ruins, Nakazato village, lava causeway. >> Naha.

● **Oki Islands** Unspoilt backwater. Aug 16 launch of festival boats. *YH* in Fuse village, NE coast of Daigo. ☎ 08512-74321. >>Sakai near Matsue.

● **Okinawa** (Main Island). Bombed treeless in WW2. Beaches scarred with big tourist hotels. US military presence (good pizza, cheap dive courses). Least spoilt area is far N. tip near Oku. Naha city very cosmopolitan. *Naha YH*'s: ☎ 98-857 0073 & 867 3218 >>Kagoshima, Fukuoka, Shibushi, Osaka, Taiwan.

● **Rebun** 'Island of flowers'. Cliff walks on west coast. Jizo-

Iwa rock pillar: 3 *YHs*. In Kafuka (port) ☎ 01638-61608 >>Wakkanai (Hokkaido).

● **Rishiri** Seal pool and lakes, S coast. Quaint fishing villages. Views from 1719m peak, 6hr summer hike from Oshidomari (port, YH ☎ 01638-22507).

● **Sado** Famous Taiko drummers (often away on tour), Shukunegi village. 5 *YH*'s. >>Niigata, Naoetsu.

● **Shikoku** Famed for fish paste.

● **Taketomi** Flowers, castle ruin, old houses. *Takana R/YH* ☎ 09808-52151.

● **Tanegashima** Space centre.

● **Tsushima** Spectacular Aso Bay islets. Views flying to/from Mitsushima airport. *Izuhara YH* in Seizan-ji temple. >>Fukuoka, Iki. Charters to Korea.

● **Yakushima** Dramatic volcanic cone draped in lush cedar forests. Shrines. Bring rain gear. Hot water rockpools on SW coast. Car/motorbike hire or lucky hitch hike necessary to reach sites and trailheads from the port. >>Kagoshima only.

● **Yoron** Star sand on Yurigahama Beach.

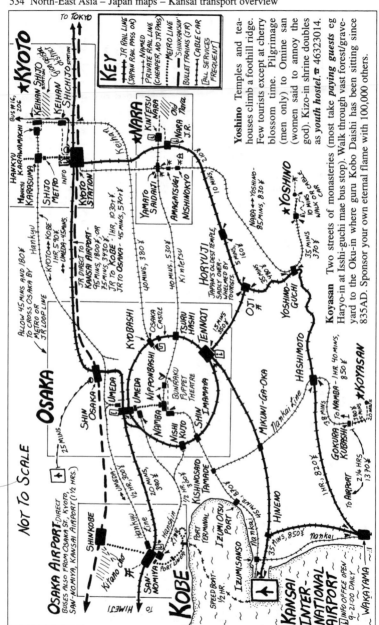

KEY

- ━━━ JR RAIL LINE (JAPAN RAIL PASS OK)
- ━ ━ PRIVATE RAIL LINE (CHEAPER, NO JR PASS)
- ·········· METRO LINE
- ═══ SHINKANSEN
- ━ ━ ━ BULLET TRAINS (JR)
- ▬▬ CABLE CAR
- ⊞ ALL SERVICES FREQUENT

Yoshino Temples and tea-houses climb a foothill ridge. Few tourists except at cherry blossom time. Pilgrimage (men only) to Omine san (women said to annoy the god). Kizo-in shrine doubles as *youth hostel.* ☎ 46323014.

Koyasan Two streets of monasteries (most take *paying guests* eg Haryo-in at Isshi-guchi mae bus stop). Walk through vast forest/grave-yard to the Oku-in where guru Kobo Daishi has been sitting since 835AD. Sponsor your own eternal flame with 100,000 others.

KYOTO STATION AREA

MATSUBAYA - 4500¥ ☎351-4268 — other cheap ryokans in area

KYOKA ☎331-2791 & MURAYAMA ☎331-1260 - BOTH ARE 4000¥

OHTO 4000¥ ☎541-7803

KEIHAN TO OSAKA

HIGASHI HONGANJI TEMPLE

KEIHAN SHICHIJO (TRACK UNDERGROUND)

KYOTO STATION

5 MINS WALK

SEIKI - MODERN TATAMI ROOMS WITH TV 5500¥/SNGL, 8-9000¥/DBL

9-17:00 M-F, 9-12:00 Sa

KYOTO TOWER

LUGGAGE LOCKERS

BUS TO AIRPORT

JR TRAINS

KINKI NIPPON TRAINS TO NARA

Japan stopover tips: Kansai

Getting to and travelling around Japan can appear dauntingly expensive, especially after a sojourn in the rest of Asia. Fortunately it is often possible to visit Japan as a free stopover between Asia and North America. Even if you have to choose Tokyo (in our opinion one of the least interesting Japanese cities), any visit to Japan is memorable. With luck you will be able to choose to stopover at the brand new Kansai airport, Japan's first 24hr entry point, built on an artificial island off Osaka. The Kansai region packs Japan's multiple facets into a conveniently small area. Kyoto and Nara, Japan's two historic (and still cultural) capitals rub shoulders with industrial giant Osaka whose modern towers are more impressive than any in Tokyo. Nearby in the surrounding mountains are peaceful temple villages (Yoshino is a personal favourite) and some excellent hikes. The area is criss-crossed with the very frequent services of a dozen different rail companies making exploration convenient if sometimes confusing.

● **Information** The JNTO information office at the airport (9am-9pm daily) can help with accommodation and gives away excellent free area and city maps. Their impressive *Map of Kansai* shows every single rail line – initially rather overwhelming. We have simplified the network to show key stations only (see p537).

● **Airport transport** Kansai airport to Kyoto takes only 75 mins, ¥3200 by JR Haruka LEX train; 95 mins, ¥1800 on direct JR express; or 2-2½hrs, ¥1430 using private rail lines (with two changes and photo stop at Osaka castle).

● **Possible transport confusions** Osaka has dozens of stations. The station name 'Osaka' is used only by JR: other companies use the name Umeda (mostly prefixed by the name of the company eg Hankyu Umeda) for stations within 10 mins walk of JR Osaka. There are also several Namba stations within walking distance from the 'Giant crab claw', the entertainment area and Bunraku puppet theatre. Kobe's main stations (private and JR) are all called Sannomiya not Kobe. In Kyoto many stations take the street name (eg Shijo (metro) and Keihan Shijo) can be a long walk apart.

Kyoto is Japan's cultural heart. There are almost numberless ancient temples and gardens dotted throughout a sprawling modern city and in its wooded mountainous fringes. Ginkaku-ji (silver), Kinkaku-ji (gold) and Kiyomizu (sacred water) temples are somewhat tourist trampled; escape on the Philosophers' Walk or head for the hills (Hiei-zan, Ohara village).

To visit the Royal Palace apply 1-2 hours ahead (with passport) to the Imperial Agency Office. Glimpse geisha and maiko girls, early evening around the ancient **teahouses** of Hanami Koji (Gion area).

YH ☎ 075 462 2288, nearly 1hr by bus #26 from station (stop C1). Other cheap hotels are marked above.

Japan stopover tips: Tokyo daytrips

Map labels:
YUMOTO · ★NIKKO ☆YH · TSUCHITARU ☆YH · Ryuzu Falls · Lake Chuzenji · Kegan Falls · 12 KM · 1½ HRS · 9HRS WALK · 2½ HRS 2840¥ · 1HR 55 MINS, 2350¥ OR 2 HRS 10MINS, 1330¥ SOBU FREE PASSES (2 DAYS RETURN - 4400¥, 4 DAYS 5760¥) ALL ON TOBU-NIKKO LINE. JR COSTS MORE, REQ CHANGE (UTSUNOMIYA) · TO TOKYO DISNEYLAND · 53 MINS, 890¥ · KITA-KAMAKURA · KAMAKURA · Big Buddha · ☆YH · Mt MITSUMINE TEMPLE ★ 1 820¥CABLECAR · OWA · MITSU-MINE GUCHI · HIKE 10HRS OVER 3 PEAKS, 5KM HUTS EN ROUTE · ★ Mt Tanigawa 3 HRS WALK · CHICHIBU · Seibu Line · DOAI ☆YH · 1½ HR · 710¥ VIA HOMO · 1½–2 HRS · ½ HR · MITAKE · 15MINS · HINATA-WADA · 40 MINS 310¥ · ☆YH · 2 MINS 240¥ · 15 MINS · 4KM · 3 HRS · 4 HRS MITAKESAN ★ · OKUTAMA · OMATSURI · 45 MINS · ☆田 KOMADORI SANSO - IN AN OLD CHICHIBU LODGE, 4000¥ ☎0428-788-472 · Chuo Line · TACHIKAWA · 2 HRS · 1 HR · 5th STAGE · Mt FUJI · KAWAGUCHI KO. BASE FOR 5 LAKES REGION · 4–5 HRS · DOWN ONLY · GOTEMBA · HAKONE! WONDERFUL HIKES BUT MANY TOURISTS. LAKE... VARIOUS TRANSPORT OPTIONS · 70 MINS 1550¥ ODAKYU LINE · ½ HR, 1400¥ (OR BY SHINKANSEN 3600¥, 40 MINS) · ODAWARA · 1 HR, W CHANGE · 45 MINS · 5th STAGE · TOKYO

Tokyo may be one of the biggest cities in the world but it's short on visible history and culture. Also, being a disparate assemblage of smaller centres, it lacks the imposing army of skyscrapers that mass on the skylines of cities like Hong Kong, New York or even Osaka. However, cheap airline stopovers usually limit you to Tokyo – and if you are unable to visit anywhere else in the country, Tokyo is still fascinating.

● **Tokyo airports** Only China Airlines (the Taiwanese carrier) uses conveniently central Haneda airport. All other international services are from Narita airport (still anachronistically known as New Tokyo International Airport though it is neither new nor, in fact, in Tokyo). On arrival at Narita, head for the JNTO information offices for useful free maps and accommodation help (open daily 9am-8pm; if closed in one terminal, try in the other). The much touted ¥2890 NEX train to Tokyo takes only 53 mins but by the time you've made the compulsory reservation, you might as well have taken the little advertised Keisei commuter train to Tokyo Ueno (¥980, 1¼hrs) or the Skyliner, (¥1880, 1hr). Avoid Narita-Tokyo buses which cost ¥2800 and get snared for hours in heavy traffic. Left luggage costs ¥500/bag/day.

● **Narita** This is a typical, if unspectacular, smaller Japanese city only 10 mins from the airport on very frequent trains: ideal for stopovers of only a few hours. Its Shinshoji temple is impressively large (if not especially old) with a three-storey pagoda. *Kirinoya ryokan* (¥5000, 1km from Narita station, ☎ 0476-230674) is a handy place to stay before an early flight. Or try the slightly more distant *BB hotel* ¥5000 (☎ 043-462 1865), 10mins walk from Shizu station, 9 Keisei line stops from airport.

● **Tokyo transportation** The city has two different metro companies. Within Tokyo's city limits (NB Narita is too far out) the go-as-you-please Tokyo Furii Kippu allows unlimited rides on JR trains, both metro systems, and most buses. However at ¥1460 (about ten times the cheapest metro fare) the cost is hard to recoup. If sticking to the central area, walking and ¥120 hops on the Yamanote loop line should suffice. Day passes for any single company's lines cost around ¥700.

This map shows a few selected stations and areas only. **Tokyo info** ☎ 03-3503 4400. Cheaper accommodation (some conveniently located options below) is worth booking ahead. Love hotels that are cheap in other cities (inc Narita) are rarely below ¥7000 in central Tokyo for 10pm–10 am 'sleep'.

1) **Youth hostel** 18th floor, Central Plaza Bldg Iidabashi. V. good ☎ 03-3235-1107. Beds ¥2800-4100.

2) **Youth hostel** Mouldering dorms built for 1964 Olympics.at 3-1 Kami-zono cho, Shibuya. ☎ 03-3467 9163. Beds ¥2800-4100.

3) **Suzuki**, 7-15-23 Yanaka, ☎ 03-3821 4944. ¥4000 pp.

4) **Sawanoya**, 3-11 Yanaka 2, Taito. ☎ 03-3822 2251. ¥4600. Other cheapies around Nezu metro station.

5) **Kikuya**, 2-18-9 Nishi Asakusa, Taito. ☎ 38414051. ¥4800

6) **Shigetsu**, 1-31-11 Asakusa, Taito. ☎ 03-3843 2345. ¥7000

7) **Happo Kaku**, 2-15-10 Minami Ikebukuro ☎ 03-3982 1181.¥6000.

NARITA (INT'L)

TO

1½ HRS, 1260 ¥ — OR — 1 HR, 2890¥ (NEX)

1½ HRS, 970¥ — OR — 1 HR, 1880¥ (SKYLINER)

Kesei Line

AOTA

OSHIAGE

ASAKUSA — SOME INTERESTING OLDER STREETS ★NAKAMISE/ SENSOJI TEMPLE.

SUMO VENUE & MUSEUM

EDO TOKYO – HISTORICAL MUSEUM, SOME RECONSTRUCTED BLDGS.

RYOGOKU

NIPPORI

NATIONAL MUSEUM

UENO

5 MINS

12 MINS

10 MINS

AKIHABARA ELECTRONICS SHOPS (BUT FEW BARGAINS)

Yamanote Loop

13 MINS

NEZU

4

25 MINS

SHITAMACHI RECONSTRUCTED OLD STREET

TOSHUGU SHRINE

Ueno Park MANY GALLERIES

11 MINS

IIDABASHI

3

SHINJUKU HUGE TV-SCREEN. NEON: SEEDY BARS.

TOSHUGU SHRINE

IMPERIAL PALACE MASSIVE CITY WALLS. ¥ FOR ENTRY. MUST BOOK.

JNTO INFO FOR ALL OF JAPAN

TOKYO STATION

Tokyo City Info.

5 MIN

YURAKUCHO CHEAP SNACKS IN ARCHES.

10 MINS

HIGASHI GINZA

KABUKI-ZA ONE ACT OF CLASSIC JAPANESE THEATRE FOR ONLY ¥900

GINZA NEON DEPT STORES, THE WORLD'S MOST EXPENSIVE BARS.

FUJITA VIRTUAL REALITY AMUSEMENTS IN THE COMPANY HQ BUILDING.

YOYOGI

HARA-JUKU

8 MINS

2 MINS

5 MIN

TOKYO TOWER (DULL EIFFEL IMITATION)

HAMA-MATSU-CHO

4 MINS

HANEDA (MOSTLY DOMESTIC)

23 MINS

20 MINS

IKEBUKURO

12 MINS

SKYSCRAPERS AROUND CITY HALL ★VIEWS FROM THE CHEAPISH RESTAURANT ON THE TOP FLOOR OF THE SUMITOMO BLDG.

SUNSHINE CITY- GIANT SHOPPING TOWER

8 MINS

MEIJI SHRINE

Yoyogi Park

15 MINS

10 MINS

★ AT SUNDAY LUNCHTIME WITNESS 'MASS INDIV- IDUALITY'- A CACOPHANY OF BANDS, BUSKERS, & ROCKABILLY DANCE SQUADS ON A SPECIALLY CLOSED STREET IN YOYOGI PARK.

Central Tokyo

KEY

MONORAIL

JR LINE- JAPAN RAIL PASS ACCEPTED

PRIVATE RAIL LINE/ METRO - MOST OMITTED

— SHORT OR INTERESTING WALK

Ⓧ TRANSFER STATION FOR 'EXCURSION'

South Korea

The World Fair, held at Taejon back in 1994, highlighted the clashing coexistence of peasant past and techno-future that makes this country so intriguing. Riding in spacecraft simulator modules and gawking at abstract conceptual art were villagers in traditional Hanbok costume, the design of which harks back to 13th-century Mongol court fashion. Amidst all the technology, a mother unfolded a cloth-wrapped container of *kimch'i* (home-made in the time-honoured way) and handed it to her sandwich-nibbling child as they picnicked beneath the futuristic 'Tower of Light'.

Here was an ancient country with a clear, apparently successful national goal; shooting itself from feudal backwardness to world pre-eminence in a single generation. Success has been slightly delayed. At the end of 1997, the economic miracle collapsed with accountants pointing long overdue fingers at the cronyism and corruption of the bloated conglomerates. Banks crashed and companies were left top heavy with debt.

But the IMF is charging to the rescue. And it's a great time to visit Korea yourself: the *won*'s value has suddenly halved making everything relatively cheap. Though its only land border (with North Korea) remains closed, South Korea is a convenient boat hop between China and Japan. Alternatively, many discount tickets with Korean or Asiana airlines allow you a free Seoul stopover. Once here, your reaction to the Korean people will depend greatly on where you've come from. After China they'll seem charming and helpful. After Japan they're harsh and direct, if refreshingly 'human'. Crash or no crash, the cultural gulf between young and old will remain fascinating. So will the jarring mismatch between the quaint old courtyard homes and the stark platoons of numbered concrete towers which overshadow them – even in the smallest country towns across this craggy-green land of garlic and ginseng.

❏ **W&M's country ratings – South Korea**
- **Expense $$$$** $20/day at least despite currency drops. It's easy to spend more. Prices have increased steadily over the past decade.
- **Value for money ✔✔✔** Good value in comparison to its neighbours (Japan and east coast China) but not compared to South East Asia.
- **Getting around ✔✔✔** Transport is efficient and buses are very frequent. But bus and train stations are often inconveniently far apart; some ticket vending machines have instructions only in Korean.
- **English spoken ✔✔✔** A phrase book is very useful though university students often speak some English.
- **Woman alone ✔✔✔✔✔** No particular problem.
- **For vegetarians ✔✔✔** A vegetarian option is usually available. I am a vegetarian – *ch'aeshik juwi imnida.*

PRACTICAL INFORMATION
Visas and formalities

If you need a visa (see Essential information box) you may also be required to provide tickets or a letter from a travel agent confirming onward flights. Nationalities who normally need visas may visit Cheju Island visa free for up to 15 days.

48-hour transit visas are available on arrival for passengers changing planes at Seoul's Kimpo Airport.

● **Extensions** Neither tourist visas nor the visa-free period (both usually three months) are extendible – a restriction which was designed to cut down on the increasing number of English teachers working without correct documentation. Changing visa type requires you to leave the country.

Money

Travellers' cheques are generally easy to change (US$ and yen are the most accepted) and get slightly better rates than cash.

There are many ATMs but few have international links, most operate business hours only and many have instructions only in Korean.

Cash advances are commission free, though finding a bank which offers the service for your card may not be easy.

Banks are open Monday to Friday 9.30am-4.30pm, Saturday 9.30am-1.30pm. It's hard to change money when the banks are closed.

Transport

● **Bus** The Korean bus system is efficient and extensive – there is at least one bus a

---

❑ **Geo-political information – South Korea**

Population: 45 million (1997), 43.4m (1990), 34.7m (1974).

Area: 219,000 sq km.

Capital: Seoul (10.6 million, 1990).

Other major cities: Pusan (3.8m), Taegu (2.2m), Incheon (1.8m), Kwangju (1.1m), Taejon (1m), Ulsan, Suwon, Songnam, Chonju, Chongju, Masan (400,000+), Chinju, Cheju, Mokpo, Kunsan (300,000+) and 21 more cities over 100,000.

GNP per capita: $8200 (1994), $4124 (1988), $2238 (1984).

Currency history: Won/US$1 — Feb 1998: W1690, Oct 1997: W910, July 1996: W810.8, Jan 1996: W786.8, Jan 1995: W791.2, Jan 1994: W811.9, 1991: W733, 1986: W881, 1980: W659.

Major exports/economy: Heavy industry, footwear, cars. Rapid industrialisation.

Ethnic mix: Korean.

Official languages: Hanguk (Korean).

Religious mix: Confucian (10m – but only 233 temples), Buddhist (11m, 85% Mahayana), Christian (17.5m, of which 80% protestant), Chundo Kyo (uniquely Korean shamanistic religion).

Landmarks of national history: **676AD**: Silla Kingdom unified Korea. **936**: Koryo kingdom dominated the peninsula. **1234**: Printing developed. **1392**: Yi dynasty replaced Buddhism with Confucianism. **1443**: Hangul alphabet invented under King Sejong. **1592-7**: Much of Korea was torched by the Japanese invasion. **1905**: Became a Japanese protectorate. **1941**: Japanese language made compulsory. **1945**: US and Soviet invasions resulted in the division of Korea at the 38th parallel. **1950-53**: Korean war killed around four million.

Leader: President Kim Dae Yung. Former presidents Chun Doo Hwan and Roh Tae Woo face treason charges over the 1979 coup and the suppression of an uprising in Kwangju.

Pressing political issues: Corruption, continuing worries about the collapse of the North – the south would be flooded with refugees. Stockmarket crash.

day between every city; almost every town with a bus station has a direct bus to Seoul. Buses leave frequently and are reasonably priced. Tickets are bought in the station beforehand (often each destination will have its own ticket-selling window). Classes include: de luxe (plush seats, drinks on board, a reserved seat), express (similar to de luxe but less leg room), and local (no guarantee of a seat and slow as there are stops all along the way).

In big cities there may be up to four regional bus stations (north, south, east and west) each of which serves local towns in that particular direction. These stations are connected by city buses. The long distance bus station which serves places further afield is usually attached to one of these.

● **Train** Train types include *t'ongil* which is not air conditioned, *mugungwha* which is, and *saemaul-ho* which is both air conditioned and faster than the other two. An even faster TGV-style bullet train is under construction. Bookings are advised at least a few hours ahead, and even more during busy periods, to ensure a seat.

● **Air** The domestic air system is very extensive, check-in is quick (we caught a Cheju-Seoul flight despite arriving at the airport only 15 minutes before departure). Allow two hours to reach Pusan's airport; the traffic can be appalling.

International departure tax: W8000. Domestic: W2000.

● **Boat** Many boat services ply between the islands of Korea's south and west coasts. See p14-15 for international routes.

Departure tax on international boats: W2000.

● **Hitchhiking** Koreans apparently never hitch. But if you are standing at the side of the road looking as if you need a ride a passing driver is likely to help you out. Indeed, on our first experience of hitching in Korea, we were astounded at how easy it was – each car stopped for us until we found one going to our destination.

● **Underground** Pusan and Seoul have underground railways. The one in Seoul feeds directly into the suburban rail lines to Incheon, Suwon etc.

● **Taxis** Prices go up at night; many drivers want to know where you're going and will only take you if it's the way that they're already headed.

Accommodation

Almost every town or village has at least one *yogwan,* a traditional Korean inn with simple rooms, a blanket and thin mattress on the floor (the average cost is W12-15,000 for a room). A *yoinsuk* is of a slightly lower quality and price than a *yogwan* (W10-12,000). A room in a private house – *minbak* – is cheaper still (W7-10,000) though these are usually found only in rural areas and in national/provincial parks. Bargaining is acceptable, especially in the low season. A *minbak* on the outskirts of a national park charged W10,000 in the high season but only W5000 in the low; no one else was staying there, so we managed to bargain the rate down to W2500/day for a three-day stay (meals are not included).

In towns and villages, most locals should know where cheap accommodation is: ask for a *bee-sah-gee ahn-noon-bahng* (inexpensive hotel room) – the word for 'cheap' is even more difficult to say.

Food and drink

Korean food packs a garlic-chilli punch without the fruity moderation of Thai cuisine. The halitosis atmosphere in buses and

❏ Essential information for travellers – South Korea

● **Visa** Most Europeans can stay for three months without a visa and Japanese for 15 days. Visas are required for Canadians, Americans, Australians and New Zealanders.

● **Currency** Won. US$1=W1690. (NB The prices quoted in this chapter are from our pre-crash research when US$1=W900.)

● **Time zone** 9 hours ahead of GMT (same as Japan, 1hr ahead of China).

● **Religious tone** A spiritual feel definitely exists but it has been smothered by modernisation. The Christian influence is strong. Active Shamanistic ('Mugang') worship.

● **Health factors** Tap water is safe to drink. There's no malarial risk.

● **Special dangers** If you're staying in an *ondol* (under floor)-heated room don't leave cameras, film or heat sensitive material on the floor and leave the window open – carbon monoxide from burning coal can seep through old porous floors.

● **Social conventions** Koreans sometimes appear rude. A Korean who bumps into you as you walk down the street is unlikely to offer an apology. This is largely because, linguistically and culturally, Koreans should know where you are on a social hierarchy to apologise appropriately (or, in some cases, to even acknowledge your presence). Once introduced, however, Koreans make charming company. Koreans show respect when shaking hands (or when giving/receiving) by supporting their right forearm with the left hand. When someone pours a beer for you, it is polite to receive it by holding your glass with two hands. As in Japan, outdoor shoes are only worn outdoors and special slippers are provided for the toilet. As it is correct to address people by the first syllable of their family name, you'll find that a remarkable number of your friends are called Kim or Park.

● **Typical traveller destinations** Kyongju, Cheju Island and Seoul.

● **Highlights** Hiking/exploring the national parks (eg Soraksan). Drunken talks with university students. Kapsa, Ullung-do, Tongdosa, Pulguksa (Kyongju) if you can lose the tour groups.

● **When to go** Trying to find the narrow gap between the sweltering summer and the freezing winter is the key to an enjoyable visit. Autumn (particularly October and November) is beautiful with cool evenings, leaves changing colour in the mountains and clear air. Spring and summer see frequent heavy rain, sometimes for prolonged periods, especially in July when typhoons can hit.

● **Pulse of the country** City centre coffee shops (besuited yuppies call from table to table on their mobile phones); P'anmunjom (a tense border post with North Korea), Kyongju (a cultural centre).

● **Key tips** Some command of spoken and written Korean is very useful and not as difficult to pick up as it would appear.

　　United Service Organization (USO) (Seoul ☎ 795 3063; Pusan ☎ 462 3732) is the entertainment branch of the US army but you don't have to be a marine to take part in their very reasonably priced tours. Options include tours to the demilitarised zone and skiing holidays in the winter.

● **Festivals** Around Chusok (in summer) public transport is fully booked as everyone heads back to their families for a type of thanksgiving. Most shops are closed. Lunar new year is also a major holiday (kites are flown to release last year's bad luck to the heavens).

❏ **Some national and provincial parks**

● **Odaesan National Park**

Nearby towns   Wolchongsa (main gateway to park); Kangnung (nearest city).

Getting there   1½hrs on several buses between Wolchongsa and Kangnung.

Accommodation Several possibilities around the Kangnung bus terminal.

What's there/notes Hiking but no camping. Highest peak is Pirobong (1563m).

● **Kayasan National Park**

Nearby towns   Kayasan village, Taegu is the nearest large city.

Getting there   Several buses from Taegu (1hr), direct buses to Haeinsa from
                  Pusan and Chinju.

Accommodation Several places in Kayasan – the cheapest are W14,000/sgl in
                  the high season and W9000 in the low.

What's there/notes Haeinsa – where thousands of wooden carved blocks with
                  Buddhist scripture is housed in the temple. Hiking.

● **Ch'ongnyangsan Provincial Park**

Nearby towns   Ch'ongsong (gateway), Andong.

Getting there   Occasional buses go from Seoul (Tong terminal) to
                  Ch'ongsong, but there are plenty from Andong.

Accommodation Several *yogwan* in the park – W13,000/sgl. No camping.

What's there/notes Mountains and hiking, though the park is often crowded

● **Chirisan National Park**

Nearby towns   Taewonsa at the east end of the park (the most popular gate
                  way), Ssanggyesa (southern gateway), Chinju (nearest city).

Getting there   Bus services run frequently to Taewonsa and Ssanggyesa
                  from Chinju (2½hrs). Direct to Ssanggyesa from Pusan
                  (West terminal: 5½hrs).

Accommodation Camping in the wilds of the park and in Taewonsa. Both
                  Taewonsa and Ssanggyesa have *minbak* for around W10,000.

What's there/notes Hiking and camping. A Buddhist temple in Ssanggyese.

● **Soraksan Park**

Nearby towns   Sokch'o and Wont'ong (both gateways).

Getting there   Direct bus from Seoul to the park entrance (Sangbong
                  Terminal, 5hrs). Shuttles from Sokch'o and Wont'ong (both
                  30 mins).

Accommodation Plenty of *minbak* at the base of the park (Sorak-dong) and
                  shelters in it (you need your own sleeping bag and food).

What's there/notes Taech'ongbong Peak (1708m) – walks to the peak take
                  between 4½ and 7 hours but it is closed from mid-March to the
                  end of May, and in November; waterfalls, rocky peaks.

● **Songnisan Park**

Nearby towns   Songni-dong (at entrance of park), Taejon (nearest city).

Getting there   Several direct buses from Seoul daily (3hrs), Taejon (very
                  frequent, 1¾hrs) and other cities.

Accommodation Several *minbak* in the town; the cheapest is one block to the
                  left of the main street as you face the park entrance.

What's there/notes   Popju giant bronze Buddha statue (built in 1989) beside an
                  ancient wooden pagoda. The day hike to the top becomes
                  very muddy in the rain.

commuter trains is nature's retribution. To enjoy the food fully, help is needed choosing as the menus are normally in Korean script. Whatever you order (or think you've ordered) it is likely to come with a side dish of *kimch'i* (spicy fermented cabbage). Chefs and women are judged by their *kimch'i* – look for the large, glazed brown earthenware urns outside any traditional home.

Typical dishes include *bibimbap* (which can be virtually anything – *bibim* means mix – but is often vegetarian), *pulgogi* (marinated beef strips that you grill yourself on a charcoal burner), *kalbi* (similarly treated ribs) and *kamja puch'im* (a potato pancake seasoned with soy sauce).

Staying in touch
● **Mail** Sending mail is reliable if expensive. Major post offices have a convenient boxing service for parcels.

American Express (☎ 398-0114) is at 3/F, Hankook Kumbak Building, 181-2 Buam-Dong, Chongro-Ku, Seoul.
● **Phone** Dial 001 to place an international call, 007 to make a collect call. International country code: +82. Seoul: 02, Pusan: 051, Taejon: 042, Cheju: 064.

Activities
● **Skiing** See box below.
● **Taekwon-do** Non-Koreans can partici-
pate in Taekwon-do (Korean martial arts) training sessions at universities during the summer and winter breaks. Advance booking is advised.
● **Hiking and outdoor activities** There are some beautiful national parks and mountain walks. Be aware, however, that these get extremely full of other walkers – especially in school holidays when the innumerable parties of loud, over-friendly children can destroy the atmosphere extremely effectively. Summits to well-known mountains are frequently scaled by flights of steps up which queues of smoking and drinking septuagenarians splutter noisily. That said, during the week and low season, parks can be nearly deserted. See box opposite.
● **Watersports** Chungmun and other beaches on Cheju-do are pleasant but somewhat over-hyped. On the mainland, the west coast beaches are generally preferred to the east. Summer is the only season when it is warm enough to go swimming.
● **Work** Pre-crash, the combination of low start-up costs and high wages made Korea one of the best countries for finding an English teaching job. Average pay was $25-35 an hour; some schools offered free or cheap housing. Teachers with contracted positions typically work 20-30 hours a week for a salary of $1700-2300/month.

❏ Skiing in South Korea
Korea has some of the best value and most easily accessible skiing in Asia. Most slopes open sometime in November and close in March. Skis etc can be hired for about W16,000 a day and a lift ticket costs W16,700; half-day options available.

Resort	Slopes	Lifts	Vertical	How to get there
Yongpyeong	13	16	715m	Local bus Kanghung to Hoenggye (W600, 10 mins), then taxi (10 mins). Seoul office (☎ 561-6255).
Alps	8	5	1780m	Daily shuttle bus from Seoul (W16,000) or a free shuttle bus twice a day from Sokch'o. Seoul office (☎ 756-5481).
Daemyung	7	5	1357m	Shuttle bus from Seoul (30-45 mins), or taxi from Hongch'on (W5000, 30min).

Other smaller resorts (each within an hour of Seoul) include: Bear Town, Chonmasan, Yangji, and Suanbo.

❏ Korean script – Hangul

At first sight Korean script looks as dauntingly unreadable as Chinese. It isn't. In fact, Hangul is one of the world's most elegantly logical writing systems. Despite its inscrutable appearance, it's surprisingly easy to learn and you'll quickly be able to wow your friends with your esoteric knowledge. Like English it is an alphabet and letters represent sounds (not ideas as in Chinese).

		(SHORT "A")	("EE")		(SHORT "O")	("ŏŏ")	(SHORT "OO")
SIMPLE VOWELS (0 or 1 dot)	A	AE	E	I	O	Ŏ	U	Ŭ
	ㅏ	ㅐ	ㅔ	ㅣ	ㅗ	ㅓ	ㅜ	ㅡ
	ma**r**k	m**a**p	m**e**t	m**ee**t	b**oa**t	b**o**ttle/ b**u**t	b**oo**t	b**oo**k

"Y" VOWELS (2 DOTS)	YA	YAE	YE	✕	YO	YŎ	YU	✕
	ㅑ	ㅒ	ㅖ		ㅛ	ㅕ	ㅠ	

"W" VOWEL COMBINATIONS	WA	WAE	WE	WI	OE (WÉ)	WO	w**ai**t	ŬI
	ㅘ	ㅙ	ㅞ	ㅟ	ㅚ	ㅝ	Lou**i**se	ㅢ
	(O+A)	(O+AE)	(U+E)	(U+I)	(O+I)	(U+Ŏ)		(Ŭ+I)

CONSONANTS	B see P	Ch/J/т ㅈ	Ch'/т ㅊ	D see T	G see K or Ng	H ㅎ	J see Ch	K/G ㄱ	K' ㅋ	KK ㄲ	L/R ㄹ
M ㅁ	N ㄴ	Ng/silent* ㅇ	P/B ㅂ	P' ㅍ	PP ㅃ	R see L	S/Sh ㅅ	SS ㅆ	T/D ㄷ	T' ㅌ	Tch ㅊ	TT ㅍ	TT ㄸ	W, Y see vowels

These letters are arranged into crunchy little syllable clusters. Typically this means putting a consonant before a vowel and (optionally) jamming another consonant underneath. Using Hangul writing logic you might write

London as: and **taxi** as:

Lŏ Dŏ 래〉 런 던   TAXI "AE" 택 시

The exact letter positions vary – horizontal, vertical or clumped according to what fits best: eg vertical in Kongju (a Korean town):

Every cluster must start with a consonant. However, since many Korean syllables actually begin with a vowel, the issue is fudged by using a silent 'ng' consonant. Seoul station (phonetically Sôul Yok) is:

NB ㅈ = Ch   ㄱ = ㅅ

Consonants change slightly according to where in the sylla-

Sŏ ㅓ 러 챵 래〉 서 울 역

ble the letter occurs. In Korean K and G, Ch and J etc don't actually sound so different so mumble slightly like the locals do, and no one will notice*. Similarly beginners needn't worry about the difference between unaspirated and aspirated consonants (eg Ch versus Ch'). If you see a rare double consonant at a word's end, one will be silent.

*Exceptions: Ch, Ch' and S all become T at the end of a word. L/R becomes N after an M, N or Ng.

Americans seem to be the preferred nationality for English teaching jobs – they have the accent Koreans are most familiar with. However, the recent drop in the supply of foreign teachers, following scares over the North's nuclear capabilities, means jobs are easier to come by for all nationalities. The easiest place to find work is at a *hakwan* (foreign language institute), though universities and occasionally private individuals will also hire. The best time to find work is late December and mid to late June. A professional appearance and smart CV are especially important for landing a good job.

Other jobs in Korea of interest to travellers include modelling, film work, editing and proofreading. Some background in your prospective field would be helpful.

The *Korea Super Job Catalog* ($25), sold by Bonus Books (US toll free ☎ 800-225-3775), 160 E Illinois, Chicago, IL 60611, has extensive listings of jobs if you prefer to look for one before you go.

Korea Services Group, 147-7 Bum Jeon Dong, Jin-ku, Pusan 614-060, hires English teachers, helps foreigners find work and arranges visas. The **ELS International Language Institute** hires English teachers from abroad. The USA office (for US and Australian citizens) is at: 5761 Buckingham Parkway, Culber City, CA 90230, (US ☎ 310-642-0988, fax 310-410-4688). The Korea office is at: 649-1 Yeoksam-dong, Kangnam-gu, Seoul 135-081, (☎ 2-554 9191/4, fax 2-553-1290).

• **Volunteering** The **Korean National Commission for UNESCO**, PO Box Central 64, Seoul 100, runs a work camp in Korea though you have to pay to participate. Many Christian-based NGOs also do work in Korea.

Further information

● **Books and maps** A good up-to-date guidebook is extremely useful if you're expecting to go to out of the way places. After years of very mediocre attempts, Lonely Planet has finally published an

---

❏ Meeting the locals

● **The people** Koreans are generally helpful and forthright. Most topics are open to discussion with younger Koreans (one even asked us how easy it was to find sexual partners while travelling). Issues of Korean nationalism, however, can sometimes draw a heavy response. Koreans are extremely keen to present a positive image of their country and for their country to be viewed as culturally unique and dynamic. What other country celebrates the creation of its alphabet as a holiday?

University students are especially open to talking with foreigners. As in Western countries, a good place to meet them is at their student union (*hahksehng-hweh-gwahn*) on any college campus.

Attitudes to Japan are often antagonistic. Many Koreans claim to hate the Japanese, though not on an individual level. Admitting that you are simply transiting through Korea between China and Japan may cause mild disappointment.

• **Some phrases in Korean**

Greeting (to younger person) – *Anyong ha se yo*
Response – *Ye, anyong ha shim nika*
Greeting (to an older person) – *Anyong ha shim nika*
Response – *Ye, anyong ha se yo*
Thank you – *Kamsa hamnida* or *ko map sumni da*
It's good – *Chon imnida*
Toasts – *Kuhn-beh* (cheers); *wee-hah-yeh* (to us or to you)
Let's go (together)! – *Kahp-shee-dah*

excellent *Korea* guide (4th edition). It includes Hangul script and has extensive listings of cheap accommodation, as well as in-depth background information. For cultural background information, *Culture Shock! Korea* is recommended.

Many excellent background books on Korea (in English) are available locally. Indeed, some are difficult to find outside Korea. Good books widely available include *A History of Korea* by Woo-Keun Han (University of Hawaii Press), a well-written historical account of Korea through the 1970s, and *To Dream of Pigs: Travels in South and North Korea* by Clive Leatherday (Desert Island Books). Guidebooks are available at bookstores in Korea, but are difficult to find used.

● **Maps** It is worth noting that maps produced in Korea rarely show the division of North and South. There is also tremendous potential for confusion in roman script – Kyongju, Gyongju and Gyeongchu are all transliterations of the same place while Kyongju, Kongju and Kwangju are all different major towns. However, place name differences show up clearly in the local Hangul script which is easy to learn.

● **Information offices Korea National Tourism Corporation** (KNTC) Head Office (☎ 729-9600, fax 757-5997), 10 Ta-dong, Chung-gu, Seoul 100-180, the government's tourist information service is phenomenal. They have free maps and brochures for almost every city and area of the country, often with bus and train times as well as prices. Most towns of tourist interest have a least one KNTC office and, in our experience, their staff were eager to do what they could to help (that is, when they spoke English – their Pusan office seems more geared towards Russians).

KNTC doesn't know so much about cheap accommodation outside major tourist centres.

Web sites

Korea Help Page:Some travel information, but most of it is basic
http://soback.kornet.nm.kr/~wharms/rok-help.html

Korean Celebrities (a good place to get a feel for the constantly changing Korean pop culture).
http://www.cris.com/~dna2/koreans.html

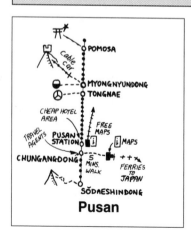

Pusan

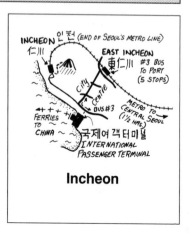

Incheon

Seoul

●**Accommodation** The cheapest option is still the famous *Inn Daewon*. Other cheap hotels (some around the Inn Daewon) have singles for W10-12,000, though these are often full of English teachers renting long term. The City Hall tourist office may be willing to call around for you to find a vacant room. If you arrive late, the Inn Daewon will also help you find a cheap place (around W12,000) if they are full.

● **Getting to Central Seoul**

From	To Central Seoul/Inn Daewon
Kimpo Int'l Airport	Local bus (incl. #1002) or express bus (dep every 10 mins).
Seoul train station	Subway (line 1) to Chonggak.
Ch'ongnyangni stn	Subway (line 1) to Chonggak.
Incheon (China boats)	City bus to Incheon subway station then direct to Chonggak (on line 1).
Tong bus stn	Subway (line2, Kangbyon stn) to Shimsoldong, then line1
Sobu bus stn	Subway (line 3) to Chongno 3-ga, then transfer to line 1.
Sangbong bus stn	City bus to Ch'ongnyangni Station.

● **Sights and entertainment** The most common tourist activity is shopping. Seoul has several glitzy urban shopping malls and slightly less glitzy markets. Markets include: It'aewan (also an entertainment centre with bars, discos, and fast food joints; take a taxi or walk around 1km west of Samgakchi subway station), Namdaemum (one of the cheapest; caters to Russians; take subway line 4 to Hoehyon), and Yongsan (Korean, Chinese and Taiwanese electronics; take subway line 1 to Yangon).

Seoul has several royal palaces surrounded by the traffic and the trappings of modern life, so you need an active imagination to pretend you are back in the 12-16th centuries (when most were built). All the palaces are all marked on the KNTC tourist map; the most dramatic include: Ch'anggyonggung (closed Tuesday), Toksugung, and Kyongbokkung.

● **Two recommended subway stops from where to start exploring** 1) Ahpkujong-dong (line 3): ritzy, expensive, and friendly if Westernised; 'home of the beautiful people'.
2) Shinchon (line 2): fun, less pretentious than Ahpkujong-dong, with lots of drinking places and hangouts; good place to meet people.

● **Cheju-do (Island)** Korea's beach resort and 'Honeymoon Island'. Cheju City (sprawling city, transport hub, cheapest *yogwans* near port). Mt Halla (though Korea's highest mountain, its gentle rise through moorland lacks the drama of Taedun San or Sorak San). Sogwipo (comically dour newly wed couples queue to be photographed at the Chongbang waterfall which dribbles over a cliff onto the beach). Songsan Po (village at a distinctive pinnacle of rocky headland, cliffs, nice sunrise view). Songup ('Folk village' preserves unique thatched traditional Cheju houses and 'Easter Island' megalithic heads).

● **Chinju** Old Choksongnu pavilion lost in this dull sprawl. Flight to Cheju.

● **Haein Sa** Temple complex of 90 holy buildings scattered across Kayasan national park, holding the original Triptakata Koreana scriptures carved on 80,000 wooden blocks. >>Taegu

● **Hallyo Waterway** Several daily hydrofoils Yosu-Chungmu-Pusan weave between the many islands. Views attractive. Boats enclosed; can't stand on deck.

● **Kanghwa** Over-hyped castle/palace.

● **Kapsa** Ancient temple complex. Highlight of a trip is the 3-5hr hike to Tonghaksa on an easy to follow, popular forest/mountain trail. Small shrines and a tiny monastery en route.>> Kongju.

● **Kongju** Attractive smaller town. Very ruined ruins of castle cover a whole hilltop at the old-town entrance (walk across long river bridge from the bus station). Tumuli. The *Samuron Yoinsuk* has basic rooms round an atmospheric courtyard.

● **Kyongju** Ancient capital of Silla, grassy park full of tumuli: one tomb is open: burial treasures on display. Traditional houses, and surrounding hills full of tombs, temples, hikes. Tourist info at bus station but nearby Hanjin Yogwan (traveller hangout) is better for tips.

● **Maisan** 'Horse's ears' (mountain). Curious cairns between the 'ears'. >>Ch'onju, Kwangju

● **Mokpo** Base for ferries to dramatic offshore islands (eg Huksando, Hongdo).

7hr ferry via inner islands to Wando.

● **Odaesan** Nat park (see p542), Sari-ra reliquaries – as on Laos' Plain of Jars.

● **Pomunsa** 'Eyebrow rock Buddha'.

● **Panmunjon** Border village straddling the de-militarised zone (DMZ). Here tentative re-unification noises are occasionally voiced. Visits restricted to tours: typically $50 from Seoul, but cheaper with US forces groups (book ahead). Contrast visits from the North Korean side!

● **Popju** Oldest wooden pagoda in Korea, huge bronze Buddha, short walk from Sogni-dong where you can buy good hiking maps for the surrounding Sognisan national park.

● **Pulguksa** Korea's grandest temple. Majestic with ginko trees and reflecting pond, but swarms with tourists. >>City buses from Kyongju.

● **Pusok Sa** Ancient temples and the 'floating rock' – a holy geological curiosity. >>Andong

● **Suwon** 'Walled city' makes the place sound too exciting. The remnant gate is a traffic circle. However the excellent (folk village is worth the W3500. Dancers and artisans demonstrate traditional crafts in an extensive wooded 'village' of re-assembled buildings from all over Korea. Free bus (from office across from Suwon railway station). Direct buses to Seoul.

● **Taedun San** Dramatic rocky pinnacles scaled via cablecar or brightly painted steep stairways by gaggles of kimchee picnickers. >>Taejon.

● **Taejon** The futuristic 'tower of light' remains from the World Expo. *Yogwans* near the main station.

● **Tongdo Sa** Village on the Pusan-Kyongju highway. Walk 3km west to the extensive temple set in beautiful streamside woodland. Peaceful except when tour coaches roll in. >>Hitching is easy.

● **Tonghak Sa** Extensive, beautifully set monastery complex on city bus line from Taejon.

● **Ullung Do** Quaint fishing villages cling to steep coast. Round-island ferry rec.

● **Yosu** No 'sights' but pleasant town to wander while awaiting Hallyo hydrofoil.

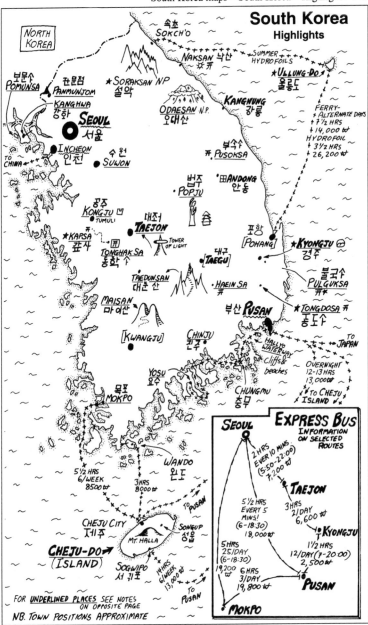

South Korea
Highlights

NORTH KOREA

속초 SOKCH'O

NAKSAN 낙산 ☆☀开

SUMMER HYDROFOILS

★ULLUNG-DO 울릉도

보문 POMUNSA

판문점 PANMUNJOM

SORAKSAN NP 설악

KANGNUNG 강릉

ODAESAN N.P. 오대산

FERRY ALTERNATE DAYS 7½ HRS 14,000₩ HYDROFOIL 3½ HRS 26,200₩

강화 KANGHWA

SEOUL 서울

TO CHINA

INCHEON 인천

수원 SUWON

부석 PUSOKSA 开

田ANDONG 안동

공주 KONGJU 田 TUMULI

법주 POPJU

포항 POHANG

★KYONGJU ☯ 경주

대전 TAEJON

TOWER OF LIGHT

★KAPSA 갑사

TONGHAK SA 동학사 ☆

대구 TAEGU

불국 PULGUKSA 开★

TAEDUNSAN 대둔산

HAEIN SA 개 ★TONGDOSA 开 통도사

MAISAN 마이산

PUSAN 부산

[KWANGJU]

CHINJU 진주

HALLYO WATERWAY

TO JAPAN

YOSU 여수

CHUNGMU 충무

OVERNIGHT 12-13 HRS 13,000₩

Cliffs & beaches

TO CHEJU ISLAND

목포 MOKPO

WANDO 완도

5½ HRS 6/WEEK 8500₩

3 HRS 8000₩

TO PUSAN

CHEJU CITY 제주

SONGUP 성읍

MT. HALLA

CHEJU-DO (ISLAND)

SOGWIPO 서귀포

1 HRS 6/WEEK 13,000₩

TO PUSAN

FOR UNDERLINED PLACES SEE NOTES ON OPPOSITE PAGE

NB. TOWN POSITIONS APPROXIMATE

EXPRESS BUS
INFORMATION ON SELECTED ROUTES

SEOUL

2 HRS EVERY 10 MINS (5:50-22:00) 7,200₩

TAEJON

3 HRS 21/DAY 6,600₩

5½ HRS EVERY 5 MINS! (6-18:30) 18,000₩

KYONGJU

1½ HRS 12/DAY (7-20:00) 2,500₩

5 HRS 25/DAY (6-18:30) 19,200₩

6 HRS 3/DAY 19,800₩

PUSAN

MOKPO

North Korea

The North Korean Government is usually classified as Marxist or Communist, but authoritarian, reclusive, and bizarre would be more accurate descriptions. From 1953, when war divided Korea, until 1994 the northern half of the peninsula was ruled by Kim Il-Sung and his 'far-sighted, immortal' *Juche* ideology. The entire country was, and still is, run like a sort of Kim Il-Sung fan club. Portraits and statues of the 'Great Leader' are omnipresent. Superlatives continue to flow from the North Korean propaganda machine; in a 1996 article wishing him a happy birthday he was described as the 'Greatest leader in the history of the universe who never once made a mistake' – reading it you'd hardly have guessed that he'd been dead for two years.

The Great Leader died in July 1994, leaving his son, the 'Dear Leader' (a playboy by the dour standards of North Korea) in command. The change in leadership has yet to translate into an opening of the country. The reforms of Russia, China and the Eastern European countries are seen as selling out socialism rather than examples to be followed. One of the largest liberalisations in recent years is that bicycles are once again allowed in Pyongyang.

Meanwhile, the North Korean economy – proclaiming itself the most industrialised in the world – is on the verge of collapse. Factories are idle and North Korea is receiving emergency food aid following disastrous harvests.

❏ **Essential information for travellers – North Korea**

• **Visa** Required. You can only obtain a visa if you join a tour (the average cost is $130 a day). The North Korean International Tourist Company in Macau and the North Korean embassy in Beijing are the cheapest places in Asia to arrange tours.

NB Japanese passports are not valid for travel to North Korea. US passports are theoretically valid though tour agents usually will not accept Americans. Travellers are occasionally refused entry into North Korea by border guards, even though they have valid visas (eg when Kim Il Sung died).

• **Currency** Won. US$1=W2.14. Despite the artificially fixed exchange rate, the government ensures there is no black market. Most costs are included in the tour price but some $1 notes would be useful for small items, such as meals on the train coming into North Korea.

• **Time zone** 9 hours ahead of GMT (1hr ahead of China; same as South Korea and Japan).

• **Religious tone** None. Religion is frowned upon by the government though much of the population is thought to harbour traditional Buddhist, Confucian or Shamanist leanings.

● **When to go** April, May, October and November are relatively dry and neither unduly hot nor cold. 16 February (Kim Jong Il's Birthday), 15 April (Kim Il Sung's birthday) and 1 May are all times to witness the splendour of the choreographed victory march and mass displays.

Analysts predict the imminent demise of the government but they have been predicting that for years. The country's few visitors report little visible unrest in a people who have been led to believe that their country has developed faster than anywhere else on earth. With no chance of going abroad (Koreans studying in eastern European universities were recalled when the Berlin Wall started teetering) and with most foreign radio and TV broadcasts blocked, the North Korean people's ignorance has been carefully contrived – but it won't last forever.

Despite the cost, a visit to this unique historical quirk is worth doing soon. When the world's most heavily fortified border opens, the empty dead-end highway between Seoul and Pyongyang will swarm with millions of South Korean trippers and the spooky feeling of isolation will be lost.

❏ **W&M's country ratings – North Korea**
● **Expense $$$$$** Because it is tour or nothing.
● **Value for money** Such bourgeois ratings don't apply here.

❏ **Geo-political information – North Korea**
Population: 24.3 million (1997).
Area: 120,000 sq km.
Capital: Pyongyang (2 million, 1986).
Other major cities: Hamhung (670,000), Chongjin (530,000), Sinuiju (330,000), Kaesong (310,000), Anju (200,000).
GNP per capita: $910 (1988). The economy is thought to be reducing by 5% annually.
Currency history: Won/US$1 – Feb 1998: W2.14, Oct 1997: W2.14, 1995: W2.15, 1994: W2.15, 1992: W2.15, 1990: W0.97.
Major exports/economy: The biggest foreign exchange receipts are the remittances of Korean Japanese pachinko tycoons to their relatives in North Korea. Plans to export Manganese. The threat of nuclear arms was swapped for 500,000 tonnes of oil a year.
Official language: Korean.
Religious mix: Officially there are 25,000 Christians (using 500 house churches), 10,000 Buddhists and an unspecified number of adherents to Chundo Kyo.
Landmarks of national history: **1945**: Japanese occupation ended, replaced by a Soviet one as far as the 38th parallel – this became the border with the US occupied south. **1947**: UN resolution to create a unified Korea was rejected by the USSR. **1950-53**: Korean War. **June 1994**: Meeting planned between the leaders of the North and South but Kim Il Sung died before it convened.
Leaders: President Kim Il Sung died in July 1994 (though his death may not be immediately apparent). No president has officially taken the Great Leader's place though his son the Dear Leader, Kim Jong Il, has been increasingly referred to as 'Great'. In October 1997 he was confirmed as party chairman.
Pressing political issues: Survival.

PRACTICAL INFORMATION
Taking a tour

Obligatory tours are the North Korean government's way of controlling your movements and watching what you do. Undoubtedly these tours do limit your freedom and give you an artificial view of the country but they are an incredible experience. And with accommodation so scarce and the paranoia of talking to foreigners so high, it is unlikely you'd be able to travel around the country independently, even if you were allowed to. One diplomat in Pyongyang who tried to buy a train ticket found that absolutely no one would help her, even though she spoke fluent Korean.

It seems possible, at least in some cases, to spontaneously change your tour itinerary after arriving in North Korea – travellers we met had talked their guides into taking them to local eating establishments, to schools, and to towns that were not on the schedule. Theoretically, you are allowed to wander around on your own during free times in the tour, though guides will often insist they join you in case you get lost. Some private travel agencies:

VNC Travel (Netherlands ☎ 0302-613844, fax 0302-627734, e-mail: VNC.Travel@inter.nl.net), Mississippi-dreef 95, PO Box 79, 3500 AB Utrecht, Netherlands. A one-week tour costs NLG1675 (Netherlands guilders) per person for two people sharing and taking the train from Beijing.

Regent Holidays (UK ☎ 0117-921 1711, fax 0117-925 4866), 15 John St, Bristol BS1 2HR, England. A six-day tour from Beijing including visa, train in and flight back costs around £1200.

Wallem Travel, (Hong Kong ☎ 2876 8231, email: wtlhk@wallem.com), 46th Floor, Hopewell Centre, 183 Queen's Rd E, Wanchai, Hong Kong.

Destinations that are generally included on a tour are:

● **Pyongyang**, the capital and showcase of North Korea, where everything is supposed to be bigger (13-lane streets, a 150,000-seat stadium) and better (an Arc de Triomphe 16m higher than in Paris) than anywhere else. Most tours take you to the circus and to Mangyongdae (the birthplace of Kim Il Sung).

● **P'anmunjom** (in the demilitarised zone, opposite the village of the same name in South Korea) and nearby Kaesong (the ancient capital that escaped the war).

● **Myoyangsan** (International Friendship Exhibition – a museum of gifts given to North Korea from world leaders).

● **Nanpo** – the irrigation system that the North says is a wonder of agricultural engineering and which the South says was built to flood its territory).

● The craggy **Kumgang** mountains and the areas around Mt Paekdusan (2744m) – the highest point on the Korean peninsula and thought to be the birthplace of the Korean race. North Koreans claim it's also the birthplace of Kim Jong Il.

Further information

Ryohaengsa (Korean International Tourist Bureau) (☎ 2-3817201 fax 2-3817607), Central District, Pyongyang – though we never received a reply. **North Korea International Tourism Company** (☎ 33-3355, fax 33-3939), 23rd floor, Nam Van Commercial Centre, 57-9 Rua da Praia Grande, Macau. Or through the North Korean embassy in Beijing.

❏ **Some things to know about North Korea**

Photographs, except of sensitive military subjects, can be taken relatively freely – ask your guide. Statues of the Great Leader should be photographed complete (no photos of just his head or any other part of his body). Bringing binoculars, radios, and any written material printed in South Korea are strictly forbidden. Talking politics with your guide is not only allowed, it is probably the most fascinating part of the tour. Does your guide really believe the stories he/she tells you: like the one about the peasants who, during the Korean War, formed a human bridge to allow tanks to cross a river, by driving on their backs? You may be surprised.

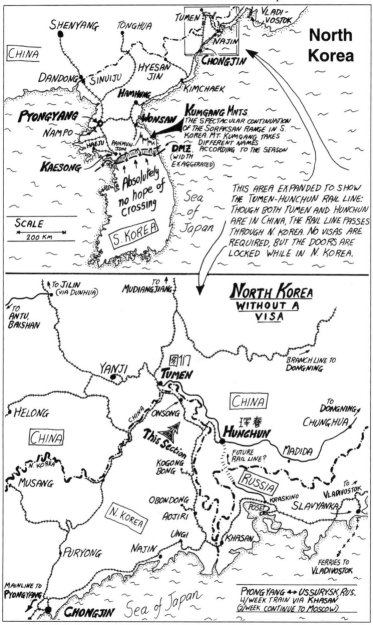

North Korea

CHINA

SHENYANG TONGHUA TUMEN VLADI-VOSTOK

NAJIN

CHONGJIN

DANDONG SINUIJU HYESAN JIN KIMCHAEK

HAMHUNG

PYONGYANG WONSAN **KUMGANG MNTS.**
THE SPECTACULAR CONTINUATION
OF THE SORAKSAN RANGE IN S.
NAMPO KOREA. MT. KUMGANG TAKES
HAEJU PANMUNJOM DIFFERENT NAMES
ACCORDING TO THE SEASON

DMZ (WIDTH EXAGGERATED)

KAESONG

Absolutely
no hope of
crossing

S. KOREA

Sea
of
Japan

SCALE
200 KM

THIS AREA EXPANDED TO SHOW
THE TUMEN-HUNCHUN RAIL LINE:
THOUGH BOTH TUMEN AND HUNCHUN
ARE IN CHINA, THE RAIL LINE PASSES
THROUGH N. KOREA. NO VISAS ARE
REQUIRED, BUT THE DOORS ARE
LOCKED WHILE IN N. KOREA.

NORTH KOREA WITHOUT A VISA

To JILIN (VIA DUNHUA) TO MUDIANGJIANG

TO ANTU, BAISHAN

YANJI 图们 TUMEN BRANCH LINE TO DONGNING

HELONG CHINA ONSONG CHINA 珲春 HUNCHUN TO DONGNING CHUNGHUA

This Section

KOGONG BONG MADIDA

N. KOREA MUSANG FUTURE RAIL LINE? RUSSIA

OBONDONG TO VLADIVOSTOK

N. KOREA AOJIRI KRASKINO SLAVYANKA

PURYONG UNGI POSET KHASAN

NAJIN

FERRIES TO VLADIVOSTOK

MAINLINE TO PYONGYANG

CHONGJIN Sea of Japan

PYONGYANG ↔ USSURYSK, RUS.
4/WEEK TRAIN VIA KHASAN
(2/WEEK CONTINUE TO MOSCOW)

Taiwan

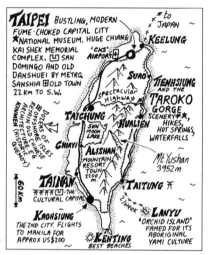

TAIPEI BUSTLING, MODERN
FUME-CHOKED CAPITAL CITY
✗NATIONAL MUSEUM. HUGE CHIANG
KAI SHEK MEMORIAL
COMPLEX. ⌂ SAN
DOMINGO AND OLD
DANSHUEI BY METRO.
SANSHIA ⊞ OLD TOWN
22 KM TO S.W.

DOZENS OF OFFSHORE
RETAIN OLD CHINESE
ARCHITECTURE (e.g.
KINMEN (HISTORIC
QUEMOY)

✗ to
JAPAN
✦KEELUNG
'CKS'
AIRPORT
SUAO
spectacular
Highway
TIENHSIUNG
AND THE
TAROKO
GORGE
SCENERY★★,
HIKES,
HOT SPRINGS
WATERFALLS

TAICHUNG
SUN
MOON
LAKE
HUALIEN

CHIAYI
ALISHAN
MOUNTAIN
RESORT
TOWN
2200 M.
Mt Yushan
3952m

60 Km

TAINAN
卅卅卅⌂-THE
CULTURAL CAPITAL
TAITUNG 禾

KAOHSIUNG
THE 2ND CITY. FLIGHTS
TO MANILA FOR
APPROX US$200

✗creek
LANYU
'ORCHID ISLAND'
FAMED FOR ITS
ABORIGINAL
YAMI CULTURE
KENTING
BEST BEACHES

Taiwan, named Formosa (beautiful isle) by 16th century Portuguese sailors, prefers the soubriquet Republic of China. It considers mainland China to be temporarily under rebel control (as it has been since 1949). This doesn't stop Taiwanese investors pouring money into the People's Republic while hoping that the PRC will not pour back troops. Conflict is threatened every time there's any talk of Taiwan declaring outright independence. And, with the nearest Taiwanese isles (the Pescadores) a mere 4km off the Fujian coast, there wouldn't be far for the troops to come.

❏ **Essential information for travellers – Taiwan**
● **Visa** 14 days without a visa for 16 Western nationalities.
● **Currency** New Taiwan dollar NT$. US$1=NT$32.2. Reasonably stable.
• **Time zone** 8 hours ahead of GMT. Same as mainland China, 1hr behind Japan.
● **Religious tone** Despite great modernisation, there's a heavy undercurrent of superstitious Taoism, and ritualistic Buddhism. There's a special God for most aspects of life, but Kuan Yin (mercy) has a special following – her birthday is the 19th day of the second moon. As there's been no cultural revolution, many splendid temples survive. There's also a vocal Christian minority. As in Japan the number 4 is considered unlucky.
● **Highlights** Tainan (temples, cultural heart), mountain hikes, the Taroko Gorge.
● **When to go** Summers are miserably hot and humid in the lowlands, and prone to rain everywhere, especially in the colder mountains. Winter is rainy but mild in the north east, warm in the south and snowy in the high mountains. Chinese New Year (Feb) is extremely difficult for finding accommodation and air tickets. October and November are the most pleasant months, but October is also the high season for domestic tourism. Don't expect any serenity at weekends.
● **Key tips** If you want to work in Taiwan, Tainan is better than Taipei as it's cheaper to live, more cultured and less polluted but wages are similar.
● **Festivals** Apart from the fireworks on National Day (10 October) all major festivals are linked to the lunar calendar: two weeks after Chinese new year, the lantern festival in the Luerhmen district of Tainan is especially impressive.

y not ward off invasion, potions made from body parts of
are said to have powerful properties. The drinking of
a green snake's venom chaser is supposed to improve
nake alley' in Taipei's red light district was something of
ntil pressure from animal rights' lobbyists abroad forced
ground. There's now only a couple of snake shops left in

the world's most densely populated countries, most of
lle down the west coast. The east is harsher but the great
dding, mountainous spine of truly alpine proportions.

PRACTICAL INFORMATION
Visas and formalities
Most but not all Western nationals get a
14-day visa free stay on arrival by boat or
plane, though you may be required to show
onward tickets. The same nationals could
opt for a 30-day 'landing visa' (NT$1500)
available at international airports (but not
harbours). For longer stays or for other
nationals (eg Irish, Norwegians, Danes,
East Europeans, South Africans) you'll
need to apply in advance for a tourist visa
(easy, but $40 fee). Taiwan is not officially
recognised by most countries so its
embassies lurk under such pseudonyms as
Taipei Board of Trade, Taiwan Cultural
Centre. Tourist visas are valid for 60 days
and extendible up to six months.

Transport
Bigger towns may have several bus stations according to destination (for government buses) or company. Private buses are
slightly cheaper than public ones. Buses
and trains run very frequently along the
populous west coast, but less so along the
rugged east. Cross-mountain routes are
spectacular but there are only a few buses
a day (mostly morning departures). Bus
transfers from Taipei's Chiang Kai Shek
international airport cost from NT$110.
There's a separate airport for domestic
flights. A second line of the Taipei metro is
now operating.

Accommodation
There are various hostels which offer dorm
beds or tatami floor-space for under
US$10, but these fill up fast during week-
ends and holidays and are rare to non-exis-
tent on the smaller islands. Booking ahead
is advisable. In Taipei try the *Amigo* (☎ 02-
571 0612) 3rd Floor, 286 Chilin Rd; it's
close to the Meilihuda Fandian stop on the
inter-airport bus.

Information
There's a very handy tourist English language help line in Taipei – call ☎ 02-2717
3737 between 8am and 8pm any day of the
year. They can help with virtually any
question. Maps and tourist information are
available from Floor 9, 280 Chunghsiao E
Rd section 4 or at the airports. For general
Taiwan travel info try: http://travel.cyber-
taiwan.com/index.htm.

❏ **Geo-political information – Taiwan**
Population: 21.5 million (1997).
Area: 35,600 sq km.
Capital: Taipei (Taibei) 2.6 million.
GNP per capita: $10,500 (1994).
Leaders: President Lee Teng-Hui, Prime minister Vincent Siew.
Pressing political issues: Independence and how openly such a sensitive sub-
ject can be discussed without inviting a Chinese invasion. Knock on effect of the
Korean and South-East Asian stock market crashes.

APPENDIX A: VISA STRATEGY

The border crossings below are all quite possible. However, in the directions shown, planning well ahead for visas is essential. See country chapters for more information.

● **[1] Kalimantan, Indonesia to Eastern Malaysia** If you entered Indonesia on the two-month visa waiver, you will not be allowed to exit into Sabah, Malaysia (in contrast, the road from Pontiniak to Kuching, Sarawak is officially OK except when closed for political reasons as in early 1997). There is no way to change visa type so get a full Indonesian visa in advance. Heading south is easier as the Indonesian consuls in Kota Kinabalu, Sabah and in Kuching, Sarawak will usually give the necessary visa.

● **[2] China to Vietnam** There's no Vietnamese embassy in Kunming or Nanning. You must either divert to Guangzhou or Hong Kong or take a very long loop through Laos and apply in Vientiane. Lao transit visas in Kunming give five days, non-extendible though a few days extra for a $5/day fine are possible. Remember to state the correct entry/exit points for Vietnam.

● **[3] Yunnan to Burma** Burmese visas are clearly marked 'Land route prohibited'. (Two lucky travellers did somehow manage to use such visas to cross at Ruli).

● **[4] Nepal-Tibet** crossing rules are ever changing. One consistent fact: Chinese visas issued in Kathmandu are valid only for entering as part of a tour group so apply before arrival in Nepal. Delhi is usually OK but if possible apply outside the subcontinent. Don't mention Tibet when applying.

● **[5] China to Central Asia** One option for getting a Kazakh visa in W China is a long-shot in Urumqi, and it's potentially very expensive. The only other option is Beijing where five-day transit visas are usually easy to obtain. Don't worry about the obvious insufficiency of five or even two days transit: as soon as you arrive in Almaty dash to the Kyrgyzstan embassy where a one month visa is available with minimal formalities. The Kyrgyz visa ironically allows you to stay a further three days in Kazakhstan. See the visa shuffle (opposite). When applying for the initial transit visa you unfortunately have to give the exact dates – annoyingly these cannot usually be changed. If heading eastbound, Chinese visas are usually available in Almaty (though **not** in Bishkek). Nonetheless, get the Chinese visa before getting this far. It's a long way back to Europe!

● **[6] The Karakoram Highway** Although the road is now open almost year-round, Chinese visas are only available in Islamabad during the official season (April-Oct) or with a confirmed air ticket. Coming from Xinjiang note that the nearest Pakistan embassies are a very long way away: Beijing or Almaty (Kaz).

● **[7] Kyrgyzstan to Tajikistan** The physically challenging Pamir Highway route is especially difficult to organise southbound as you'll normally need a special permit which is only available in Dushanbe.

● **[8] Turkmenistan** visas easy to get in Turkey but impossible once in the Caucasus.

● **[9] Russia** Visas, never easy to get, are especially hard in Tbilisi/Baku: your only hope is to get an Armenian visa in Tbilisi and do the Visa Shuffle to transit Russia in 3 days.

● **[10] Syria** strictly refuses entry to anyone who has been to/is going to Israel. Heading in claim that you're planning to take the boat from Jordan to Egypt. Coming the other way, a trip via Israel can be hard to disguise. Even if your Israeli visa was on a separate slip of paper the border post on entry/exit stamps of Jordan/Egypt can give you away. At the border your bag may be examined for Israeli air/bus tickets, money, postcards etc.

● **[11] Iran** Always changing policy. Ask travellers for the latest news. The most helpful consulate en route was at Erzurum, Turkey but he has just been replaced.

● **[12] Australia** Western travellers sometimes forget that a visa is needed for Australia. There is no Australian consulate in Kupang, Timor where cheapest flights depart. Best to apply at home before departure.

APPENDIX B: THE VISA SHUFFLE

The information which follows applies only to **Armenia, Belarus, Kazakhstan, Kyrgyzstan, Russia, Tajikistan and Uzbekistan**. These seven signed a little publicised 1992 reciprocal visa agreement which we've dubbed the 'Visa Shuffle'. Now, using the visa of any signatory nation, you may transit any of the others. This is of enormous significance to the independent traveller. It can save considerably on fees for visas as well as on wasted time applying for them. Most importantly, it means you can get into countries where visas are very tough, using visas (like that of Kyrgyzstan) that are relatively easy to procure. The shuffle theoretically allows a transit of three days, though each country interprets the rule slightly differently.

Typically, shuffle signatory nations have loosely controlled (or uncontrolled) borders. As no one is likely to stamp your passport within the shuffle zone, nobody actually knows when you entered a specific country. So you could easily stay longer than the three days allowed without being detected. The exception is Armenia. Since it has no direct borders with any other shuffle nation, you will be stamped out when you leave, invalidating a single entry visa. However, an Armenian visa is one of the easiest to procure, and worth having in your passport in case of emergencies.

Some problems with the shuffle

● Hotels which need to register you with the local police (eg in Belarus, Uzbekistan) won't let you in if you don't have a 'real' visa. The solution is to stay on overnight trains or with private individuals.
● Many border guards and police either don't know about the agreement or choose to feign ignorance in the hope of a bribe. In Uzbekistan we were once locked up for an hour for lack of a proper visa. Eventually we were released when we politely stuck to our convictions. Fortunately not all officials are as awkward as the notorious Uzbeks. In Russia, Belarus and Kazakhstan, when challenged for lack of a local visa we showed guards a Kyrgyz visa and a copy of the original 'Shuffle' agreement. This worked so effectively that we have include the relevant first and last pages of this same (sadly poor quality) copy here (overleaf). Hopefully it will prove as useful to you.
● In Tajikistan the shuffle only works reliably in the 'Khojent Periscope'.
● In Uzbekistan the shuffle is supposed to be for transits directly through Tashkent. If, as we did, you try to stop en route in Bukhara or Samarkand, there may be a small fine ($20) to pay. Given this and the generally unpleasant nature of Uzbek police, it is worth paying a little extra to get a full Uzbek visa (easiest in Kazakhstan or Turkmenistan).

Example of the visa shuffle in action

Take a traveller who wants to visit Central Asia by train via Belarus, Russia and Kazakhstan. The trip can easily involve more than a dozen border crossings. Yet through the shuffle, a two month trip is possible on just two visas if she plans carefully. In London or Brussels she applies for a Kyrgyz visa timed to start the day she enters Belarus. Then on arrival in Almaty, Kazakhstan (direct train from Moscow) she can apply for a one month Uzbek visa to start the day the Kyrgyz one finishes. This would be enough to take her all the way back to the Belarus-Poland border, or, should she choose, to the Chinese frontier via Kazakhstan or Kyrgyzstan. Once within Central Asia other visas are easy to get eg a Kazakh visa in Tashkent or a second Kyrgyz visa in Almaty or Bishkek, should she wish to stay longer.

Other notes about the visa shuffle

● Russian embassies will theoretically issue visas for other shuffle countries when there is no embassy of that country nearby. If you do get a visa this way it will be a Russian loose leaf visa even though it's actually valid for another country altogether. However, Russian consuls are strict about issuing such visas and unlikely to do so without directly faxed instructions from the relevant ministry of Foreign Affairs.

● Shuffling with a Russian visa is generally easier than with any of the others. That's because Russian visas look just like the old USSR visas to which police and border guards are already accustomed.

● The shuffle isn't well publicised locally.

Officials may be more confused than you are, and may be honestly unaware of the agreement. To avoid confrontation and loss of face, tell them confidently about the validity of the shuffle before you're asked. If there's any doubt, explain to guards in garbled Russian that you've called (*telefon*) Mr. X and Mrs. Y at the embassy (*pasolsva*) who say it's all fine and dandy (*harrashow*). Smile and show off the copy of the agreement (relevant sections below).

СОГЛАШЕНИЕ

о взаимном признании виз государств - участников Содружества Независимых Государств

Правительства государств - участников Содружества Независимых Государств, подписавшие настоящее Соглашение, именуемые в дальнейшем Сторонами

руководствуясь желанием развивать дружественные добрососедские отношения и способствовать взаимному обеспечению безопасности,

считая необходимым создавать оптимальные условия для въезда, передвижения и выезда граждан третьих государств и лиц без гражданства, в дальнейшем именуемых иностранными гражданами, на их территориях,

признавая, что одним из эффективных средств достижения этих целей является сотрудничество и оперативное взаимодействие консульских служб государств Содружества;

согласились о нижеследующем:

Статья 1

Каждая Сторона признает въездные, выездные и транзитные визы, выдаваемые иностранным гражданам компетентными органами Сторон. Указанные визы, выдаваемые одной из Сторон для въезда на ее территорию, пребывания и выезда, дают право их владельцам беспрепятственно следовать транзитом через территории других Сторон к месту назначения или пункту выезда в третью страну.

Статья 2

Порядок пребывания и передвижения иностранных граждан, временно находящихся на территории Сторон, в том числе с целью транзитного проезда, определяется компетентными органами Сторон в соответствии с национальным законодательством этих Сторон.

Customs declaration form (CDF)

Wherever you enter the CIS you are still required to complete the Soviet-style customs declaration form stating, amongst other valuables, the total foreign currency you are carrying. When you finally exit the CIS, the amount of hard currency you leave with should be less than the sum you entered with, so if you get a cash advance en route keep receipts. The CDF can be a great excuse for customs officers to strut their egos and look avariciously through your wallet. Worse, if you happen to lose the form, the rules theoretically allow unscrupulous guards at your exit point to confiscate any cash you are carrying. At major points like the airports in Moscow, St P and Tashkent (particularly notorious) they may actually do just that, or 'let you off' with a $200 fine. Note that not everywhere is so harsh but it's worth keeping photocopies of the CDF in case of loss.

Статья 8

Настоящее Соглашение открыто для присоединения любого государства с согласия всех Сторон.

Статья 9

Настоящее Соглашение вступает в силу на 30-й день с момента подписания.

Совершено в городе Москве 13 ноября 1992 года в одном подлинном экземпляре на русском языке. Подлинный экземпляр хранится в Архиве Правительства Республики Беларусь, которое направит государствам, подписавшим настоящее Соглашение, его заверенную копию.

За Правительство
Республики Армения

За Правительство
Российской Федерации

За Правительство
Республики Беларусь

За Правительство
Республики Таджикистан

За Правительство
Республики Казахстан

За Правительство
Туркменистана

За Правительство
Республики Кыргызстан

За Правительство
Республики Узбекистан

За Правительство
Республики Молдова

За Правительство
Украины

APPENDIX C: RUSSIAN WORDS & PHRASES

Though no longer the official language in much of the ex-USSR, Russian remains commonly spoken throughout. Stringing a couple of mangled words into a sentence of DIY Ruskii works surprisingly well especially if pronounced with a lugubrious Boris Karlov accent. Some of our renderings below are far from the dictionary translitterations. For example 'Do you understand?' should be *Vy panimayitye* but since in reality people seem to say something more like 'pani maish?' to our less cultured ears, we note the latter. A proper phrase book is, however, invaluable. Some phrases to get you started:

Phrases you're likely to hear and possible responses

Pani maish	(Do you) understand(?)	(I don't) understand	*(ne) pani mayu*
Mozhna?	May I?	You may	*Mozhna*
....*nada?*	Do I need....	Yes/No you do/don't	*nada/ ni nada*
Iz vinyitse	Sorry/excuse me	Doesn't matter	*Nichi vo*
Davai	Come on/go ahead/drink that!	OK//cheers	*Harra show//*
Shpees	(Let's) eat	It's delicious	
Choo choot	Just a bit (or a triple vodka)	Just a tiny bit	*Mnozhka*
Kakvas zavoot?	What's your name?	My name's...	*Mnya zavoot...*
At kuda?	Where do you come from?	I'm from UK/USA	*Yaiz Anglia/Amerika*
Kuda?	Where are you going?		
...*yist*	Do you have...?/are you...?		
Adin? (to a man)/*Adna* (to a woman)		Are you single/alone?	
Zakreet?	Do you want a cigarette?	I don't smoke	*Ne zakryu*

Other useful words

without...(meat)	*bez....(myasa)*	money	*dyengi*
guest	*ghosti*	friend	*droog*
Thanks (very much)	*Spaseeba bolshoi*	big	*bolshoi*
What (is that)?	*Shto (eta)?*	small/kids	*malinki*
far	*daliko*	near	*bliska*
If...	*yesli...*	late	*pazna*
early	*rana*	now	*sichas*
Not....	*ne....*	The train's late	*poezd apazdevet*
Maybe...	*mozhit beet...*	Good/That's OK	*narmal/harra show*
Good ...	*Dobri*	Goodbye	*Dus vi-danya*
morning	...*utram*	yesterday	*fchira*
day/afternoon	...*dyen/dnyom*	today	*sivodni*
evening	...*vyechr*	tomorrow/manyana	*zavtra*
The day after tomorrow *Pasli zavtra*		The day before yesterday *paza fchira*	
How much (does it cost)? *Skolka (stoit)?*		per hour/day/week *za chas/dyen/nidelnya*	
How long (in hours)? *Skolka chasov?*		When? *Kagda*	Why? *Pachimu?*
Where is....?	*Gdye....?*	hotel *(gostinyitsa)*, bath house/sauna *(banya)*,	

cheap restaurant *(stalovar)*, embassy *(pasolstsva)*, station *(vokzal)*, bus station *(avto vokzal)*, town/city *(gorod)*, old town area *(stary gorod)*, country cottage/hut *(datcha)*

On timetables

departure	От	*at prav layitsa*	arrival	Пр	*pribyvat*
Monday *pani delnik*		Tuesday *ftornik*	Wednesday *srida*	
Thursday *chetverk*		Friday *pyatnitsa*	Saturday *subota*	Sunday *vas krisenye*
Runs weekdays *ezhednyevo* раб			public holidays/weekends вых	
alternate days:	even *chetneem* Чет		odd *nechetneem* Неч	

The Cyrillic alphabet (including variants for non-Russian areas)

CYRILLIC	ENGLISH EQUIVALENT	CYRILLIC	ENGLISH EQUIVALENT
В	V (AN ENGLISH B IS ACTUALLY Ƃ IN)	Ə	A (UNVOICED, C.ASIA)
Ƃ	SILENT	Ч	CH
bI	Y/I	Д	D
C	S	Э	E (COMPARE Ƹ = Z)
E	YE (COULD BE E, TOO)	Ф	F
Ë	Yo (AND OFTEN THE ¨ ARE OMITTED)	Г	G (H IN UKRAINE)
H	N (H, = NG)	Ғ	GH (AZERI, C.ASIA)
m	t (M = M, m = t, T = T)	Ө	Ö (C.ASIA)
И	I (NOT BACKWARDS N)	П	P
Р	R	К,	Q (C.ASIA)
Я	YA (Ɏ IN TURKMENISTAN)	Ш	SH (OR $ IN TURKMENISTAN)
ʒ	g (G = Г)	Щ	SHCH
Х	KH	Ц	TS
У	U (ÿ = W IN BELARUS)	Ю	Yu
		Ɜ	Z
A, K, O AND **T** AS IN ENGLISH. (ALSO **I** IN UKRAINE/BELARUS)		Ж	ZH (J IN C.ASIA)

Major numbering systems in Asia

1	2	3	4	5	6	7	8	9	10	237 (ie random number)	
١	٢	٣	٤	٥	٦	٧	٨	٩	١٠	٢٣٧	ARABIC, FARSI, URDU...
			۴	۵	۶						(ALTERNATIVES)
९	२	३	४	५	६	७	८	९	९०	२३७	DEVANAGRI (HINDI, NEPALI..)
১	২	৩	৪	৫	৬	৭	৮	৯	১০	২৬৯	BENGALI, BANGLA
૧	૨	૩	૪	૫	૬	૭	૮	૯	૧૦	૨૩૭	GUJERATI
๑	๒	๓	๔	๕	๖	๗	๘	๙	๑๐	๒๓๗	THAI
໑	໒	໓	໔	໕	໖	໗	໘	໙	໑໐	໒໓໗	LAO
၁	၂	၃	၄	၅	၆	၇	၈	၉	၁၀	၂၃၇	BURMESE
一	二	三	四	五	六	七	八	九	十	二百三十七	CHINESE/ JAPANESE

NB 100 = 百 1000 = 千 10,000 = 万 THUS 900,000 IS 九十万 (9×10×10,000)

PLASTIC MONEY
IN THE FORMER USSR AND TURKEY

Plastic cash-substitutes, already very useful in Europe, are quickly gaining importance across Asia. In Turkey, a key bridge between the continents, both credit and debit cards are well established with close to 65,000 merchants presently accepting Eurocard/MasterCard. In the former Soviet Union, credit cards are relatively new, but are increasingly useful. The map shows where in the region Eurocard/MasterCard is accepted. The approximate number of participating outlets is given by country (except in Central Asia and the Caucasus where rapid development makes figures unrepresentative).

Cirrus and Maestro have the added advantage of being debit cards. Travelling in Turkey you can pay directly from your account through some 30,000 Maestro terminals or make convenient cash withdrawals from 5000 Cirrus ATMs (even the smallest Turkish towns seem to have one). Cirrus/Maestro, also widespread in much of Central and Eastern Europe, is starting to be introduced into the ex-Soviet countries with Moscow and Kiev already on line.

Information kindly provided by Europay International

INDEX

Note Bold print indicates a town plan

Aba Grasslands (CChina) 228
Abakan (Rus) 305
Abashiri (Jap) 533
Abbottabad (Pak) 330
Aberdeen (HK) 231
Abkhazia (Geo) 82, 115
Achal (Xin) 262, 265
Adam's Peak/Sri Pada (SL) 412, 413
Adana (Tky) 29
Adgeya Adog (Rus) 288
Adilcevaz (Tky) 39
Adjaria (Geo) 82
Afghanistan 76
Aflatun (Kyr) 161
Afrasiab (Uzbek) 193
Agdash (Azer) 101
Agra (Ind) **367**
Ahar (Iran) 62
Ahlat (Tky) 39
Ahmadabad (Ind) 360
Ahwaz (Iran) 61, 70
Ajmer (Ind) 361
Ak Suu Pass (Kyrgyz) 142
Akademgorok (Rus) 305
Akdamar Island (Tky) 39
Akhalsikhe (Geo) 116
Akhmeta (Geo) 117
Akihabara (Jap) 537
Akiyoshidai (Jap) 530
Aksaray (Tky) 38
Ala Archa (Kyrgyz) 154
Alamut Ruins (Iran) 65
Alanya (Tky) 29, 37
Alashankou (Xin) 143
Alaverdi (Armen) 91
Albania 28
Ali (Tibet) 257
Ali Sadr Caves (Iran) 63
Alkhalkalaki (Geo) 84, 116
Allahabad (Ind) 368
Alma Arasan Sanitorium (Kazakh) 142
Alma Arasan (Kazakh) 141
Almaty (Kazakh) 139, 143
Alor Setar (Mal) 436
Alupka (Ukr) 287
Alverdi Cathedral (Geo) 117
Amami Oshima (Jap) 533
Amarapura (Brm) 464
Amherst (Brm) 466
Ananuri (Geo) 118
Andaman Islands (Ind) 353, **371**
Andizhan (Uzbek) 157, 158, 187, 190

Angkor Wat (Cam) 494
Angren (Uzbek) 190
Ani (Tky) 41
Ankara (Tky) 29, 37
Annapurna Trek (Nep) 390
Anousavari Monument (Laos) 506
Antakya (Tky) 37
Anuradhapura (SL) 412, 413
Aokata (Jap) 523
Apsherson Peninsula (Azer) 100, **104**
Aragac Mt. (Armen) 91
Aragats (Armen) 91
Aral Sea (Kazakh-Uzbek) 195, 196
Arbil (Hariem) 45
Archal (Xin) **163**
Ardahan (Tky) 41, 116
Ardanuc (Tky) 41
Ardehil (Iran) 64
Ark, The Bam (Iran) 75
Ark, Bukhara's (Uzbek) 194
Arkit (Kyrgyz) 158, 159, 160, 161
Armenia 86
Arnavutkoy (Tky) 35
Arshan (Rus) 308
Arslanbob/Astanbap (Kyrgyz) 157
Artashat (Armen) 91
Artux, Little (Xin) 163
Artux (Xin) **265**
Artvin (Tky) 29, 41
Arugam Bay (SL) 412, 413
Arunachal Pradesh (Ind) 353
Asbesdos Deposit/Shemienquan (Xin) 263
Ashgabat (Trkstn) 175, **176**, 177
Asia's longest suspension bridge (KKH) 340
Aso (Jap) 531
Assam (Ind) 353
Assassin's Castles (Iran) 65
Astanbap/Arslanbob (Kyrgyz) 157
Astara (Iran) 61
Astara (Azer) 101
Astor Valley (KKH) 341
Astrakhan (Rus) 311
At Bashi (Kyrgyz) 163
Atashgah (Azer) 104
Ateshkade (Iran) 74
Attapu (Laos) 511
Attock (Pak) 330

Aungban (Brm) 465
Austria 28
Autthaya (Thai) 448
Ava (Brm) 464
Aya Sofia Mosque (Tky) 35
Ayodhya (Ind) 368
Azad Sq. (Azer) 102
Azerbaijan 93

Ba Ba Lakes (Viet) 478
Babur's Hut (Kyrgyz) 157
Babushkin (Rus) 308
Badaling (CChina) 217
Badgirs 75
Bagerhat (Bang) 406
Baghdad (Iraq) 45
Baglung (Nep) 390
Bago (Brm) **463**, 466
Bagrot Valley (KKH) 341
Baguio City (Phi) 515
Bahawalpur (Pak) 333
Bai Chi (Viet) **479**
Bairam Ali (Trkstn) 175, **178**
Bajgiran (Trkstn) 175
Bajgiran (Iran) 72
Bakharden (Trkstn) 177
Bakhchiserai (Ukr) 287
Bakhtaran/Kermanshar (Iran) 63
Baku (Azer) 82, 84, 101, **102**, **103**, 104
Balakan (Azer) 101,105, 106, 117
Balbai Village (Kyrgyz) 142, 155
Bali (Indo) **423**
Balikchee (Kyrgyz) 155, 156
Balkh (Afg) 81
Baltistan Valley (KKH) 338
Baluchistan (Pak) 328
Bam (Iran) 61, 73, **75**
Bam Railway (Rus) 13, 213, 308
Bamai Temple (CChina) 224
Bamda (Tibet) 256
Bamian (Afg) 81
Ban Thakho (Laos) 511
Ban Houayxay (Laos) 505, 509
Ban Na Som (Laos) 510
Ban Hat Lek (Thai) 496
Ban Chiang (Thai) 448
Banaue (Phi) 515
Band e Amir (Iran) 71
Band-i-Amir Lakes (Afg) 81
Bandar Abbas (Iran) 61, 73, **75**
Bandar Anzali (Iran) 64

Banepa (Nep) 393
Bangaon (Ind) 406
Bangkok (Thai) 445, 447, 448, 449
Bangladesh 396
Bannu (Pak) 333
Banpo (CChina) 223
Baodai Bridge (CChina) 221
Baoding caves (CChina) 225
Baoguo (CChina) 225
Baoshan (Yun) 240
Baotou (CChina) 215
Bardia NP (Nep) 390
Baren (Xin) 265
Barguzin Valley (Rus) 308
Barisal (Bang) 406
Barkam (CChina) 256
Barkhor Square, Lhasa's (Tibet) 255
Barkol (Xin) 263
Barnaul (Rus) 304
Barskoon (Kyrgyz) 155
Basantapur (Nep) 391
Bashkortistan (Rus) 288
Basilan (Phi) 515
Basseini (Brm) 462
Basuangas Is. (Phi) 515
Bat Pagoda (Viet) 486
Batdambang (Cam) 494, 495
Batticaloa (SL) 412, 413
Battle Potemkin Mutineers 106
Batumi (Geo) 84, 116, **122**
Bayan Buluk (Xin) 266, 267
Bazaar Kurgan (Kyrgyz) 157
Bazaar, Istanbul Covered (Tky) 35
Behai (CChina) 219
Beidaihe (CChina) 218
Beijing (CChina) 13, **216**, 217, 218
Beishan Cliff Temple (CChina) 227
Belgorsk (Rus) 13
Belarus 275
Belisirma Village (Tky) 38
Ben Tre (Viet) 486
Benopol (Bang) 406
Beo (Viet) 479
Beppu (Jap) 523, 531
Berincang (Mal) 436
Bert's Books (Cam) 493
Beruni (Uzbek) 195, 196
Besiktas (Tky) 26
Bethume's Tomb (CChina) 224
Bezeklik Caves (Xin) 263
Bhaktapur (Nep) **392**, 393
Bharatpur (Nep) 388
Bhubaneswar (Ind) 369
Bhuj (Ind) 360
Biak (Indo) 423
Bib Khanym Mosque (Uzbek) 192
Big Goose Pagoda (CChina) 223
Bihar (Ind) 353
Bikaner (Ind) 361, 362
Biratnagar (Nep) 391
Birganj (Nep) 389, 391
Birobidzhan (Rus) 307
Biryard (Iran) 72
Bishkek (Kyrgyz) **152**, **153**, 154, 156, 158
Bistotun (Iran) 63
Biyara (Hariem) 45
Biyisk (Rus) 305
Black Coffee Cafe (CChina) 225
Blagovashchensk (Rus) 13, 213
Blue Area (Pak) 332
Blue Mosque, Istanbul (Tky) 35
Bodh Gaya (Ind) 369
Bodrum (Tky) 29
Bogale (Brm) 462
Bogazkale (Tky) 37
Bogdo Khan Palace (Mong) 318
Bohol Is. (Phi) 515
Bokombaeva (Kyrgyz) 155
Bolovens Plateau (Laos) 511
Bolshoi Koty (Rus) 309
Bolshoi Goloustnoye (Rus) 308
Bolshoi Listivanka (Rus) 308, 309
Bombay (Ind) **360**
Boracay Is. (Phi) 515
Borit Lake (KKH) 340
Borjomi (Geo) 122
Borobadur (Indo) 424
Borodino 303
Borzhomi (Geo) 116
Bosnia-Herzegovina 28
Bosphorous, Boats on the (Tky) 35
Boten (Laos) 505, 509
Boyuk-Kasik (Azer) 101
Braldo Valley (KKH) 341
Brastagi (Indo) 426
Bratsk (Rus) 13, 307
Brest (Belarus) 274, 284
Brezengy (Trkstn) 176
Bucas Is. (Phi) 515
Buddha Cave, Golden (Laos) 510
Budhankantha (Nep) 393
Bukhara (Uzbek) 175, 187, 191, **193**, **194**, 196
Bukhta Peschanya (Rus) 309
Bulaksu (Xin) 265
Bulgaria 28
Bund, The (CChina) 221
Bundala (SL) 412, 413
Bungamati (Nep) 393
Buon Ma Thot (Viet) 484
Burana Tower (Kyrgyz) 154
Burang (Tibet) 257
Buratiya (Rus) 288
Burma 450
Burmese characters 456
Burning Ghat (Ind) 368
Bursa (Tky) 29, 36
Bushehr (Iran) **71**
Bushet Church (Geo) 117
Bustan (Uzbek) 195, 196
Butterfly Valley (Tky) 36
Butterworth (Mal) 436, 437
Butwal (Nep) 388, 390
Buzovna (Azer) 104

Ca Na (Viet) 484
Ca Mau (Viet) 486
Calcuit Is. (Phi) 515
Calcutta (Ind) 369, **370**, 389
Cambodia 488
Cameroon Highlands (Mal) 436
Camiguin Is. (Phi) 515
Camp Nusa (Mal) 436
Cannakale (Tky) 29
Cantho (Viet) 486
Canton/Guangzhou 14, 219, **220**, 230
Cao Bang (Viet) 478
Cappadocia (Tky) **38**
Carmen (Phi) 515
Caspian Sea, crossing the 127
Cat Ba (Viet) 479
Cat Co Beach (Viet) 479
Cat Hai Isd. (Viet) 479
Catanduandes Is. (Phi) 515
Caucasus 83
Cebu City (Phi) 515
Chabahar (Iran) 73
Chaika (Azer) 104
Chainpur (Nep) 390
Chak Chak (Iran) 73
Chalus (Iran) 64
Chamdo (Tibet) 256
Chandpur (Bang) 406
Changchun (CChina) 214
Changunarayan (Nep) 393
Charbak Lake (Uzbek) 190
Chardzhou (Trkstn) 175, **177**
Charkilik (Xin) 264
Charkilik/Ruoqiang (Xin) 263
Chat Bazaar (Kyrgyz) 159
Chau Doc (Viet) 486
Chaungtha Beach (Brm) 462
Chechnya (Rus) 82, 288
Chegdomyn (Rus) 307
Cheju Is. (SKor) 548
Cheliken (Trkstn) 175
Chelyabinsk (Rus) 305
Chengde (CChina) 218
Chengdu to/from Lhasa 251, 256
Chengdu (CChina) **225**, 228, 240

Cherchen/Qiemo (Xin) 263
Chernehiv (Ukr) 284
Chernevitsi (Ukr) 284
Chernobyl (Ukr) 274, 284
Cheug Chau Is. (HK) 231
Chi Chi Is. (Jap) 533
Chiang Mai (Thai) Tai, **446**, 448, 449
Chiang Rai (Thai) 448, 449
Chilas (KKH) 338
Chiliharti (Bang) 406
Chimbulak (Kazakh) 141
China, People's Republic of 197
China Beach (Viet) 483
Chinese phrases 206/7
Chinju (SKor) 548
Chiriya Tapu (Ind) 371
Chita (Rus) 13, 307, 317
Chitral Valley (Pak) 330, 331
Chittagong (Bang) 404, **407**
Chittagong Hill Tracts (Bang) 407
Chitwan NP (Nep) 390
Chiu Gompa (Tibet) 257
Choeung Ek (Cam) 493
Chogha Zambil (Iran) 70
Choibalsan (Mong) 317
Cholon (Viet) **485**
Cholpan Ata (Kyrgyz) 156
Cholpan-Ata #1 (Kyrgyz) 155
Cholpon Ata #2 (Kyrgyz) 158, 159
Chongqing (CChina) **222**, 225
Chop (Ukr) 284
Chor Minor (Uzbek) 193
Chorsu Market (Uzbek) 189
Chow Yadgar (Pak) 330
Chufutkale (Ukr) 287
Chuli (Trkstn) 177
Chungking Mansions (HK) 231
Chuvash (Rus) 288
Coal Mines, Dickensian (Xin) 267
Colombo (SL) 412, 413
Comilla (Bang) 407
Con Phung (Viet) **486**
Connaught Place, Delhi (Ind) **359**
Cox's Bazaar (Bang) 404, **407**
Crescent Moon Lake (CChina) 226
Crimea, The (Ukr) 285
Crimea (Ukr) **287**
Croatia 28
Crown Jewels (Iran) 66
Ctesiphon (Iraq) 45
Culion Is. (Phi) 515
Cuyo Is. (Phi) 515
Czech Republic 28

Dacca (Bang) **408**

Daewon, Inn (SKor) 547
Dagestan (Rus) 82, 105, 288
Dagomys (Rus) 82
Dai Linh (Viet) 483
Daju (Yun) 240
Dakhme (Iran) 73, 75
Dakshinkali (Nep) 393
Dalat (Viet) **484**
Dali (Yun) 240
Dalian (CChina) 218
Daluo (Yun) 241
Daman (Nep) 391
Damenglong (Yun) 241
Damghan (Iran) 72
Damside (Nep) 395
Damxung (Tibet) 255
Danang (Viet) **483**
Dandong (CChina) 218
Danigrad (Rus) 310
Danubyu (Brm) 462
Darband (Iran) 67
Darchen (Tibet) 257
Darjeeling (Ind) 389
Darra Adem Khel (Pak) 328, 330
Dartsendo/Kanding (CChina) 256
Dauki (Ind) 406
Daw Aung San Suu Kyi (Brm) 461
Dayehan (Xin) 263
Dazu (CChina) **225**
Dean's Hotel (Pak) 330
Debland (Uzbek) 191
Dege (Tibet) 256
Dejeti-Oguz (Kyrgyz) 155
Delhi (Ind) **359**, 368, 389
Denizli (Tky) 29, 36
Densapar (Indo) 423
Deosai Plains (KKH) 341
Deqin (Yun) 240
Derbent (Rus) 82
Derinkuyu (Tky) 38
Devanagri 362
Dezful (Iran) 70
Dhaka (Bang) 389, 404, 406, 407, **408**
Dhangmari (Bang) 406
Dhankuta (Nep) 391
Dhulikhel (Nep) 253, 391, 393
Dhunche (Nep) 391
Dien Bien Phu (Viet) 478
Diger Rostam (Iran) 73
Diglipur (Ind) 371
Dilizhan (Armen) 91
Dinajpur (Bang) 404, 406
Dingshan (CChina) 221
Diu (Ind) 360
Diyabarbakir (Tky) 29, 40
Djavari (Geo) 118
Doai (Jap) 536

Dogubayazit (Tky) 29, 39, 52
Dolpo Trek (Nep) 390
Don Khong (Laos) 511
Dong Dang (Viet) 219, 478
Dong Hoi (Viet) 482
Dong Ha (Viet) 482
Dongjingcheng (CChina) 214
Dongxing (CChina) 219, 479
Dostoyevsky's House (Rus) 303
Dostyk/Druzhba (Kazakh) 139, 143
Dostyk Trekking (Kyrgyz) 152
Dragon Lakes (Xin) 267
Dragon's Head (CChina) 217
Dreamland (Bang) 406
Drigungtil Monastery (Tibet) 255
Druzhba/Dostyk (Kazakh) 139, 143
Druzhba (Trkstn) 195
Dudinka (Rus) 299
Dumre (Nep) 390
Dunhuang (CChina) **226**, 263, 264
Durbar Square, Kathmandu (Nep) 394
Dushanbe (Tajik) 164
Dzelinga (Rus) 308
Dzhalalabad (Kyrgyz) **157**, 158
Dzhambul (Kazakh) 158

Ebino Kogen (Jap) 530
Ecbatan Ruins (Iran) 63
Echmiadzin (Armen) 39, 91
Eco Centre (Uzbek) 191
Edirane (Tky) 29
Egyptian Market, Istanbul (Tky) 35
Eidelweiss Pub (Kazakh) 141
Einme (Brm) 462
Ejinhoroqi (CChina) 215
Ekaterinburg (Rus) 13, 304, **305**
El Nido (Phi) 515
Emei Shan (CChina) 225
Eminonu (Tky) 26
Erzerum (Tky) **39**, 41
Esendere (Tky) 39
Estonia 28, 274
Everest Base Camp Trek (Nep) 391
Everest, Mt. (Nep-Tibet) 253
Evpatoria (Ukr) 287
Extremely unhealthy place (Xin) 263
Eyup Mosque (Tky) 26

Fairy Meadows (KKH) 341
Fangcheng (CChina) 219
Fansipan Mt. (Viet) 478
Farsi 59
Fatehpur Sikri (Ind) 367
Fener (Tky) 26

Feodosia (Ukr) 287
Fergana (Uzbek) 190
Feroz Shah Kotla (Ind) 359
Fethiye (Tky) 29
Fevralsk (Rus) 13
Fin (Iran) 68
Finland 28, 278
Firuza (Trkstn) 177
Fish Sandwiches (Tky) 35
Fish Market, Cox's Bazaar
  (Bang) 407
Fishtail Lodge (Nep) 395
Flores (Indo) **423**
Forbidden City, Beijing
  (CChina) 216
Forest of Pagodas (CChina) 224
Foros (Ukr) 287
Fort Monro (Pak) 333
Four Thousand Islands (Laos)
  511
Friendship Bridge (Lao-Thai)
  448, **507**, 510
Friendship Bridge (Nep-Tibet)
  253
Fuji, Mt. (Jap) 531, 536
Fukang (Xin) 263
Fukue (Jap) 523, 533
Fukuoka (Jap) 14, 523, 531
Fukushima (Jap) 533
Full moon party (Thai) 449
Fuman (Iran) 64
Fushiki (Jap) 14
FYROM/Macedonia 28

Gabala (Azer) 100, 101
Gagarin (Rus) 303
Gahar Lake (Iran) 63
Galipoli (Tky) 29
Galle (SL) 412, 413
Ganden Monastery (Mong) 318
Ganden (Tibet) 255
Ganesh Himal Trek (Nep) 390
Gangtok (Ind) 373
Ganja (Azer) 100, 101
Ganja Road (Azer) 107
Ganjala Trek (Nep) 391
Gansu bus insurance (CChina)
  227
Gaochang/Kara Khoja (Xin) 263
Gardabani (Geo) 117
Garni (Armen) 91
Gateway to Hell/Ozoresan (Jap)
  530
Gateway of India (Ind) 360
Gaur (Bang) 406
Gaya (Ind) **369**
Gechard (Armen) 91
Gelati (Geo) 116
Geli Ali Bakh (Hariem) 45
Gengis Khuree (Mong) 318
Genting Highlands (Mal) 435

Geok Tepe (Trkstn) 177
Georgia 108
Georgetown (Mal) **436**
Gergeti (Geo) 119
Germany 28
Gerze (Tibet) 253, 257
Geyzing (Ind) 373
Ghazni (Afg) 81
Ghengis Khan's Mausoleum
  (CChina) 215
Ghulmet (KKH) 338
Giariahat (Ind) 370
Gilgit (KKH) 338, 339, **341**
Gizhduvan (Uzbek) 191
Goa (Ind) 353
Gobi Dessert (Mong) 317
Gobustan (Azer) 100, 101, 103
Godwari (Nep) 393
Golaghra-e-Shohada (Iran) 69
Golden Horn, The (Tky) 26
Golden Buddha Cave (Laos)
  510
Golden Rock (Brm) 466
Golinka (Tibet) **256**
Golmud (CChina) 226, 251
Golzar-e-Shohada (Iran) 69
Gombori Pass (Geo) 117
Gonbad-e-Kavuz (Iran) 72
Gongkar Airport (Tibet) 255
Gongshan (Yun) 240
Gongxiang (CChina) 224
Gonoura (Jap) 532
Gorakpur (Ind) 368
Goreme (Tky) 29, 38
Gorgan (Iran) 72
Gorges, The Three (CChina) 222
Gori (Geo) 122
Gorka (Nep) 390
Gorkii/Nizhny Novgorod (Rus)
  303, 311
Gorkpur (Ind) 389
Gorno Altai (Rus) 288
Gosainkund Trek (Nep) 391
Goto Islands (Jap) **532**, 533
Great Wall of China (CChina)
  217
Greece 28
Gregorevka (Kyrgyz) 142, 155
Gremi (Geo) 117
Grodno (Belarus) 274
Guangzhou/Canton (CChina) 14,
  219, **220**, 230
Guanxian (CChina) 228
Guba/Quba (Azer) 100, 101
Gudauri (Geo) 118
Gudong (Yun) 240
Guilin (CChina) 219
Gujarat (Ind) 353
Gulag Archipelago, The (Rus)
  304
Guldursun (Uzbek) 195
Guma (Xin) 262

Gumri (Armen) 84, 90, 91
Gurvan Nuur (Mong) 317
Gurzuf (Ukr) 287
Gusar (Azer) 101
Gutsuo (Tibet) 253
Gwa (Brm) 462
Gyaki (Tibet) 257
Gyantse (Tibet) 255

Ha Tien (Viet) 486
Haein Sa (SKor) 548
Haft Tappeh (Iran) 70
Haiphong (Viet) **479**
Hakim Tower (Uzbek) 193
Hakkiri (Tky) 39
Hakodate (Jap) 533
Hakone (Jap) 536
Halabja (Hariem) 45
Hallyo Waterway (SKor) 548
Halong City (Viet) **479**
Halong Bay (Viet) 476, **479**
Hamadan (Iran) 61, **63**
Hami (Xin) 263
Hamza Mausoleum (Uzbek) 190
Hanami Koji (Jap) 535
Haneda Airport (Jap) 536
Hangul, how to read 544
Hangzhou (CChina) 221
Hankou/Wuhan (CChina) **222**
Hanoi (Viet) 478, 479, **480**, **481**
Haputale (SL) 412, 413
Harbin (CChina) 13, 214
Hardiwar (Ind) 368
Harem (Tky) 26
Harhoria/Karakoram (Mong)
  318
Haridaspur (Ind) 369, 406
Hariem 43
Harrah (Tky) 40
Haryana (Ind) 353
Hat Yai (Thai) 445, 449
Hatxaykoun (Laos) 511
Havelock Is. (Ind) 371
Heavenly Lake (Xin) 263
Heho (Brm) 465
Heihe (CChina) 13, 214
Hekou (CChina) 478
Hekou (Yun) 241
Helan Shan (CChina) 215
Helicopter, bar in a (Kyrgyz)
  154
Hell, ride from (Laos) 509
Hell, ride (Uzbek-Kazakh) 195
Hellambu Trek (Nep) 391
Hemkumari (Ind) 406
Hemu (Tibet) 255
Heng Shan Bei/North (CChina)
  215
Herat (Afg) **81**
Hermitage, The (Rus) 302
Hezuo (CChina) 228

Hichinohe (Jap) 523
Hida Takayama (Jap) 531
Higasi Honganji Temple (Jap) 535
Hikkaduwa (SL) 412, 413
Hille (Nep) 391
Himachal Pradesh (Ind) 353
Hiragana characters 526
Hiroshima (Jap) 523, 531, 533
Hispar Valley (KKH) 340
Ho Chi Mihn City (Viet) **485**
Ho Chi Minh (Viet) 486
Ho Chi Minh Mausoleum (Viet) 480
Hoa Binh (Viet) 478
Hoan Kiem Lake (Viet) 481
Hohot (CChina) **215**
Hoi An (Viet) 483
Hokkaido (Jap) 532, 533
Homel/Gomel (Belarus) 274, 284
Hon Chong (Viet) 486
Hong Kong 14, 219, 229 **230**, **231**
Hong Gai (Viet) **479**
Hongshan Hotel (Xin) 268
Hopa (Tky) 29
Hopar (KKH) 340
Hope (Tky) 84
Hore (Tibet) 257
Hormuz Is. (Iran) 73
Horton Plains (SL) 412, 413
Horyuji Temple (Jap) 534
Hosap Castle (Tky) 39
Hotan (Xin) 262
Hovshol Nuur (Mong) 317
Howrah Station (Ind) 370
Hsipaw (Brm) 464
Huang Shan (CChina) 215, 221
Huangzhong, Taer-Si (CChina) 226
Huashan (CChina) 223
Hue (Viet) **482**
Humla Trek (Nep) 390
Hunchun (CChina) 214, 553
Hungary 28
Hunza Valley (KKH) 338
Hushe Valley (KKH) 341

Idzhevan (Armen) 90, 91
Igdir (Tky) 29, 39, 84
Ihlara Valley & Village (Tky) **38**
Ikalto (Geo) 117
Iki Is. (Jap) 533
Ilam (Nep) 391
Ilisu (Azer) 105
Imamadze Borajim Shrine (Iran) 65
Imperial Palace, Tokyo's (Jap) 537
Inani Beach (Bang) 407

Incheon (SKor) 14, **546**
India 342
Indonesia 416
Ingushetia (Rus) 82, 288
Inland Sea (Jap) 533
Inle Lake 465
Iran 47
Irian Jaya (Indo) 424
Iriomote (Jap) 533
Irkestam Route (Kyrgyz-Xin) 127
Irkestam (Kyrgyz) 157
Irkutsk (Rus) 13, 308, **309**
Isak Pasa Palace (Tky) 39
Ise (Jap) 531
Isfahan (Iran) 52, 61, 68, **69**
Ishankala (Uzbek) 195
Ishigaki (Jap) 14, 533
Islamabad (Pak) 330, **332**
Islami Is. (Iran) 62
Islamka (Afg) 81
Issyk Alta Valley (Kyrgyz) 154
Istanbul (Tky) **26**, 29, 36
Istikal St. (Tky) 26
Istra (Rus) 303
Isvestkovy (Rus) 13
Italy 28
Ivangorod (Rus) 274, 303
Ivolginsk (Rus) 308
Iwani (Jap) 523
Izborsk (Rus) 274, 303
Izmir/Smyrna (Tky) 36
Izmir (Tky) 29

Jafflong (Bang) 407
Jafna (SL) 412, 413
Jaipur (Ind) 361, 362
Jaipurhat (Bang) 406
Jaisalmer (Ind) 361, 362
Jaiyuguan (CChina) 217, 226
Jakarta (Indo) 424
Jal Binayak (Nep) 393
Jalalabad (Afg) 81
Jam Minaret (Afgh) 80, 81
Jame Mosque (Mal) 437
Jammu & Kashmir (Ind) 353
Janakpur (Nep) 391
Japan 517
Jars, Plain of (Laos) 505, 510
Java (Indo) **424**
Jayanagar (Ind) 391
Jelentut (Mal) 436
Jenge-Jol (Kyrgyz) 161
Jerry Rubin Club (Rus) 301
Jerusalem, New (Rus) 303
Jessore (Bang) 406
Jevlakh (Azer) 101
Jiaxing (CChina) 221
Jilgen Turbaza (Kyrgyz) 161
Jinghong (Yun) **241**, 509
Jingpo Lake (CChina) 214

Jingshan Park (CChina) 216
Jingzhou (CChina) 222
Jinjiang (Yun) 240
Jinshanling (CChina) 217
Jiohe/Yarkhoto (Xin) 263
Jiri (Nep) 391
Jodpur (Ind) 361, 362
John's Cafe (Xin) 265
Johor Bahru (Mal) 437
Jokang (Tibet) 255
Jolfa (Azer) 101
Jomson (Nep) 390
Jon Aryk (Kyrgyz) 154
Jonda (Tibet) 256
Jorethang/Yoretan (Ind) 373
Jukhari Eskipara (Azer) 100
Juma Bazaar (Uzbek) 191
Jumla (Nep) 390
Jun (Viet) 484

K. Kermanshan (Iran) 61
Kabali (Geo) 117
Kabardino Balkaria (Rus) 82, 288
Kabul (Afg) 81
Kackar Mountains (Tky) 41
Kagan (Uzbek) 175, 191
Kagan Valley (Pak) 330, 331
Kagoshima (Jap) 523, 531
Kai Yuan (Yun) 241
Kaifeng (CChina) **224**
Kailash, Mt. (Tibet) 257
Kakani (Nep) 393
Kakarbitta (Nep) 389, 391
Kal Oya (SL) 412, 413
Kalabakh (Pak) 330
Kalardasht (Iran) 64
Kalaw (Brm) 465
Kalimantan (Indo) 424
Kaliningrad (Rus) 274
Kalmyk (Rus) 288
Kam Tin (HK) 231
Kamnetspodilskii (Ukr) 284
Kampot (Cam) 494
Kanazawa (Jap) 531
Kanchenjunga Trek (Nep) 391
Kandahar (Afg) **81**
Kanding/Dartsendo (CChina) 256
Kandy (SL) 412, 413
Kangding (CChina) 225
Kanghwa (SKor) 548
Kansai Airport (Jap) 534, 535
Kantan (Xin) 267
Kapati (Bang) 407
Kapong Chhnang (Cam) 494
Kapsa (SKor) 548
Kara Khoja/Gaochang (Xin) 263
Kara Kum Desert (Trkstn) 174
Kara Balta (Kyrgyz) **154**, 158
Kara Kul (Kyrgyz) 158, 159

Kara Bogaz Gol (Trkstn) 174
Karachay Cherkess (Rus) 82, 288
Karachi, dangers in (Pak) 328
Karajigach (Kyrgyz) 161
Karakol (Kyrgyz) 155, 156
Karakoram/Harhoria (Mong) 318
Karakoy (Tky) 26
Karakul Lake (Xin) 339
Karasu (Kyrgyz) 163
Karavan/Kerben (Kyrgyz) 157, 158, **160**, 161, 190
Karbudi Is. (Iran) 62
Karelia (Rus) 288
Karimabad (KKH) 338, 339
Kars (Tky) 29, 41, 84
Kashan (Iran) **68**
Kashgar to/from Lhasa 251
Kashgar (Xin) 264, 339
Kashgar, Kashi (Xin) 262, **265**
Kasi (Laos) 510
Katakana characters 526
Katex 105
Kathgodam (Ind) 389
Kathmandu (Nep) 253, 388, 390, 391, 389, 393, **394**
Kathmandu to/from Lhasa 251, 389
Kawaguchi (Jap) 536
Kayseri (Tky) 38
Kazakh/Qazak (Azer) 101
Kazakhstan 132
Kazan (Rus) 311
Kazbegi (Geo) **119**
Kep (Cam) 494
Kerala (Ind) 353
Kerama (Jap) 533
Kerbala (Iraq) 45
Kerben/Karavan (Kyrgyz) 157, 158, **160**, 161, 190
Kergeti Valley (Kyrgyz) 154
Keriya/Yutian (Xin) 262
Kerki (Trkstn) 175
Kerman (Iran) 61, **74**
Kermanshar/Bakhtaran (Iran) 63
Khabarovsk (Rus) 13, **310**
Khachmas (Azer) 101
Khakassia (Rus) 288
Khan's Palace (Azer) 105
Khandoskevi (Geo) 118
Khani (Rus) 307
Khankendi/Stepanakert (Armen) 90, 91
Khao San Road 447
Khao Sam Roi Yot NP (Thai) 449
Khaplu (KKH) 338
Khaptada NP (Nep) 390
Kharkov (Ukr) 127, 284, **287**
Khe Sahn (Viet) 482

Khevkhurtopeli (Geo) 117
Khevsureti Region (Geo) 118
Khiva (Uzbek) 175, 187, 195, **196**
Khlong Yai (Thai) 496
Khojeli (Trkstn) 195
Khojeli (Uzbek) 195
Khojent/Leninabad (Tajik) 164, 190
Kholodnaya (Rus) 308
Khome Waterfall (Lao) 511
Khomeini Sq, Tehran (Iran) **66**
Khomeni's Tomb (Iran) 67
Khomolsk (Rus) 13, 14
Khone Waterfall (Laos) 511
Khoramabad (Iran) 63
Khoramshahr (Iran) 70
Khorg (Tajik) 164
Khorgas Border Crossing (Kazakh-Xin) 143
Khorgas (Xin) 262, 266
Khudat (Azer) 101
Khujurt (Mong) 317
Khulna (Bang) 404, **406**
Khunjerab Pass (KKH) 338
Khuzestan (Iran) **70**
Khuzyr (Rus) 308, 309
Khvetera (Geo) 117
Khyber Pass (Afgh-Pak) 80
Kiev (Ukr) 284, 286
Kilik Pass (Afgh-China) 80
Killing Fields, The (Cam) 493
Kim Lien (Viet) 482
Kirov (Rus) 13, 305
Kitipur (Nep) 393
Kizhy (Rus) 303
Klin (Rus) 303
Ko Phangan (Thai) 449
Ko Samui (Thai) 449
Ko Phi Phi (Thai) 449
Ko Lanta (Thai) 449
Ko Samet (Thai) 449
Ko Chang (Thai) 449, 496
Kobe (Jap) 14, 523, 531, 534
Kobuleti (Geo) 116
Kochi (Jap) 523
Kodari (Nep) 253, 391
Kokand (Uzbek) 187, **190**
Komi (Rus) 288
Komodo (Indo) 424
Komsolsk-na-Amure (Rus) 13
Komsomolskaya Sq. (Rus) 310
Komsomosk-na-Amure (Rus) 307
Konarak/Konark (Ind) 369
Kong Xedong (Laos) 511
Kongju (SKor) 548
Kontum (Viet) 483
Koormintoo (Kyrgyz) 155
Kopyure Bazaar (Kyrgyz) 159
Korea, South 538

Korea, North 550
Korla (Xin) 263, 266
Korsakov (Rus) 13, 14
Koshi Tappu NP (Nep) 391
Kostroma (Rus) 303, 311
Kot Diji (Pak) 333
Kota Bharu (Mal) 437
Koty, Bolshoi (Rus) 309
Kowloon (HK) 230, **231**
Koya San (Jap) 531, 534
Krabi (Thai) 449
Krakatoa (Indo) 424
Kransnovodsk/Turkmenbashi (Trkstn) 175
Kraskino (Rus) 214
Krasnoyarsk (Rus) 13, 304, 305
Kratie (Cam) 494
Kremlin, The (Rus) 301
Krivirog (Ukr) 285
Krong Kaoh Kong (Cam) 494, 495, 496
Kuala Tahan (Mal) 436
Kuala Lipis (Mal) 437
Kuala Lumpur (Mal) **437**
Kuan Yin Temple (Mal) 436
Kuanda (Rus) 307
Kuantan (Mal) 437
Kulai lakes hike (Kazakh-Kyrgyz) 142
Kumamoto (Jap) 531
Kume (Jap) 533
Kumgang Mountains (NKor) 553
Kumkapi (Tky) 26
Kunes (Xin) 267, 266
Kunming (Yun) **239**, 240, 241
Kunya Urgench (Trkstn) 175, 195
Kupe 271
Kuqa (Xin) 262, **266**, 267
Kurashiki (Jap) 531
Kurdamir (Azer) 101
Kurgan (Rus) 305
Kurram Valley (Pak) 330, 331
Kursk (Rus) 303
Kushka (Trkstn) 175, 81
Kutaisi (Geo) 116
Kuzun (Azer) 101
Kwai, Bridge over the River (Thai) 448
Kyaikpin Pagoda (Brm) 461
Kyaikto (Brm) 466
Kyanjin Gompa (Nep) 391
Kyaukme (Brm) 464
Kyaukpadaung (Brm) 463
Kyaukse (Brm) 464
Kyauktaw (Brm) 462
Kyber Pass (Afghan-Pak) 330, 81
Kyongju (SKor) 548, 549
Kyoto (Jap) **535**

Kyrgyzstan 144
Kyzyl Kul (Kyrgyz) 159, 160, 161
Kyzyl (Rus) 306, 317
Kyzyl Ungar (Kyrgyz) 157

Labutta (Brm) 462
Laem Ngop (Thai) 496
Lagodekhi (Geo) 117
Lahitan (Iran) 64
Lahore (Pak) **331**, hostel rip offs 328
Lai Chau (Viet) 478
Lake Orumiyeh (Iran) 62
Lake Kara-Kol (Tajik) 164
Lake Paravani (Geo) 116
Lakeside (Nep) 395
Lalbagh Fort (Bang) 408
Lam Cafe (Viet) 481
Lama Temple (CChina) 216
Lamma Is. (HK) 231
Lancang (Yun) 241
Lang Son (Viet) 478
Lang Co (Viet) 483
Langar (Uzbek) 191
Langkawi Is. (Mal) 436
Langmusi (CChina) **228**
Langtang Trek (Nep) 391
Lantau Is. (HK) 231
Lanzhou (CChina) 223, 226, **227**, 228
Lao Pako Resort (Laos) 510
Lao Bao (Viet) 482, 511
Lao Cao (Viet) **478**
Lao Cai (Viet) 241
Laos 497
Lashio (Brm) 464
Latvia 28, 274
Lavra (Geo) 117
Lavra, The (Ukr) 286
Lena (Rus) 13, **307**
Lena, Source of River (Rus) 308
Lenin, huge head (Rus) 309
Lenin museum (Kyrg) 152
Lenin's Train (Rus) 301
Lenin's Hut (Rus) 302
Leninabad/Khojent (Tajik) 164, 190
Leninopol (Kyrgyz) 158, 159
Lenkoran (Azer) 100, 101
Lerik (Azer) 101
Leshan (CChina) 225
Leyte Is. (Phi) 515
Lhasa (Tibet) **255**, 256
Lhaze (Tibet) 253
Lianjiang (CChina) 219
Lijiang (Yun) 240
Lin Chung (Xin) 267
Line of Control (India-Pak) 328
Linxia (CChina) 226, 228
Lithuania 28, 274

Little Siberia (Xin) 263
Liuyuan (Xin) 263
Livadia (Ukr) 287
Lo Wu (HK) 230, 231
Loi Kaw (Brm) 465
Lomatong (Nep) 390
Lombok (Indo) 424
Long Hai (Viet) 484
Long Is. (Ind) 371
Long Hoa (Viet) 484
Long Xuyen (Viet) 486
Longmen Caves (CChina) 224
Lotte World (SKor) 547
Louang Prabang (Laos) 505, **508**, 509, 510
Love Valley (Viet) 484
Lu Shan (CChina) 222
Lubang (Phi) 515
Lucknow (Ind) 368, 389
Luizhou (CChina) 219
Lukla (Nep) 391
Lumbini (Nep) 390
Lumphat (Cam) 494
Lunan (Yun) 241
Luomen (CChina) 223
Luoyang (CChina) 224
Luqu (CChina) 228
Lushun (CChina) 218
Luzon Is. (Phi) 515
Lvov (Ukr) 28, **284**
Lyab-i-Khauz Teahouse & Pool (Uzbek) 194

Macau 234
Macedonia/FYROM 28
Macuni (CChina) 225
Madhya Pradesh (Ind) 353
Madura (Indo) 425
Mae Hong Son (Thai) 448, 449
Mae Sot (Thai) 448, 460
Magome (Jap) 531
Magway (Brm) 462, 463
Maha Aung Mye Bonzan Monastery (Brm) 464
Macau 14, 219, 230
Mahan (Iran) 73
Maharashtra (Ind) 353
Mahastanagar (Bang) 406
Mahendranagar (Nep) 388, 389, 390
Mai Khao beach (Thai) 449
Mai Chau (Viet) 478
Mai Sai (Thai) 448, 460
Maiden's Tower (Azer) 102
Mainamati (Bang) 407
Maisan (SKor) 548
Majishan (CChina) 223
Makhachkala (Rus) 82, 84
Makran (Pak) 328
Maku (Iran) 61, 62
Malacca (Mal) 437

Malapascua Is. (Phi) 515
Malaysia 431
Maluku (Indo) **425**
Manas Park (Bhu-India) 375
Manaslu Trek (Nep) 390
Manchir Monastery (Mong) 318
Mandalay (Brm) 460, **464**
Mandian (Yun) 241
Mandvi (Ind) 360
Mangup (Ukr) 287
Manila (Phi) 515
Manipur (Ind) 353
Maowen (CChina) 228
Maragheh (Iran) 63
Marble Mountains (Viet) 483
Mardakan (Azer) **103**, 104
Mardan (Pak) 330
Margilan (Uzbek) 190
Mari El (Rus) 288
Maritui (Rus) 308
Markam (Tibet) **256**
Marmaris (Tky) 36
Martaban (Brm) 466
Martinduque Is. (Phi) 515
Mary (Trkstn) 175, **178**
Masbate Is. (Phi) 515
Mashad (Iran) 61
Mashhad (Iran) **72**
Masirabad (Bang) 407
Masjid Imam Mosque (Iran) 69
Masule (Iran) 64
Matale (SL) 412, 413
Matara (SL) 412, 413
Mati (CChina) 226
Mawlamyine/Moulmein (Brm) 460, 466
Maymyo (Brm) 464
Mayon Volcano (Phi) 515
Mazar-i-Sherif (Afg) 81
Mazhang (Yun) 240
Medeo (Kazakh) 141
Meghalaya (Ind) 353
Megri (Armen) 90, 91
Meiji Shrine (Jap) 537
Meishan (CChina) 225
Mekong Delta (Viet) 476
Melihkovo (Rus) 303
Mencer (Tibet) 257
Menghai (Yun) 241
Mengla (Yun) 241, 509
Menglian (Yun) 241
Menglianggu (CChina) 218
Mengyuan (CChina) 223
Mergui Archipeligo (Brm) 460
Merv (Trkstn) 175, 178
Mesta (Geo) 116
Mikolaev (Ukr) 284, 285
Min Vodi (Rus) 82
Mindanao Is. (Phi) 515
Mindoro (Phi) 515
Mindroling (Tibet) 255

Mingun (Brm) 464
Minsk (Belarus) 28, **278**, 284
Minusinsk (Rus) 317
Mirador Mansions (HK) 231
Miran (Xin) 263
Mirjave (Iran) 61, 73
Mirjave Village (Iran) 333
Mitakesan (Jap) 536
Mitok San (Jap) 531
Mitsumine Temple (Jap) 536
Miyako (Jap) 14, 533
Mizoram (Ind) 353
Moc Bai (Viet) 484
Moc Chau (Viet) 477
Moenjodaro (Pak) 333
Mogao Caves (CChina) 226
Mogok (Brm) 464
Mohammad Kashgari, Tomb of
   (Xin) 265
Mohan (Yun) 241, 509
Mokpo (SKor) 548, 549
Moldova 28, 284
Mongolia 312
Mong Hsan (Brm) 465
Mong Kai (Brm) **479**
Mong Cai (Viet) 219
Mongla (Bang) 406
Monywa (Brm) 464
Mordva (Rus) 288
Moron (Mong) 317
Moscow (Rus) 13, **300**, 301, 303
Mostiska (Ukr) 284
Motsameta (Geo) 116
Moulmein/Mawlamyine (Brm)
   460, 466
Moulmeingyun (Brm) 462
Moulvi Bazaar (Bang) 407
Mount Popa (Brm) 463
Mount Victoria (Brm) 463
Mrauk-Oo/Myohaung (Brm)
   462
Mt Elbruz (Rus) 82
Mt. Bromo (Indo) 424
Mt. Harriet (Ind) 371
Mt. Ilandag (Azer) 100
Mt. Goyazan (Azer) 100
Mt. Ararat (Tky) 39
Mt. Everest (Nep-Tibet) 253
Mt. Apo (Phi) 515
Mt. Songshan (CChina) 224
Mt. Pinatubo (Phi) 515
Mtskheta (Geo) **118**, 116
Muang Xepon (Laos) 511
Muang Pakxong (Laos) 511
Muang Khong (Laos) 511
Muang Keo/Ngoy/Nang Kio
   (Laos) 509, 510
Muang Hiap (Laos) 510
Muang Khoua (Laos) 509
Muang Sing (Laos) 509
Mubinjon's GH (Uzbek) 194

Mubinjon's B&B (Uzbek) 193
Mudiangjiang (CChina) 214
Mudon (Brm) 466
Mugling (Nep) 388, 390, 391
Mui Ne Beaches (Viet) 484
Mukadan (Thai) 511
Mukdahan (Thai) 448, 449
Munich 28
Munyak (Uzbek) 195, 196
Muq (Xin) 265
Muree & the Gali's (Pak) 331
Muroran (Jap) 523
Muse (Brm) 240, 464
Mushima (Jap) 533
Muslim Hotel, Quetta's (Pak)
   333
Mustagh Ata (Xin) 339
Mutiyan (CChina) 217
My Son (Viet) 483
My Ly (Viet) 483
My Tho (Viet) 486
Mymensing (Bang) 407
Myitkyina (Brm) 464
Myohaung/Mrauk-Oo (Brm)
   462

Nagaland (Ind) 353
Nagano (Jap) 531
Nagar Valley (KKH) 340
Nagasaki (Jap) 14, 531
Nagchu (Tibet) 256
Naghsh e Rosta (Iran) 71
Nagorno Karabakh (Armen) 90
Nagoro-Karabakh (Azer-Armen)
   100
Nagoya (Jap) 531
Naha (Jap) 14
Nain (Iran) 68
Najaf (Iraq) 45
Nakhchivan (Azer) 82, 84, 100,
   101
Nakhodka (Rus) 310
Nakhon Phanom (Thai) 449
Nalqe 75
Naltar Valley (KKH) 340
Nam Tso Lake (Tibet) 255
Nam Nun (Laos) 510
Namangan (Uzbek) 158, 161,
   190
Nambak (Laos) 509
Namchee Bazaar (Nep) 391
Namtha (Laos) 509
Nan (Thai) 448
Nanai (Uzbek) 161, 190
Nang Kio/Ngoy/Muang Keo
   (Laos) 509, 510
Nanjing (CChina) 215, 221
Nanning (CChina) **219**
Nanping (CChina) 228
Nara (Jap) 531, 534
Narat (Xin) 266, 267

Nardaran (Azer) 104
Nargarkot (Nep) 393
Narita Airport (Jap) 536
Narkil Fortress (Geo) 121
Narva (Belarus) 274, 303
Naryn (Kyrgyz) 163
Nebit Dag (Trkstn) 175
Negombo (SL) 412, 413
Negros Is. (Phi) 515
Neil Is. (Ind) 371
Nekresi (Geo) 117
Nemrut Dag #1 (Tky) 40
Nepal 378
Nepalganj (Nep) 388, 390
Nerchinsk (Rus) 306, 307
Neryungri (Rus) 307
Nevsehir (Tky) 38
New Territories (HK) 230
Ngapali (Brm) 462
Ngor Monastery (Tibet) 255
Ngoy/Muang Keo/Nang Kio
   (Laos) 510, 509
Nha Trang (Viet) **483**, 484
Nias (Indo) 425
Niigata (Jap) 523, 14
Nikitski (Ukr) 287
Nikko (Jap) 531, 536
Nikolaevsk-na-Amure (Rus) 13
Ninglang (Yun) 240
Ninh Binh (Viet) **480,** 482
Ninotsuminda (Sakarejo) (Geo)
   117
Nisa (Trkstn) 177
Nishapur/Neishabur (Iran) 72
Niya (Xin) 262
Nizami Library (Azer) 102
Nizhin (Ukr) 284
Nizhny Novgorod/Gorkii (Rus)
   303, 311
Nododevinchi Convent (Rus)
   301
Nom (Xin) 263
Nomal (KKH) 338
Nong Kai (Thai) 448, 449, **507**,
   510
North Korea 550
North Ossetia (Rus) 82, 288
North West Frontier Province
   (Pak) 328
Novaya Chara (Rus) 307
Novgorod (Rus) 303
Novo-Selenginsk (Rus) 308
Novosibirsk (Rus) 13, **305**
Novy Urgal (Rus) 13, 307
Nuakot Palace (Nep) 393
Nukus (Uzbek) 195, 196
Nurata (Uzbek) 191
Nuristan (Afgh) 80
Nuwara Eliya (SL) 412, 413
NWFP (Pak) 328

Nyalam (Tibet) 253
Nyaung-Oo (Brm) 463

O'Kim's Pub (SKor) 547
Odaesan (SKor) 548
Odessa (Ukr) 284
Oil rigs (Azer) 104
Oil Route, The (Turkmen-Iran) 127
Ok Mok Pass (Kyrgyz) 158, 159
Oki Islands (Jap) 533
Okinawa (Jap) 14, 533
Old Miran (Xin) 263
Old Merv (Trkstn) 175, 178
Olgii (Mong) 127, 317
Oludeniz (Tky) 36
Olympos (Tky) 36
Omsk (Rus) 13
One Hundred and Eight Dagobas (CChina) 215
Onta (Jap) 531
Opal (Xin) 265, 339
Opera, Sichuan (CChina) 225
Orenburg (Rus) 304
Orient Hostel (Tky) 35
Orissa (Ind) 353
Ortakoy (Tky) 26
Orumiyeh (Iran) 61, **62**, 63
Osaka (Jap) 14, 523, 531, 534
Osh (Kyrgyz) **157,** 190
Osh Bazaar (Kyrgyz) 152
Oshu Bulak Police Post (Kyrgyz) 159
Otaru (Jap) 14, 523, 533
Otaru (Rus) 306
Ozerni route (Kazakh-Kyrgyz) 142
Ozkonak (Tky) 38
Ozoresan (Jap) 530

P2/ Phnom Pénh (Cam) 493
Pa-an (Brm) 466
Pac Bo Cave (Viet) 478
Pagan (Brm) 460, **463**
Pahardur (Bang) 406
Pahartali Lake (Bang) 407
Pak-ou Caves (Laos) 509
Pakbeng (Laos) 509
Pakistan 320
Pakokka (Brm) 463
Pakxe (Laos) 505, 511
Palanpur (Ind) 360
Palawan Is. (Phi) 515
Palpung Monastery (Tibet) 256
Pamir Highway & Mountains (Tajik) 157, 164
Pamukkale (Tky) 36
Panay Is. (Phi) 515
Panda Reserve, Giant (CChina) 225
Panfilov (Kazakh) 139, 143

Panglong (Brm) 465
Panmunjon (SKor) 548
Pantheon (Geo) 121
Panzhihua (Yun) 240
Parkmellat (Iran) 67
Paro (Bhu) 375
Party, full moon (Thai) 449
Paryang (Tibet) 257
Pasanauri (Geo) 118
Pasargad (Iran) 71
Passu (KKH) 338, 339
Patan (Nep) 393
Patna (Ind) 369, 389
Pattaya (Thai) 449
Pechory (Rus) 303
Pedang Besar (Mal) **436**
Pelling (Ind) 373
Penang Is. (Mal) 436
Peng Lai (CChina) 218
Peng Chau Is. (HK) 231
Penjikent (Tajik) 191
Perm (Rus) 305
Persepolis (Iran) 71
Pescadorls (Phi) 515
Peshawar (Pak) **330**
Petrodvarets (Rus) 302
Petropavlosk Kamchatsky (Rus) 299
Petrushevicha Sq. (Ukr) **284**
Phan Rang (Viet) 484
Phan Thiet (Viet) 484
Pharping (Nep) 393
Philippines, The 512
Phimai (Thai) 448
Phitsanulok (Thai) 448
Phnom Penh (Cam) **493**, 494, 495
Phong Tho (Viet) 478
Phongsali (Laos) 509
Phonsavan (Laos) 510
Phuket (Thai) 449
Phunsholing (Bhu) 375
Pigeon Tower 75
Pindaya (Brm) 465
Pindi/Rawalpindi (Pak) 330
Pingxiang (CChina) 219
Plain of Jars (Laos) 505, 510
Platscart 271
Playku (Viet) 483
Plover Bay (HK) 231
Plyos (Rus) 311
Podil (Ukr) 286
Pogranichi (Rus) 214
Point Ron Beaches (Viet) 482
Pokhara (Nep) 388, 390, **395**
Pokrovka (Rus) 214
Poland 28, 278
Polonnaruwa (SL) 412, 413
Poltask (Belarus) 274
Poltiava (Ukr) 285
Pomunsa (SKor) 548

Popju (SKor) 548
Port Blair (Ind) 371
Port Baikal (Rus) 308, 309
Port Aurthur/Lushun (CChina) 218
Potala, fake (CChina) 218
Potala, real (Tibet) 255
Poti (Geo) 116
Pottery Towns (Jap) 530
Prambanan (Indo) 424
Prasat Preah Vihear (Cam) 448, 494
Princes Islands (Tky) 35
Prome/Pyay (Brm) 460, 462
Pskov (Rus) 274, 303
Pudong (CChina) 221
Puerto Galera (Phi) 515
Pulau Perhentian (Mal) 435
Pulguksa (SKor) 548
Punakha (Bhu) 375
Punjab (Ind) 353
Puri (Ind) 369
Pusan (SKor) 14, 549, **546**
Pushkin Art Museum (Rus) 301
Pushkin (Rus) 302
Pusok Sa (SKor) 548
Putuo Shan (CChina) 221
Pyatgorsk (Rus) 82
Pyay/Prome (Brm) 460, 462
Pyongyang (NKor) 553

Qax (Azer) 105
Qax Corridor (Azer) 100, **105, 106**
Qazak/Kazakh (Azer) 101
Qazax (Azer) 107
Qazvin (Iran) 61, 64, **65**
Qeshm Is. (Iran) 73
Qiaotou (Yun) 240
Qiemo/Cherchen (Xin) 263
Qingchengshan (CChina) 225
Qingdao (CChina) 14, 218
Qinghai Lake (CChina) 226
Qingshihe (Xin) 143, 262
Qingtongxia (CChina) 215
Qinibagh Hotel (Xin) 265
Qinping Market (CChina) **220**
Qinzhou (CChina) 219
Qom (Iran) 68
Qomolungma/Mt. Everest (Nep-Tibet) 253
Quba/Guba (Azer) 100, 101
Quetta (Pak) 52, 333
Qufu (CChina) 218
Qujing (Yun) 241

Rach Gia (Viet) 486
Raffles Hotel (Sgn) 427
Raikomol (Kyrgyz) 161
Raj's Sandwich Corner (Nep)

394
Rajasthan (Ind) 353
Rajbiraj (Nep) 391
Rajshahi (Bang) 406
Raketa Terminal (Rus) 309
Ramah Lake (KKH) 341
Ramana (Azer) 104
Ranchi (Ind) 369
Rangamati (Bang) 407
Rangoon (Brm) 460, **461**, 462
Rangphu (Tibet) 253
Rangpur (Bang) 406
Rann of Kutch, The (Ind) 360
Ranong (Thai) 449
Rasht (Iran) 61, 64, **65**
Ratanapura (SL) 413
Ravar (Iran) 73
Rawaling Trek (Nep) 391
Rawalpindi (Pak) 330, **332**
Rawu (Tibet) 256
Raxaul (Ind) 389
Red Square, Moscow (Rus) 301
Red Square, The East is
   (CChina) 227
Registan, The (Uzbek) 192
Reibun (Jap) 533
Repulse Bay (HK) 231
Riakot Bridge (KKH) 338
Riga (Latvia) 274
Rinca (Indo) 424
Ringo Guest House (Ind) 359
Rishikesh (Ind) 368, 389
Rishiri (Jap) 533
Ritan Park Embassy Area
   (CChina) 216
Rivne (Ukr) 284
Rocket Boat, The (Bang) 406
Rohtas Fort (Pak) 330
Romania 28
Romblon Is. (Phi) 515
Rongxar Valley (Tibet) 253
Ross Is. (Ind) 371
Rostov-on-Don (Rus) 311
Royal Palace (Brm) 464
Royal Palace (Nep) 394
Rudbar (Iran) 64
Rumtek Monastery (Ind) 373
Ruoqiang/Charkilik (Xin) 263
Russia 289
Russian phrases 560
Rustavi (Geo) 117

Sa Huynh (Viet) 483
Sadakhlo (Geo) 116
Sadatabad (Iran) 71
Sado (Jap) 533
Safdarjang Tomb (Ind) 359
Safranbolu (Tky) 29, 37
Saga (Tibet) 257
Sagada (Phi) 515
Sagaing (Brm) 464

Saigon (Viet) 484, **485**, 486
Sairam (Xin) 143
Sakha (Rus) 288
Sakya (Tibet) 255
Salavan (Laos) 511
Salt Range (Pak) 330, 331
Sam Son (Viet) 482
Samar Is. (Phi) 515
Samara (Rus) 311
Samarkand (Uzbek) 187, 191,
   192, 193, 196
Sambor (Cam) 494
Sameba (Geo) 119
Samsun (Tky) 29
Samye (Tibet) 255
Sangkhlaburi (Thai) 448
Sangsang (Tibet) 257
Sankhu (Nep) 393
Sanli Urfa (Tky) 29
Sanlitun Embassy Area
   (CChina) 216
Santipar Is. (Laos) 510
Sapa (Viet) 478
Sapporo (Jap) 533
Saratov (Rus) 311
Sari (Iran) 72
Sarkhs (Trkstn) 175
Sary Kumysh Lake
   (Trkstn/Uzbek) 174
Sary Chelek Lake (Kyrgyz) 159,
   161
Sary Tash (Kyrgyz) 157
Sasaram (Ind) 369
Sasebo (Jap) 531
Sasha&Lena's (Uzbek) 193, 194
Satpara Lake (KKH) 341
Saturn (Thai) 436
Saty (Kazakh) 142
Savannakhet (Laos) 505, **511**
Sekong (Laos) 511
Selcuk (Tky) 29
Selenga Delta (Rus) 308
Seman Hotel (Xin) 265
Seminovka (Kyrgyz) 142, 155
Semnan (Iran) 72
Sendai (Jap) 533
Seoul (SKor) 14, 549, **547**
Sera Monastery (Tibet) 255
Serbia/Yugoslavia 28
Sero (Iran) 61
Sevan Lake (Armen) 91
Sevastopol (Ukr) 287
Shah-i-Zinda (Uzbek) 192
Shakhidlar Khiabana (Azer) 102
Shakhimardan (Uzbek) 190
Shakhrisabz (Uzbek) 191
Shamian Island (CChina) **220**
Shanghai (CChina) 14, 215, **221**
Shangyang (Yun) 241
Shanhaiguan (CChina) **217**, 218
Shaolin (CChina) 224

Shaoxing (CChina) 221
She Dor Madrassa (Uzbek) 192
Sheki (Azer) 84, 101, **105**
Shemakha (Azer) 100, 101
Shemienquan/Asbesdos Deposit
   (Xin) 263
Shenjianmen (CChina) 221
Shenyang (CChina) 214, 218,
   220, 230
Sheung Shui (HK) 231
Shewdagon Pagoda (Brm) 461
Shigatse, Xigatse (Tibet) 255
Shijiangzhang (CChina) **224**
Shikoku Is. (Jap) **532**, 533
Shilin (Yun) **241**
Shimshal Valley (KKH) 340
Shin (Azer) 105
Shinjuku (Jap) 537
Shinmoji (Jap) 523
Shiraoi (Jap) 533
Shiraz (Iran) 61, **71**
Shirkusu Temple (CChina) 224
Shivapuri (Nep) 393
Shush/Susa (Iran) 70
Shuya (Rus) 303
Shwayambhunath/Monkey
   Temple (Nep) 392, 394
Shwenyaung (Brm) 465
Si-O-Sepol Bridge teahouse
   (Iran) 69
Sialkot (Pak) 330
Siberia, Little (Xin) 263
Siberia, hitching to 127, 154
Siberut (Indo) 425
Sibyan Is. (Phi) 515
Sichuan Opera (CChina) 225
Siem Reap (Cam) 494, 495
Sigar Valley (KKH) 341
Sigiriya (SL) 412, 413
Signaghi (Geo) 117
Sihanoukville (Cam) 494, 495,
   496
Sikkim (Ind) 353
Siliguri (Ind) 389
Silk Railway (China-C.Asia-
   Rus) 13, 127
Silver Pagoda, Phnom Pénh
   (Cam) 493
Silvermine Bay (HK) 231
Simao (Yun) 241
Simbirsk (Rus) 311
Simferolpol (Ukr) 284, 285, 287
Simiez (Ukr) 287
Similan Is. (Thai) 449
Simitai (CChina) 217
Simonoseki (Jap) 14
Sind, The (Pak) 328
Singapore **427**
Singu (Brm) 463
Sioni (Geo) 117, 119
Sirjan (Iran) 61

Sittaw (Brm) 462
Skardu (KKH) 338
Skovorodino (Rus) 13
Slavyanka (Rus) 214, 310
Slovakia 28
Slovenia 28
Sludyanka (Rus) 308, 309
Smith Is. (Ind) 371
Smolensk (Rus) 274, 303
Smyrna/Izmir (Tky) 36
Sno (Geo) 119
Snowlands Guesthouse (Tibet) 255
Soc Trang (Viet) 486
Sochi (Rus) 82, 84, 285
Sohotan NP (Phi) 515
Sokh (Uzbek) 190
Sokollu Mosque (Tky) 35
Sokulak Valley (Kyrgyz) 154
Solevki (Rus) 304
Solovensk (Rus) 317
Son La (Viet) 478
Songpan (CChina) 228
Sosnovka (Kyrgyz) 154, 158
South Korea, 538
South Ossetia (Geo) 82
Sri Lanka 409
Sri Pada/Adam's Peak (SL) 412, 413
Sri Ksetra (Brm) 462
Srimangal (Bang) 407
St. Hripsime Cathedral (Armen) 91
St. Petersburg (Rus) 28, **302**, 303
St. Martin's Island (Bang) 407
St. Basils Cathedral (Rus) 301
Stalin Museum (Geo) 122
Stanley (HK) 231
Staraya Russa (Rus) 303
Starocherkassk (Rus) 311
Stary Krym (Ukr) 287
Stepanakert/Khankendi (Armen) 90, 91
Stepanovan (Armen) **91**
Stone Forest (Yun) **241**
Strand Hotel (Brm) 461
Stung Treng (Cam) 494, 495
Sudak (Ukr) 287
Suifenhe (CChina) 214
Sukhe Baator Sq. (Mong) 318
Sukhotai (Thai) 448, 449
Sukhumi (Geo) 84
Sukkur (Pak) 333
Sule Pagoda (Brm) 461
Suleiman Gora (Kyr) 157
Sulawesi (Indo) **425**
Sultanahmet (Tky) **35**
Sulu Archipelego (Phi) 515
Sumatra (Indo) **426**
Sumba (Indo) 426

Sumbawa (Indo) 426
Sumela Cliff Monastery (Tky) 40
Sumela Monastery (Tky) 42
Sumgait (Azer) 104
Summer Palace, Bukhara (Uzbek) 193
Summer Palace, Beijing (CChina) 216
Summer Palace, St. Petersburg (Rus) 302
Sunauli (Nep-Ind) 389, 390
Sundarbans, The (India-Bang) 369, 406
Sundarjal (Nep) 391, 393
Sunday Antique Market (CChina) 221
Sunday Market (Trkstn) 176-7
Sunday Market (Xin) 265
Surakhany (Azer) 103, 104
Surat (Ind) 360
Susa/Shush (Iran) 70
Sust (KKH) 338, 339
Suwon (SKor) 548
Suzhou (CChina) 221
Severobaikalsk (Rus) 13, 307, **308**
Sviyzhsk (Rus) 311
Swallow's Nest (Ukr) 287
Swanetia (Geo) 115
Swat Valley (Pak) 330, 331
Swayambhunath Temple (Nep) 394
Sylhet (Bang) 407
Syriam (Brm) 461
Syzran (Rus) 311

Taal Volcano (Phi) 515
Tabas (Iran) 72
Tablas Is. (Phi) 515
Tabriz (Iran) 52, 61, **62**, 63
Tachilek (Brm) 448
Tad Phan Waterfall (Laos) 511
Taejon (SKor) 548, 549
Taer-Si/ Huangzhong (CChina) 226
Taesun San (SKor) 548
Taft (Iran) 73
Taftan (Pak) 333
Taganrog (Rus) 311
Tai Po (HK) 231
Taian (CChina) 218
Taihu Lake (CChina) 221
Taipei (Taiwan) 14, 554
Taishan (CChina) 218
Taiwan 14, 554
Taiyuan (CChina) **224**
Tajikistan 164
Taketomi (Jap) 533
Takht-e-Soleiman (Iran) 63
Takht-i-Bahi (Pak) 330

Takushima (Jap) 533
Talas (Kyr) 158, **159**
Taldi Bazaar (Nep) 390
Taldy Bulak (Kyr) 158, 159
Tallinn (Estonia) 274
Tam Dao (Viet) 478
Taman Negara NP (Mal) 436
Tamil Nadu (Ind) 353
Tanah Toraja (Indo) 425
Tanegashima (Jap) 533
Tangawa, Mt. (Jap) 536
Tangkou (CChina) 221
Tapah Rd. (Mal) 436
Taplejung (Nep) 391
Taq-e-Bostam (Iran) 63
Tash Kurgan (Afg) 81
Tash Kumyr (Kyr) **157**, 158, 159, 160, 161
Tash Rabat (Kyr) 163
Tashauz (Trkstn) 175, 195, 196
Tashigang (Bhu) 375
Tashir (Armen) 91
Tashkent (Uzbek) 187, **188**, **189**, 190
Tashkurgan (Xin) **339**
Tashling (Nep) 395
Tashmilek (Xin) 265
Tataristan (Rus) 288
Tatopani (Nep) 253
Tatvan (Tky) 39
Taungdwingyi (Brm) 462
Taunggyi (Brm) 465
Tawella (Hariem) 45
Taxila (Pak) 330
Tay Ninh (Viet) 484
Tayedbad (Iran) 72
Tayshet (Rus) 13
Tbilisi (Geo) 84, 116, **121**
Tegene (Kyr) 161
Tehran (Iran) 61, 63, **66**, **67**, 68
Tekke Bazaar (Trkstn) 176
Teknaf (Bang) 407
Telavi (Geo) 117
Tembling (Mal) 436
Temple of Heaven, Beijing (CChina) 216
Tepliye Kluche Sanitorium (Kyr) 154
Teploklyuchenka (Kyr) 156
Terai, The (Nep) 388
Terdrom Monastery (Tibet) 255
Terelj (Mong) 318
Termez (Uzbek) 187
Terracotta Warriors (CChina) 223
Tha River (Laos) 509
Tha Deua (Laos) 510
Tha Teng (Laos) 511
Thailand 439
Thai Nguyen (Viet) 478
Thamel (Nep) 393, **394**

Than Lyin (Brm) 461
Thanbyuzayat (Brm) 466
Thanh Hoa (Viet) 482
Thanton (Brm) 466
That Phanom (Thai) 448
That Luang Stupa (Laos) 506
Thai characters 443
Thazi (Brm) 465
Thimphu (Bhu) 375
Three Gorges (CChina) 222
Three Pagoda Pass (Brm-Tai)
  449, 460
Thuan An (Viet) 482
Tianchi/Heavenly Lake (Xin)
  263
Tianchi Lake (CChina-NK) 214
Tianjin (CChina) 14, 218
Tiansui (CChina) 223
Tibet, 242 routes to 251
Ticlin Is. (Phi) 515
Tiger Leaping Gorge (Yun) 240
Tilla Kari Madrassa (Uzbek)
  192
Timor (Indo) 426
Tingri (Tibet) 253
Tioman Is. (Mal) 435
Toba Lake (Indo) 426
Tobolsk (Rus) 304, 305
Tokmak (Kyr) 154
Toksugung Palace (SKor) 547
Toktogul (Kyr) 158, **159**
Tokur (Rus) 306
Tokyo (Jap) 523, 536, **537**
Tolguchka Market (Trkstn) 176,
  177
Toling Tsada (Tibet) 257
Tollygunge Club (Ind) 370
Tolyati (Rus) 311
Tomsk (Rus) 305
Tongdo Sa (SKor) 548
Tonghak Sa (SKor) 548
Tongsa (Bhu) 375
Toop (Kyr) 155
Topkapi Palace (Tky) 35
Toprak Kala (Uzbek) 195
Tortoise&Violin (Uzbek) 189
Torugart Pass (Kyrgyz-Xin) 127,
  163, 262
Torzhok (Rus) 303
Tottori (Jap) 531
Tower of Death (Uzbek) 193,
  194
Trabzon (Tky) 29, 40, 42, 84
Trac Co (Viet) 479
Traffic Hotel (CChina) 225
Trans-Siberian Railway (Rus)
  13, 213, 308
Tram Tau Pine Forests (Viet)
  477
Trans Dniestr Region (Ukr) 284
Trans-Manchurian Railway

(China-Rus) 13, 213
Trans-Mongolian Railway
  (China-Mon-Rus) 13, 213, 317
Trat (Thai) 449, **496**
Traveller's Guest House,
  Moscow (Rus) 300
Tretyakov Gallery (Rus) 301
Trincomalee (SL) 413
Trisuli Bazaar (Nep) 390
Trowulan (Indo) 424
Tsada/Toling (Tibet) 257
Tsakhkadzor (Armen) 91
Tsangu Lake (Ind) 373
Tsaparang (Tibet) 257
Tsarskoe Seto (Rus) 302
Tsethang (Tibet) 255
Tsezerleg (Mong) 317
Tsim Sha Tsui (HK) 231
Tsinandali (Geo) 117
Tsingtao beer, home of (CChina)
  218
Tskhneti (Geo) 116
Tsnori (Geo) 117
Tsochen (Tibet) 257
Tsumago (Jap) 531
Tsushima (Jap) 533
Tuergate (Xin) 163
Tumen (CChina) 214, 553
Tunxi (CChina) 221
Turakurgan (Uzbek) 190
Turkmenbashi/Kransnovodsk
  (Trkstn) 175
Turkmenistan 169
Turpan (Xin) 263
Tus (Iran) 72
Tuva (Rus) 288, 306
Tver (Rus) 303
Tynda (Rus) 13, 307
Tyu Ash Pass (Kyr) 158
Tyumen (Rus) 13, 305, 304

U Minh Forest (Viet) 486
UB/Ulaan Baator (Mong) **318**
Ubambar 75
Ubon Ratchathan (Thai) 445,
  448, 449
Uch Kurgan (Uzbek) 161
Uchisar (Tky) 38
Uchkuduk (Uzbek) 191
Udmurt (Rus) 288
Udom Xay (Laos) **509**
Ufa (Rus) 305
Uglich (Rus) 303, 311
Ujang Pandang (Indo) 425
Ukraine 279
Ulaan Baator/UB (Mong) 13,
  318
Ulan Ude (Rus) 13, 308, **309**
Ultar Glacier (KKH) 340
Ulugbek Madrassa (Uzbek) 192
Ulugchat (Xin) 265

Ulung Do (SKor) 548
Umeda Station (Jap) 534, 535
Unawatuna (SL) 412, 413
Undur Dov (Mong) 318
Uplitshikhe (Geo) 116
Ural Mountains (Rus) 304
Urgench (Uzbek) 175, 187, **195**
Urgup (Tky) 38
Urgut (Uzbek) 191
Urumqi (Xin) 13, 143, 263, **264**
  266, **268**
Ushguli Village (Geo) 116
Ussurisk (Rus) 13, 214, 553
Ust Barguzin (Rus) 308
Uttar Pradesh (Ind) 353
Uvs Nurr, Lake (Mong) 317
Uzbekistan 179
Uzgen (Kyr) **157**, 158
Uzhgorod (Ukr) 28, 284

Vabkent (Uzbek) 191
Van (Tky) 29, **39**
Vangvieng (Laos) **510**
Vanino (Rus) 307
Varanasi (Ind) **368,** 369, 389
Vardzia Caves (Geo) 116
Veraval (Ind) 360
Victoria Memorial (Ind) 370
Vidubitski Monastery (Ukr) 286
Vientiane (Laos) 505, **506**
Viet Cong Tunnels (Viet) 484
Vietnam 467
Vigan (Phi) 515
Vilnius (Lithuania) 274
Vinh Long (Viet) 486
Vinh (Viet) **482**
Vishnupur (Ind) 369
Vitsebsk (Belarus) 274
Vladikavkaz (Rus) 84
Vladimir (Rus) 303
Vladivostok (Rus) 13, 14, 214,
  310
Volgagrad (Rus) **311**
Volgoda (Rus) 303
Voronezh (Rus) 303
Vostok 5 (Kyr) 152
Vung Tau (Viet) **484**
Vyborg (Rus) 28, 303

Wakanai (Rus) 306
Wakhan Corridor (Afgh) 80
Wakkanai (Jap) 14
Wanding (Yun) 240
Wandoor (Ind) 371
Wanxian (CChina) 222
Wat Phu (Laos) 511
We Is. (Indo) 426
Weihai (CChina) 14, 218
West Bengal (Ind) 353
Wolong Nature Reserve
  (CChina) 228

World's most expensive bars 537
World's first tea factory 221
World's longest trolley route 287
World's longest beach 404
World's highest minaret 81
World's coldest capital city 318
World's largest uncracked bell 464
World's deepest and largest lake 308
World's biggest Buddha 225
World's wettest area 404
World's End (SL) 413
Wu Wei (CChina) 217, **226**
Wudangzhou Monastery (CChina) 215
Wuhan (CChina) **222**
Wuhu (CChina) 222
Wushan (CChina) 222
Wutai Temple (CChina) 215
Wutaishan (CChina) 215
Wuxi #1 (CChina) 221
Wuxi #2 (CChina) 222
Wuzhou (CChina) 219

Xam Nua (Laos) 510
Xanlar (Azer) 107
Xegar (Tibet) 253
Xiagnburi (Laos) 509
Xiahe (CChina) **228**
Xian (CChina) **223**
Xigatse, Shigatse (Tibet) 255
Xining (CChina) 226, **227**, 228
Xinjuiang 258
Xinyang (CChina) 223
Xishuangbanna (Yun) 238

Yakutsk (Rus) 13, 307
Yala Park (SL) 413
Yalta (Ukr) **285**, 287
Yan an (CChina) 223
Yandoon (Brm) 462
Yangon/Rangoon (Brm) 460, **461**, 462
Yangqing Temple (CChina) 224
Yangshuo (CChina) 219, 221
Yanji (CChina) 214
Yaprakhisar Village (Tky) 38
Yarkand (Xin) 262
Yarkhoto/Jiohe (Xin) 263
Yaroslavl (Rus) 13, 303, 311
Yasnaya Polyana (Rus) 303
Yaunghwe (Brm) 465
Yazd (Iran) 61, 73, **74**
Yeni Mosque (Tky) 35
Yerevan (Armen) 84, 90, 91, **92**
Yildiz Park (Tky) 26
Yincheng (CChina) 222
Yinchuan (CChina) 215
Yingxian (CChina) 215
Yining (Xin) 143, 262, **266**
Yok Don Park (Viet) 484
Yokohama (Jap) 14
Yoksom (Ind) 373
Yongning (Yun) 240
Yoretan/Jorethang (Ind) 373
Yoron (Jap) 533
Yoshino (Jap) 534
Yosu (SKor) 548
Youshahan (Xin) 263
Youyiguan (CChina) 478
Yukesekova (Tky) 29, 39
Yulin (CChina) 223
Yumoto (Jap) 536
Yunnan 235

Yunggan Caves (CChina) 215
Yuri Gagarin's House (Rus) 303
Yutian/Keriya (Xin) 262
Yuzhno Sakhalinsk (Rus) 13
Ywama (Brm) 465

Zagatala (Azer) 101, 106
Zagorsk (Rus) 303
Zagulban beach (Azer) 104
Zahedan (Iran) 61, 73
Zaisan (Mong) 318
Zakatala (Azer) 105
Zakho (Hariem) 45
Zangmu (Tibet) 253
Zaporizhzhya (Ukr) 284, 285
Zenkov Wooden Cathedral (Kazakh) 141
Zhalu (Tibet) 255
Zhamo (Tibet) 256
Zhangye (CChina) 217, 226
Zhanjiang (CChina) 219
Zhengzhou (CChina) 224
Zhiglovo (Rus) 306
Zhinvali (Geo) 116, 118
Zhongdian (Yun) 240, 256
Ziar (Iran) **68**
Ziarat (Pak) 333
Zibo Tombs (CChina) 218
Zikhter (Xin) 267
Zindam (Uzbek) 194
Znamensky Monastery (Rus) 309
Zoige (CChina) 228
Zongwei (CChina) 215
Zugdidi (Geo) 84, 116
Zuhai (CChina) 219, 230
Zuunmod (Mong) 318
Zvartnots (Armen) 91

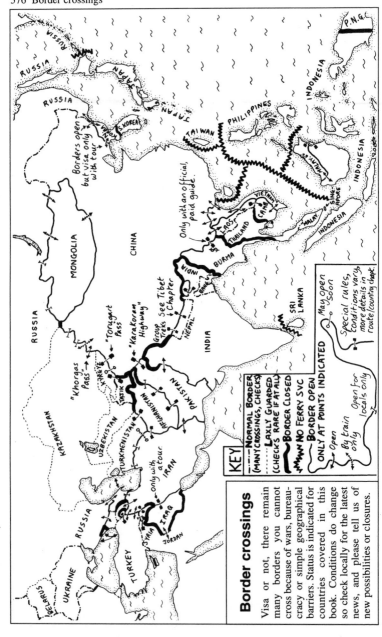

Border crossings

Visa or not, there remain many borders you cannot cross because of wars, bureaucracy or simple geographical barriers. Status is indicated for countries covered in this book. Conditions do change so check locally for the latest news, and please tell us of new possibilities or closures.

KEY

━━━ NORMAL BORDER (MANY CROSSINGS, CHECKS)

------- LAXLY GUARDED (CHECKS RARE IF AT ALL)

▬▬▬ BORDER CLOSED

〰〰〰 NO FERRY SVC

━━━ BORDER OPEN ONLY AT POINTS INDICATED

Open

By train only

Open for locals only

May open soon

Special rules, conditions vary, more details in route/country chap.